Kaufman's New Repertoire for Black and White

Larry Kaufman

Kaufman's New Repertoire for Black and White

A Complete, Sound and User-friendly Chess Opening Repertoire

New In Chess 2019

© 2019 New In Chess

Published by New In Chess, Alkmaar, The Netherlands
www.newinchess.com

Cover design: Volken Beck
Supervision: Peter Boel
Editing and typesetting: René Olthof
Proofreading: Dennis Keetman
Production: Anton Schermer

Have you found any errors in this book?
Please send your remarks to editors@newinchess.com. We will
collect all relevant corrections on the Errata page of our website
www.newinchess.com and implement them in a possible next edition.

ISBN: 978-90-5691-862-0

Contents

Explanation of symbols

The chessboard
with its coordinates:

a b c d e f g h

☐ White to move
■ Black to move
♔ King
♕ Queen
♖ Rook
♗ Bishop
♘ Knight

± White stands slightly better
∓ Black stands slightly better
± White stands better
∓ Black stands better
+− White has a decisive advantage
−+ Black has a decisive advantage
= balanced position
! good move
!! excellent move
? bad move
?? blunder
!? interesting move
?! dubious move
N novelty
↑ initiative
→ attack
⇄ counterplay
⊜ compensation
∞ unclear

General introduction

In 2013 I wrote *The Kaufman Repertoire for Black and White*. The Black half of this book is an update of the Black half of that one, mostly updated in 2018 with some further updates in 2019, with the addition of the Marshall Attack being the biggest change. The White half however is completely new; it had to be, because in KRBW I recommended 1.d4, whereas here I recommend 1.e4. Many of the games, and most of the analysis, for the White book are from 2019.

The main theme of the book, especially the White portion, is that you can obtain good positions, meaning slightly favorable ones as White and only slightly worse ones as Black, without having to play the most complex, theory-heavy lines in most cases. I was pleasantly surprised to see how little White gives up by avoiding the most critical lines. Apparently the elite GMs agree with me as they have been playing many of my White sidelines against each other in 2019. White can usually maintain a plus even in these sidelines well into the endgame. It won't be enough to win many correspondence games when your opponent is using an engine, but for over-the-board play, you will generally emerge from the opening as White with good winning chances if you are the stronger player, and with black should at least obtain positions where you won't just be fighting a one-sided battle for a draw. Although this is a repertoire book, I have made a much greater effort than in my previous books to give alternatives for the chosen side, especially in the White book, as I really don't want the book to become obsolete just because one or two variations prove to be dead draws or otherwise dubious. The price for this is less coverage of rare moves by the opposing side. Usually inferior moves by Black can be rather easily refuted with any modern engine. I can't cover everything!

Although I am the oldest active GM in the U.S. and no longer play near GM level, I do have some real advantages for writing a book like this. Computer chess is having a revolution now, based on Monte-Carlo Tree Search and Neural Networks, inspired by the success of AlphaZero. This is not a book on computers, so you'll have to look elsewhere for more information about these terms, but suffice it to say that I am very much involved with these developments as a partner in KomodoChess, which has a very strong Monte-Carlo version already, and so I know what engines to use, what hardware to buy, and how to use them effectively. In March of 2019 I purchased a computer with a very powerful GPU (RTX 2080 for the tech-minded) and 8 very fast CPU cores. My method for working on this book is to run each position on the latest Lc0 (which is a neural network designed to roughly replicate Alpha Zero, rather successfully I would say) on my GPU and 2 CPU cores while running Komodo 13 MCTS on the other 6 CPU cores. These two engines complement each other quite well. Lc0 is in general stronger due to the extremely powerful GPU (which has almost 3000 cores!!). But it has no chess knowledge except what it taught itself by playing games, whereas Komodo MCTS has ten years of refinement of its chess knowledge behind it. Also Lc0 is relatively weaker in the endgame, and rather blind to perpetual checks in many positions. Note that both of these engines can be used in 'MultiPV' mode to display the top 5 (or more) moves without any loss of quality, which is not at all true of normal (non Monte-Carlo) engines, nor do the two engines have to share resources.

The result is a quality of analysis that vastly exceeds what most people will get using normal engines on normal pcs with shared resources and MultiPV displays. Aside from using these two engines, I also keep an eye on analysis done by others using Stockfish, Houdini, and normal Komodo, as well as database statistics using two databases. One is the Hiarcs Powerbook (mostly engine vs engine games I believe), and the other is a combination of the ChessBase MegaBase and a database of correspondence games. Of course I also consult books and magazines (especially New In Chess *Yearbook*), but due to the amazing developments mentioned above I consider anything older than 2018 to be unreliable so looking at older books was not a priority. One book I did consult on several lines for White was *Keep It Simple* by Christof Sielecki, both because it is new enough (2018) and because we chose some of the same lines, since simplicity was also one of my goals in this book. But I wanted my book to be suitable even for grandmasters, so in general my choices are not as simple as his; I'm really trying to prove an edge for White, not just interesting lines with surprise value. Although the variations chosen are aimed at reasonably strong players, my explanations are at a more elementary level, so even if some of the lines are a bit difficult, I hope that less advanced players will learn how to evaluate positions from my comments.

My role in choosing which moves to give is primarily as a referee. When the two engines (plus other analysis and database stats when applicable) agree, I will very rarely argue. These engines play somewhere in the 3400 to 3600 Elo range, and only in special circumstances would I ignore them. But when they disagree, which is pretty often, I have to decide which one is right, and here my chess understanding and knowledge of chess engines both play a role. The default assumption is that Lc0 is right, but if Komodo MCTS strongly prefers a move that is only slightly below the best according to Lc0, or if Lc0 seems to be blind to some feature of the position or to a perpetual check, I'll probably go with Komodo's choice. I also consider whether the move is easy or difficult to understand; it is common that Komodo will pick the same move that I would pick, while Lc0 prefers one that just doesn't seem as good. Lc0 may be correct, but if I can't figure out why, probably the reader will also have difficulty, so I do consider this factor.

I generally quote the evaluation shown by Komodo (example: (+0.26) – between brackets) because until recently the Lc0 evaluations +0.27 were unrealistic, and I try to put into words the factors that justify the assessment shown. I tend to use symbols showing advantages a bit more aggressively than is customary, because if both engines show around +0.15 (for example), the position is almost surely favorable for White, if only slightly, and calling it equal just seems wrong.

The book is full of novelties, which I mark with an N, although it often happens that someone plays one of these moves shortly after I wrote up the game, so don't be surprised if you see games with my 'novelty'. When I refer to material advantages, I use the scale that I have promoted (see the chapter called 'Material values', namely pawn = 1, knight or bishop = 3½ (with a slight preference for the bishop in general), rook = 5¼, queen = 10, and the bishop pair earns a half point bonus. Checkmate may be the nominal object of the game, but nowadays it seems as if the rules have been changed to say that being the sole possessor of the bishop pair wins! It's an exaggeration, but if you don't believe that winning the bishop pair for nothing is generally a serious advantage, a lot of the White book won't make much sense. All modern computers and top GMs accept this.

Writing this book has made me feel like a time traveler. It is full of the latest games and novelties, many in 2019, and features some games by players born in the 21st century. Yet I also have ties to the distant past. My first chess teacher, Harold Phillips, was Greater New York champion in 1895, and played twice against the first World Champion, Wilhelm Steinitz, in 1894!! I met Edward Lasker, whose most famous game was played in 1912, and had some instruction from Norman Whitaker, a top player around 1920. I played against Sam Reshevsky and Al Horowitz in the U.S. Championship, and won a ten game rapid match from Arnold Denker, three of the four top American players during World War II. My first big success was winning the American Open championship in 1966, but I didn't earn the Grandmaster title until I won the World Senior Championship in 2008. I was part of the team that created MacHack, the first chess computer to earn a rating in human tournaments, in 1967, and 52 years later I'm still working on chess computers and playing in tournaments! In short, I have had a very long chess career!

I would like to thank Daniel Clancy for the correspondence database, Hiarcs for their database, Mark Lefler and the late Don Dailey for their roles in KomodoChess, the late Steve Brandwein for teaching me a lot about chess so long ago, Christopher Gallardo for encouraging me to write this book, and New In Chess for publishing it.

Big changes are happening in the chess world, in an effort to combat excessive draws and to minimize the role of preparation for specific games. One top event introduced 'Armageddon' playoff games after every draw, and FIDE is organizing a serious World Championship of 'Chess960' aka 'Fischerandom' with most of the elite players. I don't know where these changes will take us, but I hope to be involved in these new developments. Despite my age, I'm receptive to new ideas.

Larry Kaufman
Bethesda, USA,
October 2019

Material values

Throughout this book you will find positions with unbalanced material. I believe it is very important to evaluate the material situation properly before even considering the position of the pieces on the board (once tactics have been resolved), because you must know how much one side has sacrificed in return for whatever positional compensation the other side has obtained.

Most beginners are taught that the values of the pieces (given that a pawn is 1) are: Knight 3, Bishop 3 (or perhaps 3+ or 3¼), Rook 5, Queen 9. These values are surprisingly reliable in reduced endgames, primarily those in which at least one side has no more than one piece (plus pawns). But they are increasingly wrong as you add pieces to the board, and can give quite misleading results on a fairly full board. As this is a book on openings, not on endgames, I felt I must address this issue.

Having researched this issue more than almost anyone on earth, using all kinds of computer analysis, here are some of my conclusions:

1. There are some differences between the best values for humans and the best values for computers. In particular, the best values for computers seem to give slightly higher values to the major pieces relative to the minor pieces than the best values for humans, and computers prefer (unpaired) bishops over knights more clearly than humans do.

2. The bishop pair is worth half a pawn! This rule, first given with supporting data by me in a 1999 *Chess Life* article, has proven to be quite reliable. Most of the top computer programs use something close to this rule, with the clarification that this half-pawn includes any superiority assumed for single bishop over knight. It does not seem to matter very much what phase of the game you are in, although the two bishops do gain slightly in value as the pieces come off, so the half-pawn value is a slight exaggeration in the opening. Surprisingly, it does not even matter very much whether the position is open or closed. It's just that in closed positions the knights are worth more than bishops, but having both bishops still deserves the half-pawn bonus. In other words, even in a very closed position if you have bishop and knight vs two bishops, you gain a lot by trading bishops. Whether you would trade a knight for one of the two bishops in a closed position is a closer call, as you are giving up the stronger piece to kill the half-pawn advantage of the pair. I think it is only a slight exaggeration to say that the main goal of the opening is to obtain the two-bishop advantage; certainly that is the main goal for many of the lines recommended for White in this book.

3. For human players, I think the most reliable values to use for the pieces in the middlegame are:

Piece	Value
Knight	3½
Bishop (unpaired)	3½
Rook	5¼
Two bishops	7½
Queen	10

This will give the right answers to exchange decisions almost all of the time, assuming neither side has significant positional advantages. Any reference I make in the book to a numerical material advantage is based on this table.

4. On a crowded board, the minor pieces and queen are worth a bit more relative to rooks and pawns than the above scale indicates, and on a fairly empty board the converse is true.
Some conclusions from the above table:

Two pawns are usually a bit better than the exchange, and one pawn plus the bishop pair is almost but not quite enough for the exchange.

Two minor pieces are a bit inferior to rook and two pawns (much inferior on a fairly empty board), but if the side with the two minor pieces has the bishop pair, they are a bit superior.

Two rooks are on average better than a queen (but not on a crowded board) but worse than a queen plus pawn (not on an otherwise nearly empty board).

Two rooks are equal to three minor pieces without the bishop pair but inferior to same with the bishop pair.

Queen is a bit stronger than rook plus minor piece plus pawn, but a bit weaker if the minor piece gives a bishop pair advantage.

Queen is inferior to three minor pieces even without the bishop pair, and if the three minors include the bishop pair they are equal to queen and pawn (on a crowded board they are superior).

This should give you a good starting point for an evaluation. The hard part is to judge whether some positional advantage(s) is (are) worth ¼ pawn, half a pawn, or whatever the material gap might be. I hope that my comments in the games will help the reader to acquire or improve this skill.

Part I – White repertoire

1.e4: safe lines for a modest edge

Way back in 1940, U.S. Master Weaver Adams published a book called *White to play and win*, in which he tried to prove a win for White starting with 1.e4. Unfortunately he totally failed, since he resorted to dubious gambits that were often just winning for Black.

I don't believe that White has a forced win in chess, but I do believe that if he starts with 1.e4 and makes no mistakes, he can retain at least the preferable position without allowing an obvious draw for 30 to 40 moves or so, beyond the point to which openings can generally be analyzed. He should normally get positions where it is fairly easy to explain why White is better, even if in many cases a grandmaster can expect to hold the draw against a similar opponent. Black should at least be the one who has to be careful to get the draw. There are a great many lines in this White book where White's advantage is the bishop pair, so I'm tempted to call the White book 'White to play and win the bishop pair', but of course that wouldn't be accurate.

When I was learning chess back in the 1960s we didn't have chess computers to tell us what moves were good in the opening; the first rated chess computer was MacHack in 1967, of which I was a team member, and it was only rated in the low 1500s. What we did have then was Bobby Fischer. Whatever he played or said about the opening was treated with the same awe that we now reserve for the opinions of top players who use 3500 rated engines to prepare. Fischer's views on the opening were pretty clear; Black had multiple ways to equalize against 1.d4 but only one way, the Najdorf Sicilian, to equalize against 1.e4. He almost always opened 1.e4 except for his use (to avoid prep) of 1.c4 in his title match with Boris Spassky in 1972.

Like other Fischer disciples (notably including the late six time U.S. Champion Walter Browne), I also played 1.e4 in the 60s (I learned a lot of my White openings by simply watching all 70+ games of Fischer's 1964 simul in Washington D.C., there being no databases or internet back then) but eventually turned to 1.d4 due primarily to the success and popularity of the Najdorf. It seemed impossible to get any edge against the Najdorf, which was the most popular defense among strong players. Garry Kasparov was also mostly a Najdorf exponent, and also turned away from 1.e4 for much of his career although he may have had other reasons as well.

Due to the influence of Fischer and Kasparov, I have pretty much held the lifelong view that 1.e4 is the best opening move if we know that Black will not play the Najdorf, but that without such knowledge, 1.d4 is better. In my first opening book in 2003 I went for 1.e4 for White based on avoiding the Najdorf by the 3.♗b5 check. Unfortunately, right after my final deadline GM Ivanchuk introduced a surprising new move for Black (a seemingly unplayable 11...d5!!) in the main line of 3.♗b5 check that gave Black total equality rather easily. With the Najdorf still very difficult to crack, I returned to 1.d4 in my second opening book; the Black portion of this book is an update from that one. But this time I again reverted to 1.e4 for the White book, because it seems that White can avoid Ivanchuk's brilliant move in more than one way, still retaining the better chances. This 3.♗b5 check line has become quite popular among elite GMs, and it seems to give White rather clearly the better chances in all lines, although there is no denying that Black's chances to draw are higher than in sharper Sicilian lines. It seems that I got it right in my first book, only the details were wrong! White usually aims for the Maroczy Bind with the bishop check, something that he cannot reach with 3.d4 in most Sicilian variations. Of course there are other Sicilians besides 2...d6, but 3.♗b5 has remained in good standing against 2...♘c6, and both 3.c3 and 3.c4 are decent ways to aim for a slight edge vs. 2...e6.

In order to give White a second option, I decided to include 2.♘c3, intending to meet 2...d6 with 3.d4 cxd4 4.♕xd4 ♘c6 5.♕d2!?, which has recently caught fire in elite play. Of course I include answers to the other second moves for Black here.

The big concern for 1.e4 players in recent years has been the Berlin Defense to the Spanish, which I recommended for Black in my first book. The line I gave in that book for White (4.0-0 ♘xe4 5.♖e1) is definitely more pleasant for White than for Black, though somewhat drawish, and remains my recommendation, varying only on move 9. Against the Morphy Defense (3...a6) I changed my recommendation from the Exchange Variation (which looks just too equal) to the 6.d3 line, playing d2-d3 only after 5...♗e7. This has become popular with the elite, even appearing in the World Championship Karjakin vs. Carlsen, primarily as a way to avoid the Marshall Attack, although as I show there is a real possibility of play transposing to an Anti-Marshall line usually arising from the normal 6.♖e1. This time, I decided to offer the Italian (3.♗c4) as an alternative to the Spanish. Many elite GMs are choosing the Italian, perhaps on the grounds that if White has to settle for an early d2-d3 in the Spanish, why should it be better than the Italian? Well, it's not really that simple, but it seems to me that White can count on at least a small plus without giving Black a draw too easily in the Italian (as well as in the d2-d3 Spanish). I give both quiet (d2-d3) and sharp (4.c3 ♘f6 5.d4) options for White.

The Petroff (Russian) Defense (1.e4 e5 2.♘f3 ♘f6) is quite important and was the main choice of World Number 2 Caruana until 2019, when he seems to have moved on. Perhaps the lines I give here are the reason, although I don't know this. It seems that White can get a small edge in the former main line by simply offering a swap of knights by 8.♘bd2. Black can avoid that line by playing more symmetrically, but even this doesn't give him problem-free life. I also give an alternative with 5.♕e2, which tended to be used only as a drawing line, but now seems to be a valid way to play for a small advantage. I also cover in this chapter the Philidor Defense (2...d6 or 1...d6 with an early ...e7-e5) which was somewhat popular a few years ago but seems to be fading now, as well as the two Black gambits on move 2, Latvian and Elephant.

The Caro-Kann is one of the best replies to 1.e4, and not easy to refute. The traditional main lines where White meets 4...♗f5 with 5.♘g3 seem to be very close to equal, and the fashionable 3.e5 often leads to positions where White has more space but few winning prospects. I decided to make the Two Knights Variation my main line, based partly on a single recent game that seems to overturn the theory of the 3...♘f6 defense. I also give a rare line recommended in an SOS article in *New in Chess*, meeting 4...♗f5 by 5.♕f3, which usually results in White's winning the bishop pair at some cost in time. Since the position is open, the bishop pair should be worth something, and it is hard to find full equality for Black. For a third option, I give the Exchange Variation, which seems to have been improved by the move 6.h3. Black either has to play ...g7-g6 and ...♗f5, not a good combination of moves, or else settle for a rather inactive light-squared bishop.

Against the French I stuck with the Tarrasch Variation (3.♘d2), as in my first book. One reason for this is that there is a fairly important transposition possible between the Sicilian with 2...e6 3.c3 d5 4.exd5 exd5 and the Tarrasch French, as explained in the notes to the Sicilian game with that opening. More generally, the Tarrasch is more in line with the theme of this White book, which is to aim for small but clear advantages rather than the possibly larger but less clear advantages of sharp main lines such as 3.♘c3 in the French. 3...c5 against the Tarrasch is considered the main line, and I think that with 4.♘gf3 (rather than 4.exd5), as also given in my first book, Black doesn't get total equality. Other third move options for Black are playable and analyzed here, but White usually keeps a normal plus.

Black has several other reasonable first moves against 1.e4 besides the 'big four', which I analyze in the Other First Moves chapter. All of them give White a larger advantage than he gets against the 'big four', but you have to know what you are doing! Alekhine's Defense is met by an accelerated Exchange Variation, the Nimzowitsch Defense by offering transposition to the Spanish/Italian, the Scandinavian with 2...♕d5 by the usual 3.♘c3, the Modern by an early ♗e3, and the Pirc by a surprising early ♗f4 which has only recently come to my attention.

So how much of an edge can you get as White with my repertoire? Here are the Elo advantages for White after my preferred response to the main lines (per Hiarcs db):
- Caro-Kann Two Knights +40;
- French Tarrasch +45;
- Sicilian 2...♘c6 3.♗b5 +37;
- Sicilian 2...d6 3.♗b5+ +40;
- Petroff main line +37;
- Italian +30;
- Spanish Berlin 5.♖e1 with ♗f1 +42;
- Spanish 6.d3 +26.

So to sum up, if Black plays the defenses given in the Black book White is held to a 26 to 30 Elo plus, otherwise he gets at least 37 Elo in every line! Lc0 evaluations of these lines are reasonably consistent with these statistics. White isn't giving up much by playing these lines, which in general require much less memorization than the traditional main lines.

CHAPTER 1

Less common Black first moves

Four first moves against **1.e4** are considered fully acceptable for Black among grandmasters: 1...e5, the Sicilian, the Caro-Kann, and the French (although some would exclude the French). In this chapter I consider all the other sensible Black initial moves.

I start with Owen's Defense, **1...b6**. Although it is reasonable, Black isn't able to prevent White from creating the perfect center and defending it by 3.♗d3 and when needed ♕e2. Sometimes play transposes to an inferior (for Black) variation of the French Defense. See Game 1.1.

Next comes Alekhine's Defense, **1...♘f6**. It has faded somewhat in popularity mainly due to the 4.♘f3 line, but against that 4...dxe5 5.♘xe5 c6 has proven to be at least playable, though not equal, so I opted for the Exchange Variation but with a rare and seemingly inferior move order preferred by 2018 U.S. Champion Sam Shankland. I explain why his move order actually makes good sense and leads to a better than par advantage for White. See Game 1.2.

The Nimzowitsch Defense **1...♘c6** is met here by 2.♘f3 (rather than 2.d4), allowing Black to 'correct his mistake' by 2....e5 but giving White a larger advantage than with 2.d4 if Black avoids this transposition. See Game 1.3.

In the Scandinavian Defense **(1...d5 2.exd5)**, **2...♘f6** is met by 3.♘f3 ♘xd5 4.d4 or 3.d4 ♘xd5 4.♘f3, which differ if Black chooses 3...♗g4. I would choose 3.d4 for correspondence games or when fully prepared, 3.♘f3 otherwise. Black has problems. See Game 1.4.

The Scandinavian with **2...♕xd5** is met by **3.♘c3.**

Now the older **3...♕a5** (but with a new twist by Black) is Game 1.5. It may limit White to a favorable but probably not winning bishop vs knight endgame (though I give a White option to avoid this), so it might be playable for Black by those willing to suffer a long endgame in hopes of a draw. The newer **3...♕d6** (Tiviakov's Variation) is Game 1.6. In both cases White usually wins the bishop pair in the opening, which seems to be the theme for White in this book.

Next I cover the now rare Pribyl Defense (**1...d6 2.d4 ♞f6 3.♞c3 c6**) which I recommend meeting aggressively by **4.f4** to avoid getting 'move-ordered' out of my repertoire in case of 4.♞f3 g6. As usual, White's edge is the bishop pair. See Game 1.7.

The Modern Defense (which is far too old now for that name!) **1...g6 2.d4 ♝g7 3.♞c3 d6** is met by **4.♝e3**, and if 4...a6 5.f4. Since Black has already played ...♝g7, it makes sense to play for ♕d2 and ♝h6. I also cover 3...c5 4.dxc5 here. See Game 1.8.

The Pirc Defense (**1...d6 2.d4 ♞f6 3.♞c3 g6**) is slightly different in that Black can meet 4.♝e3 by deferring ...♝g7 to make ♝h6 less inviting. Instead, I give the rare but growing line with **4.♝f4** in this case, a line that can arise from the London System as well.

White usually achieves an exchange of bishops on g7 when the ...g7-g6 move looks rather weakening. See Game 1.9.

Game 1.1   Various Openings – Owen
Othmar Zenker   2173
Frank Bendig   2209

Correspondence game, 2008

1.e4 b6

This is called Owen's Defense, named after one of Morphy's opponents in the mid 1800s.

2.d4 e6

2...♗b7 3.♗d3 e6 4.♘f3 is the more usual move order, transposing.

3.♘f3 ♗b7 4.♗d3

White refrains from ♘c3 to avoid the pin.

4...c5 5.c3 ♘f6 6.♕e2

6...♗e7

6...d5 7.e5 ♘fd7 8.0-0 ♗e7 resembles an Advanced Variation of the French Defense where Black has played quite passively, but Black has scored pretty well from this position. 9.a3 c4 10.♗c2 b5 11.♘e1 h5 12.♕e3 ♘c6 13.♕g3 g5 14.f4 g4 15.f5 ♕b6 16.♗e3 0-0-0 17.h4 ♔b8 18.♘d2± (+0.39), but Lc0 gives a much higher score. White has a space advantage and plans of b2-b3 or b2-b4. He can either close off the kingside or open the f-file as conditions warrant.

7.0-0 ♘c6 8.e5 ♘d5 9.dxc5

9...♗xc5

9...bxc5 10.c4 ♘b6 11.♘c3 0-0 12.♕e4 g6 13.♗h6 f5 14.♕f4 ♖f7 15.♖ad1± (+0.67). White has space, pressure on d7, and attacking chances on the kingside.

10.♗e4 0-0 11.♖d1 a5

11...f5 avoids the following combination, so it is probably best: 12.♗xd5 exd5 13.♖xd5 ♕e8 14.b4 ♗e7 15.♖d1 ♖c8 16.♘a3± (+0.35). Black will have to make concessions to regain his pawn.

12.♗xh7+!

12.a3 is also good but the game move is much more exciting and probably better.

12...♔xh7 13.♘g5+ ♔g6 14.h4 ♘xe5!

The best chance.

15.♕xe5 ♖h8

15...f5 16.h5+ ♔xh5 17.♕xg7 ♕f6
18.♕h7+ ♕h6 19.♕xh6+ ♔xh6
20.♘xe6+ ♔h5 21.♘xf8+− (+1.85).
Black has enough compensation for
the pawn, but he is also down the
exchange.

**16.♖xd5 ♗xd5 17.♕g3 ♕e8 18.c4
♗c6 19.♘xe6+ ♔f6 20.♘xc5 bxc5
21.♘c3 ♔e7 22.♕xg7±** (+1.04)

With two pawns for the exchange
and a huge advantage in king safety,
White is close to winning.

**22...d6 23.♕g4 ♔f8 24.♗g5 ♕e5
25.♖d1 ♖e8 26.f4 ♕e3+ 27.♔h2
♕f2 28.♖xd6 ♗g2 29.♕g3 ♕xg3+
30.♔xg3 ♗f1 31.b3+− ♖g8 32.f5
♗xc4 33.♔f4**

33.bxc4 ♖xg5+ 34.hxg5 ♖e3+
35.♔f4 ♖xc3 36.♔e5 ♖xc4 37.♔f6
♔e8 38.♖d5 a4 39.♖e5+ ♔f8
40.♖e7+−.

**33...♗e2 34.♘d5 ♔g7 35.h5 ♗xh5
36.♖h6 ♗e2 37.f6+ ♔f8 38.♖h2
♖xg5 39.♔xg5 ♖e5+ 40.♔f4 ♖h5
41.♖xh5 ♗xh5 42.♔e5 ♗e2 43.♘b6
♔e8 44.♔d5 ♗d1 45.♔xc5 ♔d8
46.♔d6 ♗e2 47.♘d7 ♗b5 48.♘e5
♔e8 49.a4 ♗e2 50.♘c6 ♗d1
51.♘xa5**
Black resigned.

Game 1.2 Alekhine's Defense

Samuel Shankland 2731
Richard Rapport 2735

St Louis rapid 2019 (6)

1.e4 ♘f6

Alekhine's Defense, a fighting
choice but fading in elite
popularity.

2.e5 ♘d5 3.d4 d6

4.exd6

This rare trade followed by c2-c4
looks like novice play since it gives
Black extra plausible options for
knight retreats as compared to 4.c4
♘b6 and only then 5.exd6. But 2018
U.S. Champion Sam Shankland
is no novice, he would never do
this without good reason. So here
is my explanation. White wants
to know which way Black will
recapture. If he chooses the e-pawn
as in this game, White has indeed
accomplished nothing by his move-
order and has permitted the game
option, which may possibly be a tad
better than ...♘b6. But it seems Sam
was concerned about the recapture
with the c-pawn, in which case he
would presumably have refrained
from c2-c4 and just developed with

♘f3, ♗e2, and 0-0, since ...♗g4 at
any time can be met by h2-h3 when
a trade on f3 will favor White due
to the loose d5-knight. If White
had already played c4 ♘b6 then
he would probably have to spend a
tempo on h2-h3 to prevent ...♗g4.
I think that Sam is right and that
this move-order will catch on.
The real main line is 4.♘f3, when
4...dxe5 5.♘xe5 c6 has become
the main line, with just a small
white plus. It's hard to say which
line gives more, 4.exd6 or 4.♘f3,
but there is less to learn and more
surprise value with the exchange so
I'm going with that.

4...exd6 5.c4 ♘f6

The novelty 5...♘e7 may be the best
move: 6.h3 g6 7.♘f3 ♗g7 8.♗d3 0-0
9.0-0 d5 10.cxd5 ♘xd5 11.♗g5 ♕d6
12.♘c3± (+0.25). White's superior
development defines his advantage.
5...♘b6 normally arises from 4.c4
♘b6 5.exd6 exd6 so it is far more
common in the database than the
game move, but probably not better
than the game move in the given
position. 6.♘c3 ♗e7 7.♗d3 ♘c6
8.♘ge2 0-0 9.0-0

analysis diagram

9...♖e8 (9...♘b4?! 10.♗b1 ♘xc4??
11.a3 ♘c6 12.♕d3 – this well-known
trap wins a knight; 9...♗g4 10.f3
♗h5 11.b3 ♖e8 12.♗e4± (+0.32).
White's space advantage counts
extra when all the pieces are on the
board) 10.b3 a5 11.♗e3 ♘b4 12.♗b1
a4 13.a3 axb3 14.♕xb3 ♘c6 15.c5
dxc5 16.dxc5 ♘d7 17.♖d1 ♗g5 18.♘f4
♗xf4 19.♗xf4 ♕h4 20.♘d5 ♘xc5
21.♕c3 ♘e6 22.♗g3 ♕h5 23.♗e4
♖a4 24.♗f3 ♕g6 25.♘xc7 ♘xc7
26.♗xc7± (+0.30). White is up the
bishop pair.

**6.♘f3 ♗e7 7.♘c3 0-0 8.d5 ♗g4
9.♗e2 ♘fd7 10.0-0 ♘a6**

11.♗e3

11.a3 ♖e8 12.♗e3 ♗f6 13.♖c1 ♘ac5
14.b4 ♘e4 15.♘xe4 ♖xe4 was a later
game between the same players
in the same event, when 16.c5 was
good and favorable (+0.33). I prefer
the current game.

**11...♖e8 12.♕d2 ♗f6 13.♖ae1 ♘ac5
14.b3**

14.b4 ♘e4 15.♘xe4 ♖xe4 16.c5±
(+0.26). White has a large space
advantage and initiative.

**14...a5 15.♘d4 ♗xe2 16.♖xe2 ♘e5
17.♘db5 ♘ed7**

18.♖fe1

White has more space, so preventing a knight trade on e4 by 18.♕c2 is natural: 18...h6 19.h3 ♗g5 20.f4 ♗f6 21.♔h2 g6 22.♗f2 ♖xe2 23.♕xe2± (+0.58). White has a nice space advantage and Black lacks a good plan.

18...♘e4 19.♘xe4 ♖xe4 20.f3

20.♕c2 ♖e8 21.h3 h6 22.♗f4± (+0.68). White has a nice space advantage and control of the open file.

20...♖e8 21.♗f2

21.♘c3±.

21...♖xe2 22.♕xe2 ♘e5 23.f4 ♘g6 24.g3

24.♕e4±.

24...c6 25.dxc6 bxc6 26.♘d4 ♕d7 27.♕d3 ♘e7 28.♘f3 d5 29.♗c5 h6 30.♔g2 ♕f5 31.♕xf5 ♘xf5 32.cxd5 cxd5 33.♖d1 d4 34.♖d2 ♖d8 35.g4

35.♗b6±.

35...♘e3+ 36.♔h3 ♘d5 37.♗xd4 ♘xf4+ 38.♔g3 ♘e2+ 39.♖xe2 ♗xd4 40.♘xd4 ♖xd4 41.♖e8+ ♔h7 42.♖a8 ♖d5 43.♔f4 h5 44.h3 f6 45.♖a7

Draw agreed.

**Game 1.3   Various Openings –
Nimzowitsch Defense**

Magnus Carlsen   2851
Tigran L. Petrosian   2611

Internet blitz 3 + 2 2016 (11)

1.e4

I rarely choose blitz games, but this is the World Champion and I couldn't find a recent high level standard game with the line I wanted.

1...♘c6

The Nimzowitsch Defense, sometimes used by 1...e5 players to aim for the main lines while avoiding the King's Gambit. But why avoid the King's Gambit as Black?

2.♘f3

2.d4 is objectively the best move, to avoid letting Black transpose back to main line Spanish. But if you believe your opponent actually wants to stick to the Nimzowitsch, 2.♘f3 is best.

2...d6

The only serious alternative to the transposition 2...e5.

3.d4 ♘f6 4.♘c3 ♗g4 5.d5

5...♘b8

5...♘e5 6.♗b5+ (6.♘xe5 ♗xd1
7.♗b5+ c6 8.dxc6 dxe5 9.c7+ ♕d7
10.♗xd7+± (+0.30) is a sound
queen sacrifice which leads to a
slightly better endgame for White
due to a healthy vs crippled pawn
majority, but the bishop check
seems to give White more) 6...♘ed7
(6...c6 7.dxc6 ♘xc6 (7...bxc6?
8.♘xe5+−) 8.e5 dxe5 9.♗xc6+ bxc6
10.♕xd8+ ♖xd8 11.♘xe5± (+0.50).
White will emerge with better
development and a better pawn
structure) 7.a4 g6 8.a5 a6 9.♗e2
♗g7 10.0-0 0-0 11.♗e3 c6 12.h3
♗xf3 13.♗xf3 ♕c7 14.♖e1± (+0.27).
White has the bishops and a hole
on b6 to utilize.

**6.h3 ♗xf3 7.♕xf3 ♘bd7 8.g4 g6
9.♗e3 ♗g7 10.0-0-0**

10...c5
10...c6 11.♔b1 ♖c8 12.♗e2 0-0 13.h4±
(+0.78). White has a strong attack
plus the bishop pair.

11.♕e2?!
11.♕g2! ♖b8 12.f4 ♕a5 (12...b5
13.♗xb5 0-0 14.♗d2± (+0.44). Both
sides have an attack, but White
has a pawn; 12...0-0 13.h4± (+1.35).
White has a probably winning
attack) 13.e5 dxe5 14.f5 b5 15.d6 b4

16.♘d5 ♕xa2 17.♘c7+ ♔d8 18.♘a6
c4 19.♗xc4 ♕xc4 20.♘xb8 ♘xb8
21.♕b7 ♘fd7 22.♗xa7+−.

11...b5 12.g5
12.♕xb5! 0-0 13.♕a6± (+0.80).
Attacking chances are balanced, but
White is up 1.5 pawns.

12...♘h5 13.♘xb5
13.♕xb5!±.

13...♖b8 14.c3 ♕a5 15.a4

15...♘b6?
15...♕xa4 16.♕c2 ♕a5 17.♘a3 0-0=.

16.♘c7+ ♔d8 17.♕a6
17.♕b5!±.

17...♕xa4
17...♗xc3!.

**18.♗b5 ♕xa6 19.♘xa6 ♖b7 20.♗c6
♔c8**

21.b4
21.♔c2+− (+2.62). White aims for
♖a1.

21...♘c4 22.bxc5 ♘xe3?
22...♖b2!=.
23.fxe3+− ♖b3 24.♖d4??
24.♔c2!.
24...dxc5?
24...♗xd4 25.exd4 ♖a3∓.
**25.♔c2 cxd4 26.♔xb3 dxe3 27.♔c2
♗e5 28.♖b1 e2 29.♔d2 ♘g3 30.♖b7
♗xc3+ 31.♔d3 ♗e5 32.♖xa7 ♗b8
33.♖a8 e1♕ 34.♖xb8**
Mate.

Game 1.4   Scandinavian Defense –
            Marshall Variation
David Baramidze   2614
Zbigniew Pakleza   2508
Germany Bundesliga 2018/19 (8)

1.e4 d5
The Scandinavian (aka Center
Counter) Defense.
2.exd5 ♘f6

3.d4
3.♘f3 is a safer route to the same
position on move four, to avoid the
Portuguese Variation 3.d4 ♗g4.
3...♗g4 (3...♘xd5 4.d4 transposes to
the game) 4.♗b5+ ♘bd7 5.h3 ♗h5
6.♘c3 a6 7.♗e2 ♘b6 8.0-0 ♘fxd5
9.♘xd5 ♘xd5 10.d4 e6 11.c4 ♘f6

12.♗f4 ♗d6 13.♘e5 ♗xe2 14.♕xe2
0-0 15.♖ad1 (+0.60).

analysis diagram

White has more space and superior
development.
3...♘xd5
3...♗g4 4.f3 ♗f5 5.g4 ♗g6 6.c4
e6 7.♘c3 exd5 8.g5 ♘fd7 9.♘xd5
♘c6 10.h4 ♘b6 11.♕e2+ ♗e7 12.h5
♗f5 13.♘xe7 ♘xd4 14.♘xf5+ ♘xe2
15.♘xe2 0-0 16.♖h4 ♖e8 17.♔f2±
(+1.11).

Three minor pieces are generally
stronger than a queen, especially
when the rooks are on the board
and when the minors include the
bishop pair. So objectively 3.d4
is probably best, but 3.♘f3 gets
a smaller advantage in a much
simpler way when Black plays
3...♗g4.

4.♘f3 ♗g4

A) 4...g6 5.c4 ♘b6 6.♘c3 ♗g7 7.h3 0-0 8.♗e2 ♘c6 9.♗e3 e5 10.d5 ♘e7 11.g4 f5 12.♕b3 e4 13.♘g5 f4 14.♗c5 ♗xc3+ 15.bxc3 f3 16.♗f1 ♘exd5 17.h4 ♘e7 18.♗e3 c6 19.♖g1 ♕c7 20.0-0-0 c5 21.♘xe4+− (+1.50). White has a strong attack and c5 is doomed;

B) 4...♗f5 5.♗d3 ♗xd3 6.♕xd3 e6 7.0-0 c6 8.c4 ♘f6 9.♘c3 ♗e7 10.♗f4 0-0 11.♖ad1 ♘bd7 12.♕e2 ♖e8 13.♖d3± (+0.36). White has a space advantage and more active pieces.

5.c4 ♘b6 6.c5 ♘6d7 7.♗e2 e6

7...♘c6 8.0-0 e6 9.h3 ♗f5 10.♘c3 ♗e7 11.♗b5 0-0 12.♗xc6 bxc6 13.♕a4 ♘b8 14.♘e5 ♗f6 15.♖d1 ♕e7 16.♘c4± (+1.00). White's advantage in development and pawn structure is obvious.

8.♕b3

8...b6

8...♕c8 9.h3 ♗f5 10.♘c3 ♗e7 11.♗e3 ♘c6 12.g4 ♗g6 13.0-0-0 a5 14.a3 a4 15.♕c4 b6 16.h4 h5 17.gxh5 ♗xh5 18.d5 ♘a5 19.♕xa4 ♔f8 20.dxe6 ♘xc5 21.♗xc5 bxc5 22.exf7 ♕e6 23.♔b1 ♕xf7 24.♘e5 ♕f5+ 25.♕c2± (+1.21). White will remain a healthy pawn up with the better position.

9.0-0 ♗e7 10.♖d1 0-0 11.♘c3 c6 12.♗f4

Inserting 12.h3 first might be even a bit better.

12...♘f6

13.♖ac1

13.h3! ♗xf3 (13...♗h5 14.g4 ♗g6 15.♘e5±) 14.♗xf3 ♘d5 15.♘xd5 cxd5 16.♖ac1 bxc5 17.dxc5± (+0.52). White has the bishops and the more dangerous passed pawn.

13...b5?

13...♘bd7 14.h3 ♗h5 15.♕a4 b5 16.♕a6 ♕c8 17.♕xc8 ♖fxc8 18.g4 ♗g6 19.♗f1± (+0.38). White has space and a target on c6, with various plans to choose from.

14.a4+− (+1.42)

Since I can't find any meaningful improvements for Black after this, White is probably winning. Black can't complete his development without losses.

**14...a6 15.♕a3 ♘d5 16.♘xd5 ♕xd5
17.h3 ♗f5 18.axb5 cxb5 19.♕e3
♘c6 20.♘e5 ♗e4 21.f3 ♗g6
22.♘xc6 ♕xc6 23.d5 exd5 24.♕xe7
♖fe8 25.♕d6 ♕xd6 26.cxd6 1-0**

Game 1.5   Scandinavian Defense –
                Main Line
Shiyam Thavandiran   2410
Daniel Naroditsky   2616
Burlingame 2019 (2)

1.e4 d5 2.exd5 ♕xd5 3.♘c3 ♕a5
This (rather than 3...♕d6) may
be making a comeback due to the
line shown in this game, although
White retains an edge.
4.d4 ♘f6
4...c6 5.♘f3 ♗f5 6.♗c4 e6 7.♗d2
♘f6 see note to move 7.
5.♘f3 ♗f5
For 5...c6 6.♗c4 ♗f5 see next note.
6.♗c4

6...e6
6...c6 7.♗d2 ♕c7 8.♘e5 e6 9.g4 ♗e4
10.♘xe4 ♘xe4 11.♗f4 ♘d7 12.♕f3
♕a5+ 13.c3 ♘xe5 14.♗xe5 ♘d6
15.♗b3± (+0.57). White has the
bishop pair in an open position plus
better development.

7.♗d2

7...♗b4
Everyone used to play ...c7-c6 here
(or earlier), but lately the game
move is more popular, French GM
Eric Prié being its biggest advocate.
Black loses the bishop pair but
avoids worse problems as shown in
the note.
7...c6 8.♘d5 ♕d8 9.♘xf6+ ♕xf6 (9...
gxf6 10.0-0 ♘d7 11.♖e1 ♕c7 12.♘h4
♗g6 13.g3 0-0-0 14.c3 ♗d6 15.b4±
(+0.92). White has space, attack,
and better pawn structure, and
potentially the bishop pair) 10.♕e2
♘d7 11.0-0-0 ♘b6 12.♗g5 ♕g6
13.h4 ♗e7 14.♗xe7 ♔xe7 15.♗d3
♖hd8 16.♔b1± (+0.45). Black's king
in the center and space are White's
advantages.
8.a3 ♗xc3 9.♗xc3 ♕b6

10.d5

10.0-0 is the way to play if you don't want to play a favorable but drawish endgame: 10...♘c6 (10...0-0 11.a4 ♖d8 12.b3 ♕d6 13.♗b2± (+0.11), Lc0 +0.33. The position is not very open, which limits the value of the bishops, but they are still an asset) 11.b4 0-0 12.♖e1 ♗g4 13.h3 ♗xf3 14.♕xf3 ♘xd4 15.♕f4 ♘xc2 16.♗xf6 gxf6 17.♖e4 e5 18.♕g3+ ♔h8 19.♖h4 ♘d4 20.♗d3 e4 21.♖xe4 ♖g8 22.♕f4 ♖ad8 23.♖e7 f5 24.♗f1 ♕f6 25.♖ae1 ± (+0.01), Lc0 +0.40. White will regain his pawn with the better pawn structure.

10...♘bd7

10...exd5 11.♗xd5 0-0 12.♗xf6 gxf6 13.0-0 ♘c6 14.♗xc6 ♕xc6 15.♘d4± (+0.60). White's pawn structure advantage is for free.

11.dxe6

11.0-0! 0-0 (11...0-0-0 12.♗d4 c5 13.dxc6 ♕xc6 14.♕e2 ♗g4 15.♗b5 ♗xf3 16.gxf3 ♕d5 17.♖ad1 ♕f5 18.♔h1 ♖hg8 19.♖g1 g5 20.a4± (+0.88). White has two bishops for two knights and the stronger attacking chances. Or 11...exd5 12.♖e1+ ♗e6 13.♗xd5 ♘xd5

14.♕xd5 0-0-0 was played and held twice in 2018-19 by Eric Prié as Black, but neither opponent found 15.♕g5!, which ultimately seems to win a pawn for nothing according to all the top engines, though this is far from obvious) 12.dxe6 ♗xe6 13.♗xe6 ♕xe6 14.♖e1 ♕f5 15.♘h4 ♕d5 16.♕d4 ♕xd4 17.♗xd4 g6 18.♘f3 ♖fe8 19.♔f1± (+0.27). With a strong bishop for a knight in an open position White must be for choice, but the symmetrical pawn structure gives Black good drawing chances. The weakened long diagonal helps White though.

11...♗xe6 12.♗xe6 ♕xe6+ 13.♕e2 ♕xe2+ 14.♔xe2 0-0-0 15.♖he1

15...♘d5?!

Black should play 15...♖hg8 to avoid the capture of g7.

16.♗d2?!

16.♗xg7! ♖hg8 17.♗h6 ♖xg2 18.♖ad1 ♖g6 19.♗g5±.

16...♘c5 17.♔f1 ♖he8 18.♖xe8 ♖xe8 19.♖e1 ♖xe1+ 20.♔xe1 ♔d7= 21.♔e2 f6 22.c4 ♘b6 23.♗e3 ♘e6

White has the better side of a probable draw after 24.♗xb6.

½-½

Game 1.6   Scandianavian Defence –
Tiviakov Variation

Ivan Saric 2690

Wojciech Moranda 2593

Pro League Stage 2019 (10)

1.e4 d5 2.exd5 ♕xd5 3.♘c3

3...♕d6

This formerly rare move,
popularized by GM Sergei Tiviakov,
has become the main line.
3...♕d8 4.d4 ♘f6 5.♘f3 ♗g4 6.h3
♗xf3 7.♕xf3 c6 8.♗e3 e6 9.♗d3
♘bd7 10.0-0-0 ♗b4 11.♘e2 ♘d5
12.♔b1 ♘xe3 13.fxe3 ♗d6 14.♖hf1±
(+0.34). White has the center, better
development, and attacking chances.
4.d4 ♘f6 5.♘f3

5...♗g4

A) 5...c6 6.g3 ♗g4 7.♗g2 e6 8.0-0
♗e7 9.♗f4 ♕d8 10.h3 ♗h5 11.g4
♗g6 12.♘e5 ♘bd7 13.♘xg6 hxg6
14.♘e2 ♘b6 15.♕d3± (+0.38). White
has the bishops in an open position
and better development;

B) 5...a6 6.g3 ♗g4 7.♗g2 ♘c6
8.0-0 0-0-0 9.d5 ♘e5 10.♗f4 ♘xf3+
11.♗xf3 ♗xf3 12.♕xf3 e5 13.dxe6
♕xe6 14.♗g5 ♗d6 15.♖ae1 ♗e5
16.♘a4 ♖he8 17.♘c5 ♕d5 18.♕xd5
♖xd5 19.♗xf6 gxf6 20.♘d3 ♖e6
21.♖e4± (+0.38). White has the
much better pawn structure;

C) 5...g6 6.♘b5 ♕b6 7.a4 c6 8.a5
♕d8 9.♘c3 ♗g7 10.h3 0-0 11.♗c4
♘d5 12.♘e4N ♗f5 13.♘g3 ♗e6
14.♘g5 ♗c8 15.0-0± (+0.48). White
has a nice space and development
advantage.

6.h3 ♗h5

6...♗xf3 7.♕xf3 c6 8.♗f4!! ♕xd4
9.♘b5 cxb5 10.♗xb5+ ♘bd7 11.♕xb7
♕e4+ 12.♕xe4 ♘xe4 13.♗c6 ♘xf2
14.♗xa8 ♘xh1 15.♗c6+− (+1.50).
White will regain the piece with a
winning position.

7.g4 ♗g6 8.♘e5 ♘bd7

9.♘xg6

9.♗f4 is also good, and was
Caruana's choice against the same
opponent the same day, but I find
the game move more convincing.

9...♘xe5 10.♗xe5 ♕b6 (10...♕b4
11.♗d3 e6 12.a3 ♕a5 13.0-0
0-0-0 14.♘b5N ♗xd3 15.♕xd3 a6
16.a4!± ♘e8 17.b4 ♗xb4 18.♖fb1
h5 19.g5± (+0.28). White's attack is
more significant than his half-pawn
deficit) 11.♕f3 0-0-0 12.0-0-0 e6
13.♗d3 ♗b4 14.♘e2± (+0.36). White
has more space and play on either
wing.

9...hxg6 10.♗g2 c6 11.d5
11.g5 ♘d5 12.0-0 ♘f4 13.♘e4 ♕c7
14.♕g4 ♘xg2 15.♔xg2 0-0-0 16.♗f4
♕a5 17.♖ad1± (+0.53). White
has space and development, and
potential queenside attack.
11...cxd5 12.♘xd5 (+0.30)
Since White is now up the bishop
pair in an open position, with
development and pawn structure
fairly equal, he is now clearly better.
**12...0-0-0 13.♗f4 e5 14.♗e3 ♘c5
15.♘xf6 ♕xd1+ 16.♖xd1 ♖xd1+
17.♔xd1 gxf6 18.♗d5 ♖h7 19.♔e2
♘e6**

20.♗xe6+
20.h4 b6 21.h5 ♔c7 22.♗c4 ♘d4+
23.♗xd4 exd4 24.f4± (+0.64). White
will probably win a pawn or at
least reach a position where Black's

doubled pawns are useless, leaving
White effectively a pawn ahead.
**20...fxe6 21.♗xa7 b6 22.♗xb6 ♖b7
23.♗e3 ♖xb2 24.h4**
24.♖a1 f5 25.a4 ♖xc2+ 26.♔d3 ♖c7
27.a5 ♗c5 28.♖c1 e4+ 29.♔e2 ♗f8
30.♖xc7+ ♔xc7 31.a6 e5 32.g5+−
(+4.97). White will win the bishop
for his extra kingside pawn.
**24...♖xa2 25.♔d3 f5 26.h5 e4+
27.♔c3 gxh5 28.gxh5 ♗g7+ 29.♗d4
♖a3+? 30.♔b2?**
30.♔b4 ♗f8+ 31.♗c5 ♗xc5+
32.♔xc5+−.
**30...♖a7 31.♗xg7 ♖xg7 32.h6 ♖h7
33.♔c3 ♔d7 34.♔d4 ♔d6 35.♖h5
e5+ 36.♔e3 ♔d5 37.c4+ ♔xc4
38.♖xf5 ♖xh6?**
38...♔d5 39.♖h5 ♔e6 40.♔xe4
♔f7±. Black should hold with
correct defense.
**39.♔xe4 ♔c5 40.♔xe5 ♔c6 41.♖f6+
1-0**

Game 1.7 Pirc Defense – Pribyl
Sergey Karjakin   2753
Tigran L. Petrosian   2598
St Petersburg Wch rapid 2018 (13)

1.e4 d6 2.d4 ♘f6 3.♘c3 c6

The Pribyl Defense, not often seen in high level play these days.

4.f4

If White 'chickens out' with 4.♘f3, Black can play the Pirc, when ♘f3 is probably not the best option for White.

4...♕a5 5.♗d3 e5 6.♘f3 ♗g4

6...exd4 7.♘xd4 g6 8.0-0 ♗g7 9.♔h1 0-0 10.f5 ♘bd7 11.♕e1 ♖e8 12.♕h4 ♘e5 13.♗e2± (+0.52). White has more space and kingside attacking prospects.

7.♗e3 ♘bd7 8.0-0 ♗e7 9.h3

9...♗xf3

9...♗h5 10.♕e1 ♗xf3 11.♖xf3 0-0 12.a3 ♕c7 13.♖d1 b5 14.♔h1± (+0.40). White has the bishops and kingside play, perhaps with the pawn push g2-g4.

10.♕xf3 0-0 11.♘e2 ♗d8

11...c5 12.c3 cxd4 13.cxd4 ♗d8 14.a3 ♕a4 15.♗f2± (+0.87). White has the bishops, space, and probably the c-file.

12.c3 b5 13.a3 ♕a4 14.♖ad1

14.♘g3± (+1.25). White has superior development, the bishops, and a kingside attack.

14...♕b3 15.♖d2

15...♘b6??

15...♗b6 16.♘g3 g6 17.fxe5 dxe5 18.♔h1+− (+1.70). White has more space, the bishop pair, and pressure down the f-file. Probably Black will lose a pawn or the exchange.

16.dxe5 dxe5 17.fxe5 ♘fd7 18.♘d4 ♕a4 19.♘xc6+− b4 20.♘xb4 ♘xe5 21.♕g3 ♕e8 22.♘d5

With two healthy extra pawns and better development, White is obviously winning, but this was a rapid game so Black didn't resign.

22...♘g6?! 23.♗c5 ♘d7 24.♗b5 ♕e5 25.♕xe5 ♘dxe5 26.♗xf8 ♘xf8 27.b4 ♘e6 28.♖f5 f6 29.♖df2 h6 30.♖f1 ♔h7 31.♖5f2 a6 32.♗e2 ♘g5 33.♗g4 ♔h8 34.♖c2 ♘xe4 35.c4 ♘d6 36.c5 ♘b5 37.a4 ♘d4 38.♖d2 ♘b3 39.♖e2 a5 40.♖xe5 fxe5 41.♖f8+ ♔h7 42.c6 ♗b6+ 43.♘xb6 ♖xf8 44.bxa5 h5 45.♗xh5 ♘xa5 46.c7 ♘c4 47.c8♕ 1-0

Game 1.8 King's Fianchetto

Arthur Pijpers   2465
Arkadij Naiditsch   2721
Porto Carras tt 2018 (2)

1.e4 g6 2.d4 ♗g7 3.♘c3 d6

The Modern Defense – although it's been around a long time now. Since Black postpones ...♘f6 it makes more sense for White to strengthen d4 with ♗e3 rather than to expose it to a later ...e7-e5 with ♗f4. In the Pirc 4.♗e3 can be met by 4...c6, but here he has already committed to ..♗g7.

3...c5 4.dxc5 ♗xc3+ (4...♕a5?! 5.♗d2 ♕xc5 6.♘d5 ♘a6 7.♘f3 e6 8.b4 ♕f8 9.♘c3 ♘xb4? (9...♘c7 10.♖b1±) 10.♘b5 ♕c5 11.c3 ♘a6 12.♗e3 ♕c6 13.♘fd4 ♕c5 14.♖c1 ♕e7 15.♘f3+– (+2.00). White has a winning bind and development lead) 5.bxc3 ♕a5 6.♕d4 ♘f6 7.♕b4 ♕c7 8.♗d3± (+0.50). White's extra pawn seems worthless with tripled pawns, but unless Black plays ...b7-b6, untripling the pawns, he will have trouble developing, and meanwhile White has the bishop pair and space.

4.♗e3

4...a6
This is called 'Tiger's Modern', named after its popularizer, GM Tiger Hillarp Persson.
4...♘f6 5.♕d2 c6 6.♗h6 ♗xh6 7.♕xh6 ♕a5 8.♗d3 c5 9.d5 ♘bd7

10.0-0-0 b5 11.♗xb5 ♖b8 12.♗xd7+ ♗xd7 13.♘ge2 ♘g4 14.♕g7 ♖f8 15.f3 ♘f2 16.e5 ♖b6 17.exd6 ♖xd6 18.♘g3 ♗f5 19.a3 ♘xh1 20.♖xh1 h5 21.♕e5+– (+1.68). White has a pawn, superior development, immediate threats, and a strong attack for the exchange, enough to win.

5.f4
This line is justified by the time Black spends on ...a7-a6 and ...b7-b5.
5...b5 6.♘f3 ♗b7 7.♗d3 ♘d7 8.e5

8...e6
  A) 8...♘h6 9.♕e2 c5 10.dxc5 dxe5 11.♘xe5 ♘xe5 12.fxe5 0-0 13.0-0-0 ♕c7 14.♖he1 ♕xe5 15.♗g1 ♕xe2 16.♖xe2 ♖fe8 17.♖de1 ♔f8 18.♗e4 ♗xe4 19.♘xe4 ♘g4 20.c3 ♘e5 21.♔c2± (0.00), but Lc0 +0.47. With a strong passed pawn and more aggressive pieces White has the better endgame;
  B) 8...c5 9.♗e4 ♗xe4 (9...♕c8 10.♗xb7 ♕xb7 11.dxc5 dxe5 12.♕d5± (+0.58). I owe my GM title in part to a crucial qualifying game I won this way) 10.♘xe4 ♘h6 11.dxc5 ♘g4 12.♕e2 dxe5 13.0-0-0 ♕c7 14.fxe5 ♘gxe5 15.♘c3 e6 16.♗d4 0-0 17.♘xe5 ♘xe5 18.♘e4

♘c4 19.♗xg7 ♕f4+ 20.♔b1 ♔xg7
21.♘d6 ♘xd6 22.♖xd6 ♖ac8 23.♖f1
♕c4 24.♕xc4 bxc4 25.♖xa6 ♖xc5
26.♖a7 g5 27.b3 cxb3 28.axb3 ♔g6
29.c4± . White's connected passers
are more dangerous than Black's
kingside majority, although Black
can probably hold with best play.
Komodo rates it just even, but Lc0
gives +0.24.

9.a4 b4

Lc0 prefers 9...bxa4 10.♖xa4, but
Black wouldn't choose this defense
if he thought that was necessary.

10.♘e4 ♘e7

This Black set-up is known as
the 'Hippopotamus'. Since Black
concedes considerable space for
very little, White is surely better,
but it's not a huge advantage.
10...♘b6 11.a5 ♘d5 12.♗d2 f5
13.♘eg5 ♕d7 14.c4 bxc3 15.bxc3
h6 (Borisek-Bezold, PRO League
Stage rapid 2019) 16.♘xe6!!N ♕xe6
17.♖b1 dxe5 18.fxe5 ♗c6 19.c4 ♘ge7
20.cxd5 ♗xd5 21.♖c1 0-0 22.♖xc7± .
Black has inadequate compensation
for the pawn.

11.0-0

11...♘b6?

11...0-0 12.♕e2 a5 13.c4 bxc3 14.bxc3
♖b8 15.♗d2 ♘b6 16.g4± (+0.36).
White has a nice spatial plus having
deprived Black of the f5 outpost,
but this is playable for Black. White
plans h2-h4-h5.

12.c3

12.a5 ♘c4 13.♗c1 ♗xe4 14.♗xe4 d5
15.♗d3 c5 16.b3 ♘xa5 17.dxc5 0-0
18.♕e1 ♘ec6 19.♗e3± (+0.56). White
has the bishop pair plus pressure
down the a-file.

**12...0-0 13.a5 ♗xe4 14.♗xe4 ♘c4
15.♗c1 d5**

16.♗d3

16.♗c2 bxc3 17.b3 ♘d2 18.♘xd2 cxd2
19.♕xd2± (+0.80). White has a nice
space edge plus the bishops. He
plans ♗a3.

**16...bxc3 17.bxc3 c5 18.♗xc4 dxc4
19.dxc5 ♕c7 20.♗e3?!**

20.♕d6 ♕a7 21.♕b6 ♘d5 22.♕xa7
♖xa7 23.♘d2± .

**20...♘d5 21.♗d4 ♘xf4 22.♖a4 ♖ab8
23.♖xc4 ♕xa5 24.♕a4 ♕b5 25.g3?**

25.♖a1= .

**25...♘d3 26.c6 ♖fc8 27.♖a1 ♗xe5
28.♘xe5 ♘xe5 29.♕xb5 axb5
30.♗xe5 bxc4 31.♗xb8 ♖xb8 32.♖a4
♔f8 33.♖xc4 ♖c8∓**

Black is much better since White's c-pawns are redundant, but White did hold the draw.

34.g4 g5 35.h4 h6 36.hxg5 hxg5 37.♔f2 ♔e7 38.♔e3 ♔d6 39.♔d4 f6 40.♖a4 ♖xc6 41.c4 f5 42.gxf5 exf5 43.♖a8 g4 44.♖g8 ♔e7 45.♔e5 ♔f7 46.♖b8 g3 47.♖b7+ ♔g6 48.♖b3 ♖c5+ 49.♔f4 ♖xc4+ 50.♔xg3 ♔g5 51.♖a3 ♖g4+ 52.♔f3 ♖h4 53.♔g2 ♖h8 54.♔g3 f4+ 55.♔g2 ♔g4 56.♖b3 ♖a8 57.♔f2 ♖a2+ 58.♔f1 ♖c2 59.♖a3 f3 60.♖a8 ♖c1+ ½-½

Game 1.9 Pirc Defense
Gabor Papp   2591
Jure Skoberne   2572
Austria Bundesliga 2018/19 (5)

1.e4 d6 2.d4 ♘f6 3.♘c3 g6
The Pirc Defense, considered to be a relatively good choice for a must-win game, but it doesn't really equalize. For 3...e5 see the Philidor chapter.
4.♗f4

I didn't even know this was a serious move until recently, I always played 4.♗e3. The two may transpose if bishops are exchanged on h6, but other lines are quite different. Both give White some advantage, so I'm going with the one that has surprise value.
4...♗g7
4...c6 – the idea is to avoid wasting a move with the bishop in case White plays ♕d2 and ♗h6, and to prepare ...b7-b5 in case of queenside castling by White. 5.♘f3. So White waits for ...♗g7 before commiting to ♕d2. Now if Black plays ...b7-b5 White can play ♗d3 and castle kingside. 5...♗g7 6.♕d2 0-0 7.h3 (7.♗h6 b5 8.♗d3 ♗g4 (+0.14) is also a good line for White, but a bit risky in view of the likely exchange on f3. So White just prevents ...♗g4) and now:

A) 7...♕a5 8.♗d3 (+0.18) improves over 8.e5 as played by Maxime Vachier-Lagrave against Magnus Carlsen in Biel 2018. 8...♘bd7 9.0-0 e5 10.♗e3 ♖e8 11.dxe5 ♘xe5 12.♘xe5 dxe5

analysis diagram

13.a4!N (13.♘d5 ♕xd2 14.♘xf6+ ♗xf6 15.♗xd2 ♗e6 16.♗c3 ♗g7 17.a4. Lc0 prefers White, Komodo rates it dead even. I would say any white plus is minuscule) 13...♖d8 14.♘b1 ♕c7 15.♕c3 ♘h5 16.♖e1

♘f4 17.♗f1 ♘e6 18.♘d2 c5 19.♗c4± (+0.29). White has two good squares for his minors (d5 and c4) while Black has only one (d4), and even that one can be challenged eventually by c2-c3;

B) 7...b5 8.a3 a6 9.♗d3N ♗b7 10.♗h6 c5 11.♗xg7 ♔xg7 12.dxc5 dxc5 13.e5 ♘fd7 14.♗e4 ♗xe4 15.♘xe4 ♘c6 16.e6± (+0.46). White will emerge with better pawn structure for free.

5.♕d2 0-0 6.♗h6 e5 7.♗xg7 ♔xg7 8.♘ge2

8...c6

A) 8...c5 9.d5 b5 10.♘g3 b4 11.♘d1 ♘bd7 12.h4 h5 13.♕g5 ♘b6 14.a4 a5 15.♘e3± (+0.20). White has space and kingside threats;

B) 8...♘c6 9.f3 ♖b8 10.0-0-0 b5 11.dxe5 ♘xe5 12.♘f4 b4 13.♘cd5 ♘xd5 14.♘xd5 a5 15.h4 h5 16.♗e2 ♗e6 17.f4 ♘g4 18.♗xg4 ♗xg4 19.♖de1 c5 20.♘e3 ♕f6 21.♘xg4 hxg4 22.h5 ♕d4 23.♕xd4+ cxd4

24.♔d2± (+0.22). White's better pawn structure and better king position give him the better endgame.

9.0-0-0 ♕a5

9...♕e7 10.h4 h5 11.♘g3 b5 12.♕g5 ♖e8 13.♗e2 ♔h7 14.♖hf1±. White plans f2-f4.

10.h4 b5?!

10...h5 11.♘g3 ♘bd7 12.♗e2 exd4 13.♕xd4± (+0.66). Black must lose the d6-pawn or make serious concessions to save it.

11.dxe5 dxe5 12.h5 ♗e6?

This just drops a vital pawn for nothing.

12...♕c7 13.f3± (+0.68). White plans g2-g4 and ♘g3.

13.hxg6 fxg6 14.♕d6 ♖e8 15.♕xe5 ♘bd7 16.♕g5 ♕c7 17.♘d4 ♘e5 18.f4 ♘f7 19.♕h4 h6 20.e5 (+4.51) **1-0**

After 20...♘g8 21.♗d3 White has a winning attack and an extra pawn, so Black gave up.

CHAPTER 2

Caro-Kann

The Caro-Kann, **1.e4 c6**, followed by **2.d4 d5**, is one of the four main defenses to 1.e4, has a good reputation among top players, and is a favorite of mine as Black. It is quite difficult to demonstrate a meaningful advantage against it.

The traditional main line, where White allows the exchange on e4 and meets 4...♗f5 by 5.♘g3 followed by an early h4-h5 and castling queenside, gives White very little theoretically and practically. In the last couple decades the Advance Variation 3.e5 (as recommended in my 2003 book) has become the main line, and while it certainly gives White more space, Black has reasonable chances for counterplay or for reaching a position where progress by White is difficult. I have decided to give three (!) different systems against the Caro.

First I consider the Exchange Variation, but with a recent twist; after **3.exd5 cxd5 4.♗d3 ♘c6 5.c3 ♘f6** (or 5...♕c7) I give **6.h3** rather than the standard (5...♘f6) 6.♗f4 ♗g4.

White spends a tempo to prevent this ideal bishop development, so Black normally replies 6...g6 to prepare ...♗f5 (the only other active square for the bishop). However White can then either exchange to give Black damaged pawns, or, perhaps better, avoid the exchange by ♗e2 since the bishop on f5 is rather unstable with a pawn on g6 blocking its retreat. Basically White is playing the Black side of the Queen's Gambit Declined Exchange Variation, but with the opponent unable to post his bishop actively without a concession, as well as an extra tempo. See Game 2.1.

Next I go for a rare line (from the SOS column in *New In Chess*) where White allows the usual trade on e4 (**3.♘c3/d2 dxe4 4.♘xe4**)

but meets **4...♗f5** by **5.♕f3!?**. First I cover the less common **4...♘f6**, allowing White to double his pawns, which we do, meeting the now usual 5...exf6 by aiming to castle queenside and attack. See Game 2.2. Then comes the Smyslov Variation **4...♘d7**, which I meet by a plan I saw Bobby Fischer play 55 years ago! It still looks pretty good with the latest engines. See Game 2.3. After that is the 5.♕f3 line, which usually results in winning the bishop pair (a huge theme in this book). Game 2.4 shows that this can lead to a real advantage, not just a nominal one.

My main line against the Caro is the Two Knights Variation (**2.♘c3 d5 3.♘f3**), also a Fischer favorite.

It aims to win the bishop pair. I was a bit reluctant to include this as a lot of the lines are similar to those in Sielecki's *Keep It Simple* (New In Chess 2018), but I came across a game with a huge novelty that significantly alters the theory in White's favor. First I cover **the exchange on e4** in Game 2.5, which transposes to Game 2.3 if Black plays 4...♘d7, but is much better for White than the normal Caro if Black plays the dubious 4...♗f5 here, and is also different and perhaps better for White than normal in case of **4...♘f6**, since here White can play **5.♕e2** rather effectively since d4 doesn't hang. Next comes what has become the main line recently (or close to it anyway), **3...♘f6**. This is Game 2.6 with the above novelty, when White recaptures on g3 with the f-pawn rather than the h-pawn! This looks like a beginner's error at first, but the engines convinced me that it is correct and favors White.

The final two games feature **3...♗g4**, the usual move against the Two Knights until recently. After **4.h3**, Black must choose.

If he **retreats to h5**, White has a forcing sequence that usually results in White winning a bishop for three pawns (so half a pawn by my count), unless Black goes for a dubious pawn gambit. See Game 2.7. Therefore Black usually **takes on f3**, after which it's not so clear what Black has for the bishop pair ('half pawn'). White is usually able to achieve d2-d4 at some point, after which Black normally trades on e4 even though this opens the game for the bishop pair. The only tricky part is that you must play accurately to get in d2-d4 without losing the d4-pawn or losing too much time. See Game 2.8.

Game 2.1 Caro-Kann Defense –
Exchange Variation

Fabiano Caruana 2828
Samuel Shankland 2725

PRO League Stage rapid 2019 (4)

1.e4 c6 2.d4 d5 3.exd5 cxd5 4.♗d3
I decided to include this Exchange
Variation as a White alternative
when I saw that 6.h3 had some
sting to it. It looks fairly promising.
4...♘c6 5.c3 ♘f6
5...♕c7 6.h3 ♘f6 7.♘f3 g6 8.0-0
♗g7 (8...♗f5 9.♗e2 ♗g7 transposes
to the note to move 9 below)
9.♖e1 0-0 10.♘bd2 ♖e8 11.♘f1
(11.♘b3± (+0.35)) 11...♘h5 12.♘e3
♘f4 (12...♘f6 13.♘c2± (+0.32). Black
is unlikely to achieve a minority
attack) 13.♗f1 ♗d7

analysis diagram

14.h4?! (14.♘g4 ♖ad8 15.♘ge5±
(+0.64). White will have a real
advantage in space and piece
placement) 14...♕d6 15.g3 ♘h5 16.♗g2
± ♘f6 17.♘c2 ♘h5 18.b3 ♗f5 19.a4
♕c7 20.♘e3 ♗e4 21.♗a3 ♖ad8 22.b4
e5 23.b5 exd4 24.cxd4 ♗xf3 25.♗xf3
♘xd4 26.♗xh5 gxh5 27.♗b2 ♖e4
28.♕xh5 ♖de8 29.♔g2 ♘c2 30.♗xg7
♘xe1+ 31.♖xe1 ♔xg7 32.♕g5+ ♔h8

33.♕f6+ ♔g8 34.♘f5 1-0 Caruana-
Khamrakulov, chess.com INT 2019.

6.h3
Normal until recently was 6.♗f4
♗g4 7.♕b3, but World Number 2
Caruana and other GMs have been
playing the text move lately, and it
does seem to present more problems
for Black than the older line.
6...g6
6...e6 7.♗f4 ♗d6 8.♗xd6 ♕xd6
9.♘f3 ♘e4 10.0-0 0-0 11.♖e1 f5
12.♘bd2 ♗d7 13.♗b5 ♘b8 14.♗f1
♘c6 15.♘b3± (+0.27). Black's bad
bishop and backward e6-pawn are
White's advantage. White can aim
for ♘b3-c1-d3.
7.♘f3
7.♗f4 ♗f5 8.♗e2 ♗g7 9.♘f3 0-0
10.0-0 transposes to the game.

7...♗f5

7...♗g7 8.♗f4 0-0 9.0-0 ♘h5 10.♗h2 ♗h6 11.♖e1 ♘f4 12.♗f1 ♕b6 13.b4 ♕c7 14.♘bd2± (+0.72). The pin is very annoying, and White has a queenside initiative. It's a surprisingly large edge for White.

8.♗e2

8.0-0 is more common and probably also slightly more comfortable for White, but preserving the good bishop is logical.

8...♗g7 9.0-0 0-0

9...♕c7 10.♖e1 0-0 11.♗e3 ♘e4 12.♘bd2 ♖ad8 13.♕c1 ♖fe8 14.♗f1 h6 15.♘h4 ♔h7 16.♘xf5 gxf5 17.♘f3± (+0.20). Black has little for the bishop pair; his outposted knight is offset by broken kingside pawn structure.

10.♗f4 ♘e4 11.♘bd2

11...♖e8

11...♖c8 12.♖e1 h6 13.♗f1 g5 14.♗h2 e6 15.♘xe4 ♗xe4 16.♘d2 ♗f5 17.♘b3 ♖e8 18.♗d3± (+0.36). The exchange of the light-squared bishops will leave the black king slight weakened. Black's usual minority attack doesn't look like a realistic option here.

11...f6 12.♘xe4 ♗xe4 13.♕b3 ♕d7 14.♖fe1 ♖ad8 15.♗g3± (+0.33). White

will expel the bishop by ♘d2 and then Black will have a weak e-pawn.

12.♖e1 h6 13.♗f1 g5 14.♗h2 ♕d7

15.♘xe4

15.♘b3 e6 16.a4 ♕d8 17.♘fd2 ♘d6 18.♘c5 b6 19.♘d3± (+0.33). Black has to either allow an outpost on e5 or create a weakness with ...f7-f6.

15...♗xe4 16.♗d3

16.a4! e6 17.a5 a6 18.♘e5 ♘xe5 19.♗xe5± (+0.36). Black's king will be weaker than White's however he plays.

16...f5 17.♗f1

A) 17.♗c2 ♗xc2 18.♕xc2 f4 19.h4 e5 20.dxe5 ♘xe5 21.♘xe5 ♗xe5 22.♕g6+ ♕g7 23.♕h5 ♖e7 24.♖ad1 ♖d8 25.hxg5 hxg5 26.g3 fxg3 27.♗xg3=;

B) 17.♘e5 ♘xe5 18.♗xe5 ♗xe5 19.dxe5 ♗xd3 20.♕xd3 e6 21.c4 ♖ad8 22.♖ad1=.

17...f4 18.♗d3 ♗xf3 19.♕xf3 e5 20.♕h5 e4

20...exd4 21.cxd4 ♖e6=.

21.♗e2 ♖e7 22.♗g4

22.f3 ♖f8 23.fxe4 dxe4 24.♖f1=.

22...♕e8 23.g3? f3

23...♕xh5 24.♗xh5 f3∓.

24.♕xe8+ ♖axe8 25.♗f5 ♖d8 26.g4 b5? 27.b4 a5? 28.a4± bxa4?

**29.b5+– ♘a7 30.♖eb1 ♖b7 31.b6
♘c6 32.♗c7 ♔f7 33.♗xd8 ♘xd8
34.♖xa4 ♘c6 35.♖b5 1-0**

Game 2.2 Caro-Kann Defense

Alexander Predke 2620
Ziaur Rahman 2470

New Delhi 2019 (10)

**1.e4 c6 2.d4 d5 3.♘c3 dxe4 4.♘xe4
♘f6 5.♘xf6+**

5...exf6

White's pawn majority is now more useful than Black's, but Black will maintain equality in development and king safety so he is only slightly worse.

The 5...gxf6 recapture, a favorite of the great Bent Larsen long ago, has almost disappeared from grandmaster play, apparently because the simple plan of c2-c3, ♘f3, g2-g3, and ♗g2 leaves Black reluctant to castle queenside but with no compensation for his poor pawn structure otherwise. 6.c3 ♗f5 7.♘f3 e6 8.g3 ♕d5 9.♗g2 ♕c4 10.♘h4 ♗g6 11.♗f3 ♕d3 12.♕b3 ♕a6 13.♗e2 ♕b6 14.♕d1 ♘d7 15.0-0 ♗e7 16.a4 a5 17.♖e1 f5 18.♘g2± (+0.95). Black has a poor pawn

structure and a very bad bishop on g6, while White has good squares for his pieces.

**6.c3 ♗d6 7.♗d3 0-0 8.♕c2 ♖e8+
9.♘e2**

9...h5

Until 2018, 9...g6 and 9...h6 were preferred as the text looks risky, but computers have convinced the GMs that it is really the best move as it is not purely defensive.

10.0-0

10.♗e3 to castle queenside and 10.h3 to meet 10...♘d7 with 11.g4 are also good moves chosen by GMs, but simply castling looks like a safe route to an edge.

10...♘d7?!

10...h4 11.h3 ♘d7 12.♗e3 ♘f8 13.♖ad1 ♗c7 14.c4 ♕d6 15.♗f4 (15.♘f4 ♗e6 16.c5 ♕e7 17.b4 ♖ad8 18.♘xe6 ♘xe6 19.♗c4 ♗b8 20.d5 cxd5 21.♗xd5 ♕c7 22.f4 g6 23.♗b3± (+0.17). White has the bishop pair for an edge) 15...♖xe2 16.♗xd6 ♖xc2 17.♗a3 ♗e6 18.♗xc2 ♗xc4 19.♖fe1 ♘e6 20.♗b4 ♖d8 21.b3 ♗d5 22.♔f1 (+0.17). Black may ultimately win a second pawn (d4) for the exchange but only at the price of allowing multiple trades favoring White, and one of his two pawns is not very useful.

11.♘g3 ♕c7

12.h3

12.♘xh5!. Only a computer would find the following sequence over the board: 12...♗xh2+ 13.♔h1 ♗d6 14.♗c4 ♘f8 15.♗h6! ♗e6 16.♗d3! gxh6 17.♕d2!± (+0.90). Black has to return the piece by ...♗f4 after which his awful pawn structure around the king gives White a clear advantage.

12...♗xg3 13.fxg3 ♘f8

13...♕xg3?! 14.♗f4 ♕h4 15.g3 ♕xh3 16.♖ae1 ♖xe1 17.♖xe1 g6 18.♗xg6 ♘f8 19.♖e8 ♕g4 20.♗d3 b5 21.♕e2 ♗b7 22.♖xa8 ♗xa8 23.♕xg4+ hxg4 24.♗f5+− (+1.27). With the bishop pair, a good majority vs a crippled one, and a bad black bishop, White should win.

14.♗f4

14.♕f2 ♗e6 15.c4 ♖ad8 16.♗e3± (+0.76). White has the bishops and the more useful majority.

14...♕d8 15.♕f2 ♗e6 16.c4?!

16.♖fe1± (+0.68). Same comment as previous note.

16...♕a5

16...♘g6! 17.♗e3 ♘e5 18.dxe5 ♕xd3 19.exf6 ♗xc4 20.♖fe1 ♖e5 21.fxg7 ♖ae8± (+0.78). Here I agree with

Lc0 that White's extra pawn will not mean very much.

17.♗d2± (+1.02)

White has the bishop pair and a much more useful pawn majority, and Black's h5-pawn is potentially weak.

17...♕b6 18.♗c3 ♖ad8 19.♖ad1 ♕c7 20.b3 b5 21.♕f3 bxc4 22.bxc4 ♕d6 23.♖d2

23.♕xh5 ♕xg3 24.♖f3± (+0.70). Again, White has the bishops and the greater chance of a passed pawn.

23...♕a3 24.♖c2 ♕d6 25.♖cf2 ♘g6 26.♔h1 ♕c7 27.♖e2 ♘f8 28.♖fe1 ♗d7 29.♗e4 ♘e6? 30.♕xh5+− ♘g5 31.♔h2 ♕d6 32.♗c2 ♖xe2 33.♖xe2 ♖e8 34.♖xe8+ ♗xe8 35.♕e2 ♗d7 36.♕d3 g6 37.♕e3 ♕e6 38.♕xe6 ♗xe6 39.♗b3 ♘e4 40.♗b4 f5 41.d5 cxd5 42.cxd5 ♗d7 43.♗c2 ♔g7 44.g4 ♔f6 45.gxf5 ♔xf5 46.♗d6 1-0

Game 2.3   Caro-Kann Defense – Smyslov
Emil Sutovsky   2647
Vladimir Fedoseev   2706
Poikovsky 2018 (3)

1.e4 c6 2.d4 d5 3.♘d2 dxe4 4.♘xe4 ♘d7

This Smyslov Variation has fallen out of favor.

5.♘f3

The main line starts with 5.♘g5 but is rather complicated, and there is no need to go for that to get a modest edge.

5...♘gf6 6.♘xf6+

The alternative 6.♘c3!? was dismissed as 'obviously' inferior to 6.♘g3 in my younger days, since it disconnects c2 from d4, but it has the benefit of allowing for the placement of the dark-squared bishop on f4 or g3: 6...e6 7.♗d3 ♗e7 8.0-0 0-0 9.♕e2 c5 10.♖d1 cxd4 11.♘xd4 ♖e8 12.a4 a6 13.a5 (+0.18). This is slightly more pleasant for White, but I prefer the game continuation.

6...♘xf6 7.c3

7...♕c7

A) 7...♗f5 8.♘e5

A1) 8...♘d7 9.♘xf7 ♔xf7 10.♕f3 e6 11.g4 ♕f6 12.gxf5 ♕xf5 13.♕xf5+ exf5 14.♗c4+ ♔f6 15.h4 ♖e8+ 16.♔f1 g6 17.♗f4± (+0.70). White's bishop pair looks quite potent here;

A2) 8...♘d5 9.♕f3 g6 10.♗d3 ♕c8 11.0-0 f6 12.♘c4 ♗xd3 13.♕xd3 ♗g7

14.♖e1 0-0 15.♗d2± (+0.32). The weak pawn on e7 and weak square e6 give White an obvious though small edge;

A3) 8...e6?. This obvious move is a well-known error. I witnessed Bobby Fischer catch someone in it in a simul in 1964, and I never forgot it: 9.g4 ♗g6 10.h4 ♗d6! 11.♕e2 c5! 12.dxc5 ♗e4!? 13.cxd6 ♗xh1 14.g5 ♘d7 15.♗f4 0-0 16.0-0-0 ♘xe5 17.♕xe5 ♗d5 18.c4 ♖c8 19.♔b1± (+1.08).

analysis diagram

With a series of clever computer moves Black has avoided material loss, but with a monster passed pawn on d6 and the bishop pair and kingside attack for the exchange White is clearly much better, probably winning;

B) 7...♗e6 8.h3 (oddly, the obvious 8.♗d3 is met by the time-losing 8...♗g4 since driving the bishop to g6 no longer helps White) 8...♗d5 9.♗d3 ♗xf3 10.♕xf3 ♕d5 11.♕g3 e6 12.♗e2± (+0.37). White has a clean bishop pair plus;

C) 7...♗g4 8.h3 ♗xf3 (8...♗h5 9.g4 ♗g6 10.♘e5 ♗e4

analysis diagram

11.f3 (11.♖g1N ♘d7 12.♕e2± (+0.32).
Black has development problems
due to the endangered bishop)
11...♗d5 12.♗e3 g6 13.c4 ♗e6
14.♗d3± (+0.41). Planning ♕e2 and
0-0-0) 9.♕xf3 ♕d5 10.♗e2 ♕xf3
(10...e6 11.♕g3±) 11.♗xf3 e6 12.♗d2
♗e7 13.0-0-0± (+0.40). Black has
no compensation for the bishop
pair, but with no weaknesses and a
good bishop has quite good drawing
chances.

8.♘e5 ♗e6 9.♗f4 ♕b6 10.♗c4

10.♕d2!± (+0.50). Black has
problems getting developed.

**10...♗xc4 11.♘xc4 ♕b5 12.♕e2 e6
13.♗d6?!**

13.a4 ♕d5 14.0-0 ♗e7 15.a5 0-0
16.a6 b6 17.♘e5± (+0.30). White has
a nice space edge, and the c6-pawn
is weak.

13...♖d8

13...♕d5! 14.♗xf8 ♕xg2 15.♗xg7
♕xh1+ 16.♕f1 ♕xf1+ 17.♔xf1 ♔e7
18.♗xh8 ♖xh8=.

**14.♗xf8 ♔xf8 15.a4 ♕d5 16.0-0 h5
17.♘e3**

17.♘e5 g6 18.a5 ♔g7 19.a6 b6 20.h3±
(+0.16). Again White has space and a
c6 target.

**17...♕e4 18.♕c4 ♔g8 19.♕b4 ♖d7
20.♕c5**

20.♖ae1 ♕f4 21.h3 h4 22.♕b3=.

20...a6

20...b6=.

21.♕e5?

21.♘c4 h4 22.♕e5±.

**21...♕xe5 22.dxe5 ♘g4 23.♘c4 b5
24.axb5 axb5 25.h3 bxc4 26.hxg4
hxg4 27.♖a4 ♖h5 28.♖xc4 g3
29.fxg3 ♖xe5 30.♖xc6 ♖e2 31.b4
g5 32.♔h1 g4 33.b5 ♖dd2 34.♖c4
f5 35.♖g1 ♔f7 36.♖b4 ♖d8 37.♖gb1
♖dd2 38.♖g1 ♖d8 39.♖f1 ♖dd2
40.♖g1 ½-½**

Game 2.4   Caro-Kann Defense – Classical
Anton Demchenko   2679
Kacper Piorun   2634
Germany Bundesliga 2018/19 (8)

**1.e4 c6 2.d4 d5 3.♘d2 dxe4 4.♘xe4
♗f5**

5.♕f3

This rare line, played regularly
by only one top-level GM
(Demchenko), was not even
analyzed by Bologan in his recent
book on the Caro-Kann, but was
analyzed in 'S.O.S.' in New In Chess.
It aims simply to win the bishop

pair or extract some concession from Black to avoid this outcome. I expect this line to catch on, as it seems difficult to prove full equality for Black.

5...e6 6.♘e2 ♗e7

A) 6...♕d5 7.♘2g3 ♗xe4 8.♕xe4 ♘f6 9.♕xd5 cxd5 10.♗d3 ♘c6 11.c3± (+0.17). Black is down the bishop pair for only slight compensation;

B) 6...♘f6 7.♘xf6+ ♕xf6 8.♕b3 ♕e7 9.♘g3 ♗g6 10.h4 h5 11.♗d2± (+0.22). White is better developed than in the normal main line Caro, and the pawn on h5 can be a target;

C) 6...h5 7.c3 ♘d7 8.♘2g3 ♗g6 9.h4 ♘gf6 10.♗d3 ♘xe4 11.♗xe4 ♗xe4 12.♘xe4 ♘f6 13.♗g5 ♗e7 14.♗xf6 gxf6 15.0-0-0± f5 16.♘c5 ♕d5 17.♘xb7 ♖g8 18.♘c5 ♗xc5 19.dxc5 ♕xc5 20.g3±. Lc0 gives White a normal plus presumably due to his much better pawn structure, while Komodo thinks that Black's more active pieces give full compensation. I'm inclined to favor White myself.

7.c3

7...♘f6

After 7...♗xe4 8.♕xe4 ♘f6 9.♕f3 0-0 Black has an ephemeral lead in

development for the bishop pair, but the bishops are forever and the position is open: 10.g3 (10.g4!? is an Lc0 suggestion, claiming a small White edge. Obviously it is double-edged) 10...♘bd7 11.♗g2 e5 12.0-0 ♖e8 13.♕f5 exd4 14.♘xd4 ♗c5 15.♗e3.

analysis diagram

Already here Lc0 is quite happy. 15...♖e5 (15...g6 16.♕d3 ♘d5 (16...♘e5 17.♕d1±) 17.♗xd5 cxd5 18.♗f4 ♗b6 19.♖ad1± (+0.30). White has traded his bishop pair for a superior pawn structure) 16.♕d3 ♘d5 17.♗d2 ♖e8 18.♘f3 ♘7f6 19.b4 (White actually erred in Demchenko-Erenburg, chess. com 2019, by playing ♖ae1 first, which after the rook trade allowed ...♕b6 forking b2 and f2, and Black eventually won) 19...♗b6 20.♖ae1 ♖xe1 21.♖xe1 a5 22.b5 cxb5 23.♕xb5 ♖c8 24.♘g5± (+0.40). White has the bishop pair in an open position.

8.♘xf6+ ♗xf6 9.♘g3

9.♘f4 0-0 10.g4 ♗c2 11.♕e2 ♗a4 12.♘h5 ♘d7 13.♘xf6+ ♘xf6 14.♗g2± (+0.35). White has the bishops for free.

9...♗g6 10.♗e2

A) 10.♗c4 ♘d7 11.♘e4 0-0
12.♘xf6+ ♘xf6 13.a4± (+0.20). Black
has little to offset the bishops;

B) 10.♘e4 ♗e7 11.♗d3 0-0
12.h4!? ♗xh4 13.♘c5 b6 14.♗xg6
fxg6 15.♕h3 bxc5 16.♕xh4 ♕xh4
17.♖xh4± (+0.25). This is a pleasant
endgame for White despite being a
pawn down, both Komodo and Lc0
agree.

10...♕d5

10...0-0 11.♘h5 ♘d7 12.♘xf6+ ♘xf6
13.♕f4 ♗h5 14.g4 (+0.10). Lc0 gives
only +0.03, so perhaps you should
choose one of the move ten options.
Black has compensation for the
bishops here.

11.♗e3

11.♘h5 ♗xh5 12.♕xd5 exd5
13.♗xh5 g6 14.♗e2 h5 15.♗e3± is
similar to the game.

**11...♘d7 12.♘h5 ♗xh5 13.♕xd5
exd5 14.♗xh5 g6 15.♗e2 ♗g7
16.0-0-0**

16.g4± (+0.27). White avoids the
...h7-h5 defense played in the game.

**16...h5 17.♖de1 ♘f6 18.♔c2 ♔d7
19.f3 ♘e8**

20.h4

20.♗d3 ♗h6 21.♗f2± (+0.23). No
compensation for the bishop pair,

except that the symmetrical pawn
structure means good drawing
chances for Black.

**20...♘c7 21.g4 ♖ae8 22.♔d2 ♘e6
23.gxh5 ♖xh5 24.f4 ♖h7 25.h5
gxh5 26.♖xh5 ♖xh5 27.♗xh5 ♘d8
28.♗g4+ ♔d6 29.f5 ♖e4 30.♖g1 ♗f6
31.♔d3 b5 32.b3?!**

32.♗f2 ♘b7 33.♗g3+ ♔d7 34.♗h5
♖e7 35.♖e1±.

**32...♘b7 33.c4?! bxc4+ 34.bxc4 c5∓
35.dxc5+ ½-½**

Game 2.5   Caro-Kann Defense –
            Two Knights Variation

Sebastien Mazé   2578
Pavel Eljanov   2682

Skopje 2019 (8)

1.e4 c6 2.♘c3 d5

2...e5 3.♘f3 d6 4.d4 ♘d7 5.♗c4 ♗e7
6.a4 ♘gf6 7.0-0 0-0 transposes to
our line in the Philidor Defense.

3.♘f3

3...dxe4

3...g6 4.d4 ♗g7 (note that this
position can and often does arise
by 1.e4 g6 2.d4 ♗g7 3.♘c3 c6 4.♘f3
d5) 5.h3 ♘f6 (5...dxe4 6.♘xe4 ♘f6
7.♘xf6+ exf6 8.♗d3 0-0 9.0-0 ♖e8

10.♗e3± (+0.27). White has a healthy vs crippled pawn majority and better center control; 5...♘h6 6.♗d3 0-0 7.0-0 f6 8.♖e1 ♘f7 9.♗f1 b6 10.a4 a6 11.b4 ♗b7 12.♗a3 ♖e8 13.b5 axb5 14.axb5± (+0.63). White will emerge with a large space advantage and more active pieces) 6.♗d3 dxe4 7.♘xe4 ♘xe4 8.♗xe4 0-0 9.0-0 c5 10.dxc5 ♕c7 11.♕d5!N ♘a6 12.♗e3 ♗xb2 13.♖ab1 ♖d8 14.♕g5 ♗f6 15.♕g3 ♕xg3 16.fxg3 ♘c7 17.♖fd1 ♖xd1+ 18.♖xd1 ♘e6 19.♖d3 ♔g7 20.g4± (+1.20). Black just can't complete development, and White has a crushing space advantage.

4.♘xe4

4...♘f6

Here, with ♘f3 replacing the usual d2-d4, the move 4...♗f5?! loses the bishop pair for nothing: 5.♘g3 ♗g4 (although 5...♗g6? is normal and best with d2-d4 replacing ♘f3, here it falls into a well-known trap: 6.h4 h6 7.♘e5 ♕d6 (7...♗h7? 8.♕h5 g6 9.♗c4 e6 10.♕e2+− (+1.15). The imprisonment of the bishop on h7 makes this position clearly winning for White) 8.d4 ♘d7 9.♘xg6 ♕xg6 10.c3 ♕d6 11.♗c4 e6 12.♕f3± (+0.60). White has the bishop pair

and superior development and space) 6.c3 ♘f6 7.d4 e6 8.♗d3 ♕d5 9.♗e2 ♘bd7 10.0-0 ♗e7 11.♖e1 0-0 12.♗f4 ♕a5 13.h3± (+0.38). White wins the bishop pair for free. 4...♘d7 5.d4 transposes to Game 2.3.

5.♕e2

The exchange on f6 is not quite as attractive for White here as with d2-d4 replacing ♘f3, because the recommended plan in that position puts the knight on e2. But here ♕e2 is a good move, whereas with d2-d4 replacing ♘f3 it would just lose the d4-pawn.

5...♘xe4

A) 5...♗f5 6.♘xf6+ (White is more inclined to trade knights when Black cannot recapture with his e-pawn, which is now thought to be the better recapture on move 5) 6...gxf6 7.d3 ♘d7 8.g3 ♘e5 9.♘xe5 ♕a5+ 10.♗d2 ♕xe5 11.♗c3 ♕xe2+ 12.♗xe2± (+0.35). Black has no offset for his damaged pawn structure;

B) 5...♗g4 6.h3 ♗h5 7.♘xf6+ gxf6 8.d3 e6 9.♗d2 ♘a6 10.a3 ♘c5 11.g3N ♘a4 12.♗g2 ♗g7 13.0-0 0-0 14.♖ab1 ♘b6 15.♕d1 f5 16.♕c1 ♖e8 17.♗g5 ♗f6 18.♗xf6 ♕xf6 19.♘h4 e5 20.♕d2

± (+0.31). White has the better pawn structure and safer king.

6.♕xe4 ♗e6

A) 6...♕d5 7.♕h4 ♕e6+ 8.♗e2 ♕g4 9.♕g3 ♕xg3 10.hxg3 ♗f5 11.b3 ♘d7 12.♗b2 e6 13.0-0-0± (+0.37). White leads in development and piece activity;

B) 6...♘d7 7.♗c4 ♘f6 8.♘e5 e6 9.♕e2 b5 10.♗d3 ♗b7 11.b3 ♗d6 12.♗b2 0-0 13.0-0 ♕c7 14.♖fe1± (+0.32). White's kingside attack potential is obvious and for free.

7.b3 ♘d7 8.♗b2 ♘f6

9.♕e2

9.♕e3 ♗f5 10.♘d4 ♗g6 11.f4 ♕a5 12.♗c4 e6 13.f5 ♗xf5 14.0-0 0-0-0 15.♘xf5 exf5 16.♗xf7 ♕xd2 17.♗e6+ ♔b8 18.♕xd2 ♖xd2 19.♗xf5 ♘d5 20.♗d3 ♗c5+ 21.♔h1 ♘e3 22.♗xg7 ♖d8 23.♗e5+ ♗d6 24.♗xd6+ ♖xd6 25.♖f8+ ♔c7 26.♖f7+ ♔b6 27.a4 a5 28.♖e1 (+0.02), but Lc0 gives +0.31. It's a drawish endgame, but Black has to be more careful than White.

9...♗g4 10.h3 ♗xf3 11.♕xf3 g6 12.d4

12.g4 ♗g7 13.0-0-0 0-0 14.h4 ♕d5 15.♗e2 ♖ad8 16.h5 ♕xf3 17.♗xf3 ♘d5 18.c3 ♘f4 19.♗a3 ♘d3+ 20.♔c2 ♗f6 21.♖df1 ♗g5 22.♗e4

♘f4 23.d4± (+0.17). White has the bishops but Black does have a rather strongly posted knight.

12...♗g7 13.♗e2 ♕a5+ 14.c3 0-0 15.0-0 ♖fd8 16.♖fe1 e6 17.♗f1 ♘d5 18.a3 ♕b6 19.♗c4 ♕c7 20.a4 a5 21.♖ad1 ♖ab8 22.♗c1 ♕d7 23.♗g5 ♖e8 24.♗f1 h6 25.♗h4 ♘e7

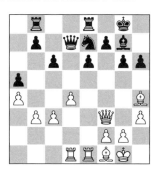

26.♗xe7?!

26.♗g3!. Don't give up the bishop pair needlessly! Of course 2600 rated GMs know this, I suppose White thought it was necessary or else thought trading was the best way to draw a higher rated opponent. 26...♖bd8 27.♖d3 (+0.12). White is up the bishop pair, but everything else about Black's position is ideal, so White's edge is quite small.

26...♕xe7 27.♕e4

Having given up his only advantage, the bishop pair, White now has to play carefully for the draw.

27...♕a3 28.♕c2 ♖bd8 29.♗d3 ♖e7 30.h4 h5 31.g3 ♕d6 32.♖e3 ♕d7 33.♕e2 ♕c7 34.♔g2 ♖d6 35.♗e4 ♖ed7 36.♗f3 ♕b6 37.♕c4 ♗f6 38.♖ee1 ♔g7 39.♖b1 ♕a7 40.♖e2 ♖c7 41.♖e3 ♖dd7 42.♖a1 ♗e7 43.♖a2 ♖d8 44.♕e2 ♗f6 45.♖d2

♕b8 46.♖a2 ♖dd7 47.♖d3 ♕d8
48.♗e4 ♖d6 49.♖f3 ♔g8 50.♕c4
♗g7 51.♕c5 ♖cd7 52.♕c4 ♔h8
53.♕c5 f5 54.♗b1 ♖d5 55.♕c4 c5
56.♖e2 cxd4 57.♖xe6 ♖7d6 58.♖xd6
♕xd6 59.♕c8+ ♕d8 60.♕xd8+
♖xd8 61.cxd4 ♖xd4 ½-½

Game 2.6   Caro-Kann Defense –
                Two Knights Variation

Francesco Rambaldi   2559
Alexander Shimanov   2642

New York 2017 (3)

1.e4 c6 2.♘f3 d5 3.♘c3 ♘f6
Until I analyzed this game I
thought 3...♘f6 was Black's best
move in the Two Knights Caro,
as it avoids the loss of the bishop
pair that happens with 3...♗g4. But
maybe 3...♗g4 is Black's best after
all.
4.e5 ♘e4

5.♘e2
5.d4 would be my choice if the line
in this game turns unpromising:
5...♘xc3 6.bxc3 c5 (6...e6 7.c4 c5
8.cxd5 ♕xd5 9.c4 ♕e4+ 10.♗e3
cxd4 11.♗d3 ♕c6 12.♘xd4 ♕xg2
13.♔e2 ♕h3 14.♖g1± (+0.19). White
has a huge lead in development for

the pawn) 7.c4 ♘c6 8.♗e2 e6 9.cxd5
exd5 10.0-0 c4 11.c3 b5 12.a3 ♗e7
13.♘e1 0-0 14.♘c2 f6 15.f4 (+0.11).
White's kingside majority is more
dangerous than Black's queenside
majority.
5...♕b6
5...♗g4?! 6.♘fg1! ♘c5 7.d4 ♘e6 8.f3
♗f5 9.♘g3 g6 10.c3 c5 11.♘xf5 gxf5
12.f4 ♘c6 13.♗e3± (+0.53). White
has a better pawn structure, the
bishop pair, and a target on f5.
6.d4 e6
6...c5 7.dxc5 ♕xc5 8.♘ed4 ♘c6
9.c3± (+0.55). White plans ♗e3 with
much better development.
7.♘g3 c5
7...♘xg3 8.hxg3 c5 9.c3 ♘c6 10.dxc5
♗xc5 11.♕c2 a5 12.♗d3 ♗d7
13.♕e2± (+0.40). Black's king has no
safe home.
8.♗d3!
Sielecki in *Keep it Simple* considers
this a mistake and gives the '!' to
8.c3, but see move 9.
8...♘xg3

9.fxg3!
This novelty is not only stronger
than the usual 9.hxg3, but seems to
change the verdict on 3...♘f6 from
equal to favoring White!

Everyone else played the 'obviously better' capture 9.hxg3 before, but White has nothing after 9...cxd4=. That's why everyone thought 8.c3 was best.

9...h6

9...♘c6 10.0-0 cxd4 11.♕e2 h6 12.a3 ♗e7 13.b4 ♗d7 14.g4 0-0-0 15.♔h1 ♔b8 16.♗b2 ♖c8 17.h3 was Miettinen-Millett, ICCF 2018, wrongly cited in New In Chess *Yearbook* 132 as the stem game for 9.fxg3, but we agree that White is clearly better here (+0.38), Lc0 +0.63, and that this 9.fxg3! novelty changes the verdict on 3...♘f6 in White's favor. White will regain the pawn on d4 with a nice space advantage and a queenside attack. 9...cxd4 10.0-0 ♘c6 would just transpose.

10.0-0 ♘c6?

10...♗d7 11.c3 ♗b5 12.♗xb5+ ♕xb5 13.g4 cxd4 14.♘xd4 ♕d7 15.♕f3 ♗c5 16.♔h1 ♘c6 17.♘xc6 bxc6 18.g5 hxg5 19.♗xg5± (+0.17), but Lc0 +0.38. Black's king has no safe place. 19...♔f8 is probably best but White can triple on the f-file.

11.dxc5 ♗xc5+ 12.♔h1 ♕c7

13.♕e2?!

Why surrender the bishop pair here?

13.c3! a6 14.♕e2 ♗d7 15.♗d2± (+1.00). Black lacks a safe place for his king. if he castles kingside, g3-g4 starts an attack, and if he castles queenside, b2-b4 does the same. If he does neither, a queenside advance should work.

13...♘b4 14.a3 ♘xd3 15.cxd3 ♕d8 16.♘h4 ♕e7 17.♕h5?!

17.♕g4! g5 18.♘f3 ♗d7 19.b4 ♗b6 20.a4± (+0.70). Again Black's king is unsafe on either wing.

17...♗d7 18.♗d2?!

18.a4!± (+0.50). White should prevent ...♗b5.

18...♗b5 19.♖f3?!

19.♕e2± (+0.24). White plans h2-h3, ♖ac1, and ♘f3, to meet ...0-0 by g3-g4.

19...♖f8?

20.♖af1?

20.d4! ♗xd4 21.♕g4 ♗xe5 22.♖e1!+− (+3.11). Bishop retreats run into ♘f5 or ♗b4. Probably only a computer could find this double-pawn sacrifice.

20...0-0-0 21.b4 ♗b6 22.♖xf7 ♖xf7 23.♕xf7 ♕xf7 24.♖xf7 ♖d7 25.♖f8+

🗒d8 26.🗒f7 g5 27.♘f3 ♗xd3 28.h3
🗒g8 ½-½

Game 2.7   Caro-Kann Defense –
Two Knights Variation
Yuri Solodovnichenko   2587
Davit Magalashvili   2488
Konya 2016 (6)

─────────────────────────

**1.e4 c6 2.♘f3 d5 3.♘c3 ♗g4 4.h3
♗h5**

This is rather uncommon as it
allows White to win either bishop
for three pawns or a pawn by force.
But taking the knight also loses
'half a pawn', so it's not clearly
worse to retreat.
**5.exd5 cxd5 6.♗b5+ ♘c6 7.g4 ♗g6
8.♘e5 🗒c8 9.d4 e6 10.♕e2**

Now Black must choose between the
game continuation, which loses a

piece for three pawns, or the dubious
gambit of a pawn by 10...♗d6.
10...♗b4
10...♗d6 11.♗xc6+ (this is probably
better than the simpler pawn win
given in the note: 11.♘xg6 hxg6
12.♘xd5 ♔f8 (12...a6 13.♗xc6+
🗒xc6 14.c4± (+0.22). Black has
more active pieces for the pawn)
13.♗xc6 🗒xc6 14.♘e3 ♘f6 15.c3±
(+0.21). Again, Black has more active
pieces for the pawn) 11...bxc6 12.h4
f6 13.♘xg6 hxg6 14.♕xe6+ ♕e7
15.♕xe7+ ♘xe7 16.♗d2 g5 17.h5 g6
18.h6 🗒h7 19.0-0-0 ♘g8 20.♘a4
🗒xh6 21.♘c5± (+0.35). White has
the healthier pawn majority and
better piece placement.
11.h4 ♘ge7 12.h5 ♗e4 13.f3 0-0

14.♘xc6
14.♗xc6 is an alternative way to win
the bishop for several pawns, but I
would choose the game variation.
14...♘xc6 15.♘xc6 🗒xc6 16.0-0-0!N
♗xc3 17.bxc3 🗒xc3 18.♗d2 🗒xc2
19.🗒f2 ♕b6 20.♕e3 ♗xf3 21.🗒xf3
h6 22.🗒af1 f6 23.♕d3 🗒xa2 24.🗒3f2
(+0.15). Black is up half a pawn
by my count, but White has some
kingside attacking prospects and so
I'd say White is slightly for choice.

14...♘xc6 15.♗e3 ♕f6 16.fxe4
♘xd4 17.♗xd4 ♕xd4 18.♖d1
♗xc3+ 19.bxc3 ♕xc3+ 20.♔f1 dxe4
21.♕xe4 ♕xc2

22.♕xc2

22.♕e2!. With bishop for three
pawns White is clearly better, and
since the exchange of queens as
played in the game looks rather
drawish it is probably better to
play this way. 22...♕c5 (22...♕xe2+
23.♔xe2 ♖c2+ 24.♖d2 ♖fc8
25.♗d3± (+0.84). Since White
retains his a2-pawn here, his
winning chances are much higher
than in the game) 23.♗d3 ♕g5
24.♔g2 ♖fd8 25.♕e4 g6 26.h6±
(+0.93). White is up by a bishop for
three pawns, so half a pawn net,
and the 'thorn' pawn on h6 is a
constant worry for Black.

**22...♖xc2 23.a4 a6 24.♗e2 ♖a2
25.♖d7 ♖xa4 26.♖xb7 ♖a1+ 27.♔g2
♖xh1 28.♔xh1 h6 29.♗xa6 ♖a8
30.♗c4**

30.♗d3 ♔f8 31.♔g2± (+0.81), but
Lc0 only +0.30. With a bishop for
two pawns White has the only
winning chances, but the game
suggests that White doesn't have a
winning plan.

30...♖c8 31.♗b3 ♔f8 32.♔g2 ♖c3
33.♗d1 ♖d3 34.♗e2 ♖c3 35.♗f3
♖a3 36.♔g3 ♖a4 37.♔f2 ♖a3
38.♖c7 ♖b3 39.♖a7 ♖c3 40.♔e2
♖b3 41.♗e4 ♖c3 42.♗d3 ♖c5
43.♔e3 ♖e5+ 44.♔f4 ♖d5 45.♗e4
♖c5 46.♗h7 ♖c4+ 47.♔g3 ♖c3+
48.♔h2 ♖c8 49.♔g2 ♖b8 50.♔f2
♖b2+ 51.♔e3 ♖b3+ 52.♔d2 ♖b4
53.♖a8+ ♔e7 54.♗g8 ♖b7 55.♔e3
♔f6 56.♔f4 g5+ 57.hxg6 ♔xg6
58.♖e8 ♖b4+ 59.♔g3 ♔g7 60.♔f3
♖a4 ½-½

Game 2.8   Caro-Kann Defense –
Two Knights Variation
Maxime Vachier-Lagrave   2780
Quinten Ducarmon   2479
PRO League Stage rapid 2019 (1)

**1.e4 c6 2.♘f3 d5 3.♘c3 ♗g4 4.h3
♗xf3 5.♕xf3**

5...♘f6

5...e6 6.♗e2 ♘f6 (6...♘d7 7.d4 ♕b6
8.♕d3 dxe4 9.♘xe4 ♘gf6 10.c3±
(+0.36). White has achieved his
goal (bishop pair in open position)
without loss of time; 6...g6 7.d4 ♗g7
8.♗e3 ♘f6 9.0-0-0± (+0.20). White
has a better development, the
bishop pair, and attacking chances)

7.d3 transposes to the game, while 7.0-0 transposes to the move 6 note.

6.d3

A) 6.d4 is a decent line, but not my first choice: 6...e6 7.a3N. This novelty was suggested to me by GM Alex Lenderman and also by Stockfish and Komodo. The idea is to prevent ...♗b4 after 7...dxe4 8.♕e3. Usual is 7.♗d3 when White gets full compensation for the d4-pawn, but not more than that with accurate play by Black: 7...dxe4 8.♕e3. White will regain his pawn and have the same type of bishop pair with open center edge as in the game, but the time spent on a2-a3 and ♕e3 makes this less appealing than the game;

B) 6.♗e2 e6 7.0-0 seems more precise to me, and MVL switched to this in a newer game.

analysis diagram

B1) 7...♘bd7 or 7...♗d6 can now be met by d2-d4 without tempo loss;

B2) If Black plays 7...♗e7 then the two lines may transpose: 7...♗e7 8.♖d1 (8.d4 dxe4 9.♕e3 ♘bd7 10.♘xe4± (+0.24). White gets his goal position, but at the price of having made a now useless

♕e3 move) 8...d4 9.♘b1 0-0 10.d3 transposes to 7...♗e7 in the game;

B3) 7...♗c5 8.♖d1 (this favors White) 8...♗d4

analysis diagram

9.♕f4 (9.exd5 keeps the bishop pair edge safely but makes a draw more likely) 9...e5?! (9...♗xc3 10.bxc3 ♘xe4 11.♖b1 ♕e7 12.♗f3 ♘g5 13.♗h5 g6 14.♗e2 0-0 15.d3 f6 16.♖e1± (+0.06), but Lc0 +0.34. Two bishops vs two knights isn't enough for a pawn, but White also has much more active rooks) 10.♕g3± dxe4?! 11.d3 exd3 12.♗xd3 ♘bd7?! (12...0-0 13.♘e2 ♘bd7 is the better way to transpose to the game) 13.♘e2 (13.♕xg7 ♖g8 14.♕h6±) 13...0-0 14.♗f5 ♘c5 15.♗h6 ♘h5?! (15...♘e6 16.♗xe6 ♘h5 17.♕g4 fxe6 18.♘xd4 exd4 19.♕xh5 gxh6 20.♕g4+ ♔h8 21.♕xe6 c5 22.♕xh6± (+1.00). White is a clear pawn up) 16.♕g4 ♕d6 17.♕xh5 ♕xh6 18.♕xh6 gxh6 19.c3 1-0 Vachier-Lagrave-Navara, Riga 2019.

6...e6 7.♗e2 ♘bd7

A) 7...♗c5 8.0-0 0-0 9.♖d1 ♗d4 (9...♘bd7 transposes to the game) 10.♕f4 ♗b6 11.d4± (+0.17). White will have the typical bishop pair with open center edge if Black trades off on e4;

B) 7...♗d6 8.d4 dxe4 9.♘xe4 ♘xe4 10.♕xe4 ♘d7 11.c3 0-0 12.♗d2 ♘f6 13.♕f3± (+0.31). White aims to castle queenside, but if Black prevents this by ...♕a5 he will castle kingside with a clean bishop pair edge;

C) 7...♗e7 8.0-0 0-0 9.♖d1 d4 10.♘b1 c5 11.♕g3 ♘fd7 12.♘d2 ♘c6 13.♘f3± (+0.16). White has a rather favorable King's Indian reversed, because Black is missing the more valuable bishop here.

8.0-0

8.♕g3 is good here, but Black can avoid it by 7...♗c5 8.0-0 ♘bd7, transposing to the game. 8...g6 9.0-0 ♗g7 10.a4N a5 11.♔h1± (+0.15) Lc0 +0.30. White plans f2-f4, which will give a space advantage on top of the bishop pair.

8...♗c5

9.♖d1

9.♕g3 0-0 10.♗f4 ♔h8 11.♖ad1± (+0.15). White has the bishops and kingside plans.

9...0-0

9...♗d4!=. White's ♖d1 move was good with Black's knight still on b8

(Black would have castled instead), because then ♕f4 is hard to answer. Here it would be met by ...♗e5, so 9.♖d1 is dubious in the game position.

10.d4

Now White will be up the bishop pair for nothing, with a good center.

10...dxe4 11.♘xe4 ♗e7 12.♘d2 ♕a5 13.♘c4 ♕d5 14.♕b3 ♘b6

15.a4

15.♘e5!± (+0.78). It seems Black has to trade queens here, after which the half-open a-file plus the bishop pair and a strongly outposted knight add up to a serious advantage.

15...♖fd8 16.a5 ♘xc4 17.♗xc4 ♕h5 18.♖e1 ♖d7 19.c3 ♖ad8

19...♗d6 20.a6 b6 21.♕c2± (+0.30). It's just the bishop pair here.

20.♖e5 ♕h4??

20...♕g6 21.♕d1 ♘d5 22.♗d3 f5 23.♕e2 ♔f7 24.♕f3+− (+1.00). With Black's weak king and weaker e6-pawn together with White's bishop pair, White should win.

21.♗g5

Black resigned.

CHAPTER 3

French Tarrasch

The French Defense (**1.e4 e6 2.d4 d5**) is one that conventional engines tend to like or at least respect, but one that doesn't score very well in high level human play or engine vs engine play. Most top players consider it slightly inferior to 1...e5, the Sicilian, and the Caro, primarily because the queen's bishop is often a bad piece in the French. However it is fairly popular in amateur play, because White has to play some very complicated sharp lines if he hopes to refute it.

In my 2003 book, I recommended the Tarrasch (3.♘d2) against the French, and I still do. While 3.♘c3 may give a larger edge with perfect play, you need to know a lot, and you tend to get very closed positions which don't give much chance to demonstrate tactical skills. With **3.♘d2** you can be more confident of getting at least a small pull with less risk.

Normally White will get to play against either an isolated pawn on d5 or a backward one on e6, although there are other lines. The French is the only major defense in this book against which I give only one line, as 3.♘c3 would just take too much space, I don't believe in the Advance Variation (3.e5), and the exchange is just too insipid for this book. I'll just say here that if I did include 3.♘c3 as an option, I would probably recommend the exchange against the Winawer (3...♗b4) because it is much more effect there than on move 3, and the Steinitz (4.e5) against 3...♘f6, but the Steinitz has many variations.

    Black can transpose out of the Tarrasch by **3...dxe4 4.♘xe4**, the Rubinstein Defense. Although it doesn't fully equalize, it comes reasonably close and deserves serious treatment. It is sufficient to develop normally, trading on f6 when legal, but of course choosing the right development scheme is the key. See Game 3.1. The notes cover the Fort Knox Variation, where Black concedes the bishop pair but nothing else.

Next comes **3...♘c6**, the Guimard Defense, which is not as silly as it looks, blocking the c-pawn. The line I give features a rather amusing maneuver ♘b1-d2-b1-a3-b5 to get the edge! See Game 3.2.

Black can choose to postpone commitments by **3...♗e7**, the Morozevich Variation, a formerly obscure move which has risen to become very respectable, and is my personal favorite as Black.

I go for **4.♘gf3**, which leads to a position that could arise from 3...♘f6 but only if Black chose to play ...♗e7 at a point where another move was probably better. So White deserves a small plus. See Game 3.3. White can try a crazy Lc0 inspired sacrifice given in the notes or settle for a safe but modest edge.

Black's main option when playing for a win is **3...♘f6**.

It usually leads to positions with an isolated d4-pawn for White on a closed file against a backward e6-pawn on a half-open file, which is in principle favorable to White. White usually aims to exchange dark-squared bishops and is usually better once he does so as White retains his 'good' bishop while Black is stuck with his 'bad' one. See Game 3.4.

The main move for Black was and still is **3...c5**.

White can play 4.exd5, aiming to leave Black with an isolated pawn on d5 after 4...exd5, but the recapture with the queen on move four is rather popular now and quite close to equal. So I stuck with **4.♘gf3** as in my first book, which avoids that line but does allow other ones. After 4...♘f6 or 4...♘c6 we can exchange on d5 without the queen recapture being a good one, although the knight recapture is reasonable in the former case; see Game 3.5 for that and for 4...♘c6. For **4...♘f6 5.exd5 exd5** see Game 3.6, which deviates from the main line of the past half century on move ten as explained there. Black's isolated pawn on d5 defines White's edge. The main line is **4...cxd4**. Now 5.exd5 ♕xd5 would again be the line we're trying to avoid, so we play **5.♘xd4**.

Then one main line is **5...♘c6**, when **6.♗b5** is our choice, and after **6...♗d7 7.♘xc6** both recaptures are serious lines for Black, leading to rather different play with White looking a bit better in both cases. See Game 3.7. Finally we look at **5...♘f6 6.exd5 ♕xd5** in Game 3.8. Black avoids structural concessions, but has to play for a while with a knight on a6, obviously not a good square.

Game 3.1 French Defense – Rubinstein

Levon Aronian   2765

Georg Meier   2622

Germany Bundesliga 2018/19 (9)

1.e4 e6 2.d4 d5 3.♘c3 dxe4

The Rubinstein Variation, a reasonable choice for Black when a draw is the goal.

4.♘xe4

We would get here by 3.♘d2 dxe4 4.♘xe4.

4...♘d7

A) 4...♘f6 5.♘xf6+ ♕xf6 6.♘f3 h6 7.♗d3 ♗d6 8.♕e2 ♘c6 9.c3 0-0 10.h4 ♖e8 11.♗g5 hxg5 12.hxg5 ♕d8 13.♕e4 f5 14.♕h4 ♘e7 15.♕h8+ ♔f7 16.♕h5+ ♔f8 17.0-0-0 ♗d7 18.♗c4 ♕c8 19.♖de1 c5 20.♖h4 ♘g8 21.♕h8 ♖e7 22.g6 ♕e8 23.dxc5 ♗xc5 24.♘e5 ♗xf2 25.♖h5 ♗xe1 26.♖xf5+ wins. Black has many other ways to play after the piece sacrifice, but White has more than enough pressure and attack in all cases;

B) 4...♗d7 is the 'Fort Knox' Variation, supposedly because it is unbreakable, but if that were so, it would be popular with the elite, and it is not. 5.♘f3 ♗c6 6.♗d3 ♘d7 7.0-0 ♘gf6 8.♘g3 ♗e7 9.♕e2

analysis diagram

9...♗xf3. This surrender of the bishop pair is played here to avoid a suffocating space disadvantage in the next note. If White postponed ♕e2, Black would postpone ...♗xf3 until the queen move was played (if 9...0-0 10.♘e5 ♘xe5 11.dxe5 ♘d7 12.♖d1 ♕e8 13.c3 a5 14.♗f4 ♔h8 15.♗c2 ♘c5 16.♕g4± (+1.20). White's kingside space advantage and attacking potential are likely decisive), 10.♕xf3 c6 11.♖e1 0-0 12.c3 ♖e8 13.♗c2 ♕b6 14.♖b1 ♖ad8 15.h3± (+0.45). White is up the bishop pair (half a pawn, I say) in a fairly open position, otherwise the position is equal.

5.♘f3 ♘gf6 6.♘xf6+ ♘xf6 7.c3 c5 8.♗f4 a6 9.♗e2 ♗d6 10.♘e5 ♕c7 11.♗f3

I think the move 11.0-0 is more precise than the game move, to avoid the note to move 14. 11...0-0 (11...♘d7 12.♖e1 0-0 13.♗d3± (+0.55). Black has problems developing due to his vulnerable king) 12.♗f3 ♖b8 13.♕e2 c4 14.b3 b5 15.bxc4 bxc4 16.♗g3± (+0.22). White has the better pawn structure and an outposted knight.

11...♘d7 12.0-0 ♘xe5 13.dxe5 ♗xe5 14.♕a4+

14...b5

After 14...♗d7! 15.♗xe5 ♕xe5 16.♕a5 ♗c6 17.♗xc6+ bxc6 18.♖ad1 0-0 19.b3 h6 20.c4 ♕g5 21.♖d6 ♖fd8 22.♖xc6 ♕d2 23.♖xc5 ♕c2 24.g3 Black has full compensation for the pawn according to Komodo, while Lc0 still gives White (+0.15).

15.♗xe5 ♕xe5 16.♕a5

16...♖a7?

16...♖b8 17.♗c6+ ♗d7 18.♗xd7+ ♔xd7 19.♖fe1 ♕f4 20.♖ad1+ ♔e7 21.g3 ♕f5 22.♕c7+ ♔f6 23.♖d7 ♔g6 24.♔g2± (+0.45). With majors doubled on the 7th rank and an exposed black king, White obviously has more than enough for one pawn.

17.♗c6++− ♔e7 18.♕b6 ♖c7? 19.♖ad1 ♖d8 20.f4 ♕e3+ 21.♔h1 ♖dd7 22.♗xd7 ♖xd7 23.♖xd7+ ♗xd7 24.♖d1 1-0

Game 3.2 French Defense – Guimard
Liviu Nisipeanu   2687
Michael Richter   2505
Germany Bundesliga 2016/17 (6)

1.e4 e6 2.d4 d5 3.♘d2 ♘c6
This is the Guimard Variation. It looks wrong to block the c-pawn, but it has its points and does exploit ♘d2 a bit.
4.♘gf3 ♘f6 5.e5 ♘d7 6.♗d3
6.♘b3 is the most frequent move historically, but the game move is 'hot'. 6...a5 7.a4 ♗e7 8.c3± (+0.30). White has a nice space advantage, but choosing the right plan after castling may be a bit difficult.

6...♘b4

6...f6 7.exf6 (7.♘g5 ♘dxe5 8.dxe5 fxg5 9.♕h5+ is also somewhat favorable for White but rather messy, and since 7.exf6 seems to give a simple edge I choose it as my main line) 7...♕xf6 8.♘f1 e5 (8...♗d6 9.♘e3±) 9.♘e3 ♘xd4 10.♘xd4 exd4 11.♘xd5 ♕e5+ 12.♕e2 ♔d8 13.♘f4

♗b4+ 14.♔d1 ♕xe2+ 15.♘xe2 ♘e5
16.♗g5+ ♗e7 17.♗xe7+ ♔xe7 18.♖e1
♔f6 19.♔d2 ♖d8 20.♘g3 ♘xd3
21.cxd3 b6 22.♖ac1 c5 23.b4 cxb4
24.♖c7 ♖d7 25.♘e4+ ♔e7 26.♖c4
♔f8 27.♖xb4± (+0.40). White has
better rooks and a safer king.
**7.♗e2 c5 8.c3 ♘c6 9.0-0 a5 10.a4
♗e7 11.♘b1!**
Komodo loves this retreat, heading
for b5.
**11...0-0 12.♘a3 cxd4 13.cxd4 f6
14.exf6 ♘xf6 15.♘b5 ♗d7**

16.♖e1?!
16.♗d3 ♖c8 17.♖e1 ♘b4 18.♗b1 ♘e4
19.♕e2 ♕e8 20.♖a3 ♘c6 21.♖e3 ♗b4
22.♖d1± (+0.35). Black will either
lose a pawn or make concessions to
save it.
16...♘e4
16...♗b4 17.♗d2 ♘e4 18.♗xb4
♘xb4 19.♖c1 (+0.02). Black's strong
knights offset his inferior bishop.
**17.♗d3 ♘b4 18.♗xe4 dxe4 19.♖xe4
♗c6 20.♖xe6 ♗d5?**
20...♖c8 21.♗d2 ♗d5 22.♖e5 ♖c6
23.♖a3 ♕d7 24.♖ae3 ♗f6 25.♖h5
♘c2 26.♖c3 ♗xf3 27.♖xf3 ♘xd4
28.♖d3 ♕f7 29.g4± (+0.71). Black
doesn't have much for the pawn.
21.♖e3+− (+1.42)

White is up 1.5 pawns for very little.
**21...♗f6 22.♗d2 ♘c6 23.♕e2 ♗xf3
24.♖xf3 ♘xd4 25.♕c4+ 1-0**

Game 3.3   French Defense –
          Morozevich Variation
Fabien Libiszewski   2540
Matthew Sadler   2687

England tt 2017/18 (6)

1.e4 e6 2.d4 d5 3.♘d2 ♗e7
This once obscure move is now the
third choice. Black is just trying
not to commit yet. It is sometimes
called the Morozevich Variation,
and has been my own choice many
times as Black.
4.♘gf3
4.e5 and 4.♗d3 are good
alternatives.
4...♘f6 5.e5 ♘fd7 6.♗d3 c5 7.c3

7...♘c6
7...b6 8.0-0 ♗a6 This trade is
strategically desirable for Black,
but White gets too much space and
development. 9.♘e1 ♗xd3 10.♘xd3
♘c6 11.♕g4 g6 12.♘f3 h5 13.♕g3
c4 14.♘de1 h4 15.♕g4 ♖h5 16.g3N
(+1.00). White will eventually break
in on the kingside.
8.0-0 g5

A) 8...a5 9.a4 0-0 10.♖e1 cxd4 11.cxd4 ♘b4 12.♗b1 b6 13.♖a3 ♗a6 14.h4 ♖c8 15.♘f1 h6 16.♘g3± (+1.48). Lc0 showed a winning score well before this. White just has a decisive kingside attack with no counterplay;

B) 8...♕b6 9.dxc5 ♘xc5 10.♗c2 ♕c7 11.♖e1 ♘d7 12.♕e2 0-0 13.♘b3± (+0.64). White has much more space and better development, and can plan a kingside attack.

9.dxc5

9.♘b1!?N is a ridiculous-looking untried Lc0 suggestion, but I couldn't prove it wrong: 9...♕b6 (not the only move, but White just wants to play ♗e3 before Black can win the d-pawn for free) 10.♘xg5 ♗xg5 11.♗xg5 ♕xb2 12.♗e3!! cxd4 13.cxd4 ♘dxe5 14.♘c3! ♕xc3 15.dxe5 ♕xe5 16.♖e1± (+0.28), but Lc0 rates it much higher for White. After all these crazy sacrifices, both engines agree that White has more than enough compensation for two pawns!!
Don't try this without a lot of preparation!

9...♘dxe5 10.♘xe5 ♘xe5

11.♘b3

11.♗c2N ♘xc5 12.c4 ♗e7 13.♖e1 ♘g6 14.♕h5 ♘f4 15.♕f3 ♕c7 16.g3 ♘g6 17.♕c3 d4 18.♕xd4 0-0 19.♘f3± (+0.10). Black has nothing to offset his slightly damaged kingside pawn structure.

11...♘xd3 12.♕xd3 f6 13.f4

13.♕e2N 0-0 14.h4 gxh4 15.♗h6 ♖f7 16.♖ae1 ♘d7 17.♕h5 ♗f8 18.♖e3 (0.00) Lc0 +0.13, but it looks easier to play White.

13...gxf4 14.♗xf4 e5

15.♗h6

15.♕g3!? is a crazy piece sacrifice by Lc0 which apparently leads to an equal endgame! 15...exf4 16.♕g7 ♖f8 17.♘d4 ♕c7 18.b4 a5 19.♖ae1 ♔d8 20.a3 axb4 21.axb4 ♖a6 22.♖f2 ♗xc5 23.♕xc7+ ♔xc7 24.bxc5 ♖f7 25.♖xf4=. Komodo says zero, Lc0

still gives White a slight edge.
White has the better side of a
probable draw.

15...♖g8 16.♕xh7 ♗e6 17.♗g7?
17.♗e3 ♕d7 18.♖f2=.
17...♕d7∓ 18.♔h1? ♗d8−+
**19.♕g6+ ♗f7 20.♕g3 ♗e7 21.♘a5
b6 22.cxb6 axb6 23.♘b3 ♖a4 24.h3
♖e4 25.a4 d4 26.cxd4 ♕d5 27.a5
♕xb3 28.♕xb3 ♗xb3 29.dxe5 fxe5
30.axb6 ♖xg7 31.b7 ♗d6 32.♖a8+
♔e7**
White resigned.

Game 3.4 French Defense – Tarrasch
Aleksandar Berelowitsch   2521
Bart Michiels   2554

Belgium tt 2018/19 (5)

1.e4 e6
The stats for the French are poor for
Black, +57 Elo for White compared
to just +38 in the initial position
or +39 after 1.e4. This is why it is a
rather rare choice among the elite
GMs. Computers tend to rate it
more favorably.
2.d4 d5 3.♘d2 ♘f6
This is the second most popular
move and the usual choice of
players wanting to play for a win.
It avoids structural concessions but
concedes a lot of space.
4.e5 ♘fd7 5.♗d3 c5 6.c3 ♘c6 7.♘e2
This set-up allows for adequate
defense of d4.
7.♘gf3 is a riskier gambit line. The
stats in Hiarcs powerbook are +59
Elo for White with 7.♘e2, way above
par.

**7...cxd4 8.cxd4 f6 9.exf6 ♘xf6 10.0-0
♗d6 11.♘f3**

11...0-0
  A) 11...♕c7 12.h3 (12.♗g5 0-0
13.♖c1 ♗d7 14.♖e1± (+0.42). This
is also good but perhaps more
complex than the 12.h3 line)
12...0-0 13.♗e3 ♗d7 14.♖e1 ♗e8
15.♘g5 ♗f7 16.♖c1. This plan was
recommended in *Yearbook* 130. It
seems pretty convincing as a safe
route to an edge: 16...h6 17.♘xf7
♕xf7 18.a3 a6 19.♗b1± (+0.30).
Black has no compensation for the
bishop pair;
  B) 11...♕b6 12.♗f4 is not a real
gambit: 12...♗xf4 13.♘xf4 ♕xb2
14.♖e1 0-0 15.g3!? (15.♘xe6 ♗xe6
16.♖xe6 ♖ae8 17.♖xe8 ♖xe8 18.♖b1
(18.♕c1 ♕xc1+ 19.♖xc1 – I played
this way as White in the 2019

Maryland Open and won, but if Black had played 19...♖c8 my edge would have been tiny) 18...♕xa2 19.♖xb7 ♘e4 20.♕f1 h6 21.h3± (+0.26), due to White's safer king, but practical results are just even in a dozen games) 15...g6 16.♖b1!?. What follows is a crazy computer line that no human would ever find over the board, but it may be the only path to a serious advantage: 16...♕xa2 17.h4 ♖b8 18.♘e5 ♘xe5 19.♖xe5 ♗d7 20.h5 ♘xh5 21.♖xh5 gxh5 22.♗xh7+ ♔xh7 23.♕xh5+ ♔g8 24.♕g6+ ♔h8 25.♔g2 ♕xb1 26.♕xb1 ♖xf4 27.gxf4± (+1.92), but Lc0 gives only about half that. I won't try to guess whether White wins or Black draws with perfect play.

12.♗f4 ♗xf4 13.♘xf4

13...♘e4

A) 13...♘g4 14.♕d2 ♕f6 15.♘h5 ♕h6 16.♕xh6 ♘xh6 17.♖ac1 a6 18.♖fe1 ♗d7 19.♘g3 ♘f7 20.♘e2± (+0.20). White has a good vs bad bishop, and e6 is weaker than d4;

B) 13...♕b6 14.♖e1 ♕xb2 15.g3 ♖b8 16.h4 ♗d7 17.♖b1 ♕xa2 18.♘e5 ♔h8 19.♖e2 ♕a5 20.♘xd7 ♘xd7 21.♘xe6 ♖f6 22.♖e3 ♘f8 23.♖b5 ♕a3 24.♘f4

♕a2 25.h5± (+0.62). White has much more active pieces and a safer king for the pawn.

14.♕c1 ♘g5
The rare move 14...♕f6 sets a very nasty trap.

analysis diagram

15.♘e2! (15.♘h5?? ♕g6 16.♘f4 (if 16.♘g3? ♘xg3 17.♗xg6 ♘e2+ Black wins a bishop) 16...♕g4 17.g3 g5 18.h3 ♕f5 19.♘xg5 ♕xg5–+ is a tournament game I played as White against a higher-rated opponent in 2018; I saw the queen sacrifice trick only after making my 15th move. White has lost a knight for just a pawn. I decided not to resign, and, incredibly, saved a draw by somehow reaching rook vs rook and bishop, and eventually claimed the fifty move rule just as he threatened an unstoppable checkmate! This was the most amazing save of my very long career in chess) 15...♘d6 16.♕e3 ♘f5 17.♗xf5 ♕xf5 18.♖ac1 (18.♘e5 ♘xe5 19.dxe5 ♗d7 20.♘d4 ♕f4 21.g3 ♕xe3 22.fxe3± (+0.35). The strong outpost knight vs bad bishop is more significant than the bad white pawn structure) 18...♗d7 19.♖fe1 (+0.60). White has knight vs bad bishop, and Black's weak pawn is on a half-open file while White's is not.

15.♘xg5 ♕xg5

16.♘e2

I recommended the spectacular shot 16.♗xh7+ in my first book, which trades bishop and knight for rook and two pawns. While statistics and Lc0 favor White, with a few accurate moves Black should hold comfortably, so I'm now recommending the game move. 16...♔xh7 17.♘xe6 ♕f5 18.♘xf8+ ♕xf8 19.♕g5 ♕f5 20.♕h4+ ♔g8 21.♖ae1 ♗e6 22.♖e3 ♖f8 23.h3 ♕g6 24.♖fe1=. Lc0 gives White a normal edge, while Komodo rates it dead even. Rook and two pawns for bishop and knight is a small material plus, a quarter pawn by my count, but the two extra pawns can only create isolated passers at best. I would choose White if given the choice, but I don't see a realistic plan to play for a win.

16...♕xc1

16...♕f6 17.♕d2 ♗d7 18.♗b5 ♘b8 (else White gets knight vs bad bishop) 19.a4 ♗xb5 20.axb5 ♘d7 21.g3 ♘b6 22.♘f4 ♘c4 23.♕e2 ♖fe8

24.♖fd1 ♘d6 25.h4 ♖e7 26.♖a3 ♖f8 27.♖xa7 ♘f5 28.♕e5 ♘xh4 29.♕xf6 ♖xf6 30.♖a8+ ♔f7 31.♘d3 ♘f3+ 32.♔g2 g5 33.b6± (+0.16). White aims to target b7.

17.♖axc1 a6

This prevents ♗b5 aiming for knight vs bad bishop.

18.f3 ♗d7 19.♔f2 ♖ac8 20.♖fd1

20.♔e3! ♔f7 21.h4± (+0.18). White has the better bishop, better king, and more space.

20...♔f7 21.♔e3 ♔e7 22.f4 ♖f6?!

22...♗e8!.

23.♘g1 ♗e8 24.♖d2

24.♖f1!.

24...♗g6 25.♗xg6 ♖xg6 26.♘f3 ♔d8 27.♘e5

27.♖c5± (+0.46). White has several advantages – better king, better rooks, better pawns.

27...♘xe5 28.♖xc8+ ♔xc8

29.fxe5?

White settles for just a cosmetic advantage; the symmetry makes a draw very likely. The other capture offers some real winning chances; a sample line follows:

29.dxe5! ♔d7 30.g3 h5 31.♖d3 h4 32.♔f3 hxg3 33.hxg3 ♖h6 34.♖b3 ♔c6 35.♖c3+ ♔d7 36.♔g4 ♖h2

37.♖b3 ♔c6 38.♔g5 d4 39.♔g6
♔d5 40.♖xb7 ♔e4 41.♖xg7 d3
42.♖d7 ♖h3 43.♔f6±. White's two
extra pawns should probably win,
although the advanced black passed
pawn gives him some small hope
for a draw.

**29...♔d8 30.♖f2 ♔e8 31.♖c2 ♔d8
32.♖f2 ♔e8 33.♖c2 ½-½**

Game 3.5 French Defense – Tarrasch

Wolfgang Klewe   2325
Holger Elias   2361

Correspondence game, 2018

1.e4 e6 2.d4 d5 3.♘d2 c5 4.♘gf3

4...♘f6

A) 4...♘c6 5.exd5 exd5 6.♗b5
♗d6 7.dxc5 ♗xc5 8.0-0 ♘ge7 9.♘b3
♗d6 10.♖e1 0-0 11.♗d3 h6 12.h3
♘f5 13.c3± transposes to analysis
in Rozentalis-Stocek in the Anti-
Sicilian chapter below;

B) 4...a6 5.exd5 exd5 6.♗e2 ♘f6
7.0-0 ♗e7 8.c4 0-0 (8...cxd4 9.cxd5
0-0 10.♘xd4 ♘xd5 11.♗f3 ♗f6
12.♘e4 ♗e5 13.♗g5 ♘f6 14.♘b3
♘c6 15.♕e2± (+0.25). White has
better development and a nice pin)
9.cxd5 ♖e8 10.♖e1 cxd4 11.♘xd4

♘xd5 12.♗f3 ♘c6 13.♘xc6 bxc6
14.♘c4 ♗f6 15.♗d2 ♖xe1+ 16.♕xe1
♗e6 17.♖c1± (+0.22). Black has no
compensation for his inferior pawn
structure.

5.exd5 ♘xd5 6.dxc5 ♗xc5

6...♘d7 7.♘b3 ♘xc5 8.♕d4 ♘b4
9.♕xd8+ ♔xd8 10.♘bd4 f6 11.a3
♘d5 12.♗c4 ♘b6 13.♗a2± (+0.10),
but Lc0 gives White a normal
advantage, around +0.15 on
Komodo's scale. White has some
edge in development and king
safety.

7.♘e4 ♗e7 8.c4 ♘b4 9.♕xd8+ ♔xd8

10.♔d1

Lc0 prefers 10.♔d2 so as to have
♖d1 later in some lines.

**10...♘4c6 11.♗e3 e5 12.♘c3 f6
13.♗d3 f5 14.♗c2 h6 15.♔e2 ♗e6
16.♖ad1+ ♘d7 17.b3 g5± (+0.28)**

Black apparently gave up this correspondence game for personal reasons, since White has only a small edge after 19.h3, based on the d-file and the d5 outpost for his knight. **1-0**

Game 3.6 French Defense – Tarrasch
Sergey Rublevsky   2683
Boris Savchenko   2585
Sochi rapid 2017 (5)

1.e4 e6 2.d4 d5 3.♘d2 c5 4.♘gf3 ♘f6 5.exd5 exd5 6.♗b5+ ♗d7 7.♗xd7+ ♘bxd7 8.0-0 ♗e7 9.dxc5 ♘xc5

10.♖e1
This is newly popular since the main line with 10.♘b3 doesn't appear to give any edge.
10.♘b3 ♘ce4 11.♘fd4 ♘d6! was found by Rybka around 2007. Previously 11...0-0 12.♘f5 and 11...♕d7 12.f3 ♘d6 13.♘c5 were the main lines which kept a small White plus. 12.♖e1 0-0 13.c3 ♖e8 14.♗g5 h6 15.♗h4 ♕b6 16.♕c2 ♘c4 17.♖ad1 g5 18.♗g3 ♗f8 19.h3=. The knight outpost on c4 and the potential one on e4 offset the weak d5-pawn.

10...0-0 11.♘f1 ♖e8 12.♗e3 ♕d7
12...a5 13.c3 a4 14.a3 ♘b3 15.♖b1 ♕d7 16.♕c2 ♗d6 17.♘1d2 ♘xd2 18.♕xd2± (+0.23). The exchange of two pairs of minors accentuates the weakness of the isolated d-pawn.
13.c3 a5 14.♗d4 ♖ac8 15.♘e3 ♘fe4

16.♘e5
16.♕c2! ♗f8 17.♖ad1± (+0.64). Black has nothing better than trading queens with 17...♕a4, after which d5 is very weak.
16...♕d8 17.♕h5 g6 18.♕f3 f5

19.♘xf5!?
19.♖ad1 ♘e6 20.♕e2 ♗f6 21.♘f3 ♘xd4 22.♘xd4 ♘xc3 23.bxc3 f4 24.♕d2 fxe3 25.♖xe3 ♖xe3 26.♕xe3± (+0.17). White's edge is the weak d5-pawn.
19...gxf5 20.♕xf5 ♗f6 21.f3 ♘d6?

21...♗xe5 22.♗xe5 ♘d3 23.♖xe4
dxe4 24.♕g4+ ♔f7 25.♗d4 ♕d6
26.fxe4 ♘e5 27.♖f1+ ♔e7 28.♗xe5
♕xe5 29.♖f5 ♕h8 30.♕h4+ ♔e6
31.♕h6+ ♔e7 32.♕h4+=; perpetual
check.

22.♕g4+ ♔f8

23.♖ad1

23.♗xc5 ♗xe5 24.♗a3 ♕f6 25.f4
♗xf4 26.g3 ♖c4 27.gxf4 ♖ce4
28.♖xe4 ♖xe4 29.♖d1 ♖xf4 30.♕g2
d4 31.♕d5 ♖g4+ 32.♔h1 ♖g6
33.♕xb7±. White's extra pawn is
probably enough to win the game.
**23...♘e6 24.♘d7+ ♕xd7 25.♗xf6
♕f7 26.♖xd5 ♕xf6 27.♖xd6
♖c6 28.♖d5 ♕g6 29.♖f5+ ♔g7
30.♕xg6+ ♔xg6 31.♖xa5 ♖d8
32.♖ae5?!**

32.♖b5 b6 33.♖e4±. Four good
pawns for a knight obviously
favors White, though Black should
probably hold.
**32...♘f4 33.♖5e4 ♖f6 34.g3 ♘h3+
35.♔g2 ♘g5 36.♖4e3 ♘xf3 37.♖1e2
♖d2 38.♖xd2 ♘xd2 39.b3?**

39.a4=.

**39...♖a6∓ 40.♖e7 ♖xa2 41.♖xb7
♘xb3+ 42.♔h3 ♘c5 43.♖b6+ ♔g7
44.g4 h6 45.♔g3 ♖c2 46.h4 ♖xc3+
47.♔f4 ♖c1 48.g5 h5 49.♖h6 ♖c4+**

**50.♔g3 ♘e4+ 51.♔g2 ♖c2+ 52.♔f3
♘d2+ 53.♔e3 ♘f1+ 54.♔d3 ♖d2+
55.♔c3 ♖h2 56.♖xh5**

Now the draw is clear, since rook
+ knight vs rook does not set the
difficult problems of rook + bishop
vs rook.

**56...♘g3 57.♖h6 ♘f5 58.♖a6 ♖xh4
59.g6 ♖g4 60.♔d3 ♘h4 61.♖a7+
♔xg6 62.♖a8 ♔f6 63.♖f8+ ♔e7
64.♖a8 ♘f5 65.♖a6 ♖d4+ 66.♔c3
♖d7 67.♖a8 ♔e6 68.♖e8+ ♔d5
69.♔d3 ♘d6 70.♖h8 ♔e5 71.♔e2
♘f5 72.♖e8+ ♔f4 73.♖f8 ♔e4
74.♖e8+ ♘e7 75.♖a8 ♘c6 76.♖e8+
♘e5 77.♖e6 ♖d8 78.♖e7 ♖a8
79.♔e1 ♔d4 80.♔f1 ♖a2 81.♖e8
♘g6 82.♖d8+ ♔e3 83.♖e8+ ♔f3
84.♔e1 ♖b2 85.♔d1 ♘f4 86.♖f8
♖b6 87.♔d2 ♖d6+ 88.♔c3 ♔e3
89.♖e8+ ♘e6 90.♔c4 ♔e4 91.♔c3
♔e5 ½-½**

Game 3.7   French Defense – Tarrasch
Daniel Naroditsky   2616
Varuzhan Akobian   2643
chess.com INT 2019 (4)

**1.e4 e6 2.d4 d5 3.♘d2 c5 4.♘gf3
cxd4**

5.♘xd4

I recommended this line, rather than 4.exd5 or 5.exd5, in my first book in 2003, and still do. It avoids the 4...♛xd5 (or 5...♛xd5) line which is extremely difficult to show an edge against.

5...♘c6 6.♗b5 ♗d7 7.♘xc6 bxc6

7...♗xc6 8.♗xc6+ bxc6 9.c4 ♘f6 10.♕a4 ♕c7 11.exd5 exd5 12.0-0 ♗e7 13.b3 0-0 14.♗b2 ♖ab8 15.cxd5 ♘xd5 16.♕g4 ♗f6 17.♗xf6 ♘xf6 18.♕c4± (+0.20). Black has no compensation for having two isolated pawns.

8.♗d3 ♗d6

8...♕c7 9.♕e2 ♘e7 (for 9...♗d6 see game) 10.0-0 ♘g6 11.♘f3 ♗d6 12.♖e1 ♘f4 13.♗xf4 ♗xf4 14.e5 0-0 15.g3 ♗h6 16.h4± (+0.18). White's kingside initiative looks more relevant than Black's bishop pair.

9.♕e2

9...♕c7

A) 9...e5 10.exd5 cxd5 11.c4 ♘e7 12.cxd5 ♘xd5 13.♘f3 0-0 14.0-0 ♘f6 15.♘xe5 ♖e8 16.f4 ♘g4 17.♗xh7+ ♔xh7 18.♕d3+ ♔g8 19.♕xd6 ♗b5 20.♕xd8 ♖axd8 21.♖e1 f6 22.h3 ♘xe5 23.fxe5 ♖xe5 24.♗f4± (+0.37). Black should be able to draw this pawn down rook and bishops of

opposite color endgame, but only White can hope to win;

B) 9...♘e7 10.e5 ♗c7 11.0-0 c5 12.b3

analysis diagram

12...♗a5 (12...♘g6 13.♗b2 ♗a5 (13...♘f4 14.♕e3 ♘xd3 15.cxd3 ♗a5 16.♗a3 ♗b4 17.♗xb4 cxb4 18.♖fc1± (+0.27). White has knight vs bad bishop and control of the open file) 14.g3 0-0 15.h4 h6 16.♖ad1± (+0.07), but I agree with Lc0 that White's kingside advantage is worth more than this) 13.♗b2 ♘g6 14.g3 0-0 15.♖ad1 ♕c7 16.h4± (+0.11), but I think that White's space advantage and kingside initiative deserve more than this.

10.♘f3 e5?

10...dxe4 11.♕xe4 ♘f6 12.♕h4 h6 13.0-0 c5 14.♖e1 ♗c6 15.♘d2 ♘d5 16.♘c4 ♗f4 17.♗xf4 ♘xf4 18.♗e4 g5 19.♕g3 ♖d8 20.♘e5 ♗xe4 21.♖xe4± (+0.28), and Lc0 really likes White, who has the better pawn structure and safer king.

11.exd5 cxd5?! 12.♘xe5+− ♗xe5 13.f4 f6 14.fxe5 ♕xe5 15.♗f4 ♕xe2+ 16.♗xe2 ♘e7 17.0-0-0 ♔f7 18.♗f3 ♗e6 19.♖he1 ♖ac8 20.♖d2 ♖c6 21.b3 ♖d8 22.♔b2 g5 23.♗e3 a6 24.c4 g4 25.♗e2 ♖dc8 26.c5 h5

27.b4 ♖b8 28.a3 ♘f5 29.♔g1 d4
30.♗xd4 a5 31.♔c3 axb4+ 32.axb4
♖a8 33.♔c4 ♗xc4 34.♔xc4 ♖c7
35.♗c3 ♔g6 36.b5 ♖a4+ 37.♔b4
♖c8 38.b6 ♖b8 39.♔b5 ♖aa8 40.c6
h4 41.c7 ♖b7 42.♔c6 1-0

Game 3.8 French Defense – Tarrasch
Csaba Balogh   2632
Tomas Petrik   2473

Czech Republic tt 2017/18 (6)

**1.e4 e6 2.d4 d5 3.♘d2 c5 4.♘gf3
cxd4 5.♘xd4 ♘f6 6.exd5**

6...♕xd5
This may be the best defense to the
Tarrasch, it keeps White's edge to a
minimum.
6...♘xd5 7.♘2f3 ♗b4+ 8.♗d2 0-0
9.♗xb4 ♘xb4 10.c3 ♘d5 11.♗c4
b6 12.0-0 ♗b7 13.♖e1 ♘c6 14.♘xc6
♗xc6 15.♘e5 ♗b7 16.a4 ♕c7 17.a5
♖ad8 18.♕a4 ♘f6 19.axb6 axb6
20.♗f1± (+0.17). White has better
pawn structure and a better placed
knight.
7.♘b5 ♘a6
7...♕d8 8.♘c4 ♘d5 9.♘e3 a6
10.♘xd5 exd5 11.♘d4 ♘c6 12.♗e3±
(+0.14). The exchange of knights
makes this isolated d-pawn position

favorable for White, as Black has no
prospect of getting a knight to its
natural outpost on e4.
8.a3 ♗d7
8...♗e7 9.♘c3 ♕d8 10.♕f3± (+0.23).
Black will have trouble completing
his development safely.
9.♘c3 ♕d6

10.♕e2!
Alternatives are less convincing.
  A) 10.♕f3 ♗c6 11.♕g3 ♕xg3
12.hxg3 ♘c7 13.♘c4 (+0.04). White's
only edge is his active rook on h1,
not much here;
  B) 10.♘c4 ♕xd1+ 11.♘xd1 ♘c5
12.♘c3 ♘a4 13.♘xa4 ♗xa4 14.b3
♗b5 15.♗b2 (+0.08). White has just
a slight plus in piece placement.
**10...♗e7 11.♘c4 ♕c7 12.♕e5 0-0
13.♗f4**

13...♖fc8

13...♕c8? 14.0-0-0 ♗c6 15.♘d6± (+0.42). White wins the bishop pair while Black still has an offside knight.

14.0-0-0?!

14.♗e2! ♕xe5 15.♘xe5 ♗e8 16.♗f3± (+0.34). White's minor pieces are all superior to Black's.

14...♕xe5 15.♗xe5

15...♗e8?

Needlessly giving up the bishop pair.

15...♘c5! 16.♗e2 ♗c6 17.f3 ♘d5 18.♖he1 (+0.10). White is better developed but not by much.

16.♘d6 ♗xd6 17.♗xd6± (+0.38)

Black has no compensation for the bishop pair.

17...♘c5 18.♖d4

18.f3 a6 19.♔b1± (+0.38) was perhaps even better.

18...♘d5 19.♘xd5 ♘b3+ 20.♔b1 ♘xd4 21.♘e7+ ♔h8 22.♘xc8 ♖xc8 23.♗d3 ♗c6 24.f3 ♖d8

24...♘f5 25.♗f4 f6 26.♖e1 ♖e8 27.b4± (+0.30). It's the bishop pair, nothing else.

25.♗g3 a6 26.♖e1 ♗b5? 27.♗xb5 ♘xb5 28.a4

28.c4! ♘d4 29.♖d1 ♘c6 30.♖xd8+ ♘xd8 31.♔c2+− (+1.40). This ending looks won for white, with his pawn majority looking far more dangerous than Black's. With opposite side passed pawns, bishop vs knight is a real edge.

28...♘a7 29.c3 ♔g8 30.♔c2 ♔f8 31.b4 ♔e7 32.♗f2 ♘c8 33.c4 f6 34.♔c3 g5 35.h4

35...♖g8?

35...gxh4 36.♖h1±.

36.hxg5 ♖xg5 37.g4 ♔f7 38.♖d1+− ♔e8 39.♖h1 ♖g7 40.♖h6 ♖f7 41.♗h4 ♔e7 42.c5 e5 43.g5 fxg5 44.♗xg5+ ♔d7 45.♔c4 ♘e7 46.♖d6+ ♔c7 47.b5 axb5+ 48.axb5 ♔c8 49.♔b4 ♖g7 50.♗f6 ♖f7 51.♔c4 h5 52.♗g5 h4 53.♖h6 ♘f5 54.♖h8+ ♔c7 55.♔d5 ♖d7+ 56.♔e4 ♘e7 57.♗f6 ♘g6 58.♖g8 ♖d4+ 59.♔e3

Black resigned.

CHAPTER 4

Petroff, Philidor, and Black gambits

In this chapter I cover Black's sensible alternatives to 2...♘c6 after **1.e4 e5 2.♘f3**. There are several more or less silly moves here that I don't cover, such as Damiano's 2...f6?, met by 3.♘xe5!. I do cover two unsound but at least tricky gambits, the Elephant Gambit **2...d5** and the Latvian Gambit **2...f5**, of which the Latvian is more popular while the Elephant is less clearly losing. See Game 4.1.

The Philidor (**2...d6**) comes in two varieties.

Black can give up the center by taking on d4 at the first chance (Game 4.2), or can support the e5-pawn by ...♘d7 (called the Hanham Variation, named after a top American player of the later 1800s who lost a game with it to my first chess teacher in 1898!). The Hanham is now almost always reached by a different move order starting with 1...d6, but the same position may arise after four moves. See Game 4.3. Both of these are serious openings which are played from time to time by grandmasters (including myself), but in both cases White gets a bigger advantage with proper play than in the Petroff or the other four main defenses to 1.e4. I recommend castling queenside in the first case and an early a2-a4 in the second one. The Game 4.2 line is a pretty reasonable choice for Black in a must-win situation, because although White is better, both sides have play, and the chances of a draw are fairly low. I selected this defense for Black repeatedly and successfully for the computer program Rybka in a match where it gave draw and White odds in every game to GM Joel Benjamin.

The Petroff (**2...♘f6**) is a very major defense and was featured in the latest World Championship by Caruana, the main advocate (until 2019 anyway) of it at top level.

It used to be considered almost as a sure way to get a draw as Black, but I think that the Berlin has taken its place in that category. After **3.♘xe5 d6 4.♘f3 ♘xe4** I first give the **5.♕e2** line, which has been somewhat rehabilitated from its former status as a drawing line only, as well as the related version with 4.♘d3 in the notes (Game 4.4), and then give as my main recommendation trading off Black's e4-knight in the main line **5.d4 d5 6.♗d3**

... by a timely ♘bd2 (Games 4.5 and 4.6). I think this was also formerly thought to be just a way to draw but now seems quite promising as a winning try, and the Petroff doesn't look quite so safe to me now. In both of these games White had a pretty clear edge by around move 15. Caruana avoided this line by playing symmetrically (**6...♗d6**) in most of his Petroff games, with a recent counter to that idea shown in Game 4.7, where White seems to have had a small but clear endgame advantage around move 17. Finally, in Game 4.8 Yu Yangyi just plays **6...♗e7** and castles, avoiding ...♘c6 in case ...c7-c6 looks like a better option. The game looks like a boring grandmaster draw at first glance, but it seems that White had at least two chances to get a serious advantage, and even in the final position he could have played on with a slight pull. Although the Petroff may be a good way to play for a draw, it doesn't look fully equal to me, there always seem to be ways to make Black suffer to get the draw.

Game 4.1 King's Pawn Opening –
Latvian Gambit

Giorgio Ruggeri Laderchi 2438
Alfredo Dutra 2431

Correspondence game, 2018

1.e4 e5 2.♘f3 f5?

The Latvian Gambit, but I would call it the Latvian Blunder, since Black gets absolutely nothing for the pawn in the game line or else suffers an awful position to regain it.

2...d5? is the Elephant Gambit. It is not as bad as the Latvian it seems, because at least Black can get some compensation for the pawn in the Elephant. 3.exd5 and now:

analysis diagram

A) 3...♗d6 4.d4 e4 5.♘e5 ♘f6 6.♗b5+ c6 7.dxc6 bxc6 8.♗a4N 0-0 9.♘c3 ♗a6 10.♗g5 ♗b4 11.♕d2 ♕c8 12.♗xf6 gxf6 13.h4+− (+0.90). White has a winning attack with ideas of ♖h3 and 0-0-0;

B) 3...e4 4.♕e2 ♘f6 5.♘c3 ♗e7 6.♘xe4 ♘xd5 7.♕d1 0-0 8.♗c4 ♘c6 9.h3 ♘f4 10.0-0 ♘a5 11.♗e2 ♗f5 12.d3 ♘xe2+ 13.♕xe2± (+0.70). Black has the bishop pair for the pawn, but nothing else;

C) 3...♕xd5 4.♘c3 ♕e6 5.♗b5+ c6 6.♗a4 ♕g6 7.♗b3 ♗e6 8.0-0 ♘d7 9.d4 0-0-0 10.♕e2 exd4 11.♘xd4 ♗xb3 12.axb3 ♗c5 13.♕c4 ♘e7 14.♗f4 ♕f6 15.♘f3 b5 16.♕e4 ♖he8 17.♗g5 ♕g6 18.♕xg6 hxg6 19.♘e4 f6 20.♗d2 ♘f5 21.♘xc5 ♘xc5 22.♖xa7+− (+1.01). White has won a pawn for nothing.

3.♘xe5

3...♕f6

3...♘f6 4.♗c4 ♕e7 5.d4 ♘c6 6.0-0 fxe4 7.♗f4 d5 8.♗b3 ♗e6 9.c4 dxc4 10.♗a4 ♗d7 11.♘c3 0-0-0 12.♗xc6 ♗xc6 13.♘xc6 bxc6 14.♖b1 ♕b4 15.♗e5 ♗e7 16.♕e2 ♖he8 17.♘xe4+− (+1.08). White has regained the pawn and has an obviously huge advantage in pawn structure and king safety, and will surely win a pawn.

4.d4 d6 5.♘c4 fxe4 6.♘c3 ♕g6 7.f3

7...♗e7

7...exf3 8.♕xf3 ♘f6 9.♘e3 ♘c6
10.♗d3 ♕f7 11.♗c4 ♕g6 12.♘ed5
♗g4 13.♕e3+ ♔d7 14.0-0 ♖e8
15.♕f2 ♘xd5 16.♘xd5+– (+1.70).
White has a winning advantage in
development and king safety.
**8.♘xe4 d5 9.♘e5 ♕b6 10.♘c3 ♘f6
11.♗e2+– (+1.14)**

White has a nice outposted knight
and an extra pawn for nothing.
11...0-0

11...c5 12.dxc5 ♕xc5 13.♗f4+–.
**12.♘a4 ♕a5+ 13.c3 c6 14.0-0 ♘bd7
15.♘d3 ♖e8 16.♖e1 ♘f8 17.b4 ♕d8
18.♘e5 ♗f5 19.♘c5 ♕c7 20.♗d3
♗xd3 21.♘cxd3 ♗d6 22.♗f4 a5
23.a3 ♘h5 24.♗g5 ♘f6 25.♕d2
♘8d7 26.♔h1 ♗e7 27.a4 axb4
28.cxb4 ♘f8 29.a5 ♘e6 30.♗e3 ♗d6
31.♖ec1 ♕b8 32.a6 ♘d8 33.♗g5
♗e7 34.♖e1 ♕c7 35.a7 ♘e6
36.♗e3 ♗d6 37.♕a2 ♖e7 38.g4 h6
39.♘g6 ♖ee8 40.♘h4 ♗f8 41.♘f5 b5
42.♕a6 ♘d8 43.♗d2 g6 44.♘xh6+
♔h7 45.g5 ♖xe1+ 46.♗xe1 ♘h5
47.♘e5 ♗e7 48.♗d2 ♗d6 49.♘hg4
♗xe5 50.dxe5 ♘e6 51.♘f6+ ♘xf6
52.exf6 ♔g8 53.♕a3 d4 54.♕d3
♔f7 55.f4 ♖xa7 56.♖e1 ♕d7 57.♔g1
1-0**

Game 4.2   King's Pawn Opening –
Philidor Defense
Jürgen Krebs 2258
Hans-Georg Koch 2257
Correspondence game, 2015

1.e4 e5 2.♘f3 d6 3.d4

3...exd4

A) 3...♗g4 4.dxe5 ♘d7 (Black
gets only a tempo for the pawn,
but the alternative is even worse:
4...♗xf3 5.♕xf3 dxe5 6.♕b3!N,
improving over 6.♗c4 (which is
close to winning) from Morphy vs
Duke of Brunswick, 1858, perhaps
the most famous chess game of all!
6...b6 7.♗c4± (+1.41). White has a
lead in development, threats, and
the bishop pair, while Black has
weakened his position with ...b7-b6.
White should win) 5.exd6 ♗xd6
6.♗e2 ♘gf6 7.♘d4 ♗xe2 8.♕xe2 0-0
9.f3 ♗e5 10.♘f5± (+1.00). White is a
clean pawn up;

B) 3...f5? was popular in the
mid 1800s, even though all four
plausible replies are probably
winning for White! 4.exf5 e4 5.♘g5
♗xf5 6.♘c3 d5 7.f3 e3 8.♗xe3 h6
9.g4 hxg5 10.gxf5 ♘c6 11.♕d2 ♗e7
12.0-0-0+– (+1.32). White has

an extra 1.5 pawns with a good position;

C) 3...♘c6 4.♗b5 transposes to the Spanish Steinitz Defense. 4.c3 (+0.43) is also good.

4.♘xd4 ♘f6 5.♘c3

5...♗e7

This line, credited to Antoshin, works reasonably well against routine play by White, but the text line with queenside castling is pretty much a refutation of it. 5...g6 6.♗e3 ♗g7 7.♕d2 0-0 8.0-0-0 ♖e8 9.f3. So it's essentially a Yugoslav Attack vs the Sicilian Dragon, except that the c7-pawn should be on e7. The difference is in White's favor here as Black lacks the usual counterplay on the c-file. 9...♘c6 10.g4 a6 11.♗e2 ♘e5 12.g5 ♘h5 13.f4 ♘g4 14.♗g1 c5 15.♘b3 ♗xc3 16.bxc3 ♖xe4 17.h3 ♘g3 18.♗f3 ♖a4 19.hxg4 ♘xh1 20.♘xc5 ♖xa2 21.♘e4+− (+4.42). White's attack will at least leave him with two bishops for a rook and pawn with a continuing attack.

6.♗f4!

6.g3 is a good alternative if you prefer same-side castling, but it is less convincing than the plan with

castling queenside: 6...0-0 7.♗g2 ♘c6 8.♘xc6 bxc6 9.0-0 ♘d7 10.b3 ♗f6 11.♗b2 ♖b8 12.f4± (+0.50). White has more space and better pawn structure, but no easy way to win.

6...0-0 7.♕d2

7...c6

7...♘c6 8.0-0-0 ♘xd4 9.♕xd4 ♗e6 10.f3 a6 11.g4 b5 12.h4 c5 13.♕e3 b4 14.♘a4 ♕c7 15.b3 ♕c6 16.♖h2 ♖fe8 17.h5 d5 18.g5 ♘d7 19.g6± (+0.40). White's attack is faster than Black's.

8.0-0-0 b5 9.f3 b4 10.♘a4 ♗d7

11.g4!

This piece 'sacrifice' seems to be only played in correspondence games, but since it actually wins rook and two pawns for two minors it is not a real sacrifice, and the resultant position is great for White.

This seems to be the refutation of the Philidor with 3..exd4.
11.b3 d5 12.h4 (this Lc0 gambit novelty is strong, but it's better to play 11.g4 the move before) 12...dxe4 13.fxe4 ♘xe4 14.♕e3 ♘f6 15.♘f5 ♖e8 16.♕g3 ♗xf5 17.♖xd8 ♖xd8 18.♗e2± (+1.28). Queen is usually stronger than rook, knight and pawn, and White still has some kingside attack.

11...c5 12.♘f5 ♗xa4 13.♘xe7+ ♕xe7 14.♗xd6 ♕e8

A) 14...♕e6 15.b3 ♖d8 16.♗c4 ♕e8 17.e5 ♘fd7 18.e6 fxe6 19.♖he1 ♘f8 20.bxa4+−;

B) 14...♕b7 15.♗xf8 ♔xf8 16.e5 ♘e8 17.e6 ♘c6 18.b3 ♖d8 19.♕f4 ♖xd1+ 20.♔xd1 ♘d8 21.exf7 ♕d7+ 22.♗d3 ♘xf7 23.bxa4+−.

15.♗xc5 a5 16.♗xf8 ♕xf8 17.e5 ♘fd7

18.♕d6
The equally strong move 18.♕e3 has been played twice in correspondence games: 18...♘c5 19.♗c4 ♘bd7 20.b3 ♗c6 21.♖d6 ♖c8 22.♖hd1 ♕e7 23.e6 ♔h8 24.f4± (+1.12). White has a strong attack and a slight material plus (quarter of a pawn).

18...♕xd6 19.♖xd6 ♔f8 20.f4
20.e6! fxe6 21.♖xe6 ♘c6 22.b3 ♘d8 23.♖a6 ♗c6 24.♖xa8 ♗xa8 25.♗b5 ♗c6 26.♗xc6 ♘xc6 27.♖e1± (+0.96). With no other pieces, a rook and pawn are generally a bit better than two knights, so here White is really more than a full pawn ahead, and should win. But the move played is also fine.

20...♗c6 21.♖g1 ♔e7 22.♗d3 g6
22...♘f8 23.♖e1± (+1.00). White has rook and two pawns for two knights, while Black still has development problems.

23.♖g3 ♖a7 24.♖h3 ♘f8 25.f5 ♖d7 26.f6+ ♔d8 27.♖e3 h6 28.♗c4 ♖xd6 29.exd6 ♘bd7 30.♖e7 ♘xf6 31.♖xf7 ♘8d7 32.♗e6 a4 33.♗xd7 ♘xd7 34.♖h7 ♘f6 35.♖xh6 ♘xg4 36.♖h4 ♘e5 37.♖xb4 ♔d7 38.h4 ♔xd6 39.♔d2 ♘d7 40.b3 1-0

Game 4.3   King's Pawn Opening –
           Philidor Defense
Jorden van Foreest   2614
Denis Khismatullin   2621
St Petersburg rapid 2018 (10)

1.e4 d6
1...e5 2.♘f3 d6 3.d4 ♘d7 was the normal move order long ago (3...♘f6 4.♘c3 ♘bd7 is another move order to reach the Hanham, but it gives White a good option of 4.dxe5 ♘xe4 5.♕d5. Whether it is better for White than the current game is hard to say, so no need to learn it) 4.♗c4 c6 So far Harold Phillips vs J.M.Hanham, 1898. Amazingly, Mr. Phillips, who won that game,

was my first chess teacher!! 5.0-0 ♗e7 (here 6.♘c3 could transpose to the current game, but due to the line given, which wins the bishop pair for nothing, the 1...d6 move order is now standard) 6.dxe5 dxe5 7.♘g5 ♗xg5 8.♕h5 ♕e7 9.♕xg5± (+0.94). The open position favors the bishop pair, and White leads in development as well.

2.d4 ♘f6 3.♘c3 e5

3...♘bd7 4.♘f3 e5 transposes to the game. This move order has the advantage for Black of avoiding the 4.dxe5 dxe5 5.♕xd8+ line, but allows 4.f4. In either case I prefer the line in the game for White.

4.♘f3 ♘bd7

The Hanham Defense, a good choice to play for a win against a weaker opponent who might not know it well (not the case here!). I've often played it myself.

5.♗c4 ♗e7 6.a4

Castling first is usual, but it seems White wants to discourage 6...♘b6. If White intends 7.a4 anyway, why not play it now?

6...0-0 7.0-0

Unfortunately for those like myself who might like to play this line for

Black, both engines evaluate this position around (+0.30), nearly double White's initial edge. My database stats are also quite good for White, plus 56 Elo (par for 1.e4 is 38 Elo).

7...c6

8.h3

8.a5 is also good, e.g. 8...h6 (8...♖b8 9.♕e2 b5 10.axb6 axb6 11.d5 b5 12.dxc6 bxc4 13.cxd7 ♗xd7 14.♕xc4± (+0.32). White is up half a pawn (pawn for bishop pair) without much compensation for Black) 9.h3 exd4 (9...♖b8 10.dxe5 dxe5 11.♘h4± (+0.28). The knight heading for f5 or g6 will at least win the bishop pair for free) 10.♘xd4 ♘c5 11.♕f3 ♘cxe4 12.♘xe4 ♘xe4 13.♕xe4 d5 14.♗xd5 ♕xd5 15.♕xe7 ♕xd4 16.♖a3 ♕d8 17.♖e1± (+1.02). The rook on the 7th rank (after the queen trade) plus the other mobile rook would normally win, but bishops of opposite colors leave Black with some hope for a draw.

8...exd4

A) 8...a5 9.♖e1 ♘b6 10.♗b3 ♘fd7 11.♗e3 exd4 12.♘xd4 ♘c5 13.♕e2 ♘xb3 14.♘xb3 ♖e8 15.♖ad1 ♗f8 16.♕d3 ♘d7 17.f4 b6 18.♗f2±

(+0.30). White's huge development advantage and space are surely worth more than the bishop pair;

B) 8...♘xe4 9.♘xe4 d5 10.♖e1 exd4 11.♗xd5 cxd5 12.♘g3 d3 13.♕xd3 ♘c5 14.♕d1± (+0.33). Black has the bishop pair but probably can't retain it since the light-squared bishop will probably have to take a knight on f5 or be taken on e6. Black lacks any activity to offset the isolated d-pawn since his knight can't safely reach e4.

9.♕xd4 ♘c5 10.♖e1 ♗e6 11.♗f4 d5 12.exd5 cxd5 13.♗a2 ♘ce4 14.♘xe4 dxe4

14...♘xe4 15.♕d1 ♖e8 16.♘d4 ♗c5 17.c3 ♕b6 18.♖e2± (+0.54). White has pressure on the isolated d-pawn, and will probably win the bishop pair at some point.

15.♕xd8 ♖axd8 16.♗xe6 fxe6 17.♘g5 ♘d5 18.♘xe6 ♘xf4 19.♘xd8 ♖xd8 20.♖xe4 ♘g6

21.♖ae1

After the better move 21.♔f1!± (+0.42) White is up by rook and two pawns for bishop and knight, roughly a quarter pawn plus, but nearly a full pawn plus if he can exchange rooks. With two rooks vs rook and two minors, the side with the extra rook strives to exchange the other pair of rooks, so ♔g1-f1–e1 and ♖d1 makes sense.

21...♔f7 22.g3 ♖d5 23.♔g2 ♗f6 24.♖b4 b6 25.♖e2 ♘e7 26.♖b5?
The exchange of rooks is strategically good for White, but not worth a pawn.
26.c3± (+0.18). With little hope for a rook exchange White's tiny material plus is hard to exploit.

26...♖xb5 27.axb5

27...♘f5?
27...♗xb2 28.c4 ♗f6=. Rook and pawn vs bishop and knight is about even with no other pieces on the board.

28.c4±
Very strange that Black didn't take the free pawn on b2.

28...♘d4 29.♖e3 ♘c2 30.♖e4 ♘b4 31.♖e2 ♘d3 32.b3 ♘c1 33.♖e3 ♗d4 34.♖f3+ ♔e6 35.♔f1 ♔e5 36.b4 ♔e4 37.♖a3 ♘d3 38.♖xa7 ♘xb4 39.♔e2 ♗f6 40.♖d7 ♔e5 41.♔e3 ♘c2+ 42.♔d3 ♘b4+ 43.♔e3 ♘c2+ 44.♔d2 ♘b4 45.c5 bxc5 46.b6 ♔e6 47.b7 ♘a6 48.♖c7 ♘b8 49.♖xc5 ♔d7 50.♔d3 ♘a6 51.♖c8 ♗e5 52.♔e4 ♗c7 53.♖g8 1-0

Game 4.4 Russian Game/Petroff

Vladimir Onischuk 2623
Andrey Vovk 2624

Hungary tt 2018/19 (4)

1.e4 e5 2.♘f3 ♘f6 3.♘xe5 d6 4.♘f3
The rare move 4.♘d3 leads to
similar play to our game: 4...♘xe4
5.♕e2 ♕e7 6.♘f4

analysis diagram

A) 6...♘f6 7.d4 ♕xe2+ 8.♗xe2
♘c6 (8...♗f5 9.c3 ♘bd7 10.f3 h5
11.h4 d5 12.♗d3 ♗xd3 13.♘xd3
♗d6 14.♔f2± Motylev. (+0.18). The
white king and white d3-knight
are better placed than their black
counterparts) 9.c3 g6 10.f3 ♗g7
11.h4 h5 12.a4 0-0 13.a5 ♗d7
14.♔f2± (+0.19). White has more
space and a better placed king for
the endgame;
B) 6...♘c6 7.♘d5 ♘d4 8.♘xe7
♘xe2 9.♘d5 ♘d4 10.♘a3 ♘e6
11.f3 ♘4c5 12.d4 ♘d7 13.c3 c6
14.♘f4 ♘b6 15.♗d3 d5 16.♘c2
♗d6 17.♘xe6 (17.♘e2 (Motylev)
17...0-0 18.♔f2 a5 19.a4 ♘d7 20.h4
b6 21.♘e3 g6 22.g4 ♘f6 23.h5 ♗a6
24.♗xa6 ♖xa6 25.♗g2± (+0.13).
White has space and some kingside
pressure) 17...♗xe6 18.♔f2 h5 19.h4

♘c8 20.♖e1 (this is Motylev's
improvement over Carlsen-
Caruana, London 2018) 20...♘e7
21.g3 ♔d7 22.♘e3 g6 23.♘g2 ♗f5
24.♗e2 f6 25.♖h1 ♖ae8 26.♗f4 ♘c8
27.♗xd6 ♘xd6 28.♘e3± (+0.16). The
bishop is a 'hostage'. White can take
it when it suits him to do so.
4...♘xe4

5.♕e2
This move used to be considered to
be a drawing line, but it now seems
like a legitimate try for a small
white edge. It's not my first choice
though.
5...♕e7 6.d3 ♘f6 7.♗g5 ♕xe2+
7...♘bd7 8.♘c3 ♕xe2+ 9.♗xe2 h6
10.♗d2 c6 11.0-0-0 d5 12.♖de1 ♗d6
13.♗d1+ ♔d8 14.h3 ♔c7 15.♘e2 ♘e5
16.♘xe5 ♗xe5 17.g4± (+0.26). White
will likely win the bishop pair by
♘e2-g3-f5.
8.♗xe2 ♗e7
So White has the extra developing
move ♗g5 in addition to his normal
first move advantage. Of course
the symmetry and the queen trade
makes a draw somewhat likely, but
the tempo gained should cause
Black at least some problems.
9.♘c3

9...♘c6

9...c6 10.0-0-0 h6 11.♗d2 ♘a6
12.♖de1 ♘c7 13.♗d1 ♗d7 14.h3 ♘e6
15.♘h4 0-0-0 16.f4 ♖he8 17.♘f3 ♗f8
18.g4 ♘c7 19.f5 (19.♖eg1 g6 20.g5±
(+0.25). White has an initiative and
a space advantage) 19...♖xe1 20.♖xe1
♖e8 21.♘e4 ♘xe4 22.dxe4 g6 23.c4
d5 24.exd5 (24.cxd5 cxd5 25.fxg6
fxg6 26.e5 g5 27.♗c2 ♗c5 28.♗f5
♘e6 29.♗e3 d4 30.♗g1± (+0.12).
White has pressure on the d4-pawn,
but Black should draw) 24...♖xe1
25.♗xe1 cxd5 26.fxg6 fxg6 27.♘e5
♗e8 28.♗c2 g5 29.♗f5+ (29.♗g3
(+0.05) would keep a tiny edge,
though the game is headed towards
a likely draw) 29...♔d8 30.♗g3 dxc4
31.♘xc4 ♗c6 32.♔d2 ♗g2 33.h4
gxh4 34.♗xh4+ ♗e7 35.♗g3 ♗g5+
36.♔e2 ♗d5 37.b3 ♘e6 38.♗e5
♔e7 39.♗d6+ ♔f6 40.♗e5+ ♔e7
41.♗d6+ ♔f6 42.♗e5+ ♔e7 ½-½
Ponomariov-Bu Xiangzhi, Batumi
2018.

10.♘b5 ♔d8 11.c4

11.h3 a6 12.♘bd4 ♘xd4 13.♘xd4
♖e8 14.0-0-0 ♘d5 15.♗xe7+ (+0.12).
Black's awkward king is White's
small plus.

11...h6 12.♗f4

12.♗e3 ♘g4 13.d4 ♖e8 14.h3 ♘xe3
15.fxe3 a5 16.♔d2 a4 17.♖hf1 (+0.10).
White has better king placement,
better development, and more
space while Black has the bishop
pair. White is for choice, but not by
much.

12...♖e8 13.h3 a6 14.♘c3

14...♗f5

14...b5 15.a3=.

15.g4 ♗h7 16.♔d2

16.♗e3 b5 17.a3± (+0.13), but Lc0
rates it much higher. White has a
more active queen's bishop than
Black.

16...♘d7

16...b5=.

17.g5 hxg5?!

17...b5 18.gxh6 bxc4 19.dxc4 ♖b8
20.b3 ♗f6 21.♖ae1 ♖b4 22.♗d1 ♖xe1
23.♘xe1 gxh6 24.♗xh6 ♘c5 25.♖g1
♔d7 26.♗e3 ♗f5 27.♘c2 ♗xc3+
28.♔xc3 ♘e4+ 29.♔b2 ♘d3+ 30.♔a3
c5 31.♗e2± (+0.20). Black has only
partial compensation for the pawn.

18.♘xg5 ♗g8 19.♗e3 ♗f8?! 20.h4± ♘e7 21.♗h5 g6 22.♗e2 ♘f5 23.h5 ♘f6 24.♘ge4 ♘xe4+ 25.♘xe4 ♘xe3 26.fxe3 ♗e7 27.♖af1 b5 28.h6 f5 29.h7 ♗xh7 30.♖xh7 fxe4 31.d4 ♖f8 32.♖xf8+ ♗xf8 33.♗g4 c5 34.♗e6

♖b8 35.b3 ♗e7 36.♖g7 g5 37.♔e2 a5 38.cxb5 ♖xb5 39.♖g8+ ♔c7 40.♖c8+ ♔b7 41.♖e8 ♗f6 42.♖f8 cxd4 43.♖xf6 d3+ 44.♔d1 ♖c5 45.♖f5 ♔c6 46.♖xc5+ ♔xc5 47.♔d2 d5 48.♔c3 ♔d6 49.♗g4 ♔e5 50.a3 d4+ 51.exd4+ ♔f4 52.d5 e3 53.d6 ♔g3 54.♔xd3 1-0

Game 4.5   Russian Game/Petroff –
Jaenisch Variation

Alexandra Kosteniuk   2537
Ottomar Ladva   2497

PRO League Stage rapid 2019 (3)

1.e4 e5 2.♘f3 ♘f6 3.♘xe5 d6 4.♘f3 ♘xe4 5.d4 d5 6.♗d3 ♘c6 7.0-0 ♗e7 8.♘bd2

This is not so common but good for a small edge. Perhaps this is why Caruana, the top Petroff specialist, avoids this ...♘c6 line.

8...♗f5

   A) 8...♘d6 9.c3 ♗f5 10.♘b3 (10.♗c2± (+0.31). The idea is to provoke the exchange of bishops by 'threatening' ♗b3) 10...♗xd3 11.♕xd3 0-0 12.♗f4 a5 13.♘bd2 a4 14.♖fe1 ♕d7 15.♖e2 ♘d8 16.♖ae1 ♘e6 17.♗g3 ♗f6 18.♘e5 ♗xe5 19.♗xe5 c6 20.h4 ♖ae8 21.♕h3 ♖e7

22.♕g4± (+0.30). White has bishop for knight and some kingside pressure;

   B) 8...♘xd2 9.♗xd2 ♗g4 10.c3 0-0 11.h3 ♗h5 12.g3 ♕d7 13.♔g2 ♗g6 14.♗xg6 fxg6 15.♕c2 ♖ae8 16.♖ae1 ♗d6 17.♕d3 a6 18.h4 (18.b3 ♕f7 19.h4± (+0.27). White plans c3-c4) 18...♘d8 19.c4 dxc4 20.♕xc4+ ♕f7 21.♕xf7+ ♘xf7 22.♗c3± (+0.25). Black can't easily exchange all the rooks, while White can bring his knight to c4 or e4 or e5.

9.♖e1 ♘xd2 10.♕xd2 ♗xd3 11.♕xd3 0-0 12.♖e2 ♕d7 13.♗f4 ♖ae8 14.♖ae1 a6 15.h3

15.♕b3± (+0.55) is similar to the game.

15...h6 16.♕b3

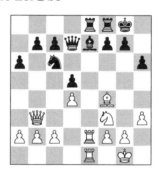

16...♘a5?

16...b5 17.c3 ♖d8 18.♕c2 ♖fe8 19.♖e3 ♗d6 20.♗xd6 ♖xe3 21.♖xe3 ♕xd6 22.♕e2± (+0.46). White has control of the open file and ideas like ♘f3-e1-d3 or a2-a4 or b2-b4.

17.♘e5+– ♕f5 18.♕g3

18.♕xd5+–.

18...♗g5 19.♗xg5 ♕xg5 20.♕f3 ♕d8 21.♕c3 c6 22.b3 ♖e7 23.♘d3 ♖xe2 24.♖xe2 b6 25.♕e1

25.♘b4+–; 25.♖e1+–.

25...♕f6?

25...♘b7 26.♘b4 ♕f6 27.♖e7±.

26.♘e5

26.♕b4!.

26...♖d8? 27.♖e3 ♖e8?? 28.♘d7 1-0

Game 4.6   Russian Game/Petroff –
               Jaenisch Variation

Alireza Firouzja   2657

Alexander Lenderman   2637

Astana Wch-tt 2019 (9)

1.e4 e5 2.♘f3 ♘f6 3.♘xe5 d6 4.♘f3 ♘xe4 5.d4 d5 6.♗d3 ♗f5

This obscure line has caught on a bit lately.

7.0-0 ♗e7 8.♖e1 ♘c6 9.♘bd2

Now we have transposed back to the previous game, so for us the unusual sixth move doesn't make any difference.

9...♘xd2 10.♕xd2 ♗xd3 11.♕xd3 0-0 12.c3

12.♖e2 as in the previous game also gives some edge. I would probably choose 12.c3, but it's debatable.

12...♕d7

12...h6 13.♗f4 ♗d6 14.♗xd6 ♕xd6 15.♖e3± (+0.34). Black can't easily exchange all the rooks, so White keeps control of the only open file.

Black's knight wants to move to permit ...c7-c6 but that would allow ♘e5.

13.♗f4

White has scored well from here and is obviously better developed with the black knight preventing ...c7-c6. Lc0 really likes White, but the pawn symmetry does give Black decent drawing chances. It is instructive to see how a strong GM like Lenderman is unable to hold.

13...♖fe8 14.♖e2

14.h4 a6 15.h5 h6 16.♖e3 ♗d6 17.♗xd6 ♖xe3 18.♕xe3 ♕xd6 19.♖e1 ♔f8 20.♕d3± (+0.44) illustrates the point of h4-h5; if Black challenges on the open file the queen invades on h7 after trading rooks.

14...♗d6 15.♗xd6 ♖xe2 16.♕xe2 ♕xd6 17.♖e1 g6 18.h4 h5 19.b4 ♖f8 20.♘g5 a5

21.b5

21.bxa5 ♘xa5 22.♕e7± (+0.33). White's rook and knight are invading, while Black must defend passively.

21...♘a7 22.g3 ♘c8?!

22...♕d7 23.a4 ♘c8 24.♕f3 – Komodo says dead even, but Lc0 shows +0.17, and it does look easier to play for White since Black cannot challenge on the open file.

23.♘h3 ♕f6 24.♘f4 ♘b6 25.♕d3 ♖d8 26.♖e5 ♔f8 27.♕e2 a4

28.♖e3± ♔g7? 29.♖e7+−

Winning a pawn due to the threat of 30.♘e6+, with more to follow.

29...♔f8 30.♖xc7 ♖e8 31.♕f3 ♖e4? 32.♔g2 ♕f5 33.♖xb7 ♘c4 34.♘d3 1-0

Game 4.7   Russian Game/Petroff –
           Jaenisch Variation

Alexander Grischuk   2771
Eltaj Safarli   2662

Astana Wch-tt 2019 (6)

1.e4 e5 2.♘f3 ♘f6 3.♘xe5 d6 4.♘f3 ♘xe4 5.d4 d5 6.♗d3

6...♗d6

This used to be considered inferior to ...♘c6 and ...♗e7, but Caruana has brought it back to top popularity. It is probably the better choice, but still not fully equal.

7.0-0 0-0 8.♖e1 ♗f5 9.c4 c6 10.♕b3 ♕d7

10...♘a6 11.cxd5 cxd5 12.♘c3 ♗e6 (12...♘b4 13.♗xe4 dxe4 14.♗g5 ♕b6 15.♘xe4 ♗e6 16.♕a3 ♖fe8 17.♘xd6 ♕xd6 18.♗d2 a5 19.♖e5 ♕b6 20.♗xb4 axb4 21.♕d3 f6 22.♖e3± (+0.50). Black's pressure on a2 and bishop vs knight offer just partial compensation for the pawn) 13.a3 ♘c7 14.♗e3 f5 15.♖ad1 ♔h8 16.♗c1 ♕e7 17.♕c2 ♖ac8 18.♘e5± (+0.21). White's pieces are a bit more mobile than Black's, and the black outpost may be expelled.

11.♘c3 ♘xc3 12.♗xf5 ♕xf5

13.♕xb7!

13.bxc3 b6 14.cxd5 cxd5 15.♕b5 ♕d7 16.a4 ♕xb5 17.axb5 a5 18.bxa6 ♘xa6 19.♗a3 ♗xa3 20.♖xa3 ♘c7 21.♖b3 b5 22.g3 (+0.10). White has one fewer weak pawns than Black does and a more active knight, but the endgame is rather drawish.

13...♕d7 14.♕xd7 ♘xd7 15.c5 ♗xh2+ 16.♘xh2 ♘e4

17.♘f1
17.♗f4 ♖fe8 18.♘g4 g5 19.♗h2 ♔g7
20.f3 ♘ef6 21.♖xe8 ♖xe8 22.♗e5
♘xe5 23.♘xe5 ♖e6 24.a4 (+0.40).
White plans b2-b4-b5, Black will
struggle to draw.
17...♖fe8 18.f3 ♘ef6 19.♖xe8+
19.♗g5 h6 20.♗h4 ♘h5 21.♘e3 ♘f8
22.♘f5 ♘g6 23.♗f2 ♘hf4 24.♔f1±
(+0.37).
White's queenside majority looks
much more useful than Black's
kingside majority, and the knight
on f5 looks very strong.
19...♖xe8

20.♗d2
20.♘g3 g6 21.♗f4± (+0.20). White's
queenside expansion plan gives him
the easier game.
**20...♘f8 21.♘e3 ♘e6 22.♘c2 h5
23.♖e1?!**

The rook needs to support the
queenside advance.
**23...g5 24.a4 ♔h7 25.♘b4 ♖c8
26.♘d3 ♘d7 27.b4 a6 28.f4 gxf4
29.♘xf4 ♘df8 30.♘xh5 ♘xd4 31.♖e7
♘fe6 32.♘f4 ♘xf4 33.♗xf4 ♔g6
34.♔f2 a5 35.bxa5 ♘e6 36.♗d6 ♖a8**

37.♖b7?
37.♗c7=.
**37...♖xa5 38.♖b6 ♘xc5 39.♖xc6
♘e4+ 40.♔f3 ♖xa4 41.♗f4+ f6
42.♗e3 ♖a3 43.♔e2 ♔f5 44.♖c8
♘d6 45.♖d8 ♔e6 46.♗c5 ♖a2+
47.♔f3 ♘c4 48.♖e8+ ♔f5 49.g4+
♔g6 50.♖g8+ ♔f7 51.♖f8+ ♔g7
52.♖d8 ♘e5+ 53.♔e3 ♖a5 54.♖xd5
♔g6 55.♔d4 ♖a4+ 56.♔c3 ♖xg4
57.♗e7 ♖g3+ 58.♔c2 ♔f7 59.♗xf6
♔xf6**

Black gets a 'moral victory', but this
endgame is much easier to draw

than the rook and bishop vs rook endgame.

60.♖d8 ♔f5 61.♔d1 ♔e4 62.♖e8 ♖g2 63.♔e1 ♖a2 64.♔d1 ♔d4 65.♖d8+ ♔e3 66.♖e8 ♖d2+ 67.♔c1 ♖d5 68.♔c2 ½-½

Game 4.8   Russian Game/Petroff –
                    Jaenisch Variation

Viswanathan Anand   2767
Yu Yangyi   2738

Stavanger 2019 (6)

1.e4 e5 2.♘f3 ♘f6 3.♘xe5 d6 4.♘f3 ♘xe4 5.d4 d5 6.♗d3 ♗e7 7.0-0 0-0

8.♖e1

8.c4 is a decent alternative, but I'll prefer Anand's move. 8...♘f6 9.♘c3 ♘c6 10.h3 ♘b4 11.♗e2 dxc4 12.♗xc4 c6 13.♖e1 ♘bd5 14.♗g5 ♗e6 15.♕b3 h6 16.♗xd5 ♘xd5 17.♗xe7 ♕xe7 18.♘xd5 cxd5 19.♕xd5 ♗xd5 20.♖xe7 ♖fe8 21.♖e3 (+0.27). White is a pawn up but a draw is likely.

8...♗f5 9.♘bd2

9.c4 is okay here too, although I'm sticking with the game. 9...♘c6 10.cxd5 ♕xd5 11.♘c3 ♘xc3 12.bxc3 ♖ae8 13.♗f4 ♗xd3 14.♕xd3 ♗d6 15.c4 ♕h5 16.♗e3 b6 17.♖ad1 h6

18.h3± (+0.23). White has the advantage of center pawn vs wing pawn, and may aim for c4-c5.

9...♘d6 10.♗xf5 ♘xf5 11.♘f1 c6 12.♕d3 ♘d6 13.♗f4 ♘a6 14.♘e3 ♘c7 15.♖e2 ♘e6 16.♗xd6 ♗xd6 17.g3 ♕d7 18.♖ae1 ♖ae8 19.b3 ♘c7 20.c4

It looks pretty balanced and drawish, but White has already doubled rooks on the open file, and knight vs bishop is good with pawn symmetry.

20...♗b4 21.♖a1 f6 22.a3 ♗e7 23.♖ae1 ♗d8 24.♔g2 ♖e6 25.cxd5 cxd5

26.♖c1?!

26.b4 ♖e4 27.♕b3 ♔h8 28.a4 a6 29.h4 g6 30.♖d2 ♔g7 31.♖c1 ♖f7 32.♖dc2 ♘e6 33.♖d1 ♘c7 34.h5± (+0.65), but Lc0 says +1.32. White has ideas like hxg6 and ♖h1, or h5-h6, or b4-b5, with strong pressure on the king and on the d5-pawn. The knight is better than the passive bishop here, with pawn symmetry favoring the knight.

26...♖c6 27.♖ec2 ♖xc2 28.♕xc2 ♖e8 29.♕c5?!

29.b4 ♖e6 30.♕b3 ♖c6 31.♖d1± (+0.30), but Lc0 +0.72. White plans to expand on both wings with a3-a4 and h2-h4. Most engines worry about conceding the open c-file, but NN engines like AlphaZero and Lc0 don't care about that if it doesn't seem relevant. Keeping one rook on the board is often key to playing for a win, even if it means conceding a not too useful file. The main point here is that a central knight is superior to a bishop in a mid-

back rank square, usually its worst possible post.

29...a6 30.a4 ♖e6 31.♕b4 (+0.11)

Although the normal engines rate it close to equal, Lc0 shows +0.40, with ideas like h2-h4-h5 or ♘f3-e1-d3. The pawn symmetry suggests a draw, but the knight is better than the bishop here. Perhaps time was a factor in Anand's decision to call it a draw.

CHAPTER 5

Italian Game

The Italian (**1.e4 e5 2.♘f3 ♘c6 3.♗c4**) is the most popular opening among novice players, but until quite recently it was a rather rare choice in elite-level games.

However, due to Marshall/Berlin phobia, it has become a serious alternative to the Spanish recently, with former World Champion Anand being perhaps the leading practitioner of the Italian; his recent games play a big role in this chapter.

There are basically two main ways to play the Italian, at least against the main reply 3...♗c5. I exclude the lines where all four knights come out to their natural squares early as they are a bit drawish, and Evans' Gambit (4.b4) which both Fischer and Kasparov liked on occasion but which doesn't look so good with modern computer analysis. Note that after 3...♗c5, common sense says that not only is White better because it is his turn, but his advantage should at least be more than just that because the knight on f3 blocks a pawn that has much less need to move than the one Black has blocked with his ♘c6, since the c7-pawn hems in the queen. Whether White's edge is more or less than in the Spanish is not at all clear. So I give both.

First we consider lines where White is ambitious and doesn't settle for meeting ...♘f6 by d2-d3. If Black plays the Two Knights Defense, **3...♘f6**, one way to get an exciting game is the ancient and crude **4.♘g5**.

After the nearly forced **4...d5** (the Traxler Counter-Gambit 4...♝c5 isn't a blunder but is now considered dubious) **5.exd5 ♞a5** (5...♞xd5 is also considered dubious) **6.♝b5+ c6 7.dxc6 bxc6 8.♛f3** is an old line that I played well over fifty years ago which virtually forces Black to gambit a second pawn, which we refuse. Analysis indicates that White retains slightly better chances though the resultant endgames should be drawn. See Game 5.1.

After **3...♝c5 4.c3 ♞f6 5.d4 exd4 6.e5** is a sharp line analyzed recently in New In Chess *Yearbook* with the conclusion that Black can equalize in one or two lines with very accurate play. I found some improvements for White that at least seem to keep the slightly better chances, though it's quite close to equal in a couple of lines. See Game 5.2, which includes in the notes a very recent game in which Anand adopted this idea at the highest level and did obtain some advantage.

Next we come to meeting **3...♞f6** by the safe but unexciting **4.d3**.

First we'll look at **4...h6**, intending ...d7-d6 (without fear of ♞g5) and either ...g7-g6 or the recently popular ...g7-g5. White seems to keep a normal edge in this line by avoiding d2-d4 when the reply ...g5-g4 would win a pawn. See Game 5.3. If Black just plays **4...♝e7** we get play somewhat like the Spanish with d2-d3, where White is at least for choice. White gets a space advantage and generally meets ...♗e6 by trading bishops and playing b2-b4. See Game 5.4.

Finally we come to the critical **3...♘f6 4.d3 ♗c5 5.0-0**, or 3...♗c5 4.0-0 ♘f6 5.d3, transposing.

Play primarily depends on whether Black responds to c2-c3 by ...a7-a5 (Game 5.5) or by ...a7-a6 (Game 5.6). It's hard to say which is better for Black; ...a7-a5 gives Black more space than ...a7-a6, but freezing the queenside gives Black less counterplay there in case of an all-out kingside attack by White. In case Black plans a quick ...♗e6 (not fearing doubled e-pawns), as is fashionable, there is a big difference. If Black has played ...a7-a6, then the exchange of bishops followed by b2-b4 and ♕b3 usually gives at least a pull. If he has played ...a7-a5, the exchange is much less enticing without b2-b4 as an option, but on the other hand the reply ♗b5 is usually a good one. Game 5.5 features an early ♗g5 to 'punish' ...a7-a5, but the notes feature a game (also by Anand) in which White plays quietly with h2-h3 and ♘bd2 instead of ♗g5. It seems that both ways of playing for White offer chances for an edge.

In Game 5.6, White meets ...a7-a6 by a2-a4 (this has largely replaced the older response ♗b3), and gets the advantage of pawns on d4 and e4 vs d6 and e5. It's not much, but it is something. Whether Black plays ...a7-a5 or ...a7-a6 White should always get the preferable position, but most likely his advantage is less than with any other defense to 1.e4, and most games between top players at standard time limits in the Italian are drawn.

Well, what can I say, White's advantage in chess is not enough to win by force. But against a weaker opponent or one with less time after the opening White should get a decent percentage of wins.

Game 5.1   King's Pawn Opening –
          Two Knights Defense

Valery Lebedev   2474

Carlos Martin Sanchez   2471

Correspondence game, RUS-RoW 2018

1.e4 e5 2.♘f3 ♘c6 3.♗c4 ♘f6 4.♘g5

This almost forces Black to gambit
a pawn.
4...d5
4...♗c5?! 5.♗xf7+ ♔e7 is the Traxler
Counter-Gambit. 6.♗c4 is less
frequent than the other bishop
retreats, but looks best: 6...♕e8
7.♘c3 ♖f8 8.0-0 h6 9.♘f3 d6 10.♗e2
(+0.92). White is up a pawn for
nothing. The bishop retreat makes
d2-d3 possible without fear of the
reply ...♗g4.
5.exd5 ♘a5
   A) 5...♘xd5 6.d4 (6.♘xf7, the
famous Fegatello or Fried Liver
Attack, also gives White the edge)
6...♗e6 7.0-0 ♘xd4 8.♘xe6 fxe6
9.♕h5+ g6 10.♕xe5 ♕f6 11.♕xf6
♘xf6 12.♘c3 0-0-0 13.♗g5 ♗g7
14.♖ae1 ♔b8 15.♗d3± (+0.73).
White has the bishops and better
pawns. Dan Heisman has promoted
6...♘xd4 7.c3 b5!, e.g. 8.♗d3 h6
9.♘xf7 ♔xf7 10.cxd4 exd4 11.0-0

♖b8 12.a4 ♘b4 13.♗xb5 ♗d6
(recommended by José Lopez Senra
in *Yearbook* 132) 14.♗d2 ♖f8 15.♗xb4
♗xb4 16.♕b3+ ♗e6 17.♕xb4 c6
18.♘a3 a5 19.♕c5 cxb5 20.♘xb5
(+0.53), Lc0 +0.44 and Black may be
able to hold with perfect play, but it
won't be easy;
   B) 5...♘d4 (the Fritz Variation)
6.c3 b5 7.♗f1 ♘xd5 8.cxd4 ♕xg5
9.♗xb5+ ♔d8 10.0-0 ♗b7 11.♕f3
♖b8 12.dxe5 ♘e3 13.♕h3 ♕xg2+
14.♕xg2 ♘xg2 15.d4 ♗e7 16.♗e2
♘h4 17.♖d1 ♘f3+ 18.♗xf3 ♗xf3
19.♖d3± (+0.57). Black has only
the bishop pair for the pawn, not
enough;
   C) 5...b5 (the Ulvestad Variation)
transposes to the Fritz Variation
after 6.♗f1 ♘d4 7.c3.
6.♗b5+ c6
6...♗d7 7.♕e2 ♗e7 8.♘f3 ♘xd5
9.♘xe5 c6 10.♗d3 ♗e6 11.♘c3 ♘f4
12.♕e4 ♘xd3+ 13.♘xd3 0-0 14.♘f4±
(+0.23). Black has the bishop pair
and a little development for the
pawn, not quite enough.
7.dxc6 bxc6

8.♕f3
I played this line as White in the
mid 1960s, and it still looks pretty

good. White isn't really intending to win a second pawn, just to inconvenience Black slightly.
8.♗d3 is a popular move in recent years, of about equal merit: 8...♘d5 9.♘f3 ♗d6 10.0-0 ♘f4 11.♖e1 (11.♘c3 ♘xd3 12.cxd3 0-0 13.b3 c5 14.♗a3 ♘c6 15.♘e4 ♘b4 16.♗xb4 cxb4 17.♖e1 gave White an edge in Aronian-Ding Liren, St Louis 2019 but 13...♖e8 14.♖e1 f6 is fully equal according to the engines and has scored 6 out of 10 for Black in my database) 11...♘xd3 12.cxd3 0-0 13.♘xe5 c5 14.♘c3 ♗b7 15.b3 ♖e8 16.♘c4 ♖xe1+ 17.♕xe1 ♘xc4 18.bxc4 ♕g5 19.g3 ♕g4 20.♘d5 ♗xd5 21.cxd5 ♕d4 22.♗a3 ♕xd3 23.♗b2 ♕xd5 24.♗c3 (+0.05), Lc0 +0.16. White's bishop is more active than Black's here, but it's a pretty tiny edge.

8...♗e7

8...♖b8 9.♗e2 ♗e7 10.♘e4 ♘d5 11.d4 f5 12.♘ed2 exd4 13.♕g3 ♗e6 14.♕xg7 ♖g8 15.♕e5 ♔d7 16.♕xd4 ♗f6 17.♕d3 ♖xb2 18.c3 ♖b7 19.0-0± (+0.36). Black has better development for the pawn, but his king is unsafe.

9.♗d3

9.♗xc6+ is more common but probably inferior. Why solve all of Black's problems for him just to win half a pawn (pawn minus bishop pair)?

9...0-0 10.♘c3 h6

10...♖b8 11.♗f5 ♗xf5 12.♕xf5 g6 13.♕f3 ♘d5 14.♘h3 f5 15.d3 ♘b7 16.♘xd5 cxd5 17.0-0 ♘c5 18.b3 ♖e8 19.d4 exd4 20.♘f4 ♗f6 21.♘xd5 ♗g7 22.♗f4 ♖c8 23.♖ad1 ♘e6 24.♗d2

♖xc2 25.♘b4 ♖c8 26.♖c1 ♕d7 27.♘d3± (+0.13), but Lc0 thinks White has a serious advantage. The blockading knight does favor White, but I think Lc0 overstates the case.
11.♘ge4 ♘d5 12.♘g3 ♘b4 13.♘f5 ♗g5 14.h4 ♘xd3+ 15.cxd3 ♗e7 16.b3 ♗xf5 17.♕xf5 c5 18.♗b2 ♘c6 19.♔f1 ♘d4 20.♕xe5
20.♕e4 ♖e8 21.♖h3 ♗f8 22.♕d5 favors White by +0.30 per Lc0 but only +0.03 per Komodo, I would split the difference.
20...♗f6 21.♕d5 ♘c2

22.♖b1

A) 22.♕xd8 ♖fxd8 23.♖b1 ♘b4 24.♘a4 ♗xb2 25.♘xb2 ♘xa2 26.♖h3 (+0.04). With an extra but doubled isolated pawn White is for choice but a draw is likely;

B) 22.♖c1 ♘b4 23.♕xd8 ♖fxd8 24.♘a4 ♗xb2 25.♘xb2 ♘xa2 26.♖xc5 ♖ab8 27.g3 ♖xb3 28.♘c4 ♖b7 29.♔e2 ♖e7+ 30.♘e3 ♘b4 31.♖b1 ♘xd3 32.♖c4 (+0.03) is a drawn endgame although Lc0 prefers White.

22...♘b4 23.♕c4

23.♕f5 ♘xd3 24.♗a1 ♘f4 25.g3 ♘e6 26.♔g2. Here Komodo says Black has full compensation for the pawn, while Lc0 says White is still for choice. I would say Black has almost enough to claim equality.

23...♘xd3 24.♖h3 ♘xb2 25.♖xb2 ♗d4 26.♖c2 ♕f6 27.d3 ♖ae8 28.♘e4 ♕e5 29.♔g1 a5 30.♖e2 ♕h5 31.♔f1 ♖e6 32.♘g3 ♖xe2 33.♘xe2 ♖e8 34.♖f3 ½-½

Game 5.2 Italian Game
Awonder Liang   2590
Hikaru Nakamura   2746
St Louis ch-USA 2019 (4)

1.e4 e5 2.♘f3 ♘c6 3.♗c4 ♗c5 4.c3 ♘f6 5.d4 exd4 6.e5!
6.cxd4 ♗b4+ 7.♗d2 ♘xe4 is fully equal for Black if he knows the lines in the Black book.
6...d5 7.♗b5 ♘e4 8.cxd4 ♗b6
8...♗b4+ 9.♗d2 ♘xd2 10.♘bxd2 0-0 11.♗xc6 bxc6 12.♖c1 ♗a6 13.♕a4 ♗xd2+ 14.♔xd2 ♗b5 15.♕a3 a5 16.♖c2± (+0.12), Lc0 +0.27. White's king will be safe on c1, after which his much better pawn structure should give him the better chances.
9.♘c3 0-0 10.♗e3 ♗g4 11.h3 ♗h5 12.♕c2

Note how White postpones the decision on where to castle. This scores a whopping +68 Elo for White in my database, nearly double 'par'.

12...♗g6

A) 12...♗xf3 13.gxf3 ♘g5 14.0-0-0 (14.♗xc6 ♘xf3+ 15.♔e2 ♘xd4+ 16.♗xd4 ♗xd4 17.♗xb7 ♖b8 18.♗c6 ♖b6 19.♗a4 ♕g5 (19...♗xe5 20.♗b3 ♖e8 21.♔f1 ♖d6 22.♖e1 c6 23.♖g1 ♖de6 24.♖e3 ♕e7 25.♘e2± (+0.68). Black has the better king safety and pawn structure, but it's not enough for a 1.5 pawn (knight for two pawns) deficit) 20.♖ae1 c5 21.♘d1N ♕xe5+ 22.♔f1 ♕f4 23.♖g1 g6 24.♖g3± (+0.12), but Lc0 +0.64. Here Black has more compensation for the 1.5 pawns, but perhaps not enough. I would avoid this with 14.0-0-0, but this is our fall-back line) 14...♘xf3 15.♗xc6 bxc6 16.♕e2 ♘h4 17.♖hg1 ♕d7 (17...f6 18.♕g4 ♘g6 19.h4± (+0.46). White's attack is worth more than Black's extra doubled pawn) 18.♗g5 ♘f5 19.♗f6 g6 20.♕g4± (+1.10). White has a powerful attack for just a pawn;

B) 12...♘xc3 13.bxc3 f6 14.exf6 ♕xf6 15.♗e2 and now:

analysis diagram

B1) 15...♖ae8 16.0-0± (+0.20). Black's bishop on b6 is a bit out of play, and his knight is tied to defending e5;

B2) 15...♕g6 16.♕xg6 ♗xg6 17.0-0 ♖ae8 18.a4± (+0.18). White can play on either flank as appropriate. He may play ♖a1-a2-b2 or g2-g4 and ♔g1-h2-g3;

B3) 15...♘a5 16.0-0 ♗xf3 (16...♖ae8 17.♘e5 ♗xe2 18.♕xe2 ♕e6 19.♖ae1 ♘c4 (so far the game Aronian vs So, Zagreb 2019) 20.f4 ♘d6 21.♕c2 c6 22.♖f3± (0.04), but Stockfish and Lc0 give White around +0.16. The white kingside majority looks more useful than the black queenside majority) 17.♗xf3 c6 18.♖ae1 ♘c4 19.♗c1 ♖ae8 20.♗e2 ♖e6

analysis diagram

21.♗d3 (21.♗g4 ♖ee8 22.g3± (+0.20). Black's outposted knight partly offsets White's bishop pair) 21...g6 22.♖e2 (22.g3 ♗c7 23.h4 ♖fe8 24.♕d1± (+0.20). Again the bishop pair is only partly offset by the strong knight) 22...♖xe2 23.♕xe2 ♘d6 24.♖e1. Play went on, but after the exchange of rooks the draw looked inevitable, ½-½ (36) Anand-Aronian, Stavanger 2019 (24.g3± (+0.43). It's only human to contest

the open file, but engines see that it isn't too relevant here and that White needs to keep a rook to have winning chances. AlphaZero was also noted for giving up open files to retain a rook for use elsewhere;

B4) 15...♗g6 16.♕b3 ♕d6 17.0-0 ♗e4 (17...♖ae8 18.♖ae1 ♘a5 19.♕a4± ♗e4 20.♘g5 ♗g6 21.♗c1 ♕f6 22.♘f3 ♖e4 23.♕d1 c6 24.♗a3 ♖fe8 25.♘e5 ♗c7 26.♘xg6 ♕xg6 27.♗d3 ♖xe1 28.♖xe1 ♕f7 29.♕b1 g6 30.g3± (+0.16). White has the bishop pair, which has extra value with opposing pawn majorities) 18.♘d2 ♗g6 19.a4± (+0.11), but Lc0 +0.33. White may exchange queens by ♕a3 with queenside play. His minor pieces are slightly better;

C) 12...♖b8 13.♘xe4 ♘b4 (13...dxe4 14.♕xe4 ♗xf3 15.gxf3 f5 16.♕f4 ♕d5 17.♗xc6 ♕xc6 18.0-0 ♖bd8 19.♖ad1± (+0.34). White is a pawn up. His bad pawn structure is at least partly offset by the half-open g-file to pressure the black king) 14.♘f6+ gxf6 15.♕d2 a6 16.♗a4 ♗a5 17.0-0 ♗xf3 18.a3 ♘c6 19.b4 ♗b6 20.gxf3 fxe5 21.♗xc6 bxc6 22.♗h6 ♖e8 23.♔h2 ♖e6 24.dxe5 ♕h4 25.♖g1+ ♖g6 26.♖af1 ♖e8 27.♗f4 ♕h5 28.♕d3 a5 29.♖g4± (+0.45) is a messy position, but White has the better prospects with his extra kingside pawns here;

D) The somewhat odd move 12...♗a5! may be Black's only path to roughly equal chances:

D1) 13.♗e2 is the safe line for White: 13...f5 (13...f6 14.exf6 transposes) 14.exf6 ♘xf6 15.0-0

♗b6 16.♖ad1 ♕d6 17.♖fe1 ♖ae8
18.a3 (0.00).

analysis diagram

It's objectively equal, but I think it
is a tad easier to play White, who
has ideas like ♘h4, ♘g5, ♘h2, ♘a4,
♕c1 etc. Lc0 has only a minuscule
preference for White;

D2) 13.0-0 ♗xf3 14.gxf3 and now:

analysis diagram

D21) 14...♘xc3 15.bxc3 ♕d7
16.♔h2 ♘xd4 17.cxd4 ♕xb5 18.♖g1
g6 19.♖ad1± (0.00). White has
attacking prospects for the pawn.
Lc0 naturally likes White +0.28,
conventional engines consider it
pretty balanced;

D22) 14...♘xd4 15.♗xd4 ♕g5+
16.♔h1 ♗xc3 17.bxc3 ♕f5 18.♔g2
♕g5+ 19.♔h1 ♕f5 20.♖fc1 ♕xh3+
21.♔g1 ♘g5 22.♗e2 ♘xf3+ 23.♗xf3

♕xf3 24.♖d1 ♕g4+ 25.♔f1 b6
26.♖d3 ♕f5 27.♕d1 ♖fe8 28.♕f3
♕xf3 29.♖xf3 c5 30.♗e3 ♖xe5 31.a4
f6 32.a5 (+0.16). White is half a
pawn down (bishop for four pawns),
but will probably win a pawn
shortly and have the better of a
likely draw;

D23) 14...♘g5 15.♔g2 ♗xc3 16.bxc3
♘e6 17.f4 f5 18.♕a4 ♕d7 19.♕d1
a6 20.♗d3 b5 21.♔h2 (+0.16), Lc0
agrees. White has the bishop pair,
protected passed pawn, more
space, and potential pressure
down the half-open g-file, but
his damaged kingside and Black's
blockading knight give Black some
compensation. Stockfish also likes
White. I would prefer White, but
only slightly.

13.♕b3 ♘e7 14.0-0 c6 15.♗d3

15...♘d2

15...♘f5 16.♖fe1 ♘xe3 (16...♘xd4
17.♗xd4 ♗xd4 18.♘xe4 dxe4
19.♗xe4 ♗xe4 20.♖xe4 ♗b6 21.a4
♖b8 22.♕c2 (22.e6 ♕d5 23.♕xd5
cxd5 24.exf7+ ♖xf7 25.♖e5 ♖d8
26.♔f1 ♖f4 27.a5 ♗c5) 22...a5
(to stop a2-a4-a5-a6) 23.e6 fxe6
24.♖xe6 ♕d5 25.♖ae1 ♕c5 26.♕b3
♔h8 27.♖1e2± (+0.32). White's

domination of the open file and extra king-protecting pawn are his advantages) 17.♖xe3 ♘g5 18.♗xg6 fxg6 (18...♘xf3+ 19.♖xf3 hxg6 (19...fxg6 20.♘e2±) 20.♖d1 f6 21.exf6 ♖xf6 22.♘a4 ♖xf3 23.♕xf3 ♕f6 24.♕e3 ♗a5 25.♖d3 ♕f7 26.♕e2 ♖e8 27.♖e3 ♖xe3 28.♕xe3 (0.00), but White does have the supposed advantage of queen and knight vs queen and bishop, plus better pawn structure) 19.♘xg5 ♕xg5 20.♘e2± (+0.30). White's protected passed pawn is his advantage; Black lacks a suitable blockader.

16.♘xd2 ♗xd3 17.♖fe1

17...♗g6

A) 17...♘g6 18.♘a4 ♗f5 19.♘xb6 axb6 20.f4 ♕d7 21.♘f3± (+0.10), Lc0 +0.30. Space is White's advantage. He aims to play g2-g4 or perhaps take on b6;

B) 17...♘f5 18.♘a4± (+0.33). White has more space and may take on b6 or aim for ♘c5.

18.♘f3 ♘f5 19.♘a4

New In Chess *Yearbook* calls this equal without further analysis, but I think White is at least still for choice.

19...f6?!

A) 19...♗a5 20.♖e2 ♘xe3 (20...♕e7 21.♗d2±) 21.♕xe3± (+0.19). White can expect to trade a knight for one of Black's bishops, perhaps by a timely ♘h4 or ♘c5-d3-f4, after which his space advantage on the kingside gives him a plus;

B) 19...h6 20.a3 ♖e8 21.♘xb6 axb6 22.♖ad1 ♘xe3 23.♖xe3± (+0.09), but Lc0 +0.61. I think the truth is in between. White has more space and can maneuver his knight around and possibly organize a kingside advance, but Black has a sound position.

20.♘xb6 ♕xb6 21.♕c3 ♖ae8 22.♗f4 fxe5 23.♗xe5 ♕d8 24.♖e2

24.a4 a6 25.a5± (+0.55). Black's extra queenside pawn is almost useless, while White has real prospects of using his extra kingside pawn for attack.

24...♖f7 25.♖ae1 ♖fe7 26.♕d2 ♘h6 27.♗f4 ♘f7 28.♖xe7 ♖xe7 29.♘e5 ♘xe5 30.♗xe5 ♕d7 31.♖e3 h6 32.♕c3± (+0.64) ½-½

Presumably a reputation draw, since White is surely for choice with his powerful outposted bishop and potential to attack on the kingside, although I think that Lc0's claim of

73% expected score for White is way too high...

Game 5.3 Italian Game – Giuoco Piano
Sergey Karjakin   2782
Shakhriyar Mamedyarov   2808
Paris rapid 2018 (5)

1.e4 e5 2.♘f3 ♘c6 3.♗c4 ♘f6 4.d3 h6

This was formerly played with the idea to follow up with ...g7-g6 (before or after ...d7-d6) without allowing ♘g5. But lately it has been played with the idea of ...g7-g5 (especially after White plays c2-c3), planning ...♗g7 and ...♘c6-e7-g6. It doesn't fully equalize, but it does seem like a rather good choice for Black when a draw just won't do.
5.0-0 d6
Black waits to see one more White move before choosing between ...g7-g6 and ...g7-g5.
6.c3 g5
Logical now since the natural 7.d4 (striking in the center to answer a flank attack) means gambiting a pawn. But White need not hurry. 6...g6 7.d4 ♕e7 was the standard way to play the line until recently,

but it doesn't equalize: 8.♖e1 ♗g7 9.♘bd2 0-0 10.h3 ♗d7 11.♘f1 ♖ae8 12.♘g3 ♕d8 13.♗b3± (+0.68).

analysis diagram

Black has no compensation for his space disadvantage, but at least his position is solid. But the computers have taught us that other things being equal, space matters.

7.a4!
White preserves the bishop on a strong diagonal and gains space.
7...♗g7 8.♖e1 0-0 9.h3
Note that White only does this after Black castles, since otherwise the reply ...g5-g4 might be a bit dangerous for White.
9...d5?!
9...♘e7 10.♘bd2 ♘g6 11.♘f1 c6 12.♘g3± (+0.22). The position is almost symmetrical, but White's

dark-squared bishop is superior to the black one, and he has a lead in development.

10.exd5 ♘xd5 11.♘bd2 a6 12.♘e4 ♘f4 13.a5 b5 14.axb6 cxb6

15.b4?!

15.♗e3! ♘a5 (15...♖b8 16.d4 exd4 17.cxd4± (+0.80). The threats of 18.♗xa6 and 18.♗xf4 followed by d4-d5 are hard to meet) 16.♗a2± ♘xd3? 17.♘fxg5! hxg5 18.♕h5+−.

15...♘e7?

15...♖a7 16.♗e3 ♔h8 17.b5 axb5 18.♗xb5 ♖xa1 19.♕xa1 ♕c7 20.♕a3± (+0.25). White has the better pawn structure and invasion plans on d6.

16.d4

16.b5! a5 17.♗a3± (+0.85).

16...♕c7 17.♗xf4 gxf4 18.♕e2

18.♗b3±.

18...exd4 19.cxd4 ♘f5 20.♖ac1 ♕d8 21.♕d2 ♘xd4 22.♕xf4 ♘xf3+ 23.♕xf3 ♗b7

23...♖a7 24.♖cd1±.

24.♕f5

24.♖cd1±.

24...♗xe4 25.♕xe4 a5 26.bxa5 bxa5 27.♖e3 ♖c8 28.♕f5 ♖c7? 29.♖g3+− ♕d6 30.♔h2 ♖d8 31.♖cc3 ♔f8 32.♕h7 ♕e5 33.♖ce3 ♕a1 34.♖g4 ♗e5+ 35.g3 ♗g7 36.♖f4 ♖d1

37.♕e4 ♗f6 38.h4 h5 39.♕a8+ ♖d8 40.♕f3 ♖d6 41.♕xh5 ♖d2 42.♗xf7 ♖xf7 43.♕h6+ 1-0

Game 5.4   Italian Game – Giuoco Piano
Surya Ganguly   2633
Murtas Kazhgaleev   2587
Astana 2019 (6)

1.e4 e5 2.♘f3 ♘c6 3.♗c4 ♘f6 4.d3 ♗e7 5.0-0 0-0 6.♖e1

This is pretty much automatic, to rule out ...d7-d5 while playing a very useful move.

6...d6 7.a4

This has become the preferred way to meet Black's threat of ...♘a5.

7...♔h8

Black plans ...♘g8 and ...f7-f5, but it doesn't equalize.

A) 7...♗e6 8.♗xe6 (this trade in similar positions used to be considered bad, but now it's generally believed that the damage to Black's pawn structure and king shelter exceeds the benefit of the half-open f-file, at least when White can achieve c2-c3 and b2-b4) 8...fxe6 9.c3 ♕d7 10.b4 a6 11.♘bd2 h6 12.♘f1± (+0.33). White's better bishop and queenside initiative give him the edge;

B) 7...♞a5 8.♝a2 c5 9.♞a3 ♞c6
10.c3 ♝e6 11.♝xe6 fxe6 12.♝d2 a6
13.h3 ♛e8 14.b4 cxb4 15.cxb4 h6
16.♞c4 b5 17.axb5 axb5 18.♖xa8
♛xa8 19.♞a5 ♖c8 20.♛b3 ♞d8
21.♝e3± (+0.24). White has better
pieces and better pawns.
**8.a5 a6 9.♞c3 ♞g8 10.♞d5 f5
11.h3 fxe4 12.dxe4 ♞f6 13.c3 ♞xd5
14.exd5 ♞b8 15.♞d2**
15.♝d3 ♛e8 16.c4 ♞d7 17.b4 ♞f6
18.♞g5± (+0.78). White has more
space and will probably win the
bishop pair on e6.
15...♞d7 16.♞e4± (+0.38)
White has more space.
**16...♞f6?! 17.♞xf6± ♝xf6 18.♝d3
g6 19.♝h6 ♖f7 20.♛d2 ♝f5 21.♝e2
♛e7 22.c4 ♖g8 23.♖a3 ♝h4
24.♝e3 ♝c8 25.♖f1 ♖gf8 26.b4±
h6? 27.♝xh6+– ♝xf2+ 28.♔h1 ♖g8
29.♝g5 ♛f8 30.♖f3 ♖xf3 31.♝xf3
♝d4 32.♝e2 ♝f5 33.g4 ♝e4+
34.♔h2 ♛e8 35.♝f6+ ♔h7 36.♛g5
♛f8 37.♝e7 ♝e3 38.♛xe3 1-0**

Game 5.5 Italian Game – Giuoco Piano
Anish Giri   2790
Pavel Eljanov   2765
Stavanger 2016 (1)

1.e4 e5 2.♞f3 ♞c6 3.♝c4 ♝c5 4.c3
I prefer the move-order 4.0-0 ♞f6
5.d3 0-0 6.♖e1 d6 7.c3 or 5...d6 6.c3
0-0 7.♖e1 to cut out 6...d5 as in the
game.
4.0-0 ♞f6 5.d3 0-0 (5...d6 6.c3 was
the move-order in Vachier-Lagrave-
Ding Liren, Zagreb 2019, see below)
6.♖e1 (6.h3 is also a good move as

explained in the next game notes,
but it doesn't go with the quick
♝g5 plan of this game) 6...♞g4 (6...
d6 7.c3 transposes to the game)
7.♖e2 ♞d4 8.♞xd4 ♝xd4 9.h3 ♞f6
10.♞d2 d6 11.a4 c6 12.a5 a6 13.♞f3
♝a7 14.♝e3 ♝xe3 15.♖xe3 ♖e8 16.d4
exd4 17.♛xd4 ♝e6 18.♝f1 (+0.15),
Lc0 +0.34. White has more space
and pressure on d6.
4...♞f6 5.d3 0-0 6.0-0 d6
6...d5 7.exd5 ♞xd5 8.a4 a6 9.♖e1
♝g4 10.♞bd2 ♞b6 11.h3 ♝h5
12.♝a2 ♛xd3 13.a5 ♝xf3 14.♞xf3
♛xd1 15.♖xd1 ♞c8 16.b4 (+0.04),
Lc0 +0.34. White is down half a
pawn, but has space, the d-file,
and a great diagonal for the light-
squared bishop. Certainly White
has full compensation, but whether
he has an actual advantage is not
clear.
7.♖e1 a5

This spoils White's queenside play
but makes the pin more attractive
as Black will lack queenside play
himself.
8.♝g5
8.h3 can be considered the main
line, which I'm trying to avoid by

8.♗g5. Of course 8.h3 is not bad: 8...
h6 9.♘bd2 ♗e6

analysis diagram

10.♗b5 (this move shows the
downside of ...a7-a5; 10.a4 ♗xc4
11.♘xc4 ♖e8 12.♗e3 ♗xe3 13.♘xe3
b6 14.♕b3 ♘e7 15.g3 ♘g6 16.♔g2
♕d7 17.♖ad1 (+0.12). White is still
for choice due to his better knight
placement, but it's very close to
equal) 10...♕b8 11.♘f1 ♕a7 12.d4
exd4 13.♗xc6 dxc3 14.♗a4 ♗xf2+
15.♔h2

analysis diagram

15...d5 (15...♗xe1 16.♕xe1 d5
17.e5 cxb2 18.♗xb2 ♘e4 19.♗c2
♕f2 20.♕xf2 ♘xf2 21.♘1d2 ♖ad8
22.♘d4 ♘e4 23.♘xe4 dxe4 24.♘xe6
fxe6 25.♗b3 ♖fe8 26.♗c3 b6 27.♗c4
♔f7 28.♔g3± (+0.15). White will
pick up the e4-pawn and be up ¼

pawn by my count – two bishops
for rook and two pawns) 16.e5 (16.
exd5 ♘xd5 17.♖e5 ♖ad8 18.♕e2
♗c5 19.♔h1 ♕b6 20.♗b3 cxb2
21.♕xb2± (+0.66). White is up
half a pawn (knight for 3 pawns);
Black is better developed, but with
all the other pieces still on the
board, a minor piece is close to
four pawns in value. Pawns gain
in value in the endgame) 16...♘e4
17.♗e3 (17.♖e2 c6 18.♗c2 f5 19.a4
(+0.17), Lc0 +0.46. Again knight for
three pawns, but the outpost on e4
makes this position less appealing
for White than the previous note
to me, so here I side with Komodo
over Lc0) 17...c5 18.♗xf2 ♘xf2
19.♕c2 cxb2 20.♖ab1 (20.♕xb2
♘d3 21.♕d2 ♘xe1 22.♖xe1 ♖ad8
23.♗c2=) 20...c4 21.♕xb2 ♘d3
22.♕c3 ♘xe1 23.♖xe1 ♕c5 24.♖b1
♗f5?! 25.♖b5 ♕c7?! 26.♘e3 ½-½
(107) Anand-Ding Liren, Stavanger
2019. White gradually built up an
advantage but Black was able to
hold.

8...h6 9.♗h4 g5 10.♗g3

10...♗a7

A) 10...g4 11.♗h4 gxf3 12.♕xf3
♔g7 13.♘d2 ♗e6 14.♖ad1 ♗b6

(14...♗xc4 15.♘xc4 ♕e7 16.d4
exd4 17.♕g3+ ♔h7 18.♕f4 ♕e6
19.♗xf6 dxc3 20.♗xc3 f5 21.e5 d5
22.♘d2 ♖ad8 23.♘b3 b6 24.♖d3 ♖g8
25.♖f3 ♖df8 26.♗d2 ♗e7 27.♖c3
d4 28.♘xd4 ♘xd4 29.♕xd4 ♖d8
30.♕e3 ♗c5 31.♖xc5 bxc5 32.♗xa5
♕xa2 33.♗xc7± (-0.07), but Lc0
shows +0.14. With two pawns for
the exchange, better pawn structure
and safer king, White seems for
choice, but the active rooks should
suffice to hold the balance) 15.h3
♖h8 16.♔h1± (+0.40). It's hard to
prove a win, but Black cannot get
out of the pin and faces a difficult
struggle to save a draw. 16.b3 a4
17.d4 ♗xd4 18.cxd4 ♘xd4 19.♕c3±
(+0.30) is also good, and safer, since
White has regained his sacrificed
material;

B) 10...♘h7 11.d4 ♗b6 12.dxe5 h5
13.h4 ♗g4 14.hxg5 (14.♘bd2 ♘xe5
15.♗e2 ♘xf3+ 16.♘xf3 ♖e8 17.♕d2
♗xf3 18.♗xf3 ♕f6 19.♗e2 ♖e6
20.♖ae1 ♖ae8 21.♗xh5 gxh4 22.♗f4
♕g7 23.♔h1 ♘f6 24.♗h6 ♕h7
25.♗f3 (0.00), Lc0 +0.16. Black's
active pieces nearly compensate for
White's bishop pair and structure)
14...♘xg5 15.exd6 h4 16.♗h2 ♕f6
17.♘bd2 cxd6 18.♗e2 ♗xf3 19.♗xf3
♘e5 20.♖f1 h3 21.♗g4 d5 22.♗xh3
♖ae8 23.♔h1 dxe4 24.♗xe5 ♖xe5
25.♕g4 ♗xf2 26.♘c4 e3 27.♘xe3
♖xe3 28.♖xf2 ♕xf2 29.♕xg5+
♔h8 30.♕h6+ ♔g8 31.♕g5+ ♔h8
32.♕h6+ ♔g8 33.♕g5+ ½-½ Vachier-
Lagrave-Ding Liren, Zagreb 2019.
11.♘a3 ♗g4
  A) 11...♘h7

analysis diagram

12.♘d2 (12.d4 h5 13.h3 ♕f6 14.♘b5
♗b6 15.♗e2± (+0.34). White's
superior center is his edge; Black's
attack is not very dangerous and
also weakens his own king. White's
bishop on e2 takes the sting out
of the attack) 12...g4 13.♘b5 ♗b6
14.♗b3 a4 15.♗c2 h5 16.h4 gxh3
(16...d5? 17.d4± was Vachier-Lagrave
vs Ding Liren, Shenzhen 2018, won
by White; 16...♗e6 17.♗xa4 ♘e7
18.♗b3 ♘g6 19.♗xe6 fxe6 20.♘c4±)
17.♕xh5 ♔g7 18.♘c4 ♘g5 19.♗h4
f6 20.g3± (+0.37). White will either
take on b6 or get in d3-d4 if Black
preserves the bishop;
  B) 11...g4

B1) The piece sacrifice 12.♗h4
seems only to draw with correct
play, but it is tricky: 12...gxf3

13.♕xf3 ♔g7 14.♘c2 ♗e6 15.♗d5
♖g8 16.h3 ♘b8 17.♗xb7 ♘bd7
18.♗c6 ♖b8 19.♗xd7 ♗xd7 20.♘e3
♗xe3 21.fxe3 ♖xb2 22.♔h1 a4 23.a3
♕e7 24.♖f1 ♕e6 25.♗xf6+ ♔h7
26.♖g1 ♖d2 27.♖ad1 ♖a2 28.♖a1 ♖d2,
draw by repetition. Both sides have
other options before this;

B2) 12.♘h4 ♘h5 13.♘c2 ♕g5
14.♘e3 ♗xe3 15.♖xe3 a4 16.d4 ♘xg3
17.hxg3 ♕f6 18.♖d3 exd4 19.cxd4
♖e8 20.f3 ♕g7 21.a3 gxf3 22.♕xf3
♗e6 23.♗xe6 fxe6 24.♕d1 ♖a5
25.d5 exd5 26.♘f5 ♕g6 27.♖xd5 (27.
g4!? ♘e7 28.♖h3 ♘xf5 29.gxf5 ♕g7
30.♕e1 ♕d4+ 31.♔h1 ♖c5 32.♕h4
♕xb2 33.♖g3+ ♔h7 34.♖g1 ♖c1 and
Black should achieve a perpetual
check) 27...♖xd5 28.♕xd5+ ♕e6
29.♘xh6+ ♔h7 30.♘f5 ♕xd5 31.exd5
♖e5 32.dxc6 ♖xf5 33.♖f1 ♖b5
34.♖f7+ ♔h8 35.♖xc7 bxc6 36.♖xc6
♖xb2 37.♖c4 ♖a2 38.♖xa4 d5 39.♔f1.
Although White is two pawns up,
Black should draw comfortably.
White has many options to vary
earlier in this line, so in over-the-
board play this is no easy drawing
line for Black.

12.h3 ♗h5 13.♘c2 ♗g6 14.♗h2 ♘h5

15.d4!?

White has several options here that
offer prospects of a slight edge, such
as 15.♗b5, 15.a4, 15.♗b3, and the
recommended 15.♘e3, e.g. 15...♗xe3
16.♖xe3 (16.fxe3 ♘f6 17.♖f1± (+0.12).
With the bishop pair and some
pressure on the f-file to offset the
doubled pawns White should be for
choice) 16...♘f4 17.♕b3 ♖b8 18.a4±
(+0.20). White's edge is the bishop
pair, which gives him the option to
take on f4 at a convenient time.
**15...♘f6 16.dxe5 ♘xe4 17.♘e3
♘xe5= 18.♘xe5 dxe5 19.♘g4 h5?**
19...♔h7 20.♗d5 ♘f6 21.♗xe5 ♘xg4
22.hxg4 c6 23.♗c4 ♕xd1 24.♖axd1
♖fe8=.
**20.♖xe4 ♗xe4 21.♕xd8 ♖fxd8
22.♘f6+ ♔g7 23.♘xe4 f6 24.g4 h4
25.a4±** (+1.28), Lc0 +2.95, Stockfish
+1.15.

Pavlovic makes the curious
statement that 'engines give the
position as equal', but that certainly
isn't correct for any of the three I'm
using. White should be winning,
he's up more than a pawn by my
count and the position favors the
minors over the rook. Were engines
that weak 3 years ago? I don't think
so. I checked 5 or 6 older engines

(some much older) and none gave a lower score than 0.65, far from 'equal'.

25...c6 26.♔f1 ♔g6 27.♔e2 ♖ab8 28.♗e6 ♔g7 29.f3 ♖e8 30.♗c4 ♖ed8 31.♗d3 ♔f7 32.♘d2 ♔e7?

This drops a pawn or the exchange. 32...♖d7 33.♗g1 ♗xg1 34.♖xg1 ♖bd8 35.♗c4+ ♔e7 36.♘e4 (+1.52). White is probably winning, with ¾ pawn material plus, a great outposted knight, and lots of pawns on the board which favors minors over rooks. But it's not quite resignable.

33.♘c4 ♖d5 34.♗e4 ♖c5 35.♘d2 b5 36.♗g1 1-0

Game 5.6 Italian Game – Giuoco Piano

Markus Ragger 2701
Yury Kryvoruchko 2698
Germany Bundesliga 2018/19 (6)

1.e4 e5 2.♘f3 ♘c6 3.♗c4 ♗c5 4.c3
4.0-0 is my preferred move-order.

analysis diagram

4...♘f6 5.d3 0-0 6.h3 d6 (6...d5 7.exd5 ♘xd5 8.♖e1 ♗e6 9.c3 ♗b6 10.♗b3 ♕d7 11.♘a3 ♖ad8 12.♘c4 f6 13.d4 exd4 14.♘xb6 cxb6 15.♘xd4 ♗f7 16.♘xc6 bxc6 17.♕f3 ♖fe8 18.♖d1± (+0.13), Lc0 +0.34. Black

doesn't have much compensation for the bishop pair, just a central knight) 7.c3 a6 8.♖e1 h6 (omitting this should transpose to the game) 9.♘bd2 ♗a7 10.a4 ♖e8 11.b4 ♗e6 12.♗xe6 ♖xe6 13.♗b2 (13.♕c2 ♕d7 14.♘f1 d5 15.♗e3 ♗xe3 16.♘xe3 ♖ae8 17.b5 ♘e7 18.♖ab1 ♘g6 19.c4 d4 20.♘f5 ♖a8 21.c5 axb5 22.axb5 ♖a3 23.♖b3. Komodo says zero, Lc0 +0.18. I'd choose White, but it's nearly equal) 13...b5? (13...♘e7 14.♘f1 ♘g6 15.c4 (+0.12). White has a bit more space on the queenside) 14.d4 ♖e8 15.axb5 axb5 16.♕e2 exd4 17.♕xb5 dxc3 18.♗xc3 ♘e5 19.♕b7 (19.♘xe5! dxe5 20.♘f3 ♗d4 21.♖ad1 ♗xf2+ 22.♔xf2 ♘xe4+ 23.♖xe4 ♕xd1 24.♖xe5 ♖xe5 25.♕xe5 f6 26.♕e6+ ♔h8 27.♗d2 ♕c2 28.♕d5 c6 29.♕c5 ♕e4 30.♕d4± (+0.35). White is up half a pawn. His king is slightly weaker) 19...♖b6 20.♗xe5 dxe5 21.♖xa8 ♕xa8 22.♕xa8 ♖xa8 23.♘xe5 ♗d4 24.♘c6 ♗c3 25.♖d1 ♗xd2 26.♖xd2 ♘xe4 27.♖e2 ♘d6 28.♖c2 ♖a1+ 29.♔h2 ♘f8 30.♘e5 ♖a7 31.♘c6 ♖a1 32.♘e5 ♖a7 33.♘c6 ♖a1 ½–½ Giri-So, Zagreb 2019.

4...♘f6 5.d3

5...d6

5...0-0 6.0-0 a6 7.a4 d6 8.♘bd2 ♗a7 9.h3 ♔h8 (for 9...♘e7 10.♖e1 ♘g6 11.d4 see the note to move 11) 10.b4 ♘g8 (this move is the point of the previous one, aiming for counterplay with ...f7-f5. Note that this game was a 10' to 7' Armageddon game between two great players) 11.♗b3 f5 (11...♗d7 12.♖a2 f5 13.b5 ♘a5 14.♗c2 ♗b6 15.d4± (+0.38). Black's knight on the rim is his problem) 12.b5 axb5 13.axb5 ♗xf2+ 14.♖xf2 ♖xa1 15.bxc6 bxc6 16.♕c2 ♕e7 17.♗a2± (+0.28). White has the tiny edge of two bishops for rook and two pawns (¼ pawn by my count), while Black's rook on a1 is in some trouble. 17...♗e6 18.♘b3 (18.c4! ♖a8 19.♗b1 ♖f8 20.♕c3 ♖aa8 21.d4± (+0.25). White has the initiative in the center plus his 'quarter pawn') 18...♗xb3 19.♗xb3= ½-½ (41) Anand-Aronian, Stavanger 2019. After allowing equality, White rebuilt a winning advantage, then tossed it away and should have lost, but Black only needed a draw and got it.

6.0-0 0-0 7.♖e1 a6

8.a4

This idea to meet ...a7-a6 by a2-a4 is relatively recent, and has much to do with the resurgence of the Italian Game for White.

8.h3 ♗a7 9.a4 transposes and is fine, since 8...♘a5 is met by 9.b4.

8...♗a7 9.h3 ♘e7

9...h6 10.♘bd2 transposes to the note to move 4.

10.d4 ♘g6 11.♗d3

11.♗d3 (rather than 11.♘bd2) aims to develop the dark-squared bishop before the knight.

11.♘bd2 is the main line: 11...h6 12.a5 ♖e8 13.♕b3 ♕e7 14.♘f1 c6 15.dxe5 dxe5 16.♗d2 ♗e6 17.♗xe6 ♕xe6 18.♕xe6 ♖xe6 19.g3 ♖d8 20.♗e3 ♗xe3 21.♖xe3 ♘e8 22.♘3d2 ♖e7 23.♘c4 f6 24.♖ee1± (+0.20). White is clearly better, due to his superior knights, although the symmetrical pawn structure gives Black good drawing chances.

11...c6?!

11...♖e8 12.♕c2 ♗e6 13.♗e3 d5 14.♘bd2 exd4 15.♗xd4 dxe4 16.♘xe4 ♗xd4 17.♘xd4 ♗d5 18.♖e3 ♘f4 19.♖ae1 ♔f8 20.♘xf6 ♕xf6 21.♗f1 ♖xe3 22.♖xe3 g6 23.g3 c5 24.♘b3 ♘e6 25.♕d1 ♗c6 26.♘a5 ♖d8 27.♖d3± (+0.17). Black will have to fight for the draw. Lc0 really likes White. 27...♗e4 28.♖xd8+ ♘xd8 29.♘b3 ♘e6 30.♕d6+ ♔g7 31.♘d2 ♗c6 32.♗xa6 ♘g5 33.♕xf6+ ♔xf6 34.♗f1 ♗xa4 35.♗g2 ♗c6 36.♗xc6 bxc6 37.f4 ♘e6 38.♔f2± (+0.18). White is obviously for choice due to the pawn structure, although I think that Black should hold with proper play.

12.♗e3 ♘h5 13.♗f1 ♘hf4 14.dxe5 dxe5 15.♕xd8 ♖xd8 16.♗xa7 ♖xa7 17.♘bd2

17...♗e6?
17...f6 18.a5 ♗e6 19.♖ed1 ♖aa8 20.♘e1 ♖d7 21.♘c4± (+0.39). The weakness of b6 and the plan

of h3-h4 and g2-g3 are White's advantages.

18.♘c4± (+0.75)
Because of the twin threats of 19.♘xe5 and 19.♘b6, Black will have to take the knight and leave White with a dominating bishop vs knight in this open position.

18...♗xc4 19.♗xc4 h6 20.a5 ♘h5 21.♖ad1 ♖aa8 22.♘d2 ♘f6
22...♘hf4 23.♔f1 ♘f8 24.h4 ♖d7 25.♘f3 ♖e8 26.g3± (+0.75). White's minor pieces are superior.

23.♘b3± ♖xd1? 24.♖xd1+− ♘xe4 25.♖d7 ♖b8 26.♖xf7 ♔h7 27.♗d3 ♘g5 28.♖d7 e4 29.♗c2 b6 30.h4 ♘xh4 31.f4 ♘e6 32.♗xe4+ ♔g8 33.♗xc6 ♔h8 34.♖b7 ♖xb7 35.♗xb7 bxa5 36.g3 a4 37.♘a5 ♘f5 38.♗c8 ♘xg3 39.♗xe6 a3 40.bxa3 ♘e2+ 41.♔f2 ♘xc3 42.♗c4 ♘b1 43.♗xa6 ♘xa3 44.♗d3 g5 45.f5 ♔g7 46.♔f3 h5 47.♘c6 ♔f6 48.♔e4 g4 49.♔f4 g3 50.♘d4 g2 51.♘f3 h4 52.♘g1 ♔f7 53.♔e5 ♔e7 54.f6+ ♔f7 55.♘h3 ♔f8 56.♔e6 ♔e8 57.f7+ ♔f8 58.♘g1 1-0

CHAPTER 6

Spanish with 6.d3

The Spanish (Ruy Lopez) Opening, **1.e4 e5 2.♘f3 ♘c6 3.♗b5**, has been the main choice for White after 1.e4 e5 2.♘f3 ♘c6 for more than a century now. In most lines, White keeps a small but clear advantage, usually based on getting in the move d2-d4 before Black can achieve a similar pawn break without paying a price. Statistics are in general pretty good for White. But it has become clear in the 21st century that there are two defenses that cast some doubt on White's edge. One is the Berlin Defense (**3...♘f6**).

This was fairly obscure until Kramnik used it to wrest the World Championship from Kasparov at the start of this century. Although there are at least three paths to at least a marginal edge (4.d3, 4.0-0 ♘xe4 5.d4, and my recommendation in this chapter 4.0-0 ♘xe4 5.♖e1), the statistics are less favorable for White than in the main lines of the Spanish; the positions are just much closer to equal. Indeed, it makes sense that if White has to play d2-d3 or allow the capture of e4, he probably won't achieve the favorable center e4 + d4 vs e5 + d6 that is so typical of the main line Spanish. Still, the line given here for White is likely to give him a 'free' space advantage, and space is 'in' thanks to the engines emphasizing it.

The other main problem for White is the Marshall Attack, recommended in the Black portion of this book. The statistics for Black in the Marshall are much better than in normal Spanish lines or even in the Berlin, so close to even that White generally avoids the Marshall either by 8.a4, 8.h3 (but this is fading), or by 6.d3, my choice here. Some players even play 5.d3 to avoid the Open Variation (5...♘xe4 in response to 5.0-0), but permitting 5...♗c5 is probably a bigger problem than the Open, so I definitely prefer to wait for 5....♗e7 before settling for d2-d3. Although 6.d3 would seem to lose a tempo when d3-d4 is eventually played, there is more to it than just avoiding the Marshall Attack, as explained below. There are several possible transpositions to normal lines of the Anti-Marshall, Zaitsev, and Breyer. With all these transpositions you might well ask why play 6.d3 rather than 6.♖e1, the main line? My answer is that you have a lot less to learn with 6.d3, and have good options other than the transpositions. White doesn't get a big advantage with 6.d3, but then since 1...e5 is probably the best move objectively against 1.e4, White just isn't entitled to more than a small plus. As to whether the Spanish with 6.d3 is a better choice than the Italian (last chapter), I don't have a strong preference. Maybe I would go with the Italian against players with a lot of book knowledge and Spanish against others, but even that isn't very clear.

The 6.d3 system does allow Black to play the Open, the Archangel (5...b5 and 6...♗b7), the Neo-Archangel (5...b5 and 6...♗c5) and Anand's recent favorite the Møller (5...♗c5 6.c3 b5). The Open has been championed by Mamedyarov, ranked in the top three in the world for most of 2017-2018. Working on this chapter has given me a new respect for it, as although conventional engines generally don't like it, the NN engine Lc0 rates it as pretty much on a par with the Marshall and Berlin. I opt for the modern main line 9.♘bd2, which often leaves White with at least a superior pawn structure. Against the Neo-Archangel (which Carlsen has played), I choose a relatively new system based on an exchange sacrifice that is so effective that it is rarely accepted. The Møller is best met by a sacrificial line analyzed in more detail in the Black book. The older Archangel is met by d2-d3, when the bishop placement on b7 looks unwise when White still has the option of ♘c3.

Before we come to the above lines, we need to look at less common third moves by Black. First is the Classical Defense (**3...♗c5**), which is covered in Game 6.1 along with two rarer defenses (the Bird 3...♘d4 and the Steinitz 3...d6).

White meets 3...♝c5 by 4.c3 followed by 5.d4, which should get him a space advantage at least if not something more tangible. In Game 6.2 I look at Smyslov's 3...g6, which has caught on a bit lately; I meet it with a totally sound gambit that is generally declined and likely to transpose to a line usually arising from the Cozio Defense (3...♞ge7, not covered separately due to the transposition). The usual outcome is a big advantage in pawn structure for White. Game 6.3 features the sharp Jaenisch Variation (**3... f5**),

which is met by the simple **4.d3** rather than the very complex 4.♞c3. If Black insists on aggressive play (...♝c5 before ...d7-d6), he has to gambit a pawn, which we take. Black regains it only at the cost of an inferior position (this line is in the notes), or White can keep it for slight compensation by Black. Playing ...d7-d6 first saves the pawn, but Black has severe problems with castling, which also leaves him clearly worse. None of these defenses comes close to equalizing for Black against the lines given here.

Game 6.4 is the Berlin Defence. The 'simple' line given here leading to the exchange of e-pawns leads to a 'par' White edge according to the engines, although I can't deny that the lines do tend towards a draw. Recently White has been aiming to play d4-d5 before Black does, securing a space advantage. At least there is enough play for a stronger player with White to outplay a weaker one.

Game 6.5 features the Neo-Archangel (**3...a6 4.♝a4 ♞f6 5.0-0 b5 6.♝b3 ♝c5**), with the real Archangel (6...♝b7) covered in the notes. The game shows a recent sharp idea for White in the Neo-Archangel based on a complex but very good exchange sacrifice. Black should decline it, but even this doesn't solve all of his problems. As I show in the Black book, Black can and should prefer the Møller Variation, which is just playing 5...♝c5 first and only after 6.c3 playing 6...b5. I do cover it for White here; at the time of writing it seems that White's only try for an edge involves a long-term piece sacrifice that is good for at least a draw but perhaps not more against perfect defense. I think that the defense is too difficult for over-the-board play. If Black can find a simpler defense, well, there's always the Italian for White! The Archangel proper has faded; we have learned that it's probably best to wait for c2-c3 before playing ...♗b7.

Next comes **5...♘xe4**, the Open Spanish.

This has lately regained popularity at the top level. I meet it with **6.d4 b5 7.♗b3 d5 8.dxe5 ♗e6** and now the modern main line **9.♘bd2**, which has largely replaced the older 9.c3, perhaps due to the Dilworth Variation where Black trades bishop and knight for rook and pawn on f2 but gets enough attack to win a second pawn and equalize. In Game 6.6 Black just plays **9...♗e7** and castles, and defends his knight on e4 with ...f7-f5 when it is attacked. This is quite an old line. I give a novelty on move 26 that changes the assessment drastically in White's favor. In Game 6.7 Black plays **9...♘c5 10.c3 d4**, provoking some exchanges. I couldn't find any white edge in the main line (13.a4 after exchanges) but the second most popular line (13.♘e4) does seem to give White something. Game 6.8 has Black waiting one move with **10...♗e7 11.♗c2** before playing **11...d4 12.♘b3 d3**. White then has the choice of going for a slightly better but very drawish endgame (see the notes for this option), or accepting the complications of the game (**13.♗b1**), when White does seem to keep a meaningful edge.

Now we come to the main line of the Spanish, **5...♗e7**, which we meet by **6.d3**, threatening to take on c6 and e5.

Black has only two reasonable defenses to this threat. Game 6.9 features defending the pawn by **6...d6**, which we meet by **7.c3** giving us the option to answer ...b7-b5 at any moment by ♗c2, which often saves a tempo compared to ♗b3 ♘a5 ♗c2. Also, sometimes the bishop is needed on c2 to defend e4 before playing d3-d4. It is quite possible to transpose to main lines of the Spanish with ♖e1, since d2-d3, d3-d4 loses a tempo but so does ♗a4-b3-c2. In the game Black postpones ...b7-b5 until he has played every other useful move he can think of, and then after ♗c2 strikes with ...d7-d5. This line should allow Black to struggle to a drawn endgame if he plays perfectly, so in this sequence I recommend meeting ...b7-b5 by ♗b3 in the notes to keep an edge.

Game 6.10 has Black playing **6...b5** before White has time to get in 7.c3, and so this is the main line. The drawback is that after **7.♗b3** White is ready to play 8.a4, which is rather annoying. Black has two main ways to defend.

He can castle, meeting 8.a4 with 8...b4, when 9.♖e1 (given in the notes) transposes to a main line of the Anti-Marshall (6.♖e1 b5 7.♗b3 0-0 8.a4 b4 9.d3), while 9.♘bd2 avoids this transposition. In the game, Black plays **7... d6**, meeting **8.a4** by **8...♗d7** (probably better than 8...♗b7 staring into a strong pawn). White plays normal developing moves, and Black after doing the same chose to strike with ...d6-d5. This was probably a bad decision, although understandable as White has at least a small edge against passive play by Black. White achieved a winning material advantage but it was a rapid game and Black miraculously saved the draw.

Game 6.1 Ruy Lopez/Spanish –
Classical Defense

Tigran Gharamian 2626
Ivan Ivanisevic 2593

Heraklio Ech-tt 2017 (5)

1.e4 e5 2.♘f3 ♘c6 3.♗b5

3...♗c5

The Classical Defense.

A) 3...♘d4 is the Bird Variation.
4.♘xd4 exd4 5.0-0 ♗c5 6.♗c4
d6 7.d3 c6 8.♗b3 a5 9.a4 (+0.56).
White's king's bishop is much
stronger than Black's king bishop,
and White's kingside majority can
be used for attack while Black's
queenside majority is crippled by
the doubled pawn and not useful;

B) 3...d6 is the Steinitz Variation,
now rarely seen at high level. 4.d4
♗d7 5.♗xc6 (rarely played, but it
seems quite strong. White plans
to castle queenside and play like
the English Attack vs the Sicilian)
5...♗xc6 6.♘c3 ♘f6 7.♕d3 exd4
8.♘xd4 ♗e7 9.f3!N (humans play
9.0-0, but preparing ♗e3 and
0-0-0, suggested by Lc0, seems
better. Stockfish likes 9.b3, also
quite strong. It's funny that only an
engine suggested the human plan

of the English Attack) 9...0-0 10.♗e3
♖e8 11.0-0-0 ♗d7 12.g4± (+0.80).
White's attack is easy to play, and he
will probably regain the bishop pair
at some point by ♘f5. He has a huge
space advantage.

4.c3

I prefer this to 4.0-0 which allows
4...♘d4 slightly easing Black's
situation.

4...♘f6

4...f5 5.d4 fxe4 6.♗xc6 dxc6
7.♘xe5 ♗d6 8.♕h5+ g6 9.♕e2 ♗f5
10.♗f4 ♘f6 11.♘d2 ♕e7 12.0-0
0-0-0 13.♖ae1 ♖he8 14.♘dc4 ♘d5
15.♗g3 h5 16.f3 ♗xe5 17.♗xe5 exf3
18.♕xf3 ♕g5 19.h3 ♖f8 20.♗h2±
(+0.65). White's knight will be very
powerful on e5, whereas Black's
knight on d5 may be chased away.

5.d4 exd4 6.e5 ♘e4

6...♘d5 7.0-0 ♗e7 8.cxd4 d6 9.exd6
cxd6 10.♕b3 ♘c7 11.d5 ♘xb5
12.♕xb5 a6 13.♕e2 ♘e5 14.♘xe5
dxe5 15.♕xe5 0-0 16.♘c3± (+0.57).
White is up 'half a pawn' for
nothing.

7.cxd4

7.0-0 d5 (7...dxc3 8.♕d5 ♗xf2+
9.♖xf2 ♘xf2 10.♘xc3 ♘g4 11.♗g5
♘e7 12.♕c5 c6 13.♘e4 cxb5 14.♘d6+

♔f8 15.♘d4+− (+2.18). Although a rook and two pawns down, White has a decisive attack on the king. Both black rooks are useless) 8.cxd4 ♗b6 9.♘c3 0-0 10.h3 ♗f5 11.♖e1 h6 12.♗e3± (+0.44). White has a nice space advantage and Black will have to make concessions to develop the queen's rook.

7...♗b4+ 8.♘bd2 0-0 9.0-0 d5

9...♘xd2 10.♗xd2 ♗xd2 11.♕xd2 ♘e7 12.♗c4 d6 13.♕e3 ♗f5 14.♖ad1 ♘g6 15.h3± (+0.34). White has more space and better development.

10.♕a4 ♖b8

10...♗xd2 11.♘xd2 ♗d7 12.f3 a6 13.♗xc6 ♗xc6 14.♕c2 ♘g5 15.f4 ♘e6 16.♘f3 f5 17.♘g5 ♘xd4 18.♕f2 h6 19.♕xd4 hxg5 20.fxg5 ♕d7 21.♗d2 ♕e6 22.♖f3± (+0.33). White has kingside attacking chances and more space.

11.a3 ♗e7

12.♖e1

12.♕c2! ♗f5 13.♗d3± ♗g4 14.h3 ♗h5 15.♗xe4 dxe4 16.♕xe4± (+0.40). White has won a pawn for the bishop pair, so half a pawn.

12...♗f5 13.♘f1 f6?

13...a6 14.♗xc6 bxc6 15.♕xc6 ♖b6 16.♕c2 ♕d7= (+0.09). White is again up half a pawn, but here

Black has clear compensation with his better development and the indirect attack on the queen.

14.♘g3 fxe5 15.♗xc6 bxc6 16.♘xe5 The outposted knight on e5 shows why 13...f6 was bad.

16...♗h4 17.♖e2

17...c5?

17...♗xg3 18.hxg3 c5 19.♗f4± (+0.88). Black's outposted knight can be expelled while White's cannot.

18.♘xe4 ♗xe4 19.f3 ♗f5 20.dxc5 ♗f6? 21.♗f4+− ♕e8 22.♕d4 ♖d8 23.c6 ♖d6 24.♖c1 ♕d8 25.b4 g5 26.♗g3 ♖e8 27.♖ee1 h5 28.h3 ♗g7 29.b5 g4 30.hxg4 hxg4 31.♕f4 ♖f8 32.♘xg4 d4 33.♖c5 ♗e6 34.♕g5 d3 35.♗xd6 ♕xd6 36.♖xe6 ♕xe6 37.♖d5 ♕e1+ 38.♔h2 d2 39.♖xd2 ♕c1 40.♘f6+ 1-0

Game 6.2   Ruy Lopez/Spanish – Smyslov Defense

Arkadij Naiditsch   2721
Hikaru Nakamura   2763
Douglas 2018 (8)

1.e4 e5 2.♘f3 ♘c6 3.♗b5 g6 This Smyslov Defense has gotten rather popular of late at high level.

3...♘ge7 is the Cozio Defense, which I played in the mid 1970s. 4.0-0 g6 5.c3 ♗g7 6.d4 exd4 7.cxd4 d5 8.exd5 ♘xd5 transposes to the game by a more traditional route.

4.d4

4.c3 is most frequent and also good.

4...exd4

5.c3

This is a gambit, but a sound one. 5.♗g5 is the main line, but it's not very convincing: 5...♗e7 6.♗xe7 ♕xe7 7.♗xc6 dxc6 8.♕xd4 ♘f6 9.♘c3 ♗g4 10.♘d2 c5 11.♕e3 0-0-0 12.f3 ♗e6 13.0-0-0 b6 14.♖he1 (+0.08). White's advantage is the healthy vs crippled pawn majority, but the bishop vs knight partly compensates. If this is the best White could do, 3...g6 would be the main line of the Spanish, I think.

5...♘ge7

5...dxc3 6.♘xc3 h6 (6...♗g7 7.♗g5 ♘ge7 8.♘d5 h6 9.♗f6 ♗xf6 10.♘xf6+ ♔f8 11.♕d2 ♘g8 12.♘d5 ♘f6 13.♕c3 ♔g7 14.0-0± (+0.28). Black cannot escape the pin easily, and White has much superior development for the pawn) 7.0-0 ♗g7 8.♗e3 ♘ge7 9.♕d2 (Black's inability to castle without losing

h6 gives White full compensation for the pawn, at least) 9...d6 10.♖ac1 a6 11.♗e2 ♗d7 12.h3 ♖c8 13.b4 ♔f8 14.♖b1 ♔g8 15.a4 ♗e6 16.b5 axb5 17.axb5 ♘e5 18.♘xe5 dxe5 19.♕xd8+ ♖xd8 20.♘a4 b6 21.♖bc1 ♖c8 22.♗c4+− (+0.64).

analysis diagram

White's superior development and threats should regain the gambit pawn with interest.

6.cxd4 d5 7.exd5 ♘xd5 8.0-0 ♗g7 9.♗xc6+ bxc6 10.♗g5 ♕d6 11.♖e1+ ♗e6 12.♘bd2 0-0 13.♘e4 ♕b4 14.♕c1 ♖fe8 15.♗d2 ♕b6 16.♘c5 ♗f5 17.♘e5

17...♖ad8

17...♖e7 18.a4 ♖ae8 19.h3 h5 20.♖a3 ♕b8 21.♖b3 ♕a8 22.a5± (+0.35). White has space, powerful knight outposts, and the better pawn structure for the bishop pair – more than enough.

18.h3 ♘f6 19.♘b3

19.♕c4! ♘d5 20.g4 ♗c8 21.b4± (+1.06). White has a dominating space and pawn structure advantage.

19...♖d5? 20.♘xc6 ♖xe1+ 21.♗xe1 ♗f8 22.♘e5 ♗e6 23.♘c4

23.♗c3±.

23...♕b7 24.♘e3 ♖h5 25.♘c5 ♗xc5 26.dxc5 ♗xh3 27.c6 ♕c8 28.f3 ♗xg2 29.♘xg2 ♕h3 30.♗c3 ♘d5 31.♗d4 f6 32.♕e1 ♔f7 33.♖d1 ♖g5 34.♕e2 ♔g7 35.♗c5 ♖e5 36.♕f2?

Both 36.♕f1 and 36.♗e3 win.

36...♖g5?

36...♖h5.

37.♖d4+− ♕e6 38.♖e4 ♕xc6 39.♕d4 a5 40.a3 h5 41.♔h2 ♔h7 42.♕c4 ♕b7 43.♖e7+ ♔h8 44.♗d4 ♖f5 45.♖d7 ♕b8 46.♕c6 1-0

Game 6.3   Ruy Lopez/Spanish –
                Jaenisch Variation

| **Fabiano Caruana** | 2832 |
| **Levon Aronian** | 2765 |

London 2018 (2)

1.e4 e5 2.♘f3 ♘c6 3.♗b5 f5

The Jaenisch Variation, rather popular among players who want to go all out for a win with black, but it is risky.

4.d3

4.♘c3 was the main move historically, but 4.d3 is catching up, is much simpler, and is more consistent with the main line Spanish 6.d3.

4...fxe4 5.dxe4 ♘f6 6.0-0

6...d6

The gambit move 6...♗c5 is of about equal merit with the less popular move in the game.

A) 7.♕d3 makes it difficult for Black to castle kingside and keeps a small edge, but the acceptance of the gambit is more promising: 7...d6 8.♕c4 ♗d7 9.♘c3 ♕e7 10.♘d5 ♘xd5 11.exd5 ♘d4 12.♘xd4 ♗xd4 13.♗e3 ♗xe3 14.fxe3 0-0-0 15.♗xd7+ ♕xd7 16.♖f2 (+0.12). White keeps control of the only open file, but it's not much;

B) 7.♗xc6 bxc6 8.♘xe5 0-0 9.♘c3 d6 10.♘a4 (10.♘d3 also favors White) 10...♕e8 11.♘d3 ♗g4 12.♕e1 ♗d4 13.c3 ♗b6 14.♘xb6 axb6 15.f3 (Harikrishna-Nihal Sarin, Kolkata 2018, was eventually drawn after the weaker 15.c4) 15...♗e6 16.e5 (16. a3 ♗c4 17.♕d1 ♕g6 18.♖e1 ♘d7 19.♔h1 ♕f7 20.♗e3 c5 21.♗f2 ♗xd3 22.♕xd3 ♘e5 23.♕d2± (+0.33), but Lc0 +0.72. Black has a well placed knight, but this hardly makes up for a pawn) 16...dxe5 17.♘xe5 ♖xa2 18.♖xa2 ♗xa2 19.h3 c5 20.♗f4 ♗b3 21.♕c1± (+0.50). White has a strongly posted knight and the healthier pawn majority.

**7.♗c4 ♗g4 8.h3 ♗h5 9.♘c3 ♘d4
10.g4 ♘xf3+ 11.♕xf3 ♗g6**

12.♗e6

12.g5! ♘d7 13.h4 ♗e7 14.♕g4 ♘f8
15.f4 exf4 16.♗xf4 c6 17.♔g2 ♕a5
18.♖ad1 0-0-0 19.♗e6 ♔c7 20.♗xd7
♖xd7 21.e5 ♖xf4 22.♕xf4 ♕xe5
23.♕xe5 dxe5 24.♖xd7+ ♔xd7
25.♔f3± (+1.18). Rook and knight
for two bishops and pawn is only
a tiny edge with a rook added to
each side, but with no other majors
on the board it is a significant plus.
25...♗xc2 is met by 26.♘e4.

12...c6 13.♗e3

13.b4± (+0.16) was also strong, to
be able to retreat the bishop to b3
while aiming for b5.

13...♕e7 14.♗b3 ♗f7 15.♖fd1

15.♕g3! ♘d7 16.♖ad1 0-0-0 17.f4
♗xb3 18.axb3 h5 19.g5 exf4
20.♗xf4± (+0.35). White will either
win the d6-pawn or get an attack
on the Black king.

15...a6 16.♕g3

16.♔g2! zero, but Lc0 likes White,
who is better developed.

16...b5?

16...♘d7! 17.♔g2 h5 18.♕f3 would
have been equal.

17.f4 ♗xb3 18.axb3 g6?

18...exf4 19.♕xf4 ♘d7 20.♘a2 a5
21.♘b4 ♘e5 22.♘d3± (+0.28). White
has a serious lead in development.

19.b4

19.fxe5! dxe5 20.g5 ♘h5 21.♕g4±.

19...♕e6 20.♕f3 exf4 21.♗xf4

21.♗d4! ♗g7 22.e5 dxe5 23.♗c5!±
(+1.03). The threats of 24.♘xb5! and
24.♖d6 will win material.

21...♘d7 22.e5

22.♘e2! ♘e5 23.♕c3±.

22...d5

23.♖d4??

23.♘e2=.

**23...♗g7−+ 24.♗g3 ♗xe5 25.♖d3
♗xg3 26.♕xg3 0-0 27.♖e1 ♕f6
28.♖d2 ♖ae8 29.♖xe8 ♖xe8 30.♖f2
♕e5 31.♕xe5 ♖xe5 32.♘e2 c5
33.bxc5 ♘xc5 34.♘d4 ♔g7 35.♔g2
♘e6 36.♘xe6+ ♖xe6 37.♖d2 ♖d6
38.♔f3 ♔f6 39.c3 ♔e5 40.♖e2+ ♔f6
41.♖e8 d4 42.cxd4 ♖xd4 43.♖a8
♖d6 44.♔e4 ♔g5 45.♖h8 ♖d7
46.♖a8 ♖d6 47.♖h8 h6 48.b4 ♖c6
49.♔d5 ♖c4 50.♖a8 ♖xb4 51.♖xa6
♖b3 52.h4+ ♔xg4 53.♖xg6+ ♔h5
54.♖b6 b4 55.♔e4 ♖h3 56.♖b5+
♔g6 57.♖b6+ ♔g7 58.♖b7+ ♔f8
59.♔f5 ♖xh4 60.♔f6 ♔e8 61.♔e6
♖e4+ 62.♔f5 ♖c4 63.♖b6 h5 64.♔e6
♔d8 65.♔d6 ♔c8 66.♔d5 ♔c7**

**67.♖h6 ♖h4 68.♔c5 ♔d7 69.♔d5
b3 70.♖h7+ ♔c8 71.♔c6 ♖c4+
72.♔d5 ♖b4 73.♔c6 ♖c4+ 74.♔d5
b2 75.♔xc4 b1♕ 76.♖xh5 ♕c2+
77.♔d4 ♕d1+ 0-1**

Game 6.4   Ruy Lopez/Spanish – Berlin
Ian Nepomniachtchi   2763
Vladimir Kramnik   2777
Wijk aan Zee 2019 (3)

1.e4 e5 2.♘f3 ♘c6 3.♗b5 ♘f6

The notorious Berlin Defence,
considered by some to be the
refutation of 1.e4 as a winning try.
It is hard to crack, but it's not an
easy draw at the top level; even the
best players lose games with it still.
4.0-0
The popular move 4.d3 would
seem to be the best fit with my d3
repertoire in the main line Spanish,
but I don't play d2-d3 in the main
line until Black commits to ...♗e7.
Here 4...♗c5 is the main line, and
it is hard to prove more than a
cosmetic edge against it. Play might
continue 5.0-0 d6 (5...♘d4 is also
critical) 6.c3 0-0 7.♘bd2 a6 8.♗a4
when Black has several options.
4...♘xe4 5.♖e1

The Berlin endgame with 5.d4 ♘d6
6.♗xc6 dxc6 7.dxe5 etc. is quite
close to equal and is fading from
elite play. The 5.♖e1 line at least
keeps the queens on the board and
usually keeps a space advantage.
5...♘d6 6.♘xe5 ♗e7 7.♗f1
I recommended this in my first
book back in 2003, when almost no
one played it, and I still do.
7...♘xe5 8.♖xe5 0-0

9.d4
9.♘c3 was my choice in that book,
and it is a decent alternative to the
text, although probably a bit more
drawish: 9...♘e8 10.♘d5 ♗d6 11.♖e1
c6 12.♘e3 ♗c7 13.♘f5 d5 14.♘e7+
♔h8 15.♘xc8 ♖xc8 16.d3 (+0.26).
White is up the bishop pair and is
'better', but the pawn symmetry
results in a very high draw
percentage from here.
9...♗f6
9...♘e8 10.c4 ♗f6 11.♖e1 d5 12.cxd5
♕xd5 13.♗e3 ♕a5 14.♘c3 ♗e6
15.a3 c6 16.♘e4 ♗d5 17.♘c5 ♕c7
18.♕g4 b6 19.♘d3± (+0.20). White's
development is superior.
10.♖e1 ♖e8
10...♘f5 11.c3 d5 12.♘d2 ♘d6 13.♘f3
c6 14.♗f4 ♗f5 15.h3± (+0.26).

White's edge is the e-file and that Black's f6-bishop bites on granite. **11.c3 ♖xe1 12.♕xe1 ♘e8 13.d5** Everyone used to play 13.♗f4, when the symmetry after ...d7-d5 makes a draw quite likely. It is because of the space-gaining move in this game that I recommend 9.d4 now. In general I think the elite players are more space-conscious than in earlier times, probably because the engines love space.

13...b6
13...c6 14.♕d1 b6 15.♗f4 ♗b7
16.dxc6 dxc6 17.♘d2 c5 18.♘c4
(18.♕g4 (+0.19) keeps the queens on and is probably the best winning try, although it is also more risky)
18...♕xd1 19.♖xd1 ♖d8 20.♖xd8
♗xd8 21.♗b8 a6 So far Anand-Caruana, Karlsruhe/Baden Baden 2019. Now 22.g3 keeps a slight pull, although the endgame should be drawn (+0.18).
**14.♗f4 ♗b7 15.♕d2 h6 16.c4 c6
17.♘c3± cxd5 18.cxd5 d6 19.♖e1
♘c7 20.♗c4 ♗xc3 21.bxc3 ♕f6
22.h3 ♖c8 23.♖e4 b5?!**
23...♖e8 24.♖xe8+ ♘xe8 25.♗b3
♗c8 26.c4 ♗f5 27.♕e3± (+0.52).

White has the bishops and more space and a target on d6.
24.♗b3 a5 25.a3 ♕f5?!
25...♖e8 26.♖d4 a4 27.♗a2±.
26.♖d4
26.♕d3! ♕g6 27.f3± (+1.00). With the bishop pair, space, and control of the open file, White dominates.
**26...♕b1+ 27.♗d1 b4 28.cxb4 ♘b5
29.♕d3 ♕a1**
29...♕xd3 30.♖xd3 axb4 31.axb4
♖a8 32.♗e2 ♖a4 33.♖e3 ♖xb4
34.♖e8+ ♔h7 35.♗d2 ♖b2 36.♗d3+
g6 37.♗e3±. White will win the d6-pawn due to pins on the b-file.
**30.♖e4 ♗xd5 31.♖e1 ♗c4 32.♕f5
♖f8 33.♔h2**

33...g6?
33...♕d4 34.♗c2 g6 35.♕g4 ♘xa3
36.♖d1 ♕f6 37.♖xd6 h5 38.♕f3 ♗e6
39.♗d3 axb4 40.♕g3+−.
34.♕e4 d5 35.♕e7 axb4 36.♗e5 1-0

Game 6.5   Ruy Lopez/Spanish –
Neo-Archangel
Ray Robson   2670
Surya Ganguly   2652
Ulaanbaatar 2018 (9)

**1.e4 e5 2.♘f3 ♘c6 3.♗b5 a6 4.♗a4
♘f6 5.0-0**

5...b5

5...♗c5 is an alternate move-order designed to postpone the decision as to how to meet a2-a4 until White has committed to c3. Anand has been playing this lately, and it looks better than playing ...b7-b5 first. I played this way myself about 20 years ago. 6.c3 b5 7.♗b3 (7.♗c2 is very interesting, but not clearly in White's favor. See the Black book) 7...d6 8.a4 ♗b7 9.d4 ♗b6 10.♗g5 (10.♖e1 0-0 11.♗g5 h6 12.♗h4 g5 13.♘xg5! is way more interesting and dangerous, but probably leads to perpetual check with correct play. See the Black book. This is the way to play this for White if you know the analysis) 10...h6 11.♗xf6 ♕xf6 12.♗d5 (White has given up the bishop pair because he knows that eventually Black must move his knight and allow a bishop exchange) 12...0-0 13.♘a3 exd4 14.cxd4 ♖fb8 15.♘c2 bxa4 16.♖xa4 a5 17.♖e1 ♘e7 18.♗xb7 ♖xb7 19.♘e3 ♖ab8 20.g3 (or 20.b3, as in the Black book. Either way, White is just nominally better) 20...c6 21.♘c4 ♕e6 22.♔g2 ♗d8 23.h3 (+0.20), Lc0 +0.09. White has a better center, but

the pressure on b2 will provoke the exchange of knight and b2-pawn for bishop and a5-pawn, after which White's edge is minimal.

6.♗b3

6...♗c5

The Neo-Archangel, rather popular in modern grandmaster games. 6...♗b7 is the Archangel, which has mostly been supplanted by the Neo-Archangel as in this game: 7.d3 (7.♖e1 is also a good line, aiming for c2-c3 and d2-d4, but since we are playing d2-d3 in the main line Spanish it makes sense to play it here, where it is especially effective at walling in the b7-bishop. Black will rarely play ...♗b7 voluntarily if White has played d2-d3) 7...♗e7 8.a4 0-0 (note that we can also get this position by 5...♗e7 6.d3 b5 7.♗b3 0-0 8.a4 ♗b7) 9.♖e1 (this is the older main line of the Anti-Marshall 8.a4, which is usually met by 8...b4 nowadays) 9...d6 10.♘bd2 ♘a5 11.♗a2 c5 12.♘f1 bxa4 13.♘e3 ♗c6 14.♘h4 g6 15.♘f3 ♖b8 16.♘d5 ♘xd5 17.♗xd5 ♗d7 18.♗h6 ♖e8 19.♕d2 ♗c6 20.b3± (+0.08), but Lc0 gives +0.46. White regains the pawn on a4 with some positional edge, mainly due to the offside black knight.

7.a4

This move-order, rather than 7.c3 d6 8.a4, has the advantage of ruling out the defense ...♗g4, although that can be well met by h2-h3 anyway. Perhaps more important, in case of 7.a4 ♗b7 White can omit c2-c3 and perhaps play ♘c3 later.

7...♖b8

7...♗b7 8.d3 0-0 9.♗g5 h6 10.♗h4 ♗e7 11.axb5 axb5 12.♖xa8 ♕xa8 13.♘c3 ♘a5 14.♗xf7+ ♖xf7 15.♘xe5 ♖f8 16.♘g6 ♖f7 17.♘xe7+ ♖xe7 18.♗xf6 gxf6 19.♘xb5 ♕d8 20.♘d4± (+0.18), Lc0 +0.60. White has three pawns for the piece, so is half a pawn down, but Black has two isolated pawns, a broken king shield, and a knight on the rim, while White has f5 for his knight.

8.c3 d6 9.d4 ♗b6

10.a5!

This involves a positional exchange sacrifice, but Black rarely accepts it as the compensation looks more than adequate.

10.axb5 axb5 11.♘a3 0-0 12.♘xb5 ♗g4 was the main line until recently, with practical results

similar to other main line defenses to 1.e4. White wins a pawn but Black gets serious compensation. Most engines claim that Black's compensation isn't quite up to par, but Lc0 says that Black is no worse than in other good defenses like the Marshall.

10...♗a7

10...♘xa5?! 11.♖xa5 ♗xa5 12.dxe5 ♘g4 13.♗g5 f6 14.exf6 gxf6 15.♗h4 c5 16.h3 (16.♗d5!?) 16...h5 17.♗d5N ♘e5 18.♘xe5 dxe5 19.f4 ♗c7 20.fxe5 ♗xe5 21.♘d2 ♖b6 22.♘f3± (+1.53). White is still down the full exchange, but all of his pieces are active whereas Black's rooks are doing little, and White has a much safer king and better pawn structure as well. White is probably winning, but to prove it would take a lot of analysis.

11.h3 0-0 12.♗e3

White can play normal, calm moves now that Black's potential counterplay based on ...♘a5 has been prevented.

12...♖a8

This defends against 13.dxe5.

13.♖e1 h6 14.♘bd2 ♖e8

15.♘f1

15.♕c2 exd4 16.♗xd4 ♗d7 17.e5 dxe5 18.♗xe5 ♗e6 19.♖ad1 ♘xe5 20.♘xe5± (+0.14). White's powerful knight on e5 should be more effective than Black's bishop on a7 once the light-squared bishops vanish.

But the game line seems more convincing.

15...exd4 16.cxd4

16...♘xe4

16...♖xe4 17.♘g3 ♖e7 18.♕d2 d5 19.♖ac1 ♗d7 20.♗xh6 gxh6 21.♕xh6 ♘xd4 22.♘e5N (+2.88). White has a winning attack, though it's still a bit messy.

17.♗d5 ♗b7 18.♗xh6 gxh6 19.♖xe4 ♖xe4 20.♗xe4 d5 21.♗c2 ♕f6 22.♖a3 ♗xd4 23.♘g3

23...♗xb2

23...♖e8 24.♘h5 ♕h8 25.♘xd4 ♕xd4 26.♖g3+ ♔f8 27.♕c1 ♖e2 28.♕xh6+ ♔e7 29.♔h2 ♖xf2 30.♖e3+ ♘e5 31.b4± (+1.82), but Lc0 only +0.76. White has a safer king, better pawns, and better pieces for just one pawn. White will probably win the exchange.

24.♖b3?!

24.♘h5! ♕d6 25.♖b3 ♗h8 26.♘h4 ♔f8 27.♘f5 ♕c5 28.♕c1 ♔e8 29.♖f3+− (+2.40). White has a winning attack, although accuracy is still required.

24...♘d4?

24...♖d8! 25.♕d2 ♔f8 (+0.02). White may not have quite enough compensation for two pawns.

25.♘h5?

25.♘xd4! ♕xd4 26.♕b1 ♗a1 27.♕c1+−.

25...♘xf3+?

25...♕h8=.

26.♖xf3 ♕d4 27.♕e2 ♕c4 28.♕d2 ♕c6 29.♗h7+ ♔xh7 30.♕xb2 1-0

Game 6.6 Ruy Lopez/Spanish – Open
David Navara   2738
Wesley So   2765
St Louis 2019 (1)

1.e4 e5 2.♘f3 ♘c6 3.♗b5 a6 4.♗a4 ♘f6 5.0-0

I don't recommend avoiding the Open Spanish by 5.d3 due to 5...♗c5. I only play d2-d3 after Black has committed to 5...♗e7.

5...♘xe4 6.d4 b5

6...♗e7 7.♖e1 b5 8.♖xe4 d5 9.♘xe5 ♘xe5 10.♖xe5 bxa4.

analysis diagram

So far Caruana-Carlsen, Zagreb 2019. 11.b3 (this is simply to kill the bishop pair) 11...0-0 12.♗a3 ♗xa3 13.♘xa3 ♖e8 (13...♕d6 14.♘b1 f6 15.♖e1N axb3 16.cxb3 c5 17.♘c3 ♖d8 18.♖c1± (+0.41). Black will have two isolated pawns and a slightly bad bishop) 14.♖xe8+ ♕xe8 15.♘b1 axb3 16.cxb3N ♕c6 17.♕d2 ♗d7 18.♘c3 ♖e8 19.♖e1 ♖xe1+ 20.♕xe1± (+0.17), Lc0 +0.43. Queen and knight vs queen and bishop is considered slightly favorable, and here the bishop is a bit bad, and the lack of any pawn majorities favors knights.

7.♗b3 d5 8.dxe5 ♗e6

This position arises pretty much by force once Black takes on e4. It has occurred in thousands of games.

Aside from the ♘bd2 and c2-c3 idea, White can also play 9.♗e3 or 9.♕e2 with chances for a small plus.

9.♘bd2

9.c3 ♗c5 10.♘bd2 0-0 11.♗c2 ♘xf2 is the famous Dilworth Variation, which is rather equal. The point of the 9.♘bd2 move order is to avoid this.

9...♗e7 10.c3 0-0 11.♗c2 f5 12.♘b3 ♕d7 13.♘fd4 ♘xd4 14.♘xd4 c5 15.♘xe6 ♕xe6 16.f3 ♘g5 17.a4 ♖ad8 18.axb5 axb5 19.♖a7

19...♖d7

19...g6 20.f4 ♘e4 21.♕e2 c4 22.♗e3 ♖a8 23.♗xe4 dxe4 24.♖fa1 ♕c6 25.♖1a6 ♕xa6 26.♖xa6 ♖xa6 27.g4 ♔f7 28.♔f2 ♖a2 29.♔g3± (+0.20). Although two rooks are on average a bit better than the queen, Black's king is not safe and Black will have trouble defending f5, h7, and b5.

20.♖xd7 ♕xd7 21.f4 ♘e4 22.♗xe4 fxe4 23.f5 d4 24.f6 gxf6

24...♗d8 25.♗e3 d3 26.♗xc5 ♖f7 27.♕b3 ♕c6 28.♗d4 gxf6 29.e6 ♖e7 30.♖xf6 ♗b6 31.♕d1 ♗xd4+ 32.cxd4 e3 33.♕xd3 ♖xe6 34.♕b3± (+0.68). White will keep his extra pawn, although Black has some hope of drawing a rook endgame a pawn down.

25.♗h6 ♖f7

26.cxd4?

26.♕e1!N ♗f8 27.♕g3+ ♔h8 28.♗xf8 ♖xf8 29.exf6± (+0.93). The 'thorn' pawn on f6 makes Black's king unsafe. White is likely to win a pawn by combining threats against the king with threats against e4 or c5.

26...♕e6??

26...fxe5 27.♖xf7 ♔xf7 28.♕h5+ ♔g8 29.dxe5=.

27.d5

This wins because 27...♕xe5 is met by 28.♕g4+ and 29.♕c8+.

1-0

Game 6.7 Ruy Lopez/Spanish – Open

Frank McDermott   2151
Danny den Drijver   2052

Correspondence 2017

1.e4 e5 2.♘f3 ♘c6 3.♗b5 a6 4.♗a4 ♘f6 5.0-0 ♘xe4 6.d4 b5 7.♗b3 d5 8.dxe5 ♗e6 9.♘bd2 ♘c5 10.c3 d4
I think that this sideline is underrated and is probably Black's best option in the Open Spanish.

11.♗xe6 ♘xe6 12.cxd4 ♘cxd4 13.♘e4
13.a4 is more common but I could not prove a white edge in that line.

13...♗e7 14.♗e3 ♘f5 15.♕c2 0-0

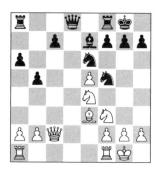

16.♘eg5
16.♖ad1 ♘xe3 17.fxe3 ♕c8 18.♘d4 ♘xd4 19.exd4 ♕e6 20.♘g3 c6 21.♘f5 ♖fe8 22.♖c1 ♖ac8 23.♘xe7+ ♖xe7 24.b4 (+0.02). White has more space, but it's almost balanced.

16...♗xg5 17.♘xg5

17...♘xg5

A) 17...h6 18.♘xe6 fxe6 19.♕e4 ♘xe3 20.♕xe3± (+0.22). White has fewer weak pawns and more space, but Black has active pieces so White's edge is modest;

B) 17...g6 18.♘xe6 fxe6 19.♕c5± (+0.45). Black has more weak pawns than White.

18.♕xf5 ♘e6 19.♕e4± f5 20.exf6 ♕xf6 21.♖ac1 c5 22.♖fd1 ♖ad8 23.♕c6 ♖de8

24.♕xa6

24.♖d2 ♕f5 25.h3± (+0.72). Black is hard-pressed to avoid losing a pawn.

24...♕xb2 25.♖b1 ♕c2 26.♕xb5

26.♖dc1 ♕a4 27.♕xa4 bxa4 28.g3 ± (+0.46). White has better pawns and bishop vs knight with opposing majorities, which favors bishops.

26...♕xa2 27.♖d2 ♕a7 28.♕c4 ♕f7 29.h3 ♖d8 30.♖xd8 ♖xd8 31.♖c1 ♖c8 32.♖d1 ♖c7 33.♖d5 ♘f8 34.♗xc5 ♘e6 35.♕b4 ♖xc5 36.♖xc5 ♘xc5 37.♕xc5 ♕f6 38.♕d5+ ♔f8 39.♕a8+ ♔f7 40.♕d5+ ♕e6??

40...♔f8±.

41.♕xe6+ ♔xe6 42.♔h2 ♔e5 43.♔g3 ♔f5 44.h4 h5 45.♔f3 g5 46.♔g3+‒ 1-0

Game 6.8 Ruy Lopez/Spanish – Open

Fabiano Caruana 2827

Shakhriyar Mamedyarov 2820

Batumi ol 2018 (8)

1.e4 e5 2.♘f3 ♘c6 3.♗b5 a6 4.♗a4 ♘f6 5.0-0 ♘xe4 6.d4 b5 7.♗b3 d5 8.dxe5 ♗e6 9.♘bd2 ♘c5 10.c3 ♗e7 11.♗c2 d4 12.♘b3 d3

13.♗b1

Or also 13.♘xc5 dxc2 14.♕xd8+ ♖xd8 15.♘xe6 fxe6 16.♗e3 ♖d5 17.♖fc1 ♘xe5 18.♘xe5 ♖xe5 19.♖xc2 ♔f7 20.c4 b4 21.♖d1 ♖d8 22.♖xd8 ♗xd8 23.♔f1 ♗g5 24.♗d4 ♖a5 25.b3 e5 26.♗a7 (+0.05) and White has the sunny side of a drawn endgame.

13...♘xb3 14.axb3 ♗f5 15.♗e3 0-0 16.♗d4 ♕d5 17.♖e1

17...d2

17...♖fd8 18.h4 d2 19.♕xd2 ♗xb1
20.♖axb1 ♕xb3 21.e6 fxe6 22.♕f4
♗d6 23.♕g4 e5 24.♗e3 ♖f8 25.♕e4
♘e7 26.♘g5 g6 27.h5 h6 28.♘f3 g5
29.♘xe5 ♕e6 30.♗d2 ♘f5 31.♘g4
♕xe4 32.♖xe4± (+0.18). The
h6-pawn is a target, and White has
the open file.

**18.♖e2 ♗xb1 19.♖xb1 ♘xd4
20.♘xd4 ♗g5 21.g3 c5 22.♘f5 ♕d3
23.♘d6 ♕g6 24.h4**

24...♗f4

24...♗xh4 25.♖xd2 ♗e7 26.♕e1 ♕e6
27.♕e4 ♗xd6 28.♖xd6 ♕xb3 29.♔g2
♕c4 30.♕xc4 bxc4 31.f4± (+0.20).
White will easily regain his pawn
with obvious positional advantages
in the endgame, though Black
should hold.

25.♘e4

25.h5 ♕e6 26.♘e4 ♗xe5 27.♖xd2
♕f5 28.♘d6± (+0.27). White is
likely to win the a6-pawn soon, but
his extra doubled pawn will be hard
to convert.

**25...f5 26.♘xd2 ♖ad8 27.♖a1
♖fe8 28.♕e1 ♗xd2 29.♖xd2 ♖xd2
30.♕xd2 ♖xe5 31.♕d8+ ♖e8
32.♕d5+ ♕e6 33.♖d1 c4 34.bxc4
bxc4 35.♕b7**

35...♖e7?!

35...♕e4 36.♖d7 ♕xb7 37.♖xb7±
(+0.63). Black's two isolated pawns
give White an obvious edge,
although Black retains drawing
chances.

**36.♖d8+ ♔f7 37.♕f3 g6?! 38.♕f4
♕c6 39.♖d1 ♖e4 40.♕h6 ♔g8
41.h5 ♖e8 42.hxg6 hxg6 43.♔f1 ♖e6
44.♕h4 ♖e8 45.♖d4 ♖c8?**

45...a5 46.g4 fxg4 47.♖xg4± (+0.66).
White has enough threats to win a
pawn shortly.

**46.♕h6+− ♕e6 47.♖h4 ♔f7
48.♕h7+ ♔f6 49.♖d4 ♕e7 50.♕h6
♔f7 51.♕d2 ♖c7 52.♖h4 ♔f6
53.♕d4+ ♕e5 54.♕b6+ ♔g7
55.♕b8 ♔f6 56.♕h8+ ♕e6 57.♕g8+
♔f6 58.♖d4 ♕e7 59.♖d8 ♔g5
60.f4+ ♔h5 61.♖d2 ♕g7 62.♖h2+
♔g4 63.♔g2 g5 64.♕e8 1-0**

Game 6.9 Ruy Lopez/Spanish
Andrei Volokitin   2639
Maxim Vavulin   2583
Batumi Ech 2018 (6)

**1.e4 e5 2.♘f3 ♘c6 3.♗b5 a6 4.♗a4
♘f6 5.0-0 ♗e7 6.d3**

This is popular primarily to avoid the Marshall Attack, but it also avoids many other Spanish lines.

6...d6

The idea of meeting the threat of 7.♗xc6 and 8.♘xe5 this way rather than by 6..b5 is to take away the quick attack on the b5-pawn by a2-a4.

The drawback is that now when White plays c2-c3 (7.c4 is a decent alternative) a later ...b7-b5 can be answered by ♗c2 instead of ♗b3, saving a tempo in many lines. But there are also drawbacks to having the bishop on c2 instead of b3 – mainly that ...d6-d5 is easier to achieve. It appears to me that if Black intends to play the Zaitsev against 6.♖e1, then 6.d3 d6 makes good sense as it may transpose directly to the Zaitsev.

7.c3 0-0 8.♖e1 ♖e8

8...b5 9.♗c2 ♖e8 (9...d5 10.♘bd2 dxe4 11.dxe4 ♗e6 12.a4 ♕b8 13.♕e2 ♕b7 14.b4 ♗d6 15.♗d3 ♖ab8 16.♖b1 ♘e7 17.c4 c6 18.c5 ♗c7 19.♘f1± (+0.25). In this line, White has a clear space advantage for free, but there is no easy way forward) 10.♘bd2 ♗f8.

analysis diagram

11.h3 is the choice if White intended ♗b3 if Black played as in this game. 11.♘f1 h6 12.♘g3 d5 transposes to the game) 11...h6 12.d4 ♗b7 13.a4 exd4 14.cxd4 ♘b4 15.♗b1 c5 16.d5 ♘d7 17.♖a3 is a transposition to a main line of the Zaitsev, where White retains his normal opening edge. White lost a move with d2-d3, then d3-d4, but saved a move getting the bishop from a4 to c2 in one turn instead of two. This is outside the scope of this book, but it is important that White has this option if Black plays ...b7-b5 early.

9.♘bd2 ♗f8 10.♘f1 h6 11.♘g3 b5

12.♗c2

12.♗b3 ♘a5 13.♗c2 c5 14.d4 cxd4 15.cxd4 exd4 16.♘xd4 ♗b7 17.b3 ♖c8 18.♗b2 ♘c6 19.♘xc6± (+0.24). White

127

has the better pawn structure and more active bishops after either recapture. Note that Black can avoid this by playing ...b7-b5 earlier if he is willing to allow a transposition to the main line of the Zaitsev.

12...d5

12...g6 13.a4 ♖b8 14.axb5 axb5 15.h3 d5 16.d4 dxe4 17.♘xe4 ♗f5 18.♘xf6+ ♕xf6 19.♗xf5 ♕xf5 20.♖a6 e4 21.♘h2 ♖e6 22.d5 ♖d8 23.dxe6 ♖xd1 24.exf7+ ♔xf7 25.♖xd1 ♘e5 26.♖a7 ♕c8 27.♖d5 ♕b8 28.♗e3 ♔e6 29.♖d2 ♗d6 30.♖a1± (+0.30), but Lc0 gives +0.48. Two rooks on open files are stronger than a queen.

13.exd5 ♕xd5

13...♘xd5 14.h3 ♗d6 15.a4± (+0.17). White has ideas of d3-d4 or ♘e4 once Black defends the b5-pawn.

14.d4

14.h3 ♗e6 15.♗e3 ♖ad8 16.♘e4 ♘xe4 17.dxe4 ♕xd1 18.♖exd1 f6 19.b4 a5 20.♗d3 axb4 21.♗xb5 ♖xd1+ 22.♖xd1 ♖d8 23.♖b1 ♘b8 24.cxb4 ♗xa2 25.♖b2 (+0.05). White's knight is better than Black's (it can aim for f5), but of course the endgame should be drawn.

14...♗g4 15.♗b3 ♕d6 16.h3 ♗xf3 17.♕xf3 exd4 18.♗f4 ♕d7 19.♗xh6 ♘a5 20.♗c2 d3 21.♗xd3 gxh6 22.b4

22...♘c6??

22...♕c6! 23.♘e4 ♗g7 24.bxa5 ♘xe4 25.♗xe4 ♕xc3 26.♗xa8 ♖xe1+ 27.♖xe1 ♕xe1+ 28.♔h2 c5 29.♗d5 ♕e7 30.g3 ♗d4 31.♔g2 ♔g7 32.♔f1 (+0.03) should be a draw, but Black has to be more careful than White due to the difference in king safety.

23.♕xf6+− ♗g7 24.♘h5! ♗h8 25.♗c2 ♖e6 26.♖xe6 ♕xe6 27.♕xe6 fxe6 28.♗e4 ♗xc3 29.♖c1 1-0

Game 6.10   Ruy Lopez/Spanish
Sergey Erenburg   2589
Wesley So   2765
PRO League Stage rapid 2019 (10)

1.e4 e5 2.♘f3 ♘c6 3.♗b5 a6 4.♗a4 ♘f6 5.0-0 ♗e7 6.d3 b5 7.♗b3

7...d6

7...0-0 8.a4 b4 and now:

A) 9.♘bd2 is the move to play if you want to show that 6.d3 is better than 6.♖e1 against the Marshall, and I think it is a good choice: 9...♗c5 (9...d6 10.a5 (10.c3 ♖b8 11.a5 ♗e6 12.♘c4 bxc3 13.bxc3 h6 14.h3± (+0.25). White has plans of ♖e1 and ♗a4 or d3-d4. Black's knight on c6 is poorly placed here) 10...♗e6 11.♗xe6 fxe6 12.c3) 10.h3 d6 11.♘c4 h6 12.♗e3 ♗xe3 13.fxe3 a5 14.♘cd2 ♘b8 15.g4= (+0.00), but Lc0 +0.45. I must agree with Lc0 here; White has much better development and kingside attacking chances, and the doubled pawns hardly matter here;

B) 9.♖e1.

analysis diagram

The point of this move, rather than 9.♘bd2, is to meet 9...♗c5 by 10.♗g5, but this transposes to an anti-Marshall line, in which case why play 6.d3 (rather than 6.♖e1) ? The answer must be that White is avoiding other Spanish lines. 9...d6 (9...♗c5 10.♗g5 h6 11.♗h4 d6 12.♘bd2 g5 13.♗g3 ♖b8 14.c3 ♗a7 15.a5 ♗e6 16.♗a4 ♘e7 17.d4 ♘g6 18.♕e2 ♕c8 19.♘f1 ♘h5 20.♘e3 (+0.12). White has the better center, but it's not much) 10.a5 ♗g4 (10...♗e6 11.♗xe6 fxe6 12.♘bd2 ♕e8 13.c3 ♖b8 14.d4 ♖b5 15.dxe5 dxe5 16.♘c4 ♗c5 17.♕e2 ♕g6 18.h3 h6 19.♗e3 bxc3 20.bxc3 ♗xe3 21.♕xe3 ♖fb8 22.g3± (+0.31). Black's doubled isolated e-pawns define White's edge; 10...♖b8 11.♘bd2 ♗e6 12.♗xe6 fxe6 13.♘b3 ♕c8 14.♕e2 ♘d7 15.♗e3 ♗f6 16.♘fd2 ♘d8 17.♕g4 ♖e8 18.♘f3±

(+0.01), but Lc0 +0.20. White has the better pawn structure, the better bishop, and some kingside ideas, but no clear path forward) 11.c3 d5? (11...♖b8 12.♘bd2 ♗e6 13.♘c4 bxc3 14.bxc3 h6 15.d4 exd4 16.♘xd4 ♗d7 17.h3± ♖e8 18.♗f4 ♗f8 19.e5 dxe5 20.♘xe5 ♘xe5 21.♗xe5 ♗d6 22.♗xd6 ♖xe1+ 23.♕xe1 cxd6 24.♗c4± (+0.17). White's minor pieces are more active and a6 is weak)

analysis diagram

12.h3 (12.exd5! ♘xd5 13.h3± is a more accurate move order to reach the game, since Black can't even get off with losing the bishop pair by 13...♗xf3? 14.♕xf3, winning) 12...♗h5?! (12...♗xf3 13.♕xf3 bxc3 14.bxc3 d4 15.♗d5 ♕d7 16.♗xc6 ♕xc6 17.cxd4 exd4 18.♗g5± (+0.28). Black's backward c7-pawn is a target, and c4 beckons for the white knight) 13.exd5 ♘xd5 14.♗a4 ♘xa5 15.♖xe5 ♗xf3 16.♕xf3 c6 17.♗xc6 ♘xc6 18.♖xd5± (+1.22) (Black has nothing for the lost pawn) 18...♕c8 19.♗f4 (19.♘d2!+–) 19...bxc3? (19...a5 20.♖a4±) 20.bxc3+– ♕b7

analysis diagram

21.♘d2 (21.♖d4!) 21...♕b2 22.♕d1 ♕xc3? 23.♘e4 ♕b4 24.♖b1 ♕a3 25.♗c1 ♕a2 26.♘c3 ♕xb1 27.♘xb1 a5 28.♕a4 ♖fc8 29.♗f4 h6 30.♘d2 ♖a7 31.♘c4 ♖b7 32.♘xa5 ♘xa5 33.♖xa5 1–0 Erenburg-Azarov, chess.com 2019.

8.a4

8.a3 is an alternative main line, but I prefer the game move. 8...0-0 9.♘c3 ♘a5 10.♗a2 ♗e6 11.b4 ♗xa2 12.♖xa2 ♘c6 13.♗g5 ♘g4 14.♗d2 ♘f6 15.♖e1 ♕d7 16.♖a1 (+0.10). White has the better bishop, but the perfect pawn and knight symmetry makes White's edge very small and a draw likely.

8...♗d7 9.c3 0-0 10.♗c2 b4 11.♖e1 ♖b8 12.♘bd2 ♖e8 13.h3 d5

13...h6 14.a5 ♗f8 15.♘c4± (+0.15). White is clearly but just slightly better due to his better knight on the c-file and better a- and c-pawns.

14.a5 ♗f8 15.♗b3 bxc3 16.bxc3 dxe4?

16...♗e6 17.♘g5 h6 18.♘xe6 ♖xe6 19.♘f3 ♗c5 20.♗d2± (+0.80). White is up the bishop pair and has strong pressure on the center, and will

have the better pawn structure after trading on d5.

17.♘g5 ♖e7 18.♗a3+−

This just wins the exchange for nothing, with the better position as well. The final drawn result was surely due to the fast time control and the rating gap, not to the current position. In a top level standard time control game Black might well resign here.

18...♗e8 19.♗xe7 ♗xe7 20.♘dxe4 ♘d5 21.♘f3 ♔h8 22.♗c4?

22.♗a4 f6 23.d4 exd4 24.♘xd4 ♘e5 25.♗xe8 ♕xe8 26.♘f3+− (+3.22). White is up by rook for bad bishop in an open position.

22...f5 23.♘g3 ♘xc3 24.♕c1 f4 25.♘f5 ♗b4 26.♘xe5 ♗xe5 27.♖xe5 ♕f6 28.d4 ♗d7

29.♕xf4??

29.♘e7!+− (+2.12). White keeps the exchange plus.

29...♖f8

Now the pinned knight can't be saved, but fortunately for White he still has a repetition draw available.

30.g4 g6 31.g5 ♕d8 32.♖c5 ♕e8 33.♖e5 ♕d8 34.♖c5 ♕e8 35.♖e5 ♕d8 ½-½

CHAPTER 7

Sicilian with 2.♘c3

In this chapter White meets the Sicilian **1.e4 c5** with **2.♘c3**, not with the idea of playing a closed Sicilian, but rather with the new idea of meeting **2...d6** (usually intending Najdorf or Dragon) by **3.d4 cxd4 4.♕xd4 ♘c6 5.♕d2**.

White plans b2-b3, ♗b2, and castling queenside, intending an English Attack kingside pawn storm. Of course I have to include counters to the other serious options for Black on move 2, which often means playing some Open Sicilian without having to meet the two 'best' ones, the Najdorf and the Sveshnikov, as I'll explain. If you don't want to play Open Sicilians at all, just skip this chapter and go to the 2.♘f3 chapter, which I consider my main line.

The most natural reply to 2.♘c3 is **2....♘c6**, as that will be the most useful move if White plays some closed Sicilian line as suggested by 2.♘c3.

Then I recommend **3.♘f3** (3.♗b5 is a decent move here, as it is after 2.♘f3, but I couldn't prove an edge in one main line). Now after **3...e6** play **4.d4**

cxd4 5.♘xd4 (we can reach this position also by 2...e6 3.♘ge2 (I prefer this move here to meet 3...a6 by 4.g3) 3...♘c6 4.d4 cxd4 5.♘xd4). Now **5...♘f6 6.♘xc6** (not 6.♘db5 as it allows a transposition to the highly respected Sveshnikov Sicilian) **6...bxc6 7.e5** is Game 7.1. It is very sharp and requires memorizing, so I also include a simpler alternative, 4.♗b5, in the notes. For **5...♕c7**, the Taimanov Sicilian, see Game 7.2 for **6.g3**, a fairly simple path to a normal opening edge for White.

Next we come to **2...a6**, which is often the choice of a would-be Najdorf player but can also be chosen by Taimanov or Kan players, although they are more likely to choose 2...♘c6 or 2...e6.

We play **3.♘ge2** (intending 4.g3, or else 3.g3 first, transposing once ♘ge2 is played). The idea is that we will postpone deciding between d2-d3 and d2-d4 until we have played g2-g3 and ♗g2 to see what set-up Black chooses. If he plays ...e7-e6 we choose d2-d4, if he plays ...d7-d6 and ...g7-g6 we choose d2-d3, arguing that in closed Sicilian lines the move ...a7-a6 is somewhat wasted, as Black would normally prepare ...b7-b5 by ...♖b8. For lines in which Black plays ...e7-e6 or ...d7-d6 but not the other, see Game 7.3, which also covers 2...g6, which we meet by 3.d4 cxd4 4.♕xd4 planning to castle queenside with strategies similar to the Yugoslav Attack against the Dragon, but the details are different so your opponent will likely be out of book. The actual game features a pawn sacrifice on move 9 that is totally sound and quite strong.

For a Scheveningen set-up (...e7-e6 and ...d7-d6) see Game 7.4, which shows that the ♗g2 set-up has some sting when Black delays the development of his kingside too long.

Now comes **2.♘c3 ♘c6 3.♘f3 ♘f6 4.♗b5**, which could just as easily have gone into the Rossolimo portion of the other Anti-Sicilian chapter, via 2.♘f3 ♘c6 3.♗b5 ♘f6 4.♘c3. See Game 7.5, which includes in the notes a game between the world's two highest rated players played in June 2019.

This defense is not so popular for Black in either move-order as it seems to give White an above-par edge.

In Game 7.6 we look at the very important **2.♘c3 ♘c6 3.♘f3 e5**.

This is the usual choice of those players who intended to play the Sveshnikov, such as World Champion Magnus Carlsen, who played Black in this game. Black wins this game rather quickly, but I would credit the player, not the opening, as my notes show a normal White edge with an improvement on move 13.

Finally we come to the idea after **2...d6** described in the first paragraph, to foil the Najdorf. As explained in Game 7.7, it was an idea of a Greek FIDE Master, brought to the world's attention by Carlsen, and then later also taken up by his last challenger Caruana. Although it looks a bit silly at first glance, it carries some real venom and is a legitimate try for a white edge.

Game 7.1   Sicilian Defense –
Four Knights Variation

Wei Yi   2733
Alexandr Fier   2561

Moscow 2019 (2)

1.e4 c5 2.♘f3

2.♘c3 ♘c6 3.♘f3 e6 4.♗b5 would
be the way to avoid the game
complications: 4...♘ge7 5.0-0 a6
6.♗xc6 ♘xc6 7.d4 cxd4 8.♘xd4
♕c7 9.♘xc6 dxc6 (9...bxc6 10.♕g4
♗d6 11.♕xg7 ♗xh2+ 12.♔h1 ♗e5
13.♗f4 ♗xg7 14.♗xc7 d5 15.♖fe1 ♖a7
16.♗d6± (+0.17). White's superior
development more than offsets the
bishop pair) 10.♕h5 b5 11.♖d1 e5
12.♗g5 ♗e7 13.♗xe7 ♕xe7 14.♖d2
0-0 15.♖ad1 g6 16.♕f3 ♗e6 17.♕g3
f6 18.♕d3± (+0.00), but Lc0 thinks
Black must give two rooks for the
queen for a +0.42 score. 18.♕e3 is
also slightly better for White.

**2...e6 3.d4 cxd4 4.♘xd4 ♘f6 5.♘c3
♘c6**

Our likely move order to reach this
position is 2.♘c3 ♘c6 3.♘f3 e6 4.d4
cxd4 5.♘xd4 ♘f6.

Now 6.♘db5 is often played,
but it allows Black to reach the
Sveshnikov by 6...d6 7.♗f4 e5

8.♗g5, when Black has avoided what
may be the best line against the
Svesh proper, namely 7.♘d5. 6.a3 is
safe and not bad, but it is obviously
a concession, so the forcing line in
this game is really the only critical
test of the variation.

6.♘xc6 bxc6 7.e5 ♘d5 8.♘e4

8...♕c7

8...♗b7 9.♗e2 c5 10.0-0 ♕c7
11.♘d6+ ♗xd6 12.exd6 ♕c6 13.f3 c4
14.♕d4 0-0 15.♗xc4 ♕xd6 16.♖d1
♖fc8 17.b3 ♕b6 18.♕xb6± (+0.34).
Whichever way Black recaptures,
White will have a solid bishop pair
endgame advantage.

9.f4

This is a very sharp line which you
must memorize.

9...♕b6

9...♕a5+ 10.♗d2 ♕b6 11.♗d3 ♘b4
12.♕e2 ♘xd3+ 13.♕xd3 ♕xb2
14.0-0 ♕a3 15.♕e2 ♕b2 16.♗e3
♗e7 17.♖ab1 ♕a3 18.♖b3± (+0.77).
White's huge lead in development
and space are clearly worth more
than Black's extra pawn.

10.c4 ♗b4+

10...♘e3 11.♕d3 ♗b4+ 12.♗d2 ♗a6
13.♗xb4 ♕xb4+ 14.♔f2 ♕xb2+
15.♗e2 ♘xc4 16.♖hd1 ♕b6+ 17.♕d4

♘b2 18.♗xa6 ♘xd1+ 19.♖xd1 ♕xd4+
20.♖xd4 ♖b8 21.♖a4 ♔e7 22.♔e3
♖b2 23.♘d2 ♖hb8 24.♗d3± (+0.25).
Although rook and two pawns are a
tad better than bishop and knight
with queens off, the presence of
the extra pair of rooks, the weak
a7-pawn, the backward d7-pawn,
and the great white king position
give him the better chances.

**11.♔e2 f5 12.exf6 ♘xf6 13.♗e3
♕d8 14.♘d6+ ♗xd6 15.♕xd6 ♗b7
16.♖d1**

16.♔d1 c5 17.♕xc5 ♗e4 18.♗e2 ♖c8
19.♕xa7 0-0 20.♕d4±.

16...♖c8 17.♖g1 c5 18.g4

18...♖c6

18...♕b6 19.g5 ♕xd6 20.♖xd6 ♘e4
21.♖d3 d5 22.♖a3 d4 23.♖xa7 ♘d6
24.♗c1 ♖c7 25.♔e1 ♔d7 26.♗d3 g6
27.♖a5 ♘f5 28.h3 h6 29.gxh6 ♖xh6
30.♗f1 ♗e4 31.b3± (+0.25). Black
has considerable compensation for
the pawn in this endgame, but he is
also down the bishop pair.

**19.♕e5 0-0 20.g5 ♘h5 21.♗h3 d6
22.♕xe6+ ♔h8 23.♖gf1 ♖b6 24.b3
♖a6 25.♖d2**

25.♕d7 ♖xa2+ 26.♖d2 ♖xd2+
27.♗xd2 ♕a8 28.♕g4 ♕e8+ 29.♔d1
♕e4 30.♕xh5 ♕d3 31.f5 ♕xb3+

32.♔e1 g6 33.♕e2 ♕xh3 34.♕e7
♕h4+ 35.♖f2 ♕e4+ 36.♕xe4 ♗xe4
37.f6± (+0.10), Lc0 +0.31. Black
should hold this opposite bishops
endgame despite the dangerous
passed pawn.

**25...d5 26.♕e5 ♖e8 27.cxd5 ♖xe5
28.fxe5**

28...♗xd5

28...c4 29.bxc4 ♖a3 30.♗c5 and now:

A) 30...♖xh3 31.♔d1 ♖h4 32.♖f8+
♕xf8 33.♗xf8 ♔g8 34.♗a3 ♗c8
35.e6 ♖xc4 36.♖e2 ♖d4+ 37.♔c2
♖xd5 38.e7 ♗d7 39.e8♕+ ♗xe8
40.♖xe8+ ♔f7 41.♖e7+ ♔g6 42.♖xa7
♖xg5 43.♗d6 ♖d5 44.♗c7± (+0.55).
Black might be able to draw, but not
easily;

B) 30...♗a6!? 31.♖f8+ (Black
should also hold after 31.♔d1 with
perfect play) is analyzed to a likely
draw in New In Chess *Yearbook* 131,
page 19. As with many lines in this
book, this is a problem only for the
correspondence player; as long as
Black has to find many good moves
in multiple lines to hold the draw,
White can be satisfied with the
opening for over-the-board play,
even at grandmaster level.

29.♗g2 c4?

29...♖xa2! 30.♗xd5 ♖xd2+ 31.♗xd2 ♘f6. Now both captures allow perpetual check: 32.exf6 ♕xd5 33.f7 ♕e4+ 34.♔f2 ♕f5+ 35.♔g2 ♕g4+ or 32.gxf6 ♕xd5 33.f7 ♕e4+.

30.♗xd5 c3 31.♗b7 cxd2 32.♗xa6 ♕e8 33.♗c4 g6 34.e6 1-0

Game 7.2   Sicilian Defense – Taimanov
Magnus Carlsen   2835
Richard Rapport   2731
Wijk aan Zee 2019 (8)

1.e4 c5 2.♘f3

2.♘c3 ♘c6 3.♘f3 e6 4.d4 cxd4 5.♘xd4 would be the likely move order for us to reach the game (Black's second and third moves could be transposed).

2...e6 3.d4 cxd4 4.♘xd4 ♘c6

The Taimanov Sicilian, which I played often as Black in 1962!

5.♘c3 ♕c7

5...a6 6.g3 ♕c7 transposes.

6.g3

This positional line has some sting to it when Black has played (or will need to play) ...a7-a6.

6...a6

6...♘f6? was already known to be bad half a century ago: 7.♘db5 ♕b8

8.♗f4 ♘e5? (8...e5 9.♗g5 a6 10.♗xf6 gxf6 11.♘a3 ♗xa3 12.bxa3 ♘e7 13.♕d3± (+0.30). Black has more serious pawn weaknesses and less space) 9.♗e2 ♗c5 10.♗xe5 ♕xe5 11.f4 ♕b8 12.e5 a6 13.exf6 axb5 14.♘e4 ♗f8 15.♕d4+−.

7.♗g2 ♘f6 8.0-0

8...d6

  A) 8...♘xd4 9.♕xd4 ♗c5 10.♗f4 d6 11.♕d2 h6 12.♖ad1 e5 13.♗e3 ♗e6 14.♗xc5 dxc5 15.♘d5 ♗xd5 16.exd5 ♕d6 17.c4 0-0 18.♗h3 (18.♖fe1 ♘d7 19.♗h3 f5 20.f3 b5 21.♕c2 (21.b3± (+0.16). The protected passed pawn and pressure on f5 and e5 are White's edge) 21...g6 22.g4 fxg4 23.♗xg4± (+0.12). The protected passer and threats to Black's king give White a plus) 18...♖fe8 19.♖fe1 ♖e7 20.♖e3 b6 21.a3 ♖ae8 22.b4 (22.♕c2± (+0.32). White active bishop and protected passed pawn are his edge) 22...♖c7 23.♖b3 (23.♕e2±) 23...b5 24.♗f1 bxc4 25.♗xc4 cxb4 26.♕xb4 ♕xb4 27.♖xb4 a5 28.d6 ♖c5 29.♖a4 ♖d8 30.♗b3 ♘e8 31.♖d5 ♖c3 32.♗c4 ♘xd6 33.♗f1 f6 34.♖axa5 ♖c6 35.♖a7 ♖b8 36.♖d1 ♘f5 37.♗g2 ♖c3 38.♗d5+ ♔h8 39.♗e4 ♘d4 40.♗g6 f5 41.h4 f4 42.♔g2 ♖f8 43.h5 (43. g4±) 43...fxg3 44.fxg3 ♘f5 45.♖f7 (45.♖dd7±) 45...♘e3+ 46.♔h3 ♔g8 47.♖xf8+ ♔xf8 48.♖a1 ♘d5 49.♔g2 ♖c5 50.♖b1 ♖a5 51.♖b8+ ½-½ Adams-Spoelman, Germany Bundesliga 2017/18;

B) 8...♗e7 9.♖e1 0-0 10.♘xc6 dxc6 11.e5 ♖d8 12.♕f3 ♘d5 13.h4 ♗d7 14.♗g5 ♗xg5 15.hxg5 ♘xc3 16.♕xc3 ♗e8 17.♖ad1 a5 18.♕c5 (18. a3 ♖ab8 19.♕c5 b6 20.♕e3± 1-0 (60) Wang Hao-Andreikin, China tt 2019 (+0.22)) 18...b6 19.♕a3± ♖xd1 20.♖xd1 ♕xe5 21.♕e7 ♕b8 22.c4 (+0.50). White's total board domination is obviously worth more than Black's extra pawn, though the game still has to be won.

9.♘xc6

This is rather rare, but may be even better than the usual 9.♖e1:

analysis diagram

A) 9...♗d7 10.♘xc6 bxc6 11.♘a4 ♖b8 12.b3 e5 13.♕d3 a5 14.♗d2 ♗e7 15.c4 0-0 16.♖ac1± (+0.62). White has space and weak pawns to target;

B) 9...♗e7 10.♘xc6 bxc6 11.e5 dxe5 12.♖xe5 0-0 13.♖e1 ♗b7 14.♗f4 ♕a5 15.a3 ♖ad8 16.♕e2± (+0.41). Black has a problem bishop on b7;

C) 9...♖b8 10.♘xc6 bxc6 11.e5 dxe5 12.♖xe5 ♗d6 (12...♕xe5 13.♗f4 ♕c5 14.♗xb8 ♗e7 15.♗c7 0-0 16.♘a4 ♕f5 17.♕d2± (+0.60). White has the better pawn structure and better development) 13.♖e1 0-0 14.b3 c5 15.♘a4 c4 16.♘b2 cxb3 17.axb3 ♖d8 18.♕e2 ♗d7 19.♕c4 ♗b5 20.♕xc7 ♗xc7 21.♖d1± (+0.28) is a decent alternative, with White's better pawn structure giving him a small endgame plus, but probably the game move is stronger.

9...bxc6 10.♘a4 ♖b8 11.c4 c5 12.b3 ♗e7 13.♗b2 0-0

14.♕e1

14.f4 ♘d7 15.♕d2N ♗b7 16.♖ad1 transposes to move 20 of the game while cutting out the ...♘e5 option.

14...♘d7 15.♖d1 ♗b7

15...♘e5 16.♕c3 ♗f6 17.♕d2 ♗d7 18.♘c3± (+0.40). White has space and pressure on d6.

16.♕c3 ♗f6 17.♕d2 ♗e7 18.♕c3 ♗f6 19.♕d2 ♗e7 20.f4 e5 21.♗c3 ♗c6 22.♗a5 ♕b7 23.♘c3± (+0.56) White can aim for ♘d5 or f4-f5 if Black just waits.

23...exf4 24.gxf4 ♖fe8 25.e5 ♗xg2 26.♕xg2 dxe5 27.♘d5 e4 28.♗c3 f6 29.♔h1

29.♖fe1 ♔h8 30.♖xe4+– was the surer way to win, regaining the pawn with a crushing positional advantage, but Carlsen's way is fine too.

29...♔h8 30.♖g1 ♗f8 31.♘e3 ♕c6 32.♖d5 ♕e6 33.♖h5 ♕f7 34.♕h3 g6 35.♖h4 ♖b6 36.f5 ♘e5 37.♘d5 ♖d6 38.fxg6 ♘xg6 39.♗xf6+ ♖xf6 40.♖xh7+ 1-0

Game 7.3   Sicilian Defense –
           Paulsen/Kan Variation

Dmitry Andreikin   2710
Denis Khismatullin   2634

Satka 2018 (1)

1.e4 c5 2.♘c3 a6
  A) 2...g6 3.d4 cxd4 4.♕xd4 ♘f6 5.♗e3 ♘c6 6.♕d2 ♗g7 7.f3 0-0 8.0-0-0 d6 9.♘ge2.

So it looks like the Yugoslav Attack vs the Dragon, but because the knight is on e2 instead of d4 all theory is out the window. 9...♕a5 10.♔b1 b5 11.♗h6N (everyone has played ♘c1 or ♘f4 here, both good moves, but it makes sense to exploit the fact that ♗h6 can be played without losing a knight on d4) 11...♗e6 12.♗xg7 ♔xg7 13.♘c1

♖ab8 14.g4 ♘e5 15.g5 ♘h5 16.f4 ♘c4 17.♕d4+ f6 18.f5 ♗f7 19.♗e2 ♕b6 20.♕xb6 ♖xb6 21.♗xh5 gxh5 22.♖hg1± (+0.14). White has a better pawn structure and initiative;
  B) 2...e6 3.♘ge2 a6 transposes to the note to move 3, while 3...♘c6 4.d4 cxd4 5.♘xd4 transposes to the Four Knights (5...♘f6 – Game 7.1) or the Taimanov (5...♕c7 – Game 7.2).
3.g3
3.♘ge2 e6 4.g3 b5 5.♗g2 ♗b7 transposes to the game. The 3.♘ge2 move order allows White to refrain from g2-g3 in case of 3...♘c6: he can switch to the Taimanov by 4.d4. Note that we can't avoid having to learn the Taimanov since Black may choose the move order 2...♘c6 3.♘f3 e6. We only want to play g2-g3 after ...a7-a6 is on the board.
3...b5
3...♘c6 4.♗g2 g6 5.♘ge2 ♗g7 6.d3 d6 7.0-0 ♘f6

analysis diagram

8.♘d5N 0-0 9.c3± (+0.24). The move ...a7-a6 looks rather like a wasted move here.
4.♗g2 ♗b7 5.♘ge2 e6 6.d4 cxd4 7.♘xd4 b4
7...♘f6 8.a3 ♕c7 9.0-0 d6 10.♖e1 ♘bd7 11.a4 b4 12.♘a2 ♘c5 13.c3 b3

14.♘xb3 ♘cxe4 15.♗f4 ♗e7 16.♕d3 ♕b6 17.♕c2 d5 18.a5 ♕d8 19.♖ad1 ♕c8 20.♘ac1 0-0 21.♘d3± (+0.00). Lc0 likes White due to his more active pieces, Komodo considers the center pawns adequate compensation. I prefer White.

8.♘a4 ♘f6 9.c4!

9...d6

A) 9...♗xe4 10.♗xe4 ♘xe4 11.♕f3 f5 12.g4 ♘c6 13.♘xc6 dxc6 14.gxf5 exf5 15.♕xf5 ♘d6 16.♕h5+ g6 17.♕f3 ♕e7+ 18.♗e3 ♕e4 19.♕xe4+ ♘xe4 20.0-0-0 ♗e7 21.♖he1 0-0 22.♗d2 ♘xf2 23.♖xe7 ♘xd1 24.♔xd1 ♖ae8 25.♖xe8 ♖xe8 26.♘c5± (+0.71). Bishop and knight vs rook and pawn with no other pieces on the board is just a slight edge, but the weak black queenside makes White's edge significant;

B) 9...♘xe4 10.0-0 ♗e7 11.♗e3 0-0 12.♘b3 a5 13.♗b6 ♕c8 14.♘xa5 f5 15.♘xb7 ♕xb7 16.♗e3 ♘c6 17.c5± (+0.56). White has a good bishop pair plus and also targets on d7 and e4.

10.0-0 ♘bd7 11.♕e2 e5 12.♘f5 g6 13.♘e3 ♗c6 14.b3
14.♕c2 ♖b8 15.♗d2 ♗e7 16.♘d5 a5 17.♘xe7 ♕xe7 18.f3 0-0

19.♗e3± (+0.14). White has the bishop pair, Black has slightly better development.

14...♗xa4 15.bxa4 ♘c5 16.f4 ♗g7

17.f5?
17.♖b1! 0-0 18.fxe5 dxe5 19.♘d5 ♘xd5 20.cxd5 ♘xa4 21.♖xb4 ♘c3 22.♕b2 ♘b5 23.♗e3± (+0.42). Black lacks compensation for the bishop pair.

17...0-0 18.♘d5 ♘xa4?
18...♘xd5 19.cxd5 ♘xa4∓.

19.♗g5 ♘c3 20.♘xc3 bxc3 21.♖ac1 h6 22.♗e3 ♕a5 23.♕d3 ♘g4 24.♕xc3 ♕xc3 25.♖xc3 ♘xe3 26.♖xe3 ♗f6 27.♖d3 ♖ad8 28.fxg6 fxg6 29.♗h3 ♔g7 30.♗e6 ♖fe8 31.♗d5± ♖b8 32.♖a3 ♖b6 33.h4 h5 34.♔g2 ♖eb8 35.♔h3 ♗f8 36.♖f2 ♖fb8 37.♖ff3 ♖f8 38.♖fb3 ♗d8 39.c5 ♖xb3 40.♗xb3 dxc5 41.♖xa6 ♖f3 42.♖a8 ♗e7 43.♖a7 ♔f8 44.♖a8+ ♔g7 45.♖a7 ♔f8 46.♗d5 g5 47.hxg5 ♗xg5 48.♔g2 ♖c3 49.♖f7+ ♔e8 50.♖f5 ♖c2+ 51.♔h3 ♗e7 52.♖xh5 c4 53.♖xe5 c3 54.♖e6 ♔d7 55.♖c6 ♗d6 56.a4 ♗c7 57.♔g4 ♖c1 58.♖c4 ♔d8 59.♔f5 ♔d7?
59...♗xg3 60.♔e6 ♘c7 61.♗b7±.

60.♗e6+ ♔d8 61.♔f6 ♖f1+ 62.♗f5 ♖f3 63.g4 1-0

Game 7.4 Sicilian Defense –
Scheveningen Variation

Levon Aronian 2763
Vincent Keymer 2516

Karlsruhe/Baden Baden 2019 (6)

1.e4 c5 2.♘c3 a6 3.♘ge2 d6
Black has to play this way if he
intends the Najdorf and wants
to avoid the line 2...d6 3.d4 cxd4
4.♕xd4. The move ...a7-a6 will turn
out to be more useful than 2...d6 if
White insists on playing this way.
4.g3
White is willing to play quietly
here, hoping that ...a7-a6 will prove
to be a wasted move. Normally in
closed Sicilians Black prepares ...b7-
b5 by ...♖b8, not by ...a7-a6.
**4...♘f6 5.♗g2 ♘c6 6.0-0 e6 7.d4
cxd4 8.♘xd4**

8...♗d7
If 8...♕c7 9.♘xc6 bxc6 10.♘a4 the
white sequence attempts to prove
...a7-a6 to be a useless or even
harmful move: 10...♗b7 11.c4 c5
12.♕e2 ♗e7 13.b3 0-0 14.♗b2 ♘d7
15.♖ad1 ♗c6 16.♘c3 ♗f6 17.♘b1±
(+0.10). White has more space and
Black has two weak pawns. Lc0 likes
White more than Komodo does.

9.♖e1
9.♘xc6 ♗xc6 10.♗f4 ♗e7 11.e5
dxe5 12.♗xc6+ bxc6 13.♗xe5 0-0
14.♕xd8 ♖fxd8 15.♖fd1 ♘d5 16.♘a4
(+0.10) is very similar to the game.
9...♗e7 10.♘xc6 ♗xc6 11.e5
11.a4 ♕c7 12.a5 0-0 13.♗e3 ♘d7
14.♘a4 ♖ae8 15.♘b6 f5 16.♘xd7
♕xd7 17.♕d3 fxe4 18.♗xe4 ♗xe4
19.♕xe4± (+0.22). White has fewer
weak pawns.
**11...dxe5 12.♗xc6+ bxc6 13.♖xe5
0-0 14.♕xd8 ♖fxd8 15.♖e2 c5
16.♘a4 ♖d1+ 17.♔g2 ♖ad8 18.b3
♘d5**

19.c3
19.♘b2 ♘c3 20.♖e3 ♗f6 21.♘xd1
♘xd1 22.♖b1 ♘xe3+ 23.♗xe3 ♗e7
24.f4 h6 25.♔f3 (+0.06). White has
the much better pawn structure, but
it's very hard to exploit this here.
**19...♖c8 20.♖e4 ♘f6 21.♖e2 ♘d5
22.♖d2 ♖xd2 23.♗xd2 c4 24.♘b2
♗f6 25.♘xc4 ♗xc3 26.♖d1 ♗xd2
27.♖xd2 g5 28.♔f3 ♔g7 29.♘e3 ♖c3
30.♖c2?!**
30.♔e4 ♘xe3 31.fxe3 (+0.02).White
has the better side of a drawn rook
endgame.
**30...f5 31.♖xc3 ♘xc3 32.a4 g4+
33.♔g2 ♔f6 34.♘c2 ♘e4 35.b4 ♘c3**

**36.b5 axb5 37.a5 ♘d5 38.a6 ♘c7
39.a7 ♔e5 40.♔f1 ♔d5 41.♘b4+
♔c4 42.♘c6 ♔d3 43.♔e1 ♘a8
44.♘d8 e5 45.♘c6 ♔e4 46.♔d2
♔d5 47.♘b4+ ♔c4 48.♘c6 ♔d5
49.♘b4+ ♔e4 50.♘c6 f4 51.♔c3
♔d5 52.♘b4+ ♔e4 ½-½**

Game 7.5 Sicilian Defense – Rossolimo
Pentala Harikrishna   2730
Jan-Krzysztof Duda   2731
Prague 2019 (3)

___

1.e4 c5 2.♘f3 ♘c6 3.♘c3
3.♗b5 ♘f6 4.♘c3 would be our
move-order to reach the game via
the Rossolimo, or we could reach it
via 2.♘c3 ♘c6 3.♘f3.
3...♘f6
  A) 3...g6 4.♗b5 ♘d4 (4...♘f6 is
the note to move 4; 4...♗g7 5.0-0
transposes to the Rossolimo
Sicilian proper) 5.♘xd4 cxd4 6.♘e2
♗g7 7.0-0 ♘f6 8.e5 ♘g4 9.♘xd4
♘xe5 10.♘b3 a6 11.♗e2 d5 12.c3
0-0 13.♖e1 ♖e8 14.d3 ♗d7 15.♗e3
(+0.09). White's development is
smoother, Black's pieces are a bit in
the way of each other;
  B) 3...d6 4.d4 cxd4 5.♘xd4 ♘f6 (so
we have transposed to the Classical
Sicilian) 6.f3 (fortunately it seems
that simply playing the English
Attack works well here, no need
for the complex Richter-Rauzer –
6.♗g5) and now:
  B1) 6...e6 7.♗e3 ♗e7 8.♕d2 0-0
9.0-0-0 a6 (9...d5 10.♗e2!±) 10.g4
♘xd4 11.♗xd4 b5 12.g5 ♘d7 13.h4
b4 14.♘a4 ♕a5 15.b3 ♘c5 16.♘xc5
dxc5 17.♗b2 ♖d8 18.♕f4 ♖xd1+

19.♔xd1 ♕xa2 20.♔c1 ♕a5 21.♕e5
f6 22.♕g3+− (+3.55). White has a
decisive attack;
  B2) 6...e5 7.♘b3 ♗e7 8.♗e3 0-0
9.♕d2 a5 10.♗b5 ♗e6 11.0-0-0 ♘a7

analysis diagram

12.♗xa7 was formerly overlooked
due to the strong belief against
trading off the better of two bishops
for a knight, but it works well here:
12...♖xa7 13.♔b1 ♖a8 14.a4 ♕b6
15.♕d3 ♖fd8 16.♘d5 ♘xd5 17.exd5
♗d7 18.♗xd7 ♖xd7 19.♘d2 ♕b4
20.♖he1 ♖c8 21.♖e4 ♕b6 22.♘c4
♕a6 23.♘a3 ♕xd3 24.♖xd3± (+0.23).
This knight vs bad bishop endgame
clearly favors White.
4.♗b5

4...♕c7
  A) 4...g6 5.0-0 ♗g7 6.e5 ♘g4
7.♗xc6 dxc6 8.♖e1 0-0 9.d3 ♘h6

10.♘e4 b6 11.a4± (+0.30). White has space and the initiative on both wings for the bishop pair;

B) 4...♘d4 5.e5 ♘xb5 6.♘xb5 ♘d5 7.♘g5 f6

analysis diagram

8.♘e4 (8.♕h5+ g6 9.♕f3 fxg5 10.♕xd5 a6 11.♘c3 ♕c7 12.d3 ♗g7 13.♗e3 ♕xe5 14.0-0 ♕f5 15.♖fe1± (+0.20). White will regain his pawn with a sizable lead in development. Black is unlikely to retain his bishop pair edge) 8...f5 9.♘bc3 (9.c4! ♘c7 10.♘xc5 ♘xb5 11.cxb5 d6 12.exd6 exd6 13.♘a4 ♕e7+ 14.♕e2 ♕xe2+ 15.♔xe2 ♗e7 16.d3 ♗f6 17.♗f4 ♗e6 18.♖hc1 ♔d7 19.♗e3 ♖he8 20.♔d2 ± (+0.43). White aims to play b5-b6 strongly) 9...♘xc3 10.♘xc3 d6 11.0-0 dxe5 12.♕e2 e6 and White managed to win this balanced position. It was only a 10 to 7 minute Armageddon game, but one with a lot at stake between the world's top two ranked players: 1-0 (52) Caruana-Carlsen, Stavanger 2019.

5.0-0 ♘d4 6.♖e1 a6 7.♗f1 ♘g4

7...e5 8.♘d5 ♘xd5 9.exd5 ♗d6 10.b3 0-0 11.♗b2 b5 12.c3 ♘xf3+ 13.♕xf3± (+0.45). White has space and better development.

8.e5

This is a gambit, but quite a good one.

8.g3 is the normal, safe move. 8...♘xf3+ 9.♕xf3 ♘e5 10.♕e2 e6 11.b3 d6 12.♗b2 ♗e7 13.♗g2 ♘c6 14.♘d1 ♘d4 15.♕d3 0-0 16.c3± (+0.38). White will have more space and better development once he gets in d2-d4.

8...♘xf3+ 9.♕xf3 ♘xe5 10.♕h5

10...♘g6?!

10...d6 11.f4 ♘c6 12.♘d5 ♕d8 13.b3 e6 14.♗b2 ♘d4 15.c3! ♘c2 16.c4! ♘d4 (in this position the knight would rather trade itself for the powerful bishop than for the out of play rook on a1) 17.♗xd4 cxd4 18.f5 g6 19.fxg6 fxg6 20.♕f3 ♗e7 21.♘xe7 ♕xe7 22.♗d3 ♖f8 23.♕e4 ♖f7 24.♕xd4± (+0.32).

White has healthier pawns, better development, and the safer king.
11.♘d5 ♕d6 12.d4 cxd4 13.♗d2

13...e6??

13...b6 14.♗b4 ♕c6 15.g3N ♗b7
16.♗g2 ♔d8 17.♗e4 e6 18.♘e7 ♕c7
19.♘xg6 fxg6 20.♕h4+ ♔e8 21.♗xf8
♖xf8 22.♕xh7 ♗xe4 23.♖xe4
♕xc2 24.♕xg6+ ♔d8 25.♖f1 ♕xb2
26.♕g5+ ♖f6 27.♖ee1± (+0.65).
White will win back one of his two
pawn deficit and will continue to
have a strong attack on the exposed
king.

14.♗a5+− b6 15.♗xb6 ♘f4 16.♕h4
The mate threat on d8 wins.

**16...♗e7 17.♘xe7 ♕xb6 18.♘xc8
♖xc8 19.♕xf4 ♖xc2 20.b3 0-0
21.♖ed1 ♕a5 22.♕xd4 ♖xa2
23.♖xa2 ♕xa2 24.♕a4 ♕c2
25.♖xd7 g6 26.g3 a5 27.♖a7 ♖b8
28.♖xf7 1-0**

Game 7.6   Sicilian Defense –
            Anti-Sveshnikov

Peter Svidler   2735
Magnus Carlsen   2845

Karlsruhe/Baden Baden 2019 (8)

1.e4 c5 2.♘f3 ♘c6 3.♘c3

Note we can reach this by 2.♘c3
♘c6 3.♘f3 so it's important for
2.♘c3 players.

3...e5
Black can play the Accelerated
Dragon by 3...g6 or the Taimanov
by 3...e6, but the text is necessary
if you only intend the Sveshnikov
against 3.d4. It is perfectly valid to
play 3...g6 if you are willing to play
the Accelerated Dragon provided
White 'promises' (as here) not to
play the Maroczy Bind.
4.♗c4

In my youth, analysis stopped here
since White is 'obviously' better, but
later Black in effect said 'prove it!'.
4...♗e7

4...g6 5.d3 h6 6.h4 (6.a3 d6 7.b4 ♗g7
8.♗e3 b6 9.♘d5 ♘ge7 10.c3 ♗d7
11.d4 cxd4 12.cxd4 exd4 13.♘xd4
0-0 14.♘xc6 ♗xc6 15.♖c1± (+0.13),
Lc0 +0.32. White has a space and
center advantage) 6...d6 7.h5 g5
8.♘h2 ♗g7 9.♘g4 ♘ge7 10.♘e3 0-0
11.♗d2 ♔h8 12.g4 ♖b8 13.a4 ♘d4
14.♘cd5 ♘xd5 15.♘xd5 (15.♗xd5!
♘e6 16.b4 ♘f4 17.0-0 ♗e6 18.bxc5
dxc5 19.♕f3 b6 20.♗c4±) 15...♘e6
16.f3?! ♘f4 17.♕b1 ♗e6 18.♕a2 ♕d7
19.♖g1 b6 20.♗c3 ♗xd5 21.♗xd5 a6

22.♗d2 ♕e7 23.♖f1 b5 24.axb5 axb5 25.♔f2 c4 26.♗xf4 exf4 27.♖ad1 f5

analysis diagram

28.gxf5? (surprisingly White didn't take long to reply to Black's stunning move and faltered) 28...g4 (the white king is totally helpless in this line) 29.d4 ♕h4+ 30.♔e2 ♕h2+ 31.♖f2 gxf3+ 0-1 Nepomniachtchi-Carlsen, Zagreb 2019.

What both players missed after 28.exf5! ♗d4+ 29.♔g2 ♕e2+ 30.♔h1 ♗f2 is the miraculous escape ploy 31.b4! and there is no good way to defend against the perpetual of ♕a1+ and ♕a7+. As a matter of fact they also missed 30.♔h3!.

5.d3 d6

5...♘f6 6.♘d2 (6.♗g5!?) 6...d6 transposes to the game.

6.♘d2 ♘f6 7.♘f1! ♘d7

The ...♗g5 option is Black's justification in playing this line. I suspect that Carlsen would rather play White here, but he is willing to take on slightly worse positions as Black in order to play for the win, and in any case what defense to 1.e4 is not slightly worse for Black?

8.♘d5

8.♘e3 may give a little something, but I prefer the game move: 8...♘b6 9.0-0 0-0 10.♘ed5 ♘xd5 11.♘xd5 ♗g5 12.♗xg5 ♕xg5 13.a4 ♖b8 14.♕c1± (+0.20). The endgame is more pleasant for White.

8...♘b6 9.♘xb6

9.♘fe3 is again not bad but I like the game line: 9...0-0 10.0-0 ♗g5 11.♘xb6 axb6 12.a4 ♗xe3 13.♗xe3 ♕e7 14.b3 ♗e6 15.♕h5 ♖fd8 16.♖ae1± (+0.20). Black can't eliminate the bishop pair without giving himself a weak backward pawn.

9...axb6 10.c3 0-0 11.♘e3 ♗g5 12.0-0

Although White lost this game badly, his position is fine at this stage.

12...♔h8

A) 12...♗xe3 13.♗xe3 ♕e7 14.f4 exf4 15.♗xf4 ♗e6 16.♗b5!± (+0.20). Black has little compensation for the bishop pair;

B) 12...♗e6 13.♗xe6 fxe6 14.♕b3 d5 15.a4 ♘a5 16.♕a2 c4 17.dxc4 d4 18.♘c2 ♗xc1 19.♖axc1 dxc3 20.bxc3 ♕d2 21.♖b1± (+0.15). White will have fewer weak pawns and a better knight after Black recoups his pawn deficit.

13.a3

13.♘d5!N ♗xc1 14.♕xc1 ♘e7 (14...f5 15.exf5 ♗xf5 16.♕e3± (+0.33). White has the better queen, better knight, better pawns) 15.♕d1 ♘xd5 16.♗xd5 ♕c7 17.b4± (+0.15). White has better pawns and can play on both flanks or even in the center.

13...f5 14.♘xf5 ♗xc1 15.♖xc1

15.♕xc1 ♗xf5 16.exf5 d5 17.♗b3 ♖xf5 18.f4 ♕d6 19.fxe5 ♖xf1+ 20.♕xf1 ♘xe5 21.d4 cxd4 22.cxd4 ♖f8 23.♕e2 ♘c6 24.♕e3 g6 25.♖f1 ♖xf1+ 26.♔xf1 (+0.01). White has the sunny side of a likely draw.

15...♗xf5 16.exf5 d5 17.♗a2 ♖xf5 18.♕g4 ♖f6

19.f4?!

19.♖ce1 ♕d6 20.♕d1 ♖af8 21.a4= (-0.05). Black has more activity, White has the static edge.

19...exf4 20.♕g5 ♕f8∓ 21.♕xd5 ♖d8 22.♕f3?! ♘e5 23.♕e4 ♘g4 24.♖ce1 ♘e3 25.♖f2 ♖e8 26.♕xb7?! g5∓ 27.♖fe2? g4

27...f3!–+.

28.♖f2 ♕h6 29.♕c7 ♖ef8 30.h3 gxh3 31.g3 fxg3 32.♖xf6 h2+ 33.♔h1 g2# 0-1

Game 7.7   Sicilian Defense –
               Anti-Najdorf

Fabiano Caruana   2819
Maxime Vachier-Lagrave   2773
Karlsruhe/Baden Baden 2019 (2)

1.e4 c5 2.♘c3 d6

Players aiming for the Najdorf have mostly switched to 2...a6 lately, presumably out of fear of the line shown here, even though it may be a wasted tempo in some closed lines.

3.d4 cxd4 4.♕xd4 ♘c6 5.♕d2

This time-losing move is actually quite strong, is scoring very well at top level, and is favored by the world's top two players. The idea is simply to castle queenside with the bishop on b2 defending the king. It is credited to Greek FM Ioannis Simeonidis, and it was brought to the world's attention when Magnus

Carlsen adopted it in 2018 to defeat GM Wojtaszek. I don't see any clear equalizer for Black.

5...♘f6

5...g6 6.b3 ♗h6 7.f4 ♘f6 (7...f5 8.♗b2 ♘f6 9.♗d3 ♕a5 10.exf5 ♗xf5 11.♘ge2 0-0-0 12.a3 ♖he8 13.0-0-0 d5 14.♗xf5+ gxf5 15.♕e3 e6 16.♔b1 ♘e4 17.♖hg1 ♘xc3+ 18.♕xc3 ♕xc3 19.♗xc3± (+0.18). White's slightly better pawn structure and control of the long diagonal give him the more pleasant endgame) 8.♗b2 e5 9.g3 0-0 10.0-0-0

analysis diagram

A) 10...♘d4 11.♔b1 ♗g4 12.♗e2 ♘xe2 13.♘gxe2 ♖e8 14.♕d3 (14.♕xd6 exf4 15.♕xd8 ♖exd8 16.♖xd8+ ♖xd8 17.♘xf4 ♗f3 18.♖e1 ♖e8 19.♘fd5 ♘xd5 20.♘xd5 ♗g7 21.♗xg7 ♔xg7 22.♘c3 f5 23.e5 ♗c6 24.♔c1 (0.00), Lc0 +0.10. White's extra pawn will probably not survive, but it has some nuisance value so White has the sunny side of the draw) 14...exf4 (14...♗g7 15.h3 ♗xe2 16.♕xe2 exf4 17.gxf4 ♘xe4 18.♘xe4 ♗xb2 19.♔xb2 d5 20.♕b5 ♖xe4 21.♕xb7 ♕f6+ 22.♔b1 ♖ae8 23.♕xa7 ♕c3 24.♕a3 ♖e2 25.♕b2 ♕f3 26.♖hf1 ♕xh3 27.f5

♖c8 28.fxg6 hxg6 29.♕f6 ♕e6 30.♕xe6 fxe6 31.♖c1 (+0.05), Lc0 +0.16. White has two connected passed pawns while Black's are disconnected, but this shouldn't be enough to win here) 15.gxf4 ♖c8 16.♖hf1 ♖xc3 17.♘xc3 ♗xd1 18.♘xd1 ♗g7 19.♘c3 ♕e7 20.♖e1± (+0.34). White has the better pawn structure and the center;

B) 10...♖e8 11.♔b1 ♘d4 12.♕f2 ♗g4 13.♖e1 ♗g7 14.♗d3 ♖c8 15.h3 ♗d7 16.g4 ♕a5 17.fxe5 dxe5 18.♘ge2 ♘xe2 19.♘xe2 b5 20.♖d1 ♗e6 21.♘g3±. Komodo only gives +0.08, but Lc0 gives White a larger edge. White's knight can reroute to e3; Black lacks an equivalent plan.

6.b3 e6

A) 6...e5 7.♗b2 ♗e7 8.0-0-0 0-0 9.♔b1± (+0.28). White has the usual English Attack plan of f2-f3, g2-g4, and in some lines the option of ♘d5 is useful;

B) 6...g6 7.♗b2 ♗g7 8.0-0-0 0-0 9.♔b1 ♕a5 10.f3± (+0.31). As usual the white king is safe and he has the standard g2-g4, h2-h4 attack.

7.♗b2 d5

A) 7...a6 8.0-0-0 b5 9.f3 ♗e7 10.♔b1

analysis diagram

10...♗b7 (10...h5 (in the Carlsen game Black played this a move earlier, but the inclusion of ...♗e7 ♔b1 slightly helps Black) 11.♘h3 ♗b7 12.♘g5± (+0.25). White plans f4 and ♗e2. This is better for White than normal English Attack lines in the Najdorf) 11.g4± (+0.32). White has an attack and a safe king;

B) 7...♗e7 8.0-0-0 0-0 9.f4 a6 10.g4 ♘xg4 11.♘f3 ♘f6 12.♖g1±. White's attack is surely worth more than the pawn.

8.exd5 exd5 9.0-0-0 ♗e6

10.a3

10.♔b1 ♕a5 11.♘b5 ♕xd2 12.♖xd2 ♗b4 13.♖d3 0-0 14.♗xf6 gxf6 15.♘e2 ♖ad8 16.♘bd4 (+0.21). White is for choice, but this is less convincing than the game move.

10...♗c5 11.♘f3 0-0 12.♗d3 ♖c8

13.♖he1

13.♔b1! is safer than the game move: 13...a6 (13...♕e7 14.♔a2± (+0.11). White can attack while his own king is fairly safe) 14.♖he1 ♕a5 15.♘a4 ♕xd2 16.♖xd2 ♗a7 17.♘g5 ♖fe8 18.♘xe6 fxe6 19.♘c3 ♗d4 20.f3 ♔f7 21.♘d1 ♗xb2 22.♔xb2± (+0.10). White has fewer pawn islands and bishop vs knight with pawns on both sides.

13...♖e8

13...♕e7 is probably the best practical try but extremely complicated. White should probably avoid it unless he has prepared very well. I don't claim to know what should really happen: 14.b4 ♘xb4 15.axb4 ♗xb4∞ 16.♕e3 (16.♔b1 ♖c7 17.♕e3 ♖xc3 18.♗xc3 ♗xc3 19.♗xh7+ ♔xh7 20.♘g5+ ♔g8 21.♕xc3 ♕d6 22.♘xe6 fxe6 23.f3± (+0.43). White has the exchange for a pawn. But Black has alternatives before this, so this is a very risky line for both players) 16...♗xc3 17.♗xc3 ♖xc3 18.♗xh7+ ♔xh7 19.♘g5+ ♔g6 20.♕xc3 ♔xg5 21.f4+ ♔h6 22.f5 ♘e4 23.♕h3+ ♔g5 24.♖f1 ♕c5 25.fxe6 fxe6 26.♖xf8 ♕xf8 (+0.09). Queens will probably come off, leaving an endgame where Black has two pawns for the exchange with a draw likely.

14.h3

14.♘b5 ♕e7 15.b4 ♗b6 16.♘h4± (+0.62). White will probably win the d5-pawn.

14...♕a5 15.♘b5 ♕xd2+ 16.♖xd2 a6 17.♘bd4

17.b4 ♗f8 18.♘bd4± (+0.23). White
has a good endgame against the
isolated pawn.

17...♘e4

18.♖de2

18.♗xe4 dxe4 19.♖xe4 ♘xd4
20.♘xd4 ♗d5 21.♖xe8+ ♖xe8 22.f3
♖e1+ 23.♖d1 ♖xd1+ 24.♔xd1 ♗xd4
25.♗xd4 (+0.67), but I don't agree.
Black should draw despite being
a clear pawn down due to the
opposite-colored bishops.

**18...♗d7 19.♔d1 f6 20.♘xc6 ♗xc6
21.♘d4 ♗d7 22.f3**

22.c4± (+0.47). White is winning
the d5-pawn for inadequate
compensation.

**22...♘g3 23.♖xe8+ ♖xe8 24.c4 dxc4
25.♗xc4+ ♔f8 26.b4**

26.♖xe8+ ♔xe8 27.♘e6 ♗xe6
28.♗xe6± (+0.43). White has a clear
bishop pair plus, although the pawn
symmetry gives Black drawing
chances.

**26...♗d6 27.♘e6+ ♗xe6 28.♖xe6
♖d8 29.♔c2 ♘h5**

30.♖e4

30.♗f1 (+0.11). White's bishop pair
is not so effective here, but it's
something.

**30...b5 31.♗d3 ♘f4 32.♗f1 ♖e8
33.♔b3 ♖xe4 34.fxe4 ♘e6 35.a4
♘c7 36.♗d4 ♔e7 37.♗e2 ♔d7
38.♗e3 ♗e5 39.h4 g6 40.h5 gxh5
41.♗xh5 ♘e6 42.♗g4 ♔d6 43.a5
♘d4+ 44.♔a2 ♗c7 45.♗f2 ♘c2
46.♔b3 ♘d4+ 47.♔a2 ♘c2 48.♔b3
♘d4+ 49.♔a2 ½-½**

CHAPTER 8

Sicilian with 2.♞f3

While 1...e5 is the dominant reply to 1.e4 in both elite GM and novice play, the Sicilian remains very popular at pretty much all levels in between. The reason is not hard to understand; after 1.e4 e5 it is obvious that White is at least slightly better due to moving first, whereas after **1.e4 c5** it is at least possible to imagine that Black is equal or even better, since the natural plan for White to play d2-d4 quickly involves losing a center pawn for a bishop's pawn, a small concession, at least when the bishop's pawn is blocked by a knight on c3 and therefore not involved in the fight for the center. White does get better development in return, but at least you can argue about which side is better.

In this chapter I will try to show that White can get some advantage without having to make this concession. He will either play c2-c3 before d2-d4, or will play c2-c4 and d2-d4 to get the Maroczy Bind, where the pawn on c4 is no less valuable than the black pawn on d6, or else will dispense with d2-d4 entirely.

We will play 2.♞f3, in order to see one black move before committing to a plan.

Black has three main replies (2...d6, 2...♞c6, and 2...e6) and two other somewhat reasonable moves (2...g6 and 2...♞f6). Other moves can mostly be met by 3.c3 with better chances for White than in the above lines. We meet **2...g6** by **3.c3** in Game 8.1, c2-c3 being in general especially suitable as a counter to a bishop on g7. In the notes we cover the Nimzowitsch Variation 2...♞f6 3.e5 ♞d5 4.♞c3 e6 and now the rather rare but good 5.♞e4.

Against **2...e6** first I give the rare but rising **3.c4**, aiming for the Maroczy Bind. This was generally thought to be a poor version for White, but that view is changing, and Magnus Carlsen chose it for a critical playoff game in his last title defense. See Game 8.2 and notes.

My main line option is **3.c3**.

White simply plays the Alapin (2.c3) Sicilian, now that Black has forfeited some of his best options against the Alapin that involve an early ...♗g4 (or ...♗f5 or even ...♗e6). I consider the Alapin on move 2 to be just too equal to recommend, but after 2...e6 it seems White has at least a small pull. Game 8.3 features **3...d5 4.exd5 exd5**, which is likely to transpose to the French Tarrasch, so check the relevant games there. In the game Black avoids the transposition by an early ...a7-a6 to prevent ♗b5, in which case posting the bishop on g2 makes sense to target the d5-pawn. In Game 8.4 Black takes back with the queen (**4...♕xd5**), when we play an early ♗e3 to provoke an exchange on d4, resulting in a reasonably pleasant (for White) isolated d4-pawn game where White gets better development to offset the pawn weakness. Game 8.5 has Black playing **3...♘f6** which we meet with an early ♗c4, generally leading to positions with a 'free' space advantage for White.

Against **2...♘c6** we play the Rossolimo **3.♗b5** (personal note: I drew a game with GM Nicolas Rossolimo back in the 1960s in Puerto Rico).

The idea is that we will either take the knight or just castle, aiming for ♖e1 and c2-c3 and d2-d4, depending on circumstances. It may feel a bit strange to be forced to take the knight if Black plays **3...a6**, whereas in the Spanish (Ruy Lopez) most strong players don't take the knight after 3...a6. The theoretical justification is that doubled pawns are weaker when the rear one has advanced. Black usually replies by 3...g6 (the choice in the last World Championship in multiple games) or 3...e6; note that **3...d6**, analyzed in Game 8.6, can also arise via 2...d6 3.♗b5+ ♘c6. Although at one time this was a major line, it now seems that White has multiple paths to a normal edge. The fourth reasonable move is **3...♘f6**, when we play 4.♘c3, transposing to a line covered in the 2.♘c3 chapter, which also seems to offer White something. In Game 8.7 I analyze **3...e6 4.0-0 ♘ge7**, when the game features the rather odd-looking but effective 5.d4 (aiming for an Open Sicilian with c2-c4 still an option since Black cannot provoke ♘c3 by ...♘f6), while the notes cover the standard 5.♖e1, the safe choice for a slight edge, meeting **5...a6** by **6.♗f1**. This rook and bishop maneuver is quite common and good for both colors in many openings. As an alternative, Game 8.8 looks at **3...e6 4.♗xc6 bxc6 5.d3**, meeting **5...♘e7** by the unusual but logical **6.h4** as in the recent game Giri-Carlsen. As usual, even with black Carlsen won, but not from a good opening position.

Now we come to the main line of the Rossolimo, **3...g6**.

First I give the uncommon but rather good **4.0-0 ♗g7 5.♘c3**, which can also arise from 2.♘c3 ♘c6 3.♘f3 g6 4.0-0 ♗g7 5.♗b5, and is thus crucial to the 2.♘c3 chapter. See Game 8.9. After the usual **5...e5**, we play **6.a3** intending to gambit a pawn by 7.b4, but the gambit is really too strong to be accepted. I really don't know why this 5.♘c3 line isn't more popular. If White chooses **5.♖e1** instead of 5.♘c3, the reply **5...♘f6** is much more reasonable than after 5.♘c3. See Game 8.10, where it seems that with perfect defense Black can reach an inferior but drawn endgame. Game 8.11 features the similar gambit to Game 8.9, **5.♖e1 e5 6.b4**, which is more forcing since White hasn't spent a tempo on a2-a3. It may not give any objective advantage against the very best defense, but even in that line the positions are more pleasant to play for White. Game 8.12 opts for **6.♗xc6 dxc6 7.d3**, which may be good for a tiny edge, but it's not clear that the rook is needed on e1 in this line. It's more popular nowadays to capture the knight on move 4 (**4.♗xc6**), waiting to see which way Black recaptures before committing the king.

If Black **recaptures with the b-pawn** (Game 8.13), castle kingside, since with the b-file open castling queenside is not logical. White plans to play ♖e1, c2-c3, h2-h3, and d2-d4, but if Black plays ...f7-f5 White switches to e4-e5 and d2-d3. Although White got no edge in that recent game, the notes show how he could have gotten one on move 14.

If Black chooses the more popular recapture **4...dxc6**, we postpone castling, playing **5.d3 ♗g7 6.h3** (played before ♘c3 since White wants to meet ...♗g4 by ♘bd2) in Game 8.14. This is the main line of the Rossolimo now, with Carlsen repeatedly defending the Black side. As the analysis shows, he generally does not fully equalize, but he aims for the Sveshnikov so he has to meet the Rossolimo, and I suppose he would say if asked, 'What defense does fully equalize?' I recommend spending a lot of time on this game and notes.

Against **2...d6**, perhaps planning the dreaded Najdorf, we give check with **3.♗b5+**, the so-called Moscow Variation.

If it's a blitz game he might not see it and forfeit with an illegal move! Seriously, the motivation is primarily to be able to achieve the Maroczy Bind or force some other concession. If Black blocks by ...♘d7 (directly or after a bishop exchange on d7) that is a concession as long as Black retains his c5-pawn, since knight directly behind pawn (here ♘c6) is ideal shape. In the open Sicilian with the c5-pawn traded for the d4-pawn, the knight is quite often better on d7 than on c6 to avoid blocking the c-file for a rook and to avoid blocking a bishop on b7. Against **3...♗d7** (the main line), 4.♗xd7+ ♕xd7 5.c4 appears to give White a slight pull, but the immediate **4.c4** has caught on lately and looks even better. Either way we normally get a Maroczy Bind, but some details favor the 4.c4 version. Both are covered in Game 8.15.

In recent years **3...♘d7** has become rather popular, especially when Black doesn't want a draw.

The immediate **4.c3** is Game 8.16 (with 4.0-0 in the notes), preparing a nice home for the bishop on c2, which should give at least a slight edge. The more subtle **4.♗a4** in Game 8.17, aiming to play c2-c4 against ...a7-a6 or c2-c3 otherwise, is based on a surprising but totally sound gambit. Most lines are pretty good for White, but Black can limit White to a small space advantage in one line.

Finally, since this 3...♘d7 line is so critical for the whole repertoire, Game 8.18 features a third option, **4.d4 cxd4 5.♕xd4**, aiming either for quick development or for a Maroczy Bind depending on how Black develops. This line looks pretty promising to me, based on the move 9 note with a move 11 novelty.

Game 8.1 Sicilian Defense –
Hyper-Accelerated Dragon

Wang Hao 2730

Roderick Nava 2392

Makati 2018 (4)

1.e4 c5 2.♘f3 g6

2...♘f6 is called the Nimzowitsch
Variation.

analysis diagram

3.e5 ♘d5 4.♘c3 e6 (4...♘xc3 5.dxc3
♘c6 6.♗f4 e6 7.♕d2 ♕c7 8.h4
h6 9.h5 b6 10.0-0-0 ♗b7 11.♖h3±
(+0.45). White has a large space
advantage, plus pressure on d7 and
g7) 5.♘e4 f5 6.♘c3 ♘e7 7.♘b5 ♘g6
8.b3 a6 9.♘d6+ ♗xd6 10.exd6 ♕b6
11.h4 ♕xd6 12.h5 ♘e7 13.♗b2 0-0
14.h6 g6 15.♗d4± (+0.12), but Lc0
+0.55. White has the bishop pair,
development, and a 'thorn pawn' on
h6 for the pawn, more than enough.
Black is left with the 'wrong'
bishop.

3.c3

This is especially appropriate after
2...g6, so that the bishop will bite on
granite.

3...♗g7

3...d5 4.exd5 (4.e5 is also good and
may transpose to the game, but it

does allow Black other options)
4...♕xd5 5.d4 ♗g7 6.♘a3 cxd4 7.♘b5
♘a6 8.♘bxd4 ♘f6 9.♗b5+ ♗d7
10.♗xa6 bxa6 11.0-0 0-0 12.♖e1
♖fe8 13.♘e5 ♖ac8 14.h3 a5 15.c4
(+0.20).

analysis diagram

White will eliminate Black's bishop
pair at a suitable moment and will
remain with the superior pawn
structure.

4.d4 cxd4 5.cxd4 d5 6.e5

6...♘c6

6...♗g4 7.♗b5+ ♘d7 (7...♘c6
8.♗xc6+ bxc6 9.♘bd2 e6 10.h3
♗xf3 11.♘xf3 ♘e7 12.0-0 0-0
13.♕c2 ♕b6 14.b3± (+0.60). White
was 5 out of 5 from here. He has
more space and pressure against
the backward c-pawn, and a great
diagonal for his bishop (a3 to f8))

8.0-0 a6 9.♗e2 e6 10.♘bd2 ♘e7
11.h3 ♗xf3 12.♘xf3 0-0 13.♗d3
♘c6 14.♗e3 ♘b4 15.♗e2 ♖c8 16.a3
♘c6 17.♗d3± (+0.53). White has the
bishop pair and more space with no
offsetting factors.

7.h3 ♘h6 8.♘c3 0-0 9.♗b5 f6 10.0-0

10...♘f7

10...fxe5 11.dxe5 e6 12.♖e1 ♕c7
13.♗xc6 ♕xc6 14.♗g5 ♗d7 15.♖c1
♘f7 16.♗f6 ♖ac8 17.♗xg7 ♔xg7
18.♕d2± (+0.92). White has a 5½ out
of 6 score in my database from here.
He has knight vs bad bishop and a
much safer king.

11.exf6 ♗xf6 12.♖e1 ♕d6

12...♘a5 13.♗f4 a6 14.♗f1± (+0.75).
White has better development and
pressure on the backward e-pawn.

13.♗e3 a6 14.♗f1 b5 15.♕d2 e6

16.g3

16.a4 b4 17.♘a2 ♗b7 18.♖ad1 ♕e7
19.♘c1 ♘d6 20.♗h6 ♖fe8 21.♘b3±
(+1.00). White has two great outpost
squares and pressure on e6.

**16...♕d8 17.♖ac1 ♗d7 18.b3 ♖c8
19.♗g2 ♘d6 20.♗h6 ♖e8**

21.g4?!

21.♘e5 ♘xd4 22.♕xd4 ♘f5 23.♕d2
♘xh6 24.♘xd7 ♕xd7 25.♘e4
♗e7 26.♕xh6 dxe4 27.♖cd1 ♕a7
28.♗xe4± (+0.34). White has better
pawn structure and attacking
chances.
21.h4! ♘f5 22.♗g5 ♘cxd4 23.♘xd4
♘xd4 24.♘xd5 exd5 25.♖xe8+
♗xe8 26.♖xc8 ♕xc8 27.♗xf6
♕c1+ 28.♕xc1 ♘e2+ 29.♔f1
♘xc1 30.♗xd5+ ♗f7 31.♗xf7+
♔xf7 32.♗g5 ♘xa2 33.♗d2 ♔e6
34.♔e2+− (+1.50). Black will
ultimately pay a pawn to save his
knight when the extra kingside
white pawn should win.

21...b4

21...♘f7 22.♗f4 ♗e7=.

**22.♘a4 ♘e4 23.♕d3 a5 24.♗e3?!
♕c7?! 25.♘d2 ♘xd2 26.♕xd2 ♕d8
27.♖c2 ♘a7 28.♖xc8 ♕xc8 29.♘c5
♘b5 30.♗f1 ♘c3 31.♗f4 ♗b5
32.♗g2? ♗c6? 33.♗e5± ♗e7 34.a4
♗f8?! 35.♕f4+− ♗e7 36.♗d6 ♗d8**

37.♕e5 ♗d7 38.♖e3 ♕c6 39.♔h1
♗f6 40.♕xf6 ♕xd6 41.♖f3 ♕e7
42.♕e5 ♘e4 43.♘xe4 dxe4 44.♖e3
♖f8 45.♔g1 ♕f6 46.♕xf6 ♖xf6
47.♖xe4 ♔f8 48.♖e5 ♖f4 49.♗e4 1-0

Game 8.2 Sicilian Defense – Taimanov
Sergey Karjakin   2782
Maxime Vachier-Lagrave   2789
Paris rapid 2018 (1)

1.c4
1.e4 c5 2.♘f3 e6 3.c4 ♘c6 4.d4 cxd4
5.♘xd4 ♘f6 6.♘c3 would be our
move-order to reach the game.
1...c5 2.♘f3 ♘c6 3.d4 cxd4 4.♘xd4
♘f6 5.♘c3 e6 6.e4

6...♗b4
6...♗c5 7.♘c2 (7.♘b3 is much more
common but not necessarily better
than Carlsen's choice. Either way
White has his Maroczy Bind:
7...♗b4 8.♗d3 0-0 9.0-0 d6 10.♘a4
b6 11.a3 ♗c5 12.♘c3± (+0.24). The
bishop on c5 is uncomfortable.
White can take it whenever he
chooses to win the bishop pair,
or try for more) 7...0-0 8.♗e3 b6
9.♗e2 (9.♕d2 ♕e7 10.0-0-0 ♗b7
11.♗g5 h6 12.♗h4± (+0.44) was the
way to go all-out for the win, but

in the actual game, in the rapid
playoff of the Classical World
Championship, Carlsen needed
only a draw so of course he just
castled kingside) 9...♗b7 10.0-0
♕e7 11.♕d2 ♖fd8

analysis diagram

12.♖fd1 (12.♖ad1 d6 13.a3 a5
14.f3± (+0.22). Since White cannot
advance on the queenside, he
should probably place his rooks
on d1 and e1 for possible kingside
action) 12...♘e5 (12...d6=) 13.♗xc5
bxc5 14.f4 ♘g6 15.♕e3 d6 16.♖d2
a6 17.♖ad1 ♕c7 18.b3 h6 19.g3 ♖d7
20.♗f3 ♖e8 21.♕f2 ♘e7 22.h3 ♖ed8
23.♔g2 ♘c6 24.g4 ♕a5 25.♘a4 ♕c7
26.e5 (26.♘c3±) 26...dxe5 27.♘xc5
♖xd2 28.♖xd2 ♖xd2 29.♕xd2 ♗a8
30.fxe5 ♕xe5 31.♘d7 ♕b2 32.♕d6
♘xd7 33.♕xd7 ♕xc2 34.♕e8+
♔h7 35.♕xa8 ♕d1+ 36.♔h2 ♕d6+
37.♔h1 ♘d4 38.♕e4+ f5 39.gxf5 exf5
(39...♘xf5=) 40.♕e3 ♘e6 41.b4 ♘g5
42.c5 ♕f6 43.c6 ♘e6 44.a4 ♘c7
45.♕f4 ♘e6 46.♕d6 ♕a1+ 47.♔h2
♘d4 48.c7 ♕c3 49.♕c5 ♕e3 50.c8♕
f4 51.♕g4 1-0 Carlsen-Caruana,
London 2018.
7.♘xc6 bxc6 8.♗d3 e5 9.0-0 0-0
10.♕e2

This move, rare until 2018, has been played more than once each by the World Champion and his 2016 challenger. White keeps his options open.

10...d6

A) 10...♖e8 11.♘a4 d5 12.a3 ♗d6 (12...♗f8 13.♗g5 h6 14.♗xf6 ♕xf6 15.cxd5 cxd5 16.exd5 e4 17.♘c3 ♗f5 18.♗b5 ♖e5 19.♖ae1± (+0.32). Black has the bishop pair for the pawn, but not much else. White has the option to play f2-f4) 13.♗g5 h6 (13...d4 14.c5 ♗c7 15.b4±: Although Komodo rates it even, I share Lc0s preference for White. He has all the active plans) 14.♗xf6 ♕xf6 15.cxd5 cxd5.

analysis diagram

So far Carlsen-Gelfand, St Petersburg Wch blitz 2018. 16.♗b5±

(+0.50). White will win the pawn by ♗c6xd5, after which the powerful outpost bishop minimizes the value of Black's bishop pair, his only compensation for the pawn;

B) 10...♗xc3 11.bxc3 d6 12.c5 dxc5

analysis diagram

13.♗c4 (White avoided this obvious move in Carlsen-Anand, St Petersburg Wch rapid 2018, presumably to avoid the exchange of his paired bishop by a later ...♗e6, but since Black can only achieve this exchange reasonably by returning the extra (doubled isolated) pawn, White is asking too much of the position to refrain from ♗c4) 13...♕e7 14.♗a3 ♗e6 15.♗xe6 ♕xe6 16.♗xc5± (+0.30). The bishop is a bit better than the knight is this fairly open position, but I would say that White's edge is rather small.

11.♘a4 d5

11...c5 is the most frequent move but probably not a good one: 12.♖d1 h6 13.♗c2 ♕e7 14.♕d3 ♖d8 15.a3 ♗a5 16.♖b1± (+0.30). White has pressure on the weak d6-pawn and expansion with b2-b4 or rerouting the knight to c3.

12.a3 &d6 13.&g5 h6

13...d4 14.c5 &c7 15.b4. Here Lc0 really likes White, Komodo calls it even. I think White has a small plus; normal engines tend to over-value a blocked passed pawn in the middlegame.

14.&xf6

14.&h4 罝b8 15.cxd5 cxd5 16.exd5 e4 17.&c4± (+0.20). Black has some but not full compensation for the pawn.

14...豐xf6 15.cxd5 cxd5 16.exd5

16...豐f4

16...豐h4 17.&c2 &g4 18.f3 &d7 19.©c3 f5 20.g3 (+0.47). Lc0 thinks Black has enough compensation for the pawn, Komodo disagrees. Probably the truth is in between, meaning Black has nearly enough.

17.&b5 &g4 18.豐e3 豐xe3 19.fxe3 罝ab8 20.©c3 罝fc8 21.a4 &c5 22.罝ae1 &h5 23.h3 &g6 24.g4 罝d8 25.罝f2

25.罝e2± (+0.24). Better to reserve f2 for the king here.

25...罝d6 26.當g2 a6 27.&c6

27.&c4=.

27...罝b4 28.a5 h5 29.當g3 罝d8 30.©a4 &e7 31.罝c1 hxg4 32.hxg4 f5 33.罝xf5 &xf5 34.gxf5 當f7 35.©b6

罝xb2 36.©c4 罝b4 37.©xe5+ 當f6 38.©d3 罝b3 39.罝d1 &d6+ 40.當g4 罝g8 41.e4 g6 42.fxg6 罝xg6+ 43.當f3 罝a3 44.當e3 &e5 45.罝f1+ 當e7 46.罝f3 &g7 47.罝h3 當d6 48.當f4 罝f6+ 49.當e3 罝f7 50.罝g3 &e5 51.罝g6+ 罝f6 52.罝xf6+ &xf6 53.&b7 &g5+ 54.當e2 當c7 55.&xa6 罝a5 56.&c4 罝a4 57.©c5 罝xc4 58.©e6+ 當d6 59.©xg5 罝xe4+ 60.©xe4+ 當xd5 ½-½

Game 8.3 Sicilian Defense – Alapin
Eduardas Rozentalis 2508
Jiri Stocek 2581
Germany Bundesliga 2017/18 (2)

1.e4 c5 2.©f3 e6 3.c3 d5 4.exd5 exd5 5.d4 a6

5...©c6 6.&b5 is now almost the same as the French Tarrasch variation, except c2-c3 has been played rather than ©bd2. Transposition is likely: 6...&d6 7.dxc5 &xc5 8.0-0 ©ge7 9.©bd2 0-0 10.©b3 &d6 (10...&b6 11.罝e1 ©f5 avoids the exchange of the dark-squared bishops by &e3, which would favor White, e.g. 12.&d3 h6 13.&c2 &e6 14.豐d3 豐f6 15.&e3 &xe3 16.罝xe3 罝ad8 17.罝ee1 g6 18.©c5 &c8 19.&a4± (+0.30). White has both the better development and the better pawn structure) 11.&d3! h6 (not 11...&g4? 12.&xh7+!) 12.h3 ©f5 13.罝e1 (this is a transposition to a variation from the French Tarrasch. Black lacks compensation for the isolated pawn because he can't get a knight

to the e4 outpost) 13...♛f6 14.♗c2
♖d8 15.♕d3 g6 16.♗d2 a5 17.a4 b6
18.♕e2 ♗a6 19.♕d1 ♖e8 20.♗xf5
gxf5 21.♘bd4 ♘xd4 22.♖xe8+ ♖xe8
23.♘xd4± (+0.40). Black's bishop
pair can't offset four isolated
pawns.

6.g3

I played the usual 6.♗d3 against
Russian GM Igor Glek long ago and
lost. I concluded afterwards that
the rare 6.g3, targeting the weak
d5-pawn, is probably best, and this
game supports this conclusion.
6...♘c6 7.♗g2 ♗g4
7...♘f6 8.0-0 ♗e7 9.dxc5 ♗xc5
10.♖e1+ ♗e6 11.♘bd2 0-0 12.♘b3
♗b6 13.♘bd4± (+0.32). White can
win the bishop pair at a time of his
choosing.
8.0-0 cxd4

9.♕b3

  A) 9.h3± (+0.32). White wins the
bishop pair;
  B) 9.♖e1+ ♗e7 10.♕b3± (+0.41).
This looks like the best of several
good options.
**9...♗c5 10.♘xd4 ♘ge7 11.♗e3
♗xd4 12.cxd4 0-0 13.♘c3±** (+0.31)
White has the bishop pair for free.
13...♘a5 14.♕c2
14.♕b4± (+0.34). White has a clean
bishop pair plus.
**14...♖c8 15.♖fe1 h6 16.b3 b5?!
17.♕d2 ♘ac6 18.♖ac1 ♕d7 19.♘e2
♗h3 20.♗h1 ♗f5 21.♘f4 ♗e4 22.f3
♗h7 23.♗g2 ♘f5 24.♗f2 ♖fe8
25.♖xe8+**
25.♗h3± (+0.80). The pin plus the
bishops should be close to winning.
25...♖xe8 26.♘d3
26.h4± (+0.93). White can combine
pressure on the c-file with the pin
♗h3.
**26...♕d6 27.♘c5 ♕f6 28.♖d1 h5
29.♕f4?**
29.f4 ♕d6 30.♗f3± (+0.87). With
the powerful outposted knight
and the bishops, White is close to
winning.
29...♖c8?
29...♖e2=.
**30.h4 ♘b4?! 31.g4 ♕h6 32.♕d2
♕xd2 33.♖xd2 ♘e7 34.gxh5±
a5? 35.♗f1 ♖b8? 36.♗g3 ♖a8
37.♗xb5+−**
With an extra pawn (plus the
useless one on the kingside) and the
bishop pair, White is winning.
**37...♘f5 38.♗f2 ♘d6 39.♗a4 ♗b1
40.a3 ♘c2 41.♗c6 ♖a7 42.♗xd5**

♞xa3 43.♗e4 a4 44.bxa4 f5
45.♗d5+ ♚h7 46.♖b2 1-0

Game 8.4 Sicilian Defense – Alapin
Husein Nezad 2425
Evgeny Romanov 2636
Biel 2018 (4)

**1.e4 c5 2.♞f3 e6 3.c3 d5 4.exd5
♕xd5 5.d4 ♞f6**

6.♗e3

6.♞a3 ♞c6 7.♗e2 cxd4 8.♞b5 ♕d8
9.♞bxd4 ♞xd4 10.♕xd4 ♕xd4
11.♞xd4 ♗c5 12.♞b3 ♗b6 13.♗f3
e5 14.0-0 0-0 15.♖e1 e4 16.♗d1 ♖e8
17.♗e3 ♗xe3 18.♖xe3 b6 19.♞d4
(+0.05). White is slightly for choice
in a drawish endgame due to his
better bishop.
6...cxd4

6...♗e7 7.c4 ♕d8 8.♞c3 0-0 9.♗e2
♞g4 10.♗c1 cxd4 11.♕xd4 ♞f6
12.0-0 ♞c6 13.♕e3 ♕c7 14.♖d1±
(+0.16). White's queenside pawn
majority is a little more useful than
Black's kingside majority.
**7.cxd4 ♗e7 8.♞c3 ♕d6 9.♗d3 0-0
10.0-0 ♞c6 11.a3 ♖d8**

11...b6 12.♕e2 ♗b7 13.♖ad1 ♖fd8
14.♖fe1 transposes to the game.

12.♕e2 b6 13.♖ad1 ♗b7 14.♖fe1

14...♞d5?!

14...♖ac8 15.♗b1 ♞d5 16.h4N. White
plans to play ♗g5 or to provoke
...g7-g6 and then play h4-h5.
16...♞xc3 17.bxc3 ♞a5 18.♞e5 ♕d5
19.♗xh7+ ♚xh7 20.♕h5+ ♚g8
21.♕xf7+ ♚h7 22.f3 ♕c7 23.h5 ♖f8
24.♕g6+ ♚g8 25.h6 ♗f6 26.♗f4 ♖e7
27.♕g3 ♗xe5 28.♗xe5 ♖ff7 29.♗xg7
♖xg7 30.♕b8+ ♚h7 31.hxg7 ♖xg7
32.♖e4± (+0.25). White is half a
pawn up and can expect to get the
queens off soon.
15.♞g5 ♗xg5

15...h6 16.♗h7+ ♚f8 17.♞ge4 ♞xc3
18.bxc3 ♕d5 19.c4 ♕a5 20.♞g3 ♗f6
21.♗e4± (+1.30). White's threats of
♞h5 and perhaps ♕g4 or d4-d5 are
hard to meet.
16.♗xg5 ♖e8 17.♕h5 g6

18.♘e4

18.♕h4! ♕f8 19.♘xd5 exd5 20.b4+− (+1.95). With Black's weakness on the dark squares and White's bishop pair and ideal development, White should win.

18...♕f8 19.♕h4 f5 20.♘f6+ ♘xf6 21.♗xf6 ♘b8

21...♖ac8 22.h3 ♕f7 23.♖c1 ♘b8 24.♗c4+− (+1.66). White's pressure on e6 and on the dark squares should win.

22.d5 ♗xd5 23.♗c3 ♘c6 24.♗b5 ♖ec8

25.♗xc6

25.♖xd5! exd5 26.♖e6 ♕c5 27.♗xc6 ♖xc6 28.♖e7 h5 29.♖g7+ ♔f8 30.♕g5 ♖ac8 31.g3+− (+7.46). White has a winning attack.

25...♖xc6 26.♕d4 ♖xc3 27.♕xc3 ♖c8 28.♕e5 ♕c5 29.h3+− (+1.76) White has the exchange for a pawn with a good position, which should be decisive with the rooks being active.

29...a5 30.♕f4 ♕b5 31.♖c1 ♖c5 32.b4 axb4 33.axb4 ♖c4 34.♖xc4 ♕xc4 35.♕b8+ ♔g7 36.♕a7+ ♔h6 37.♕xb6 g5 38.♕c5 ♕b3 39.h4 gxh4 40.♕e3+ ♕xe3 41.♖xe3
And Black resigned.

Game 8.5 Sicilian Defense – Alapin
Gawain Jones   2640
Peter Svidler   2768
Wijk aan Zee 2018 (7)

1.e4 c5 2.c3

2.♘f3 e6 3.c3 ♘f6 4.e5 ♘d5 would be our move-order to reach the game. I think that this game is Black's best bet against the Alapin given that he has already played ...e7-e6.

2...♘f6 3.e5 ♘d5 4.♘f3 e6 5.♗c4 d6 6.d4 cxd4 7.cxd4

7...♘c6

7...♗e7 8.0-0 0-0 9.♖e1 (White should defer the capture on d6 until Black has played ...♘c6 as otherwise ...b7-b6 and ...♗b7 solves Black's problems) 9...dxe5 (9...♘c6 10.exd6 ♕xd6 11.♘c3 ♖d8 transposes to the game) 10.dxe5 a6 11.a3 b5 12.♗xd5± (+0.22). White's edge is the isolated d-pawn. Black probably won't be able to retain both his bishop pair and his weak pawn.

8.0-0 ♗e7 9.exd6

9.♕e2 is the usual move but is not very convincing (9.a3 and 9.♗d2 are also serious options but Black can reach rough equality with accurate play): 9...0-0 10.♘c3 ♘xc3 11.bxc3 dxe5 12.dxe5 b6 13.♗d3 ♕c7 14.♗g5 ♗b7 15.♕e4 g6 16.♕h4 ♗xg5 17.♘xg5 h5 18.♖ae1 (+0.02). White has some attacking prospects, but the weak c3-pawn is an equalizer.

9...♕xd6 10.♘c3 0-0 11.♖e1 ♖d8 12.a3 a6

13.♗e3

13.♗a2 ♘f6 14.♗e3 b5 15.♕e2 ♗b7 16.♖ad1 b4 17.d5 (17.♘a4 ♕c7 18.♘c5 bxa3 19.bxa3 ♗xc5 20.dxc5=) 17...bxc3 18.dxe6 ♕c7 19.exf7+ ♔h8 20.♖xd8+ ♖xd8 21.bxc3 ♗xa3 22.♘g5 (22.♗g5!? ♗f8 23.h4∞) 22...♗c8 23.♕c4 ♗f8 24.♗b1 h6 25.♘f3 ♗g4 26.♘h4 ♗h5 27.♗g6 ♗xg6 28.♘xg6+ ♔h7 29.♘f4 ♕d7 30.♘e6 ♘e5 31.♕d4 ♕xe6 32.♕xd8 ♕xf7 33.h3.

analysis diagram

Although two knights are in general somewhat stronger than rook and pawn, White has more active pieces and a safer king. Komodo rates it even, while I am inclined to agree with Lc0 in having a slight preference for White.

13...♘xe3 14.fxe3 b6

15.♖c1

15.♖f1! ♗b7 16.♗a2 h6 17.♕e2 b5 18.♘e4 ♕d7 19.♖ac1± (+0.42). White can aim for ♗b1 and ♕d3, or double rooks on either the c- or the f-file, or play a timely ♘c5, or even possibly g2-g4-g5.

15...♗b7 16.♗a2 ♖ac8 17.♘e4

17.♖f1± (+0.25). White plans ♕d3 and ♗b1.

White's superior center and the semi-open f-file more than offset the bishop pair.

17...♕d7 18.♘fg5 ♗xg5 19.♘xg5 h6 20.♘f3 ♕d6 21.♖f1 ♖c7 22.♕e2 ♖dc8 23.♖cd1 ♘a5 24.♗b1 ♘c4 25.♗d3 b5 26.♖f2 f5 27.e4 fxe4 28.♗xe4 ♗xe4 29.♕xe4 ♕d5 30.♖e1 ♕xe4 31.♖xe4 ♖c6 32.♖fe2 a5 33.♘e5 ♖d6 34.♘xc4

Draw agreed.

Game 8.6 Sicilian Defense – Rossolimo

Michael Adams   2709

Alan Pichot   2552

Gibraltar 2018 (4)

1.e4 c5 2.♘f3 ♘c6 3.♗b5 d6

This was once a main line, arising
out of both 2...♘c6 3.♗b5 and 2...d6
3.♗b5+ ♘c6. But it seems that Black
has to surrender the bishop pair
for minimal compensation to avoid
an unpleasant position. White has
three promising lines on move 7.

4.0-0 ♗d7 5.♖e1

5.c3 ♘f6 6.♖e1 was the move order
in Giri-Mamedyarov, Zagreb 2019,
by transposition from 1.♘f3 c5.

5...♘f6

5...a6 6.♗xc6 ♗xc6 7.d4 cxd4
8.♘xd4 ♖c8 9.c4 ♘f6 10.♘c3 e6
11.♗f4N ♗e7 12.♘d5! 0-0 13.♘xc6
♖xc6 14.♘xe7+ ♕xe7 15.b3 b5
16.cxb5 axb5 17.♕d3 ♕b7 18.♗xd6
♖d8 19.e5 ♘e8 20.♖ed1 b4 21.h3±.
Komodo says equal, but Lc0 gives
+0.28. Black can only regain his
pawn at the cost of two rooks for
a queen. With no other pieces
remaining, this favors White,
although Black may hold.

6.c3 a6

7.♗f1

A) 7.♗c4!? ♗g4 (7...b5 8.♗f1
♗g4 9.a4 b4 10.d4 cxd4 11.cxd4 e5
12.dxe5 ♘xe5 13.♘bd2± (+1.09).
White has better development and
a better pawn structure, and will
probably win the bishop as well)
8.d4 cxd4 9.cxd4 ♗xf3 10.gxf3 ♖c8
11.♗e3 g6 12.♗f1 ♗g7 13.♗h3 0-0
14.♗xc8 ♕xc8 15.♔h1± (+0.63).
Black's superior pawn structure
offers only partial compensation
for the exchange. Black could have
avoided the exchange sacrifice, but
then White's bishop pair would
have been active and strong;

B) 7.♗a4 b5 8.♗c2 e5 (8...♗g4 9.h3
♗xf3 10.♕xf3 g6 11.d3 ♗g7 12.♗e3
0-0 13.a3 ♖c8 14.♕d1 ♕c7 15.♘d2
♖fd8 16.♖c1± (+0.27). White is
gradually consolidating his bishop
pair edge) 9.h3 ♗e7 10.d4 0-0 11.d5
♘a5 12.b3 ♕c7 13.♗e3± (+0.43) is
very similar to some lines of the
Spanish where White enjoys a large
spatial edge for free.

7...♗g4

8.h3

8.d4 is also favorable for White,
scoring even better than 8.h3, e.g.
8...cxd4 9.cxd4 d5 10.exd5 ♘xd5

11.♘c3 e6 12.h3 ♗h5 (12...♗xf3
13.♕xf3 ♗e7 14.♘xd5 ♕xd5
15.♕xd5 exd5 16.♗e3 0-0 17.g3±
(+0.38). White is up the bishop pair
for free) 13.g4 ♗g6 14.♘xd5 ♕xd5
15.♗g2 0-0-0? (15...♗b4 16.♘e5
♕b5 17.a4 ♕b6 18.a5 ♘xa5 19.♕a4+
♕b5 20.♕xb5+ axb5 21.♘xg6 hxg6
22.♖e5 0-0 23.♖xb5 ♘c6 24.♖b1
♗d6 25.♗e3 ♘b4 26.♗d2 ♘c6
27.d5 ♘d4 28.♖xb7 e5 29.♔h1±
(+0.77). Black's outposted knight
offsets the bishop pair, but White
is a pawn ahead) 16.♘e5!+− ♕xd4
17.♕f3 ♖d5 18.♗xf7 ♖g8 19.♘g5 ♗d6
20.♘xe6 ♕b4 21.♗e3 ♖e5 22.a3
♕xb2 23.♖ac1 ♖xe6 24.♖xc6+ ♔d7
25.♖xa6 ♖b8 26.♖a7 ♗e4 27.♕f7+
♖e7 28.♕c4 ♖c8 29.♕a4+ ♗c6
30.♗xc6+ ♖xc6 31.♖c1 1-0 Giri-
Mamedyarov, Zagreb 2019.

8...♗xf3 9.♕xf3

9...e6

9...g6 10.d3 ♗g7 11.♗e3 0-0 12.♘d2
♘d7 13.♕d1 b5 14.♘f3 ♘de5 15.♘xe5
(15.♘h2 ♕c7 16.♖c1 ♖ac8 17.h4N
h5 18.♖c2 e6 19.f4 ♘d7 20.g4 hxg4
21.♘xg4± (+0.45). White has the
bishops and attacking prospects)
15...♘xe5 16.a4 ♕c7 17.♕b3 c4
18.♕a2 ♕b7 19.d4 ♘d3 20.♗xd3

cxd3 21.♕d5 ♕xd5 22.exd5 ♖fc8
23.♗d2 ♗f6 24.axb5 axb5 25.g3±
(+0.95).

analysis diagram

White can expect to win the
d3-pawn.

10.d3 ♗e7 11.♘d2 0-0 12.♕e2 b5

12...d5 13.♘f3 b5 14.g3± (+0.26).
White has the bishops and some
hope for attack.

13.a3

13.♘f3 ♕b6 14.♗e3 ♖ac8 15.a3±
(+0.20). White has the bishop pair
and plans b2-b4 and/or g2-g3, ♗g2.

13...d5 14.g3 ♕b6 15.♗g2 ♖fd8

15...♖fe8 16.♔h2 ♕c7 17.e5 ♘d7
18.f4± (+0.16). White can develop a
kingside attack with the bishop pair
as a long-term plus.

16.e5

16.exd5 ♘xd5 (16...exd5 17.♘f1±
(+0.40). The position has opened
up for the bishop pair) 17.♘f1 ♖ac8
18.♘e3 ♘f6 19.a4± (+0.20). Black has
little compensation for the bishops.

16...♘d7 17.f4 a5 18.♘f3 d4?
19.cxd4 cxd4 20.f5 ♘c5 21.f6 gxf6
22.exf6 ♗xf6 23.♗g5

23.♘g5! h6 24.♕g4+−.

23...♗g7 24.♗xd8 ♖xd8 25.♘g5 h6
26.♘e4

26.♘xf7! ♔xf7 27.♗xc6 ♕xc6
28.♖ac1 ♕d6 29.♖xc5+–.
**26...♘b3 27.♖ad1± ♘e7 28.♖f1 ♘d5
29.♕h5 ♕c7 30.g4 ♘e3 31.g5 ♖d5
32.h4 ♖f5 33.♖xf5 exf5 34.gxh6 fxe4
35.hxg7 ♔xg7 36.♕g5+ ♔f8 37.♖e1
exd3 38.♕h6+ ♔g8 39.♕g5+ ½-½**

Game 8.7 Sicilian Defense – Rossolimo
Lucas van Foreest   2502
Anton Korobov   2699
Wijk aan Zee 2019 (13)

**1.e4 c5 2.♘f3 ♘c6 3.♗b5 e6 4.0-0
♘ge7**

5.d4
This looks like just a weird open
Sicilian, but White plans to get in
c2-c4 before ♘c3, so it is justified.
5.♖e1 is the standard route to a
small plus.

analysis diagram

A) 5...♘d4 6.♘xd4 cxd4 7.c3 a6
8.♗f1 ♘c6 9.b4 ♗e7 10.a4 0-0
11.♘a3 dxc3 12.dxc3 ♗f6 13.♕b3
d5 14.♗e3 d4 15.♖ad1 e5 16.♘c2
♗g4 17.♖d2 ♕e7 18.cxd4 exd4
19.♗f4 (19.♘xd4N ♕xe4 20.♘xc6
♕xc6 21.♗c4 b5 22.♗d5 ♕c3
23.♕b1± (+0.18). White has better
placed pieces) 19...♗e6 20.♕g3
♖fd8 21.♖ed1 h5 22.h3± (+0.19).
White has a useful kingside pawn
majority;

B) 5...♘g6 6.c3 a6 (6...d5 7.exd5
(7.♕a4 ♗e7 8.d4 0-0 9.exd5
♕xd5 10.dxc5 ♗xc5 11.♘bd2 ♗e7
12.♘c4± (+0.37). White has superior
development and may threaten
♘b6 soon; 7.h4N dxe4 8.♖xe4 h5
9.d4± (+0.46). The inclusion of
the h-pawn moves gives White
g5 for his bishop) 7...♕xd5 8.d4
cxd4 9.♘xd4 ♗d7 10.♗d3 ♘xd4
11.♗e4± (+0.12). White has better
development) 7.♗f1 ♗e7 8.d4 cxd4
9.cxd4 d5 10.♘c3 0-0 11.♗d3N ♘b4
12.♗b1 dxe4 13.♗xe4± (+0.25).
Black has some problems with his
development;

C) 5...a6 6.♗f1 d5 7.exd5 (7.d3
d4 8.e5 (+0.02), Lc0 +0.12) is an
interesting new idea with some
chances for an edge) 7...♘xd5 8.d4
♘f6 9.♗e3 cxd4 (9...♗e7 10.c4 0-0
11.♘c3 cxd4 12.♘xd4 transposes)
10.♘xd4 ♗d7 11.c4 ♗e7 12.♘c3 ♕c7
13.h3 0-0 14.♘f3 ♖ac8 15.a3 ♘a5
16.♘d2 ♖fd8 17.b4 ♘c6 18.♘f3±
(+0.40). White has a significant
space advantage and the more
effective pawn majority.
5...cxd4 6.♘xd4

6...♕b6

A) 6...♘g6 7.♗e3 ♗e7 8.♗e2 0-0
9.c4 ♘xd4 10.♕xd4 b6 11.♘c3
♗b7 12.♖ad1 ♗c6 13.♕d2 ♘f6
14.♗d4± (+0.28). White has the
usual Maroczy plus;

B) 6...♘xd4 7.♕xd4 a6 8.♗e2 ♘c6
9.♕c3 b5 10.♗f4 ♗b7 11.♘d2 ♖c8
12.a4 ♘b4 13.♕g3 ♘xc2 14.axb5
♘d4 15.♗d3 ♘xb5 16.♖fd1± (+0.66).
White's huge lead in development
is obviously worth more than one
backward pawn;

C) 6...a6 7.♗e2 d5 8.♘xc6 bxc6
9.♗f3 (9.exd5 cxd5 10.c4 ♗b7 11.♖e1
♕c7 12.♘a3 ♖d8 13.♗g5± (+0.37).
Black has serious development
problems) 9...♕c7 10.♖e1 ♗b7
11.c4 ♖d8 12.♘d2± (+0.25). Black
will have to suffer some damage
to his pawn structure to get
castled, and will still have inferior
development.

7.♘xc6 bxc6

A) 7...dxc6 8.♗d3 ♘g6 9.♕h5 e5
10.♘d2 ♗e7 11.♗c4± (+0.25). White
has attacking chances at no cost;

B) 7...♘xc6 8.♗e2 ♗e7 9.c4 0-0
10.♘c3± (+0.43). Another good
Maroczy Bind for White.

8.♗e2 ♘g6 9.c4 ♗e7

10.♘c3

10.♗e3 c5 11.♕c2 ♖b8 12.b3 0-0
13.♘c3 ♗b7 14.♖ad1 d6 15.f4±
(+0.16). White has a useful spatial
plus.

10...c5 11.♗e3?!

This was an unnecessary pawn
sacrifice.

A) 11.f4!N 0-0 12.b3 d6 13.♗b2±
(+0.20). White has a decent space
advantage;

B) 11.♖b1! ♗b7 12.♗e3± (+0.20).
White will attack with f2-f4.

11...♕xb2 12.♘b5

12.♕e1 ♗f6 13.♖c1 ♗b7 14.♗d3 ♘e5
15.♗e2 ♘g6=.

12...0-0 13.f4 a6 14.♖b1 ♕xa2
15.♖a1 ♕b2 16.♖b1 ♕a2 17.♖a1
♕b2 18.♖b1 ½-½

Game 8.8 Sicilian Defense – Rossolimo
David Anton Guijarro   2651
Luka Lenic   2650
Heraklio Ech-tt 2017 (6)

1.♘f3 c5 2.e4

We would of course transpose the
first two moves, but note that this
shows that the Sicilian portion of
this White book is useful for 1.♘f3
players as well as 1.e4 players.

2...♘c6 3.♗b5 e6 4.♗xc6 bxc6 5.d3 ♘e7

5...♕c7 6.0-0 d6 7.♘fd2 ♘e7 8.f4 ♖b8 9.♘c3 ♘g6 10.f5 ♘e5 11.♘c4 ♘xc4 12.dxc4 ♗e7 13.♕d3 ♗f6 14.fxe6 ♗d4+ 15.♗e3 ♗xe3+ 16.♕xe3 ♗xe6 17.b3± (+0.40). White has more space, a more active queen, and a target on d6.

6.h4

This is effective against either ...g7-g6 or ...♘g6.

6...d6

If 6...h5, 7.e5 is justified by the inclusion of the h-pawn pushes, as now ♗g5 can't be met by ..h7-h6 or ...f7-f6.

analysis diagram

7...d6 (7...f6 8.♘bd2 ♘f5 9.♘e4 d6 10.exd6 ♗xd6 11.b3 ♗e7 12.a4 e5 13.♗a3 ♕d5 14.♕d2 0-0 15.0-0-0±

(+0.36). The heavy pressure on c5 should pay dividends soon) 8.exd6 ♘g6 (so far Giri-Carlsen, Zagreb 2019. If 8...♘f5 9.♘bd2 ♗xd6 10.b3 ♗e7 11.♗b2 f6 12.♕e2 e5 13.0-0-0± (+0.47) White has much better pawn structure and development for the bishop pair) 9.♘bd2 ♗xd6 10.♘c4 ♗e7 11.♕e2 ♕d5 12.b3 f6 13.♗e3 ♕d8 14.g3 ♘f8 15.♗b2 e5 16.0-0-0± (+0.76). White has a big lead in development and much better pawn structure for the bishop pair. The semi-closed nature of the position favors knights.

7.h5 e5 8.h6 ♗g4 9.hxg7 ♗xg7 10.♗h6 ♗xh6 11.♖xh6 ♘g6 12.♘bd2 0-0 13.♕e2 ♖b8 14.0-0-0 f6 15.♖dh1 ♖b7 16.♕e3 ♖g7 17.g3 ♕e7 18.♘h4 ♘xh4 19.♖1xh4 d5

20.f4

20.♖h1± (+1.03). White has pressure against the weakened king, and Black has several weak pawns.

20...exf4 21.gxf4 c4 22.dxc4 ♗f5 23.cxd5

23.b3! ♗xe4 24.cxd5 cxd5 25.♘xe4 dxe4 26.♔b2± (+0.68). White has the safer king and better pawn structure.

23...cxd5 24.♖h1

24.b3±.

24...♗xe4 25.♘xe4 ♕xe4 26.♕xe4 dxe4 27.f5 ♖c8 28.c3 ♖f7 29.♖6h4 ♖c5 30.♖xe4 ♖xf5 31.♖h2 ♖f1+ 32.♔c2 f5 33.♖ee2 ♔g7 34.b4? f4=
Drawn after another sixty moves.

Game 8.9 Sicilian Defense – Rossolimo
Constantin Lupulescu   2608
Robert Ris   2451

England tt 2018/19 (3)

1.e4 c5 2.♘f3 ♘c6 3.♗b5 g6 4.0-0 ♗g7 5.♘c3

Note that this can also arise from 2.♘c3 ♘c6 3.♘f3 g6 4.♗b5 ♗g7 5.0-0, so it is critical to the 2.♘c3 chapter as well as being a good option in the standard Rossolimo.
5...e5
5...♘f6?! 6.e5 ♘g4 (6...♘h5 7.♖e1 ♘f4 8.d4 cxd4 9.♘xd4 ♘e6 10.♘xe6 fxe6 11.♗xc6 bxc6 12.♘a4 ♕c7 13.b3 0-0 (13...♗xe5?? 14.♖xe5+−) 14.♗b2 c5 15.c4± (+0.31). White's space and pawn structure advantage more than make up for the bishop pair) 7.♗xc6 dxc6 8.♖e1 0-0 9.d3 ♘h6 10.♘e4 b6 11.a4 a5 12.c3 ♖a7 13.♗f4 ♘f5 14.♕c2 h6 15.h3 g5 16.♗h2 ♗a6 17.♖ad1 ♖d7 18.c4 ♗c8 19.e6 ♘d4

20.♘xd4 ♖xd4 21.exf7+ ♖xf7 22.f3 ♗f5 23.♘f2 ♕d7 24.♔h1± (+0.37). White has a safer king and a good square (e4) for the knight.
6.a3 ♘ge7 7.b4

7...b6
  A) 7...d6 8.bxc5 dxc5 9.♗c4 0-0 10.d3 ♘d4 11.♗g5 h6 12.♗xe7 ♕xe7 13.♘d5 ♕d8 14.c3 ♘e6 15.a4± (+0.23). White's knight outpost counts for more than the black bishop pair, especially since the unopposed bishop is bad;
  B) 7...cxb4 8.axb4 ♘xb4 9.♗a3 ♘bc6 10.♗d6 0-0 11.♗c4± (+0.90). White's hugely superior development is worth way more than the extra black edge pawn. It's like a Benko Gambit where White has played very badly, with colors reversed.
8.bxc5 bxc5 9.d3 0-0 10.♗g5

10...♕c7

10...♗b7 11.♖b1 h6 12.♗a4 ♕c8
13.♗h4± (+0.30). White's pieces
are more active, and Black has a
backward pawn on d7.

11.♗xc6 ♘xc6 12.♘d5 ♕a5

13.♘f6+

13.♖b1 d6 14.♗e7 ♘xe7 15.♘xe7+
♚h8 16.♘xc8 ♖axc8 17.♘d2±
(+0.42). The knight is much better
than the bishop here.

13...♚h8 14.♘d2 ♘d4 15.♘d5

15.♘c4 ♕a6 16.♘d5 f6 17.♗e3
♖b8 18.f4± (+0.28). White has the
initiative and better placed pieces.

15...♗b7

15...f6 16.♘c4 ♕a6 17.♗e3 (+0.22).
Similar to the previous note.

**16.♗e7 ♖fe8 17.♘c4 ♕a4 18.♗xc5
♗xd5 19.exd5 ♕xc2 20.♗xd4 ♕xd1
21.♖fxd1 exd4 22.♘d6 ♖e7 23.♖ab1
♚g8 24.♘c4 d6 25.g3±** (+0.83)
White's knight is vastly better than
the bishop here.

**25...♖c8? 26.♖b5 ♖c5 27.♖xc5 dxc5
28.♖b1+− ♖d7 29.♖b8+ ♗f8 30.a4
f6 31.a5 ♚f7 32.a6 ♚e7 33.♖a8 h5
34.f4 ♚f7 35.♚f2 ♗e7 36.♚f3 ♗d8
37.h3 ♚e7 38.g4 hxg4+ 39.hxg4
♗b6 40.f5 gxf5 41.gxf5**
Black resigned.

Game 8.10 Sicilian Defense – Rossolimo

Nils Grandelius 2688

Nihal Sarin 2598

Malmö 2019 (6)

**1.e4 c5 2.♘f3 ♘c6 3.♗b5 g6 4.0-0
♗g7 5.♖e1 ♘f6**

5...e5 is probably better. See next
game.

**6.e5 ♘d5 7.♘c3 ♘c7 8.♗xc6 dxc6
9.♘e4**

9...b6

9...♗e6 10.d3 0-0 11.♗e3 b6 12.♕d2
♘d4 13.♘xd4 cxd4 14.♗h6 c5
15.♘g3± (+0.24), Lc0 +0.54. White
plans to double rooks on the e-file
and can then play on either wing.
With all the pawns on the board,
the white knight should be no
weaker than the remaining black
bishop, and White's king will be
safer.

**10.♘f6+ ♚f8 11.♘e4 ♗g4 12.d3
♘e6**

12...♗xe5 13.♘xe5 ♗xd1 14.♗h6+
♚g8 15.♘xc6 ♗xc2 16.♘xd8 ♖xd8
17.♘xc5 bxc5 18.♖xe7 ♘e6 19.♖e1
♗a4 20.♖xa7 ♘c6 21.h4 ♖a8
22.♖xa8+N ♗xa8 23.♖e5 ♘c6 24.d4
cxd4 25.b4± (+1.05). Although
White has only a pawn for the

knight, the black rook locked in the corner is almost useless and White already has two connected outside passers.

13.♘eg5 ♘xg5 14.♗xg5 ♕d5 15.♖e4 ♗xf3 16.♕xf3 ♗xe5 17.♕e3

17...f6?

After 17...♗xb2! 18.c4 ♕f5 19.♗h6+ ♔g7 20.♖e1 ♕h5 21.♗f4 ♗f6 22.♖xe7 h6 23.♖c7 (23.h3 g5 24.♗e5 ♗xe7 25.♗xh8 ♗d6 26.♗a1 ♕g6 27.♕e2 ♖d8 28.g3 the evaluation is near zero. White has full compensation for the extra doubled black pawn, but perhaps not more than this) 23...♔g7 24.♕e6 g5 25.♗e5 ♕g6 26.h3 (26. g3 ♖hd8 27.♖e3 ♗xe5 28.♕xe5+ ♕f6 29.♕xf6+ ♔xf6 30.♖xc6+ ♔g7 31.♔f1 ♖ac8 32.♖xc8 ♖xc8 33.♖e7 ♖d8 34.♔e2 a5 35.h3± (+0.01), Lc0 +0.17. White clearly has the better side of a drawn ending) 26...♗xe5 27.♕xe5+ ♕f6 28.♕xf6+ ♔xf6 29.♖xc6+ ♔g7 30.♖e7± (0.00), Lc0 +0.16. Black can hold this ending with careful play.

18.♖e1 ♖e8 19.♗h6+ ♔g8 20.c3?

20.♕f3! ♗d6 21.g4+− (+1.78). As explained in *New In Chess*, Black has nothing useful to do here, while

White can keep improving his position.

20...♗d6 21.c4

21.g4± (+0.50).

21...♕h5 22.h4 ♗e5?? 23.♗g5+− ♗d4 24.♖xd4 fxg5 25.♖d7 ♔g7 26.♖xe7+ ♖xe7 27.♕xe7+ ♔h6 28.♖e5 ♕d1+ 29.♔h2 ♕h5 30.♕xg5+ ♕xg5 31.hxg5+ 1-0

Game 8.11 Sicilian Defense – Rossolimo
Fabiano Caruana   2832
Magnus Carlsen   2835
London Wch m 2018 (5)

1.e4 c5 2.♘f3 ♘c6 3.♗b5 g6 4.0-0 ♗g7 5.♖e1 e5 6.b4!?

This gambit is actually not very risky, and requires great accuracy by Black. Probably Black won't have much trouble holding in correspondence chess, but it's a worthy option for over-the-board play.

6...♘xb4

6...cxb4?! 7.a3 ♘ge7 8.axb4 0-0 9.♗xc6 dxc6 (9...bxc6 10.♗b2 d6 11.d4 ♕c7 12.dxe5 dxe5 13.♕d3 ♖d8 14.♕c3 f6 15.♕c4+ ♔h8 16.♘bd2± (+0.32). White's pressure on two weak black pawns and his much better queen overcome the bishops; 9...♘xc6 10.b5 ♘d4 11.c4 d6 12.♘xd4 exd4 13.d3± (+0.35). White's big space advantage, good bishop, better pawn structure, and pressure on a7 more than offset the bishop pair) 10.d3± (+0.39). White's center pawn vs edge pawn offsets the bishop pair, while his superior development (especially the rook on a1) gives the plus.

7.♗b2 a6

7...♕c7 is objectively best I think, but requires knowing a lot: 8.d4! a6 9.♗f1 exd4 and now:

analysis diagram

A) 10.c3 d3 11.♘a3 ♘c2 (11...♘h6 12.h3 ♘c6 13.♕xd3 f6 14.♘c4 ♘f7 15.♗c1 0-0 16.a4 d6 17.♗f4. White has full compensation for the pawn, with better development, more space, and two backward black pawns on half-open files. Komodo rates it just dead even, Lc0 gives White a modest plus. At least we can say it is more pleasant to play for White) 12.♘xc2 dxc2 13.♕xc2 d6 14.c4 f6 15.h4 ♘h6 16.♖ad1 ♗d7 17.h5 0-0-0 18.♘h4. White has full compensation for the pawn, since the threat on g6 is difficult to meet

without a concession. Objectively this is equal, but more pleasant to play for White;

B) 10.♕c1 (White prepares c2-c3 by defending ♗b2 so Black can't reply ...d4-d3) 10...♘c6 11.c3 ♕d8 12.cxd4 cxd4 13.♘a3 d6 14.♘c2 ♘ge7 15.♘fxd4 0-0 16.♘xc6 ♘xc6 17.♗xg7 ♔xg7 18.♘e3 ♗e6 19.♖b1 ♖b8 20.♗xa6 bxa6 21.♕xc6 ♕a5 22.♕xd6 ♖fd8 23.♕f4 ♖xb1 24.♖xb1 ♗xa2 25.♖c1. Both Komodo and Lc0 rate it equal, but probably it is easier to play White, who has some kingside prospects.

8.a3 axb5 9.axb4 ♖xa1 10.♗xa1 d6 11.bxc5 ♘e7

12.♕e2

12.cxd6 ♕xd6 13.d4 exd4 14.♗xd4 0-0 15.♗xg7 ♕xd1 16.♖xd1 ♔xg7 17.♘d4 b4 18.♘d2 (+0.25). Ivan Saric says the bishop vs knight is enough to offset the doubled pawns, but Lc0 gives White +0.14. Black should be OK, but it's easier to play for White.

12...b4 13.♕c4

13.c3 0-0 14.cxb4 dxc5 15.bxc5 ♘c6 16.♕b5± (+0.38). Black has the bishop pair for the pawn, but not much more.

13...♕a5 14.cxd6 ♗e6 15.♕c7 ♕xc7 16.dxc7 ♘c6

17.c3?!

17.♖d1! ♔d7 18.d4 b3 19.♘xe5+ ♔xc7 20.cxb3 ♖a8 21.♘d2 ♗xe5 22.dxe5 ♖a2 23.h3 b5 24.♔h2 b4 25.♔g3 Komodo shows just +0.02, but Lc0 gives +0.20. Black has enough compensation for the two (doubled) pawns to hold, but White is for choice.

17...♔d7 18.cxb4 ♖a8 19.♗c3 ♔xc7 20.d3 ♔b6

20...b5!∓.

21.♗d2 ♖d8 22.♗e3+ ♔b5 23.♘c3+ ♔xb4 24.♘d5+ ♗xd5 25.exd5 ♖xd5 26.♖b1+ ♔c3 27.♖xb7 ♘d8 28.♖c7+ ♔xd3 29.♔f1 h5 30.h3 ♔e4 31.♘g5+ ♔f5 32.♘xf7 ♘xf7 33.♖xf7+ ♗f6 34.g4+

Draw agreed.

Game 8.12 Sicilian Defense – Rossolimo

Reinhardt Semmler 2348

Vasily Eremin 2368

Correspondence game, 2017

1.e4 c5 2.♘f3 ♘c6 3.♗b5 g6 4.0-0 ♗g7 5.♖e1 e5 6.♗xc6 dxc6 7.d3 ♕e7 8.♗e3 ♘f6 9.h3 0-0 10.♕d2

10...♘d7

10...b6 11.a4 a5 12.♘a3 ♗a6 13.b3 ♖fe8 14.♖ad1± (+0.13). But Lc0 loves White here. White has ideas of ♘c4, ♗h6, and ♘h2 planning f2-f4.

11.♕c3 a5 12.a4 ♖e8 13.♘bd2 b6 14.♘c4 ♗a6 15.♗g5 ♕e6 16.♖ad1 ♗xc4

16...♖ab8 17.b3 ♘f8 18.♕d2 ♕d7 19.♗h6 f6 20.♗xg7 ♔xg7 21.c3 ♘e6 22.d4 ♖bd8 23.♕b2 ♘f4 24.♕c2 cxd4 25.cxd4 exd4 26.♘xd4± (+0.08), Lc0 +0.14. ...c6-c5 will leave Black with a much less useful pawn majority than White. The bishop does not look better than the white knight on c4 here.

17.♕xc4

17.dxc4 ♘f8 18.♖d3 f6 19.♗e3 ♕f7 20.♖ed1 ♘e6 21.♕d2 ♘d4 22.c3 ♘xf3+ 23.gxf3 ♕xc4 24.♖d7 ♕e6

25.♔h2 (+0.16). The domination of the only open file counts for more than the extra doubled pawn.
17...♘f8 18.♕xe6 ♘xe6 19.♗d2 ♖eb8 20.♖a1 f6 21.g3 ♔f7 22.♔g2 ♗f8 23.b3 ♗d6 24.h4 h5 25.♗e3 ♘d4 26.♖ec1 ♘e2 27.♖f1 ♘d4 28.♖a2 ♔e7 29.♘d2 ♖g8

30.f4
30.♘c4 ♗c7 31.f4 exf4 32.♗xf4 ♗xf4 33.gxf4 b5 34.♘e3 ♔f7 35.♔f2± (+0.03), but Lc0 +0.20. White wants to play ♖fa1 to provoke a weakening.
30...exf4 31.gxf4 ♗c7 32.♔h1
32.♘c4 ♘e6 33.♖aa1 ♔f7 34.♖f2 ♖ad8 35.♔f3 ♖ge8 36.♖g2 ♖g8 37.♖ag1± (+0.35). White has obvious positional advantages, but no clear path to progress. Black has to watch out for a timely f4-f5.
32...♖ab8 33.♖f2 ♖bf8 34.♔g2 g5 35.fxg5 ♘e6 36.♖a1 fxg5 37.♖xf8 ♔xf8 38.♖f1+ ♔e7 39.hxg5 ♘xg5 40.♔h1 ♘e6 41.♖f5 ♖h8 42.♘f3 ♖f8 43.♖xf8 ♘xf8 44.♗g5+ ♔f7 45.♗d2 ♘g6 46.♔g2 ♘f4+ 47.♔f2 ½-½
White is still for choice, but this was a correspondence game with computer use allowed, so a draw was pretty certain.

Game 8.13 Sicilian Defense – Rossolimo
Viswanathan Anand 2767
Shakhriyar Mamedyarov 2774
Stavanger 2019 (2)

1.e4 c5 2.♘f3 ♘c6 3.♗b5 g6 4.♗xc6
The point of capturing now is to see which way Black recaptures. If he captures with the b-pawn as here, White has no reason to defer castling since 0-0-0 would be too risky.
4...bxc6
It is more popular and more natural to capture with the d-pawn, but this capture has its adherents at high level. It chooses the long-term asset of gaining a center-controlling pawn over the superior piece activity after 4...dxc6.
5.0-0 ♗g7 6.♖e1 ♘h6
This move looks weird, but Black plans to place the knight on f7 or f5 since on f6 it gets kicked away by e4-e5.
7.c3 0-0

8.h3
8.d4 cxd4 9.cxd4 d5 10.e5 f6 11.♘bd2 fxe5 12.♘xe5 ♗xe5 13.dxe5 ♕b6 14.♘f3 ♘f5 15.a4 ♖b8 16.e6. Komodo calls it even, but Lc0 really

likes White: +0.31. White is for choice, but it's a bit double-edged. I prefer the game move.

8...f5 9.e5 ♘f7 10.d3 ♖b8

10...♗a6 11.c4 d6 12.e6 ♘e5 13.♘xe5 ♗xe5 14.♘d2 (+0.14). White has space and better pawns for the bishop pair, and the closed position favors knights.

11.b3 d6 12.♗f4 h6 13.h4 e6

14.exd6

14.♕d2!N ♖e8! (14...g5 15.hxg5 hxg5 16.♘xg5 ♘xe5 17.♘a3± (+0.32). White has a much safer king and better pawn structure for the bishop pair) 15.♘a3 d5 16.♘c2 a5 17.d4 cxd4 18.cxd4 ♗f8 19.♔h1 ♔h7 20.♖g1 c5 21.dxc5 ♗xc5 22.♖ac1 ♗b6 23.♖gd1 a4 24.♗e3 axb3 25.axb3 ♗c7 26.♘cd4 ♗d7 27.♔g1± (+0.18), Lc0 +0.39. White has space, a blockading knight, a mobile passed pawn, and more active pieces, all for the bishop pair.

14...g5 15.♗e5 ♘xe5 16.♘xe5 ♕xd6 17.♕e2 ♗xe5 18.♕xe5 ♕xe5 19.♖xe5 ♖d8 20.♖xc5 ♖xd3 21.♘a3 ♗d7 22.♖a5 ♖b7 23.hxg5 hxg5 24.c4

24.♔f1! ♔g7 25.♔e2 ♖d5 26.♘c4 is equal.

24...♔g7 25.c5 ♔f6 26.♘c4 e5 27.♘d6 ♖c7 28.f3 ♔e6 29.♖e1 ♖d5 30.b4 ♖d4?! 31.a3?!

31.♖a3!±.

31...g4 32.♖a6 ♔d5 33.♘f7?? e4−+ 34.fxg4? ♗c8 0-1

Game 8.14 Sicilian Defense – Rossolimo

Georg Meier   2623
Etienne Bacrot   2684

PRO League Stage rapid 2019 (2)

1.e4 c5 2.♘f3 ♘c6 3.♗b5 g6 4.♗xc6 dxc6 5.d3

White defers castling here to meet 5...♗g4 by 6.♘bd2 and to keep open the option of castling queenside.

5...♗g7

5...♕c7 and now:

A) 6.h3 is recommended by former FIDE World Champion Ruslan Ponomariov, whose comments in New In Chess *Yearbook* Vol. 132 guided the following analysis. It avoids the need for ♕e1 in the game as well as both ...♘g4 and ...♗g4 on move 8: 6...♗g7 (6...e5 7.♗e3 f6 8.♕d2±) 7.♘c3 e5 8.♗e3 b6 9.a3 ♘f6 (9...f5 10.b4±; 9...a5 10.♘a4 ♖b8 11.0–0 ♘f6 12.♕d2 0–0 13.b4±)

10.b4 ♘d7 11.0–0 0–0 12.♕b1 ♕d8 13.♕b3 ♕e7 14.♖fb1 ♖e8 15.b5 cxb5 16.♕xb5 ♘f6 17.a4 ♗d7 18.♕b3± (+0.35), Lc0 +0.53. White has more center pawns, a good bishop, good squares for his knights, and the plan of a4-a5, all for the bishop pair;

B) 6.0-0 e5 7.♗e3 ♘f6 8.♕e1

analysis diagram

8...♗g4 (8...♘g4 9.♗d2 f6 10.b4 cxb4 11.♗xb4 ♘h6 12.a4 ♘f7 13.h3 ♗e6 14.♗xf8 ♔xf8 15.♕e3± (+0.04), Lc0 +0.30. White has more center pawns, and with most of the pawns on the board the lone bishop is not superior to the knight) 9.♘bd2 ♘h5 10.a3 ♗e7 (10...a5 11.h3 ♗e6 12.c3 f6 13.d4 ♗e7 14.dxe5 fxe5 15.♕e2 a4 16.♘g5 ♗xg5 17.♗xg5± (+0.26). Black has little to offset his inferior pawn structure) 11.♕b1 ♘f4 (11...0-0 12.b4 cxb4 13.axb4 a6 14.♕b2 ♗d6 15.h3 ♗xf3 16.♘xf3± (+0.36). White is up by a center pawn for an edge pawn, and has superior pieces) 12.b4± (+0.37). Black doesn't want to activate White's rook by trading on b4, but may lose a pawn soon or get a horrible pawn structure otherwise. 12...♘e2+ 13.♔h1 ♘d4?!

14.♘g1 g5? (14...0-0-0 15.♕b2 f5 16.f3 ♗h5 17.♗f2±) 15.bxc5 ♗xc5 16.♗xg5 ♖g8 17.♗h4 ♗e7 18.♗g3 0-0-0 19.♘c4 f6 20.a4 (20.f4!± (+1.60). Black will have to sacrifice an exchange on g3 just to survive) 20...♘e6 21.f3 ♗h5 22.♗f2 ♗c5 23.♗xc5 ♘xc5 24.♘e2 ♗f7 25.♘e3 ♕a5 26.♕e1 ♕xe1 27.♖fxe1 a5 28.♔g1 h5 29.h4 ♔c7 30.♔f2 ♗e6 31.♖g1 ♖h8 32.♖h1 ♖d7 33.♖hd1 ♗f7 34.d4 exd4 35.♖xd4 ♖xd4 36.♘xd4 ♖d8 37.♘e2 ♖d2 38.♔e1 ♖d8 39.♘f5 ♖a8 40.♘c3 ♗e6 41.♘e3 ♔d6 42.♖d1+ ♔e7 43.♖d4 ♖a6 44.♔d2 ♖b6 45.♘f5+ ♗xf5 46.exf5 ♖b2 47.♖c4 ♔d6 48.♘e4+ ♘xe4+ 49.♖xe4 ♖a2 50.g4 hxg4 51.fxg4 ♔d5 52.♔d3 ♖a3+ 53.c3 b5. Now 54.g5! would have won, he played 54.h5?? and only drew, ½-½ (68) Aronian-Carlsen, Stavanger 2019.

6.h3 ♘f6

6...e5 7.0-0 ♕c7.

analysis diagram

The World Champion keeps playing this way (...♕c7) and gets away with it. He shows that it is playable, but it doesn't look equal. White has various paths to a small edge:

A) 8.a3 ♘f6 9.♗e3 c4 10.♘c3 cxd3

analysis diagram

11.♕xd3 (11.cxd3 0-0 12.♕c2 ♖d8 13.a4 ♕e7 14.a5 ♘e8 15.♘e2 ♘c7 16.♗c5 ♕e8 17.d4 exd4 18.♗xd4 ♗xd4 19.♘fxd4 ♕e7 20.f4 ♗d7 21.♖ae1± (+0.33). White has space, development, and an attack) 11...0-0 (+0.05), Lc0 +0.53 ('More or less equal,' says Ponomariov. So clearly he agrees with Komodo, not Lc0, here) 12.♖fd1 ♖e8 13.♗c5 ♗f8 14.♗xf8 ♔xf8 15.♖d2 ♗e6 16.♖ad1 (16.♕d6+ ♕xd6 17.♖xd6 ♔e7 18.♖ad1 ♘d7 19.♘g5 ♘f6 20.♘xe6 fxe6 21.f3± (+0.24). White has an obviously better pawn structure, but whether he can exploit it is questionable; 16.♕e3 ♔g7 17.♖ad1 ♘d7 18.♘g5 ♘f8 19.♘xe6+ ♖xe6 20.♘e2± (+0.20), but Lc0 +0.54. White's control of the open file is his edge) 16...♖ad8 17.♕xd8?! (17.♕e3= Komodo slightly prefers Black due to the bishop for knight, while Lc0 slightly prefers White due to the open file. It's pretty even) 17...♖xd8 18.♖xd8+ ♔g7 (-0.25). Both engines already prefer Black; with 14 pawns on the board and four minor pieces, the two rooks are not better than the

queen. Black was better, then White missed a win, finally the game was drawn, ½-½ (56) Caruana-Carlsen, Stavanger 2019 (9);

B) 8.♗e3! b6 9.♘bd2 (this has the drawback of making a later ...f7-f5 effective) 9.a3 (best per Ponomariov) 9...♘e7 (9...f5 10.exf5 gxf5 11.♖e1±) 10.b4 cxb4 11.axb4 0-0 (11...f5 12.c4! 0-0 13.c5±) 12.♕d2± ♖d8 (12...f5 13.♗h6±) 13.♖a3 f5 14.♕c1 f4 15.♗d2 h6 16.♗c3 g5 17.♕b2 ♘g6 18.♘bd2 ♗e6 19.♖fa1 ♔h7 20.♘c4 ♗xc4 21.dxc4± (+0.52), Lc0 +0.67. White has a much better bishop and pressure on two weak pawns; 9...♘e7 10.a3 0-0 11.b4 cxb4 12.axb4 f5 and now:

analysis diagram

B1) 13.♗g5 (trading off an unpaired bishop for a knight in a somewhat blocked position is reasonable. It's not the engines' first choice, but with deeper analysis it looks good as the bishop is otherwise a target) 13...h6 14.♗xe7 ♕xe7 15.c3 ♖d8 16.♕e2 c5 17.b5 f4 18.♖a3 a6 19.bxa6 ♖xa6 20.♖xa6 ♗xa6 21.c4 ♕d6 22.♖b1 g5 23.♘e1± (+0.47). The blocked pawn structure favors knights, offsetting the bishop pair edge, and Black has three weak pawns to one for White;

B2) 13.♘c4 ♗e6 14.♘g5 (14.♕c1! fxe4 15.♘g5 ♗d5 16.♘xe4 ♘f5 17.♕e1 ♖ad8 18.♘cd2 h6 19.♕e2 ♘d4 20.♕d1 ♗e6 21.c4 ♗f5 22.♗xd4 ♖xd4 23.♘f3 ♖d7 24.♕e2± (+0.58). Here too Black has two bishops for two knights but the position is not very open, the knight on e4 is great, and Black has an inferior pawn structure) 14...♗d7

analysis diagram

15.♕e2 (15.♖e1! h6 16.♘f3 ♗e6 17.♕e2 f4 18.♗c1 g5 19.♗b2 g4 20.hxg4 ♗xg4 21.d4 exd4 22.e5 ♖ad8 23.♘cd2 ♔h8 24.♕c4 ♘f5 25.♘xd4 b5 26.♕c5 ♖d5 27.♖xa7 ♕d8 28.♘xc6 ♖xc5 29.♘xd8 ♖xc2 30.♘e6 ♖xd2 31.♗c1 ♖c2 32.♖xg7 ♘xg7 33.♘xf8 ♔g8 34.♘g6± (+0.40). White is a pawn up but Black should draw after 34...f3) 15...h6 16.♘f3 f4 17.♗d2 g5 18.♗c3 ♘g6 19.d4 exd4 20.♗xd4 g4 21.hxg4 ♗xg4= 22.c3 c5 23.bxc5 bxc5 24.♗xg7 ♕xg7 25.♘d6 ♔h8 26.♘f5 ♖xf5 27.exf5 ♘h4 28.f6 ♕xf6 29.♖a6 ♕g7 30.♖xh6+ ♕xh6 31.♕e5+ ♕g7 32.♕xg7+? (32.♘xh4 ♕xe5 33.♘g6+ ♔g7 34.♘xe5 ♗f5 35.♖d1 (-0.34).

It should be noted that this was an Armageddon playoff game (10' to 7' but with a draw Black wins) so White had no incentive to seek a draw) 32...♔xg7 33.♘xh4 a5 34.♖a1 a4 35.♖a3 ♔f6 36.♔f1 ♔e5 37.♔e1 ♔d5 38.f3 ♗h5 39.♔d2 ♗e8 40.♔c1 ♔c4 41.♘f5 ♖a6 42.♘g7 ♗g6 43.♔d2 ♔d5 0-1 Aronian-Carlsen, Stavanger 2019 (Armageddon).

7.♘c3 ♘d7 8.♗e3 e5

9.♕d2

White will either kill Black's bishop pair, his only compensation for inferior pawn structure and development, or make castling difficult for Black. Database stats are an excellent +52 Elo for White here with 327 games.

9...h6

9...♕e7 10.♗h6 (once Black loses the bishop pair White has a better pawn structure 'for free') 10...f6 11.♗xg7 ♕xg7 12.♕e3 (12.♘h2 – this less common but even more successful move is Ponomariov's choice: 12...♘f8 13.f4 exf4 14.♕xf4 ♘e6 15.♕f2 0-0 16.♘f3 16.0-0 is usual and also good, but probably castling queenside is more likely to lead to a win: 16...♗d7 17.0-0-0 ♖ad8 18.h4±

177

(+0.53), Lc0 +0.61. Ponomariov says 'White's advantage is not so big, but... the first player risks nothing'. With the better pawn structure, more space, and attacking prospects, White's advantage is at least clear) 12...♕e7 13.♘d2 ♘f8 14.f4 exf4 15.♕xf4 ♘e6 16.♕h4 ♘d4 17.0-0-0 ♗e6 18.♖hf1± (+0.45), Lc0 +0.66. White's pawn center and pressure on f6 give him the edge.

10.a3

10.0-0.

analysis diagram

This is the usual move and Ponomariov's choice, planning ♘h2 and f2-f4. White wants to take advantage of Black's inability to castle without losing h6. I think that the a2-a3 plan is more promising, but both should give White a pull and the choice is difficult.

A) 10...♕e7 11.♘h2 ♘f8 12.f4 exf4 13.♗xf4 ♘e6 (13...♗e6 14.♖ae1±) 14.♗g3 ♘d4 (14...♕g5 15.♕e1 ♘d4 16.♕f2 0-0 17.♗d6 ♗xh3 18.♗f4 ♕xg2+ 19.♕xg2 ♗xg2 20.♔xg2 ♘xc2 21.♖ad1 ♖ad8 22.♖d2 ♘d4 23.♗e3± (+0.30), Lc0 +0.50. With a knight for three pawns, White

is up half a pawn. White can exchange the outposted knight now or after playing ♘f3 first) 15.♖ae1 0-0 16.e5 ♗f5 17.♘e4 ♗xe4 18.♖xe4 ♘f5 19.♗f2 b6 20.♘f3 ♕e6 21.a3± (+0.59), Lc0 +0.71. White plans b2-b4, later g2-g4. He has a substantial space advantage;

B) 10...b6 11.♘h2 ♘f8 12.f4 exf4

analysis diagram

13.♗xf4 (improving on the 13.♖xf4 ♗e6 14.♖f2 of the first match game Caruana-Carlsen, London 2018) 13...♘e6 14.♗e3 ♘d4 15.♖ae1 ♗e6 16.♘d1 (16.e5 ♘f5 (16...♗xe5?! 17.♘g4 ♗g7 18.♘xh6±) 17.♗f2 ♕c7 18.♘f3 0-0-0 19.♘e4 ♗d5 is 'complex' (Ponomariov). Lc0 still likes White, but the lines end up about equal according to Komodo and Stockfish) 16...♕d7 17.c3 ♘b5 18.♘f3 0-0-0 19.♘f2 ♘c7 (unclear per Ponomariov) 20.a3 g5 21.b4± (+0.15), Lc0 +0.25. White's queenside initiative and better center should count for more than the bishop pair, although it's close.

10...a5

10...b6 11.0-0 ♘f8 12.b4 ♘e6 13.♖ae1 ♘d4 14.♘h2 ♕d6 15.♘a4 cxb4 16.axb4 ♗e6 17.c3 ♘b5 18.♖a1 ♖d8

19.c4 ♘d4 20.♖fb1 ♖d7 21.c5 ♕c7
22.♗xd4 ♖xd4 23.♘f3 ♖d8 24.b5±
(+0.27) Lc0 +0.48. Black will have
to pay some price to avoid losing a
pawn.

**11.0-0 b6 12.♘a4 f5 13.exf5 gxf5
14.♖ae1**

Wrong rook, it seems.

14.♖fe1! ♔f7 15.♖ad1 ♖a7 16.c3
f4 17.♗xf4 exf4 18.♕xf4+ ♕f6
19.♕c4+ ♔f8 20.♖e6 ♕f7 21.♖de1
♘f6 22.♘xc5 bxc5 23.♕xc5+
♔g8 24.♖xc6 ♗xh3 25.♘e5 ♕e7
26.gxh3± (+0.46). With four pawns
for the bishop and more active
pieces, White is surely better.

14...♔f8

15.♕c1?!

  A) 15.g3 ♔g8 16.♕e2 ♔h7 17.♘h4
♘f6 18.♔h2± (+0.26). White's
pressure on Black's weak pawns
counts for more than the bishop
pair here;

  B) 15.♕e2 ♔g8 16.♘h2 ♗a6 17.f4
e4 18.c4 ♘f6 19.dxe4 ♘xe4 20.♕c2±
(+0.31). White has much better
pawn structure and development
for the bishop pair.

15...♔g8 16.c4?

16.♘h2! f4 17.♗d2 ♔h7 18.♕d1 ♖e8
19.♕f3 ♕f6 20.♗xf4 b5 21.♘c3 b4
22.♘g4 ♕xf4 23.♕xf4 exf4 24.♖xe8

bxc3 25.bxc3 h5 26.♘h2 ♗xc3 27.♖b1
♘f6 28.♖e7+ ♔h6 29.♘f3=.

16...♔h7 17.♕c2 ♖g8 18.♔h1 ♕e8?
18...♘f8∓.

**19.♘h2 ♕g6 20.f4± exf4 21.♗xf4
± b5 22.♘c3 bxc4? 23.dxc4± ♘f8
24.♘f3 ♕h5 25.♘e2 ♘e6 26.♘g3+−
♕f7?**

A tactical oversight, but 26...♕g6
27.♘h4 ♘d4 28.♕f2 is also losing.

27.♗d6?
27.♘xf5! ♘xf4 28.♘e7+ ♔h8 29.♘h4
is a more convincing win.

27...♕g6 28.♘xf5 ♘d4 29.♘3xd4?
29.♘5xd4! cxd4 30.♕xg6+ ♔xg6
31.♗e5 c5 32.♘h4+ ♔h5 33.♗xg7
♖xg7 34.♘f5 was necessary to win.

**29...cxd4 30.♖e7 ♗xf5 31.♕xf5
♖ge8?**
31...♖xf5 32.♖xf5 ♖ge8.

32.g4?
32.♖xg7+! ♔xg7 33.♗e5+ ♔h7
34.♕d7+ ♔g8 35.♖f6! is decisive.

**32...♖xe7 33.♗xe7 ♖e8= 34.♗c5
d3 35.♖d1 ♕xf5 36.gxf5 ♗xb2
37.♖xd3 ♖e5 38.♖d7+ ♔g8 39.♗d4
♗xd4 40.♖xd4 ♖xf5 41.♔g2 ♔g7
42.♔g3 ♖f6 43.♔g4 ♔g6 44.♖e4
♖d6 45.♔f4 ♖d3 46.♖e6+ ♔g7 47.h4
♖xa3 48.♖xc6 a4 49.h5 ♖a1 50.♖g6+
♔f7 51.♖a6 a3 52.♔g3 a2 53.♔g2**

♔e7 54.c5 ♔d7 55.♔h2 ♔c7 56.c6
♔d6 57.♔g2 ♔c7 58.♔h2 ♔d6
59.♔g2 ♔c7 60.♔h2 ♔d6 61.♔g2
♔c7 62.♔h2 ½-½

Game 8.15 Sicilian Defense – Moscow
Arkadij Naiditsch   2711
Aleksander Mista   2604
Linares 2018 (3)

1.e4 c5 2.♘f3 d6 3.♗b5+ ♗d7

This used to be the main line of
the Moscow (3.♗b5+) Variation, but
3...♘d7 has pretty much supplanted
it in high level play, probably
because it offers much better
winning chances for Black, though
more risk as well. Also the 4.c4
move given here has proven to be
tough to meet. Given that White's
only moved pawn is on White
while Black's moved pawns are on
Black, the exchange of light-squared
bishops favors White in principle.
If White trades on d7 (now or
later) he doesn't really lose a tempo
since both recaptures misplace the
recapturing piece.
4.c4!?
4.♗xd7+ was the main line here
and is still quite good, but the game

move has recently caught on and
avoids making Black's development
easy: 4...♕xd7 (4...♘xd7 5.0-0
♘gf6 6.♕e2 e6 7.b3 ♗e7 8.♗b2 0-0
9.c4 a6 10.d4 cxd4 11.♘xd4 ♕b6
12.♘c2 ♖ac8 13.♘c3 ♖fe8 14.♔h1
♕c5 15.♖ac1± (+0.29). White has a
normal Maroczy space advantage)
5.c4 ♘c6 6.d4 cxd4 7.♘xd4 ♘f6
8.♘c3 g6 9.f3 ♗g7 10.♗e3 0-0
transposes to the note to move 10.
4...♘f6
  A) 4...♗xb5 5.cxb5 ♘f6 6.♘c3 g6
7.d4 cxd4 8.♘xd4 ♗g7 9.0-0 0-0
10.♕e2 ♘bd7 11.♖d1 ♖c8 12.♗g5
♖e8 13.♖ac1 (+0.15). White's space
advantage is worth something, and
the huge superiority of ♖d1 vs ♖e8
easily offsets the doubled pawn;
  B) 4...♘c6 5.♘c3 g6 (5...♘f6 6.0-0
g6 7.♗xc6N ♗xc6 8.d4 ♘xe4
9.♘xe4 ♗xe4 10.♖e1 ♗f5 11.♗g5 h6
12.♗f6 ♖g8 13.b4 cxb4 14.d5 ♕c7
15.♘d4 0-0-0 16.♘b5 ♕a5 17.♗d4
a6 18.♘a7+± (+1.02). White meets
...♔d7 by ♖c1, ...♔c7 or ...♔b8 by
a2-a3!) 6.♗xc6 ♗xc6 7.d4 cxd4
8.♘xd4 ♗g7 9.♗e3 ♘f6 10.f3 0-0
11.0-0± (+0.50). It's a pretty good
Maroczy Bind for White, since
Black can only keep his bishop pair
by extreme passivity. White has
traded off his bad bishop without
losing control.
**5.♘c3 g6 6.d4 cxd4 7.♘xd4 ♗g7
8.♗e3 0-0**
8...♘c6 9.h3 0-0 10.0-0 a6 11.♗xc6
bxc6 12.♘f3 ♖b8 13.e5 ♘e8 14.♕d2
♗e6 15.exd6 ♘xd6 16.b3± (+0.30).
White has space and a superior
pawn structure for the bishop pair.

9.♗xd7 ♛xd7

9...♘bxd7 10.0-0 a6 11.♖c1 ♖c8 12.b3 ♛a5 13.♕e2 ♖fe8 14.♗d2 ♛c5 15.♘f3± (+0.30). White has a rather good Maroczy Bind here as Black is rather passive.

10.h3

10.f3 would transpose to the main line of 4.♗xd7+ ♛xd7 5.c4, which is also pleasant for White, but the game move is the main point of the 4.c4 move order. h2-h3 makes more sense than f2-f3 unless e4 really needs the protection, as White often later plays f2-f4. 10...♘c6 11.0-0 a6 12.♕d3 ♛c7 13.b3 ♖fc8 14.♘xc6 bxc6 15.♖ad1 ♘d7 16.f4 ♖e8 17.♔h1 ♖ad8 18.♗d2 (18.♘a4 ♘c5 19.♘xc5 dxc5 20.♕e2 ♖xd1 21.♕xd1 ♗d4 22.♗d2± (+0.27). Black's outposted bishop is only partial compensation for his ruined pawn structure) 18...♘c5 19.♕f3 a5 20.f5 ♗f6 21.♘e2 a4 22.b4 ♘d7 23.♘f4 ♛b6 24.♕g3± (+0.56). White has space and the initiative on both wings.

10...♖c8

10...♘c6 11.0-0 ♖fc8 12.b3 a6 13.a4 e6 14.♖c1 ♛c7 15.♕d2 ♘d7 16.♘d5 exd5 17.cxd5 ♘c5 18.dxc6 bxc6 19.b4 ♘xe4 20.♕d3 ♗xd4 21.♕xd4 ♛e7 22.♗h6 ♛e5 23.♕xe5 dxe5 24.♖fe1

f5 25.f3 ♘d6 26.♗d2 ♘f7 27.♖c5± (+0.32). White will regain the pawn on e5 or c6 with a favorable endgame.

11.b3 a6 12.a4 ♘c6 13.0-0 ♛d8 14.♘de2

14.♕d2 ♛a5 15.♘de2 ♘d7 16.♖ab1 transposes to the game.

14...♘d7 15.♖b1 ♛a5 16.♕d2 ♛b4

17.♖fc1

17.♖fd1 ♖e8 18.f4± (+0.32). White has ideas of ♘d5 or ♕c2 or ♗f2 or even g2-g4.

17...e6 18.♕d1

18.♖d1 ♖d8 19.♕c2± (+0.25). White just patiently exploits his space edge and pressure on d6.

18...♖d8 19.♗g5 ♗f6 20.♗d2 ♛b6 21.♘f4?! ♘b4?!

21...♗d4=.

22.a5 ♛a7 23.♗e3 ♛b8 24.♘a4± ♘c5?

24...♛c7 25.♗d2±.

25.♘b6

25.♕f3+−.

25...♘a2 26.b4

26.♘fd5! exd5 27.♘xd5 ♘xe4 28.♖c2+−.

26...♘xe4 27.♕c2 ♘ec3 28.♘xa8 ♛xa8 29.♗d2

29.♖b3!+−.

29...♘xc1 30.♖xc1 ♖c8 31.♗xc3 ♖xc4

32.♗xf6?!

An unnecessary queen sacrifice, though probably good enough to win. 32.♘e2 ♗xc3 33.♕b3+−.

32...♖xc2 33.♖xc2 ♕b8 34.♘d3 (+1.62)

White has only a tiny material edge (a quarter of a pawn, I reckon), but his control of the only open file together with the bishop on its ideal square near the king produce decisive threats.

34...h5 35.h4 ♔h7 36.♘f4 ♔g8 37.♘d3 ♔h7 38.g3?

38.♘e1!+−, heading to g5.

38...e5 39.♘e1 g5

39...♕e8 40.♘f3 ♕d7±.

40.hxg5 ♔g6 41.♘g2+− ♔f5 42.♘e3+ ♔e4 43.♖d2 b6 44.♔g2 bxa5 45.g6 fxg6 46.f3+ ♔xe3 47.♗g5# 1-0

Game 8.16 Sicilian Defense – Moscow

Levon Aronian	2765
Maxime Vachier-Lagrave	2781

London 2018 (1)

1.e4 c5 2.♘f3 d6 3.♗b5+ ♘d7 4.c3

I used to play 4.0-0 first, but now I see that the tempo saved gives White more options to counter Black's various set-ups.

4.0-0 a6 5.♗d3 ♘gf6 6.♖e1 e6 7.a4 (7.c3 b5 8.♗c2 c4=) 7...b6 8.c3 ♗b7 9.♘a3 ♗e7 10.♗c2 0-0 11.d3 ♖e8 12.♗f4 (+0.05). This is pretty equal, although I'd rather have White than Black due to his slightly better piece activity. Since all the pieces are on the board and nothing is blocked, it's probably a good choice for a must-win game.

4...♘gf6

4...a6 5.♗a4 ♘gf6 6.♕e2 b5 7.♗c2 ♗b7 8.d4 (the advantage of omitting castling is that White gets to play this before Black plays ...c5-c4, so there is no en passant capture) 8...e6 9.0-0 ♗e7 10.a4 0-0 11.♖e1 (11.♗f4 cxd4 12.cxd4 ♘b6 13.b3 (+0.10). White retains the better center) 11...♕b6 12.♗d3 ♖fd8 13.♘bd2 (+0.12). White has the usual two center pawns vs none edge.

5.♗d3

This is the set-up for White named after the late IM Danny Kopec, except that White has 'lost' a tempo by checking first. But the knight on d7 is misplaced now; if it were still at home Black would play ...♗g4 and ...♘c6, so it's an improved version of the Kopec System.

5...♘e5

A) 5...e6 6.♗c2 b5 (6...c4 7.♕e2 ♕c7 8.♘a3 d5 9.exd5 ♗xa3 10.dxe6 0-0 11.exd7 ♗xd7 12.0-0 ♖fe8 13.♕d1 ♗d6 14.d3± (+0.32). Black has a lead in development which offers partial compensation for the pawn) 7.d4 ♗b7 8.♕e2 ♖c8 (8...a6 9.0-0 ♗e7 transposes to the note to move 4) 9.0-0 ♗e7 10.♖e1 cxd4 11.cxd4 0-0 12.a3 a6 13.♘c3 ♘b6 14.♗d3± (+0.14). White's pawn duo on the fourth rank vs Black's on the third rank is his advantage;

B) 5...g6 6.♗c2 ♗g7 7.d4 0-0 (so far Nepomniachtchi vs Giri, Zagreb 2019) 8.a4 cxd4 9.cxd4 e5 10.d5 ♘c5 11.♘c3± (+0.24). It looks like some lines of the King's Indian. Black may play ...a7-a5 to prevent White from doing so, but then b5 and c4 are good squares for white knights.

6.♗e2 ♘xf3+

6...♘g6 7.♕c2 e6 8.d4 ♗d7 9.h4 h5 10.♗d3± (+0.26). White has ideas of e4-e5 and ♗xg6, or just ♗g5, and has the favorable fourth rank vs third rank center duo.

7.♗xf3 e5 8.d4 ♗e7

9.dxe5!

9.0-0 0-0 10.♗e3 b6 11.♘d2 ♕c7 12.♖e1 ♗d7 13.a4 a6 was the previous game between the same players, when 14.♗e2 would have preserved a small plus. White played 14.b4 and ultimately lost.

9...dxe5 10.♕xd8+ ♗xd8 11.♘d2 ♗e6

12.♗e2±

White's advantage (+0.30) is modest but clear. He has good advanced squares to use (c4, d5, d6) while Black does not.

12...♗c7 13.f3 ♔e7 14.a4

14.♘f1 ♖hd8 15.♘e3± (+0.34). White would like to play a2-a4 and ♗c4.

14...h5

15.h4

Perhaps unnecessary.

15.♘c4± (+0.60). White can proceed with ♗e3 and a4-a5 or ♗g5 and ♘e3.

15...♖hd8 16.♘c4 ♘e8 17.♗e3 b6 18.♗f2

18.g3± (+0.42). White plans ♔f2 and f3-f4, or b2-b4, or g2-g4.

18...f6 19.0-0

19.g4 hxg4 20.fxg4± (+0.40). Next g4-g5.

19...g6 20.♖fc1 ♘d6 21.♘e3 f5 22.♘d5+ ♗xd5 23.exd5 c4 24.♗e3

24.♖ab1=.

24...♔d7?!

24...♔f7=.

25.♖ab1 ♖f8 26.b3 f4 27.♗f2 e4 28.fxe4 ♖ae8?

28...♘xe4 29.♗xc4 ♘xf2 30.♗b5+ ♔d6 31.♔xf2±.

29.bxc4 ♘xe4 30.c5+− ♘xc3 31.♖xc3 ♖xe2 32.d6 ♗d8 33.c6+ ♔c8 34.a5 ♖xf2 35.♔xf2 ♖f5 36.c7 ♗xh4+ 37.♔f3 ♖d5 38.axb6 1-0

Game 8.17 Sicilian Defense – Moscow

Awonder Liang   2589

Pere Garriga Cazorla   2448

Sitges 2018 (8)

1.e4 c5 2.♘f3 d6 3.♗b5+ ♘d7 4.♗a4

White wants to play the Maroczy Bind with c2-c4, but if he plays it directly Black won't play ...a7-a6, leaving the bishop stranded on b5. If Black refuses to play ...a7-a6 White will probably choose c2-c3 after castling rather than c2-c4. I think that 4.♗a4 is probably better than 4.c3 and also has more surprise value.

4...♘gf6 5.0-0!

5...a6

A) 5...♘xe4 6.♖e1 ♘ef6 7.d4 cxd4 8.♘xd4 e6 9.♘b5± (+0.30). White regains the pawn favorably;

B) 5...e5 6.c3! ♗e7 7.♖e1 0-0 8.d4 ♕c7 9.dxe5 ♘xe5 10.♘xe5 dxe5 11.c4 ♗e6 12.♕e2 h6. Vachier-Lagrave vs Topalov, Riga 2019, was agreed drawn here, in a game that Black needed to win. After 13.♘c3 (+0.70) White is much better as he can play ♘d5 whenever he wishes. The players obviously agreed with this assessment;

C) 5...g6 is the best set-up vs the Maroczy Bind, but here White can switch to the c2-c3, d2-d4 plan which makes the bishop on g7 look a bit misplaced: 6.♖e1 ♗g7 7.c3 0-0 8.d4 e5 9.dxe5 ♘xe5 10.♘xe5 dxe5

11.c4± (+0.16). White's pieces are better placed for this symmetrical pawn structure;

D) 5...e6 6.♖e1:

analysis diagram

D1) 6...♗e7 7.c3 (strategically c2-c3 is more suitable against ...g7-g6, and c2-c4 against ...e7-e6, but Black's delay in playing ...a7-a6 makes c2-c3 work well here. 7.d4?! cxd4 8.♕xd4 0-0 9.c4 ♕c7 (-0.04). White cannot avoid making some concession here. Strategically this is ideal for White, but he has tactical problems) 7...0-0 8.d4 cxd4 9.cxd4 a6 10.♗c2 b5 11.♘bd2 ♗b7 12.♘f1± (+0.34). Black has nothing to offset White's space advantage;

D2) I think 6...a6 is Black's best line against 4.♗a4, as it forces White to commit to c2-c3 or c2-c4, when c2-c3 is not so good due to ...b7-b5 and ...c5-c4: 7.c4 ♗e7 8.d4 cxd4 9.♘xd4 0-0 10.♗c2 ♕c7 11.b3 b6 12.♗b2 (White would prefer the set-up ♘c3, f2-f3 or h2-h3, and ♗e3, but ♘c3 now is met by ...b7-b5) 12...♗b7 13.♘c3 ♖fe8 14.♕d2 ♗f8 15.♖ad1 (+0.10). White has a Maroczy Bind vs Hedgehog set-up, which is just a tad better for White.

The bishop on b2 would probably be better on e3 (with f2-f3 played). This seems to be the only drawback of 4.♗a4.

6.c4!

The discovery that White can profitably gambit the e4-pawn on both this and the previous move is what makes 4.♗a4 a good move.

6...g6

A) 6...♘xe4?! 7.♖e1 ♘ef6 8.d4 cxd4 9.♘xd4 e6 10.♘c3 (the direct rook sacrifice 10.♖xe6+ favors White, but the sacrifice a move later is a simpler path to an advantage: 10...fxe6 11.♘xe6± ♕b6 12.♗e3 ♕a5 13.♗d2 ♕f5 14.♘c7+ ♔f7 15.♘xa8 d5 16.♗c2 ♕e5 17.cxd5 ♕b8 18.d6 ♗xd6 19.♗b3+ ♔f8 20.♗e3 ♗xh2+ 21.♔h1 ♗e5 22.♘c3±) 10...♗e7 11.♖xe6 fxe6 (11...0-0 12.♖e1±) 12.♘xe6 ♕a5 13.♗d2 and White is clearly better;

B) 6...e6 7.♘c3 ♗e7 8.d4 cxd4 9.♘xd4 ♕c7 10.♕e2N 0-0 11.♔h1 ♘b6 12.♗b3 ♗d7 13.♘c2 ♖ac8 14.♘e3 ♗c6 15.f3 ♖fe8 16.♗d2 ♘bd7 17.♖ad1 ♗f8 18.♗e1± (+0.22). White has achieved a good version of the Maroczy Bind.

7.♘c3 ♗g7 8.d3 0-0 9.h3 ♘e8

A) 9...罝b8 10.奧e3 營a5 11.奧d2 營c7
12.罝b1 (+0.13). White plans b2-b4
with space and initiative;

B) 9...b6 10.罝b1 奧b7 11.奧e3 e6
12.b4 營c7 13.營d2± (+0.23). White
has space and queenside play.

10.奧e3

10.d4 ᗺc7 11.奧xd7 (11.奧e3! ᗺe6
(11...cxd4 12.奧xd4 ᗺe6 13.奧xg7
含xg7 14.奧xd7 奧xd7 15.ᗺd5±
(+0.34). White has a good Maroczy
Bind, a nice space advantage) 12.d5
ᗺc7 13.奧xd7 奧xd7 14.e5 ᗺe8
15.奧f4 b5 16.b3± (+0.36). White
has a huge space and development
advantage for the bishop pair) 11...
cxd4 12.奧xc8 dxc3 13.奧xb7 罝b8
14.bxc3 罝xb7 15.奧e3= ½–½ (43)
Nakamura-Vachier-Lagrave, Zagreb
2019.

10...ᗺc7 11.d4 ᗺe6

12.營d2

12.奧b3! is probably better to avoid
the next note, e.g. 12...營b6 13.ᗺd5
營d8 14.罝e1 b5 15.a3 奧b7 16.罝c1±
(+0.12). White has a modest space
advantage.

12...cxd4 13.ᗺxd4 ᗺe5

13...營b6! 14.奧b3 a5 15.ᗺdb5
奧d7 16.ᗺa3 罝c8 17.f4 a4 18.f5
axb3 19.fxe6 奧xe6 20.axb3 ᗺd7

21.ᗺab5 (+0.08). White's damaged
pawn structure offsets his space
advantage.

14.奧b3

14.b3! (+0.55) is a hard move to
make as a human, since the bishop
on a4 looks vulnerable.

But the computer insists that there
is no way to exploit this, and White
can avoid doubled pawns on b3 this
way.

**14...ᗺc6 15.ᗺxe6 奧xe6 16.ᗺd5
奧xd5 17.cxd5**

17.exd5 also gives White a slight
pull.

**17...ᗺa5 18.罝fc1 ᗺxb3 19.axb3 營d7
20.罝c4 罝fc8 21.罝ac1 罝xc4**

22.罝xc4

22.bxc4 a5 23.罝a1± (+0.22). White
is for choice but it's hard to make
progress.

22...罝c8?!

Not a good move as it leads to
White's much improved pawn
structure.

22...f5 23.奧d4 奧xd4 24.罝xd4 fxe4
25.罝xe4 罝f8± (+0.26). White's
pressure on e7 and space gives him
a plus, but it looks manageable for
Black.

23.營c2 罝xc4 24.bxc4 營c7

24...e6 25.b4 exd5 26.exd5 ♗e5± (+0.38). White's space advantage is not as crushing as in the game.
25.b4 h5 26.c5 dxc5 27.bxc5 ♕a5
27...♗e5 28.♕d2± (+0.74). White's powerful center is a near-decisive advantage.
28.g3+− ♗e5 29.♕b3 ♕b5 30.♕xb5 axb5 31.♗f4 ♗xf4 32.gxf4 ♔f8 33.♔f1 f6 34.♔e2 e5 35.fxe5 fxe5 36.♔d2 g5 37.♔c3 h4 38.f3 1-0

Game 8.18 Sicilian Defence – Moscow
Andreas Heimann 2578
Radoslaw Wojtaszek 2737
Germany Bundesliga 2017/18 (2)

1.e4 c5 2.♘f3 d6 3.♗b5+ ♘d7 4.d4
This may be objectively the best line, although probably it is a bit harder to play than the moves in the previous two games.
4...cxd4 5.♕xd4

5...a6
A) 5...♘gf6 6.♗g5 a6 7.♗xd7+ ♘xd7 8.♘c3 h6 9.♗h4 e5 10.♕e3 g5 11.♗g3 h5 12.h3± (+0.22). White's king is safer than Black's;
B) 5...e5 6.♕e3 ♘gf6 7.0-0 ♗e7 8.♗d3N 0-0 9.c4 ♘c5 10.♘c3± (+0.18). White has a good Maroczy

Bind. The move ...e7-e5 is generally not helpful for Black in the Maroczy with his bishop on e7.
6.♗e2
This formerly rare move is catching on and scoring well. Normal was to surrender the bishop pair by 6.♗xd7+, but that looks pretty equal.
6...♘gf6
6...e5 7.♕e3 ♘gf6 8.c4 ♗e7 9.♘c3 0-0 10.0-0 b6 11.♖b1 ♘c5 12.b4 ♘e6 13.♖d1 ♗d7 14.♕d3± (+0.55). White has a good Maroczy, with a queenside initiative already underway and the hole on d5.
7.0-0
7.c4 is popular and sensible, but 7...g6 is hard to punish.

7...e5
7...g6 8.♘c3 ♗g7 9.♖d1 0-0 (9...♕c7 10.a4 0-0 11.a5 ♖e8 12.♕b4 ♖b8 13.♗e3 b6 14.axb6 ♘xb6 15.♕a5± (+0.13). White has better piece activity and a better pawn structure) 10.e5 ♘h5 11.♕h4 dxe5 12.♗g5 f6 13.♗e3 e6 14.♖d6 ♘f4 15.♗xf4 exf4 16.♖ad1± (+0.98). White will regain his pawn with a huge lead in development.
8.♕e3 ♘c5

9.♘c3

9.♘fd2! (White wants the Maroczy Bind. This rare move is a good one) 9...♗e7 10.c4 0-0

analysis diagram

11.♘c3!N (11.h3? b5!) 11...♗d7 12.h3 h6 13.b4 ♘e6 14.♘b3 ♘f4 15.♖d1 ♖c8 16.♗f1 ♗e6 17.♕f3 ♘g6 18.c5 ♕c7 19.♗e3 ♖fd8 20.♖ac1 dxc5 21.♘xc5± (+0.40). White wins the bishop pair for free.

9...♗e7

9...♘g4 10.♕d2 ♘f6 11.♖d1N ♗e7 12.♕e1 ♕c7 13.♘d2 0-0 14.a4 ♗d7 15.a5 ♗c6 16.♗f3 ♘e6 17.♘b3±

(+0.28). Black has holes on b6 and d5 while White's hole on d4 is under his control. White plans ♗e3 and g2-g3.

10.b3

After this move it's hard for White to avoid the draw. Since Black was much higher rated here, White was probably happy with this result. 10.♖d1 ♗d7 (10...♘g4 11.♕d2 ♘f6 12.♕e1± transposes to note to 9...♗e7) 11.a4 0-0 12.♘d2 (if 12.b4 ♘e6 13.a5 ♖c8 14.♗f1 ♖e8 15.h3 ♕c7 16.♗d2 (+0.02) White has a bit more space, it's pretty even) 12...♗c6 13.a5 d5 14.exd5 ♘xd5 15.♘xd5 ♕xd5 16.♗f3 ♕e6 17.b3 ♗xf3 18.♕xf3 e4 19.♕e2 f5 20.♗a3 (0.00). It's virtually equal, but I would choose White if forced to choose; he does have the idea of ♘d2-c4-b6.

10...♘g4 11.♕d2 ♘f6 12.♕e3 ♘g4 13.♕d2 ♘f6 14.♕e3 ♘g4 15.♕d2 ♘f6 ½-½

Index of variations (White)

1.e4 – Less common Black first moves

1.e4 c6 – Caro-Kann

1.e4 e6 2.d4 d5 3.♘d2 – French Tarrasch

1.e4 e5 2.♘f3 – Petroff, Philidor, and Black gambits

1.e4 e5 2.♘f3 ♘c6 3.♗c4 – Italian Game

1.e4 e5 2.♘f3 ♘c6 3.♗b5 – Spanish (Ruy Lopez)

1.e4 c5 2.♘c3 – Sicilian Defense

1.e4 c5 2.♘f3 – Sicilian Defense

Index of names (White)

(numbers refer to pages)

Part II – Black repertoire

Defenses of the Superstars

In KRBW I recommended meeting 1.e4 with 1...e5, aiming for the Breyer Defense to the Spanish Opening, and meeting 1.d4 with the Grünfeld Defense. In the present volume I have kept those choices, except that I now give the Marshall Attack as my preferred defense to 1.e4, keeping the Breyer as a reserve or for those who just don't like to gambit pawns or those who won't play a defense that allows forced draws. The Breyer was Magnus Carlsen's favorite shortly before KRBW was published, but after that both he and frequent World number 2 Aronian usually aimed for the Marshall Attack (until Carlsen took up the Sveshnikov Sicilian in 2018). The Breyer keeps all the pieces on the board, concedes very little to White (just a slight central advantage of pawns on d4 and e4 vs d6 and e5), and is in good shape theoretically, but it cannot be denied that even though it may be the best defense on move 9, White still has the better chances. The database statistics show that White's results are quite a bit better than Black's in all lines after 9.h3, even the Breyer, but are much less convincing against the Marshall. Regardless of whether White allows the Marshall or avoids it on move 8, his statistical edge is well below par after 7...0-0. I also added a chapter on the Møller Defense, which seems to be ideal except in one line. Against earlier deviations in the Spanish and against non-Spanish lines, I have mostly stuck to KRBW lines, with many theory updates of course. The other satisfactory option for Black, as given in my first book, is the Berlin, but playing for a slightly worse but drawn endgame is not to everyone's liking.

Against 1.d4, I stayed with the Grünfeld, a favorite of two of the world's top five players, Caruana and Vachier-Lagrave. I considered the Semi-Slav, but there are some problems in the 5.♗g5 lines and also a big problem of reaching the Semi-Slav without allowing unpleasant options like the Catalan or the Slav Exchange. The QGD is the safest choice, but like the Breyer it leaves White with at least somewhat the better chances in general. The Grünfeld is in good shape, and it seems that finding an advantage against it is an extremely challenging task, although Carlsen has been quite successful as White playing the Exchange Variation with ♗e3.

I was pleasantly surprised to learn while working on KRBW that the English Opening, 1.c4, is not much of a problem for the Grünfeld player, contrary to my opinion years earlier. I show how the move 1...g6! either transposes to the Grünfeld or leads to near-equality in all cases.

As for 1.♘f3, we can play the Grünfeld anyway, covered in the Anti-Grünfeld chapter, but in this volume my recommendation is to play the Symmetrical English with 3...d5, which avoids committing to ...g7-g6 prematurely. Black has to walk a narrow path to reach near-equality, but he does achieve the goal with the given lines. Most of the elite Grünfeld players now meet 1.♘f3 this way. In the Réti chapter I give some alternatives for Black. So my overall conclusion is that the Grünfeld does not have major move-order problems.

Many players are reluctant to meet 1.e4 with 1...e5 because there are so many ways White can vary before we get to play our own line (in this case the Marshall, on move 8 of the Spanish). This is true, but almost all of them are inferior. In fact I would say that only the Italian, the Anti-Marshall 8.a4, and the Spanish with 6.d3 lead to positions (with best play) where White is clearly for choice, and just marginally so. Quite a few of the white options that I actually face in tournaments fail even to equalize the game. When people try to take me out of book early, I am usually quite content! In this book I don't take the attitude that Black is always happy with a draw; once White makes one or two second-rate moves I start to look for a black advantage.

In updating this Black portion of the book, I made substantial use of Lc0 running on my powerful 2080 GPU, together with Komodo 13 MCTS; quoted evals such as (+0.26) are Komodo unless otherwise stated +0.27. Lc0 tends to love space, and so most mainline openings tend to show rather significant white advantages since White can almost always achieve at least a space advantage if all else fails. This made the task of showing near-equality for Black much more difficult with this update, and the reader will note that in some cases I had to recommend something other than what was the main line in the first edition. Although Lc0 is certainly too optimistic for White in general, I cannot deny that it has convinced me that White's advantage after 1.e4, 1.d4, or 1.♘f3 is larger than I had previously believed; we just have to accept that no matter what we play as Black, 'White is slightly better' is an outcome we cannot avoid if White knows everything. Grandmaster Adorjan has made a career out of writing *Black is OK* books, in which he generally argues that with the right choices of defenses Black should have roughly equal chances. I have to disagree with him on this, although he is correct in the sense that Black need not lose just because he moves second. But I think that you will find that if you know the lines in this book well enough, most opponents you face won't get any noticeable edge with white, and even when they do you should still generally be able to hold the draw with careful play or even to aim for a win if you are the stronger player that day.

CHAPTER 9

Unusual opening moves

In this chapter we'll cover less common but still moderately popular White first moves not covered elsewhere in this book. I leave out 1.g3, which after 1...g6 is extremely likely to transpose to the Neo-Grünfeld or English chapters, and also the opening 1.♘c3, which is also likely to transpose elsewhere after 1...♘f6, for example 2.e4 e5 is the Vienna, while 2.d4 d5 is the Veresov.

First we consider the Sokolsky Opening (a.k.a. Orangutan or Polish), **1.b4**.

Black can easily equalize in many ways, such as 1...d5 2.♗b2 ♗g4, but I recommend in Game 9.1 playing for the advantage with the pawn exchange **1...e5 2.♗b2 ♗xb4 3.♗xe5 ♘f6**. Black ends up two tempi ahead, which easily trumps the slight profit White made from the pawn exchange. Simply put, if three tempi equal a pawn, surely two are worth more than the modest difference in value between these pawns. The important point to remember is not to play ...♘c6 until after ...0-0, ...d7-d5, and ...c7-c5. Black's ultimate aim is ...d5-d4. Black is already a tad better (+12 Elo) in the Hiarcs Powerbook after 3...♘f6, and Lc0 really likes Black here.

Next we come to the similar but far more respectable Larsen's Opening, **1.b3**. Aside from the late great Danish grandmaster (whom I played three times, getting one draw), this was also played by Bobby Fischer and recently by the American star Hikaru Nakamura, who especially likes to play it in blitz chess, as well as by elite GMs Artemiev, Jobava, and Rapport. Its main drawback is that the knight on b1 becomes a problem piece, as its natural development to c3 blocks the bishop. For this reason, 1.b3 is an excellent first move when giving knight odds!

In normal chess, Black can equalize by playing a reverse Queen's Indian with 1...d5 2.♗b2 c5 3.e3 a6 4.♘f3 ♘c6, but I prefer to try for a small advantage by **1...e5 2.♗b2 ♘c6 3.e3 ♘f6 4.♗b5 ♗d6**, as recommended in *Chess Advantage*, but I now recommend answering the usual (but strange-looking) **5.♘a3** by the equally strange-looking **5...♘a5**. Black's main plan is ...0-0, ...♖e8, and ...♗f8, or in the 5...♘a5 line ...c7-c6, ...♗c7, and ...d7-d5. Black can also meet 5.♘a3 by 5..e4 as I show in the notes. In the Hiarcs Powerbook Black is +15 Elo after 4...♗d6, but the alternative line 4.c4 d5 5.cxd5 ♘xd5 does keep a token +7 Elo for White. See Game 9.2.

Finally we look at Bird's Opening, **1.f4**, which could also be called a reversed Dutch.

If White aims for a Leningrad by **1...♘f6 2.♘f3 d5 3.g3** I recommend the rare **3...c6 4.♗g2 ♕b6!** to provoke the undesirable move e2-e3, which permits ...♗g4. Black aims to clear all the minor pieces off except his knight and one white bishop, on the grounds that knights are better than unpaired bishops on a crowded board. If White goes for a normal Dutch with **3.e3** we pin immediately, with ideas of ...♘d7, ...♗xf3, and ...e7-e5. All this is covered in Game 9.3. Komodo rates the position dead even after 5...♕b6, and the stats (few games though) are also about even. All in all, I prefer Black's chances by a smidgeon after 1.f4.

Game 9.1 Various Openings – Sokolsky
Richard Bitoon
Wesley So   2577
Manila 2008 (6)

1.b4

The Orangutan or Polish or Sokolsky Opening. It is quite a weak opening in my opinion; White can't even equalize.

1....e5

My second choice would be 1...d5 2.♗b2 ♗g4. Such an early bishop development is logical when White can no longer attack the b7-pawn by ♕b3.

But I still prefer the game move, as I did in *Chess Advantage*.

2.♗b2 ♗xb4 3.♗xe5

If White plays 3.f4 d6 4.fxe5 dxe5 5.♗xe5 ♘f6 6.♘f3 0-0 7.e3 ♘c6 8.♗b2 ♖e8 9.♗e2 ♖xe3N 10.c3 ♖xf3 11.♗xf3 ♗d6 12.0-0 ♘e5 13.d4 ♘eg4, White must play 14.g3, when the knight fork will leave Black a pawn up with the better position as well.

3....♘f6 4.c4

4.♘f3 0-0 5.e3 d5 6.♗e2 c5 7.0-0 ♘c6 8.♗b2 ♗a5!N, planning ...d5-d4, is better than the immediate 8...

d4 given in *Chess Advantage*, which is answered by 9.c3.

4....0-0 5.♘f3 d5 6.e3 ♖e8 7.a3 ♗a5 8.♗e2 c5 9.cxd5 ♘xd5 10.0-0 ♘c6 11.♗g3

11.♗b2 ♗f5 12.♕b3 a6!.

11....♕f6N

The **actual game** continued 11...♗e6 12.♗h4 f6? (12...♕d7!) 13.♕c2= ♖c8 14.♗d3 h6 15.♘c3 ♔h8 16.♗g6 ♖e7 17.♗g3 ♗c7 18.♖fc1 ♗xg3 19.hxg3 ♘xc3 20.♕xc3 b6 21.♗b1 ♖d7 22.♕c2 ♗g8 23.♕g6 ♖d6 24.♕g4 ♖c7 25.♗f5 ♘e5 26.♘xe5 fxe5 27.d3 ♕f6 28.♗e4 ♗e6 29.♕h5 ♗f7 30.♕g4 ♖cd7 31.♖c3 ♗e6 32.♕g6? ♕xg6 33.♗xg6 ♗g4 34.♗e4 ♗e2 (Black wins a pawn) 35.♗f5 ♖d8 36.a4 g6 37.♗e4 ♗xd3 38.♗xd3 ♖xd3 39.♖cc1 a5 40.♖ab1 ♖8d6 41.♔h2 ♖f6 42.♖b2 g5 43.g4 ♔g7 44.♖c4 ♖fd6 45.♔g3 ♖d2 46.♖cc2 ♖xc2 47.♖xc2 e4 48.♖c4 ♖e6 49.♖c3 ♔f6 50.f4 gxf4+ 51.♔xf4 ♔e7 52.g5 hxg5+ 53.♔xg5 ♔d6 54.♔f5 ♖e5+ 55.♔f6 ♖d5 56.♖c2 ♖d3 57.♖e2 c4 58.g4 c3 59.g5 ♖d2 and White resigned.

12.♖a2 ♗c7 13.♗xc7 ♘xc7 14.♘c3 ♗f5 15.♖a1 ♖ad8 16.♖c1 ♘e5 17.♘xe5 ♕xe5

White has more center pawns, but they are under pressure and Black has far superior piece activity.

Game 9.2 Various Openings – Larsen
Vladimir Kostic   2440
Philipp Schlosser   2567
Austria Bundesliga 2010/11 (9)

1.b3
Larsen's Opening.
1....e5 2.♗b2 ♘c6 3.e3
Or 3.c4 ♘f6 4.e3 d5 5.cxd5 ♘xd5 6.a3 ♗d6.

analysis diagram

White is playing the Kan Sicilian with colors reversed, but having played b2-b3 rather than b2-b4 is a concession. 7.♕c2 (7.b4 would transpose directly to a main line of the Kan with reversed colors, where White has wasted his initial

extra move by playing b3-b4 in two turns. Therefore Black has the normal white advantage in this opening) 7...0-0 8.♘f3 ♕e7 9.d3 f5 10.♘bd2 ♔h8 11.♗e2 ♗d7 12.0-0 ♖ae8. Black is +12 Elo in HPB and Komodo rates it dead even. The move b3-b4 on any of the last several moves would still be the Kan with reversed colors and no extra tempo for White. Refraining from b3-b4 doesn't change much. Black is fine.
3....♘f6 4.♗b5 ♗d6

I really like this move here. It answers the threat against e5, and envisions castling, ...♖e8, and ...♗f8. In case of ♗xc6 at any time, after ...dxc6 the bishop will no longer be blocking a pawn and will be well-placed on d6.
5.♘a3
  A) In case of 5.♗xc6 dxc6 6.d3 0-0 7.♘d2 ♖e8 8.e4 (so far Nakamura-Ponomariov, St Louis 2011) 8...a5!N 9.a4 ♗g4 10.♘gf3 ♗b4 11.h3 ♗h5 I prefer Black thanks to the bishop pair and the two pins;
  B) 5.♘e2 0-0 6.0-0 ♖e8 (I think it's useful for Black to delay ...a7-a6 so that ♘a3 can still be met by

...♘a5) 7.♘g3 a6 8.♗e2 ♗f8 (this is typical of this system. The bishop avoids blocking pawn, rook, or queen, and defends the king) 9.f4 d5 10.fxe5 ♘xe5 11.♕e1 ♗d6!N 12.♘f5 ♗xf5 13.♖xf5 c5 14.♕f1 d4! 15.exd4 ♘eg4 16.g3 (after 16.h3 ♗h2+ 17.♔h1 ♗c7 18.♗xg4 ♕d6 Black wins) 16...cxd4 – Black's superior development and much safer king give him the edge despite White's two bishops.

5....♘a5

I called this 'too weird' in *Chess Advantage*, but I've changed my opinion. It cancels the threat of ♘c4 and prepares ...c7-c6. The fact that Nakamura against Ponomariov refrained from 5.♘a3 in favor of 5.♗xc6 followed by 6.d3 and 7. ♘d2 suggests that he feared 5.♘a3 ♘a5. But also good is 5...e4 6.♘c4 ♗e7 7.♗xc6 bxc6 8.♗e2 0-0 9.0-0 a5 10.d3 a4 11.♘g3 d5 12.♘e5 ♕e8 (-0.22) due to the bishop pair.

6.♘f3

In case of 6.♘c4 ♘xc4 7.♗xc4 0-0 8.♘e2 c6 9.♘g3 ♗c7 10.0-0 d5 11.♗e2 ♖e8 12.c4 a5 13.a3 ♗e6 Black has a nice pawn center without suffering too much pressure against it.

Or 6.♗e2 (now the main line) 6... a6 7.c4 0-0 8.♘c2 ♖e8 9.d3 (9.g4?! b5 (-0.52)) 9...b5 10.♘f3 (Granda Zuniga-Almagro Llamas, Linares 2017) and now 10...c5 11.0-0 ♖b8 12.♖b1 ♗c7 is a bit more pleasant for Black (-0.06).

6....♕e7 7.♘c4

Or 7.♕c1 0-0 8.♗e2 c5 9.d3 ♘c6 10.♘b5 ♗b8 11.c4 d5 12.cxd5N ♘xd5 13.0-0 ♗e6 – Black is playing the Maroczy Bind against the Scheveningen Sicilian, with colors reversed. In general the Bind is effective in this situation, more so than against the Dragon set-up.

7....♘xc4 8.♗xc4 0-0

9.♘h4?!

In the event of 9.0-0 c6 10.♗e2 ♗c7 11.c4 d5 12.♕c2 ♖e8, Black is already better here (-0.34), with more space and ideas like ...e5-e4.

9....g6 10.♕f3 c6 11.♕g3 ♘h5 12.♕h3 ♘g7 13.g4?! ♗a3 14.♗xa3 ♕xa3 15.e4 ♖d8

Black already has a likely winning advantage. He has the center, while White's pieces are randomly scattered.

16.♕f3 ♕e7 17.♘g2 d5 18.exd5 e4 19.♕g3 cxd5 20.♗e2

20....d4

20...b6!N 21.0-0 ♗b7 22.♖fe1 ♖ac8 23.c3 d4 looks even stronger.

21.0-0 b6 22.♖fe1 ♗b7 23.♗c4

23.♗d3! ♕c5 24.♗xe4 ♗xe4 25.♖xe4 ♕xc2 favors Black only slightly.

23....♕c5

23...♕d7! 24.a4 a6 was better.

24.♕f4? ♘e6 25.♗xe6 fxe6 26.c3?! e5

26...e3! 27.fxe3 dxc3 28.♖f1 ♖f8 29.♕d4 ♕c6 30.e4 cxd2 31.♕xd2 ♕xe4 wins a clean pawn.

27.♕g3?! ♖ac8 28.b4 ♕d5 29.cxd4 exd4 30.♘f4 ♕d6

31.♘h5??

White resigned after making this blunder (Black can just take the knight), but his position is probably lost anyway.

Game 9.3 Various Openings – Bird

Henrik Danielsen	2545
Pablo Lafuente	2555

Odense 2011 (7)

1.f4

Bird's Opening, a reversed Dutch once Black plays ...d7-d5. In my opinion it's strictly 'for the birds'.

1....♘f6 2.♘f3 d5

3.g3

White seeks a Leningrad reversed. If 3.e3 ♗g4 4.♗e2 ♘bd7 and now:

analysis diagram

A) 5.d4 e6 6.0-0 c5 7.♘c3 ♗d6 8.a4 0-0 9.h3 ♗xf3 10.♗xf3 a6 – although White has the bishops, his set-up calls for ♘e5, which is impossible. Black has the initiative on the queenside and the right bishop;

B) 5.b3 ♗xf3 6.♗xf3 e5 7.fxe5
♘xe5 8.♗b2 ♗d6 9.0-0 0-0 10.♘c3
c6 11.♘e2 ♕e7 12.♘d4 g6 – White's
king is weakened, e4 may be a
home for a knight, and Black will
regain the bishop pair since 13.♗e2
is too passive;

C) 5.0-0 ♗xf3 (5...c6 may be
better) 6.♗xf3 e5 7.d4 e4 8.♗e2
♗d6. In such a very closed position
Black's good bishop plus knight
may be nearly equal to White's two
bishops, and Black has more space.

3....c6

This is rare but strong. Black takes
advantage of the fact that the
pawn has not yet advanced to c5,
as it might have already advanced
to c4 if we were White against a
Leningrad Dutch.

4.♗g2 ♕b6

I like this idea. It forces White to
play e2-e3 soon in order to castle,
which allows the pin ...♗g4. The
point is that the move f2-f4 makes
the ♘f3 an important piece worth
exchanging off.

5.b3

5.e3 ♗g4 6.b3 ♘bd7 (6...g6N 7.♗b2
♗g7 transposes to the game) 7.♗b2
e6 8.h3 ♗xf3 9.♕xf3 a5 10.a4 ♗b4=.

5....g6

Instead 5...♗f5 is also satisfactory,
but I like the game move because
Black plans to give up the bishop
pair with ...♗g4 and ...♗xf3, so he
will want to exchange bishops on
the long diagonal to kill White's
bishop pair.

6.♗b2 ♗g7 7.e3 ♗g4

More accurate is 7...0-0 8.0-0 ♗g4
9.h3 (9.♘c3 ♘e4 10.♘a4 ♕a5 favors
Black slightly. Note that this doesn't
work without castling first to
protect the bishop) 9...♗xf3 10.♕xf3
♘bd7, transposing to the game.
White can equalize by 9.♕e1 ♘bd7
with a zero score per Komodo.

8.h3

8.♘c3=.

8....♗xf3 9.♕xf3 ♘bd7 10.0-0 0-0

11.g4?!

11.♕e2 ♘h5 (or 11...e5! 12.fxe5 ♘h5)
12.♗xg7 ♘xg7 13.g4 f5 – in general
knights are superior to unpaired
bishops when the board is full of
pawns, so I slightly prefer Black.
Komodo say dead even, Lc0 loves
Black.

**11....♘e4 12.♗xg7 ♔xg7 13.d3 ♘d6
14.♘d2 f5**

14...a5N 15.a3 f5 is also good. Either way Black is already for choice.

15.d4 ♘f6

15...fxg4N 16.hxg4 e5 17.dxe5 ♘xe5 18.♕g3 ♘ef7 19.♖ae1 ♖ae8 favors Black due to the pressure on the backward e3-pawn.

16.c3

16....fxg4?!

16...c5!N 17.♖ac1 cxd4 18.exd4 e6 19.g5 ♘fe4 and Black's powerful knight outpost plus queenside play with ...a7-a5 and pressure on c3 give him a clear advantage.

17.hxg4 ♘de4 18.♘xe4 ♘xe4 19.♖fc1?!

19.♕h3! ♘xc3 20.♖f2 c5 21.♖c1 cxd4 22.exd4 ♘e4 23.♗xe4 dxe4 24.♖c5 ♖ad8 25.♕e3 ♕b4 26.♖c4 ♕d6 27.♕xe4 b5=.

19....e5 20.♖c2 exf4 21.exf4 ♕c7 22.♖f1 ♖ae8 23.♗h1?

In case of 23.c4 dxc4 24.bxc4 ♕d6 White has weak pawns all over the board.

23....♘g5 24.♕g3 ♖xf4

24...♘e6! is winning.

25.♖cf2 ♖ef8 26.♖xf4 ♖xf4 27.♔g2 ♖f7

27...♘e6! 28.♖e1 ♖f6 29.♕xc7+ ♘xc7 30.c4 ♖e6 and Black is a clean pawn up in the ending.

28.♖xf7 ♕xf7 29.♕e5+ ♕f6 30.♕c7+ ♔g8 31.♔g3 b5

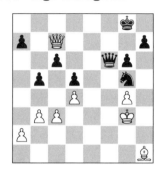

32.c4?

Passive play gives White drawing chances. Whoever said that a bad plan was better than no plan at all was wrong!

32....bxc4 33.bxc4 dxc4 34.♗xc6?! ♕xd4 35.♕b7 ♕e3+ 36.♔g2 ♕d2+ 37.♔f1 ♕d1+ 38.♔f2 ♕d2+ 39.♔f1 ♕f4+ 40.♔e1 ♕e3+ 41.♔d1 c3 42.♕d7 ♘f7 43.♔c2

43....♕d2+ 44.♕xd2 cxd2 45.♗f3 ♔g7 46.♔xd2 ♔f6 47.♔c3 ♘e5 48.♗e2 ♔g5 49.♔b4 ♘xg4

Black wins easily now.

50.♔a5 h5 51.♔a6 h4 52.♔xa7 h3 53.♗f3 ♔f4 54.♗b7 ♘f2 55.a4 ♘e4

White resigned.

CHAPTER 10

English Opening

I used to regard the English Opening (**1.c4**) as a major problem for a would-be Grünfeld player. The best move is supposed to be **1...e5**, but if I'm not keen to take on the Sicilian as White with 1.e4 how happy can I be playing against it a tempo down? The Symmetrical Defense **1...c5** is a serious option which is covered with the moves 2.♘f3 ♘f6 played in the Anti-Grünfeld chapter, while 2.♘c3 ♘c6 3.♘f3 g6 transposes to this chapter. Simply playing Grünfeld moves doesn't work as after 1.c4 ♘f6 2.♘c3 g6 3.e4 we are tricked into playing the King's Indian, while 2...d5 3.cxd5 ♘xd5 4.g3 g6 5.♗g2 is probably a bit favorable to White.

Over the past few years I have come to appreciate that **1.c4** is very well met by **1...g6!** if you hope to reach the Grünfeld.

The idea is this: Black meets ♘c3 by ...c7-c5, meets e2-e4 by ...e7-e5, and meets d2-d4 by ...♘f6. Let's look at some possible move-orders after 1.c4 g6:

If **2.d4 ♘f6** we are on track towards the Grünfeld.

If **2.♘c3 c5!** it's a rather good version of the Symmetrical Defense.

Now if **3.♘f3 ♗g7 4.d4 cxd4 5.♘xd4 ♘c6** White cannot play e2-e4 to get the Maroczy Bind. Or if **3.g3 ♗g7 4.♗g2 ♘c6 5.♘f3** Black need not play 5...♘f6?!; instead I recommend **5...d6**, planning ...♗f5 and ...♕d7. See Game 10.1.

If **2.♘f3 ♗g7 3.♘c3 c5!** as above, or **3.d4 ♘f6** (see Grünfeld), or **3.e4 e5! 4.d4 exd4 5.♘xd4 ♘f6 6.♘c3 0-0**, Black will benefit from the omission of ...d7-d6 (comparing to the King's Indian) by playing ...c7-c6 and ...d7-d5 in most lines. Alternatively Black can play **2...♘f6**, transposing to the anti-Grünfeld chapter.

If **2.e4 e5! 3.d4 ♘f6! 4.♘f3! exd4 5.e5 ♘e4** (new analysis in 2019 suggests that 5...♗b4+ is probably better and equal) **6.♕xd4 ♗b4+**

This line was not thought to be good for Black, but computer analysis suggested that Black was fully equal, though it no longer seems so. See Game 10.2.

For the Réti (**1.♘f3 ♘f6 2.g3 d5 3.♗g2 g6 4.c4 dxc4**) and the King's Indian Reversed (**4.0-0 ♗g7 5.d3 0-0 6.♘bd2 d4!?**) see Game 10.3.

Unfortunately this simple solution to the English problem does not work against 1.♘f3, because after 1...g6 White can play 2.e4!. However, after 1.♘f3 the Anti-Grünfeld (or 1...♘f6 2.c4 c5) is OK for Black. For alternative solutions to the 1.♘f3 move order, see the Réti chapter.

Game 10.1   English Opening
Zhou Jianchao   2668
Vladimir Malakhov   2732
Ningbo 2010 (14)

1.c4 c5
We would play 1...g6 and only play
...c7-c5 after ♘c3 or g2-g3 has been
played.
2.♘f3 g6 3.g3 ♗g7 4.♗g2 ♘c6

5.0-0
In the event of 5.♘c3 d6 6.d3 ♖b8
7.0-0 a6 8.a4 ♘f6, the insertion of
a2-a4 and ...a7-a6 favors Black due
to the holes on b4 and a5.
5....d6
I have played 5...♘h6 here, heading
towards d4, but I don't recommend
it as 6.h4! is rather strong.
6.♘c3 ♗f5
This system, played repeatedly by
Vladimir Malakhov, makes a lot of
sense. Black aims to exchange the
important bishop on g2.
6...♘h6 7.d4 cxd4 8.♗xh6 ♗xh6
9.♘xd4 seems to be a bit better for
White, so I have given up on the
...♘h6 idea.
7.d3
Or 7.b3 ♕d7 8.♗b2 e5 9.e3 ♗g4
10.d3 ♘ge7= (+0.07). The ...e7-e5

idea is effective against a bishop on
b2.
Should White play 7.h3 e5 8.a3
♘ge7 9.d3 0-0 10.♗d2 a5 equalizes
(+0.07).
**7....♕d7 8.♖b1 ♗h3 9.♗xh3 ♕xh3
10.♘d5 ♕d7 11.♕a4**
In G.Shahade-Kaufman, Crystal
City 2011, 11.♗d2 was played.
Now, after 11...♘f6 12.♘xf6+ ♗xf6
13.♗h6 ♕h3 14.♕d2 b6= (0.00)
Black's temporary inability to castle
is offset by the fact that the bishop
on h6 does not support any positive
plan for White.
**11....♖c8 12.a3 e6 13.♘e3 ♘ge7
14.b4 0-0 15.♗b2**

15.... ♗xb2
15...b6 directly was more precise, as
Black's king will be perfectly happy
on g7. Anyway, chances are even.
**16.♖xb2 b6 17.d4 cxd4 18.♘xd4
♖fd8 19.♘xc6 ♕xc6 20.♕xc6 ♘xc6
21.♖d1 ♔f8 22.f4 ♔e7 23.♔f2 ♖d7
24.♖d3 a5 25.bxa5 ♘xa5 26.♖xb6
♘xc4 27.♘xc4 ♖xc4= 28.♖db3?! ♖a4
29.♖6b4 ♖da7 30.♖xa4 ♖xa4 31.♔f3
h5 32.e3 ♔f6 33.h3 g5 34.e4?! h4**
With 34...gxf4! 35.gxf4 ♔g6 36.♖d3
f5 37.exf5+ ♔xf5 38.♖xd6 ♖xa3+
39.♔g2 ♖a4 Black wins a pawn,
though not necessarily the game.

35.gxh4 gxf4 36.♔xf4 ♔g6 37.♖b6 f5 38.♖xd6 ♖xe4+ 39.♔g3 ♔f6 40.♖d3 ♖a4 41.h5 ♔g5 42.h6 ♔xh6 43.♖d6 ♖e4 44.a4 ♔g5 45.h4+ ♔h5 46.a5 e5 47.a6 f4+ 48.♔f2 ♔g4 49.h5 ♔xh5 50.♖d5 ♖a4 51.♖xe5+ ♔g4 52.♖e2 ♖xa6 53.♖b2 ♖a3 54.♖c2 ♖h3 55.♔g2 f3+ 56.♔g1 ♔g3

57.♖g2+ fxg2
Stalemate.

Game 10.2   English Opening
Evgeny Tomashevsky   2701
Emil Sutovsky   2665
Plovdiv Ech 2010 (3)

1.c4 g6 2.e4
2.♘f3 ♗g7 3.e4 e5 transposes to the next note.
2....e5

3.d4

3.♘f3 ♗g7 4.d4 exd4 5.♘xd4 ♘f6 (5...♘c6 is also satisfactory) 6.♘c3 0-0 7.♗e2 ♖e8 8.f3 c6 (Black would transpose to a King's Indian line if he played ...d7-d6 now or on the next move. In that line Black often plays ...d6-d5, but here he plans to play it in one go, thus saving a vital tempo. Therefore this line should be fine for Black) 9.♗g5 ♕b6 10.♘b3 d5 11.cxd5 cxd5=.

3....♘f6! 4.♘f3
4.dxe5 ♘xe4 5.♗d3 ♘c5 6.♘f3 d6 7.♗e2 ♗g7= is fine for Black.

4....exd4 5.e5 ♘e4
Another option is 5...♗b4+! 6.♗d2 ♕e7 7.♗xb4 ♕xb4+ 8.♕d2 ♕xd2+ 9.♘bxd2 ♘h5 10.♘xd4 ♘c6 11.♘2f3 b6 (+0.03). Because of the new discovery in the 7.♔d1 line below, I now recommend this check for Black instead of the game move.
6.♕xd4 ♗b4+

7.♘bd2
A) 7.♘c3 ♘xc3 8.bxc3 ♘c6 9.♕d3 (9.♕e3 ♗e7=) 9...♗e7 10.♗h6 ♗f8 11.♗g5 ♗e7 leads to a draw by repetition. Black can avoid this by 9...♗a5!? 10.♗h6 ♕e7 11.♗e2 ♘xe5 with balanced chances if he wants a real fight.

B) 7.♔d1! f5 8.exf6 ♘xf6 9.♗h6!
(9.♗g5 0-0 or 9.♕h4 ♘c6 10.♗g5
0-0 11.♔c2 ♗e7! 12.♘c3 ♘h5
13.♗xe7 ♘xe7= (0.00)) 9...♘c6
10.♕e3+ ♔f7 11.c5 d5 12.cxd6 cxd6
13.a3!N ♗a5 14.♘g5+ ♔g8 15.♘c3
♘e5 (+0.40).

7....♘g5

7...♘xd2 8.♗xd2 ♘c6 9.♕e3 (or
9.♕f4 ♗xd2+) 9...♗xd2+ is also
about equal.

8.♗e2 ♘c6 9.♕e3

9.♕f4 ♘e6 10.♕g3 ♗g7=.

9....♘xf3+ 10.♗xf3

10....0-0N

The **actual game** continued
10...♕e7 11.♗xc6 dxc6 12.0-0 0-0
13.a3 ♗c5 14.♕g3 with a modest
white advantage, though Black
still drew. Castling is a computer
improvement.

11.0-0 ♖e8 12.♗xc6

12.♗d5! d6 13.♘e4 ♖xe5 14.♕f4 ♗e6
(+0.09).

dxc6 13.h3

13.♘f3 ♗g4=.

13....♗f5

In this position, Black's bishop pair
more than offsets his crippled pawn
majority.

Game 10.3   Réti Opening
Tomasz Markowski   2603
Oleg Romanishin   2537
Moscow 2004 (6)

1.g3 d5 2.♘f3 ♘f6

We would be more likely to reach
this position by 1.♘f3 ♘f6 2.g3 d5.

3.♗g2 g6

Black is aiming to transpose to the
Neo-Grünfeld lines in this book.
He will take any time White plays
c2-c4, unless a pawn can recapture.

4.c4

4.0-0 ♗g7 5.d3 (the King's Indian
Reversed) 5...0-0 6.♘bd2 d4 – I like
this rare move here. Black will take
e2-e4 or c2-c4 en passant.

analysis diagram

After 7.♘b3 (7.e4 dxe3 8.fxe3 c5
9.♕e2 ♘c6 10.♘b3 ♕b6 and Black's
position is more pleasant; 7.♘c4
♘d5 8.e4 dxe3 9.fxe3 c5 10.e4
♘b6=) 7...♘c6 8.♗d2 e5 9.c3 dxc3
10.♗xc3 ♘d5 11.♗d2 b6 12.♖c1
♗b7 13.♖c4 a5 14.a3 ♕d7 Black is
already for choice, due mostly to
the unfortunate position of the
b3-knight.

4....dxc4

5.♘a3

5.♕a4+ c6 6.♕xc4 ♗g7 7.0-0 0-0
8.d4 ♗f5 9.♘c3 ♘bd7 10.e3 ♘e4
11.♕e2 ♕a5=.

5....♗e6 6.0-0

6.♕c2! ♗g7 7.♘xc4 0-0 8.b3 (8.0-0
transposes to the game) 8...c5 9.♗b2
♘c6 10.0-0 ♖c8 11.♖ac1 b5N 12.♘ce5
♘xe5 13.♗xe5 ♗h6=.

6....♗g7

6...♗d5! is more accurate here to
avoid 7.♘g5.

7.♕c2

7.♘g5!.

7...0-0 8.♘xc4

8....c5!

The **actual game** went 8...♘c6
9.d3 ♗d5 10.e4 and now Black

needlessly gave up the bishop pair
by 10...♗xc4?! and went on to lose.
10...♗e6 was still close to equal.

**9.d3 ♘c6 10.♗e3 ♖c8! 11.♗xc5 b6
12.♗e3 b5 13.♘a3 ♘d5** (-0.46)
Black has huge compensation for
the pawn.

14.♗c1

Else Black regains the pawn
favorably.

14....a6 15.♕b1 ♘db4

15...♘b6 may be even better.

**16.♗d2 ♗g4 17.♖c1 ♕d7 18.♗c3
♗h6 19.♖d1 ♕e6**

This was just a sample continuation
of the gambit. White's shut-in rook
and offside knight are good value
for the pawn.

CHAPTER 11

Queen's Indian versus Réti

This chapter covers a defense to 1.♘f3, primarily either as an attempt
to reach Queen's Gambit positions while avoiding the Grünfeld, or else
intending the King's Indian Attack, where White just plays g2-g3, ♗g2,
0-0, and d2-d3 without looking at what Black is doing.

The idea of 1.♘f3 to avoid the Grünfeld is this: after **1.♘f3 ♘f6 2.c4 g6
3.♘c3**

and now **3...d5**, White does not have to play 4.d4, transposing to the
Grünfeld. He can instead play **4.cxd5 ♘xd5** and then **5.♕a4+** or **5.♕b3**
or **5.e4** or **5.g3** or **5.♕c2**, all of which pose some problems for Black. I
think that Black should not fear these lines, and I give adequate responses
in the anti-Grünfeld chapter. In this chapter I cover some alternate
solutions to this move-order, in case Black is not happy with one of the
anti-Grünfeld lines. Feel free to skip this chapter if you are following my
primary recommendation, although the first game can also be used as an
alternative to playing the Neo-Grünfeld against an early g2-g3.

So what can Black do if he fears the Anti-Grünfeld? One solution is to
answer **3.♘c3** by **3...♗g7**, then when White plays **4.e4** (4.d4 d5 is the
Grünfeld), play **4...c5** (otherwise you must play the King's Indian). Now
White's only try for advantage is **5.d4**, hoping to get a variation of the
Maroczy Bind vs Accelerated Dragon after Black takes. But Black may
surprise him with **5...♕a5**, as I played in a World Senior Championship
game against IM Rukavina in 2009, getting a winning game but only
drawing it. This should lead to positions similar to the Accelerated Dragon
Maroczy Bind if White plays accurately; perhaps Black is a tad better off
here than in the line with 5...cxd4. Still, unless you are an Accelerated

Dragon fan, these options leave something to be desired, and don't fit with the 1...e5 defense to 1.e4 given in this repertoire.

The next option is to play **1...g6**,

hoping for **2.c4 ♗g7 3.e4 e5!** as analysed in the previous (English) chapter. Of course, if **2.d4** we play **2...♘f6** and we are back on track for the Grünfeld. This is a solution favored by Peter Svidler, one of the strongest consistent Grünfeld players in recent years. The only problem with 1...g6 is **2.e4!**, after which we either have to play a Pirc or a Modern Defense with **2...d6** or **2...♗g7**, or else play **2...c5** when we are playing the Hyper-Accelerated Dragon. So the choice of this line or 1...♘f6 may come down to whether you prefer 2...♘c6 or 2..g6 in the Sicilian! Again, this won't work for our repertoire, only for those who don't fear the Maroczy Bind. However the option to play the Pirc or Modern makes some sense, as White has already played ♘f3 so he cannot play the dangerous lines with an early f2-f4 or ♗e3 with f2-f3 or ♗g5. This is often Svidler's preference.

Perhaps the best practical option for many players is **1.♘f3 c5**.

Here the idea is to meet **2.c4** by **2...♘c6**, and then answer **3.♘c3** by **3...e5**, as Grischuk played repeatedly against Gelfand in their 2011 Candidates' match. This would be my main recommendation, except that White can play **2.e4** and we must play the Sicilian. At least this time Black can choose any Sicilian, not just the Accelerated Dragon. As a practical matter, few players open with 1.♘f3 and then transpose to the Sicilian, since if they wanted to play against the Sicilian they would probably invite it by opening 1.e4. So this can be your solution if you at least have the Sicilian as a second defense. But I can't make it my choice for this book as I can't assume a knowledge of the Sicilian by the reader.

The solution I came up with is original, to my knowledge. I don't mean that the moves are original, just the concept of using the Queen's Indian as a companion to the Grünfeld. The idea is to meet **1.♘f3 ♘f6 2.c4** by **2...b6**.

Now if **3.d4 ♗b7 4.♘c3 e6** we are in the Queen's Indian, but not White's most recommended option with 4.g3. So you might say why not 4.g3 e6, the main line Queen's Indian? My answer is that if White plays **4.g3** (or 3.g3 ♗b7 4.d4 or 4.♗g2) we don't play 4...e6 but instead choose **4...g6**. This double fianchetto against the white fianchetto was recommended in a New in Chess *Yearbook* article by the very strong grandmaster Sergey Tiviakov, and I used his analysis as the starting point for my own in this book. I must admit that the computers are not too fond of this Tiviakov Variation, but as the positions are closed it is reasonable to question their judgment. I feel that this choice is the most in the spirit of the Grünfeld, as we do fianchetto the king's bishop in both lines, and it is not unusual in some Grünfeld lines to fianchetto the queen's bishop as well.

So in this chapter you will find both the Tiviakov Variation and the regular Queen's Indian lines without g3. I hope you find this solution (or one of the above-mentioned ones) acceptable. But my preferred option is the Anti-Grünfeld.

If you believe as I do (and some elite GMs) that 1...e5 and the Grünfeld are the best answers to 1.e4 and 1.d4, then it follows from the above that White's optimum opening play, if he prefers the Anti-Grünfeld to the real one, might be 1.♘f3 d5 2.d4 or 1...♘f6 2.c4 or 1...g6 2.e4 or 1...c5 2.e4. But very few players are equally at home on the white side of the Sicilian, the Queen's Gambit, the Queen's Indian, and the Symmetrical English! If you are one of them, see the 1.♘f3 chapter in the White side of this book!

Now for the games. First we look at the Tiviakov Variation **1.♘f3 ♘f6 2.c4 b6 3.g3 ♗b7 4.♗g2 g6 5.d4 ♗g7**. Note that this position can also be reached by **1.d4 ♘f6 2.c4 g6 3.♘f3 ♗g7 4.g3 b6 5.♗g2 ♗b7** (as actually played in Game 11.1) if Black doesn't like the Neo-Grünfeld 4...d5. However this is not so important because White can avoid it by playing 3.g3 first (before ♘f3), after which 3...b6? doesn't work. The resultant positions are similar to the King's Indian. The computer doesn't like Black either here or in the King's Indian, but it seems that the Tiviakov line is better than a normal King's Indian so it may be fine for Black even if the computer doesn't agree.

Next we come to **1.♘f3 ♘f6 2.c4 b6 3.d4 ♗b7 4.♘c3 e6 5.♗g5 h6 6.♗h4 ♗e7** (Game 11.2). Black equalizes without much difficulty.

The remainder of this chapter deals with the Petrosian/Kasparov Variation **5.a3** in the above sequence. It is the main line of the Queen's Indian excluding 4.g3 (which we meet with the Tiviakov Variation in Game 11.1). After **5...d5 6.cxd5 ♘xd5** White has three serious choices.

The move **7.♗d2** is met by **7...♘d7** in Game 11.3, when White can isolate the Black d5-pawn but only at the cost of the bishop pair. In Game 11.4 we examine the traditional **7.e3**, when I deviate from the recommendation of most books (7...g6), preferring **7...♗e7**, which appears to equalize comfortably thanks to a 2010 novelty. Finally we cover the most popular **7.♕c2**, which we meet by trading knights, playing 8...h6 next to prevent 9.♗g5 if White takes with the queen, or 8...c5 if he takes with the pawn. See Game 11.5. In all cases it seems that Black can equalize the game.

Game 11.1 King's Indian – Tiviakov
Sasa Martinovic   2504
Igor Kurnosov   2653

Aix-les-Bains Ech 2011 (7)

1.d4 ♘f6 2.c4 g6 3.♘f3 ♗g7 4.g3 b6
This move order shows how this system can be used instead of 4...d5 if you don't like the Neo-Grünfeld, but only if White plays ♘f3 before g2-g3.

5.♗g2 ♗b7
We might reach this position by 1.♘f3 ♘f6 2.c4 b6 3.g3 ♗b7 4.♗g2 g6 5.d4 ♗g7.
6.0-0 0-0
So it's a Queen's Indian with the bishop on g7 rather than e7. It seems to me that this difference is slightly in Black's favor.
7.d5 ♘a6
A new idea is 7...e6 8.♘c3 exd5 9.cxd5 ♖e8 10.♘d4 ♘c5 11.♗f4 ♘c5 12.♕c2 ♘h5 13.♗e3 ♖xe3! 14.fxe3 (Sadhwani-Donchenko, Porticcio 2019) and now 14...♕e7 (+0.10) gives Black excellent compensation for the exchange due to the bishop pair and White's awful pawn structure. But 12.♘db5 was better (+0.70) so I can't recommend this. Instead,

7...♘e4 8.♕c2 f5 9.♖d1 ♘a6 10.♗e3 c6 11.♗d4 was Wheeler-Berczes, Irving 2018, when 11...cxd5 12.cxd5 ♖c8 is fine for Black at +0.02. White should prefer 11.dxc6 ♘b4 12.♕c1 ♘c6 (+0.36).
8.♘c3 ♘c5

Black's light-squared bishop is restricted, but its companion is very active.
9.♘d4
A) If 9.♗e3 e6 10.♗d4 a5 11.♘e5 exd5 12.cxd5 ♖e8 13.♖c1 d6 14.♘c6 ♗xc6 15.dxc6 ♘e6 16.♗e3 a4 17.♘xa4 d5= Black's coming ...d5-d4 will leave the knight on a4 in enough trouble to guarantee the recapture of the lost pawn;
B) 9.♕c2 c6 10.e4 cxd5 11.exd5 e6 12.♖d1 exd5 13.cxd5 ♖e8 14.♘d4 ♗a6=;
C) 9.♗f4 e6 10.♘d4 exd5 11.cxd5 a5 12.♕c2 ♖e8 13.♖ad1 d6=;
D) 9.♖e1! e6 10.e4 d6 11.♕c2 exd5 12.exd5 ♖e8 13.♘d4 ♘g4 14.♘c6 ♗f5! (+0.40). White has a nice space advantage, but nothing concrete.
9....e5 10.♘b3
10.♘c2 a5 11.e4 c6 12.♖e1 cxd5 13.exd5 (13.cxd5 ♗a6∓) 13...♘e8 – though the computer says this is

equal, I prefer Black, who has ideas of ...♘d6, ...♗a6, and ...f7-f5.

10....d6 11.e4 ♗c8 12.h3?

12.♘xc5! bxc5 13.♗d2 ♘d7 14.a3 f5 15.b4 ♖b8 16.♖b1 f4 (+0.38), normally a serious advantage but perhaps not in a King's Indian-like position.

12....♘fd7

The **actual game** went 12...♘h5 13.♔h2 ♗d7 14.♗f3 ♔h8 15.♗e3 ♘f6 16.♗g2 ♘g8 17.♕d2 f5 18.exf5 gxf5 19.f4 e4 20.♘d4 with a position typical of the King's Indian. White is probably a bit better here, though Black did win the game. But it seems wrong to waste time on ....♘h5 and going back to f6, so the text is my proposed improvement.

13.♗e3

13.♘xc5 bxc5 14.♗d2 f5 15.exf5 gxf5=. Although Stockfish and Komodo slightly prefer White, Lc0 and I would rather play Black here. Usually in such positions White plays f2-f4 to induce ...e5-e4 so that he can use the d4-square, but here the c5-pawn prevents that plan.

13....f5 14.exf5 gxf5

Black has a pleasant King's Indian position, and 15.f4? can be well-

met by 15...♗a6. Lc0 already clearly prefers Black.

Game 11.2   Queen's Indian

Magnus Carlsen   2765
Peter Leko   2741

Miskolc m 2008 (8)

1.d4

1.♘f3 ♘f6 2.c4 b6 3.d4 ♗b7 4.♘c3 e6 would be the way we would reach this position.

1....♘f6 2.c4 e6 3.♘f3 b6 4.♘c3 ♗b7 5.♗g5

5.a3 would transpose to the 4.a3 games.

5....h6

6.♗h4

6.♗xf6 ♕xf6 7.e4 ♗b4 8.♗d3 c5 9.0-0 cxd4 10.♘b5 ♕d8 11.♘bxd4 0-0 12.♕e2 ♘c6 13.♖ad1 ♘xd4 14.♘xd4 a6=; Black's bishop pair offsets White's spatial advantage.

6....♗e7

This gives comfortable equality, unlike the risky 6...♗b4!?.

7.e3

For 7.♕c2 c5 8.dxc5 bxc5 9.e3 0-0 see the next note.

7....0-0 8.♗d3

8.♕c2 c5 9.dxc5 bxc5 10.♗e2 ♘c6
11.♖d1 d6 12.0-0 ♘h5 13.♗xe7
♕xe7=. White's pressure down the
d-file just offsets Black's central
pawn dominance.

8....c5

This is almost always a good move
in the Queen's Indian when White
cannot profitably respond with
d4-d5.

9.0-0

9.dxc5 bxc5 10.0-0 d6 11.♕e2 ♘bd7
12.♖fd1 ♕b6 13.b3 ♖fe8 14.♖ac1
♖ad8=. Black's pawn superiority in
the center offsets White's superior
mobility.

9....cxd4

10.exd4

10.♘xd4 ♘c6 11.♘xc6 ♗xc6 12.♕e2
♘e4 13.♗xe7 ♘xc3 14.♗xd8 ♘xe2+
15.♗xe2 ♖fxd8 16.♖fd1 d5 17.♗f3
♖ac8 18.♖ac1 ♗b7=. Black plans
...♔g8-f8-e7.

10....♘c6 11.♗c2

A) 11.♖c1 d5 12.cxd5 ♘xd5 13.♗g3
♖c8=;

B) 11.♗g3 d5 12.cxd5 ♘xd5=.

**11....d5 12.♗xf6 ♗xf6 13.cxd5
♘b4 14.dxe6 ♗xf3 15.gxf3 ♘xc2
16.♕xc2 ♕xd4 17.♖ad1**

17....♕c4!N

The **actual game** continued
17...♕h4 18.♕e4 fxe6 19.♕xe6+ ♔h8
20.♕g4 ♖ac8 21.♖d7 ♕xg4+ 22.fxg4
♗xc3 23.bxc3 ♖xc3 24.♖xa7 ♖f4
25.f3 ♖cxf3 26.♖xf3 ♖xf3 27.♔g2,
draw agreed.

**18.exf7+ ♕xf7 19.♘d5 ♗e5 20.f4
♗xf4∓**

White has little compensation for
his broken kingside.

Game 11.3   Queen's Indian – Petrosian
Baadur Jobava   2695
Zoltan Almasi   2720
Rijeka Ech 2010 (8)

**1.d4 ♘f6 2.c4 e6 3.♘f3 b6 4.a3 ♗b7
5.♘c3 d5 6.cxd5 ♘xd5 7.♗d2 ♘d7**

8.♕c2

8.♘xd5 exd5 9.g3 (if 9.b4 ♗d6
10.♗g5 f6 11.♗h4 c5 12.♗g3 ♗xg3
13.hxg3 c4 14.e3 0-0 the protected
passed pawn offsets the slightly
weakened black kingside) 9...♗d6
10.♗g5 ♘f6 11.♗g2 0-0 12.0-0 ♖e8 –
chances are balanced.

8....c5 9.♘xd5

9.e4 cxd4 10.♘xd5 exd5 11.e5 ♖c8N
12.♕d1 ♗e7 13.♗e2 0-0 14.0-0
d3 15.♗xd3 d4!. After this move,
activating his only bad piece, Black
is at least equal.

9....exd5

9...♗xd5 10.e4 ♗b7 11.d5 exd5
12.exd5 ♗d6 13.0-0-0 0-0 14.♗b5
scores too well for White though
the computer rates it as even.

10.dxc5 ♗xc5

10...bxc5 11.e3 ♗d6 12.b4 0-0 is
also okay for Black, though in this
case Black's compensation for his
isolated queen's pawn consists in
his superior development rather
than the bishop pair as in the main
line.

11.e3 0-0 12.♗d3 ♘f6 13.0-0

13....♖c8!

The text is a computer
improvement over the **actual game**,
which continued 13...♘e4?! 14.♗b4

♕e7 15.♗xc5 bxc5 16.b4! and with
a great knight to be posted on d4
vs a bad bishop White had full
compensation for the pawn and
won.

14.♕a4 ♘e4 15.♗b4

Not 15.♕xa7?? ♗c6 and the white
queen is doomed.

15....♕f6 16.♖ac1 a5 17.♗c3

After 17.♗xc5 ♘xc5 18.♕c2 ♘xd3
19.♕xd3 ♕xb2 20.♖b1 ♕f6 21.♕d4
♖c6 White's positional advantages
are not quite worth a pawn.

17....♘xc3 18.♖xc3 ♗d6

Black is not worse, as the bishop
pair easily offsets the isolated queen
pawn.

Game 11.4   Queen's Indian – Petrosian
Elina Danielian   2431
Mircea Parligras   2574
Halkis 2010 (8)

**1.d4 ♘f6 2.♘f3 e6 3.c4 b6 4.a3 ♗b7
5.♘c3 d5 6.cxd5 ♘xd5 7.e3 ♗e7**
The move 7...g6 is also okay and
is more in the Grünfeld spirit,
but this game convinced me that
7...♗e7 solves all of Black's opening
problems.

8.♗b5+

Playing 8.♗d3 should ultimately transpose to the game, with each side saving one tempo.

8....c6 9.♗d3 0-0 10.0-0

10.♕c2 h6 11.e4 ♘xc3 12.bxc3 c5 13.0-0 ♘c6 14.♗e3 ♖c8 15.♕e2 ♕c7 16.d5 ♘a5 17.c4 exd5N 18.exd5 b5 19.cxb5 ♗xd5=. The passed c-pawn offsets the split black queenside.

10....c5

11.e4

In the event of 11.♕e2 cxd4 12.exd4 ♘c6 13.♖d1 ♘a5 Black has a relatively good position compared to some other openings with the isolated white d4-pawn, since his development has been smooth and his knight eyes the b3-square. After 11.♘xd5 ♕xd5 12.e4 ♕d7 13.♗e3 cxd4 14.♗xd4 ♘c6 15.♗c3

♖fd8 16.♗c2 ♕xd1 17.♖fxd1 ♘a5 Black has the better side of equality due to the pressure on the e4-pawn.

11....♘xc3 12.bxc3 ♘c6

12...♘d7 has been more often played, but the text seems to be stronger.

13.d5

13.♗e3 cxd4 14.cxd4 ♖c8 15.♕e2 ♘a5 16.♖fd1 ♖c3 17.a4 ♘b3 18.♖ab1 ♕c7N and although the computer rates the game even, Black's position is easier to play.

13....♘a5

In previous games 13...exd5 was played, but the text move is a major improvement, giving Black full equality. After the insertion of 13... exd5?! 14.exd5 ♘a5 15.c4 b5 16.♕c2, the threat on h7 saves White a crucial tempo.

14.c4 b5

15.dxe6

A) 15.♖b1 bxc4 16.♗xc4 ♘xc4 17.♖xb7 exd5 18.exd5 ♗f6 19.♗f4 ♗d4 20.♘xd4 ♕xd5 21.♕f3 ♕xd4 – chances are balanced, with White's more active pieces offset by Black's extra pawn;

B) 15.♕c2? bxc4 just wins a pawn for Black, as now there is no ♗xh7+!.

15....bxc4 16.exf7+ ♖xf7 17.♗c2 ♕xd1 18.♖xd1 ♗f6 19.♖b1 ♖e8

20.♗e3?!

He should have played 20.♖b5! ♘b3 21.♖xb3! cxb3 22.♗xb3 ♖xe4 23.♗xf7+ ♔xf7 24.♗e3 c4 25.♘d2 ♖g4 26.f3 ♖g6 27.♘xc4 ♗xf3 28.♖d2 ♖g4 29.♘d6+ ♔g6 30.h3 ♗g5 31.♗xg5 ♖xg5. The ending is even and should be drawn.

20....♗xe4 21.♗xe4 ♖xe4 22.♖b8+ ♖f8 23.♖xf8+ ♔xf8 24.♗xc5+ ♔g8

Black's advanced passer gives him a slight edge.

25.♘d2 ♖e5 26.♗b4 ♖d5 27.♗xa5 c3 28.♗b4?! a5 29.♗xa5 ♖xa5

30.♘c4??

30.♘f1 ♖xa3 31.♘e3 would give White good drawing chances.

30....c2

Black now wins a piece and the game.

31.♖c1 ♖b5 32.♘d2 ♖c5 33.♘b3 ♖c8 34.♖e1 ♗b2 35.♔f1 ♗xa3 36.♘c1 ♖d8 37.♘a2 ♖d1 38.♔e2 ♖xe1+ 39.♔xe1 c1♕+ 40.♘xc1 ♗xc1 41.♔e2 ♔f7 42.♔f3 ♔f6 43.♔g4 ♔e5 44.h4 ♔e4 45.g3 ♗d2 46.h5 h6 47.f3+ ♔e3 48.f4 ♔e4 49.♔h4 ♗xf4 0-1

Game 11.5   Queen's Indian – Petrosian
Viacheslav Zakhartsov   2602
Stellan Brynell   2492
Cappelle-la-Grande 2011 (9)

1.d4 e6 2.c4 ♘f6 3.♘f3 b6 4.a3 ♗b7 5.♘c3 d5 6.cxd5 ♘xd5 7.♕c2 ♘xc3

8.bxc3

Or 8.♕xc3 h6 and now:

A) 9.g3 ♘d7 10.♗g2 ♗d6N 11.0-0 0-0 – White has no advantage here;

B) 9.♗f4 ♗d6 10.♗g3 (if 10.♗xd6 cxd6 11.e3 ♘d7 12.♗e2 0-0 13.0-0 ♖c8 Black's bishop is more effective than White's, with nothing to offset this) 10...0-0 11.e3 ♘d7 12.♗b5 ♗xg3 13.hxg3 c6 14.♗a4 ♖c8 15.♖d1 ♕e7 16.0-0 ♘f6 and next ...c7-c5 will give Black the edge;

C) 9.e3 ♗e7 10.♗b5+ c6 11.♗a4 0-0 12.0-0 ♘d7 13.♖d1 ♕c7 14.b4 a5 15.♗d2 ♖fc8 and with ...c6-c5 coming, Black has the edge.

8....c5 9.e4 ♘d7 10.♗f4

10.♗d3 ♕c7 11.♕b1 ♗e7 12.0-0 0-0 13.♗e3 ♖ac8 14.♖d1 ♖fd8 15.a4 h6=. Black plans ...♘f6 and perhaps ...♘f6-h5-f4.

10....cxd4 11.cxd4 ♖c8 12.♕b3

12.♕b1 ♗e7 13.♗d3 0-0 14.0-0 ♖c3 15.♖c1 ♖xc1+ 16.♗xc1 ♕a8 17.♖a2 f5 18.♗c4 ♗xe4 19.♗xe6+ ♔h8 – it's not obvious who should be better here but the computer says it is equal.

12....h6N

Playable but risky is 12...♗xe4 13.♗a6 ♗d5.

In the **actual game**, Black played 12...♗e7 13.♗d3 ♘f6 14.♕b5+ ♕d7 15.♘e5 ♕xb5 16.♗xb5+ ♔f8 17.f3 ♘e8 18.♗d7 ♖d8 19.♗c6 – White has a slight edge here, but Black held the draw eventually.

13.♗d3 g5 14.♗e3 ♗g7 15.0-0 0-0 16.♖ac1 ♘f6=

Black has a Grünfeld-like pressure against the white center. Although Black's kingside is weakened, the white queen is misplaced and the threat to e4 will provoke a concession.

CHAPTER 12

Anti-Grünfeld and Symmetrical English

The name Anti-Grünfeld is applied to the use of the opening move 1.♘f3 to aim for the usual Queen's Gambit lines without allowing the Grünfeld Defense. White plays **1.♘f3 ♘f6 2.c4 g6 3.♘c3** and if 3...♗g7, 4.e4 d6 5.d4 is the King's Indian. So a Grünfeld player will likely play **3...d5,**

after which 4.d4 would be a Grünfeld. However White can try other fourth moves instead, hoping to benefit by saving the tempo d2-d4 or in some lines by recapturing on c3 with the d-pawn instead of the b-pawn. Actually this was the hardest chapter of the book for me to write, because I believed that White had more than one path to a non-trivial advantage in the Anti-Grünfeld. However, when I really got into the analysis deeply, I found satisfactory lines for Black in each case, and my present opinion is that with best play the Anti-Grünfeld confers no larger advantage on White than he can obtain against the normal Grünfeld, which is to say very little. In several lines though, it seems that Black has hardly any choice if he wishes to stay close to equality, so you had best study this chapter rather thoroughly, unless you want to play altogether differently against 1.♘f3 – see the Réti chapter.

In Game 12.1 we look at **4.♕a4+ ♗d7 5.♕b3 dxc4 6.♕xc4 a6! 7.d4** (and other 7th moves for White). Now if 7...♗g7 8.e4 0-0 we would transpose to the Hungarian Variation of the Russian System against the Grünfeld (which I recommend in that chapter for Black), but with the difference that Black's bishop is on d7 rather than c8. This seems to be in White's favor, as he no longer can play ...♗b7 (after ...b7-b5), and also because he needs d7 as a retreat square for his knight in case of e4-e5. So we don't play this way. Instead we play **7...b5 8.♕b3 c5** (the novelty 8...♗g7 9.e4 ♘c6!? is also discussed and doesn't seem bad) **9.dxc5 ♗g7 10.e4 ♗c6** and Black doesn't seem to have any theoretical problems.

The next four games feature the exchange **4.cxd5 ♘xd5**.

In Game 12.2 White provokes an endgame by **5.e4 ♘xc3 6.dxc3 ♛xd1+ 7.♔xd1**. The novice might say that White has lost the right to castle for nothing, but with queens and a pair of knights off the board the white king will be quite happy on c2 or (after ♗c4) on e2. Black's equalizing strategy is to play ...f7-f6 and ...e7-e5, together with ...♘d7, so as to meet the natural ♗e3 by ...♗c5, exchanging off White's better bishop. It seems that this works fine, as Black has a nice plus score in grandmaster play from here in the current century.

Next we look at two queen moves, **5.♛b3** and **5.♛c2**. The first can transpose into a Grünfeld line which I recommend for White after **5....♘b6 6.d4 ♗g7 7.e4** 0-0 (recommended by Delchev) 8.♗e3 ♗g4 9.♖d1, so I don't recommend playing this way. Instead we play **7...♗g4!**. Other seventh white moves can be met by 7...♗e6, hitting the queen.

The move **5.♛c2** was unveiled by Topalov in his 2011 Candidates' match with Kamsky.

Topalov got an advantage and should have won the game but didn't. For a while I considered this novelty to be the refutation of 3...d5 in the anti-Grünfeld, but as shown in my notes to Game 12.3 I no longer consider 5.♛c2 to be any problem for Black, if he reacts in the sharp manner shown, namely **5...♘c6 6.d4 ♘db4 7.♛a4 ♗d7 8.♛d1 e5!**.

Game 12.4 features the move **5.♕a4+**. The usual reply historically was 5...♗d7, but White seems to keep a slight edge. This line bothered me quite a bit. Delchev and Agrest recommend 5...c6, and although the computers hate it I think it is playable but not quite equal. The current fad is for the computers' recommended **5...♘c6**, which leads to an endgame in which Black has an awful pawn structure. However the computers have shown that Black's superior development and piece play are enough to equalize here, and recent grandmaster games confirm this. No one would have played this way before computers, but today the motto is 'whatever works'.

Finally we come to perhaps the best of the fifth moves, namely **5.g3**.

After the natural moves **5...♗g7 6.♗g2 0-0 7.0-0** I favor **7...c5**. Now after White trades knights he can play either 9.d3 or 9.d4. The move 9.d4 is rather dangerous after 9...cxd4 10.♗e3! but the reply 10...d3! seems to lead to near-equality for Black. Instead, 9.d3 ♘c6 10.♗e3 is a dangerous gambit which gives White a pull if declined. So we take on b2 and retreat to f6 when attacked. Game 12.5 shows how Black can steer the game to the safety of an even-material bishops-of-opposite-color draw, or can play an original line I give which leads to the interesting balance of two bishops, rook, and extra pawn versus two rooks and a knight. So it seems to me that although 5.g3 should keep at least some edge, it is quite tiny with best play.

I conclude that the Anti-Grünfeld does not appear to give White any more of an edge than he gets in the real Grünfeld, but White does have a variety of interesting options here, so there is at least a reasonable case to be made for starting the game with 1.♘f3 if you expect to see the Grünfeld.

For this 2019 edition of the book, I close out this chapter with the symmetrical move 2...c5, intending to meet 3.♘c3 (or 3.g3) by 3...d5. This has become the preferred defense of the elite GMs who favor the Grünfeld. Black will usually play ...g7-g6 soon, resulting in Grünfeld or Grünfeld-like positions, but the fact that he has not yet played ...g7-g6 can work in his favor. This is now my main recommendation vs 1.♘f3. See Game 12.6.

Game 12.1 English Opening –
Anti-Grünfeld

Alojzije Jankovic 2560

Niels Grandelius 2500

Khanty-Mansiysk ol 2010 (4)

1.♘f3 ♘f6 2.c4 g6 3.♘c3 d5 4.♕a4+ ♗d7 5.♕b3 dxc4 6.♕xc4
If 6.♕xb7? ♘c6 7.♘b5 ♘d5 8.♘bd4 ♘cb4 9.a3 ♖b8 10.♕xa7 ♖a8 11.♕b7 ♗g7 12.♖b1 c5 13.axb4 ♘xb4 14.e3 ♖b8 15.♕a7 cxd4 Black wins material.
6....a6!

Very similar to the Hungarian Variation of the Grünfeld (which I recommend here) against the Russian System.
7.d4
  A) 7.e4 b5 8.♕e2 c5 9.e5 ♘h5 10.♘e4 ♘c6 11.♘xc5 ♗f5 12.d3 ♖c8 13.♗e3 (so far Ponkratov-Kurnosov, Taganrog 2011) 13...e6N 14.♖c1 ♗g4 15.♖c3 b4 16.♖c4 ♗xf3 17.♕xf3 b3! – the idea is to block the White queen's access to a4 in case of ...♘xe5 ♕d1. White is in trouble;
  B) 7.g3 b5 8.♕h4 (after 8.♕b3 c5 9.♗g2 ♘c6 10.d3 ♗g7 11.0-0 ♖c8 12.♕d1 0-0 Black's advantage in development and space easily offsets

White's extra center pawn) 8...c5 9.♗g2 ♗c6 10.d3 h6 11.0-0 ♗g7N and Black is better as White must respond to the threat of ...g6-g5;
  C) 7.d3 b5 8.♕f4 c5 9.g3 ♗c6 10.♗g2 ♗g7 11.0-0 ♘bd7N 12.a3 h6 – this permits Black to answer ♕h4 by ...g6-g5. I already prefer Black's game.
7....b5

8.♕b3
8.♕d3 ♗g7 9.e4 0-0 10.a3 (after 10.♗e3 b4 11.♘e2 ♗b5 12.♕c2 c5 13.dxc5 ♗d3 14.♕b3 ♗xe4 15.♘d2 ♘bd7 Black's lead in development is serious) 10...♗g4 11.♗e3 ♘c6 12.♖c1 ♗xf3 13.gxf3 e5 (13...♘a5 14.♕d1 ♘d7 would be the way to play if Black does not want a draw. The superior black pawn structure and development offset the bishop pair) 14.♘xb5 axb5 15.♖xc6 exd4 16.♗xd4 ♕e8 17.♖xf6 ♖d8 18.♕c3 ♖xd4 19.♕xd4 ♕e7 20.f4 ♗xf6 21.e5 c5 22.♕e4 ♗g7 23.♗xb5 ♖d8 24.0-0 ♖d4 25.♕e3 ♗h6 26.e6 ♗xf4 27.exf7+ ♕xf7 28.♕e8+ ♕xe8 29.♗xe8 ♗e5 – although White has an extra pawn, the better black pawn structure and piece placement together with bishops of opposite color make a draw almost certain.

8....c5

An interesting alternative is 8...♗g7 9.e4 ♘c6!?N (this has the intent to trade three minor pieces for the queen, which is normally bad but seems okay here) 10.e5 (10.a4 0-0) 10...♗e6 11.exf6 ♗xb3 12.fxg7 ♖g8 13.axb3 ♘b4 14.♔d1 f6 15.♗d2 ♔f7 16.♘xb5 axb5 17.♖xa8 ♕xa8 18.♗xb4 ♕e4 19.♔d2 ♔xg7. Usually three minor pieces are superior to a queen, but here White's lack of development, bad pawns, exposed king, and the reduced material all favor Black, so I would rather play Black.

9.dxc5 ♗g7 10.e4 ♗c6

11.a4

A) 11.e5 ♘fd7 12.♗e3 (in case of 12.e6 ♘xc5 13.exf7+ ♔f8 14.♕b4 ♗xf3 15.gxf3 ♘d3+ 16.♗xd3 ♕xd3 17.♕e4 ♕xe4+ 18.fxe4 ♘d7 19.♗e3 ♖c8 Black has the initiative at no cost) 12...♘xe5 13.♘xe5 ♗xe5 14.f4 ♗g7 15.♖d1 ♕a5 16.♔f2 e6 17.a3 0-0 18.♗e2 ♖c8=;

B) 11.♗e2 ♘xe4 12.♘xe4 ♗xe4 13.0-0 ♗d5 14.♕e3 ♘c6 15.♖d1 0-0 16.♖b1 ♖e8N (so as to block a later ♗b2 by ...e7-e5) 17.b4 e5 18.♗b2 ♘d4 and Black is better due to his outposted knight and threat on a2;

C) 11.♘e5N 0-0 12.f3 ♘fd7 13.♘d3 ♗b7 14.♗e3 ♘c6 15.0-0-0 ♘a5 16.♕b4 ♘c4 17.♗f2 e6 18.h4 ♕c7 – Black plans ...♘d7-b8-c6-d4 with excellent compensation for the pawn.

11....bxa4 12.♕c4 0-0 13.♗e2 ♘bd7 14.0-0

14.♘d4 ♗xe4 15.♘xe4 ♘xe4 16.♘c6 ♕c7 17.♘xe7+ (after 17.♕xe4 ♘xc5 18.♕d5 ♘b3 19.♖b1 ♖ad8 20.♕e4 ♖d6 21.♘xe7+ ♔h8 22.0-0 ♖d4 23.♕c6 ♕xe7 24.♗e3 ♖e4 25.♗xa6 f5 26.g3 ♖xe3 27.fxe3 ♘d2 28.♖be1 ♘xf1 29.♗xf1 ♕a7 Black has the better pawn structure and the initiative for free) 17...♔h8 18.♘d5 (with 18.♕xe4 ♘xc5 19.♘d5 ♕b7 20.♕f3 ♘b3 21.♖b1 ♘d4 White loses his extra piece and emerges a pawn down) 18...♕e5 19.c6 ♘d6 20.♕a2 ♘c5 21.♗e3 ♖ab8, and the threat of ...♖xb2 is hard to meet.

14....♕c7 15.♖e1

15.♘d4 ♗xe4 16.♘xe4 ♘xe4 17.♘e6 fxe6 18.♕xe6+ ♔h8 19.♕xe4 ♘xc5 20.♕c2 ♗e5 21.g3 ♖ab8 22.♗e3 ♖xb2 23.♕xc5 ♕xc5 24.♗xc5 ♖xe2 25.♖xa4 ♖f5 26.♗e3 ♗d6 27.♖xa6 ♗c5 leads to a drawn endgame.

15....♗b5!N

In the **actual game** Black played
15...♖fc8 16.♗g5 ♗b5 17.♕a2 e6
18.♖ac1 ♖ab8 19.♘xb5 axb5 20.c6
♘e5 21.♗xf6? ♗xf6 22.b3 axb3
23.♕xb3 ♕b6 24.c7 ♖xc7 25.♖xc7
♕xc7 26.♗xb5 ♕a5 27.♖b1 ♘xf3+
28.gxf3 ♗e5 29.h3 ♕d8 30.♕e3
♕h4 31.♔g2 ♖d8 32.♗f1 ♗f4
33.♕c5? ♖d2 34.♕c8+ ♔g7 35.♕c3+
♔h6 and White resigned.
**16.♕b4 ♕xc5 17.♕xc5 ♘xc5 18.e5
♘g4 19.♗f4 ♘e6 20.♗g3 ♖fb8
21.♘xa4 ♘h6**

Black is clearly better, with ...♘f5
next and threats against e5 and b2.

Game 12.2   English Opening –
              Anti-Grünfeld

Mihai Suba   2464
Vitaly Tseshkovsky   2564

Arco Wch-sen 2010 (9)

**1.♘f3 ♘f6 2.c4 g6 3.♘c3 d5 4.cxd5
♘xd5 5.e4 ♘xc3 6.dxc3**
6.bxc3 ♗g7 7.♗e2 (for 7.d4 or 8.d4,
see Chapter 8 on the Grünfeld) 7...
c5 8.0-0 ♘c6 9.♖b1 0-0 10.♕c2 b6=
or 10.♕a4 ♘e5 11.♘xe5 ♗xe5 12.f4
♗g7 13.♕b3 b6=.
6....♕xd1+ 7.♔xd1

Although this endgame was at one
time considered to favor White
slightly, White has only won a few
games at grandmaster level from
here in this century, while Black
has won several with dozens of
draws.
7....f6

Black wants to play ...e7-e5 and to
exchange dark-squared bishops
as his remaining bishop will be
slightly better than White's.
Also OK is 7...♘d7.
8.♗c4
  A) 8.♔c2 e5 9.♗e3 ♘d7 10.♘d2
♗c5 11.♗xc5 ♘xc5 12.b4 ♘e6
13.♗c4 ♔e7=;
  B) 8.e5 ♘c6 9.exf6 exf6 10.♗f4
♗c5 11.♗xc7 ♗xf2 12.♗c4 ♗f5N
13.♔e2 ♗c5 14.♖he1 ♔d7 15.♗g3
♖ae8+ 16.♔f1 ♖xe1+ 17.♖xe1 ♖e8
18.♖xe8 ♔xe8=;
  C) 8.♗e3 e5 9.♘d2 ♘d7 10.♗c4
(after 10.♘b3 a5 11.a4 b6 12.f3 ♗b7
13.♗c4 0-0-0 the b3-knight is
purely defensive) 10...♗c5 11.♗xc5
♘xc5 12.b4 ♘e6 13.♔c2 a5 14.a3 ♔e7
15.♘b3 axb4 16.axb4 ♗d7 17.♗d5 c6
18.♗xe6 ♗xe6 19.♘c5 b6 20.♘xe6
♔xe6=;

D) 8.h4! (a new idea) 8...e5 9.h5 g5 10.♗e3 ♘d7 11.♘h2 (Nisipeanu-Külaots, Dortmund 2019) and now 11...c6 to postpone the choice between ...♘c5 and ...♗c5 makes sense (+0.05), although Lc0 gives White a much larger edge which seems excessive to me.

8....e5 9.♔e2

9.♗e3 ♘d7 10.♔e2 ♗c5 11.♖hd1 ♗xe3 12.♔xe3 ♔e7 13.♘d2 a5 14.f3 ♘b6 15.♗e2 ♗e6 16.♘b3 (so far Ivanchuk-Nepomniachtchi, Havana 2010).

analysis diagram

With 16...♘d7!N Black gets the better bishop and the initiative on the queenside.

9....♘d7 10.♗e3 ♗c5 11.♖hd1 ♗xe3 12.♔xe3 ♔e7 13.♘e1 a5 14.a4 ♘b6 15.♗b3 c5 16.f4 c4 17.♗c2 ♗g4 18.♘f3 ♖ac8 19.fxe5 fxe5 20.♖d2 ♗xf3 21.gxf3 ♖hf8 22.♖g1 ♖cd8

Black is slightly better as White's kingside pawns are inferior and his bishop is slightly bad since three white pawns are stuck on light squares.

23.♖gg2 ♖xd2 24.♖xd2 ♖f6 25.h4 ♖f4 26.♖h2 ♘d7 27.♗d1 ♖f6 28.♖d2 ♖d6 29.♖xd6 ♔xd6 30.f4

♘c5 31.♗c2 exf4+ 32.♔xf4 ♘e6+ 33.♔g4 h5+ 34.♔f3 ♔e5 35.♗d1 g5 36.♗e2

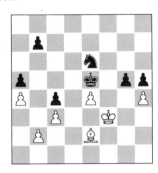

Black is much better here thanks to the outside passed pawn he will obtain and the better king position, but whether it's a forced win I don't know.

36....gxh4 37.♗xc4 ♘g5+ 38.♔g2 ♔xe4 39.b4 b6 40.♗b5 ♔e3 41.bxa5 bxa5 42.♔h2 h3 43.♗e8 h4 44.♗b5 ♔e4 45.♗f1 ♘d5 46.♗b5 ♔c5 47.♗d3 ♘e6 48.♗b5 ♘f4

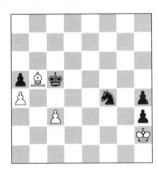

49.♗f1?

I witnessed this game in person. Suba was very upset afterward that he made this losing blunder rather than playing 49.♗e8, which appears to draw: 49...♔c4 50.♗d7 ♗xc3 51.♗b5 ♔b4 52.♗c6 ♘d3 53.♔xh3 ♘c5 54.♔xh4 ♘xa4 55.♔g3.

analysis diagram

This is a tablebase drawn position. For example: 55...♘c3 56.♔f3 ♘b5 57.♔e3 a4 58.♔d2 a3 59.♔c1 ♘c3 60.♔c2 ♔c4 61.♗e8.
49....♘d5 50.♗b5 ♘xc3 51.♗e8 ♔b4 52.♔xh3 ♘xa4 53.♔xh4 ♘c3 54.♔g4 ♘b5 55.♔f5 a5-a4 56.♔f4-e5 ♔b4-c3 57.♗e8-f7 ♘b5-d4
And White resigned.

Game 12.3   English Opening –
Anti-Grünfeld
Josif Dorfman   2578
Maxime Vachier-Lagrave   2722
Caen ch-FRA 2011 (7)

1.♘f3 ♘f6 2.c4 g6 3.♘c3 d5 4.cxd5 ♘xd5 5.♕c2!?
Topalov's brilliant new idea with which he got a winning position against Kamsky in the 2011 Candidates tournament, although Kamsky saved the draw. I thought for a while that it refuted Black's attempt to play the Grünfeld when White omits d2-d4, but this game and the analysis shows that this is not so.
5.♕b3 ♘b6 6.d4 ♗g7 and now:

analysis diagram

A) 7.♗f4 ♗e6:
A1) 8.♕c2 ♘c6 9.♖d1 (in case of 9.e3 ♘b4 10.♕d1 0-0 11.♗e2 c5 12.0-0 ♖c8 13.♗e5 ♗xe5 14.♘xe5 cxd4 15.exd4 ♘4d5N White has no attack to offset his isolani. I would prefer to play Black) 9...♘b4 10.♕b1 ♘4d5 11.♘xd5 ♕xd5 12.e4 ♕xa2 13.d5 ♕xb1 14.♖xb1 ♗d7 15.♗xc7 0-0 16.♗d3 f5 17.0-0 fxe4 18.♗xe4 ♗f5. Black is for choice, as White's pawns are weaker than Black's;
A2) 8.♕a3 ♘c6 9.e3 0-0 10.♗e2 a5 11.♕c5 a4 12.♘b5 ♖a5 13.♕c1 ♘d5 14.♗g3 ♗g4.

analysis diagram

White has an extra center pawn, but lags a bit in development. Black will aim for ...e7-e5. Chances are nearly balanced: 15.♘c3 a3 16.0-0 e5

231

17.♘xe5 ♘xe5 18.dxe5 ♗xe2 19.♘xe2
♕e7 20.♖b1 ♗xe5 21.♕d2 ♖fa8
22.b4 ♖b5 (+0.22), Lc0 +0.17. White's
kingside majority is more useful
than Black's queenside majority, but
not by much;

B) 7.♗g5 ♗e6 8.♕c2 ♘c6 9.♖d1
h6 10.♗h4 0-0 11.e3 ♘b4 12.♕b1
♗f5 13.e4 ♗g4 14.d5 f5 15.a3 g5
16.♗g3 f4 17.axb4 ♕d6 18.b5 fxg3N
19.hxg3 ♖xf3 20.gxf3 ♗xf3 21.♖h2
♗xd1 22.♔xd1 ♖f8 – Black is clearly
better. His pieces are all working
together while White's are not.
White's king in the center is not so
happy;

C) 7.e4

analysis diagram

7...♗g4 (note that if Black plays
Delchev's recommendation 7...0-0
then 8.♗e3 ♗g4 9.♖d1 transposes to
my White recommendation against
the Grünfeld (the move count is off
by one though, as here each side has
saved a tempo). Since this is not a
line either of us recommends for
Black in the Grünfeld, it is illogical
to recommend it here. Fortunately
7...♗g4 works) 8.d5 0-0 9.♗e2 c6
10.0-0 cxd5 11.exd5 ♘8d7 12.♖d1

♘e5 and White has more space but
an isolated d-pawn, so it's equal.

5....♘c6 6.d4
Topical is 6.♕b3 ♘b6 7.d4 ♗e6
8.♕d1 ♗g7 9.e3 0-0 10.♗e2 ♗c4
11.♗xc4 ♘xc4 12.0-0 ♘b6 13.b3
e5= Ipatov-Swiercz, St Louis 2017
(+0.02).
6...♘db4 7.♕a4 ♗d7 8.♕d1 e5!

9.a3?!
9.dxe5! ♗f5 10.♗g5 ♗e7 11.e4 ♗g4
12.♗xe7 ♕xe7 13.a3 ♗xf3 14.gxf3
♖d8 15.♕a4 ♘d3+ 16.♗xd3 ♖xd3
17.♕b5 ♖d4 18.♘d5 ♕xe5 19.♕xb7
♖xe4+ 20.♔f1 ♕xd5 21.fxe4 ♕c4+
22.♔g1 ♕xe4 23.♕c8+ ♔e7 24.♕xh8
♘d4 25.♕c8 ♘f3+ 26.♔g2 ♘d2+
27.♔g1 ♘f3+ leads to a draw by
perpetual check.
9....exd4 10.♘b5

10.axb4 dxc3 11.bxc3 ♗g7 12.♗d2
0-0 13.e3. So far Alexeev-Kurnosov,
Taganrog 2011. Now after either
13...♗f5 or 13...♘e5 Black is clearly
better, due to White's imprisoned
bishop on d2 and lagging
development.

**10....a6 11.♘bxd4 ♘xd4 12.♘xd4
♘c6 13.♘f3**

13....♕f6!N
The **actual game** went 13...♗e6
14.♕xd8+ ♖xd8 15.♗g5 ♗e7 16.♗xe7
♔xe7 17.e3 ♖d6 18.♖c1 ♖hd8 19.♗e2
♗f5 and draw agreed.
14.e3
After 14.♖b1 ♗g7 15.♗g5 ♕f5
16.e3 h6 17.♗h4 ♕a5+ 18.♕d2 ♗f5
19.♕xa5 ♘xa5 20.♖c1 ♗xb2 21.♖xc7
♗xa3 Black has won a pawn and has
two connected passers.

**14....0-0-0 15.♗e2 ♗g7 16.0-0 ♖he8
17.♕a4 ♔b8**

Black is much better. White's queen
is not secure and his development
is severely lagging.

Game 12.4   English Opening –
                        Anti-Grünfeld
Jan Markos   2585
Li Chao   2669
Shenzhen 2011 (4)

**1.♘f3 ♘f6 2.c4 g6 3.♘c3 d5 4.cxd5
♘xd5 5.♕a4+**

5....♘c6
Few people played this way until
computers started recommending
it, because Black gets ugly pawns. In
return though, he gets active piece
play.

Delchev recommends 5...c6, but two of his lines may not be quite equal for Black, as shown. Usual was 5...♗d7, but lately the knight move has taken over.

After 5...c6 the lines split:

A) 6.♕d4 f6 7.e4 e5 8.♘xe5 ♘xc3 9.♕xc3 ♕e7 10.♘f3 ♕xe4+ 11.♗e2 ♘d7 ('Balanced,' says Delchev) 12.d3N ♕b4 13.0-0 ♕xc3 14.bxc3 ♘b6 15.♖e1 ♔f7 and White enjoys better development for free here, though Black is not in real trouble;

B) 6.♘xd5 ♕xd5 7.e4 ♕d6 8.d4 ♘d7 9.♗e2 ♘b6 10.♕c2 ♗g4 11.♗e3 ♗g7 12.0-0 ♗xf3 13.e5N (13.♗xf3 ♗xd4 14.♖ad1 e5 15.♗xd4 exd4 16.e5 ♕e6 17.♕c5 0-0-0 and Black is for choice, Miton-Vachier-Lagrave, France tt 2010) 13...♕d7 14.♗xf3 ♘d5.

analysis diagram

Delchev calls this equal, while the computers love White due to the bishop pair (after 15.♗d2) and the obstructed black bishop. I would prefer White but only slightly. Black will activate his bishop by ...f7-f6, after which the strong knight should offer at least partial compensation for the bishops.

6.♘e5

6.♘d4 ♕d7 7.♘xd5 ♕xd5 8.♘xc6 ♕xc6 9.♕xc6+ bxc6 10.g3 was Rapport-Mikhalevski, Gibraltar 2018 and is similar. 10...a5 (+0.11) is best according to both engines and looks sensible.

6...♕d6

This is popular. In earlier days Black played 6...♘b4 here, e.g. 7.a3 ♗g7 8.axb4 ♗xe5 9.b5.

7.♘xc6 ♕xc6 8.♕xc6+

8.♕d4 ♘xc3 9.dxc3 (in case of 9.♕xh8? ♘xa2 10.b3 ♘xc1 11.♕b2 ♘xe2 12.♔xe2 ♗e6 Black has way too much for the exchange, namely two pawns, better development, the bishop pair, the better pawn structure, and a safer king!) 9...f6 10.e4 ♗e6N 11.♗e3 ♖d8 12.♕xa7 ♕xe4=.

8....bxc6

9.g3

A) 9.b3 ♘xc3 10.dxc3 (10.♗b2 ♗g7 11.♗xc3 ♗xc3 12.dxc3 was Ni Hua-Wei Yi, Shanghai 2015. Now 12...a5 looks best and equal (+0.02)) 10...♗g7 11.♗b2 a5 12.g3 a4 13.♗g2 0-0 14.bxa4 ♗b7 15.0-0 ♖xa4 16.♖fc1 ♖b8 17.♖c2 c5 18.♗xb7 ♖xb7 19.♖d1 ♗e5 20.♗c1 f6 21.♗e3 ♗d6 22.♔g2 ♖ba7 23.♖dd2 ♔f7 – the computers love Black here, despite White's passed pawn and Black's doubled pawns, due to the far more active rooks. I don't see a black advantage myself, but Black should have no trouble making a draw as White can hardly do anything but 'pass';

B) 9.e4 ♘b4 10.♔d1 ♗e6 11.d3 ♗g7 12.♗e3 a5 This was Panchanathan-Bacallao Alonso, Badalona 2011. Black is clearly better with the initiative and much better development.

9....♗g7 10.♗g2 ♗e6 11.b3

Or 11.a3 ♖b8 12.e3 0-0 13.♘a4 ♗c8 14.♘c5 (so far Vitiugov-Areschenko, Olginka tt 2011) 14...♖b5N 15.d4 e5 16.a4 ♖b8 17.dxe5 ♘b4 18.0-0 ♗xe5 19.♖d1 ♘c2 20.♖b1 ♘a3 21.♖a1 ♘c2 with a draw by repetition.

11....0-0-0

With 11...0-0 12.♗b2 ♘b4 13.0-0 ♖fd8 14.d3 ♗g4 15.♖ab1 ♖ab8 16.♖fe1 a5 Black should get enough activity to offset his inferior pawn structure.

12.♗b2 ♘xc3

13.♗xc3

13.♗xc6 ♖d6 (if 13...♘xe2 14.♗xg7 ♘d4 15.♗xh8 ♖xh8 16.♗e4 f5

17.♗d3 ♗d5 18.♖f1 ♗g2 19.♖g1 ♘f3+ 20.♔e2 ♘xg1+ 21.♖xg1 ♗d5 22.♖c1 e6 White has a cosmetic edge due to Black having one more isolated pawn, but Black should have no problems thanks to his strong bishop) 14.♗g2 ♖a6 15.dxc3 ♖d8 16.♗e4 ♖ad6 17.♗d3 ♗f5 18.0-0-0 ♗xd3 19.♖xd3 ♖xd3 20.exd3 ♖xd3 21.f4 ♖f3=.

13....♗xc3 14.dxc3 ♖d6 15.♖d1 ♖hd8 16.♖xd6 ♖xd6 17.♗e4 c5

17...♗d5 18.♗xd5 cxd5=.

18.♗c2 ♗f5 19.e4 ♗g4

19...♗xe4 20.♗xe4 ♖e6 21.f3 f5 22.♔d2 fxe4 23.fxe4 ♖xe4 24.♖f1 c4=.

20.f3 ♗xf3 21.♖f1 ♗xe4 22.♗xe4 ♖e6 23.♖xf7 ♖xe4+ 24.♔d2 h5 25.♔d3 ♖e6 26.a4 ♔d7 27.♖f8 ♖f6

28.♖a8?! ♖d6+ 29.♔c4 e5 30.♖f8 ♔e7 31.♖f2 ♔e6 32.♔xc5 e4 33.♖f8 g5 34.♖e8+ ♔f5 35.♖e7 h4 36.gxh4 gxh4 37.♖xc7? ♖e6 38.♔d5 ♖e8 39.♔c5 ♖e6

39...e3 40.♖f7+ ♔e4 41.♖f1 e2 42.♖e1 ♔f3 wins for Black.

40.♔d5 ♖e8

White resigned, seeing no defense to the advance of the passed pawn. The computer says '41.♔c5=', because computers are told to assume that if they can repeat a position once, they can do so again. But of course, having made the time control, Black would avoid repeating a third time.

Game 12.5   English Opening –
Anti-Grünfeld

Georg Meier   2659
Wesley So   2668
Lubbock 2010 (9)

1.♘f3 ♘f6 2.c4 g6 3.♘c3 d5 4.cxd5 ♘xd5 5.g3 ♗g7 6.♗g2 0-0

7.0-0

In the event of 7.♕b3 c6 8.0-0 ♕b6N 9.♘xd5 cxd5 10.♕xd5 ♘c6 White's development problems and exposed queen insure Black adequate compensation for the pawn.

7....c5 8.♘xd5

A) 8.♕a4 ♘c6 9.♕c4 ♘xc3 10.dxc3 ♕b6 11.♕h4 ♖d8=. Black's control of the open file and the threat on b2 if the c1-bishop moves offset White's mild kingside pressure;

B) 8.♕b3 e6 9.d3 ♘c6 10.♗g5 ♕d7 11.♖ac1 b6 12.♖fe1 ♗b7=. Black is

almost caught up in development and has a slight edge in space.

8....♕xd5

9.d3

9.d4 cxd4 10.♗e3 d3! 11.♘e1 ♕d6 12.♘xd3 ♘c6 13.♗c5 (13.♖c1 ♘d4 14.♘c5 ♖b8 15.♖e1 ♗f5 16.♘b3 ♖fd8=) 13...♕c7 14.♖c1 ♖d8N 15.b4 ♗f5 16.♕a4 ♗h6 17.f4 ♗g7 18.b5 ♘d4 19.♗xd4 ♖xd4 20.♖xc7 ♖xa4 21.♖xb7 ♗d4+ 22.♔h1 ♔f8 23.♖xe7 ♖b8=.

9....♘c6 10.♗e3

After 10.a3 ♕d6 11.♖b1?! c4! 12.b4 cxd3 13.b5 dxe2 14.♕xe2 ♘d4 15.♘xd4 ♗xd4 16.♗h6 ♖d8 White has little for the pawn.

10....♗xb2

Declining the gambit gives White an edge.

11.♖b1

In case of 11.♘d4 ♕d7 12.♘xc6 ♗xa1 13.♕xa1 bxc6 14.♗h6 ♕d4 15.♗xf8 ♔xf8 16.♕b1 ♗g4 17.♗xc6 ♖c8 18.e3 ♕e5 19.♗e4N c4 20.dxc4 ♖xc4 Black has the better of a probable draw.

11....♗f6 12.♕a4

After 12.♘d4 ♕xa2 13.♘xc6 bxc6 14.♗xc5 ♗g4 15.f3 ♗e6 16.d4 ♖fb8 17.♖a1 ♕c4N White doesn't have enough for the pawn.

12....♕d7 13.♕b5

13.♗xc5 b6 14.♗xb6 ♘d4 15.♕d1 axb6 16.♘xd4 ♖xa2 17.♕b3 ♖d2 18.♕b4 ♖a2 19.♕b3 ♖d2 with a draw by repetition.

13....♕e6

I analyzed the novelty 13...b6 14.♘d2 ♘d4 15.♗xd4 ♕xb5 16.♖xb5 ♗xd4 17.♗xa8 ♗d7 18.♖b3 ♖xa8.

analysis diagram

At first I wanted to recommend this, because two bishops, a rook, and an extra pawn are virtually equal in strength to two rooks and a knight. However White seems to have the initiative here, so now I would make this only a second choice in case you don't like the game continuation.

19.e3 ♗g7 20.♖fb1 ♖c8 21.♖a3 ♖c7 22.f4 e5 23.♘c4 exf4 24.gxf4 ♗f8 25.♔f2 f6 26.e4 ♔f7 – Black should be okay here, although he must be careful. White's active rooks give him the sunny side of a probable draw.

14.♕xc5 ♕xa2

Black is under pressure on the queenside, but his extra pawn offsets this.

15.♖fe1

15.♘d2N ♖d8 16.♖fe1 ♗f5 17.♖xb7 ♘d4 18.♖c7 ♖ac8 19.♕xa7 ♕xa7 20.♖xa7 ♖c1 21.♔f1 ♘xe2 22.♘e4 ♖xe1+ 23.♔xe1 ♗xe4 24.dxe4 ♘d4 25.♔f1 ♖b8 26.♗h3 h5=. The two bishops are not much of a plus with all the pawns on one side, and Black's ideally posted knight gives him equality.

15....♕a5 16.♕xa5 ♘xa5 17.♘d2 ♗c3

If Black doesn't want a draw he could try 17...♘c6 18.♘e4 a5 19.♘xf6+ exf6, but I think White keeps an edge.

18.♖ec1 ♗xd2 19.♗xd2 ♘c6 20.♗xc6 bxc6 21.♗a5 ♗e6 22.♖xc6 ♖fc8 23.♖xc8+ ♖xc8

White is 'better' according to the computers, but of course with equal material and bishops of opposite color it's almost sure to be a draw.

24.f3 ♗d5 25.♔f2 ♗c6 26.g4 f6 27.h4 ♔f7 28.♗d2 h5 29.g5 f5 30.♖a1 ♖a8 31.♖a5 a6 32.♖c5 ♖c8 33.♗b4 ♗d7 34.♖e5 e6 35.e4 ♖b8 36.♗c3 ♖b5 37.exf5 ♖xe5 38.fxg6+ ♔xg6 39.♗xe5 a5

Draw agreed. Black doesn't even need the a-pawn to draw here.

Game 12.6   English Opening –
              Symmetrical Variation

Levon Aronian   2799
Ian Nepomniachtchi   2751

St Louis rapid 2017 (2)

1.♘f3 ♘f6 2.c4 c5

This has become the main choice of Grünfeld aficionados. Black avoids committing to ...g7-g6 prematurely.

3.♘c3 d5 4.cxd5 ♘xd5

5.e3

5.d4 ♘xc3 6.bxc3 g6 7.e3 (7.e4 ♗g7 transposes to the Grünfeld; 7.♗f4 ♗g7 8.e3 ♕a5 9.♕d2 0-0 10.♖b1 b6 11.♗d3 ♘c6 12.0–0 ♗a6= (0.00). This bishop trade should make White's space advantage negligible) 7...♗g7 8.♗b5+ ♗d7 9.♗d3 0-0 10.0-0 ♘c6 11.♖b1 ♕c7 12.h3 ♖fd8= (+0.05). A typical Grünfeld position, but White is less developed than he should be.

5...♘xc3

5...e6 is normal and usually leads to the Semi-Tarrasch, but the rare line 6.♘xd5 exd5 7.b4! is pretty strong and annoying here, so I recommend the Grünfeld-like text move instead, which is the usual choice of GMs who play the Grünfeld.

6.bxc3

6.dxc3 looks odd, forfeiting castling, but if the white pawn were on e4 here White would be better, with a safe square for the king on c2 and more active bishops. Since e3-e4 cannot be stopped the dxc3 capture is a serious move even here. I think Black does best to avoid the endgame by 6...♕c7. Then 7.e4 e6

8.♗e3 ♗e7 9.♘d2 0-0 10.♕f3 ♖d8 11.♕g3 aims to open the h-file if Black trades queens, so he replies 11...♗d6. 12.f4 ♗f8!N 13.♗e2 b6 14.0-0 ♗a6! 15.♕f3 ♗xe2 16.♕xe2 ♘c5 (+0.11). White has just a small space edge.

6...g6

7.h4!

This seems to be the only way to pose problems for Black.

A) 7.d4 ♗g7 8.♗b5+! (this avoids a later ...♗b7; 8.♗d3 0-0 9.0-0 ♕c7 10.♕e2 b6= is a typical Grünfeld position with a pleasant game for Black (0.00)) 8...♗d7 9.♗d3 0-0 10.0-0 ♕c7 11.♖b1 b6 12.e4 ♘c6 13.♗e3 ♗g4 14.♗e2 ♖ad8 15.♖c1 ♕b8 16.d5 ♘e5 17.♗g5 ♗xf3 18.♗xf3 f6 19.♗f4 f5 20.g3 ♘xf3+ 21.♕xf3 ♗e5 22.♗h6 ♖f7 23.exf5 ♖xf5 24.♕e4 ♕d6 25.c4 b5 26.♗e3 bxc4 27.♕xc4 ♕xd5 28.♕xc5 ♕xc5 29.♖xc5 ♗d4 30.♗xd4 ♖xd4 31.♖c8+ ♖f8 32.♖c7 ♖a4 33.♖a1 e6= (+0.03). This is a drawn ending, White's edge is only cosmetic;

B) 7.♗b5+ ♗d7 8.♗e2 ♗g7 9.0-0 0-0 10.d4 ♕a5 11.♕b3 ♗c6 12.♗d2 ♘d7 13.c4 ♕a6 14.♘c3 ♖ab8 15.♖ac1 ♖fd8= (0.00). Another typical

Grünfeld-style position where Black has few problems.

7...♗g7

7...h6 has scored well enough for Black but Komodo considers it an unnecessary concession, and the elite GMs seem to agree.

8.h5 ♘c6

9.♗e2

A) 9.♕b3 b6!N 10.♗b5 ♕c7= (0.00). Black need not fear to castle kingside;

B) 9.♖b1 b6 10.d4 0-0 11.♕c2 cxd4 12.cxd4 ♕d6 13.♗d2 ♗f5 14.♗d3 ♗xd3 15.♕xd3 ♖fd8= (0.00). The bishop exchange has eased Black's game. I'd rather play Black in this equal position.

9...b6

9...e5! 10.e4 ♕d6 11.♖b1 0-0=, Black's active queen and space fully offset the slight white pressure on the black king (0.00).

10.♔f1 ♕d6?!

10...♗b7! 11.♕a4 ♕d7 12.d4 ♘e5 13.♗b5 ♗c6 14.♗xc6 ♘xc6 15.g3 h6 16.♔g2 g5= (0.00).

11.d4± 0-0 12.♗a3 ♗f5 13.♔g1

13.hxg6 hxg6 14.♘g5±.

13...♖fd8 14.♕a4 ♕f6 15.hxg6 hxg6 16.♖f1?! ♖ac8 17.♗b2 ♘a5 18.♗a1

18...c4?!

18...♕c6!∓.

19.♘e5

19.♖e1.

19...♕e6 20.♘f3 ♗d3

20...♗f6.

21.♕d1 ♕f5 22.♗xd3 ♕xd3

23.♕c1 ♘c6

23...e5.

24.♖d1 ♕f5 25.♖e1 ♕a5 26.e4 e6

27.g3 ♕xa2

28.e5

28.♕g5±.

28...♘e7 29.♘g5 ♘d5 30.♘e4 b5

31.♕g5 b4 32.cxb4 ♕a3 33.♖c1

♕f3 34.♖h4 ♖f8 35.♕d2 ♕d3

36.♗c3 ♕f3 37.♕g5 ♖c7 38.♗e1

♖b8 39.♘c5 c3 40.♘a6 ♖cc8

41.♘xb8 ♖xb8 42.♕g4 ♕xg4

43.♖xg4 ♖c8 44.♖e4 ♗f8 45.b5 ♗a3

46.♖c2 ♖c4 47.♖ee2 ♗b4 48.♖a2

♘c7 49.♖xa7 ♘xb5 50.♖a8+ ♔g7

51.♗xc3??

51.♔g2 should hold the draw. White lost patience here.

51...♗xc3 52.♔g2 ♖xd4 53.f4 ♖d3

54.♖f2 ♗d4–+

Note that the two minor pieces beat the rook here because of the presence of the extra pair of rooks; if they were traded it should be an easy draw. This is an important but not so widely known chess principle.

55.♖f3 ♖d2+ 56.♔h3 ♘c3 57.♖a1

♘e4 58.♖af1 ♘f2+ 59.♔h4 ♗c5

60.g4 ♘e4 61.g5 ♖h2+ 62.♖h3 ♖g2

63.♖b3 ♘f2 0-1

CHAPTER 13

Queen's Pawn Openings

In this chapter we consider openings White may choose if he starts with 1.d4 but refrains from an early c2-c4. These openings are not very popular at grandmaster level but are much more so at amateur level, because they can be played with relatively little study. As a general rule these lines don't promise White an advantage, but Black needs to know how to respond to each of them.

First we look at the Veresov Attack, **1.d4 ♘f6 2.♘c3 d5 3.♗g5**,

which we meet by **3...h6**, welcoming the bishop for knight exchange. White has to make the trade or play a bad French Defense. I think that the exchange results in a very pleasant game for Black, who can use his unopposed bishop to pin the c3-knight. See Game 13.1.

Next comes the fairly popular Trompowsky Attack, **1.d4 ♘f6 2.♗g5**,

which we meet by **2...d5**. The exchange on f6 is not to be feared, as it would happen without loss of tempo by Black. Otherwise Black will probably continue with 3...c5 and perhaps 4...♕b6, targeting the b2-pawn. See Game 13.2.

The Barry Attack, **1.d4 ♘f6 2.♘f3 g6 3.♘c3 d5 4.♗f4**,

aims at ♕d2 and 0-0-0. The remedy seems to be a timely ...♘e4. See Game 13.3.

After **1.d4 ♘f6 2.♘f3 g6** White has three popular options, all covered in Game 13.4. He can choose the Colle 3.e3, which is considered ineffective against the king's fianchetto, the Torre **3.♗g5 ♗g7 4.♘bd2** and now **4...0-0**, ready to meet 5.e4 or 5.c3 by 5...d5, or the London System **3.♗f4 ♗g7 4.e3 d6 5.h3 0-0 6.♗e2** when I like **6...c5 7.c3 ♕b6**.

I have added two games, first a game with the Jobava System, **1.d4 ♘f6 2.♘c3 d5 3.♗f4**, which is well met by the unusual but powerful **3...a6** in Game 13.5. Second is what I call the 'Fast London System', playing **♗f4 on move 2** without ♘f3. It is well met by 2...c5, planning to meet 3.d5 with either 3...b5 or 3...d6 planning ...e7-e5, and meeting **3.e3** with **3...♕b6** when **4.♘c3** can be met by taking the pawn if you don't mind a draw (Game 13.6) or by 4...d6 if you do. So don't fear these systems, but be prepared!

Game 13.1 Queen's Pawn Openings –
  Veresov Attack

Nicholas Pert   2555
Michael Adams   2715

Sheffield ch-GBR 2011 (10)

1.d4 ♘f6 2.♘c3 d5 3.♗g5

The Veresov Attack. I don't think
it's very good.

The attempt to reach the Blackmar-
Diemer Gambit by 3.e4?! fails here:
3...♘xe4! 4.♘xe4 dxe4 5.♗c4 ♘c6
6.c3 e5 7.d5 ♘e7 8.f3 (8.♗e2 c6)
8...♘g6 9.♗b5+ ♗d7 10.♗xd7+ ♕xd7
11.fxe4 ♗c5 12.♘f3 10.0-0. Black has
returned the pawn to achieve a nice
lead in development, and White
cannot castle. Black plans ...f7-f5
with a big advantage.

3....h6

This move is rare but good. It
seems wrong to spend a tempo to
force the exchange, but the point
is that White's knight on c3 is then
misplaced, because White would
want to play c3-c4 after the trade.
More usual is 3...♘bd7, but why
guard against a bad trade?

4.♗xf6
Or 4.♗h4 e6 5.e4.

Without the insertion of ...h6 ♗h4
this would be a transposition to a
mainline French Defense, where
White should keep his normal
edge. Here however, e2-e4 gives
nothing. On the other hand, a quiet
move like e2-e3 creates a position
in which the move ♘c3 just looks
stupid, blocking the otherwise
desirable c2-c4) 5...♗b4 (after 5...
g5 6.♗g3 ♘xe4 7.♘xe4 dxe4 8.h4
♘c6N 9.c3 ♖g8 10.hxg5 hxg5 White
has yet to prove full compensation
for the pawn) 6.e5 g5 7.♗g3 ♘e4
is an inferior line (for White) of
the MacCutcheon French. Black is
already equal.

4....exf6 5.e3

5.e4 ♗b4 (5...dxe4 6.♘xe4 f5 7.♘g3
♗d6 8.♕e2+ ♕e7 9.♕xe7+ ♗xe7
10.♗d3 g6 is also pleasant for Black,
because the bishop pair is a bigger
factor than the crippled majority)
6.exd5 ♕xd5 7.♘f3 0-0 8.♗e2 ♕a5
9.♕d2 ♘d7 10.a3 ♘b6 11.♖b1 ♗xc3
12.♕xc3 ♕xc3+ 13.bxc3 ♖e8N.

analysis diagram

Both sides have crippled majorities,
but White has three weak pawns
(a3, c2, c3) while Black has none.

5....♗b4 6.♗d3

If 6.♘e2 c6N 7.a3 ♗d6 it's hard to see much to offset Black's bishop pair here.

6....c5 7.dxc5

7.♕f3 ♗xc3+ 8.bxc3 0-0 9.♘e2 ♘c6=.

7....♗xc3+ 8.bxc3 0-0 9.♘e2

9....♗e6

A good alternative was 9...♘d7 10.c4 ♕a5+ 11.♕d2 ♕xd2+ 12.♔xd2 dxc4 13.♗xc4 ♘xc5 14.♖hd1 ♗e6. Black has a superior pawn structure on the queenside at no cost. His doubled pawns do not cripple a majority or fall in any 'bad' category.

10.♖b1 ♕c7 11.0-0 ♘d7 12.♖b4 ♘xc5 13.♖h4?!

White is just 'passing', so Black is already better. He has only one bad pawn while White has three.

13....♖ac8 14.♖d4 ♖fd8 15.♕c1 a6 16.♖d1 b5 17.♕a3 ♘a4 18.♖b1 ♕a7 19.h3 ♖d7 20.♖b3 ♘c5 21.♖b1 ♖dc7

21...♘a4 22.♕b4 ♕c7 23.♖f4 ♖dd8 – Black can win the pawn on c3 any time, though doing so will give White some counterplay with a2-a4. Black is obviously better.

22.♖d1 ♘a4 23.c4 dxc4 24.♗f5 ♖e8

Certainly not 24...♗xf5 in view of 25.♖d8+ and 26.♕f8.

25.♗xe6 fxe6 26.e4 ♔h7?!

26...♘c5 27.♕e3 ♖f7, and although White controls the open file and has a safer king, this does not nearly offset his pawn minus.

27.♕g3 ♘b2 28.♖1d2

28....c3 29.♘xc3 ♘c4 30.♖d1 ♘b2 31.♖1d2 ♘c4 32.♖d1 ♘e5 33.♔h2 ♖ec8 34.♘e2 ♖e7

34...♖xc2 35.f4 ♖xe2 36.fxe5 ♖cc2 37.exf6 ♖xg2+ 38.♕xg2 ♕c7+ 39.♔h1 ♖xg2 40.♔xg2 ♔g6 41.fxg7 ♕xg7 – queen and pawn are in general a bit stronger than two rooks, although here I expect that White can draw.

35.c3 ♕c7 36.♔h1 ♘c4 37.♕g4 ♘e5 38.♕g3 ♘c4 39.♕g4 ♘e5 ½-½

Game 13.2   Queen's Pawn Openings –
Trompowsky Attack

Igor Miladinovic   2561
Dragan Solak   2588
Valjevo 2011 (7)

1.d4 ♘f6 2.♗g5

This is the Trompowsky Attack, which has a few exponents among grandmasters and quite a decent following among amateurs. I think it is fading now though.

2....d5

I like this reply, because I don't consider 3.♗xf6 to be in White's favor, and otherwise the move ...d7-d5 is without drawbacks.

3.e3

A) 3.♘d2 c5 4.dxc5 e6 5.♘b3 ♘bd7 6.e3 ♘xc5 7.♘xc5 ♗xc5 8.♗b5+ ♔f8 9.♗d3 e5;

B) 3.♘c3 transposes to the Veresov;

C) 3.♘f3 transposes to the Torre;

D) 3.♗xf6 exf6 4.e3 ♗e6 (4...c5 transposes to the note to move 4) 5.♗d3 f5 (5...c5 6.dxc5 ♗xc5 7.c3 ♘c6 8.♘d2 0-0 9.♘b3 ♗d6 10.♘e2 ♖c8 and Black's bishops more than offset his isolated d-pawn) 6.♕f3 g6 7.♘e2 c6 8.0-0 ♘d7 9.♘f4 ♗d6 10.♘d2N (not 10.c4? ♗xf4 11.cxd5 ♗xh2+ 12.♔xh2 ♕h4+ and Black wins a pawn) 10...♕c7 11.♘xe6 fxe6 12.♕h3 0-0 – the Stonewall formation is great for Black when his light-squared bishop has already been exchanged, as here.

3....c5

4.♘c3

A) 4.c3 ♘c6 5.♘f3 ♕b6 6.♕c1 (after 6.♕b3 c4 7.♕c2 ♗f5 8.♕c1 ♘e4 9.♗f4 h6 10.♘bd2 g5 11.♗g3 ♘xg3 12.hxg3 ♗g7 13.♗e2 ♕d8 White has little for the bishop pair lost) 6...♘e4 7.♗f4 ♗f5 8.♘bd2 e6 9.♘xe4 ♗xe4 10.♗e2 ♗e7 11.0-0 0-0 and Black has more space at no cost;

B) 4.♘d2 h6N 5.♗xf6 exf6 – although White will isolate Black's d-pawn to compensate for Black's bishops, his knight on d2 is misplaced for putting pressure on d5.

C) After 4.♗xf6 gxf6 (now this is probably better than exf6 which would usually lead to d5 becoming isolated) 5.dxc5 e6 6.e3 ♗xc5 7.♗e2 ♘c6 8.0-0 0-0 9.c4 d4 10.b4 ♗xb4 11.exd4 f5 12.♕b3 ♕f6 13.♘c3 ♗e7 14.♖ad1 b6= (-0.06). White's better development and pawn structure compensate for the bishop pair.

4....♘c6 5.dxc5

5.♗b5 e6 6.♘f3 ♗e7 7.0-0 0-0 8.dxc5 ♗xc5 9.♕e2 ♗e7 10.♖fd1 a6 11.♗d3 ♘d7 12.♗xe7 ♕xe7 13.e4 d4 14.♘b1 e5 – Black has more space, the better bishop, and a great square (c5) for his knight.

5....e6 6.♘f3 ♗xc5 7.♗d3

White is playing a slightly dubious variation of the Queen's Gambit Accepted with colors reversed and an extra tempo, which at best may give him equality.

In case of 7.a3 0-0 8.♗d3 ♗e7 9.0-0 h6 10.♗h4 a6 11.♕e2 b5 12.h3 ♗b7 Black has more space and an extra pawn in the center.

7....h6 8.♗h4

8.♗xf6 ♛xf6 9.0-0 0-0 10.a3 ♗b6 and Black is already better thanks to the bishops and the extra center pawn.

8....g5

Also after 8...0-0 9.0-0 ♗e7 Black is at least equal.

9.♗g3 ♘h5 10.♗e5 ♘xe5 11.♘xe5 ♘f6 12.h4 ♗d6 13.♗b5+ ♚e7 14.♛d4 a6

15.hxg5?!

Better is 15.♗e2 ♛c7 16.hxg5 ♗xe5 17.gxf6+ ♗xf6 18.♛b4+ ♚e8 19.♖d1 ♗d7 20.e4 d4 21.♖xd4 ♗xd4 22.♛xd4 ♚e7 23.e5 ♗c6. White has a pawn and a safer king for the exchange. It's a close game but I'd rather play Black.

15....hxg5 16.♖xh8 ♛xh8 17.♗f1 ♗d7 18.0-0-0 ♖c8

19.♘xd7?!

In the event of 19.g3 ♗c5 20.♛d2 ♛h2 21.♘xd7 ♚xd7 22.a3 ♚c7 23.♚b1 ♚b8 Black is better with an extra center pawn and better development.

19....♘xd7 20.♛xh8 ♖xh8 21.e4 dxe4 22.♘xe4 ♗f4+ 23.♚b1 f5 24.♘c3 ♗e5 25.♘e2 ♘f6

Black is obviously better here. His bishop, knight, and king are each better positioned than their white counterparts. Moreover, his pawn majority is more advanced.

26.♘c1 ♘g4 27.♘d3 ♗d4 28.♗e2 ♘xf2 29.♘xf2 ♗xf2 30.♗f3 b6

With rooks on the board and Black having the hope of obtaining two connected passed pawns, the fact that there are bishops of opposite color isn't likely to save White.

31.b4 g4 32.♗c6 f4 33.♖d2 ♗e3
34.♖d3 ♘f6 35.♔b2 ♔g5 36.♖d7
♔h4 37.♔b3 ♔g3 38.♖g7 ♗d4
39.♖g6

39....♖c8 40.b5 axb5 41.♗d7
♖c3+ 42.♔b4 ♖xc2 43.♔xb5 ♖xg2
44.♗xe6 ♔h4 45.♔c4 ♗c5 46.a4 f3
47.♗d5 ♖g1 0-1

Game 13.3   Queen's Pawn Openings –
              Barry Attack
Antoaneta Stefanova   2524
Katerina Lahno   2536
Rostov-on-Don 2011 (10)

1.d4 ♘f6 2.♘f3 g6 3.♘c3 d5 4.♗f4
This is known as the Barry Attack,
which according to New In Chess
Yearbook is British slang for 'rubbish'
attack, not someone's name.
4....♗g7

5.♕d2
This aims at ♗h6 and at castling
queenside, which seems logical
given that the knight on c3 blocks
the c2-pawn.
5.e3 is probably the better move, but
if White has to switch to castling
kingside like this, the opening
strikes me as illogical. The knight
on c3 is merely in the way unless
White castles queenside: 5...0-0
6.♗e2 c5 7.0-0 (7.♘e5 ♘fd7 8.♘xd7
♗xd7 9.dxc5 ♗c6 10.0-0 e5 11.♗g3
d4 12.♘b5 ♘a6 13.c3 ♘xc5= (-0.11).
Black regains his pawn with no
problems) 7...b6 (defending c5
rather than exchanging it seems
better) 8.♘e5 ♗b7 9.♕d2 ♘c6
10.♖fd1 e6 11.a4 ♕e7 (-0.28). Black
has one more pawn fighting for the
center than White.
5....0-0 6.♗h6
Logical but perhaps not good. But if
he goes 6.0-0-0 ♘e4N 7.♘xe4 dxe4
8.♘e5 (after 8.♘g5 ♕d5 9.♔b1 h6
10.c4 ♕f5 11.♘h3 e3+ 12.♔d3 ♘c6
Black should win something due to
the threat of 13...♘b4) 8...♕d5 9.c4
♕e6 10.h3 (else ...f7-f6) 10...♗xe5
11.♗xe5 ♘c6 12.♗h2 ♕xc4+
13.♔b1 e3! 14.b3 ♘xd4 15.bxc4 exd2
16.♖xd2 c5 17.e3 ♘c6 White has
only the bishop pair for the pawn,
so he is just down half a pawn for
nothing.
6....♘e4 7.♘xe4
7.♕e3N ♕d6 8.♗xg7 ♔xg7 9.0-0-0
♘xc3 10.♕xc3 ♗f5 11.♔b1 ♘d7=
(0.00).
7....dxe4 8.♗xg7 ♔xg7

9.♘g5

In case of 9.♘e5 c5 10.e3 ♕c7 11.0-0-0 ♖d8 12.♕c3 f6 13.♘c4 ♗g4N 14.♖d2 ♘a6 Black has the better development and the initiative.

9....e5 10.0-0-0

If 10.dxe5 ♕xd2+ 11.♔xd2 ♖d8+ 12.♔e3 ♘c6 13.♘xe4 ♘xe5 Black's superior development and threats, plus safer king, are surely worth a pawn, e.g. 14.♔f4 f6 15.f3 ♗f5= (0.00).

10.... ♕xd4 11.♕xd4 exd4 12.♖xd4 e3 13.fxe3 h6 14.♘f3 ♖e8

White's bottled-up kingside and doubled isolated pawns on a half-open file are more than enough compensation for a pawn.

15.♖d3 ♘a6

16.g3?!

In case of 16.a3 b6 17.g3 ♘c5 18.♖c3 ♗b7 19.♗g2 ♖e7 Black is clearly for choice despite his pawn minus.

16....♘b4 17.♖b3 c5 18.a3 ♘d5 19.e4 c4 20.♖b5 ♘e3 21.♖c5? ♖d8 22.♘d2 ♗e6 23.b3 ♖d7 24.bxc4 ♖ad8 25.♖d5 ♗xd5 26.exd5

Although White has two pawns for the exchange, he can't keep them and is clearly losing.

26....♖c7

26...b5! won more easily.

27.♖g1 b5 28.♗g2 bxc4 29.♗f3 ♘xd5 30.♘b1 ♘e3 31.♘c3 h5 32.h4 ♖cd7 33.♘e4

33....f5

33...c3!.

34.♘c5 ♖d1+ 35.♖xd1 ♖xd1+ 36.♔b2 ♖d2 37.♔c3 ♖xc2+ 38.♔d4 ♘f1 39.e4 fxe4 40.♗xe4 ♖a2 41.♘e6+ ♔f6 42.♘f4 ♘xg3 43.♗xg6

♘e2+ 44.♘xe2 ♔xg6 45.♘f4+ ♔h6
46.♔xc4 ♖xa3 47.♔b5 ♖g3
White resigned.

Game 13.4   Queen's Pawn Openings –
London System

Nikolay Legky   2436
Andrei Istratescu   2617

Malakoff 2011 (6)

1.d4 ♘f6 2.♘f3 g6 3.♗f4
The London System, which has
enjoyed a surge in popularity since
the last edition of this book.
  A) 3.e3, the Colle System, is not
very effective against ...♗g7: 3...♗g7
4.♗e2 c5 5.0-0 0-0 and now:

analysis diagram

  A1) 6.c4 cxd4 7.exd4 (after 7.♘xd4
♘c6 8.♘c3 d5 9.cxd5 ♘xd5 10.♘xd5
♕xd5 11.♗f3 ♕c5 12.♘xc6 bxc6
13.♕a4 ♗f5N 14.♗xc6 ♗c2 15.♕b5
♕xb5 16.♗xb5 a6 17.♗e2 ♖fd8
White's development problem is
quite serious, so despite White's
extra pawn Black is for choice) 7...
d5 8.♘c3 ♘c6 transposes to the
Grünfeld system with e2-e3;
  A2) 6.b3 cxd4 7.♘xd4 (in case of
7.exd4 d5 8.♗b2 ♘c6 9.♘bd2 ♗f5

10.♘e5 ♖c8 11.c4 ♘xe5 12.dxe5
♘d7 13.f4 ♘c5 14.♘f3 dxc4 15.♗xc4
♘d3N 16.♗xd3 ♕xd3 Black's
bishop pair gives him the edge) 7...
d5 8.♗b2 ♖e8 9.c4 e5 10.♘f3 ♘c6
11.cxd5 ♘xd5 12.♗c4 ♗e6 and Black
is more comfortable, with better
development and the option to play
...e5-e4 or ...f7-f5;
  B) 3.♗g5 is the Torre Attack:
3...♗g7 4.♘bd2 0-0 and now:

analysis diagram

5.c3 (after 5.e4 d5 6.e5 ♘e4 7.♗e3
c5 8.c3 cxd4 9.cxd4 ♘c6 10.♗e2
f5 11.exf6 exf6N Black would be
already better with his outposted
knight) 5...d5 6.e3 c5 7.♗d3 ♕b6
8.♖b1 ♘c6 9.0-0 ♖e8 10.b4 cxb4
11.cxb4 a5=.

3....♗g7

4.e3

Instead, 4.♘bd2 0-0 and now:

A) 5.c3 d6 6.e4 ♘bd7 7.h3 e5 8.dxe5 dxe5 9.♗e3 (9.♘xe5 ♘xe5 10.♗xe5 ♘xe4 11.♗xg7 ♖e8 12.♘xe4 ♖xe4+ 13.♗e2 ♕xd1+ 14.♖xd1 ♔xg7=) 9...♕e7 10.♕c2 b6 11.b4 ♗b7 12.♗c4 ♘e8N 13.0-0 ♘d6 and Black is for choice with possibilities like ...c7-c5 or ...a7-a5 or...f7-f5;

B) 5.h3 c5 6.e3 cxd4 (6...d6 7.c3 b6 8.♗e2 ♗b7 9.0-0 ♘bd7 transposes to the note to move 7) 7.exd4 ♘c6 8.c3 d6 9.♗e2 e5 10.dxe5 dxe5 11.♘xe5 ♘d5 12.♘xc6 bxc6 13.♗g3 ♖e8 14.0-0 ♗xc3 15.♕c1 ♖xe2 16.bxc3 ♗f5 17.♘f3 ♖c2 18.♕h6 ♕f8 19.♕h4 ♖xc3 and White has only partial compensation for the pawn;

C) 5.e4 d5! 6.♗d3 (in case of 6.e5 ♘h5 7.♗e3 c5 8.dxc5 ♘c6 9.c3 ♘xe5 10.♘xe5 ♗xe5 Black has more center pawns and the better pawn structure) 6...c5 7.dxc5 ♘bd7 8.0-0 dxe4 9.♘xe4 ♘xe4 10.♗xe4 ♘xc5 and Black wins the bishop pair cleanly.

4....d6 5.h3

5.♗e2 0-0 6.0-0 ♘h5 7.♗g5 h6 8.♗h4 g5 9.♘fd2 gxh4 10.♗xh5 c5 11.c3 h3 12.g3 ♘d7N 13.♗f3 ♖b8 14.a4 a6 15.a5 b5 16.axb6 ♘xb6 17.♕e2 ♕c7 18.dxc5 ♕xc5= (+0.07). Black's bishop pair offsets White's better pawn structure.

5....0-0 6.♗e2 c5 7.c3

7.0-0 ♕b6 8.♘bd2 ♗e6 9.♘g5 ♗d7 10.♘c4 ♕c7 11.a4 ♘d5N 12.♗g3 ♘b6 13.b3 ♘xc4 14.♗xc4 ♘c6 15.c3 ♕a5= (+0.05).

7....♕b6

A decent alternative is 7...b6 8.0-0 ♗b7 9.♘bd2 ♘bd7 10.♗h2 ♕c7 11.a4 ♘e4 12.♘xe4 ♗xe4 13.♘d2 ♗c6 14.♗a6 ♗b7 15.♕e2 ♗xa6 16.♕xa6 ♖ab8 17.♖fe1 ♕b7 18.♕xb7 ♖xb7=.

8.♕b3

In case of 8.♕c1 ♘c6 9.0-0 ♗e6 10.♘bd2 cxd4 11.exd4 ♖ac8 12.♖e1 ♖fe8 13.♗e3 ♕d8 14.♘f1 ♗d5 I slightly prefer Black due to his extra center pawn and lead in development.

8....♗e6 9.♕a3?!

9.♕xb6 axb6 10.a3 ♗d7 (also good is 10...cxd4 11.exd4 ♘d5 12.♗g3 ♗d7 (-0.21), planning ♗c6) 11.♘bd2 ♗c6 12.0-0 ♘a6N 13.♖fe1 ♘c7 14.♗g3 ♖fd8= (+0.05); Black's active rook on a8 compensates for his slightly inferior pawn structure.

9....cxd4

10.cxd4?

Instead, after 10.exd4 ♕c6 11.♘bd2 b5 12.0-0 a5 13.♗e3 ♕b7 14.♖ac1 ♘c6 (-0.80) Black's minority attack and extra center pawn give him some advantage.

10....♘d5 11.♗g3 ♘b4 12.♔d2?!

Here, better was 12.♕a4 ♗f5 13.♘a3 ♘d3+ 14.♗xd3 ♗xd3 15.♖d1 ♗e4 16.♖d2 ♖c8 17.0-0 ♘a6 – Black has both the open file and the bishop pair.

12....♗f5 13.♖c1 e5 14.♖c4?

Also after the variation 14.dxe5 dxe5 15.♗xe5 ♗xe5 16.♘xe5 ♘d7 17.♘xd7 ♖fd8 18.♔e1 ♖xd7, Black's huge lead in development and safer king mean more than White's extra pawn.

14....♘8a6 15.♕a4?

In the event of 15.♘c3 d5 16.♖xb4 ♘xb4 Black is up the exchange with a much safer king.

15....d5

White resigned. Black will win the d-pawn with a continued attack. A sample continuation is 16.♖c3 exd4 17.exd4 ♖fc8 18.♗xa6 ♘xa6 19.♕b3 ♘b4 20.♘a3 ♗xd4 21.♘xd4 ♕xd4+ 22.♔e1 ♗d3 and Black wins more material.

Game 13.5   Queen's Pawn Openings – Jobava System

Baadur Jobava 2622

Shant Sargsyan 2488

PRO League KO Stage 2019 (2)

1.d4 d5 2.♘c3 ♘f6

We would transpose the first two black moves.

3.♗f4

This combination of ♘c3 and ♗f4 is called the Jobava System, after the player of this game. He doesn't play it so often lately, perhaps this is why.

3...a6

This is not so popular, but quite a good move. It prevents ♘b5, and prepares to answer White's intended queenside castling by ...b7-b5.

4.e3 e6

It seems to the engines and to me that White has already lost all of his opening advantage.

5.a3

A) 5.♘f3 c5 6.♗d3 (6.♗e2 b6 – so Black can develop his queen's bishop without loss of a tempo: 7.0-0 ♗b7=) 6...c4 7.♗e2 b5 8.0-0 ♗b7 9.♘e5 ♗d6 10.b3 0-0 11.♗f3

♘c6∓ (-0.20). Black has gained too much time and space. The knight is not happy on c3;

B) 5.g4 ♗b4 6.♗g2 c5 7.g5 cxd4 8.exd4 ♘e4 9.♘ge2 ♘xc3 10.♘xc3 ♘c6∓ (-0.45). White's king won't be too happy on either wing.

5...c5 6.h3

6.♘f3 ♘c6 7.♗e2 ♗d6 8.dxc5 ♗xc5 9.♕d2 0-0 10.0-0 ♕e7 11.b4 ♗a7∓ (-0.45). White's c2-pawn is much less useful than Black's d5-pawn.

6...♘c6 7.♘f3 b5 8.♗d3 c4 9.♗e2 ♗d6 10.0-0 0-0 11.♖e1 ♗b7

12.♕d2?!

12.♗f1 ♘e7 13.♘e2 ♘f5 14.c3 ♘e4∓ (-0.42). Black's space advantage is clear.

12...♖e8?!

12...♘e4 13.♘xe4 dxe4 14.♗xd6 ♕xd6 15.♘h2 e5∓ (-0.64). Black has a large space advantage.

13.♗g5 h6

13...♘e7!∓.

14.♗xf6 ♕xf6 15.e4 ♗f4 16.♕d1 dxe4 17.♘xe4 ♕e7 18.♘c5 ♖ad8 19.c3 ♗c8 20.♗f1 ♗d6 21.♘e4 ♗b8 22.b3 cxb3 23.♕xb3 ♕c7 24.a4 b4 25.♖ac1 ♕a5? 26.♖e3?! ♗f4 27.cxb4 ♕b6 28.a5 ♕b7 29.♖c5? ♗xe3

29...♘xd4!.

30.♕xe3 ♘xb4 31.♘f6+ gxf6 32.♕xh6 ♘d5 33.♗d3 f5 34.♕g5+ ♔f8 35.♕h6+ ♔e7 36.♘e5 ♖g8 37.♗f1 ♗d7 38.♕h4+ ♔e8 39.♕h7 ♖f8 40.♕g7 ♕b1 41.h4 ♖c8 42.♖xc8+ ♗xc8 43.h5 ♘f4 44.f3 ♕e1 45.g3 ♘xh5 46.♕h6 ♕xg3+ 47.♔h1 ♕h4+ 0-1

Game 13.6   Queen's Pawn Openings – Fast London System

Eric Prié 2490
Santiago Gonzalez de la Torre 2460

San Sebastian 2011 (3)

1.d4 ♘f6 2.♗f4

White tries to play the London without bothering with ♘f3, but this has a drawback.

2...c5

We're not playing the Benoni normally, but ♗f4 invites it.

3.e3

If 3.d5:

analysis diagram

A) 3...d6 4.♘f3 (4.♘c3 e5 5.dxe6 ♗xe6 6.♘f3 transposes) 4...e5 5.dxe6 ♗xe6 6.♘c3 ♘c6 7.e4 ♗e7 8.♕d2 0-0 9.♗e2 ♕b6 10.0-0 ♖ad8 11.♘g5 ♗c8= (+0.04). Black's pieces are coordinated and his only weakness on d6 is well-protected;

B) 3...b5 and now:

B1) 4.♘f3 ♕a5+ 5.♗d2 ♕b6 (5...b4 6.♗g5 ♕b6=) 6.c4 e6 7.dxe6 fxe6 8.cxb5 a6. This looks like an improved (for Black) version of the Blumenfeld Counter Gambit. Black has fair compensation for the pawn;

B2) 4.f3 a6 5.e4 d6 6.a4 b4 7.♘d2 e6 8.dxe6 ♗xe6 9.♘h3 ♘c6= (+0.14). Black is developing smoothly, although he may lose the bishop pair.;

B3) 4.c4. So now it's a Benko Gambit where White has declined with the seldom-played 4.♗f4. After 4...g6 5.cxb5 a6 6.♘c3 axb5 7.e4 ♘h5 8.♗e5 f6 9.♗xb8 b4 10.♘a4 ♖xb8 11.♘xc5 e6 12.♖c1 ♕b6 13.♕d4 ♗h6 14.♖c2 0–0 (-0.28) Black has a lot of development for just half a pawn.

3...♕b6

This is objectively the best defense to the 'Fast London System' (2.♗f4) as White has no more than a draw with proper play. But it does invite repetitions once the pawn is taken,

so I give an alternative to the pawn grab.

4.♘c3

A) 4.♘a3 ♕xb2 (4...d6 5.♘c4 ♕c7 6.♘f3 ♘h5 7.c3 ♘d7 8.♗g5 h6 9.♗h4 g5 10.♗g3 ♗g7=) 5.♘b5 transposes to the game;

B) 4.b3 g6 5.♘c3 ♗g7 6.♘f3 ♘c6 7.♕d2 d6 8.d5 ♘b4 9.♗c4 ♕a5 10.0-0 ♘h5 11.♖ac1 ♘xf4 12.exf4 ♗f5 13.♘d1 ♕xa2 14.♗b5+ ♔f8 15.♘e3 ♗c8 16.♖fd1 ♕b2∓ (-0.21). White's lead in development doesn't quite offset 1.5 pawns.

4...♕xb2

4...d6 is the critical line if you don't want to allow a quick repetition or if you can't remember the theory after the capture on b2. It seems to be satisfactory, e.g. 5.a3 g6 6.♘f3 ♗g7

analysis diagram

7.♗e2 (7.h3 0-0 8.♗e2 cxd4 9.exd4 ♗f5 10.♖b1 d5 is equal) 7...♘h5 8.♘d5 ♕a5+ 9.♕d2 ♕xd2+ 10.♘xd2 ♘xf4 11.exf4 ♔d8 12.dxc5 ♗xb2 13.♖a2 ♗e6 14.♖xb2 ♗xd5 15.♗f3 ♗xf3 16.♘xf3 ♔c7 17.cxd6+ exd6 18.0-0 ♘c6 19.♖fb1 b6 20.♖d1 ♖ad8= (+0.13). White's better piece activity offsets Black's better pawn structure.

5.♘b5 ♘d5 6.a3

A) 6.♖b1 ♕xa2 7.♗g3 (7.♖a1 ♕b2 8.♖b1 ♕a2 repeats) 7...cxd4 8.exd4 ♕a5+ 9.c3 d6 10.♗c4 e6 11.♘e2 a6 12.♖a1 ♕b6 13.♕b3 ♗d7 14.0-0 ♗e7 15.♖fb1 0-0 16.♘xd6 ♗xd6 17.♗xd5 ♕xb3 18.♖xb3 exd5 19.♗xd6 ♖e8 20.♖xb7 ♖xe2 21.♗xb8 ♗c6 22.♖b6 ♗b5 23.h4 ♗c4∓ (-0.24). The passed a-pawn is obviously worth more than the blocked, backward c-pawn, but a draw is likely due to bishops of opposite color;

B) 6.♘f3 ♕b4+ (6...cxd4 7.♖b1 ♕xa2 8.♖a1 ♕b2 9.♗d3 ♕b4+ 10.c3 dxc3 11.0-0) 7.♘d2 ♕a5N 8.♕f3 ♘xf4 9.♕xf4 d6 10.♕e4 ♔d8 11.♕h4 ♔e8 (11...f6 12.dxc5 a6 13.♘d4 ♕xc5= (0.00). White's better development and the right to castle offset Black's 1.5 pawn material plus) 12.♕e4 ♔d8 repeats.

6...a6 7.♖b1 ♕a2

8.♕c1

This wins the queen, but Black gets rook, bishop, pawn, and a very good position for it.

8.♖a1 ♕b2=; this draw by repetition has occurred many times, and is probably best play from here.

8...axb5 9.♖a1 ♕xa1 10.♕xa1

10...♘c6

10...e5! – speed in development and castling is critical here: 11.♗xe5 (11.dxe5 c4 12.♕d4 ♘xf4 13.♕xf4 ♗xa3 14.♘f3 ♗b4+ 15.♔e2 0-0 (material is about even but Black has a much safer king and better development) 16.♘d4 d5 17.exd6 ♘c6 18.♘xb5 ♖a5 19.♘d4 g5 20.♕f6 ♗c3 21.♘xc6 ♗xf6 22.♘xa5 b5 23.♘c6 ♗b7 24.♘e7+ ♔h8 25.♔d2 ♖d8 26.♘f5 ♗e4 27.♘d4 ♖xd6∓ (-0.60). Black is up the bishop pair and has better development) 11...c4 12.♗xb8 ♖xa3 13.♕b2 ♗b4+ 14.♔e2 ♖a2 15.♕c1 ♗a3 16.♕d2 ♗b4 17.♕c1 0-0 18.♔f3 d6 19.♕b1 ♖a4 20.♘e2 ♗d7 21.c3 ♗a3 22.e4 ♘e7N 23.g3 ♖xb8 24.♗h3 ♗e8 25.♔g2 b4 26.cxb4 ♗xb4∓ (-0.15), Lc0 -0.47. Black is ¼ pawn ahead by my count, and he has two connected passed pawns.

11.dxc5?

11.♗xb5! cxd4 12.♗xc6 bxc6 13.♕xd4 f6 14.c4 ♘xf4 15.exf4 e6 16.♘f3 ♗xa3 17.0-0 ♖a4± (+1.12). Although material is about even, White leads in development, and the c8-bishop is sad.

11...b4 12.a4 ♘c3

13.♘f3

13.♘e2 g5 14.♗xg5 ♖g8 15.f4 ♗g7 16.♕c1 ♘xa4 17.♕d1 ♘xc5 18.♘d4 ♘xd4 19.exd4 ♘e6−+ (-1.62). White is about to lose a pawn, with more losses to come.

13...♖xa4 14.♕c1 f6

14...e6! 15.♗d6 ♗xd6 16.cxd6 b6 17.♗c4 ♗a6∓ (-1.22). White will be up ¼ pawn, but he won't be able to castle and Black will quickly obtain a dominating superiority in piece placement.

15.e4 ♘xe4 16.♗c7 e6 17.♗d3 ♘xc5 18.♗b5 ♖a3 19.0-0 ♗e7∓ (-1.28)

19...♘e4!−+.

Black has a 2¼ pawn advantage by my count. White has some compensation in that the c8-bishop cannot yet move, but that's only worth a pawn or so.

20.♕f4 g5 21.♕c4 ♖c3 22.♕e2 g4 23.♗xc6 bxc6 24.♘h4 ♖g8 25.♖e1 ♗a6 26.♕d1 d5 27.♕a1? ♖xc2 28.♗b6 ♘d3−+ 29.♖d1 ♗b5 30.♕b1 ♖b2 31.♕a1 b3 32.h3 ♖c2 33.♕b1 ♗c4 34.♖xd3 ♗xd3 35.♕xb3 ♖c1+ 36.♔h2 ♗d6+ 37.g3 ♗e4 38.f3 gxf3 39.♗f2 ♖f1 40.♕c3 ♖xf2+ 41.♔g1 ♖c2 0-1

CHAPTER 14

Neo-Grünfeld

This name refers to lines in which Black plays the typical Grünfeld moves even though White has not played ♘c3. Usually this means that White has chosen an early kingside fianchetto, although first in Game 14.1 we consider (after **1.d4 ♘f6 2.c4 g6**) **3.f3** (which I wrote a whole book on titled *Sabotage the Grünfeld* – New In Chess 2014!).

White aims for the Sämisch Attack against the King's Indian or to exchange on d5 (after 3...d5) and then kick the knight when it has no opposing knight to capture. So I avoid the problem by playing **3...♘c6** (as also recommended by Delchev and Agrest), which although it looks a bit cheeky has the virtue of making f2-f3 look silly. Its point was to cover e4, but if Black focuses on d4 that becomes irrelevant, even harmful as ♘f3 is now illegal.

The remainder of this chapter deals with **3.g3 ♗g7** (3...c6, as recommended by Avrukh, is much safer but basically it's playing for a draw) **4.♗g2 d5**.

The obvious try for an advantage is now **5.cxd5 ♘xd5 6.e4 ♘b6 7.♘e2**. We hit back at the center with **7...c5 8.d5 0-0 9.0-0 e6**. Black should defer the exchange of pawns (which clears c4) until White has played either ♘bc3 or a2-a4. Normally Black develops his knight to a6. Computers tend to like White due to the advanced passed pawn but human experience suggests that Black has adequate piece play. See Game 14.2.

In Game 14.3 White simply ignores ...d7-d5 and just plays ♘f3 and castles. Black should take on c4, and then when White plays ♘a3 to regain the pawn, give it back by ...c4-c3! followed by ...c7-c5, giving White the same weak pawns he gets in the Grünfeld Exchange Variation but without the big center to compensate. This line is not very promising for White and not so popular any more.

In Game 14.4 White exchanges on d5 but refrains from 6.e4, just developing his knight to f3 and castling. This is the main line now of the Neo-Grünfeld. Black should voluntarily retreat his knight to b6 before castling, so as to be able to play ...♘c6 next with attack on d4 to force the rather tame defense move e2-e3. Only then both sides castle.

Now Black should refrain from 9...e5 due to 10.d5, instead playing the 'improving move' 9...♖e8 and if 10.♖e1, another improving move: 10...a5. Black needs to play sharply and accurately in this position; one sloppy move can leave him with an awful game. As of now it seems that Black is fine, but this is cutting-edge theory so I would keep abreast of developments in this line.

Game 14.1   King's Indian –
             Anti-Grünfeld

Zhang Ziyang   2442
Ni Hua   2646

Xinghua Jiangsu 2011 (3)

1.d4 ♘f6 2.c4 g6 3.f3 ♘c6

I like this move, endorsed by
Delchev and Agrest. f2-f3 just begs
for Black to attack the dark squares.
Usually an early ...♘c6 can be well
met by d4-d5, e2-e4, and f2-f4, but
here this would lose a tempo.
4.♘c3
A) 4.e4 e5 and now:

analysis diagram

A1) In case of 5.d5 ♘d4 6.♘e2 c5
I favor Black due to the monster
knight;
A2) 5.♘e2 exd4 6.♘xd4 ♗g7
7.♘xc6 bxc6 and I like Black due

to the possibility of getting in
...d7-d5 in one go, which would
be impossible if this arose from a
King's Indian Defense;
A3) 5.dxe5 ♘xe5 6.♗e3 ♗g7 7.♘c3
0-0 8.♕d2 d6 9.b3 ♖e8 10.♘ge2
a6 11.♖d1 (11.♘f4 c6 12.♗e2 b5 is
similar) 11...b5 12.cxb5 axb5 13.♘xb5
d5 and White is in trouble;
B) 4.d5 ♘e5 5.e4 d6 and now:

analysis diagram

B1) 6.f4 ♘ed7 7.♘c3 ♗g7
transposes to the next note;
B2) 6.♘c3 ♗g7 7.f4 (this is the
main line of the 3...♘c6 variation)
♘ed7 8.♘h3! (8.♘f3 0-0 9.♗e2
♘c5=) 8...0-0 9.♗e2 (9.♘f2 ♘c5
10.♗e2 transposes; Delchev prefers
9...♘b6 with one continuation
in his book being 10.a4 a5 11.g4!
e6 12.dxe6 ♗xe6 13.f5 ♗xc4
14.g5 ♘fd7 15.f6 ♘xf6. This is
an 'interesting' piece sacrifice
(+0.23), Lc0 +0.58, so the engines
prefer the normal 9...♘c5) 9...♘c5
10.♘f2 e6 11.0-0 (11.dxe6! fxe6
12.♗e3 b6 13.♕c2 ♗b7 14.0-0-
0! is recommended for White
by Delchev, who calls it 'very
dangerous'. I won't dispute that,
but after 14...♘fd7 15.h4 ♗xc3

16.bxc3 e5 17.f5 ♘f6 18.fxg6 ♘fxe4 19.♘xe4 ♗xe4 20.♕d2 hxg6 21.h5 g5 22.♗xg5 ♕d7 the position is messy with both kings unsafe. Komodo gives just +0.05, Lc0 +0.45, so on average similar to other critical White tries against the Grünfeld) 11...exd5 12.cxd5 c6 13.dxc6 bxc6 14.♗f3 ♖b8 15.♗e3 ♗a6 16.♖e1 ♖xb2 17.e5 ♘d5 18.♘xd5 cxd5 19.♕xd5 ♘e6 20.exd6 ♖b5 21.♕d1 ♗c3 22.a4 ♖b4 23.♘e4 ♗xe1 24.♕xe1 ♖b3 25.♗d2 ♖xf3! 26.gxf3 f5 (+0.15). Black will win the d6-pawn resulting in a symmetrical and balanced position with just a small space edge for White;

  B3) 6.♘e2 ♗g7 7.♘bc3 0-0 8.♘d4 c6 9.f4 ♘ed7 10.dxc6 ♘c5 11.♕f3 ♖e8 and due to the threat of ...e7-e5, White cannot keep his extra pawn so he stands worse.

4....d5

Black only plays this Grünfeld move when White has a knight on c3 to exchange.

5.cxd5

5.e4 dxe4 6.d5 ♘e5 7.fxe4 ♗g7 8.♘f3 ♘fd7 9.♗e2 0-0 10.♘xe5 ♗xe5 (10...♘xe5) 11.♗h6 ♖e8 12.0-0

c6 13.♕d2 ♘f6 14.h3 ♗d7 15.♖ad1 ♕c7=. Black's powerful outpost bishop compensates for White's space edge.

5....♘xd5 6.e4 ♘xc3 7.bxc3 e5 8.d5

In case of 8.♗b5 ♗d7 9.♘e2 ♗g7 10.♗e3 (10.♖b1 ♘a5 11.0-0 c6 12.♗d3 0-0 13.♗e3 ♗e6 is also equal) 10...0-0 11.d5 ♘a5 12.♗d3 ♗h6! 13.♗f2 (if 13.♗xh6 ♕h4+) 13... b6 is balanced. Black plans ...♕e7 and ...♘a5-b7-c5.

8....♘a5 9.h4

9.♗e3 c6=.

9....♗c5

9...♗e7 10.g3 0-0 Black intends to meet h4-h5 by ...g6-g5.

10.♗a3

10.h5 c6 11.hxg6 fxg6=.

10....♕d6 11.♗b4 ♗xb4 12.♕a4+ ♗d7 13.♕xb4 b6 14.♗a6 ♔e7

After 14...0-0 15.h5 c5 16.♕a3 f5 Black has the initiative.

15.0-0-0 ♗c8 16.♗b5 a6 17.♗a4 ♖b8

18.f4?!

18.h5 ♗d7=.

18....♗g4 19.♘f3 exf4 20.e5?! ♕xb4 21.cxb4 ♘c4 22.♖d4 ♗xf3 23.d6+ cxd6 24.exd6+ ♘xd6 25.gxf3 ♖bc8+ 26.♔b1 ♘f5 27.♖xf4 ♖hd8

Black is a clean pawn up.

28.h5 ♖d4 29.♖xd4 ♘xd4 30.hxg6 hxg6 31.♖e1+ ♔f6 32.♖e4?! ♖c4 33.♖f4+ ♔g7 34.a3 g5 35.♖g4 ♘xf3 36.♖g3 ♘d2+ 37.♔b2 ♘e4 0-1

Game 14.2   Grünfeld Indian –
         Fianchetto Variation

Lazaro Bruzon Bautista   2693
Le Quang Liem   2687

Havana 2011 (3)

1.d4 ♘f6 2.c4 g6 3.g3 ♗g7 4.♗g2 d5 5.cxd5 ♘xd5 6.e4 ♘b6 7.♘e2 c5 8.d5 0-0 9.0-0 e6

10.♘ec3

10.♘bc3 exd5 11.exd5 ♗f5 12.h3 (in case of 12.♘e4 ♗xe4 13.♗xe4 ♖e8N 14.♗g2 c4 15.♘c3 ♘a6 16.a4 ♘c5 the active black pieces and the weak squares b3 and d3 give Black ample compensation for the bishop pair)

12...h5 13.♘e4 ♗xe4 14.♗xe4 c4 15.♘c3 ♖e8 16.♗g2 ♘a6 17.♗e3 ♘b4 18.cd2 ♘d3 19.♖ad1 ♕f6= (+0.06). The Octopus (Kasparov's name for the ♘d3) offsets the bishop pair.

10....exd5?!

It is more accurate to play 10...♘a6 first, then 11.a4 exd5 12.exd5 transposes to the game. However, 11.♗f4 is perhaps best, hoping to provoke 11...e5 12.♗c1. Then I quote Delchev's line: 11...exd5 12.exd5 ♗f5 13.g4 ♗d7 14.♘d2 ♘b4! 15.♘de4 c4 16.♘d6 ♘d3 17.♗xf8 ♔xf8! – Delchev, who says that Black has fair practical chances for the exchange. (+0.15), Lc0 +0.35, roughly par evals. With the bishop pair, the 'octopus' knight, and several weak white pawns, Black seems fine to me.

11.exd5 ♘a6 12.a4?!

Better was 12.♘d2, which would not have much point had Black postponed the pawn exchange on d5.

12....♘c4

13.♘d2

13.♘a3 ♘e5 14.h3 ♘b4 15.♗e3? (15.♘e4 b6=) 15...b6 16.♕e2 ♗f5 17.♖fd1 ♕d7 was Nakamura-Topalov,

Monaco (blindfold) 2011. Black is clearly better, though White won.

13....♘xd2

13...♘e5! 14.♘de4 ♗g4 15.f3 ♗d7= (0.00) is better.

14.♗xd2 ♗f5 15.♗e3?

15.♘e4 b6 16.♕b3 h6= (0.00), Lc0 +0.22.

15...♕d7

15...c4 (+0.12) was probably better.

16.♕d2

A) 16.♕b3 b6 17.♕b5 (17.♖fd1 ♘b4=) 17...♘b4 18.♕xd7 ♗xd7=. White has an advanced passer, but it is isolated, and Black's knight has a nice home;

B) 16.a5 ♖ac8 17.♕a4 is better for White, so I recommend 13...♘e5 or ...c5-c4 on move 15.

16....b6 17.♗h6 ♘b4 18.♗xg7 ♔xg7

Although the exchange of bishops weakened Black's king, on balance I think it favored Black as his remaining bishop is superior to White's.

19.b3 ♖ad8 20.♕b2 f6 21.♖ad1 ♖fe8 22.♖d2

22....♗d3

22...h5! 23.h4 ♘d3 24.♕a1 ♖e5 favors Black as now f2-f4 would leave g3 too weak.

23.♖fd1 ♕f5 24.h3 h5 25.♘a2 ♗c2
26.♖f1 ♘xa2 27.♖xc2 ♘b4
28.♖d2 h4 29.♔h2 ♕g5

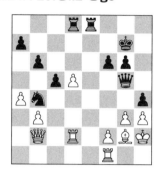

30.g4?

Apparently White had overlooked that this allows Black to transfer the knight to d4.

30....♕f4+ 31.♔h1 ♘c6!

It is headed for d4, where the knight will obviously be better than the white bishop.

32.♕c3 a5 33.♖d3 ♘d4 34.♖e3 ♘e2
35.♖xe8 ♖xe8 36.♕d3 ♘d4 37.♔g1
f5 38.gxf5 gxf5 39.♔h1 ♔h7 40.♕c4
♔h6 41.d6 ♕xd6 42.♖g1 ♕f6
43.♗f3 ♖d8 44.♕c1+ f4 45.♕c3
♖d7 46.♖g4 ♖g7

With an extra pawn and a super knight vs a bishop, Black is winning.

**47.♖xg7 ♔xg7 48.♗g4 ♕c6+
49.♔h2 ♕e4 50.♕d2 ♔g6 51.♔g1
♔g5 52.♔h2 ♔g6 53.♕c1 f3
54.♕c4 ♕e5+ 55.♔h1 ♕e1+ 0-1**

Game 14.3   Grünfeld Indian –
                     Fianchetto Variation

Nikita Maiorov   2540
Tigran Gharamian   2650

Lille 2011 (6)

1.d4 ♘f6 2.c4 g6 3.♘f3 ♗g7 4.g3 0-0
I would play 4...d5 first as explained
in the notes to Carlsen-Giri. After
5.♗g2 dxc4 6.♘a3 c3! 7.bxc3 c5 8.0-0
0-0 we are back to the current
game.
5.♗g2 d5 6.0-0 dxc4 7.♘a3 c3!
It is wise to damage White's pawn
structure this way.
8.bxc3 c5

9.e3
   A) After 9.♘e5 ♘c6 10.♘xc6
bxc6 11.♗xc6 ♗h3 12.♖e1 ♖c8
13.♗f3 ♕a5 14.♕d2 ♖fd8 Black's
compensation for the pawn is
obvious;
   B) 9.♘c4 ♘c6 10.♘fe5 ♘d5 11.♗b2
♖b8 – Black is doing fine here;
   C) 9.♖e1 (recently popular) 9...♘c6
10.♗b2 (10.e4 ♗g4 11.♗b2 ♘d7

12.h3 ♗xf3 13.♗xf3 cxd4 14.cxd4
♕b6 15.♘c4 ♕b5 16.♗e2 ♘b6=
near zero by both engines) 10...♕b6
11.♘c4 ♕a6 12.♘cd2 ♖d8 13.e4 ♗g4
14.h3 ♗xf3 15.♘f3 ♘d7 16.♗f1 ♕a5
17.d5 ♘ce5 18.♘xe5 ♘xe5 19.f4 ♘d7
20.♕c2 c4! (unclear per Delchev,
though he likes Black) 21.a4 ♖ac8=
(+0.20), Lc0 +0.12, so OK for Black;
   D) 9.♕b3 ♘c6 10.♖d1 (this scores
heavily for White) 10...♘a5 11.♕b2
♕b6 12.♘e5 ♗e6. The engines all
score it near zero, but White won all
three games from here, by chance I
think.
9....♘c6 10.♕e2
10.♗b2 ♕b6 11.♕e2 (11.♘c4 ♕a6
12.♘ce5 ♗f5=) 11...♗f5 and now:
   A) 12.♖fc1 ♖fd8 13.♘c4 (in case
of 13.♗f1 ♘a5 14.♘e5 ♖ac8 15.♘ac4
♘xc4 16.♘xc4 ♕e6 Black's more
active pieces more than offset
White's extra center pawn) 13...♕a6
14.♗f1 ♕a4=;
   B) 12.♖fd1 ♖fd8 13.♘c4 (after
13.♗f1 ♘a5 14.♘e5 ♖ac8 Black has
the initiative; White can do little)
13...♕a6 14.♗f1 ♕a4=.
10....♗f5 11.♖d1 ♕b6 12.♗d2
12.♗b2 transposes to the previous
note, while if 12.♘d2 cxd4 13.cxd4
♖ac8 14.♘b3 ♘a5! (Delchev), the
engines agree.
**12....♖fd8 13.♗e1 ♖ac8 14.♘d2
♗g4 15.f3 ♗e6 16.♔h1?**
16.♘b3! ♗xb3 17.axb3 ♕xb3 18.f4
♕e6 and White has the bishop pair
and a pawn center for the pawn. I
would prefer Black's chances, but
it's a game.

16....♕b2 17.♘ac4 ♗xc4 18.♕xc4 cxd4 19.cxd4 ♘xd4 20.♕a4

20....♕c2!N

The **actual game** went 20...♕b5?! 21.♕xb5 ♘xb5. White has only the bishop pair for the pawn, which is not enough: 22.♘f1 ♘e8 23.♖ab1 ♖xd1 24.♖xd1 ♘ed6 25.f4 ♘c3 26.♗xc3 ♖xc3 27.e4 f6 28.♖d5 ♔f7 29.e5 fxe5 30.fxe5 ♘c8 31.♗h3 ♘b6 32.e6+ ♔f6 33.♖b5 ♗h6 34.♖b2 ♗g5 35.♔g2?! ♘c4 36.♖f2+ ♔e5 37.♖e2+ ♔d6 38.♔f2 b5 39.♗g2 a5 40.h4 ♗f6 41.♗b7 a4 42.♘h2 ♔c5 43.♘f3 h6 44.♘h2 b4 45.♗e4 g5 46.hxg5 hxg5 47.♘g4 ♗g7 48.♔g2 b3 49.axb3 ♖xb3 50.♘f2 a3 51.♗c2 ♖e3 52.♘d3+ ♔b6 and White resigned.

21.♕a3 ♘e2 22.♗f1 ♘e8 23.♗xe2 ♗xa1 24.♖xa1 ♖xd2 25.♗xd2 ♕xd2 26.♕d3 ♖c2 27.♕xd2 ♖xd2 28.♗f1 ♘d6

Black has a pawn plus the dominating rook on the seventh rank. He should win.

Game 14.4   Grünfeld Indian – Fianchetto Variation

Magnus Carlsen   2814
Anish Giri   2686

Wijk aan Zee 2011 (3)

1.d4 ♘f6 2.c4 g6 3.g3 ♗g7 4.♗g2
4.♘c3 d5 5.cxd5 ♘xd5 6.♗g2 ♘b6 7.e3 0-0 8.♘ge2 (8.♘f3 transposes to the game) 8...e5 9.0-0 exd4 10.♘xd4 ♕e7=.

4....d5 5.cxd5 ♘xd5 6.♘f3 ♘b6!
It is best to play this before castling, as explained in the note to move 8.

7.♘c3
7.0-0 ♘c6 8.e3 0-0 9.♘c3 transposes to the game, but gives Black the extra option of 8...e5 which is said to be drawish, though the engine prefers White there.

7....♘c6

8.e3
If both sides had already castled White could play 9.d5 now and answer 9...♗xc3 by 10.dxc6, but as it is 8.d5? just loses a pawn to 8...♗xc3+.

8.0-0 ♘xd4 9.♘xd4 ♕xd4 10.♘b5
and now:

A) 10...♕e5 11.a4 0-0 12.♗f4 ♕xb2
13.♘xc7 (13.♖b1 ♕a2 14.♘xc7 ♖b8
15.♘d5 e5 16.♘xb6 axb6 17.♗d5 ♕a3
18.♗c1 ♕e7 19.♕b3 ♖d8) 13...♖b8
(13...♕xa1 14.♕xa1 ♗xa1 15.♖xa1
♖b8 16.♘d5 ♖a8 17.♘c7 ♖b8 with a
draw by repetition) 14.a5 (+0.16);

B) 10...♕c4 11.♕b3 0-0 12.♕xc4
♘xc4 13.♘xc7 ♖b8 14.♘d5 ♗e6
15.♘xe7+ ♔h8 16.♘d5 ♘xb2 (+0.08).

8....0-0 9.0-0 ♖e8
Black makes useful quiet moves
rather than provoke d4-d5 by ...e7-
e5.

10.♖e1
  A) 10.d5 ♘a5 11.♘d4 ♗d7 12.e4
(in the event of 12.♘b3 ♘xb3
13.axb3 c6 14.dxc6 ♗xc6 15.e4 ♗d4
White's bad pawn structure offsets
his modest mobility advantage.
12.b4 ♘ac4 13.♕c2 ♕c8 14.♖d1
♗h3 15.♗h1 (-0.30) was Jobava-
Maghsoodloo, Bandar 2017, when
15...♗g4! already favors Black)
12...♖c8 (postponing the choice
between ...c7-c6 and ...c7-c5 for one
move) 13.♖e1 c6 14.♗f4 c5 15.♘f3
♘ac4 16.♗c1 e6 17.dxe6 ♗xe6 and
Black has the advantage, due to

White's problem developing his
dark-squared bishop;

B) 10.♕e2 e5 11.dxe5 ♘xe5 12.♘xe5
♗xe5 13.♖d1 (13.e4 ♗e6 14.♖d1
♕f6=) 13...♕e7 14.e4 c6 15.♗e3 ♗e6
16.f4 ♗g7 17.e5 f6 18.exf6 ♕xf6
19.♗d4 ♕f7 20.♗xg7 ♕xg7 21.♕f2
♗f5=;

C) 10. a3 ♖b8 11.♘d2 e5 12.d5
♘e7 13.e4 c6 14.a4 (Markus-Kozul,
Zagreb 2018) 14...a5 (-0.03).

10....a5 11.♕d2?!
In case of 11.♕c2 ♘b4 (or 11...a4
12.♖d1 ♗g4N 13.h3 ♗d7 14.♕e2 ♕c8
15.♕f1 ♘b4 16.a3 ♘c6=; the weak
squares b3 and c4 give Black ample
compensation for White's extra
center pawn) 12.♕b1 ♘c6 13.♕c2
Black can now repeat for a draw or
play 13...a4 as in the last note.
11.♕e2 and now:

  A) I would avoid 11...♗g4 12.h3
♗e6 13.b3 a4 14.♖b1 axb3 15.axb3.
This was Gelfand-Grischuk, Kazan
Candidates' 2011, won nicely by
White. Now 15...♗f5 is not good due
to 16.e4, but with the pawn still on
h2 Black would have ...♗g4;

  B) 11...♗e6 and now:

analysis diagram

B1) 12.♘d2 ♘b4 (or 12...a4 13.♖d1
♕d7 14.♘de4 ♗c4 15.♕d2 ♖ed8
(+0.16), Lc0 +0.27, about par) 13.♖d1
(13.♘de4? ♗c4 14.♕d2 was seen in
Tegshuren-Kaufman, Rockville blitz
2011. After 14...e5 Black is much
better) 13...c6 14.a3 ♘4d5 15.♘ce4
♕c8 16.♘c5 ♗g4 and now:

B11) In case of 17.f3 ♗h3 18.♗xh3
♕xh3 19.♘de4 (19.♘xb7?! ♘xe3
20.♕xe3 ♕d7 21.♘c5 ♕xd4 wins
a pawn) 19...♕c8= Black's better
bishop makes up for White's better
knight on c5. For example 20.♘f2
♘d7 21.e4 ♘xc5 22.dxc5 ♘c7 23.♗e3
♕e6 24.♖d3 ♖ad8 25.♖ad1 ♕c8
(+0.13);

B12) 17.♗f3 (Bacrot-Robson,
Khanty-Mansiysk 2011) 17...h5!=
18.♘de4 ♘f6 19.♘xf6+?! exf6! 20.e4
f5 21.e5 ♘d7 22.♘xd7 ♕xd7 23.♗f4
a4. Black can develop his rook to
a5. After the bishops are traded he
will retain the better bishop and
pressure on d4;

B2) 12.b3N a4 13.♖b1 axb3 14.axb3
♗f5 15.♖b2 e5 16.dxe5 ♕e7=;

B3) 12.♖d1 ♗c4 13.♕c2 ♘b4
14.♕b1 e5 15.a3 exd4 16.axb4 dxc3
17.♖xd8 ♖axd8 18.♕c2 axb4 and
although Black has only rook and
two pawns for the queen, the threat
of ...b4-b3 is hard to meet.

**11....e5 12.d5 ♘b4 13.e4 c6 14.a3
cxd5 15.axb4 axb4 16.♖xa8 bxc3
17.bxc3 ♘xa8**

18.exd5?!
Probably Carlsen was trying to
avoid a draw against a lower-rated
opponent: 18.♕xd5 ♘b6=.
18....♘b6 19.♖d1?
19.c4 ♘xc4 20.♕b4 ♘d6 21.♗e3 ♗f8
White has some but not enough
compensation for the pawn.
19....e4

20.♘g5?
After 20.♘d4 ♕xd5 21.♕e2 ♗d7
Black is just a pawn up.
20....e3 21.♕b2?!
Better was 21.♕d3 ♗f5 22.♕b5 ♗d7
23.♕d3 ♕xg5 24.♗xe3 ♕f6 25.c4
♘a4, but White has way too little
compensation for the lost knight.
21....♕xg5 22.♗xe3 ♕g4 0-1
It's not often that Carlsen loses
in 22 moves with white, but a
poor opening followed by three
consecutive bad moves will do
the trick. I guess if you are going
to make this many errors in a
tournament, it's wise to get them all
in in one game!

265

CHAPTER 15

Grünfeld Indian – Non-Exchange lines

This chapter covers all the lines after 1.d4 ♘f6 2.c4 g6 3.♘c3 d5 in which White does not exchange pawns immediately on d5.

This includes lines with an early e2-e3, lines with ♗g5 on move 4 or 5, lines with ♗f4 on move 4 or 5, the Russian System, based on ♕b3 to recapture on c4 with the queen, and miscellaneous white tries. The one common theme in all these lines is that Black should almost never play passively. That means no early ...c7-c6 to defend d5. Usually Black will take on c4 (unless White can recapture with his f1-bishop) and/or play an early ...c7-c5. This normally forces White to play concretely, meaning he cannot just make moves by general principles, he must calculate variations.

In Game 15.1 we look at unusual white fourth moves, such as h2-h4, g2-g4, and ♕a4+. This last move intends to play the Russian System with Black's bishop on d7 rather than c8. This does spoil some of Black's options, but it creates a new one, namely a surprising ...b7-b5! on move 8. The other moves aren't very good, as 4.h4 is met by fighting in the center with 4...c5 while 4.g4 is met by 4...dxc4, clearing a square for the knight to move to if attacked.

In Game 15.2 we look at lines with **4.e3**. Lately White has been playing this with the idea of trading twice on d5 and then playing ♘g1-e2-c3 to hit the queen, which we meet by ...c7-c5 d4-d5 e7-e6 and isolating the queen's pawn. If White just develops and castles without trading on d5, Black plays a quick ...c7-c5 when White finds himself playing the Tarrasch Defense, where White's extra tempo is only enough to equalize.

Against **4.♗g5 ♘e4 5.♗h4**, we trade knights and take on c4, meeting 7.e3 by 7...♗e6 to guard the pawn. If we want equality we soon play ...c7-c5

(Game 15.3). If we want to go for the win, we defend the pawn by a quick ...♘d7-b6 as in Game 15.4.

In Game 15.5 (Gledura-Tari) we look at the recently popular idea of playing **5.h4** after **4.♘f3 ♗g7** have already been played.

This is rather dangerous if you don't know the lines, as well as covering the accelerated **h2-h4 on move 3**, against which I recommend switching to the Benko Gambit.

When ♗g5 is played on the fifth move (after **4.♘f3 ♗g7**) it is usually with the idea of meeting **5...♘e4** either by **6.cxd5**, sacrificing the bishop pair (Game 15.6), or by **6.♗f4** (Game 15.7). In the former case Black has a pleasant choice between trying to demonstrate that the bishops compensate for a possible white minority attack, or offering a gambit pawn, for which he receives rich compensation. I give both options. In case of 6.♗f4 we trade knights and play ...c7-c5, which usually leads to an early queen exchange. White retains central dominance, but in the endgame Black's queenside majority should play a role so chances are close to even.

Now we come to the lines involving 4.♗f4 ♗g7 (or 4.♘f3 ♗g7 5.♗f4, which may transpose). White can play either **5.♘f3** or **5.e3** (we meet the rare 5.♖c1 by 5...♘h5) but in both cases I recommend **castling on move 5**. Now if White plays whichever move he did not play on move 5,

we play **6...c5 7.dxc5 ♘e4** which equalizes; see Game 15.8. If White fails to defend his pawn on move 6, we take it (5.♘f3 0-0 6.♖c1 dxc4) and meet 7.e4 by ...♗g4, ...♘h5, and ...♗xf3 which sacrifices the bishop pair to inflict doubled backward pawns and an isolated pawn on White, a roughly even deal; see Game 15.9.

If White accepts the gambit after **5.e3 0-0** by taking twice on d5 and then on c7, the move 8...♘a6! regains the pawn and leaves Black with the bishop pair to offset his inferior pawn structure and inferior center. A few accurate moves give Black equality (Game 15.10).

The last line with 4.♗f4 ♗g7 is **5.e3 0-0 6.♖c1**, which I formerly believed to favour White. It now seems that **6...♗e6! 7.♕b3 c5!** leaves White with no advantage at all, while 7.♘f3 dxc4 is no better (Game 15.11). I have often played ♗f4 lines as White, as they are quite tricky and promise an edge in most variations, but apparently they yield nothing against precise play.

Finally we come to the Russian System (**4.♘f3 ♗g7 5.♕b3 dxc4 6.♕xc4 0-0 7.e4**), which was recommended line for White in the previous edition.

I concluded in the White portion of the book that only the Hungarian Variation (7...a6) gives Black near-equality, so I recommend it here. White has two main options against this. He can play the aggressive **8.e5 b5 9.♕b3 ♘fd7 10.e6! fxe6 11.♗e3**, after which White attacks the queenside after the recommended **11...♘f6** or the kingside after the dubious 11...♘b6. Black should return the pawn by **12.a4 b4!**, after which his better development and piece activity compensate fully for his inferior pawn structure (Game 15.12). Or White can play the positional **8.♗e2** which we meet by **8...b5 9.♕b3 c5! 10.dxc5 ♗e6 11.♕c2 ♘bd7!**. This leads to positions where White has won the bishop pair at the price of an isolated d-pawn and a slight inferiority in piece placement. I won't claim that Black has 100% equality here (if I did I couldn't recommend this for White), but I think he is closer to equality than in other major defenses to the Queen's Gambit. Moreover, the positions are rich enough that either side can reasonably play for a win. See Game 15.13.

Game 15.1   Grünfeld Indian

Miso Cebalo   2476

Alexander Riazantsev   2647

Biel 2009 (5)

1.d4 ♘f6 2.c4 g6 3.♘c3 d5

In this game we look at various rare lines White can try:

4.h4?!

A) 4.g4?! dxc4 5.h3 ♗g7 6.e4 c5N 7.dxc5 (after 7.d5 b5 White is already in serious trouble) 7...♕xd1+ 8.♔xd1 ♗e6 9.♘f3 ♘c6 10.♘g5 ♖d8+ 11.♔c2 ♘d4+ 12.♔b1 h5 and White is suffering;

B) 4.♕a4+ ♗d7 5.♕b3 dxc4 6.♕xc4 ♗g7 and now:

analysis diagram

B1) 7.♗f4 ♘a6 8.e4 0-0 9.♘f3 c5 10.e5 (in case of 10.d5 b5 11.♘xb5 ♘xe4 12.♕xe4 ♗xb5, Black's safer king and better development give him the edge) 10...♗e6 11.exf6 ♗xc4 12.fxg7 ♗xf1 13.gxf8♕+ ♕xf8 14.♔xf1 cxd4 15.♘xd4 ♘b4N 16.♖d1 ♖d8 17.a3 ♘d5 18.♘de2 ♘xf4 19.♘xf4 ♖xd1+ 20.♘xd1 ♕d8. Rook and two knights are a tad better than queen and two pawns, so White is effectively a bit over a pawn ahead. However White has problems getting his rook out, which gives Black a nice initiative which should equalize the chances.

B2) 7.e4 0-0 and now:

B21) 8.e5 ♗e6 9.exf6 ♗xc4 10.fxg7 ♔xg7 11.♗xc4 ♕xd4.

analysis diagram

Three minor pieces are a match for queen and pawn, but here it is queen and two pawns so Black is better;

B22) 8.♘f3 b5 9.♘xb5 ♘xe4

B221) 10.♘xc7 ♘c6 11.♘xa8 ♕a5+ 12.♗d2 ♘xd2 13.♘xd2 ♘xd4 14.♘c7 ♗c6.

analysis diagram

The c7-knight is doomed, and after its capture Black will enjoy an overwhelming position despite being the exchange down;

B222) 10.♕xc7 ♘c6 11.♗d3 ♘b4 12.♗xe4 ♗xb5 13.♕xd8 ♖axd8

269

14.♗d2 ♘d3+ 15.♗xd3 ♗xd3 16.♗c3
♗e4 17.♔e2 ♖d6 – Black's bishop
pair and pressure on the weak
d4-pawn fully offset White's extra
pawn.

4....c5!

5.dxc5

After 5.cxd5 ♘xd5 6.dxc5 ♘xc3
7.♕xd8+ ♔xd8 8.bxc3 ♗g7 9.♔d2
♘d7!N 10.♗a3 ♘f6 11.f3 ♘h5
12.♘h3 ♘g3 13.♖g1 ♔c7 14.♔c2 ♖d8
15.e4 ♘xf1 16.♖axf1 ♗e6 Black's
better development, bishop pair,
and much better pawn structure
more than offset White's extra
pawn.

5....d4 6.♘b5 e5 7.e3

The alternative 7.b4 a6 8.♕a4 ♘c6
9.♗g5 ♗d7 10.♘d6+ ♗xd6 11.cxd6
h6 12.♗xf6 ♕xf6 13.c5 e4 is awful
for White.

**7....♗xc5 8.exd4 exd4 9.♘f3 0-0
10.♗e2 ♘c6 11.♗f4?**

Better is 11.♗g5 a6 12.♘c3 dxc3
13.♕xd8 ♖xd8 14.♗xf6 cxb2
15.♗xb2 ♗f5, but Black's better
pawn structure and better
development give him a clear
advantage.

11....♗f5

White has no good answer to the
threat of ...d4-d3.

12.♗d3 ♗xd3 13.♕xd3 a6
13...♖e8+! 14.♔f1 ♘b4 15.♕b3 d3
Black has a winning attack.
**14.♘c7 ♖c8 15.a3 ♖xc7 16.♗xc7
♕xc7**

So Black 'settled' for winning two
pieces for a rook, with a clearly
winning position.

**17.b4 ♖e8+ 18.♔f1 ♗f8 19.♖d1 a5
20.b5 ♘e5 21.♘xe5 ♕xe5 22.♖h3
♗xa3 23.♕xd4 ♕e2+ 24.♔g1 ♗c5
0-1**

I owe my own Grandmaster title to
a win over the loser of this game.

Game 15.2   Grünfeld Indian
Marko Zivanic   2490
Leonid Kritz   2616
Brownsville 2010 (1)

1.d4 ♘f6 2.c4 g6 3.♘c3 d5 4.e3 ♗g7

5.cxd5

A) 5.♘f3 0-0 and now:

A1) 6.♗d2 c5 7.dxc5 ♘a6 8.cxd5 ♘xc5 9.♗c4 a6 10.a4 ♗f5 11.0-0 ♖c8 12.♘d4 ♗e4 13.♕e2 ♗xd5 14.♘xd5 ♘xd5 15.♖fd1 e6 16.♗e1 ♕g5=; Black's better piece placement and the weak squares b3 and b4 offset the bishop pair;

A2) 6.b4 c6 7.♗b2 a5 8.b5 a4 9.♗a3 ♗e6=;

A3) 6.♗e2 c5 7.0-0 (after 7.dxc5 dxc4 8.0-0 ♕a5 9.♗xc4 ♕xc5 10.♗b3 ♘c6 11.e4 ♗g4 12.♗e3 ♕a5 13.h3 ♖ad8 14.♕e2 ♗xf3 15.♕xf3 ♘d7 16.♖fd1 e6 17.♕e2 ♘c5 Black kills the bishop pair and retains the better position) 7...cxd4 8.exd4 ♘c6.

analysis diagram

We now have a position from the Tarrasch Defense to the Queen's Gambit but with colors reversed. Black is therefore down a tempo, but the Tarrasch Defense is thought to give White some advantage, so even a tempo down Black has equality here: 9.h3 ♗e6 10.c5 ♘e4 11.♗f4 ♕a5=; or 9.♖e1 ♗e6 10.c5 ♘e4=; or 9.c5 ♘e4 10.♗e3 b6=.

B) 5.♕b3 dxc4 6.♗xc4 0-0 7.♘f3 c5 8.dxc5 (the computer calls the position even after 8.d5 a6 9.a4 ♘bd7 10.0-0 ♘e8 11.e4 ♘d6 12.♗f4 ♕a5 13.♘d2 ♘e5 14.♗e2 ♗d7, but I think that the well-placed knights and mobile black queenside give Black the nod) 8...♘bd7 9.♕a3 ♕c7 10.b4 ♘e5 11.♘xe5 ♕xe5 12.♗b2 ♕g5 – since castling kingside loses the exchange here, White will have problems with his king. Black has full compensation for the pawn.

5....♘xd5 6.♘xd5

6.♗c4 ♘b6 7.♗b3 0-0 8.♘f3 c5 9.0-0 cxd4 10.exd4 ♘c6 11.d5 ♘a5 12.♖e1 ♗g4 13.h3 ♗xf3 14.♕xf3 ♖e8 15.♖d1 ♘xb3 16.axb3 ♘c8 17.♗e3 ♕d7 18.♕e2 a6=. Black's better pawn structure offsets White's space advantage. The knight will be a great blockader on d6.

6....♕xd5 7.♘e2 0-0 8.♘c3 ♕d8

8...♕d6! 9.♗e2 c5 10.d5 e6 11.e4 exd5 12.exd5 ♘d7 (-0.03) is fine.

9.♗e2 c5 10.d5 e6 11.e4 exd5 12.exd5 b6

Avrukh recommends 12...♕b6 with ideas like ...♘a6 and ...♗f5. He's probably correct, but White is a tad better after 13.0-0 ♗f5 (+0.15) so I'd go with 8...♕d6.

13.0-0 ♗b7

14.♕b3

A) 14.♗f3 ♘d7 15.♖e1 (in case of 15.d6 ♗xf3 16.♕xf3 ♕f6 17.♕d5 ♕e5= (-0.06) the advanced passer is a bit weak) 15...♘e5 16.♗e2 ♕h4 17.g3 ♕f6 (0.00);

B) 14.♗f4! ♗xc3 15.bxc3 ♕xd5 16.♕xd5 ♗xd5 17.♖fd1 ♗b7 18.♗c4 (+0.30); White is half a pawn down but with much better development. I would vary earlier.

14....♕d6

This is recommended by grandmaster Delchev. The game move 14...♘d7 wasn't bad, but it seems better to blockade the passer and to prevent ♗f4. The **actual game** went: 14...♘d7 15.♗e3 (15.♗f4 a6 16.a4 ♖e8 17.♖fe1 ♗d4=) 15...♗d4 16.♖ad1 ♗xe3 17.fxe3 ♕g5 18.e4 ♕e3+ 19.♔h1 ♘e5 20.a4 ♖ab8 21.♖de1 ♔g7 22.♗a6 ♕g5 23.♗xb7 ♖xb7 24.♘b5 ♖d7 25.♕c3 ♔g8 26.♘a3 ♖e8 27.a5 bxa5 28.♕xa5 ♘d3 29.♖d1 ♖xd5 30.♖d2 ♖xe4 31.♕xa7 ♖f5 32.♖dd1 ♖xf1+ 33.♖xf1 ♕f4 34.♖a1 ♘c1 and White resigned.

15.♖d1 ♘d7=

Black will centralize his rooks. The pressure on the d5-pawn restricts White's activity. After 16.g3 ♕f6 Komodo shows +0.05.

Game 15.3   Grünfeld Indian
Boris Gelfand   2733
Gata Kamsky   2732
Kazan 2011 (2)

1.d4 ♘f6 2.c4 g6 3.♘c3 d5 4.♗g5 ♘e4 5.♗h4 ♘xc3 6.bxc3 dxc4 7.e3 ♗e6 8.♘f3 c5

If Black wants to play for a win he can try to hold the pawn by 8...♗g7 9.♗e2 ♘b6, transposing to Avrukh-Popilski below.

9.♗e2 ♗g7 10.0-0 0-0 11.♖b1

11.♘g5 ♗d5 12.e4 h6 13.exd5 hxg5 14.♗xg5 cxd4 15.♗xc4 dxc3 16.♖e1 ♗f6 17.♗xf6 exf6 18.♖c1 ♕d6 19.♖xc3 ♘d7 (0.00). White has a good passed pawn but the black knight is better than the White bishop.

11...cxd4!

In an earlier game in the match Kamsky played 11...♗d5? and should have lost.

12.♘xd4

12.cxd4 ♕d7 13.♘g5 ♗d5 14.e4 ♗c6 15.♗xc4 ♕xd4N 16.♕b3 e6 17.♖bd1 ♕b2 18.♗xe6 ♕xb3 19.♗xb3 ♘d7∓. I would rather play Black here due to the pressure on the e4-pawn and the excellent coordination of the black minor pieces.

12....♗d5 13.♕c2 ♕d7

The move 13...♗f6 is best and equal per Lc0.

14.♖fd1

14.e4 ♗c6 15.♗xc4 ♗xd4 16.cxd4 ♕xd4 17.♖fe1 e6 18.♗e7 ♖c8 19.♖bd1 ♕e5=. White's bishop pair and

better development just offset
Black's extra pawn.
14....♗xd4 15.cxd4
15.e4 ♗e5 16.♖xd5 ♕c7 17.g3 f6
18.♕a4 ♔g7=.
15....♕e6 16.♗f3 ♗xf3 17.gxf3 ♘d7

18.♕e4
18.♖xb7 ♖fb8 19.d5 ♕h3 20.♖xb8+
♖xb8 21.♕e4 ♖b2 22.♗xe7 c3
23.♗d6 h5=. There are many
possible lines from here, but most
likely either White or Black will
end up giving perpetual check.
18.♖dc1 ♘b6 (+0.18) may be best
play.
**18....b6 19.♖dc1 ♖ac8 20.♖b4 c3
21.♖b3 ♘f6 22.♕xe6 fxe6 23.♗xf6**

Draw agreed here. A likely
continuation would have been 23...
exf6 24.♖bxc3 ♖xc3 25.♖xc3 ♖f7
26.♖c6 ♖e7 and White's more active

rook is balanced by his inferior
pawn structure. A draw is the
proper outcome.

Game 15.4   Grünfeld Indian
Boris Avrukh   2656
Gil Popilski   2449
Israel tt 2010 (9)

**1.d4 ♘f6 2.c4 g6 3.♘c3 d5 4.♗g5
♘e4 5.♗h4**
5.♗f4 ♘xc3 6.bxc3 ♗g7 7.e3 c5
8.♘f3 transposes to Game 15.7
(Eljanov-Kovchan).
5....♘xc3 6.bxc3 dxc4 7.e3
  A) If 7.♕a4+ c6 (this is a rare but
strong move) 8.♕xc4 ♕a5 9.♘f3
♗e6 10.♕d3 ♗g7 11.e3 ♘d7 12.♕c2
♘c5∓, Black plans ...♗f5 with the
initiative;
  B) 7.e4 b5 8.a4 c6 9.♘f3 ♗g7
10.♗e2 ♘d7=. White may have
enough compensation for the
pawn, but not enough to claim any
advantage.
7....♗e6

8.♗e2
  A) 8.♖b1 and now:
  A1) 8...♘d7 9.♕a4 (9.♘f3 ♘b6
is like the game but with the
inaccurate ♖b1 played; 9.♖xb7

♗d5 10.♖b2 ♖b8= as Black can later undouble by ...c7-c5) 9...♗d5 10.♗xc4 ♗xg2 11.♕b3 ♗h6 12.♗xf7+ ♔f8 13.♗d5 ♘c5 14.♗xg2 ♘xb3 15.♖xb3 b5! Black plans ...♖b8-b6 and has a winning material advantage of queen for two minor pieces;

A2) 8...c5 is an excellent alternative proposed by grandmaster Agrest:

analysis diagram

9.♘e2 (in case of 9.♖xb7 ♕a5 10.♘e2 ♗d5 11.♕b1 ♘d7 12.♖b5 ♕a3 Black is better. White will have trouble getting castled) 9...♕a5 10.♘f4 ♕xc3+ 11.♕d2 ♕xd2+ 12.♔xd2 b6 13.♘xe6 fxe6 14.dxc5 ♘d7 15.c6 ♘e5 16.c7 ♖c8 17.♗g3 ♗g7 18.♖b5 ♘f7 19.♗xc4 ♘d6 20.♗xe6 ♖xc7 21.♗xd6 exd6=. The bishops of opposite color and equal material make for an almost certain draw.

B) In the event of 8.♕b1 ♕d5 9.♘f3 ♕a5 10.♕c2 ♘d7 11.♘d2 ♘b6 12.♗e2 c5∓ White does not have much compensation for the pawn;

C) 8.♘f3 ♗g7 9.♗e2 ♘d7 10.0-0 ♘b6 transposes to the game.

8....♘d7

8...♗g7 9.♘f3 c5, transposing to Gelfand-Kamsky, is safer. The text aims to keep the pawn and is a better winning try.

9.♘f3

After 9.d5?! ♗f5 10.♕d4 ♖g8 11.♖d1 (11.e4? ♗g7 12.♕e3 ♗xe4−+) 11...b5 (against IM (now GM) Irina Krush I allowed White to regain the pawn by 11...♗g7?, though even this should equalize. After a subsequent error I lost the exchange but miraculously drew the endgame anyway!) 12.e4 g5 13.♗g3 e5! 14.dxe6 ♗xe6 White has too little compensation for the pawn.

9....♘b6 10.0-0 ♗g7 11.a4

A) For 11.e4 0-0 12.a4 (12.♕c2 ♕e8 13.♗g3 ♕a4! 14.♕d2 ♖ac8. Black has the edge (Delchev) (-0.38), Lc0 -0.24) 12...a5 13.♕c2 see the note to move 13;

B) 11.♘d2 c5=.

11....a5 12.♕c2

A) 12.♘d2 0-0 13.♗f3 ♖a7 14.♕c1 ♕d7=;

B) 12.♘g5 ♗d5 13.e4 ♗c6 14.♕c2 ♕d7∓.

12....0-0

13.♖fb1

13.e4 ♗d7 14.♗g3 e6=. White's better center and Black's doubled pawn give White enough for the pawn, but no advantage considering the weakness on a4.

13.♘d2 c5.

13....♕e8

Or 13...♗d7! 14.♘d2 ♕e8, transposing while avoiding 14.♗g3 hitting c7.

14.♘d2 ♗d7 15.♘xc4 ♗xa4 16.♕a2

16.♕e4 (Vuckovic-Sutovsky, Moscow Aeroflot 2011) 16...♘xc4N 17.♗xc4 e5 18.♕xb7 ♗c6 19.♕xc7 ♗e4 20.♘b5 ♕b8 21.♕xb8 ♖fxb8 22.♖b3 ♗c2 23.♖b2 ♗d3 24.♗c6 ♖xb2 25.♗xa8 a4 and after trading rooks on b1 Black's advanced passer should win a piece.

16....♘d5 17.♕a3

After 17.♕d2 b5 18.♘xa5 e5 19.♗f3 e4 20.♗e2 ♖xa5 21.c4 ♖a6 22.cxd5 ♕d7 23.♕c1 ♕xd5 24.♕xc7 ♖fa8 I would rather play White, but it's close to even.

17....♗c6N

The **actual game** continued 17...b5?! 18.♗f3 ♕c6? 19.♘b2? (19.♘d2! was winning) 19...♗c2 20.c4 b4 21.♕a2 ♘c3 22.♗xc6 ♘xa2 and Black

eventually won. But best is probably 17...♕c6! 18.♗xe7 ♖fb8 (0.00).

18.♗g3 e6 19.♘e5 ♗xe5 20.♗xe5 f6 21.♗g3 ♕d7 22.e4 ♘e7 23.f3 f5

This position is more or less equal. White's bishop pair and better center should roughly offset Black's extra (passed) pawn.

Game 15.5   Grünfeld Indian
Benjamin Gledura   2615
Aryan Tari   2603
Malmö 2018 (5)

1.d4 ♘f6 2.c4 g6 3.♘c3

3.h4 c5 4.d5 b5. Playing the Benko Gambit here makes sense, as attacking with h2-h4-h5 is not consistent with playing to exploit an extra pawn in the endgame. 5.cxb5 a6 6.bxa6 ♗g7 7.♘c3 ♗xa6 (+0.15). It's a normal Benko Gambit position except White has played the rather bizarre h2-h4 instead of a normal move like e2-e4, ♘f3, or g2-g3.

3...d5 4.♘f3 ♗g7 5.h4

This is a fairly dangerous line, recently popular.

5...dxc4

5...c6 is played more often, perhaps to avoid having to remember a lot of theory for a rare line, but I think it concedes White a slight plus.

6.e4 c5 7.d5 b5 8.h5 0–0 9.hxg6 fxg6 10.e5

A) 10.♘xb5 ♕a5+ 11.♘c3 ♘xe4 12.♗d2 ♘xc3 13.bxc3 ♘d7N (-0.73). It seems Black will remain a pawn ahead safely;

B) 10.♖h4 a6 (-0.04), although Lc0 gives White a par advantage. It's clearly unclear!

10...♘g4 11.d6 e6 12.♖xh7 ♖f5 13.♖h3 ♘c6

14.♘xb5

14.a4 ♘gxe5 15.axb5 ♘d4 16.♗e3 ♗b7N 17.♘xd4 cxd4 18.♗xd4 ♕xd6 19.♖xa7 ♖xa7 20.♗xa7 ♕b4 (+0.07). It's rather messy, with many lines,

but Black should recover his pawn with equality.

14...♘gxe5 15.♘xe5 ♖xe5+ 16.♗e3 ♘d4 17.♗xc4

17.♘xd4 cxd4 18.♕xd4 ♕a5+ 19.♕d2 c3 20.bxc3 ♖d5 21.♗d4 e5 22.♗b6 axb6 23.♗c4 ♗e6 24.♗xd5 ♕xd5 25.♕xd5 ♗xd5 26.♖b1 ♗f6 27.♖xb6 ♗xg2 28.♖g3 ♗e4 (-0.03). Two bishops are a tad stronger than rook and two pawns, but the advanced d6-pawn makes it equal.

17...♘xb5 18.♕d3 ♘d4 19.♕xg6 ♕f6 20.♕e8+ ♕f8 21.♕g6 ♕f6 22.♕e8+ ♕f8

Already three games have ended in draws this way.

23.♕g6 ♕f6 24.♕e8+ ♕f8 ½-½

Game 15.6   Grünfeld Indian –
            Stockholm Variation

Anatoly Shvedchikov   2421
Larry Kaufman   2413

Arco Wch-sen 2010 (11)

1.♘f3 ♘f6 2.d4 g6 3.c4 ♗g7 4.♘c3 d5 5.♗g5 ♘e4 6.cxd5 ♘xg5 7.♘xg5 e6

An excellent alternative, recommended by Delchev, is 7...0-0 8.♘f3 (8.e3 e6 9.♘f3 exd5 is similar to the next note) 8...c6 9.dxc6 ♘xc6 10.e3 e5 11.d5 (in case of 11.dxe5 ♘xe5 12.♗e2 ♘xf3+ 13.♗xf3 ♗e6 14.0-0 ♕a5 15.♕c2 ♖ab8 16.♖fd1 ♖fc8 Black's active bishop pair and the pin on the c-file are full value for the pawn) 11...e4 12.♘xe4 ♗f5 13.♘c3 ♘b4 14.♖c1 ♕a5 (or 14...♗xc3 15.♖xc3 ♘xa2 (-0.12), Lc0 0.00). The threats of ...♘xa2 and ...♘xd5 plus the bishop pair and lead in development ensure that Black is not worse despite his temporary two-pawn deficit.

8.♕d2

A) 8.♘f3 exd5 9.b4 ♕d6 10.a3 0-0 11.e3 c6 12.♗e2 ♗e6 13.0-0 ♘d7 (-0.36). The bishop pair counts for more than the minority attack;

B) 8.♕a4+ c6 (8...♗d7!? 9.♕b3 ♕xg5 10.♕xb7 ♗xd4 11.♕xa8 0-0 12.e3 ♕e5 13.♖c1 exd5 14.♕b7 ♘c6 15.♘e2 ♗xb2 16.♖xc6 ♗xc6 17.♕xc6 d4 18.♘f4 dxe3 19.g3 ♕a5+ 20.♔e2 ♕d2+ 21.♔f3 ♕xf2+ 22.♔g4 ♗e5=) 9.dxc6 ♘xc6 10.♘f3 ♗d7 11.♕d1 ♕b6 12.♕d2 ♘xd4 13.0-0-0 ♗c6 14.♘xd4 ♖d8 15.e3 e5 16.♕e1 exd4 17.exd4+ ♔f8 18.d5 ♗xd5 (18...♗d7!?=) 19.♖xd5 ♖xd5 20.♕e7+ ♔xe7 21.♘xd5+ ♔e6 22.♘xb6 axb6 is a well-known drawing line for White, but Black can vary as noted.

8....h6

Also satisfactory is 8...exd5 9.♕e3+ ♔f8, but the text is simpler.

9.♘f3

9.♘h3 exd5 10.♕e3+ (10.♘f4 0-0 11.e3 c5 12.dxc5 d4 13.exd4 ♕xd4 14.♕xd4 ♗xd4 15.0-0-0 ♘c6 16.♘fd5 ♗xc5 17.♘e4 ♗b6 18.♘xb6

axb6 19.♗c4 ♘e5=) 10...♔f8 11.♘f4 c5 12.dxc5 d4 13.♕d2 ♘a6=.

9....exd5

10.e3

White could (and perhaps should) play 10.b4 as Black could prevent this by 10...a5. For 10.b4 0-0 11.e3 see the next note.

10....0-0 11.♗e2

11.b4 c6 12.♗e2 ♗e6 13.0-0 ♘d7 14.♖fc1 ♖c8 15.♘a4 b6 16.♗a6 ♖c7= (0.00). The bishop pair offsets the weak pawn on c6.

11....a5

11...c6 12.0-0 ♕d6= is also okay, but I wanted to rule out 12.b4 and the minority attack.

12.b3

Now the minority attack is less effective, but it's hard to suggest a better plan for White.

12....c6 13.0-0 ♖e8 14.a3

14....♗f8?!

Although the computer thinks
this move, which prevents b3-b4,
is enough to equalize, I should
not have allowed the 'Stonewall'
plan of ♘e5 and f2-f4. Better was
14...♕e7 which prevents both plans
and shows -0.28 as White has
little compensation for the bishop
pair. Black can also just develop
with 14...♗f5 15.b4 ♕d6 since
the minority attack will open the
position in favor of the side with
the bishops.

15.♘e5 ♔g7?!

15...♗e6 followed by ...♘d7
was equal. Aiming for ...f7-f6
is unreasonable. Normally I
would stop the score here as the
remaining moves are not thematic,
but as I've analyzed the game
thoroughly I give my analysis.

**16.♗d3 ♗d6?! 17.f4 ♘d7 18.♕c2
♘f8 19.♖f3 c5?**

I should have admitted my earlier
mistake by playing 19...♔g8, but
White is already clearly better.

20.♘b5

20.♖g3+−.

20....cxd4 21.exd4 ♗b8

22.♖c1?!

22.♖af1!±.

22....♗d7 23.♕c5?? ♘e6!−+

24.♕c3 ♗xb5?

24...♗xe5! 25.fxe5 ♖c8 26.♕b2
♖xc1+ 27.♕xc1 ♗xb5 28.♗xb5 ♘xd4
29.♖h3 h5−+.

**25.♗xb5 ♗a7 26.♖d1 ♖c8 27.♕b2
♖f8??**

27...♘xd4! 28.♖xd4 ♖xe5! 29.fxe5
♕h4−+.

28.♘d7 ♘c7

28...♘xd4!∓.

29.♕e2?! ♖e8 30.♘e5 ♖e7?!

30...♘e6!−+.

**31.f5? f6 32.♖g3 g5 33.♕h5
♖xe5 34.♕g6+ ♔f8 35.♕xh6+
♔e7 36.♖xg5 ♘xb5 37.♖g7+ ♔d6
38.♖xb7 ♗xd4+ 39.♔h1 ♔c6 40.♖f7
♘d6 41.♖xf6 ♕xf6! 0-1**

This victory, although full of errors,
gave me a tie for first place in the
2010 World Senior Championship.

Game 15.7   Grünfeld Indian –
Stockholm Variation

Pavel Eljanov   2736
Alexander Kovchan   2595

Sochi tt 2010 (1)

**1.d4 ♘f6 2.c4 g6 3.♘c3 d5 4.♘f3
♗g7 5.♗g5 ♘e4 6.♗f4**

This is less common than 6.♗h4 or 6.cxd5, but it is played by some top players, so be advised to take it seriously. 6.♗h4 (this idea is more popular without the inclusion of 4.♘f3 ♗g7) 6...♘xc3 7.bxc3 dxc4 8.♕a4+ (after 8.e3 b5 9.a4 c6 10.♗e2 a6 White has fair compensation for the pawn, but no advantage. Black can develop his rook by ...♖a7-d7) 8...♕d7 9.♕xc4 b6 10.e3 ♗a6 11.♕b3 ♗xf1 12.♔xf1 0-0 13.♔e2 ♘c6 14.♖hd1 ♘a5 15.♕b4 e6 16.♖ac1 ♖fc8 17.c4 c5 18.dxc5 ♕b7 19.cxb6 axb6, and the exposed white king and his split queenside pawns give Black full compensation for the pawn.

6....♘xc3 7.bxc3 c5 8.e3
8.cxd5 ♕xd5 9.e3 ♘c6 transposes.
8....♘c6 9.cxd5 ♕xd5 10.♗e2
10.♕b3 ♕f5N 11.♗e2 0-0 12.0-0 cxd4 13.cxd4 ♘xd4 14.♘xd4 ♗xd4=.
10....cxd4 11.cxd4 ♕a5+ 12.♕d2 0-0 13.♕xa5
13.♖b1 b6 14.♖c1 ♕xd2+N 15.♘xd2 ♘b4 16.0-0 ♗e6=.
13....♘xa5 14.♖c1
A) 14.♗c7 ♘c6 15.♖b1 b6 16.0-0 ♗b7 17.♖fc1 ♖fc8 18.♗g3 e6 19.♗b5 ♗f8 20.a4 ♗a3 (+0.06);

B) 14.0-0 ♗e6 15.♖fc1 (15.♗c7 ♘c6= (0.00)) 15...♖fc8 16.♘d2 (16.♔f1! f6 (+0.16)) ♖xc1+ 17.♖xc1 ♗xa2 (0.00);

C) However, 14.♗d3 (to play ♔e2 next) 14...♗e6 (+0.15) Lc0 +0.25 may be White's best option, with a par score.

14....♗e6 15.e4
15.♘g5 ♖fc8 16.♖xc8+ ♗xc8 17.♗f3 ♗d7 18.♗c7 ♘c6 19.♔d2 ♖c8 20.♗g3 e5=.

15....♖ac8
15...♖fc8 16.d5 ♖xc1+ 17.♗xc1 ♗d7 18.♗d2 b6= should transpose to the main line soon.

16.d5 ♖xc1+ 17.♗xc1

17....♗d7N
This is an improvement over the **actual game**, which went 17...♖c8 18.♗d2 ♗d7 19.♗xa5 ♖c1+ 20.♗d1 ♗a4 21.♔e2 ♗b5+ 22.♔e3 ♗h6+ 23.♘g5 ♗xg5+ 24.f4 ♗h6 25.♖e1± and White later won.

18.♗d2 b6 19.♗a6
19.♗xa5 bxa5 20.0-0 ♖b8∓. Black's bishop pair and more active rook more than offset the doubled rook pawns.

19....e6 20.0-0 exd5 21.exd5 ♖d8 22.♗g5 f6 23.♗d2 ♗f8 24.♖c1

24....♗a3 25.♖c7 ♗d6 26.♖c1

26.♖xa7? ♗b8∓.

26....♗a3

Draw by repetition. Either side can avoid this, but chances are about equal as the passed d-pawn is also isolated.

Game 15.8   Grünfeld Indian

George Gabriel Grigore　　2532

Krikor Sevag Mekhitarian　2511

Arad 2010 (7)

1.d4 ♘f6 2.c4 g6 3.♘c3 d5 4.♘f3

4.♗f4 ♗g7 5.e3 0-0 6.♘f3 transposes to the game.

4....♗g7 5.♗f4 0-0 6.e3 c5 7.dxc5 ♘e4

7...♕a5 is also okay, but there is much more theory you would have to learn.

8.♖c1

8.♗e5 ♗xe5 9.♘xe5 ♘xc3 10.bxc3 ♕a5 11.♕d4 f6 12.♘f3 ♘c6 13.♕xd5+ ♔g7 14.♕d2 ♖d8N 15.♕b2 ♗g4=.

8....♘d7

This is a rare move, but apparently good for equality as it is not easy to improve on the moves of this game.

9.cxd5 ♕a5 10.♘d4 ♘xc3 11.bxc3 ♘xc5

11...♕xa2! slightly favors Black.

12.♗c4 e5

A better alternative is 12...♗d7! 13.0-0 ♘a4 14.♕b3 ♘b6 15.♗b5 ♗xd4 16.♗xd7 ♗f6 17.♗c7 ♕xd5 18.♖fd1 ♕c5 19.♗xb6 ♕xb6 20.♕xb6 axb6 21.a4 ♖fd8= (+0.09). A draw is likely due to the bishops of opposite color.

13.dxe6 ♗xe6 14.♗xe6 ♘xe6 15.♘xe6 ♗xc3+ 16.♔f1 fxe6 17.♕b3 ♕a6+ 18.♔g1 ♗f6 19.h3 ♖ad8 20.♔h2 ♖d3 21.♕b1

21....♖fd8

In the **actual game** a draw was agreed after 21...♖d2, but 22.♖hd1 would have slightly favored White. After the text move the game is even as Black's domination of the d-file offsets the slight weakness of his king.

22.♗g3 ♖3d7=

Game 15.9   Grünfeld Indian

Alexander Zubov   2574

Artyom Timofeev   2671

Moscow 2009 (1)

1.d4 ♘f6 2.c4 g6 3.♘c3 d5 4.♘f3 ♗g7 5.♗f4 0-0 6.♖c1 dxc4

Black should take advantage of White's failure to defend his c4-pawn by e2-e3.

7.e4

7.e3 ♗e6 8.♘g5 ♗d5 9.e4 h6 10.exd5 hxg5 11.♗xg5 ♘xd5 12.♗xc4 ♘b6 13.♗b3 ♘c6 14.d5 (14.♘e2 a5 15.a3 a4 16.♗a2 ♘xd4 17.♘xd4 ♕xd4 18.♕xd4 ♗xd4 19.♖xc7 ♖ac8 20.♖xc8 ♖xc8 (-0.09)) 14...♘d4 15.0-0 ♕d7 16.♖e1 ♖fe8 is equal (-0.04). White cannot keep the bishop pair. He has more space but an isolated d-pawn.

7....♗g4 8.♗xc4 ♘h5 9.♗e3 ♗xf3 10.gxf3

So we have a battle between White's bishop pair and Black's much better pawn structure.

10....e5

10...e6 11.f4 ♕h4 12.♕f3 ♘c6 13.♘e2 ♖ad8 is also reasonable but perhaps not fully equal.

11.dxe5

Some computers like 11.d5, but opening the position for the two bishops is important here. Also, in general, queen trades favor the side with the bishop pair. A good reply to 11.d5 is 11...♘f4.

11....♗xe5 12.♕xd8 ♖xd8

13.0-0

13.♘e2 ♘c6 14.0-0 ♗xb2N 15.♖b1 ♘e5 16.♖xb2 ♘xc4 17.♖xb7 ♘xe3 18.fxe3 ♖d2 19.♘c3 c6 20.♖c7 ♖ad8 21.♖xc6 ♖c2 22.♘d5 ♖xa2 is balanced.

13....♘d7

13...♘c6! 14.♘d5 (14.♘e2 ♗xb2 15.♖b1 ♘e5 transposes to the previous note) 14...♘a5 15.♗g5 ♖d7 16.♗b5 c6 17.b4 cxb5 18.bxa5 ♖e8 19.♖fd1 a6= (Delchev prefers 19...f5, but the engines disagree with him). Black's much better pawn structure offsets his inferior knight (0.00).

14.♘e2

14.♖fd1 c6 15.a4 ♗f4 16.♗e2 is a tad more pleasant for White, so I prefer the 13...♘c6 route to transpose to the game.

14....♗xb2 15.♖b1 ♘e5 16.♖xb2 ♘xc4 17.♖xb7 ♘xe3 18.fxe3 ♖d2 19.♘c3 c6 20.♖c7 ♖d3 21.♖xc6 ♖xe3 22.♘d5 ♖a3 23.♖f2 ♖e8 24.♘f6+?!

24.♔g2 ♖e6=.
**24....♘xf6 25.♖xf6 ♖e5 26.♖c6 ♔g7
27.♖c7 ♖ea5 28.♔g2 ♖xa2 29.♖xa2
♖xa2+ 30.♔g3∓**

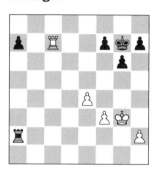

Black's extra pawn is not enough to win this endgame.
**30....a5 31.♖a7 a4 32.e5 ♔f8
33.e6 fxe6 34.♖xh7 a3 35.♖a7 ♖a1
36.♔g2 ♔e8 37.♖a6 ♔e7 38.h4 ♔d7
39.♔h2 ♔e7 40.♔g2 ♔d7 41.♔h2
♔c7 42.♖xe6 ♔b7 43.♖e3 ½-½**

Game 15.10 Grünfeld Indian
Wang Yue   2736
Dmitry Yakovenko   2742
Nanjing 2009 (7)

**1.d4 ♘f6 2.c4 g6 3.♘c3 d5 4.♗f4
♗g7 5.e3 0-0**

This is a 'gambit', but as the game shows, it is only a temporary one.

6.cxd5 ♘xd5 7.♘xd5 ♕xd5 8.♗xc7

8....♘a6!
8...♘c6 9.♘e2 ♗g4 10.f3 ♖ac8 is a wild line which unfortunately seems to win for White with correct play.
**9.♗xa6 ♕xg2 10.♕f3 ♕xf3 11.♘xf3
bxa6**
Black's bishop pair compensates for White's better pawn structure and center control.
12.♖c1 f6
This looks odd but it keeps the knight out of e5, keeps open the options of ...♗b7 or ...♗a6 or ...♗g4, and prepares ...♖f7 and ...e7-e6 or ...e7-e5.
13.♖g1
13.♔e2 a5N 14.♖c5 ♗a6+ 15.♔d2
♗b7 16.♔e2 ♗a6+ draws by repetition.
13....♗b7 14.♔e2

14....♖f7!

This is stronger than the **actual game** continuation 14...♖ac8, although that drew fairly easily, as shown: 14...♖ac8 15.♖gd1 ♖f7 16.♗a5 ♖ff8 17.♖c5 (17.♗c7 repeats) 17...e5 18.♖dc1 exd4 19.♘xd4 ♖xc5 20.♖xc5 ♖c8 21.♖xc8+ ♗xc8 22.♗b4 ♔f7 23.♗c5 f5 24.♗xa7 g5 (so White has won a pawn, but the bishop pair in this open position should draw fairly easily) 25.b3 h6 26.♗b8 f4 27.♔d3 fxe3 28.fxe3 h5 29.e4 ♔g6 30.a4 g4 31.♗f4 h4 32.e5 a5 33.e6 ♗xd4 34.e7 ♔f7 35.♔xd4 g3 36.hxg3 h3 37.g4 ♗xg4 38.♗d6 ♗d1 39.♔c3 ♔e8 40.b4 axb4+ 41.♔xb4 h2 42.♗xh2 ♔xe7 and draw agreed.

15.♖c3

Or 15.b3! ♖c8 (+0.20). Black's bishop pair offsets his poor pawn structure sufficiently to hold, though White is for choice.

15...e5 16.dxe5 ♖e8=

White must return the pawn, after which the bishop pair fully offsets Black's inferior pawn structure. 16...fxe5 17.♘g5 ♖e7 18.♖c5 h6 19.♘f3 ♖c8 20.♖gc1 ♖f7 is also equal.

Game 15.11 Grünfeld Indian
Ngoc Truongson Nguyen   2642
Li Chao   2613
China tt 2010 (4)

1.d4 ♘f6 2.c4 g6 3.♘c3 d5 4.♗f4 ♗g7 5.e3

After 5.♖c1 ♘h5 6.♗g5 (6.♗d2 c5 7.e3 cxd4 8.exd4 dxc4 9.d5 0-0 10.♗xc4 ♘d7 11.♘f3 a6 12.a4 b5

13.axb5 ♘b6=) 6...h6 7.♗h4 c5 8.e3 cxd4 9.♘xd5 ♘c6 10.exd4 ♗e6 Black will regain the pawn with an advantage in development or pawn structure.

5....0-0

5...c5 is often played and recommended, but it is safer to play this only after White has played both e2-e3 and ♘f3, to avoid dangerous lines based on a later ♘e2.

6.♖c1

In the event of 6.♕b3 c5 7.cxd5 (or 7.dxc5 ♘bd7 8.cxd5 ♘xc5 9.♕b4 b6 10.♖d1 ♘h5 11.♗g3 a5 12.♕a3 ♘xg3 13.hxg3 ♕c7 and Black has more than enough compensation for the pawn with his bishop pair, better development, more active queen, and safer king) 7...cxd4 8.exd4 ♘bd7 9.♗e2 ♘b6 10.♗f3 e6 11.d6 ♘fd5 12.♗g3 ♗xd4 13.♘ge2 ♗c5 14.0-0 ♗xd6, White can only win his pawn back at the cost of solving all Black's problems.

6....♗e6!

7.♘f3

A) 7.♕b3 c5! (grandmaster Kudrin played 7...b6 against me and drew, but I think White can keep an edge in that line with exact play) 8.♕xb7 ♕b6 9.♕xb6 axb6 10.♘f3 (10.dxc5 bxc5 11.♘f3 dxc4 transposes) 10... dxc4! 11.dxc5 bxc5 12.♘g5 ♗d5 13.♘xd5 ♘xd5 14.♗xc4 ♘xf4 15.exf4 ♗xb2 16.♖c2 ♗d4 – Black is somewhat better, mainly because he can block the white bishop by ...e7-e6 while White cannot do the same;

B) If 7.c5 c6 8.♗d3 (8.♘f3 ♗g4= or 8.h3 ♘e4) 8...b6 9.♘a4N ♘fd7 10.h3 bxc5 11.♘xc5 ♘xc5 12.♖xc5 ♕b6 13.♕c2 ♖c8 14.♘f3 ♘d7 (or 14...♘a6 (+0.03), Black will win the bishop pair to compensate for his poor pawn structure) 15.♖c3 c5 16.0-0 c4 17.b3 ♘c5 18.bxc4 ♘xd3 19.c5 ♘xc5 20.dxc5 (so far Giri-Nepomniachtchi, St Louis 2019) and now 20...♕b4 (-0.04). White can play an unclear pawn sac with 21.♘d4 or settle for equality with 21.♗e5.

7....dxc4 8.♘g5

This leads to a long forced sequence, but Black has no trouble equalizing.

8....♗d5 9.e4 h6 10.exd5 hxg5 11.♗xg5 ♘xd5

11...b5 is a decent alternative.

12.♗xc4 ♘b6 13.♗b3 ♘c6

14.d5

14.♘e2 a5 15.a3 a4 16.♗a2 ♖a5 17.♕d2 ♖b5 18.♗e3 e6 19.0-0 ♕e7=. White's isolani is restrained and under pressure and his pieces are not well placed to attack. His only plus is the bishop pair.

14....♘d4 15.0-0 ♕d7

15...♘xb3 16.♕xb3 ♗xc3 17.bxc3 ♕xd5 18.♗xe7 ♖fe8 19.c4 ♘xc4 with equality.

16.♖e1

16.♗e3 ♘xb3 17.♕xb3 ♗xc3 18.♗xb6 axb6 19.♖xc3 ♖fd8=. 16.h4 ♖fe8 17.a3 ♘xb3 18.♕xb3 ♖ad8 19.♖fd1 ♕f5!= (0.00).

16....♖fe8 17.h4

This doesn't work out well, so White should probably have just gone for the equalizing 16.♗e3 line.

17....♖ad8 18.h5 gxh5 19.♕xh5 ♕f5

White will lose the d-pawn for inadequate compensation.

20.♗d1 ♘xd5 21.♕h4 ♘f6 22.♘e4 c6 23.♖c5 ♘e2+ 24.♗xe2 ♕xe4 25.♕g3 ♕g6 26.♗f3 ♖d3 27.♕f4

In the **actual game** Black now played 27...♘d7?!, after which 28.♖a5 would have equalized. However White played 28.♗e4?!, remaining a pawn down, and lost a long endgame.

27....e6

White has only the bishop pair for the pawn, so he is half a pawn down without compensation.

Game 15.12 Grünfeld Indian –
Russian System
Alexander Shabalov 2585
Gata Kamsky 2702
Philadelphia 2010 (5)

1.d4 ♘f6 2.c4 g6 3.♘c3 d5 4.♘f3 ♗g7 5.♕b3 dxc4 6.♕xc4 0-0 7.e4 a6!

This, the Hungarian Variation, is probably the only one of many defenses that equalizes in this dangerous Russian System. It was championed from the late sixties onwards by Hungarian grandmasters like Andras Adorjan, Laszlo Barczay and Zoltan Ribli, although Alexander Alekhine was the patriarch of this move. He already adopted it before World War II – in a World Championship game against Max Euwe.

8.e5
This line has almost vanished from top play in favor of 8.♗e2 as in the next game. Or 8.♕b3 b5 9.e5, transposing.

8....b5 9.♕b3 ♘fd7

10.e6
A) 10.♗e2 c5 11.e6 cxd4! (grandmaster Peter Svidler missed this and lost to grandmaster Alexander Morozevich) 12.exd7 (12.exf7+ ♔h8 13.♘e4 ♘c6 is equal, e.g. 14.h4 h6 15.h5 g5 16.♗xg5 ♘de5 17.♗f4 ♘xf7 18.♖d1 ♗f5 19.♘c5 ♘a5 20.♕b4 ♘c6 21.♕b3 with a draw by repetition) 12...♘xd7 (12...♗b7 may be even better: 13.♘d5 ♘xd7 14.♗g5 ♘f6 15.♘xf6+ exf6 16.♗f4 ♖e8 17.♔f1 ♗d5 18.♕b4 d3 19.♗d1 f5 and with two pawns for the knight and White's rook boxed in by his king, Black is for choice) 13.♘e4 ♗b7 14.♘fd2 ♘e5 15.0-0 d3 16.♗d1 ♖c8 – although Black only has two pawns for the knight, his large development lead together with the dangerous passer offer full compensation.
B) If 10.h4 c5 11.e6 c4! 12.♕d1 ♘b6 13.exf7+ ♖xf7 14.h5 ♘c6 15.hxg6 hxg6 16.♗e3 ♘d5 (-0.15).

10....fxe6 11.♗e3
A) In the event of 11.♕xe6+ ♔h8 12.♕e4 ♘b6 13.♕h4 ♘c6 14.♗h6 e5 15.♘g5 ♕e7 Black is in good shape;

B) Or 11.h4 ♘f6 12.♗e3 (after
12.h5 ♘xh5 13.♗e3 ♘c6 White
has too little compensation for his
two-pawn deficiency; if 12.a4 ♘c6N
13.axb5 ♘xd4 14.♘xd4 ♕xd4 15.♖a4
♕e5+ Black has the initiative)
12...♘c6 (12...♕d6 also favors Black)
13.0-0-0 ♕d6 and Black's extra
pawn is of only slight value here,
but his attacking chances are not
inferior to White's;

C) 11.♘g5 ♘b6=.

11....♘f6

11...♘b6?!, as I had previously
played against Shabalov, is inferior
as the knight is needed to defend
the kingside. He won a brilliant
game.

12.a4

12.g3 ♘c6 13.♗g2 (Salgado Lopez-
McShane, Germany Bundesliga
2018/19) 13...♘a5 14.♕c2 ♗b7
(-0.04).

12...b4!

12...bxa4 is playable but not quite
equal, I think.

13.♕xb4 ♘c6 14.♕a3

After 14.♕c5?! ♕d6 15.♗c4 ♕xc5
16.dxc5 ♘g4 White must lose the
bishop pair or a pawn.

14....♕d6

15.♗e2

A) 15.♗c4 ♘b4 16.♕b3 (16.♖c1
♗b7 transposes to the 15.♖c1
line below) 16...♗b7 17.0-0 ♗xf3
18.♗xe6+ ♔h8 19.gxf3 ♖ab8
(19...♘c6 is also fine) 20.♗c4 ♕c6
21.♗e2 ♘fd5 – the broken White
kingside and poorly paced white
queen give Black enough for the
pawn (-0.15);

B) 15.♖c1 ♗b7 16.♗c4 ♘b4, and
already Black is better as White's
king is not so safe after 17.0-0 ♗xf3.

**15....♘b4 16.♖c1 ♗b7 17.0-0 ♘g4
18.h3 ♘xe3 19.fxe3**

19....♗h6

After 19...♖ab8! Black's bishop pair
and better placed pieces easily
offset his poor pawn structure.

20.♘d1 ♘d5

20...a5=.

21.♕b3 ♕g3??
21...♕b6=.
22.♕xb7 ♗xe3+ 23.♘xe3 ♘xe3
24.♖f2 ♘d5 25.♕c6 ♘f4 26.♔f1
♖ab8 27.♗c4 1-0

Game 15.13 Grünfeld Indian –
              Russian System

Alexander Riazantsev   2689
Maxim Rodshtein   2625

Moscow 2011 (5)

1.d4 ♘f6 2.c4 g6 3.♘c3 d5 4.♘f3
4.♕b3 dxc4 5.♕xc4 ♗g7 6.e4 0-0
7.♘f3 transposes to the game, as
does 7.♗e2 a6 8.♘f3; 7.♗f4 c6 8.♘f3
b5 9.♕b3 ♕a5 10.♗d3 ♗e6 11.♕d1
♗g4 12.0-0 b4 13.♘e2 ♗xf3 14.gxf3
c5 15.dxc5 ♘fd7=.
4....♗g7 5.♕b3 dxc4 6.♕xc4 0-0
7.e4 a6

8.♗e2
  A) 8.a4?! b5! 9.♕b3 c5! 10.dxc5
♗e6∓ 11.♕a3?! b4! 12.♕xb4 ♘c6∓
13.♕a3? ♖b8–+; the threat of ...♖b3
forces White to part with material.
  B) The recent fad 8.♕a4 is a
serious try here, but is well met by
8...c5! 9.dxc5 ♗d7=. Now 10.♕b4 is
met by 10...a5!, 10.♕a3 by 10...♗c6,

and 10.♕b3 or 10.♕c2 by 10...♕a5!,
in all cases with fine play for Black.
  C) 8.♕b3 b5 9.♗e2 transposes to
the game;
  D) 8.♗f4 b5 9.♕xc7 (stem
game Euwe-Alekhine, Wch m-12
Netherlands 1935) 9...♕xc7 10.♗xc7
♗b7!.
8....b5 9.♕b3 c5
9...♘c6 10.e5 ♗e6 11.exf6 ♗xb3
12.fxg7 ♔xg7 13.axb3 ♘xd4 14.♘xd4
♕xd4 15.0-0 ♕b4 16.♗f3 ♕xb3
is an interesting line but probably
more comfortable for White.
10.dxc5 ♗e6
10...♗b7 is also good, but I think
the game move is better.
11.♕c2 ♘bd7

12.♗e3
12.c6 ♘b8 13.♘g5 (13.0-0 ♘xc6
14.♘xb5 ♘xe4N 15.♕xe4 ♗d5
(-0.34)) 13...♘xc6 14.♘xe6 fxe6
15.♗e3 ♘d4 16.♕d1 ♘xe2 17.♕xe2
♕a5 18.0-0 b4 19.♘d1 ♕b5. Despite
his bad pawns, Black has all the
play here.
12....♖c8 13.♖d1
13.c6 ♖xc6 14.♘d4 ♖d6 15.♘xe6
♖xe6 16.f3 (16.0-0 ♕b8=) 16...♕c7
17.♕b3 ♖c6=. Black's pressure

and better development offset the bishop pair.

13....b4 14.♘d5

14.♘a4 ♕a5 15.0-0 ♘xe4 16.♕xe4 ♕xa4=.

14....♗xd5 15.exd5 ♘xc5 16.0-0

16....♕d6!

Previously 16...a5 was played.

17.♖c1

17.♕c4! ♘ce4 18.♕xa6 ♖c2 19.♗d4 ♘c5 20.♕xd6 exd6 21.♗b5 ♘fe4 22.♖c1 ♖xc1 23.♖xc1 ♖a8 (+0.24) was Giri-Nepomniachtchi, Moscow 2016. 'Fine for Black' – Navara. Black will soon regain the pawn with a slightly worse but drawn endgame.

17...♕b8 18.♗xc5

18.♗c4 ♖fd8 – White has the bishop pair but an isolated d-pawn, while Black has good squares for his knights on c5 and d6. 19.♖fd1 is met by 19...♘b7 (-0.09). If 18.♖fd1

a5 19.h3 ♘ce4 (+0.08). The weak d5-pawn offsets the bishop pair.

18....♘d7 19.♗xa6 ♖xc5 20.♕d2 ♖d8

20...♕d6 is a good alternative.

21.♖xc5 ♘xc5 22.♗c4 e6

Here 22...♘a4 is similar.

23.♖d1 ♘a4

24.♗b3

24.♘d4! ♗xd4 25.♕xd4 ♘b6 26.♗b3 ♘xd5 27.♕e4 (+0.20). White has some attacking ideas of h2-h4 and g2-g3, but it's not too threatening.

24....♘c5 25.♗c4 ♘a4 26.♗b3 ♘c5 27.♕e3=

27.♗c4 draws by repetition.

27....♘xb3 28.♕xb3 exd5 29.♘e1 ♕d6 30.♘d3 ♗f8 31.g3 ♖a8

31...h5=.

32.h4 ♕a6 33.♘xb4 ♗xb4 34.♕xb4 ♕xa2 35.h5 gxh5 36.♕b7 h4 37.gxh4 ♖e8 38.♖xd5 ♕b1+ 39.♔h2 ♕e4 40.♔g3 f5 41.♕b3 ½-½

CHAPTER 16

Grünfeld Exchange

In this chapter we look at lines where White exchanges pawns immediately (**4.cxd5 ♘xd5**), although 4.♘f3 ♗g7 5.cxd5 ♘xd5 will transpose to this chapter.

This usually leads to an exchange on c3 which brings White's b2-pawn to c3, where it supports the center but is itself weak. These lines tend to be more double-edged than without this exchange. With the white pawn on c3, Black always replies ...c7-c5 right after ...♗g7, but is generally reluctant to exchange on d4 without a clear motivation because it exchanges off the weak white c-pawn. Black's goal is to force White into some concession, such as moving e4-e5, taking on c5, or getting an artificially isolated pawn on d5 (for this Black must put his pawn on c4 before White does so).

In Game 16.1 we look at alternatives to the obvious 5.e4. The most important is **5.♗d2**, aiming to recapture on c3 with the bishop.

Although this trade may actually be Black's best option (see note), it is logical to move the knight to b6 when it is attacked because then the move ♗d2 is simply a wasted tempo; it almost always goes to e3 anyway to defend d4. Without the extra tempo this line is simply bad for Black, but with it Black gets nearly equal chances. Just remember after **5...♗g7 6.e4 ♘b6 7.♗e3 0-0 8.h3** (else 8...♗g4 when White plays 8.♘f3) to play **8...e5!**, and to meet the bizarre 8.♗b5 by 8...♗e6. We also look at the equally bizarre **5.♘a4**, which is better than it looks. I recommend **5...♗g7 6.e4 ♘b6**. The basic rule is that it is okay for the knight to be driven to b6 if White has paid a price for this.

Now we come to the real Exchange Grünfeld, **5.e4 ♘xc3 6.bxc3 ♗g7**.

In Game 16.2 we consider all the infrequent seventh moves. The queen check **7.♕a4+** is met by **7...♕d7**. 7...♘d7 is also playable but Black would rather not forego the option to put pressure on d4 with a timely ...♘c6). The move **7.♗a3** is similarly met by **7...♘d7**, intending ...c7-c5. Instead, 7.♗g5 is met by the immediate 7...c5, trying to provoke d4-d5. The main move in the game, **7.♗b5+**, is met by **7...c6 8.♗a4 0-0 9.♘e2 b5 10.♗b3 a5** with good counterplay. In all these sidelines Black is fine.

In Game 16.3 we consider unusual eighth moves after **7.♘f3 c5**.

Against **8.♗e2** we pressure the center by **8...♘c6 9.♗e3 ♗g4**. Against **8.h3**, pressure on d4 won't work, but after **8...0-0 9.♗e2 ♘c6 10.♗e3** we switch to an attack on e4 by **10...cxd4 11.cxd4 f5!**. As for the game move **8.♗b5+**, we block with the knight on c6, castle and play ...♗g4, leaving out the pawn exchange on d4. Again all the lines are harmless.

Now we come to the important lines with ♗e3, meaning either **7.♘f3 c5 8.♗e3 ♕a5 9.♕d2 0-0 10.♖c1** or Kramnik's preferred order **7.♗e3 c5 8.♖c1 ♕a5 9.♕d2 0-0 10.♘f3**.

I favour putting direct pressure on the center with **10...♖d8**. If White just develops we trade pawns and queens with perhaps a slightly better version of the endgame that usually arises when this trade occurs earlier. If White advances 11.d5 we play ...e7-e6. These lines are a bit complicated and must be studied carefully. Points to remember: ...♘a6 is often a good move, ...c5-c4 as a pawn sacrifice is sometimes viable, and often the a2-pawn becomes a target. See Game 16.4. It seems that both 11.♗e2 and 11.d5 give White a nominal edge, but within the bounds of what most authors would call equal. This ♗e3 line is Carlsen's main weapon against the Grünfeld, and for good reason.

The next two games feature the so-called Modern Exchange Variation, meaning **7.♘f3 c5 8.♖b1 0-0 9.♗e2**.

Game 16.5 features the popular sequence **9...cxd4 10.cxd4 ♕a5+ 11.♗d2** (11.♕d2 leads to an endgame which is covered in the notes) **11...♕xa2 12.0-0**. This is a rather dangerous (for Black) gambit by White, whose compensation for the pawn is rather obvious (several tempi and an extra

pawn in the center). The usual move here (recommended by Avrukh) is 12...♗g4, after which White generally regains his pawn and Black has to play precisely to reach an endgame that he can draw. Instead I go for the second-most popular move, **12...b6**, which intends to hold the pawn, at least for a while. After **13.♕c1 ♗b7** White can force an immediate repetition, and in any case Black doesn't have easy equality, so I give the greedy but risky **13...♕e6** in case you can't allow the repetition draw. But my preferred option, given in Game 16.6, is the same line as recommended by Delchev, namely **9...♘c6 10.d5 ♘e5 11.♘xe5 ♗xe5 12.♕d2 e6 13.f4 ♗c7!**, which prevents the normally desirable 14.c4. There are some scary lines here, but it seems that Black can hold the balance.

Now we come to the old way of playing the Exchange Variation, which has again become popular. This is **7.♗c4 c5 8.♘e2 ♘c6 9.♗e3 0-0 10.0-0**.

In Game 16.7 I give my second-string defense, **10...e6**, which aims to restrain the white d-pawn, and also gives the queen the square e7 where it is less subject to attack than on c7. Still, I prefer **10...♕c7 11.♖c1 b6** (Game 16.8), primarily because we may want to play a later ...e7-e5 without the loss of a tempo. Some of the resultant positions (after ...e7-e5 and d4-d5) are evaluated as good for White by the computers, but I don't trust computer evaluations much in highly blocked positions such as these. Computers love protected passed pawns, but when they are securely blockaded by a knight they aren't much of an asset.

I decided to include coverage of the **10...b6** gambit line as a third black option. That was Grünfeld guru Peter Svidler's choice against World Number 1 Magnus Carlsen just days before I finished the (original) book. At this writing, my analysis indicates that it may be the best choice of all for Black, since the gambit seems quite sound if accepted, while if it is declined Black has the choice transposing to 10...♕c7 or aiming instead for ...e7-e6 and ...♕e7, which is probably a bit better. See Game 16.9.

Game 16.1 Grünfeld Indian –
Exchange Variation

Alexander Evdokimov 2564

Peter Svidler 2750

Sochi tt 2010 (3)

**1.d4 ♘f6 2.c4 g6 3.♘c3 d5 4.cxd5
♘xd5**

5.♗d2

A) 5.♘a4 (Ashot Nadanian's
spectacular discovery) 5...♗g7 6.e4
♘b6 7.♗e3 0-0 8.♘f3 ♗g4 and now:

analysis diagram

A1) 9.♘c5 ♘c6 10.♘xb7 ♕b8
11.♗a6 ♘b4 12.♘c5 ♗xf3 13.gxf3
♗xd4! 14.♗xd4 (after 14.♗e2 ♖d8
15.♕b3 ♗xc5 16.♗xc5 ♘c6 17.♖c1
♘d4 18.♕e3 e5 the outposted
knight offsets the bishop pair)
14...♖d8 15.0-0 ♘xa6 16.♘xa6 ♕c8
17.♘c5 e5 18.♕c1 ♖xd4 19.♕g5 ♕d8
is equal (0.00); both sides have bad

pawns and the piece placement is
about even;

A2) 9.♗e2 ♘c6 10.d5 ♘e5
11.♘xe5 ♗xe2 12.♕xe2 ♘xa4 13.f4
e6 14.dxe6 (14.♕c2 ♘b6 15.dxe6
♗xe5 16.fxe5 fxe6 17.h4 ♖f7 18.a4
a5 (+0.13). Stockfish agrees with
Komodo that Black is nearly equal,
while Lc0 likes White. I would say
Black is fine but has to play more
carefully) 14...♗xe5 15.exf7+ ♖xf7
16.fxe5 ♕h4+ 17.♗f2 ♖xf2 18.♕xf2
♕xe4+ 19.♕e2 ♕b4+ 20.♕d2 ♕h4+
21.g3 ♕e4+ 22.♔f2 ♘xb2 23.♕xb2
♖f8+ 24.♔g1 ♕e3+ 25.♔g2 ♕f3+
results in a draw by perpetual
check;

B) Or 5.♕b3 ♘xc3 6.bxc3 ♗g7
7.♘f3 0-0 8.♗a3 b6 9.e3 c5 10.♗e2
♘c6 11.0-0 ♘a5 12.♕c2 (after
12.♕b5 ♗d7 13.♕a6 ♕c7 White's
pieces are a bit misplaced) 12...♕c7
13.♖ac1 ♗b7 14.c4 e6 15.dxc5 bxc5
with rough equality.

analysis diagram

White's knight is better placed than
Black's, but Black's bishops are
better placed than White's.

5....♗g7 6.e4 ♘b6

A good alternative is 6...♘xc3
7.♗xc3 0-0 8.♘f3 (8.♕d2 c5 9.d5 e6

293

10.♗xg7 ♔xg7 11.♗c4 ♘d7 12.♘e2 ♘b6=, and if 12.d6 then 12...♕h4 is a good reply) 8...♗g4 9.♗e2 c5 10.d5 e6 11.0-0 exd5 12.exd5 ♕d6= (the white d-pawn is passed but isolated, and Black aims for a knight vs bad bishop edge) 13.♕b3 ♘d7 (+0.11). This option now looks safer to me than the game move.

7.♗e3 0-0

8.h3

A) 8.♗b5 (this bizarre but strong move aims to provoke 8...a6 9.♗e2 as in some variations the loss of protection for the knight by the a7-pawn is important) 8...♗e6 9.♘ge2 (9.♘f3 ♗g4 10.♗e2 transposes to the 8.♘f3 line, with each side having lost a tempo. Lc0 likes the rare 10.e5 for White) 9...c6 10.♗d3 ♘c4 11.♗xc4 ♗xc4 12.0-0 ♘d7 13.♕d2 ♕a5 14.♖fd1 ♖fd8=. This is a computer improvement over 14...♖ad8, which was equal in Wang Yue-Carlsen, Medias 2010, won by Black. Presumably the idea is to retain the bishop pair if White plays ♗h6 now or later. Either way Black is fine;

B) 8.♘f3 ♗g4 9.♗e2 ♘c6 10.d5 ♗xf3 11.gxf3 (11.♗xf3 ♘e5 12.♗e2 ♘ec4 13.♗c1 c6 14.dxc6 bxc6 15.♕c2 ♕d4 16.0-0 ♖fd8 17.a4 ♕c5∓) 11...♘a5 12.♗d4 ♕d6 13.♗xg7 ♔xg7 14.♕d2 ♕f6 15.b3 ♖ad8=;

C) 8.♗e2 ♘c6 9.d5 (9.♘f3 ♗g4 transposes to the 8.♘f3 line above) 9...♘e5 10.♗d4 c5! 11.♗xc5 (11.dxc6 ♘xc6 12.♗xg7 ♔xg7∓) 11...♘ec4

analysis diagram

12.♗xc4 (12.♕b3 ♘xb2!=; note that this would be bad with Black's a-pawn on a6. This shows the point of the 8.♗b5 move) 12...♘xc4 13.♕b3 ♘xb2 14.♕xb2 ♕c7 15.♗b4 a5 16.♘ge2 axb4 17.♕xb4 f5!N (17...♕d6=; 17...♗g4=; 17...b6!N also favors Black) 18.0-0 fxe4 19.♖ac1 ♗f5 20.a4 ♕e5∓. With two bishops for two knights in a very open position, Black can afford to lose his b7- or e4-pawn and still have enough compensation. White is unlikely to hang on to both of his isolated pawns for long;

D) 8.f4 ♘c6 9.d5 ♘a5 10.♗d4 e5 11.♗xe5 ♗xe5 12.fxe5 ♕h4+ 13.g3 ♕e7 14.♕d4 ♖d8 15.b4 ♘ac4 with equality.

8....e5!

8...f5 is often played (I played it once myself) but inferior.

9.dxe5

A) 9.♘f3 exd4 10.♗xd4 ♘c6 (or 10...♕e7=) 11.♗xg7 ♔xg7 12.♗b5 ♕xd1+ 13.♖xd1 (Laylo-Navara, Khanty-Mansiysk 2009) 13...♘b4!N 14.a3 a6 15.♗e2 ♘c6 16.0-0 ♗e6 (+0.10);

B) 9.d5 c6 10.♕b3 cxd5 11.exd5 ♘a6 12.♘f3 e4 13.♘g5 ♗xc3+ 14.bxc3 ♖e8 15.d6 ♗e6 16.♕d1 h6 17.h4 ♘b8 is also equal.

9....♗xe5 10.♕c2

10.♘f3 ♗xc3+ 11.bxc3 ♕xd1+ 12.♔xd1 ♖e8 13.♗d3 ♗e6 14.♔c2 ♘c4 15.♗c1 ♘d6 16.♗f4 ♘d7 (-0.03). White can't retain his bishop pair.

10....♘c6

10...♖e8! 11.♘f3 ♗xc3+ 12.bxc3 ♕e7 13.♘d2 ♗d7 14.♗e2 ♗a4 15.♕c1 ♘8d7 16.0-0 ♖ad8 (+0.14). Black's better pawn structure and

development nearly offset the bishop pair.

11.♘f3 ♗g7 12.♗e2 ♘b4 13.♕b1 ♕e7 14.0-0 ♗e6

15.a3

A) 15.♖c1 ♘c6 16.♘b5 ♖fc8 17.♗c5 ♕f6 18.♘bd4 ♗d7 19.♕c2 ♗e8 (+0.06);

B) 15.♗g5! ♗f6 (+0.15).

15....♘c6 16.♕c2 ♖fe8

16...♖fd8 was probably better (+0.15).

17.♘b5

17.♖ad1 a6 18.♗d3 (18.♘d5!) 18...♖ad8 19.♘e2 ♖d7 20.♘f4 ♖ed8 21.♖fe1 ♘d4 22.♗xd4 ♗xd4 23.e5 c5 24.♘xe6 ♕xe6 25.♘g5 ♕e7 26.e6 ♕xg5 27.exd7 ♘xd7=. Although Black has only a pawn for the exchange, his powerful anchored bishop and the presence of the major pieces give him enough compensation.

17....a6 18.♘c3

18.♗c5 ♗b3! (probably White missed this when he played 17.♘b5) 19.♕xb3 ♕xc5 20.♘xc7 ♘a5 21.♕b4 ♕xc7 22.♕xa5 ♖xe4=.

18....♗c4 19.♗xc4 ♘xc4= 20.♗g5 ♘d4 21.♘xd4 ♕xg5 22.♘f3?!

22.♖ad1 ♕e5=.

22....♕e7 23.♖fe1 c6∓

Black's bishop is superior to White's knights.

24.♘d2 ♘xd2 25.♕xd2 ♖ad8 26.♕c2 ♕c5 27.♖ac1 a5 28.♕e2 ♕g5 29.♖cd1 ♖xd1 30.♖xd1 ♗xc3 31.bxc3 ♕c5

Black now wins a pawn.

32.♕f3 ♕xa3 33.♖d7 ♖e7 34.♖d8+ ♔g7 35.♕e3 ♖e5 36.♖d7 b5 37.♔h2? ♕c5−+ 38.♕f4 ♖e7 39.♖xe7 ♕xe7 40.e5 a4 41.♕d4 c5 0-1

Game 16.2   Grünfeld Indian –
                  Exchange Variation
Anatoli Vaisser   2507
Vlastimil Jansa   2499
Arco Wch-sen 2010 (7)

1.d4 ♘f6 2.c4 g6 3.♘c3 d5 4.cxd5 ♘xd5 5.e4 ♘xc3 6.bxc3 ♗g7

In this game I examine all the unusual moves played here. For the more regular moves 7.♘f3 and 7.♗c4, see Games 3-6 and 7-9.

7.♗b5+

A) 7.♕a4+ has become an important line.

analysis diagram

A1) In 2007 I played 7...♕d7 against IM (later GM) Irina Krush and got into trouble, but somehow I won. I now think it is the best option for Black on move 7, and it seems World Rapid #1 and Grünfeld devotee MVL agrees. Play may continue 8.♗b5 (8.♕a3 b6 9.♘f3 c5 10.♗d3 ♘c6 11.♗b5 a6 12.0-0 ♗b7 13.♗xc6 ♗xc6 was played twice by Mamedyarov vs Vachier-Lagrave, Riga 2019. The first time 14.d5 ♗b5 15.♖e1 0-0 16.♗b2 c4 17.♗c1 e6 (-0.02) was equal and soon drawn. The second game saw 14.♖e1 f5 (+0.03), which was also equal and also eventually drawn) 8...c6 9.♗d3 0-0 10.♘e2 c5 11.♕xd7 ♗xd7 (+0.05) or 9.♗e2 0-0 10.♕a3 b6 11.♘f3 c5 12.0-0 cxd4 13.cxd4 ♗b7 14.♕e3 ♘c6 15.♗b2 ♘a5 16.♖ab1 e6 (+0.06); or 8.♕b3 0-0

9.♗e3 c5 10.♘f3 cxd4 11.cxd4 ♘c6 12.♖d1 ♕d6 13.h3 ♕b4+ (-0.05);

A2) 7...♘d7 8.♘f3 0-0 9.♗g5 (9.♗e2! c5 10.0-0 cxd4 11.cxd4 ♘c5 12.dxc5! is critical and although Black should draw it is rather unpleasant for him) 9...c5 10.♖c1 (10.♖d1 ♕c7 11.♗e2 ♘f6 12.d5 ♗d7 13.♕c2 ♕a5 14.♘d2 ♗a4 15.♘b3 ♕c7 16.c4 ♕e5=; analysis by Avrukh) 10...h6 11.♗e3 a6 12.♕a3 b6 13.♗d3 e6 14.0-0 ♗b7 15.♕b3 ♕c7 16.♕d1 ♘f6 (Delchev) 17.♘d2 ♖ac8 18.a4 ♖fd8 and Black is for choice as the obvious 19.♕e2 is met by 19...cxd4 when the trade of queen for two rooks after 20.cxd4 favors Black slightly.

B) 7.♗a3 ♘d7 8.♘f3 c5 9.♕b3 0-0 10.♗e2 (10.♗d3 ♖b8 11.0-0 b5=; 10.♗c4 b5 11.♗xb5 ♖b8 12.♕a4 ♘b6 13.♕a5 cxd4 14.♘xd4 ♗b7 is also equal; White must lose back his extra pawn on e4 or on d4; 10.♖d1 ♕c7 11.♗e2 b5) 10...♖b8 (Delchev) 11.0-0 b5 and here Black has adequate counterplay;

C) 7.♗g5 c5 8.♖c1 0-0 9.♘f3 (9.d5 ♕d6 10.♗e2 f5 11.exf5 ♗xf5 12.♘f3 was Rasmussen-Andersen, Helsingør 2019. Now 12...e6 13.♗c4 b5! 14.♗xb5 exd5 15.0-0 ♘d7 (+0.06) would be equal) 9...♗g4 10.d5 ♕d6 11.♗e2 ♗xf3 12.♗xf3 b5 13.0-0 ♘d7. The plan of ...c5-c4 and ...♘d7-c5-d3 plus the weak white pawns on a2 and c3 fully offset White's bishop pair. 14.♕d2 c4 15.♕e3 ♘c5 (-0.06) (15...e5 is also equal and good). In Lysyj-Drygalov,

Russia 2019, after 16.♗e2?! e5 Black was already better (-0.40).
7....c6 8.♗a4 0-0 9.♘e2 b5
I also like 9...e5.
10.♗b3 a5

11.♗e3
In the event of 11.0-0 ♘d7 12.♗g5 a4 13.♗c2 ♘b6 14.♕c1 f6 15.♗h6 e5 16.♗xg7 ♔xg7 17.h3 ♗e6 Black stands better due to the c4 outpost for his bishop or knight and his much more mobile bishop.
Also after 11.a4 ♗a6 12.axb5 cxb5 13.0-0 ♘c6 14.♗e3 a4 Black is better, with ideas of ...♘c6-a5-c4 or ...b5-b4. Analysis by Agrest.
11....♘d7 12.h4 a4 13.♗c2 ♘b6 14.♕c1 ♘c4 15.♗h6 e5 16.♗xg7 ♔xg7 17.h5 ♕e7 18.♗d3 ♗e6

19.d5?!

19.f4 exf4 20.♕xf4 g5 21.♕g3 ♘b2 –
the white attack is dead and Black
has the initiative.

19....cxd5 20.hxg6 fxg6 21.♕h6+?!
Since there is no attack the check
should have been held in reserve.

21....♔g8 22.exd5

Here a draw was agreed, although
Black is clearly better after 22....♗f5.
White's attack has failed, his king
is in the center, and his queenside
pawns are effectively all three
isolated from each other. Curiously,
the two players in this game and I
ended up tied for 1st place (along
with one other grandmaster),
with Vaisser taking first and Jansa
second on tiebreak points. Perhaps
Jansa would have won this World
Senior Championship if he had not
agreed to a draw here.

Game 16.3   Grünfeld Indian –
              Exchange Variation

Xu Jun   2486
Wang Yue   2734

Ningbo 2011 (2)

**1.d4 ♘f6 2.c4 g6 3.♘c3 d5 4.cxd5
♘xd5 5.e4 ♘xc3 6.bxc3 ♗g7 7.♘f3
c5**

In this game we look at White's
unusual eighth moves.

8.♗b5+
This is not a promising line. White
hasn't won a single grandmaster
level game in this variation for
twelve years!

  A) 8.♗e2?! (already after this
White has no chance for even the
slightest edge) 8...♘c6 and now:

analysis diagram

  A1) After 9.d5 ♗xc3+ 10.♗d2
♗xa1 11.♕xa1 ♘d4 12.♘xd4 cxd4
13.♕xd4 0-0 14.♗h6 ♕a5+ 15.♔f1
f6 16.♗xf8 ♔xf8 White's extra
center pawn doesn't quite make
up for his loss of castling rights
and the difficulty he will have
developing his rook;

  A2) 9.♗e3 ♗g4 10.e5 (usually in
the Grünfeld when White is forced

to play this he is worse, as his d-pawn becomes backward) 10...0-0 11.0-0 ♖c8 12.h3 cxd4 13.cxd4 ♗e6 14.♕d2 ♗d5N – White has little compensation for the backward d-pawn and the resultant outpost for Black on d5.

B) 8.h3 0-0 9.♗e2 ♘c6 10.♗e3 cxd4 11.cxd4 f5! (Black scored 8 out of 10 from here in my database) 12.♗c4+ (in case of 12.exf5 ♕a5+ 13.♗d2 ♕xf5, due to the pressure on d4, Black is better) 12...♔h8 13.e5 b5 14.♗b3 ♘a5 15.0-0 ♘xb3 16.axb3 ♗b7 and here White has little compensation for the bishop pair.

8....♘c6 9.0-0 0-0

9...cxd4 first has been more popular, when White may have a microscopic edge. Now the text is catching on as Black need not fear the capture on c5, as we shall see.

10.♗e3 ♗g4

11.dxc5

11.d5 ♘e5 12.♗e2 ♘xf3+ 13.♗xf3 ♗xf3 14.♕xf3 ♕a5 15.♖ac1 c4 16.♕e2 ♖ac8=. The weak white pawns on a2 and c3 offset his extra center pawn.

11....♕c7

11...♗xc3 12.♖c1 ♗g7 13.h3 ♗xf3N 14.♕xf3 ♘d4 (-0.18).

11...♕c8 is good too.

12.♗xc6 ♕xc6 13.♕c2 ♗xf3 14.gxf3 f5 15.♖fd1 ♖f7 16.♖d5 ♖af8 17.♖ad1 fxe4 18.♕xe4 ♖xf3 19.♕xe7 ♖3f7 20.♕h4

20....♕e6

There was nothing wrong with regaining the pawn by 20...♗xc3=.

21.c4 ♗f6

Better and equal was 21...♗e5, preventing 22.♖d6 while keeping an eye on h2.

22.♕g3 ♕e4

In the **actual game** Black played to regain his pawn by 22...♕a6, but after 23.♕e4 ♕xa2 24.♖d7 he had to fight for the draw, successfully. The text equalizes, as the isolation of all five white pawns surely offsets White's one pawn lead in material.

Game 16.4   Grünfeld Indian –
                    Exchange Variation

Sipke Ernst   2587
Jan Gustafsson   2646
Germany Bundesliga 2010/11 (1)

1.d4 ♘f6 2.c4 g6 3.♘c3 d5 4.cxd5 ♘xd5 5.e4 ♘xc3 6.bxc3 ♗g7

7.♘f3

7.♗e3 c5 8.♖c1 (Kramnik's preferred move-order) 8...♕a5 9.♕d2 0-0 10.♘f3 transposes.

7....c5 8.♗e3

This variation is still popular with strong grandmasters in 2019.

8....♕a5 9.♕d2

9.♘d2 and now:

A) 9...cxd4 is a reasonable alternative to castling. It avoids the draw given below, but I consider 9...♗d7 to be the more correct move. 10.♘c4 (10.cxd4 ♘c6 11.d5 ♘d4 12.♖c1 ♗d7 13.♗d3 ♗a4 14.♕g4 ♗d7 15.♕d1 is a draw by repetition)

analysis diagram

10...♕d8 (10...dxe3?! 11.♘xa5 ♗xc3+ 12.♔e2 ♗xa5 13.♔xe3 was Aronian-Sutovsky, Ningbo Wch-tt 2011.

Black has two bishops, a pawn, and some threats against the exposed white king for his queen, but it wasn't enough and Black lost the game. The computers consider this sacrifice unsound) 11.cxd4 f5 12.♖b1 fxe4 13.♗e2 0-0 14.0-0 ♗e6 15.♖xb7 ♗d5 16.♖b5 ♘c6 17.♕d2 e6. Although Black has one more isolated pawn than White, his pieces are active and centralized. Nevertheless, the engines favor White here;

B) 9...♗d7! and now:

analysis diagram

B1) 10.♘b3 ♕xc3+ 11.♗d2 ♕b2 12.♗c1 ♕c3+ 13.♗d2 was a quick draw by repetition played in Shulman-Dominguez Perez, Lubbock 2011, and other games;

B2) 10.♗e2 ♕xc3 11.♖c1 ♕b2 12.♖c2 ♕b4 13.♖xc5 ♘c6 14.♖c4 ♕b2 15.d5 ♘d4 is also equal;

B3) 10.♖b1 ♕xc3 11.d5 b6 12.♗c4 0-0 13.0-0 ♕a5 14.♗b3 (Parligras-Baron, Skopje 2019) 14...♘a6 15.♘c4 ♕c3 16.f4 b5N 17.♖c1 ♕f6 18.♘e5 ♕d6 19.a4 ♗xe5 20.dxe5 ♕xe5 (+0.05). White has just enough compensation for his missing two pawns;

B4) 10.♖c1 cxd4 11.♘c4 ♕xa2
12.♖a1 ♕xa1 13.♕xa1 dxe3 14.♘b6
axb6 15.♕xa8 ♗xc3+ 16.♔e2
0-0 17.♔xe3 ♗d4+! 18.♔f3 ♘c6
19.♕xb7 ♘e5+ (0.00). Although two
bishops and a pawn are not enough
for the queen, Black's superior
development and threats to the
king and queen will win enough
material to equalize.

9....0-0 10.♖c1

This line is quite popular now
especially with Magnus Carlsen
playing the White side successfully.
It is perhaps the greatest threat to
the Grünfeld in 2019.

10...♖d8 11.d5

11.♗e2 cxd4 (or Delchev's line
11...♗g4 12.d5 c4! 13.0-0 ♗xf3
14.♗xf3 ♘d7, when White can try
15.h4 ♘c5 16.♖b1 ♗xc3 17.♕c2 b6
18.♗e2 ♗e5 19.♕xc4 ♖ac8 (+0.04),
Lc0 +0.22; White has the bishop
pair but otherwise the position is
pleasant for Black) 12.cxd4 ♕xd2+
13.♗xd2 ♘a6 14.♗e3 ♗g4 15.♘e5
♗xe2 16.♔xe2 f5 17.exf5 gxf5 18.♔f3
♘b4 19.♖c3 ♘d5 20.♖b1 b6 (+0.14).
White has the more active king in
the endgame, but not much more
than that.

11....e6 12.♗g5

A) 12.♗e2 exd5 13.exd5 b5!
14.♗xc5 ♗b7 15.c4 ♕xd2+ 16.♘xd2
bxc4 17.♗xc4 ♗xd5= or 14.♗g5 ♖e8
15.0-0 ♘d7 16.d6 ♗b7 17.♖fe1 ♖e4
18.♗e7 h6 19.c4 b4 20.♗d3 ♖xe1+
21.♖xe1 ♕a3 (+0.05);

B) 12.c4 ♕xd2+ 13.♘xd2 b6 14.♗e2
♘a6 15.0-0 ♘b4 16.a3 ♘a2 17.♖c2
♘c3 18.♗f3 exd5 19.cxd5?! (19.

exd5 ♗f5 20.♖cc1 ♖ac8=) 19...♗a6
20.♖fc1 ♘e2+ 21.♗xe2 ♗xe2∓. With
the bishop pair in a wide open
position and no bad pawns or pieces
Black is better.

12....f6

13.♗f4

A) 13.c4 ♘c6 14.♕xa5 ♘xa5
15.♗d2 b6 16.♗d3 ♘b7 (+0.01).
Black's knight will reach the ideal
blockading square d6;

B) 13.♗e3 ♘c6 14.♗d3 (14.♗e2
exd5 (Delchev prefers 14...♘e7 15.c4
♕xd2+, but the engines prefer
White after all three recaptures
and offer improvements over his
analysis. It probably suffices to
draw, but I wouldn't call it equal)
15.exd5 c4 16.♖d1 ♘e7 17.♗xc4 ♗e6
transposes) 14...exd5 15.exd5 c4!
16.♗xc4 ♗e6 17.♖d1 ♘e7 18.dxe6!?
(18.0-0 ♗xd5 19.♕e2 ♖ac8 20.♗b3
♗xb3 21.♖xd8+ ♕xd8 22.axb3
♘f5 (+0.07) – White has just a
nominal edge in bishop mobility)
18...♖xd2 19.♖xd2 ♕xc3 (19...♘f5!?
20.♖d3 ♖e8=, if you wish to avoid
an immediate draw) 20.♗b3 ♕c1+
21.♖d1 ♕c3+ 22.♔e2. This was
Potkin-Svidler, Moscow ch-RUS
2010 and Pashikian-Cornette, Aix-

les-Bains Ech 2011. White avoided the drawing 22.♖d2 in both games but both were drawn anyway. With a rook and bishop (and the bishop pair) for the queen White is the equivalent of a pawn down, but his strong passer evens the chances. Svidler played 22...a5, Cornette chose 22...♕b4, Delchev likes this move better; the engines agree with Svidler with both moves scored near zero.

13....♕a4 14.c4

Alternatively, 14.♕c2 ♕xc2 15.♖xc2 exd5 16.exd5 ♗f5 17.♖b2 ♗e4 18.c4 ♖e8 19.♗e2 b6 20.♖b3 g5 21.♗e3 ♘a6 22.a3 ♗c2 23.♖b2 ♗e4 24.♖a2 ♗f8 (+0.07); after ...♘c7 Black's pieces will all be working and the white passer is not dangerous.

14....exd5 15.exd5 ♘a6

15...♘c6 16.♗e3 ♘b4 17.♗xc5 a5 is probably even better.

16.♗e2 ♘b4 17.0-0 ♕xa2 18.♕e3 ♗f5 19.♕xc5

19....♘a6!

This is a computer improvement over the **actual game**, which continued 19...♘xd5?! 20.cxd5 ♕xe2 21.♖fe1?! (21.♗c7! ♖d7 22.d6±) 21...♕a2 22.♕b5 ♕a6?! (22...♖xd5

23.♕xb7 ♖ad8∓) 23.♕b3= ♕b6 24.♕a2 ♕a6 25.♕b3 ♕b6 with a draw by repetition.

20.♕b5

20.♕e7 ♕b2 21.♖ce1 ♖e8 22.♗c1 ♕xc1∓.

20....♕xe2 21.♖fe1 ♕a2 22.d6

White seems to have enough compensation for the piece with his threats against the queen and the b7-pawn to get a draw based on the following analysis, though this is far from certain.

22....♕a3 23.♕xb7 ♘b4 24.♖e7 ♗f8 25.♖xh7 ♗e6 26.♖e1 ♖ab8 27.♕e4 ♕d3 28.♕xe6+ ♔xh7 29.♕xf6 ♕f5 30.♕h4+ ♕h5 31.♕f6 ♕f5 ½-½

Game 16.5   Grünfeld Indian –
             Exchange Variation

Sipke Ernst   2497
Friso Nijboer   2556
Groningen 2002 (1)

1.d4 ♘f6 2.c4 g6 3.♘c3 d5 4.cxd5 ♘xd5 5.e4 ♘xc3 6.bxc3 ♗g7 7.♘f3 c5 8.♖b1

This, the Modern Exchange Variation, is among the most testing of White's options.

8....0-0 9.♗e2

9....cxd4

The alternatives are 9...♘c6 and 9...b6. I recommend the former (see next game) but not the latter.

10.cxd4 ♕a5+ 11.♗d2

11.♕d2 ♕xd2+ 12.♗xd2 b6 13.0-0 ♗b7 14.d5 ♗a6 15.♗xa6 ♘xa6 16.♗e3 f5 17.e5 f4 18.♗c1 ♖ad8 19.♖d1 ♘c7 20.d6 exd6 21.exd6 (21.♗a3 ♘e6 22.♗xd6 ♖f7=) 21...♘e6=.

analysis diagram

White's passer is advanced but rather weak. Black's pieces are well placed. The following moves are analysis by Avrukh: 22.♗b2 ♘c5 23.♗xg7 ♔xg7 24.♖b4 ♖f5 25.♘d4 ♖f6 26.♘b5 ♖d7 27.f3 ♔f7=.

11...♕xa2 12.0-0 b6

Other moves, especially 12...♗g4, are more popular but computer analysis says that 12...b6 is best.

13.♕c1

13.♗g5 ♗b7 14.♗d3 e6=.

13....♕e6

This avoids a quick draw. More frequent is 13...♗b7.

14.♗c4

In case of 14.♖e1 ♗b7 15.♗b5 ♕c8 16.♗g5 (16.♕a3 a6 17.♗f1 ♕d8. Komodo gives a zero score while Lc0 really likes White. It suggests that Black is OK if he plays accurately) 16...♕xc1 17.♖bxc1 ♖c8 (0.00). Both sides have dangerous passed pawns.

14....♕xe4 15.♖e1

After 15.♗xf7+ ♖xf7 16.♕xc8+ ♖f8 17.♕c4+ e6 18.♖b5 ♕c6 19.♕b3 ♘a6 20.♖c1 ♕d7 21.♘e5 ♗xe5 22.♖xe5 ♘c7 White has too little compensation for the pawn minus.

15....♗b7 16.♗b4

White can also play 16.♗h6 e6 17.♗xg7 (17.h4! looks quite dangerous) 17...♔xg7 18.♕c3 ♔g8 19.♘g5 ♕e7 20.♕g3 h6 21.♘xe6 ♗xe6 22.♗d5 ♘c6 23.♗xc6 ♖ac8 24.d5 ♕g5 25.♕f3 ♗f5 and White's strong passer gives him enough compensation for the pawn to equalize. Perhaps more dangerous is 20.♘xe6 fxe6 21.♗d5 ♗b7 22.♖xe6

303

♕f7 23.♖xg6+ hxg6 24.♗xf7+ ♖xf7 25.♕g3 ♖g7. Although with deep analysis Komodo reaches a zero score, I can't deny that White has more practical chances to win this unbalanced position than Black does. So I currently prefer 9...♘c6 as in the next game.

16....♗e6 17.♖xe6

This is the only continuation that is dangerous for Black.

A) After 17.d5?! ♗xd5 18.♖xe7 ♘d7 19.♕d2 ♗xc4 20.♖xd7 ♕c8 21.♗xf8 ♕xf8 I prefer Black's chances as he has two connected passers and the bishop pair for the exchange;

B) Or 17.♗xe6 fxe6 18.♖xe6 ♕d5 19.♖xe7 ♘c6 20.♖xg7+ ♔xg7 21.♗xf8+ ♖xf8 22.♕e3 ♖d8, and although the computer prefers White due to the large difference in king safety, I think that the secure blockade of the queen's pawn and the two connected passers should give Black about equal chances.

17....fxe6 18.♘g5

18....♘a6

This is a computer novelty. In the **actual game** Black played 18...♘c6, after which White retains chances

for an edge. The game was later drawn.

19.♘xe6

19.♕e3 ♘c7=.

19....♔h8 20.♗a3

Also after 20.♘xf8 ♖xf8 21.♗c3 ♘c7, with the black knight coming to d5 soon, White does not have enough compensation for the lost pawn.

20....♘c7

20...♖fc8 may be an improvement, when the position is equal.

21.♘xg7

21.♘xf8 ♖xf8 22.♗xe7 ♖e8 23.♗g5 ♕e4 – Black's well-placed pieces and better pawns fully offset White's bishop pair.

21....♔xg7 22.♕e1

With 22.♗xe7!?N White has full compensation for the exchange, with two strong bishops and a much safer king. I would avoid this by my suggestion on move 20.

22....e6 23.♗xf8+ ♖xf8 24.♖c1 ♔g8 25.♗b3 ♖e8 26.♕e5 ♘d5 27.♖e1 ♔f7 28.h4 h5=

White's safer king compensates for the pawn minus, but he cannot claim an advantage.

Game 16.6 Grünfeld Indian –
            Exchange Variation
Grzegorz Gajewski   2567
Emil Sutovsky   2650

Rijeka Ech 2010 (8)

**1.d4 ♞f6 2.c4 g6 3.♞c3 d5 4.cxd5
♞xd5 5.e4 ♞xc3 6.bxc3 ♝g7 7.♞f3
c5 8.♖b1 0-0 9.♝e2 ♞c6**

This line, also recommended by
Delchev and Agrest, is my first
choice. There is not so much you
need to learn here, and the line
seems to be sound.

10.d5

After 10.♝e3?! ♝g4 11.♖xb7 ♝xf3
12.♝xf3 cxd4 13.cxd4 ♝xd4
14.♝xd4 ♞xd4 15.0-0 e5 Black is
better. The outposted knight is
clearly worth more than the slightly
bad bishop. The symmetric pawn
structure also favors knights over
bishops.

10...♞e5

Accepting the pawn with 10...♝xc3+
leads after 11.♝d2 ♝xd2+ 12.♕xd2
♞d4 13.♞xd4 cxd4 14.♕xd4 to a
good endgame for White, as was
seen in Kasparov-Natsis, Malta ol
1980.

11.♞xe5

11.♞d2 f5! 12.0-0 fxe4 13.♞xe4 ♝f5
14.f3 b6=.

11...♝xe5 12.♕d2

 A) 12.♖b3 ♕c7 13.♕d2 ♝d7
14.c4N (14.f4 c4 15.♖b4 ♝d6
16.♖xc4 ♕a5=) 14...b5 15.cxb5
c4 16.♖b4 c3 17.♕c2 e6 18.dxe6
♝xe6 19.♖a4 ♖ad8= and Black is
a pawn down, but has a dangerous
advanced passed pawn and
much better coordinated and
developed pieces, so he has full
compensation;

 B) After 12.♕c2 e6 13.f4 ♝g7
14.dxe6 ♝xe6 15.♖xb7 ♕a5 16.e5
♖ab8 17.♖xb8 ♖xb8 18.♝d3?
(18.♝e3N ♝f5 19.♝d3 ♝xd3
20.♕xd3 ♖b2=) 18...♝xa2 19.0-0
♝b1 20.♕e2 ♕xc3 21.♝c4 ♝f5 Black
is just a pawn up.

12...e6 13.f4

13.0-0 exd5 14.exd5 b6 (14...♖e8
is also satisfactory) 15.c4 ♕d6
16.h3 ♖e8 17.♝b2 ♝xb2 18.♖xb2
♝d7 19.♖a1 ♝a4=. Black prevents
a2-a4-a5, leaving White with
little to do. Black's better bishop
compensates for White's blockaded
passed pawn.

13....♝c7

This is very unnatural, retreating to g7 seems 'obviously' better. However, I don't believe that 13...♗g7 equalizes, because White can play c3-c4 and e4-e5. 13...♗c7 serves to prevent c3-c4, so White can't build a big center. It's true that Black's king is a bit weakened, but White's pieces are not well placed to exploit this weakness.

14.0-0

A) 14.♗c4 a6 15.a4 b5 16.axb5 axb5 17.♗xb5 exd5 18.♗c6 ♖a6 19.♗xd5 ♖d6 20.0-0 ♗f5 21.♕c2 ♖xd5 22.exf5 ♖xf5 23.c4 ♕d4+ =;

B) 14.dxe6 ♕xd2+ 15.♗xd2 fxe6N (15...♗xe6 16.♖xb7 ♗b6 17.♔f2!N ♖fe8 18.♗b5 ♖ed8 19.♗e3 c4 20.f5 may favour White slightly) 16.0-0 b6 17.♖bd1 ♔g7 18.♗c4 ♖b8 19.e5 b5 20.♗e2 c4 21.♗e3 ♖f7 22.g3 a6=.

14....exd5 15.exd5 ♗a5

16.d6

A) 16.♖b5 ♖e8 (0.00);

B) 16.g4 ♖e8 17.f5 ♕d6 (0.00);

C) 16.♖b3 ♖e8 (0.00);

D) 16.♗a3 b6 17.♗b4 ♗xb4 18.cxb4 ♕d6 19.♖bc1 ♗d7 20.bxc5 bxc5 (0.00);

E) 16.f5 ♗xf5 17.♖xb7 ♕d6 18.♗c4 ♖fb8 19.♖b3 (or 19.♖xb8+

♖xb8 20.♕g5 ♗xc3 21.♖xf5 ♗d4+ 22.♔h1 ♖b4 23.♗d3 f6 24.♕g4 ♗e5 25.♗c4 ♗d4 26.♗d3 with a draw by repetition) 19...♖xb3 20.axb3 ♖e8 21.♖e1 ♖e5 22.♗e3 ♗c7 23.g3 h5 24.♕e2 h4 (0.00).

16....♖b8 17.♗a3

A) 17.♗b2 ♗f5 (this improves on Pelletier-Caruana, Biel 2011) 18.♖bd1 b5=;

B) 17.g4 b5=;

C) 17.♗f3 ♗f5 18.♖b5 a6 19.♖xa5 ♕xa5 20.g4 ♗d7 21.f5 ♖be8= 22.♗xb7 ♕a4 23.h3 ♗c6 24.♗xc6 ♕xc6 25.c4 ♖d8=;

D) 17.♖b5 b6 18.♗a3! ♗d7 19.♖xa5 bxa5 20.♗xc5 ♖e8 21.♗xa7 ♖b7 22.♗e3 ♕b8 23.♗f3 ♖b2 24.♕d4 ♖e6 25.♖d1 ♖b1 (+0.02). Black gets just enough counterplay to hold.

17....♗f5

18.♖b5

After 18.♖bd1 ♕f6 (18...♖c8 19.g4 ♗d7 20.f5 ♕f6 21.fxg6 ♕xg6 was Ushenina-Sutovsky, Batumi 2018, when 22.♗f3 ♕g7 23.♗b2 ♖ce8 (+0.20) is a tiny white edge) 19.♗xc5 ♗xc3 20.♗d4 ♗xd4+ 21.♕xd4 ♕xd4+ 22.♖xd4 ♖fc8 23.h3 ♗e6 (0.00). White's passed pawn is offset by his inferior pawn structure.

18....a6 19.罝xc5

In case of 19.罝b3 罠c8N 20.罝e1 b5 Black clearly has the initiative at no cost. White's queenside pieces are just targets.

19....皐b6 20.含h1 皐xc5 21.皐xc5 罠d7

According to my scale, Black is up ¼ pawn. White has some vague compensation in the weak dark squares around the black king and the advanced passed pawn, but White also has some weak pawns. Overall the engines prefer Black slightly, and I won't disagree.

22.皐b6?! 皐e4 23.罠d4 罝be8 24.皐d1 罝e6!

Black plans to return the exchange for the d-pawn and the bishop pair to get a clear positional advantage. The **actual game** went 24...皐c6? 25.f5 gxf5 26.皐c2 皐e4 27.皐b3 h6 28.罠f6 含h7 29.罝g1 罝g8 30.罠xf7+ 罝g7 31.罠xd7 罝xd7 32.罝d1 皐c6 33.含g1 罝e2 34.皐f2 含g6 35.含f1 罝e4 36.c4 a5 37.a3 含f6 38.罝d2 a4 39.皐a2 b5?! (39...含e5! 40.c5 b6 gives Black the better of a likely draw) 40.c5 b4 41.皐d4+ 罝xd4 42.罝xd4 bxa3 43.罝b4 含e5 44.罝b6 皐e4 45.含e1?! (45.c6 罝xd6 46.c7 罝d1+ 47.含f2 罝c1

48.罝e6+ 含f4 49.g3+ 含g4 50.罝g6+ 含h3 51.罝xh6+ 含g4 52.罝h7=) 45...罝a7 46.罝b4?! 皐xg2 47.皐c4?! 皐c6 48.罝c3 含d4 49.罝c4+ 含d3 50.罝b4? 罝g7 51.罝b6 含e3 52.含f1 皐g2+ 53.含e1 皐e4 and facing mate, White resigned.

25.皐c7 罠c6 26.罠d2 罝d8 27.皐b3 罝exd6 28.皐xd6 罝xd6

Black has superior pieces, the superior pawn structure, and a safer king.

Game 16.7   Grünfeld Indian –
                     Exchange Variation
Dmitry Svetushkin   2552
Zhou Jianchao   2660
Khanty-Mansiysk ol 2010 (3)

1.d4 罝f6 2.c4 g6 3.罝c3 d5 4.cxd5 罝xd5 5.e4 罝xc3 6.bxc3 皐g7 7.皐c4

This is the traditional main line of the Grünfeld.

7....c5 8.♘e2 ♘c6 9.♗e3 0-0 10.0-0
Or 10.♖c1 cxd4 11.cxd4 ♕a5+ 12.♔f1 ♕a3 13.♖c3 (13.♕b3 ♕xb3 14.♗xb3 ♖d8 15.d5 ♘a5=; Black will either win the bishop pair or get in ...f7-f5) 13...♕d6 14.h4 ♖d8 15.h5 ♗e6 16.hxg6 hxg6 17.d5 ♗g4N 18.f3 ♗xc3 19.♘xc3 ♕f6 20.♕d2 ♘e5 21.♗e2 ♗xf3 22.gxf3 ♘xf3 23.♗xf3 ♕xf3+ 24.♔g1 ♕g3+ with a draw by perpetual check.

10....e6
This is my alternate line in case 10...♕c7 turns out to have problems, or just for variety. I prefer to play it immediately rather than after 10...♕c7 11.♖c1, as the queen will often go to e7 in which case 10...♕c7 will be a wasted tempo. But I have more faith in the 10...♕c7 11.♖c1 b6 line of the next game due to Line A below.

11.♕d2
A) 11.dxc5 ♕a5 12.♗b3 b6 13.cxb6 axb6 14.♕c2 ♗a6 15.♖fd1 ♖fc8 – Black plans to bring his knight to c4 which should give him good compensation for the pawn as his pieces will be more active and White has more weak pawns than Black. Or 12.f4 ♖d8 13.♕b3 (13.♕c2 looks critical. Delchev gives 13...♗f8 14.f5 ♗c5 15.♘d4 ♘e5 16.♗e2 ♘c6, but after the engine line 17.fxg6 hxg6 18.♖ad1 ♗d7 19.♔h1 ♗e7 20.♖b1 b6 21.♘f3 Komodo gives +0.34 and Lc0 +0.54, so Black probably needs an improvement) 13...♗f8 14.f5 ♗xc5 15.♘d4 ♘xd4 16.cxd4 ♖xd4! 17.fxe6 ♖xe4;
B) 11.♖c1 can be met by 11...♕e7 12.♕d2 ♖d8 13.♗g5 ♗f6 14.h4 (Delchev's line 14.♗xf6 ♕xf6 15.♖fd1 b6 16.♕e3 ♗b7 is also equal after 17.♗b3 cxd4 18.cxd4 ♘a5 (+0.10), Lc0 +0.22) 14...b6 (+0.10);
C) 11.♖b1 cxd4 (this exchange tends to favor White, but here it is played to avoid a later dxc5 and is justified by the loss of tempo that ♖c1 would imply) 12.cxd4 b6 13.♕a4 ♗b7 14.♖fd1 (else 14...a6 will be a good move) 14...♘a5 15.♗d3 ♖c8 (+0.10). Black plans ...a7-a6 and ...b7-b5.

11....b6 12.♖ac1 ♗b7 13.♖fd1 cxd4 14.cxd4 ♘a5 15.♗d3 ♖c8 16.h4
16.♗h6 ♗xh6 17.♕xh6 ♕d6 is equal.

**16....h5 17.♗g5 ♕d7 18.e5?! ♖xc1
19.♖xc1 ♘c6 20.♗b5 ♖c8 21.♗f6
♗f8 22.♕g5 a6 23.♖xc6**

23....axb5?!

Better was 23...♗xc6! 24.♗xa6
♖a8 25.♗d3 ♖xa2 26.♗xg6 fxg6
27.♕xg6+ ♗g7 28.♘f4 ♕f7 29.♕g5
♔h7 30.♗xg7 ♕xg7 31.♕xh5+ ♔g8
32.d5 exd5 when White's attack is
not worth a rook.

24.♖d6?!

24.♖xc8 ♗xc8 25.♘f4 ♔h7 26.♘xh5
♗h6 27.♕g4 ♗b7 28.♗g5 ♗xg5
29.♕xg5 gxh5 30.♕xh5+ ♔g8
31.♕g5+ ♔f8 32.♕h6+ would have
led to a draw by perpetual check.

24....♕c7 25.♔h2 ♕c2 26.♘f4 ♕xf2

27.♖d7??

27.d5! ♖c1 28.♘e2 ♖c8 29.♘f4 was a
draw by repetition.

27....♗e4??

27...♖c1 28.♖xb7 ♕g1+ 29.♔g3 ♖c3+
is mate in four.

**28.d5 ♖c1 29.♘e2 ♖c8 30.dxe6 fxe6
31.♖d2??**

After 31.♘d4 ♕xa2 White has some
compensation for the two-pawn
deficit.

31....♗h6 0-1

Game 16.8   Grünfeld Indian –
          Exchange Variation

Alexandr Fier   2571
Fabiano Caruana   2721

Gibraltar 2011 (7)

**1.d4 ♘f6 2.c4 g6 3.♘c3 d5 4.cxd5
♘xd5 5.e4 ♘xc3 6.bxc3 ♗g7 7.♗c4
c5 8.♘e2 ♘c6 9.♗e3 0-0 10.0-0
♕c7**

The old main line with 10...♗g4
11.f3 ♘a5 has become rare although
it is still sound, probably because
White has the choice of testing
Black's preparation with a sacrifice
of the exchange or of a pawn, or
playing 12.♗xf7+, winning a pawn
for substantial compensation.
I think the line in this game is
a much simpler path to equal
chances.

11.♖c1

A) 11.♖b1 b6 12.♗f4 e5 13.♗g3 ♗b7 14.d5 ♘a5 15.♗b5 f5 16.f3 ♖ad8 (0.00);

B) 11.♗f4 e5 12.♗g3 ♕e7 13.d5 ♘a5 14.♗d3 f5 (0.00).

11....b6

This is a rare but good move, also chosen by Avrukh in his 2011 book. 11...♖d8 is much more common, but Black has ideas of ...e7-e5 d4-d5 f7-f5, so he keeps the rook on f8. Another good move is 11...e6 first, planning to play ...b7-b6, ...♗b7, and ...♖ad8 next, while reserving e7 for the queen if needed. The move ...e7-e6 is also quite reasonable on move 10. But I prefer to retain the option of ...e7-e5 in one shot as in the game.

12.♕d2

A) 12.♗f4 e5 13.♗e3 (13.♗g3 ♕e7 (+0.16); 13.dxe5 ♘xe5 14.♗d5 ♗b7 15.c4 ♗xd5 16.cxd5 ♕d7= (+0.12)) 13...exd4 14.cxd4 cxd4 15.♘xd4 ♗xd4 16.♗xd4 ♘xd4 17.♕xd4 ♕e7 18.♗d5 ♗b7= (+0.09);

B) 12.dxc5 bxc5 13.♘f4 ♘e5 14.♘d5 ♕d7 15.♗b3 e6 16.♗xc5 exd5 17.♗xf8 ♗xf8 18.♕xd5 ♘c6 19.♗a4 ♕xd5 20.exd5 ♘e5=. Two bishops are a tad better than rook

and two pawns, and although they are connected passers they are easily blockaded here on the dark squares;

C) 12.f4 e6 13.♕e1 (13.f5 exf5 14.exf5 ♕e7 15.♕d2 ♗xf5 16.♗g5 ♕d7 17.♘g3?! ♘a5 18.♗e2 ♗e6∓) 13...♗b7N 14.♕f2 ♘a5 15.♗d3 f5∓. The b7-bishop will be unchallenged on the long diagonal.

D) 12.♘f4! e6 13.♗b5 ♖d8 14.d5 ♘e5 15.c4 a6 16.♗a4 g5 is slightly better for White.

12....♗b7 13.♗h6

13....♖ad8

13...e6 14.♗xg7 ♔xg7 15.♕e3 ♖fd8= is a better equalizer than the game according to the computer, since the rook is no longer needed on f8 with the pawn on e6. But I favor Caruana's plan of ...e7-e5 and if d4-d5 then ...f7-f5, for which the rook is needed on f8.

14.♗xg7

14.♖fd1 e5 15.♗xg7 ♔xg7 16.d5 ♘a5 17.♗d3 c4 18.♗c2 ♗c8 19.♘g3 ♘b7 20.♘f1 ♘d6= is similar to the game. Here too the computer likes White due to the protected passed pawn, but I think Black is fine thanks to his ideal blockading knight.

14....♗xg7 15.♕e3

15.f4 ♕d7? (15...♕d6!=) 16.♗b5
♕e6 17.f5 was Vachier-Lagrave-
Morozevich, Biel 2011. White is
better here, but Black won. No one
has repeated 15.f4 since, probably
due to 15...♕d6!.

15....e5 16.d5

A) After 16.♗b3 ♕e7 17.d5 ♗a6!
18.c4 ♘d4= the outposted knight
offsets the protected passer;

B) 16.♕g3 ♕e7 17.d5 ♘a5 18.♗b3
♗c8 (18...c4! 19.♗c2 f6=; Black
plans ...♗c8 and ...♘a5-b7-d6) 19.c4
♘b7 20.♕c3 (20.♘c3±) 20...♘d6
and White should be better but
Black drew comfortably in Feller-
Dominguez Perez, Lubbock 2011;

C) 16.♗d5 ♘a5 17.♗xb7 ♕xb7 and
now:

analysis diagram

C1) 18.f4 exd4 19.cxd4 ♖fe8?! (19...
cxd4! 20.♘xd4 ♖fe8 21.e5 b5!=)
20.e5?! (20.d5±) 20...cxd4 21.♘xd4
♕d5?! (21...b5=) 22.♘f3?! (22.♖fd1±)
22...♘c4= and Black eventually
won in Korobov-Nepomniachtchi,
Rogaska Slatina tt 2011;

C2) 18.d5 ♘c4 19.♕d3 b5 20.a4
a6 21.♖b1 ♕d7 22.♘g3 was Zilka-
Heimann, Merlimont 2011, won by

White. 22...f6! equalizes as Black's
superior knight offsets White's
protected passed pawn.

16....♘e7

16...♘a5 17.♗d3 c4 18.♗c2 ♗c8= is
Avrukh's preference.

17.♘g3

A) 17.f3 f5 (17...♘c8=) 18.♖ce1
f4 19.♕d3 ♘c8 20.♗b3 ♘d6 21.c4
b5 22.♘c3 a6 – the computer
favors White here because of the
protected passed pawn, but I think
Black is fine with his wonderful
blockading knight and much
superior bishop, which will drop
back to c8;

B) 17.a4 f5 18.f3 ♘c8 19.♖cd1
♘d6=.

17....f6

17...f5 18.exf5 gxf5 19.♕g5+ ♔h8
20.♖cd1 ♗xd5=.

18.h4 ♘c8

18...f5=.

19.♗d3 ♘d6

19.c4! 20.♗c2 ♘d6 21.f4 exf4
22.♕xf4 ♕e7= (Avrukh).

20.f4

20.c4±.

**20....exf4 21.♕xf4 ♕e7 22.♖f2 ♕e5
23.♕xe5 fxe5 24.♘f1 c4 25.♗c2
♗c8 26.♘h2**

26....h6

26...♞b5 27.♖xf8 ♖xf8 28.♝a4 ♞d6 29.♝c2 ♞b5 would draw by repetition. Probably Black wanted to win.

27.♖xf8 ♖xf8 28.♞f3 ♖e8?!

28...♖f4 29.♖e1 ♞f7=.

29.♔f2 ♝g4 30.♞h2 ♝d7 31.♔e3 g5 32.hxg5 hxg5 33.♞f3 g4 34.♞h4 ♖f8 35.♖h1 ♖f4 36.g3 ♖f6 37.a4 ♖h6 38.♖b1 ♖h8 39.♖h1 ♞e8 40.♖f1 ♞d6 41.♖h1 ♖h6 42.♖b1 ♔f7 43.♖f1+ ♔e7 44.♖h1 a5 45.♖f1 ♖f6 46.♖b1 ♞f7 47.♞f5+ ½-½

Game 16.9   Grünfeld Indian –
                   Exchange Variation

Levon Aronian
Alexander Grischuk
Kazan ct 2011 (1.1)

1.d4 ♞f6 2.c4 g6 3.♞c3 d5 4.cxd5 ♞xd5 5.e4 ♞xc3 6.bxc3 ♝g7 7.♝c4 c5 8.♞e2 ♞c6 9.♝e3 0-0 10.0-0 b6
This is a very promising gambit alternative to 10...♛c7. If White declines, Black may later find a more useful move than ...♛c7, for example ...e7-e6 and ...♛e7. The fact that Aronian in this game and Carlsen in the game quoted on

move 12 both chose to take on c5 indicates that the top players have little faith in quiet development against 10...b6.

11.dxc5
Topalov-Anand, Sofia 2010, went 11.♛d2 (11.♖c1 ♝b7 12.♛d2 transposes, while 12.♝b5 ♖c8 13.♛d2 was Giri-Vachier-Lagrave, St Louis 2019, when 13...e6 14.♖fd1 cxd4 15.cxd4 ♞a5 16.f3 ♖xc1 17.♖xc1 a6 18.♝d3 ♞c6 (+0.02) is roughly equal, Lc0 +0.19) 11...♝b7 12.♖ac1 ♖c8 13.♖fd1 cxd4 (13...e6!= was better according to Komodo (0.00), to discourage d4-d5 and to provide a good square for the queen on e7) 14.cxd4 ♛d6 15.d5 ♞a5 16.♝b5 ♖xc1 17.♖xc1 ♖c8 and was eventually drawn. Now 18.♖xc8+ ♝xc8 19.♞d4 would have given White some edge.

11....♛c7

12.♘d4

The alternatives:

A) 12.cxb6 axb6 13.♖b1 ♘e5
14.♗d5 ♖b8.

analysis diagram

At first glance it just looks like
Black has lost a pawn. Then you
should notice the positional threat
of ...♗a6, followed by ...e7-e6 and
posting rooks on c8 and d8. Then
White will have to worry about
...♘c4, ...♘g4, or ...♘d3. Black will
almost surely regain the pawn
or else win the bishop pair with
continued play against the weak
pawns. This is a completely sound
gambit.

For example: 15.♕a4 (to prevent
...♗a6) 15...e6 16.♗b3 ♗b7 17.f3
♖a8N 18.♕b4 ♗a6 19.c4 ♖fc8
20.♗xb6 ♕b7 21.♗c5 ♕xb4
22.♗xb4 ♗xc4 23.♗xc4 ♘xc4 24.a3
♘xa3 and Black has regained his
material and has a clear advantage
in piece placement, though the
position is drawish;

B) 12.f4 bxc5 13.♖b1 ♖d8 14.♕a4
♘a5 15.♗d5 ♗d7 16.♕a3 ♖ac8 17.f5
e6 18.♗f4 ♗e5 19.fxe6 fxe6 20.♗b3
♘xb3 21.axb3 ♖f8 22.♕c1 c4 23.b4
♕b6+ 24.♔h1 ♗g7 25.e5.

analysis diagram

So far Carlsen-Svidler in the Tal
Memorial, Moscow 2011. Now
25...♖f7! favors Black due to his
bishop pair. The threat of doubling
rooks will probably provoke 26.♗g3,
after which Black trades rooks and
plays ...a7-a5, equalizing the pawn
structure and opening the game for
the bishops.

12....♘e5 13.♘b5 ♕b8 14.♗e2

14.♗d5 ♘g4 15.g3 ♘xe3 16.fxe3 a6
and now:

analysis diagram

A) 17.♘a3 ♗xc3 18.♖b1 b5 19.♕c2
♗e5 20.♗xa8 ♕xa8 21.♖bc1 ♗e6=.
Two bishops and a pawn are almost
as strong as rook and knight. Here
Black doesn't have an extra pawn,
but White's four isolated pawns to
Black's zero is almost as good as an

313

extra pawn, and Black's bishops are great while White's knight is badly out of play;

B) 17.♗xa8 axb5 18.♗d5 ♕c7 19.♕d3 e6 20.♗b3 ♕xc5 21.♖ab1 ♗b7 22.a4 bxa4 23.♗xa4 ♖c8 24.♖bd1 h5=. Due to the pressure on White's weak pawns and king, Black will surely regain a pawn for his exchange. Then he will only be down by ¼ pawn and will still have the superior pawn structure and the safer king; full compensation;

C) 17.♘d4 bxc5? was Karjakin-Vachier-Lagrave, St Louis 2019, won by White. Black needed to play 17...♗h3 here, with full equality (0.00). Then 18.♗xa8 ♕xa8 19.cxb6 ♗xf1 20.♔xf1 ♕xe4 21.♔f2 ♖b8 22.♕b3 ♗h6 23.♖e1 ♖b7 (-0.03) gives Black enough for the pawn, Lc0 +0.11.

14....bxc5 15.f4 ♘g4 16.♗xc5 a6 17.♘a3 ♕c7 18.♗d4 e5 19.fxe5 ♘xe5

In return for the pawn Black has the much superior pawn structure

and a much superior knight. This should be enough to equalize.
20.♕c1 ♗g4 21.♗xg4 ♘xg4 22.♕f4 ♕xf4 23.♖xf4 ♘e5 24.♖b1 ♖ad8 25.♘c2

25....♘c4!

This improvement seems to regain the pawn and equalize. In the **actual game** Black stayed a pawn down after 25...♘d3 26.♖ff1 ♖d7 27.♖fd1 ♘f4 28.♔f2 ♖c8 29.♘e3 and should have lost, but saved a draw due to a late endgame error by White.
26.♖b4 ♖c8 27.♖a4 ♗xd4+ 28.♘xd4 ♘e5 29.♖xa6 ♖xc3 30.♖f1 ♖e3 31.♘f3 ♖xe4 32.♘xe5 ♖xe5

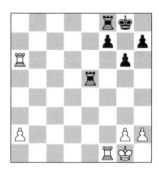

The resulting endgame is an almost certain draw.

CHAPTER 17

Center Game and Ponziani

In this chapter we consider two fairly rare white options after **1.e4 e5** that nevertheless have some devotees and so are worth studying. The Center Game involves the early development of the white queen and is often played with the idea of castling queenside and gambitting the e4-pawn for attacking chances. The Ponziani on the other hand invites Black to develop his queen early. Neither line should give White any advantage at all if you follow the lines given here.

The Center Game starts with **1.e4 e5 2.d4 exd4 3.♕xd4 ♘c6**.

Now the normal retreat for the queen is to e3, although the alternate choice of a4 has long been championed by the late IM Walter Shipman. It has the drawback of failing to defend the e4-pawn as securely though. After **4.♕e3 ♘f6 5.♘c3 ♗b4 6.♗d2 0-0 7.0-0-0 ♖e8**

White must choose between the 'safe' 8.♗c4 and the gambit 8.♕g3. In the former case Black's threats against the e4-pawn and the c4-bishop tend to put him a bit ahead in the attacking race. The gambit move **8.♕g3** can be accepted either by **8...♖xe4** (usually recommended) or by **8...♘xe4**, my choice due to the given game, which may lead to Black getting four pawns for a piece. See Game 17.1.

The Ponziani Opening starts with **1.e4 e5 2.♘f3 ♘c6 3.c3**,

after which Black can equalize either by 3...♘f6 or by **3...d5**. I choose the second move because it offers more winning chances, and also because my computer analysis actually shows a tiny edge for Black. White's best move is **4.♕a4**, after which 4...♗d7 is an exciting gambit recommended in my earlier book. However my current computer analysis makes it look less appealing than the safe **4...f6**, which seems to give Black a good position for free.

If White responds **5.d3** as in the given game, play resembles the Philidor/Hanham Defense but with colors reversed. The Hanham (1.e4 d6 2.d4 ♘f6 3.♘c3 e5 4.♘f3 ♘bd7) is not such a bad defense to 1.e4, but it does not give full equality, and even with the extra tempo of White's first move it is hardly something to avoid as Black, especially since the move ♕a4 may turn out to be inappropriate. See Game 17.2.

Game 17.1 King's Pawn Openings –
Center Game

Ian Nepomniachtchi 2587
Francisco Vallejo Pons 2679

Moscow 2007 (5)

1.e4 e5 2.d4 exd4 3.♕xd4
The Center Game.
3....♘c6

4.♕e3
4.♕a4 was IM Walter Shipman's
specialty: with 4...♘f6 5.♘c3 ♗b4
6.♗d2 0-0 7.0-0-0 d6 8.♗b5 ♗xc3N
9.♗xc3 ♘xe4 10.♕xe4 ♕g5+ Black
wins a pawn.
4....♘f6 5.♘c3 ♗b4 6.♗d2 0-0
7.0-0-0 ♖e8

8.♕g3
In case of 8.♗c4 d6 9.f3 (9.♘f3
♗e6! 10.♗xe6 ♖xe6 (-0.36)) 9...♘e5
10.♗b3 a5 11.a3 ♗c5 12.♕e1 b5

13.♘xb5 a4 14.♗a2 c6 15.♘c3 ♕b6
16.♗f4 d5 Black has a winning
attack for a pawn (-1.90).
Or 8.♕f4 (Nepo has been playing
this in rapid and blitz games,
to make Black 'pay' the bishop
pair to win the pawn) 8...♗xc3
9.♗xc3 ♖xe4 10.♕g3 d5 11.f3 ♖e6
(11...♖e8 is also OK) 12.♘e2 ♖d6
(Nepomniachtchi-Anand, St Louis
blitz 2017) 13.♘d4 ♘xd4 14.♗xd4
♗f5 15.h4 ♕d7 16.b3 ♖e8 17.h5 c5!
White has little compensation for
his half-pawn deficit.

8....♘xe4
8...♖xe4 is a good alternative which
is usually recommended here,
but 8...♘xe4 has great results and
engine scores.
8...d6 is the wimpy move. Maybe
this is good enough for equality,
but just like the computers I favor
taking pawns unless I see the
refutation.
9.♘xe4 ♖xe4 10.♗f4
A) 10.♗g5 ♗e7 11.h4 d5 12.f3 ♖e6
13.♗c4 ♘b4N 14.a3 ♗d6 15.♗xd8
♗xg3 16.♗b3 ♘c6 17.♗g5 h6 18.♗d2
♘e7. Black has traded queens and
kept his extra pawn;

B) 10.♗xb4 ♖xb4 11.a3 ♖b6 12.♘e2 d5 13.♘f4 ♗e6. White doesn't have enough for the pawn (-0.32);

C) 10.c3 ♗e7 11.♘f3 d6 12.h3 ♘e5 13.♘xe5 ♖xe5 (-0.70). White has only a more active queen for the pawn.

10....♕f6 11.♘h3 d6 12.♗d3 ♘d4
12...♖e8 13.c3 ♗xh3 14.♗g5 ♕e5 15.♗f4 ♕f6 16.♗g5 is a draw by repetition, though Black can avoid it by 15...♕h5 or 16...♕e6.

13.♔b1?!
13.♗e3 and now:

A) 13...♖g4 14.♗xd4 ♖xd4 15.c3 (after 15.♕e3 ♗f5 Black is a solid pawn up) 15...♗xc3 16.bxc3 ♖g4 17.♕f3 (or 17.♕e3 ♕xc3+ 18.♗c2 ♕xe3+ 19.fxe3 ♖xg2 20.♘f4 ♖f2 21.♖df1 ♖xf1+ 22.♖xf1 ♗d7 and with four pawns for the knight, Black is better but White may draw) 17...♕xc3+ 18.♗c2 ♕a1+ 19.♔d2 ♕xa2 (or 19...♖d4+ 20.♔e2 ♖xd1 21.♖xd1 ♕xa2 22.♖d2 ♕c4+ 23.♗d3 ♕h4 – Black has four pawns for the knight and threats, analysis by Kortchnoi) 20.♕d3 ♕a5+ 21.♕c3 ♕xc3+ 22.♔xc3 ♖xg2 and with five pawns for the knight, Black should win;

B) 13...♘f5 14.♕f3 ♖e8 15.♗g5 ♕e5 16.c3 ♗xc3 17.bxc3 ♕xc3+ 18.♗c2 ♕a1+ 19.♔d2 ♕xa2 20.♖he1 ♗d7 is another way to get four pawns for a piece with the better chances.
13....♘e2 14.♕f3?!

14....♗a3! 15.bxa3?!
Black now wins by force. On 15.c3?? ♘xc3+ wins, and after 15.♗c1 ♕xf3 16.gxf3 ♖e7 17.♘g5 ♘xc1 18.♖xc1 ♗c5 19.♖ce1 ♖xe1+ 20.♖xe1 ♗d7 21.♖e7 ♗e8 22.♗xh7+ ♔h8 23.♖xe8+ ♗xe8 24.♗e4 c6 Black has a winning endgame with the bishop pair, a much better pawn structure, and the threat on f2.
15....♘c3+ 16.♔c1 ♘xa2+ 17.♔b1 ♘c3+ 18.♔c1 ♗xh3 19.♗xe4 ♗xg2! 20.♕xg2 ♕xf4+ 21.♔b2 ♘xe4

With three pawns for the exchange and all of White's pawns isolated and his king exposed, Black is clearly winning.

22.♖d4 ♕f6

22...d5! was a more convincing win.

23.♕xe4 c5 24.♖e1 h5 25.♕f4 ♕xd4+ 26.♕xd4 cxd4 27.♖e7 b6 28.a4 g5 29.♔b3 ♔g7 30.♖c7 ♖e8 31.♖xa7 ♖e2 32.♖b7 ♖xf2 33.♖xb6 ♖xh2 34.a5 ♖e2 35.a6 ♖e8 36.a7 ♖a8

White resigned.

Game 17.2   King's Pawn Openings – Ponziani Opening

Boris Savchenko   2652
Axel Delorme   2429

Rijeka Ech 2010 (3)

1.e4 e5 2.♘f3 ♘c6 3.c3

The Ponziani Opening, which is quite rare in top level play but is seen sometimes at lower levels.

3....d5

4.♕a4

A) In case of 4.exd5 ♕xd5 5.d4 ♘f6 6.♗e2 e4 7.♘fd2 e3 8.fxe3 ♕xg2 9.♗f3 ♕h3 10.♕e2 ♗d6 11.♘c4 0-0 Black's safer king and better development will give him more than enough for the bishop pair;

B) If 4.♗b5 dxe4 5.♘xe5 ♕g5 6.♕a4 (or 6.d4 ♕xg2 7.♖f1 ♗d6 8.♕h5 g6 9.♕h4 ♗xe5 10.dxe5 ♗d7 11.♗f4 ♘ge7 and Black will castle queenside, with an extra pawn) 6...♕xg2 7.♗xc6+ bxc6 8.♕xc6+ ♔d8 9.♖f1 ♗h3 10.♕xa8+ ♔e7 11.♔d1 ♕xf1+ 12.♔c2 ♗f5 13.♘a3 f6 14.♘c6+ ♔f7 15.♘d4 ♕d3+ 16.♔b3 ♗g4 17.♘ac2 c5, Black is clearly winning here.

4....f6

In my earlier book I recommended the gambit line 4...♗d7!? here, which is quite popular and scores well. However the engines now don't consider it fully equal, whereas the text seems to give Black a good game without much risk.

5.d3

A) 5.♗b5 ♘e7 6.exd5 ♕xd5 7.d4 ♗g4 8.c4 (or 8.♗c4 ♕e4+N 9.♗e3 ♗xf3 10.♘d2 ♗d1 11.♔xd1 ♕xg2 12.♔c2 exd4 13.cxd4 ♕g6+ 14.♗d3 ♕h5 15.♖ac1 ♕a5 and White has only the bishop pair for his pawn) 8...♕e4+ 9.♗e3 ♗xf3 10.♘d2 ♕g6 11.♘xf3 ♕xg2 12.♔e2 e4 13.♘d2 ♕g4+ 14.♔f1 ♕h3+N 15.♔e2 ♕h5+ 16.♔f1 0-0-0 17.d5 ♘b8 18.♕xa7

♘f5 – here Black's king is safer than White's;

B) After 5.exd5 ♕xd5 6.d4 ♗d7 7.♗b5 a6 8.c4 ♕e4+ 9.♗e3 ♖d8! Black wins material.

5....♗e6

Or 5...♘ge7 6.♗e2 ♗e6 7.0-0 ♕d7 8.♕c2? (Nepomniachtchi-Karjakin, chess.com blitz 2017; 8.♘bd2 g5) 8... g5! and Black is clearly better.

6.♗e2

6.♘bd2 ♕d7 7.♗e2 ♗d6 8.exd5 ♗xd5 9.♘e4 ♘ge7=. White can gain the bishop pair, but Black will have better development and central control to compensate.

6...♗d6 7.b4 ♘ge7 8.♘bd2 0-0

8...a6! to prevent 9.b5 is probably better and favors Black.

9.b5 ♘b8 10.d4

After 10.0-0 ♘d7 11.♕c2 c6 Black has better central control. His formation would have been considered ideal in the 1800s.

10....exd4

Probably better than the **actual game**, which continued 10...♘d7 11.c4 c6 (after 11...dxe4 12.♘xe4 exd4 13.♘xd6 ♘c5 14.♕d1 ♕xd6

15.♕xd4 ♘f5 16.♕xd6 ♘xd6 Black would still be for choice) 12.bxc6 bxc6 13.0-0 ♗f7 14.♗b2 exd4 15.cxd5 cxd5 16.♗xd4 ♘c5 17.♗xc5 ♗xc5 18.e5 ♘g6 19.♖ac1 ♗b6 20.exf6 ♕xf6 21.♖c6 (Black is clearly better here, up the bishop pair with a good position) 21...♗e8?! 22.♖xf6 ♗xa4 23.♖xf8+ ♖xf8 24.g3 ♖c8 25.♗d3 ♖e8 26.♖c1 ♘e5 27.♘xe5 ♖xe5 28.♔f1 g6 29.♘b3 ♗xb3?! (Black plays for a draw from a better position, probably due to the huge rating difference) 30.axb3 ♖e7 31.♗e2 ♖c7 32.♖d1 ♖c3 33.♖xd5 ♖xb3 34.f4. Somehow White won from this completely equal and drawish position.

11.♘xd4

Or 11.cxd4 ♘g6 12.g3 (12.0-0 ♘f4 13.♗d1 a6 (-0.20) with play on both wings) 12...dxe4 13.♘xe4 ♗h3, and White's castling problems give Black the edge.

11....♗f7 12.0-0 ♘d7

White's pieces and pawns seem to be distributed rather randomly, while Black dominates the center.

CHAPTER 18

Bishop's Opening and Vienna Game

This chapter covers the Bishop's Opening (1.e4 e5 2.♗c4) and the Vienna
Game (1.e4 e5 2.♘c3), because they are strategically similar and because
they can easily transpose. In both cases we respond with 2...♘f6, after
which if White plays 3.♘c3 in the Bishop's Opening or 3.♗c4 in the
Vienna we reach the same position.

After **1.e4 e5 2.♗c4 ♘f6**

and now 3.♘c3 or 3.d3, I recommend avoiding the move 3...♘c6, instead
planning to put a pawn on that square. There are two reasons for this. First
of all, I don't favour placing the knight on c6 if White fails to attack the
e5-pawn, because it's generally not advisable to obstruct pawns which are
not part of the castle. After all, I like the Breyer Defense to the Spanish,
in which Black actually retreats the knight voluntarily from c6 to b8 and
then moves it to d7. Why go to c6 in the first place if you don't need to do
so? The second reason is that the moves ♗c4 and ♘c3 both invite a black
pawn to c6. In the former case it is because of the possibility of ...d7-d5 to
chase the bishop, while after ♘c3 the pawn move takes away the two most
advanced squares to which the knight might otherwise later go. In general,
it is advisable to place your pawns in front of the enemy knight with two
squares in between for precisely this reason.

When White plays **3.d3** in the Bishop's Opening, I advocate the
immediate **3...c6**, to achieve a quick ...d7-d5. White has nothing better
than **4.♘f3 d5**, when after **5.♗b3** I favour **the bishop check on b4**. The
idea is that after the obvious 6.c3 we can retreat to d6, no longer having to
fear ♘c3 with pressure on our d5-pawn. Assuming a later ♘bd2, we end
up with a position somewhat similar to the Breyer, but this time we are

playing against it! The Breyer is an excellent defense to the Spanish, but it is still not quite equal, so if we can play against it when we are Black we should have no complaint! White can instead invite a bishop trade by **6.♗d2**, but the trade is fine for Black, as a recapture by the knight again forfeits the chance to pressure d5 by ♘c3, while the queen recapture allows Black a very good pawn sacrifice option. See Game 18.1 for all of this.

If White chooses **3.♘c3** (or reverses his second and third moves), I like **3...♗c5**.

With the knight on c3 the plan with ...d7-d5 is not so inviting, as the pawn comes under heavy attack, so the move ...c7-c6 is not urgent. After **4.d3 c6 5.♘f3** we typically play ...d7-d6, ...♘bd7, ...♗b6, ...h7-h6, and ...♘d7-f8-g6, taking advantage of the delay in castling. This way we may be able to dispense with ....♖e8 later. This plan seems to give full equality. See Game 18.2.

If White does not play ♗c4 in the Vienna (after **2.♘c3 ♘f6**),

he can choose **3.f4**, which is a kind of 'King's Gambit' which Black should not accept due to 4.e5. Fortunately, the reply **3...d5!** seems to solve all problems. After the usual **4.fxe5 ♘xe4** I don't even know how White can equalize. See Game 18.3.

Game 18.1 Bishop's Opening
Viktor Bologan 2686
Yury Vovk 2539
Warsaw rapid 2010 (8)

1.e4 e5 2.♗c4 ♘f6 3.d3
For 3.d4 exd4 4.♘f3 ♗b4+ see the
game in the Gambits chapter.
3....c6 4.♘f3

4....d5
Also adequate and more consistent
with our Breyer repertoire is 4...♗e7
5.0-0 d6 6.♖e1 0-0 7.♗b3 ♘bd7.

analysis diagram

We can compare this to our
recommended Breyer. White has
saved a tempo in getting his bishop
to b3, while Black has saved two
tempi in getting his knight to d7.
White has not yet played h2-h3
or c2-c3, but probably will. Black

has not played ...a7-a6 or ...b7-b5
but may not need to do so. He has
played the useful ...c7-c6 and has
not committed his bishop to b7,
which is often not a very good
square against the d2-d3 set-up.
In short, Black is playing a much
improved Breyer Defense.
8.c3 ♘c5 9.♗c2 ♗g4 (9...♕c7 is also
okay. Black is playing the Hanham
Defense with White having played
the passive d2-d3 instead of d2-d4)
10.h3 ♗h5 11.♘bd2 ♘e6 12.♘f1 ♘d7
13.♘g3 ♗xf3 14.♕xf3 g6 15.♗h6 ♖e8
16.♖ad1 ♗g5 17.♗xg5 ♕xg5 18.d4
♘b6 19.♗b3 ♖ad8=. With all the
pawns on the board, a lone bishop
is not better than a knight.
Still, I prefer the text move 4...d5 as
it is more of a try for an advantage.
5.♗b3
5.exd5?! cxd5 6.♗b5+ ♗d7 7.♗xd7+
(7.a4 a6 helps Black as White no
longer has the Benoni move c2-c4
later due to the weak square b4)
7...♘bxd7 8.0-0 ♗d6 9.c4 0-0 10.♘c3
d4 11.♘e2 ♕c7 – Black is for choice,
thanks to his extra center pawn.
White is playing a Benoni without
the sting of the fianchettoed king's
bishop.
5...♗b4+!
I think this is better than the
usual 5...♗d6 when 6.♘c3 is rather
annoying. We just provoke 5.c3 first
to prevent this.
5...a5 is a good alternative.
6.♗d2
6.c3 ♗d6 (if Black plays 5...♗d6,
White has the better prospects after
6.♘c3) 7.♘bd2 (7.♗g5 dxe4 8.dxe4

h6 9.♗h4 ♕e7 10.♘bd2 ♘bd7 (Samuelson vs Kaufman, Arlington 2019) 11.♕e2 ♗c7 12.0-0 0-0 13.h3 ♘c5 and with ideas like ...b7-b6 and ...♗a6 or ...a7-a5 or ...♘xb3 or ...♘c5-e6-f4 Black is for choice) 7...0-0 8.0-0 ♘bd7 9.♖e1 ♖e8 10.♘f1 h6 11.♘g3 ♘f8 12.h3 ♘g6

analysis diagram

A) 13.♘h2 ♗c5 14.♘h5 (Sosa-Kaufman, Washington 2011) 14...♘xh5 15.♕xh5 ♗e6 and Black has better development and pressure on f2. White has no attack;

B) 13.♗e3 ♗e6 14.♕c2 ♕d7 15.♖ad1 a5N 16.a4 ♖ad8 – Black has a small edge due to his superior center pawns. This is the same small plus that White gets in the main lines of the Spanish due to this pawn formation.

6....♗xd2+ 7.♕xd2

7.♘bxd2 a5 8.c3 (8.a4 ♘bd7 9.0-0 0-0 10.♖e1 ♕c7 11.d4 exd4 12.exd5 cxd5 13.♘xd4 ♘c5 (+0.10). The isolated d5-pawn is safe and the b3-bishop is a hostage; or 8.a3 ♘bd7 9.0-0 a4 10.♗a2 0-0 11.♖e1 ♖e8 12.d4 exd4 13.exd5 ♖xe1+ 14.♕xe1 cxd5 15.♖b1 ♕b6 16.♘f1 ♘f8 Aronian-Caruana, Paris rapid 2018.

Black is already slightly for choice as White has to lose time just to regain his pawn) 8...♘bd7 9.0-0 0-0 10.♖e1 ♖e8= (-0.01). Black can complete development by ...♕c7 and ...♘f8 or ...♘c5.

7....a5

In the **actual game** Black played 7...♕d6, but instead I now recommend 7...a5 with the following continuation: 8.a4 0-0 9.exd5 cxd5 10.♘xe5 ♘c6 11.f4 ♖e8 12.0-0 ♘xe5 13.fxe5 ♖xe5 14.♘c3 h6 15.♖ae1 ♖g5 (0.00). Black's pressure on the kingside offsets the isolated d-pawn. Topalov-Dominguez Perez, St Louis rapid 2019, continued 16.d4 ♗h3 17.♖e2 ♗e6 18.♖ef2, when 18...♕d6 would already be more pleasant for Black, since the exchange sac on f6 is not reasonable.

Game 18.2   Vienna Game
Yge Visser   2516
Ivan Sokolov   2652
London 2006 (6)

1.e4 e5 2.♗c4
2.♘c3 ♘f6 3.♗c4 transposes.
2....♘f6 3.♘c3 ♗c5

In the 1.e4 e5 openings, if White doesn't attack e5 by ♘f3, I believe Black should not play ...♘c6. He is generally better off playing ...c7-c6, ...d7-d6, and ...♘bd7, playing a Philidor-like formation without White having played d2-d4, which is the only move that puts pressure on this formation.

4.d3

4.♘f3 d6 5.d3 c6 transposes to the game.

4....c6

5.♘f3

A) 5.f4 d6 6.♘f3 b5 7.♗b3 a5 8.a4 b4 9.♘e2 ♕c7 10.fxe5 dxe5 and White's castling problems give Black equality;

B) 5.♕f3 d6 6.h3 b5 7.♗b3 a5 8.a4 b4 9.♘b1 ♗e6 10.♘d2 ♘bd7 11.♘e2 d5 – Black has more space and better development.

5....d6 6.0-0 ♘bd7 7.a3 ♗b6

7...a5! is better and fully equal.

8.♗a2

Probably better is 8.♗e3 0-0 9.♖e1 h6 10.h3 ♖e8 11.♗xb6 ♘xb6 12.♗b3 ♗e6 13.♗xe6 ♖xe6 14.d4 ♕c7 (+0.09).

8....h6 9.♘e2 ♘f8 10.♘g3 ♘g6=

I think that Black's...c7-c6 is more useful than White's a2-a3 in this otherwise nearly symmetrical position, so White has lost the advantage of moving first.

11.d4 exd4 12.♘xd4 0-0

13.♘df5?! ♗xf5 14.exf5 ♘e5 15.♗f4 ♖e8

Black's healthy vs White's crippled majority compensates for the bishop pair. Once Black plays ...d6-d5 he should be better due to the sad bishop on a2.

16.♕d2 d5 17.♖ae1

17....♗c7

The **actual game** went 17...♘ed7 18.c4 ♘c5 19.cxd5 cxd5 20.♖d1 ♘ce4 21.♕d3 ♖c8= 22.♕f3?? ♘xf2 23.♖xf2 ♖c2 24.♘h1 ♖ee2 25.♗g3 ♘e4 26.♖f1 ♖xb2 27.♗b1 ♘xf2 28.♗xf2 ♗xf2+ 29.♘xf2 ♖xf2 and Black won.

18.♖e2 ♕d6 19.♖e3 ♖e7 20.♖fe1 ♖ae8

The white bishop on a2 is shut out of the game, so Black is better.

Game 18.3 Vienna Game
Dmitry Andreikin   2683
Vladimir Kramnik   2791
Moscow blitz 2010 (37)

1.♘c3 ♘f6 2.e4 e5
The normal move order would be 1.e4 e5 2.♘c3 ♘f6. I don't like to use blitz games, but this one shows a World Champion playing my recommended line.

3.f4
A) For 3.♘f3 ♘c6 see the chapter on the Four Knights Game;
B) 3.g3 ♗c5 4.♗g2 0-0 5.♘ge2 ♖e8 6.0-0 ♘c6 7.d3 a5 8.h3 ♘d4= is similar to the Glek System in the Four Knights chapter;
C) 3.♗c4 transposes to Game 18.2.
3...d5
Although this is a variation with a long history, played by many strong players long ago, I believe that Black is already better after three moves!
4.fxe5
4.exd5 exf4 (4...♘xd5 is an excellent pawn sacrifice, equally good) 5.d4

(in the event of 5.♗c4 c6 6.d4 cxd5 7.♗b3 ♗d6 8.♘ge2 0-0 9.0-0 g5 10.♘xd5 ♘xd5 11.♗xd5 ♘c6 12.c3 ♗g4 Black's better development outweighs his doubled pawns; 5.♘f3 transposes to the King's Gambit) 5...♘xd5 6.♘xd5 ♕xd5 7.♗xf4 ♗d6 8.♗xd6 ♕xd6 9.♕d2 0-0 10.0-0-0 ♗e6N 11.♔b1 ♘d7=.

4....♘xe4

5.♘f3
A) 5.d3 ♘xc3 6.bxc3 d4 7.♘f3 ♘c6 8.♗e2 dxc3 9.0-0 ♕d5 10.♔h1 h6 (-0.64). White has hardly any compensation for the pawn;
B) 5.♕f3 (this is now the main line) 5...♘c6 (most GMs play 5...♘xc3 here but I think it's because they were surprised. Also good is 5...f5. Then after 6.d3 ♘xc3 7.bxc3 d4! 8.♕g3 ♘c6 9.♗e2 ♗e6=) 6.♗b5 ♘xc3 7.dxc3 ♕h4+ 8.g3 ♕e4+ 9.♕xe4 dxe4 10.♗xc6+ bxc6 11.♘e2 ♗c5 Black has the bishop pair while his isolated pawns are all on closed files and not easily attacked.
5....♗c5 6.d4
6.♕e2 ♗f5 7.♘d1 ♗g4 8.d3 ♗xf3 9.♕xf3 ♘g5 (-0.47). White will have to make some concession to get castled.

6....♗b4 7.♗d2 c5

8.♘xe4

A) In case of 8.a3 ♗xc3 9.♗xc3 ♘c6 10.♗b5 cxd4 11.♕xd4 0-0 12.♗xc6 bxc6 13.♗b4 ♖e8 14.0-0 ♕b6 15.♗d6 ♗g4N Black is better thanks to his strong outposted knight;

B) If 8.♗d3 ♘xd2 9.♕xd2 cxd4 10.♘xd4 ♘c6 11.♘xc6 (11.♕f4 0-0 isn't quite as bad for White) 11...bxc6 12.0-0 0-0 13.♔h1 ♗a5 Black has the bishop pair, a pin, and White's e5-pawn is weak;

C) After 8.♗b5+ ♘c6 9.0-0 0-0 10.a3 ♗xc3N 11.♗xc3 ♕b6 12.♗xc6 bxc6 13.dxc5 ♕xc5+ 14.♗d4 ♕e7

Black is again better due to the strong knight and the option of ...c6-c5.

8....dxe4 9.♗xb4 cxb4 10.♘g1 0-0 11.♗c4 ♘c6 12.c3 bxc3 13.bxc3

13....♕c7!

In the **actual game** Kramnik actually played 13...♕g5? 14.♕e2 ♗f5 15.♘h3 ♗xh3 16.gxh3. Now 16...♘a5 would have kept the advantage. He played 16...e3? and went on to lose.

14.♗b3 ♘xe5 15.dxe5 ♕xc3+ 16.♔f2 ♕xe5 17.♖c1 ♕f6+ 18.♔e1 ♗e6

Black has three pawns for a knight, better development, and a much safer king. He should win.

CHAPTER 19

Gambits

In this chapter we consider all the lines in which White starts with 1.e4 and subsequently sacrifices a pawn, usually for development. It is said that 'the only way to refute a gambit is to accept it', and this is in most cases my advice. It is also said that having accepted a gambit, you should look for a way to return the material to achieve a good position, and this too is often my preference. But it's not good to generalize too much; each gambit should be studied independently. These gambits are mostly pretty rare in top level chess, but amateurs will often encounter them, and will be likely to fall into various traps if they have not studied the gambit in question.

The King's Gambit was really popular in the 1800s.

Black can accept (2...exf4) and then return the pawn by 3.♘f3 d5 or try to hold on to it by 3...g5 or by Bobby Fischer's recommended 3...d6. Since I believe that Black has the better chances after returning the pawn, I see no real point in learning the lines where he tries to hang on to it. However I recommend the move-order **1.e4 e5 2.f4 d5(!) 3.exd5 exf4 4.♘f3**, which transposes to 2...exf4 3.♘f3 d5 4.exd5. The point is that with the normal move order White can play the Bishop's Gambit 3.♗c4 when after 3...d5 he can choose either capture, with the bishop capture being generally considered the better one. However by playing ...d7-d5 on move 2 we cut out that option; White can still choose 4.♗c4 but he has already taken on d5 with the pawn.

Back to 4.♘f3, Black should develop by **4...♘f6** rather than expose his queen by 4...♕xd5. White has a couple ways to try to come out a pawn ahead, but they don't end well for him. If White plays normal moves he often has to surrender the bishop pair to win back his pawn on f4, which is the main reason I like this line for Black.

In Game 19.1 we look at 5.♗c4, the most popular move. In the game White manages to regain the pawn without losing the bishop pair, but he ends up with a much worse pawn structure. In Game 19.2 we consider all other fifth moves, where White's attempt to stay a pawn ahead is refuted by a novelty in the note to move 12.

The Urusov Gambit (**1.e4 e5 2.♗c4 ♘f6 3.d4 exd4 4.♘f3**)

is a rather dangerous one for Black to accept by 4...♘xe4, although the computers prefer Black. We cannot play 4...♘c6 as I'm not recommending the Two Knights Defense to the Italian. Fortunately for us the move **4...♗b4+** solves all of Black's problems quite nicely, White can't even equalize. See Game 19.3.

The Danish Gambit (**1.e4 e5 2.d4 exd4 3.c3**)

is well met by **3...♕e7!**. Technically this is 'declining' the gambit as White could play 4.♕xd4, but that clearly favours Black, so White should renew his offer by **4.cxd4 ♕xe4+**, when White struggles to prove compensation for the pawn. This line was popular around 1900 and was shown to me as a kid by an elderly Norman Whitaker, a top player from the 1920s and now known to have had a long criminal career as a swindler. But 3...♛e7 is an honest, good move. See Game 19.4.

The Göring Gambit (**1.e4 e5 2.♘f3 ♞c6 3.d4 exd4 4.c3**) had some popularity in my youth, but is fairly uncommon now. Still, it pays to know what to do.

Declining by 4...d5 gives fairly equal chances, but I think Black should try to refute this gambit by accepting **4...dxc3**. Then play branches, depending on whether White sacrifices a second pawn by **5.♗c4** or just recaptures **5.♘xc3**. In the latter case it seems to me that White lacks sufficient play for the pawn unless he chooses to head for a slightly worse endgame. See Game 19.5 for this and for the Scotch Gambit **4.♗c4**.

This is met by **4...♗c5 5.0-0 d6 6.c3 ♗g4** with only White having problems.

Perhaps the most respectable of the gambits in this chapter is the Evans Gambit. It is attributed to a Captain William Davies Evans around the year 1830, not to the late grandmaster Larry Evans. For the rest of the 1800s it was practically the main line of chess, but it almost died out around 1900 due in part to 'Lasker's Defense'. Kasparov brought it back from obscurity with a few wins in the mid-1990s, including one over his then main rival Anand. It was again revived by Nigel Short, especially with a game against Nielsen which cast doubt on the line I recommended for Black in my previous book (the game was played just weeks after I completed that book). Things are still not completely clear, but I believe I have found a way to get the better chances for the black pieces. I also give a safe line in case I'm wrong. The gambit goes: **1.e4 e5 2.♘f3 ♘c6 3.♗c4 ♗c5 4.b4!?**.

The idea is that White normally wants to play 4.c3 and 5.d4 here, but this has drawbacks, so White hopes to achieve this with a gain of a tempo at the price of the b-pawn. Normally you need at least two tempi and more typically three to justify a gambit, but the tempo is quite valuable in this position due to threats on f7. Black should accept by **4...♗xb4**, when after **5.c3 ♗a5** is the best winning try (5...♗e7 is the safest move, for which see Game 19.6) and after **6.d4** I now recommend **6...d6** rather than 6...exd4 due to the above-mentioned Short game. When White attacks f7 by **7.♕b3** we defend with **7...♕d7**.

If White then takes on e5 we return the pawn by 8...♗b6 with the idea of ...♘a5, when Black should end up slightly better. If White does not take on move 8 Black should be able to retain the pawn without conceding too much compensation. See Game 19.7.

Game 19.1 King's Gambit
Aleksander Mista 2537
Thomas Roussel Roozmon 2489
Brno 2008 (10)

1.e4 e5 2.f4 d5 3.exd5 exf4
Rather than Falkbeer's 3...e4.

4.♘f3
Or 4.♗c4 ♕h4+ 5.♔f1 ♗d6 6.♘f3
♕h6 7.♘c3 ♘e7. Black is already
clearly better as he can castle while
White cannot, other things being
fairly equal.
4....♘f6 5.♗c4 ♘xd5 6.0-0
  A) In case of 6.♗xd5 ♕xd5 7.♘c3
♕f5 8.d4 ♘c6 9.d5 (9.0-0 ♗e6
keeps the pawn) 9...♘b4 10.0-0
♗c5+ 11.♔h1 0-0 12.a3 ♘xc2 and
White won't get full compensation
for the pawn (-0.55);
  B) After 6.♘c3 ♘xc3 7.dxc3
♕xd1+ 8.♔xd1 ♗d6 9.♖e1+ ♔f8
White has little for the pawn
(-0.43).
6....♗e6
6...♗e7 7.♗xd5 (7.d4 g5 8.♘c3 is a
better try for White) 7...♕xd5 8.♘c3
♕d8 9.d4 g5 also favors Black, but
not 9...0-0 10.♗xf4 as in Carlsen-
Wang Yue, Medias 2010, won by
White.

7.♕e2
In the event of 7.♗b3 c5 8.d4 cxd4
9.♘xd4 ♗c5 10.♔h1 ♗xd4 11.♕xd4
0-0 12.♗xd5 (12.♖d1 ♘c6 13.♕f2
♕g5 14.♗xd5 ♗xd5 15.♘c3 ♗e6
16.♗xf4 ♕f5 17.♔g1 ♖fd8 with a
slight preference for Black due
to his safer king (-0.20)) 12...♘c6
13.♕xf4 ♕xd5 14.♘c3 ♕c4 15.♕f2
♖fe8 Black has better development
and a slightly safer king. The white
knight blocking his c-pawn makes
any queenside play difficult for
White.
7....♗e7 8.d4
After 8.♘c3 c6 9.d4 g5 10.♘e4 ♘d7
11.♗b3 h6 12.c4 ♘5f6 White has
only a little compensation for the
pawn.
**8....0-0 9.♘c3 ♘xc3 10.bxc3 ♗xc4
11.♕xc4 ♗d6 12.♕b5 b6 13.♘g5**

13....c5

The **actual game** went 13...♘d7 14.♗xf4 ♗xf4 15.♖xf4 and now 15...a6 would have kept the advantage, based on the superior pawn structure. He played 15...♘f6 and the game was later drawn.

14.♘e4 f3 15.gxf3

15.♖xf3? ♗xh2+ 16.♔xh2 ♕h4+ with an obvious advantage for Black.

15.♗g5 ♕c7 16.g3 ♘d7 favors Black slightly (-0.23).

15....a6 16.♕d3 ♘c6

Black's much better pawn structure and safer king give him the advantage.

Game 19.2   King's Gambit –
                      Modern Defence

Sarunas Sulskis   2559
Hrant Melkumyan   2530

Benasque 2009 (8)

1.e4 e5 2.f4 exf4 3.♘f3 d5

I prefer the move order 2...d5 3.exd5 exf4 to rule out taking on d5 with the bishop in case of ♗c4 instead of ♘f3.

4.exd5 ♘f6

5.♗b5+

A) After 5.c4 c6 6.d4 ♗b4+ 7.♘c3 0-0 8.♗xf4 cxd5 9.♗e2 (9.♗d3 dxc4 10.♗xc4 transposes) 9...dxc4 10.♗xc4 ♘c6 11.0-0 ♗g4 Black is for choice due to the heavy pressure on the weak d4-pawn;

B) Or 5.♘c3 ♘xd5 and now:

B1) 6.♗c4 ♘xc3 7.bxc3 (after 7.dxc3 ♕xd1+ 8.♔xd1 ♗d6 9.♖e1+ ♔f8 White struggles to show compensation for the pawn) 7...♗d6 8.♕e2+ ♕e7 9.♕xe7+ ♔xe7 10.0-0 ♗e6 11.♖e1 ♔d7 – again it is tough for White to prove compensation;

B2) 6.♘xd5 ♕xd5 7.d4 ♗e7 8.c4 ♕d6N 9.c5 ♕h6 10.g3 g5 11.gxf4 g4 12.♘e5 ♕h4+ 13.♔e2 0-0 – White has regained his pawn, but the price of having to advance his king was too high.

5....c6 6.dxc6 ♘xc6 7.d4 ♗d6

8.♕e2+

8.0-0 0-0 9.♘bd2 ♗g4 10.c3 (or 10.♘c4 ♗c7 11.♗xc6 bxc6 12.♘ce5 ♗xf3 13.♘xf3 ♖e8 14.♕d3 a5 15.♗d2 ♘e4 16.♖ae1 f5 and despite his inferior pawn structure, I prefer Black due to the powerful outposted knight) 10...♖e8 11.♘c4 ♗c7 12.♗d2 ♕d5 13.♘a3 ♘e4 and again the powerful e4-knight outweighs the doubled pawns.

8....♗e6 9.♘g5 0-0 10.♘xe6

Not 10.♗xc6? ♗g4.

10....fxe6 11.♗xc6 bxc6 12.0-0

12.♕xe6+ ♔h8 13.0-0 ♗c5!N 14.dxc5 (14.c3 ♗xd4+ is similar) 14...♕d4+ 15.♔h1 ♘e4 and Black's attack will win material.

12....♕c7

A greedy computer suggestion is 12...♖e8N 13.♘c3 (in case of 13.♗xf4? ♗xf4 14.♖xf4 ♕b8 15.♕f1 ♕xb2 Black will win a pawn) 13... e5 14.♕c4+ ♔h8 15.dxe5 ♗xe5 16.♗xf4 ♕b6+ 17.♔h1 ♕xb2 18.♗xe5 ♖xe5 19.♕xc6 ♖ae8 20.h3 ♕xc2. Here Black is for choice as his pieces are slightly better placed.

13.♘d2

13.♕xe6+ ♔h8 14.♕h3 (14.♘d2 ♖ae8 15.♕h3 c5 16.♘c4 f3N 17.♘xd6 ♕xd6 18.♔h1 cxd4 19.♕xf3 ♘d5 20.♕d1 ♖xf1+ 21.♕xf1 ♖f8 22.♕g1 ♘b4 23.♗d2 ♘xc2 – Black regains the pawn with advantage due to the advanced passer) 14...♖ae8 15.♘c3 ♘d5 16.♗d2 ♘e3 17.♗xe3 ♖xe3 18.♖f3 ♕b6 19.♖xe3 fxe3 20.♕xe3

♕xb2 21.♖f1 ♕xc2=. A draw is to be expected.

13....♖ae8 14.♘c4

14....g5

An alternative is 14...c5 15.♘xd6 ♕xd6 16.♗xf4 ♕xd4+ 17.♗e3 ♕xb2 18.♕c4 ♖f7=.

15.♗d2

15.b3 e5 16.dxe5 ♗xe5 17.♘xe5 ♕xe5 18.♕xe5 ♖xe5 19.♗b2 ♖e2 20.♗xf6 ♖xf6 21.♖f2 ♖fe6=. A draw is likely.

15....e5 16.dxe5 ♗xe5 17.♘xe5 ♕xe5 18.♕xe5 ♖xe5 19.♗b4 ♖fe8

19...c5!=.

20.♗c3 ♖5e6 21.♗xf6 ♖xf6 22.♖fe1 ♖fe6 23.♖xe6 ♖xe6 24.♔f2 ♖d6 25.♖e1 ♔f7 26.♖e5 ♖d2+ 27.♔f3

27....g4+ 28.♔xf4 ♖xc2 29.♔g3 ♖xb2 30.♖a5 ♔g6 31.♖xa7 h5

The game soon ended in a draw.

Game 19.3   Bishop's Opening –
Urusov Gambit

Eric Arbau   1933
Vladimir Malaniuk   2527

Bastia 2010 (5)

1.e4 e5 2.♗c4 ♘f6 3.d4 exd4 4.♘f3
This is the Urusov Gambit, a rather
dangerous one if accepted.
4....♗b4+

5.c3
If 5.♗d2 ♗xd2+ 6.♕xd2 (after
6.♘bxd2 ♘c6 7.0-0 0-0 8.♗b5 a6
9.♗xc6 dxc6 10.e5 ♘d7 11.e6 ♘c5
12.exf7+ ♖xf7 White has too little
for the pawn) 6...♘xe4 7.♕xd4 ♘f6
8.0-0 d5, here White has much less
compensation for the pawn than in
the Urusov Accepted. The exchange
of bishops has robbed White's
attack of any power.
5....dxc3 6.bxc3 d5! 7.exd5
After 7.♕a4+ ♕d7N 8.♕xb4 dxc4
9.0-0 b6 10.♖e1 ♘a6 11.♕xc4 ♘c5
Black is better due to the weak
white pawns and square d3.
7....♗c5
7...♗e7 is the move to play if you
want to keep queens on the board.
Objectively both moves are fine.
Play may continue 8.0-0 0-0 9.♗b3

♗g4 10.♗b2 ♘bd7 11.h3 ♗h5
12.♘bd2 ♖c8 13.c4 c6 14.dxc6 ♖xc6
(-0.16). Black has the better pawn
structure.
7...♗d6 8.♕e2+ ♕e7 is similar to the
game.
8.♕e2+ ♕e7 9.♕xe7+ ♔xe7
Also after 9...♗xe7 10.0-0 0-0 11.♖e1
♗d6 12.♘a3 a6 13.♗b3 ♘bd7 14.♘c4
♗c5 15.♘a5 ♗b6 16.♘c4 ♗a7 Black
is to be preferred due to the poor
white pawn structure.
10.♗f4 ♗d6
10...c6! looks even better, favouring
Black.

11.♗g3?
The computer calls the position
after 11.♗xd6+ cxd6 equal, but
I prefer Black as the c3-pawn is
weaker than the d6-pawn.
11....♖d8 12.♗h4
This implies a willingness to part
with the bishop pair, but other
moves lose the d-pawn for too little.
**12....h6 13.♗xf6+ ♔xf6 14.0-0 ♗f5
15.♘bd2 ♘d7 16.♖fe1 ♖e8 17.♘d4
♗h7**
White has no compensation for the
bishop pair.
**18.♗b5?! ♖xe1+ 19.♖xe1 ♘b6
20.♘e4+?! ♗xe4 21.♖xe4 a6 22.♗d3
♘xd5**

Bishops of opposite color do not generally draw a pawn down with knights on the board.
23.♗c4 ♘b6 24.♗b3 g6 25.g4 ♘d7 26.♗d1 ♖d8 27.h4 ♔g7 28.g5 hxg5 29.hxg5 ♘c5 30.♖g4 ♗e5 31.♗f3 c6 32.♔f1 ♔f8 33.♔e2 ♗xd4

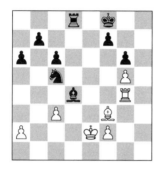

34.♖xd4?!
Taking with the pawn was the last chance to continue the fight for a draw, but Black should still win.
34....♖xd4 35.cxd4 ♘e6 36.d5 ♘d4+ 0-1

Game 19.4   King's Pawn Openings –
                    Danish Gambit

Vilmos Nogrady   2245
Konstantin Krivolapov   2325
Budapest 1996

1.e4 e5 2.d4 exd4 3.c3
The Danish Gambit.
3.♘f3?! ♗b4+ (instead 3...♘c6 transposes to the Scotch, but this is better) and now:
   A) 4.♗d2 ♗c5 5.♗c4 ♘f6N 6.e5 ♘e4 7.0-0 0-0 8.♖e1 d5 9.exd6 ♘xd2 10.♘bxd2 ♗xd6 – White cannot regain the pawn, and has only a mild lead in development for it;

B) 4.c3 dxc3 5.♘xc3 (with 5.bxc3 ♗c5 6.♗c4 d6 7.0-0 ♘c6 8.♘bd2 ♘f6 9.♘b3 ♗b6 White has a bad version of an Evans Gambit. He has only a tempo for the pawn) 5...♘f6 (or 5...♘c6, transposing to the Göring Gambit) 6.e5 ♘e4 7.♕c2 d5 8.exd6 (in case of 8.♗d3 ♘c5 9.0-0 ♘xd3 10.♗g5 ♕d7 11.♕xd3 ♗xc3 12.♕xc3 0-0 White has too little for the pawn) 8...♘xc3 9.bxc3 ♗xd6 10.♗g5 ♕d7 11.♗d3 h6 12.♗e3 ♘c6 13.0-0 0-0 14.♖fe1 ♖e8 15.♖ad1 b6 – Black will fianchetto the bishop and be a safe pawn ahead.
3....♕e7!

This is quite likely to surprise your opponent, and may very well be the best move objectively (Lc0 says so). White either loses a pawn for too little compensation or just gets an inferior game with equal material.
4.cxd4
In case of 4.♘f3 ♕xe4+ 5.♗e2 d3 6.♕xd3 ♕xd3 7.♗xd3 ♘c6 8.0-0 ♘f6 White has two tempi for the pawn, which with queens off is not enough.
After 4.♕xd4 ♘c6 5.♕e3 ♘f6 6.♗d3 d5 7.♘d2 ♗g4 Black is better, because White cannot trade on d5

without falling seriously behind in development.

4....♕xe4+ 5.♗e3

In the event of 5.♗e2 ♕xg2 6.♗f3 ♕g6 7.♘e2 ♘c6N 8.♘f4 ♕f5 9.♘c3 ♘f6 10.♕e2+ ♔d8 11.♗e3 d6 12.♘fd5 b6 13.0-0-0 ♘xd5 14.♗xd5 ♗a6! 15.♕xa6 ♘b4 16.♗e4 ♕xe4 17.♘xe4 ♘xa6 White may have compensation for a pawn, but he is down two!

5....♘f6 6.♘c3 ♗b4 7.♘f3 ♘d5 8.♕d2 ♕e7 9.♗c4

If 9.♗d3N ♘xe3 10.fxe3 d6 (perhaps even better is 10...d5 11.0-0 ♘d7) 11.0-0 ♘d7 12.e4 ♘f6 13.♔h1 0-0 14.e5 dxe5 15.dxe5 ♗xc3 16.♕xc3 ♘h5 17.♕d2 ♗g4 18.♕e3 g6 White doesn't have enough for the pawn.

9....♘xe3 10.fxe3

10....d6?!

With 10...c6!N Black plans ...d7-d5, after which White will have little compensation.

11.0-0 ♗xc3 12.bxc3 0-0 13.e4 ♗e6 14.♗d3 ♗g4 15.e5 ♗xf3 16.♖xf3 dxe5 17.dxe5?

17.♖af1=.

17....♕xe5?!

17...♘d7!.

18.♖e1 ♕c5+ 19.♔h1 ♘c6 20.♖f5 ♕d6 21.♖d5 ♕h6 22.♕e2?! ♕f6 23.♖f5

23....♕d6?!

23...♕xc3N should win. When in doubt, take stuff!

24.♗c4 g6 25.♖d5 ♕f6 26.♖d7 ♕xc3 27.♖xc7 ♖ad8 28.♖f1 ♔h8 29.♗xf7 ♕e5 30.♕f2 ♖d2 31.♕h4 ♕f5 32.♖e1?? ♖xf7 33.♕xh7+ ♔xh7 0-1

Game 19.5 Scotch Opening – Göring Gambit

Laszlo Schmikli 2289
Tamas Meszaros 2400

Hungary tt-2 2005/06 (9)

1.e4 e5 2.♘f3 ♘c6 3.d4 exd4 4.c3

4.♗c4 is the Scotch Gambit after 4...♗c5 (4...♘f6 transposes to 3.♗c4 ♘f6 4.d4 exd4) 5.0-0 (5.c3 ♘f6 transposes to the Italian Game) 5...d6 (5...♘f6 6.e5 is the Max Lange Attack) 6.c3 ♗g4 7.♕b3 ♗xf3 8.♗xf7+ ♔f8 9.gxf3 (after 9.♗xg8?! ♖xg8 10.gxf3 g5 11.♕e6 ♖g6 12.♕f5+ ♔g7 13.♔h1 ♕e7 Black has a winning attack) 9...dxc3 10.♗xg8 ♖xg8 11.♘xc3 ♘d4 12.♕d1 ♕f6 13.♘d5 ♕f7 14.♔g2 c6 15.♘e3 ♕g6+

16.♔h1 ♕h5 17.♔g2 ♖d8 18.b4 ♗b6.
The threat of ...♘d4-e6-f4 gives
Black the advantage.

4....dxc3

This is the Göring Gambit
Accepted. More popular is 4...d5,
which equalizes, but I think Black
should try for an advantage by
accepting.

5.♘xc3

Or 5.♗c4 cxb2 6.♗xb2 ♗b4+ 7.♘c3
♘f6 and now:

A) After 8.0-0 ♗xc3 9.♗xc3 0-0
10.e5 ♘e4 11.♗b2 d6 12.♕e2 (if
12.♖e1 ♗f5 13.♖c1 ♖e8 White has
insufficient compensation) 12...d5
13.♖ad1 ♗e6 Black is better. White
has the bishop pair and somewhat
better development, which is
enough for a pawn but hardly for
two;

B) 8.♕c2 d6 9.0-0-0 ♗xc3 10.♕xc3
♗e6 11.♖he1 ♗xc4 12.♕xc4 0-0
13.e5 ♘e8 14.♕c3 f6 15.♕b3+
♔h8 – here too White has plenty
of compensation for a pawn, but
probably not for two.

5....♗b4 6.♗c4 ♗xc3+

6...d6 7.♕b3 ♗xc3+ 8.bxc3 would
transpose to the game but gives
White the sensible option of

8.♕xc3, which the game order
avoids.

7.bxc3 d6

8.0-0

A) 8.♕b3 ♕e7 9.0-0 ♘f6
transposes to the game;

B) 8.♘g5 ♘e5 9.♗b3 h6 10.f4 hxg5
11.fxe5 ♕e7 12.♗d5 dxe5 13.♗a4+
♗d7 14.♕xb7 ♖d8 15.♕xa7 ♗xa4
16.♕xa4+ ♕d7 17.♕xd7+ ♖xd7
18.0-0 ♘f6 19.♖e1 g4 20.a4 ♔e7
21.a5 ♖a8=. White's passer is not
too dangerous since Black may play
...♖a6 next, and White has three
isolated pawns.

8....♘f6 9.♕b3

After 9.e5 ♘xe5 10.♘xe5 dxe5
11.♕xd8+ (instead, 11.♕b3 ♕e7
transposes to the game) 11...♔xd8
12.♗xf7 ♔e7 13.♗b3 ♗e6 14.♖e1
♗xb3 15.axb3 ♘d7 16.f4 a5 17.♗e3
♖hf8 18.fxe5 ♔e6 (-0.42). Black is
for choice, as the king is a great
blockader and the white bishop is
of the wrong color to disturb it.
Also Black has a potential outside
passed pawn.

9....♕e7

9...0-0 is even better here, White
should play 8.♕b3 or 9.e5 to force
the game line.

10.e5

10.♗g5 0-0 11.♖ae1 h6 12.♗h4 ♘a5 13.♕a4 ♘xc4 14.♕xc4 ♗e6 15.♕d3 ♖ae8 Black plans ...♗c8 next. He will eventually unpin by ...g7-g5. White doesn't have enough for the pawn.

10....♘xe5 11.♘xe5 dxe5 12.♗a3 c5 13.♗b5+

13....♗d7

13...♔f8, as recommended in *Chess Advantage*, is also okay, but riskier. The text settles for one pawn up rather than two, but permits Black to castle.

14.♗xd7+ ♕xd7 15.♗xc5

With 15.f4 0-0 16.fxe5 ♘e4 17.♖fe1 ♕c6 18.♕c4 ♘g5 19.♕xc5 ♖fc8 20.♕xc6 ♖xc6 White regains his pawn, but now he has a clearly worse endgame with three isolated pawns.

15....♘e4 16.♕b4

  A) After 16.♗a3 ♘d2 17.♕b4 0-0-0 18.♖fd1 ♖he8 19.c4 ♖e6 White has nothing for the pawn;

  B) If 16.♕a3 ♕c6 17.♗xa7 ♕xc3 18.♕a4+ ♕c6 19.♕xc6+ bxc6 20.♖fe1 ♖xa7 21.♖xe4 f6 22.f4 ♔f7 23.fxe5 ♖e8 24.a4 ♖xe5 Black stays a pawn ahead in this rook endgame, though

White's outside passer might be enough to draw.

16....♕c6 17.♗e3

17....a5

In the **actual game** Black played the inferior 17...♘d6 18.f4 (18.♖fd1 would have equalized) 18...a5 19.♕b3 ♘c4 20.♖ae1 e4 21.f5 0-0 22.f6 g6 23.♕c2 ♖fe8 24.♗d4 e3 25.♕e2 ♘e4 26.♖f3 ♖ae8 27.♕d3 ♕d5 28.♖g3 b5 29.♕e2 b4 30.♖g4 ♖xg4 31.♕xg4 bxc3 32.♕f4 g5 33.♕g4 c2 34.h4 h6 35.♕h5 ♕xd4 36.hxg5 e2+ 37.♔h1 c1♕ 38.♖xc1 e1♕+ 0-1.

18.♕b3 0-0 19.c4 a4

White is just a pawn down.

Game 19.6   Italian Game –
                  Evans Gambit
Laurent Fressinet   2707
Zahar Efimenko   2701
Wijk aan Zee B 2011 (2)

1.e4 e5 2.♘f3 ♘c6 3.♗c4 ♗c5 4.b4

The Evans Gambit is among the best gambit openings. It is sound enough, but shouldn't give any advantage to White with correct play.

4....♗xb4 5.c3 ♗e7

I give this line as a safe alternative to my main recommendation 5...♗a5, which attempts to refute the gambit.

6.d4 ♘a5

7.♘xe5

This regains the pawn but White must prove compensation for the bishop pair.

I consider 7.♗e2 to be the better move, though it is risky.

A) 7.♗d3 d6 8.dxe5 dxe5 (8...♘c6 9.exd6 ♕xd6 10.h3) 9.♘xe5 ♘f6 10.0-0 0-0 11.♕c2 ♕d6 12.♘f3 ♖d8 13.♗e2 ♕c6 14.♘bd2 h6 15.♖b1 a6 16.c4 ♕e6 17.c5 b6 (0.00);

B) 7.♗e2 d6 (safer than 7...exd4 8.♕xd4! with which Kasparov beat Anand in the Tal Memorial, Riga 1995) 8.♕a4+ (8.dxe5 dxe5 9.♕xd8+ ♗xd8 10.♘xe5 ♘f6 11.f3 0-0 12.♘a3 ♖e8 13.♘ec4 ♘xc4 14.♘xc4 ♘d7 15.♔f2 ♘b6 16.♗e3 f5=) 8...c6 9.dxe5 dxe5 10.♘xe5 ♘f6 11.0-0 ♕c7 12.♘f3 (12.f4 b5 13.♕c2 was Li Chao-Tang, chess.com rapid 2019, when 13...♗d6 14.♘d2 ♗xe5 15.fxe5 ♘g4 16.♘f3 (or 16.♗xg4) 16...♕b6+ would lead to perpetual check) 12...0-0 13.♗g5 ♖e8 14.♘bd2 ♗d7 15.♗h4 c5 16.♕c2 ♘h5 17.g3 ♖ad8 (-0.08).

7....♘xc4 8.♘xc4 d5 9.exd5 ♕xd5 10.♘e3 ♕a5

10...♕d8 11.0-0 ♘f6 was played in Kasparov-Short, London rapid 1993, but the text aims for more than equality.

11.0-0 ♘f6 12.c4 0-0 13.♗d2

13.♕d3 b5! 14.cxb5 a6 (-0.11).

13....♕a6!

In the **actual game** Black played 13...♗b4 (in Robson-Perelshteyn, Lubbock 2010, Black played 13...♕h5?? and had to resign after 14.♘d5!) 14.♗xb4 ♕xb4 15.♕d3 b6 16.♘c3 ♗d7 17.♖fd1 ♖ad8 18.a4. White was slightly better due to his central control, though Black drew. The text move is a computer improvement over both games, preserving the bishop pair.

14.♕f3

After 14.♘c3 ♖d8 the white center is under pressure and Black has the bishop pair.

14....c6 15.♖e1 ♖e8 16.♗c3 ♗e6

16...b5! favors Black.

17.♘d2 ♕a3 18.♖ac1 ♖ac8

It's hard to see much compensation for the bishop pair in this open position, so Black is somewhat better.

Game 19.7   Italian Game –
                    Evans Gambit

Nigel Short   2706
Anton Filippov   2595

Kolkata 2009 (7)

1.e4 e5 2.♘f3 ♘c6 3.♗c4 ♗c5 4.b4
Nigel Short is the top practitioner
of the Evans Gambit.
4....♗xb4 5.c3 ♗a5

This is the best attempt to refute
the Evans Gambit.
6.d4
  A) 6.0-0 d6 (6...♘f6 7.d4 exd4 8.e5
d5 9.exf6 dxc4 10.fxg7 ♖g8 11.♖e1+
♗e6 also favors Black but is more
complicated) 7.d4 transposes to the
note after 7.♕b3;
  B) Or 6.♕b3 ♕e7 7.d4 ♘f6 8.dxe5
♘xe5 9.♘xe5 ♕xe5 10.♗xf7+ ♔e7
11.0-0 ♖f8 12.♗d5 ♗b6 13.h3 d6
14.♘a3 ♗xh3 15.c4 ♘g4!N 16.♕xh3
♖xf2 17.♖xf2 ♗xf2+ 18.♔f1 ♕xa1
19.♕xg4 ♕xc1+ 20.♔xf2 ♖f8+
21.♔g3 ♕xa3+ 22.♔h2 ♕b2 and
Black wins.
6....d6!
I think this is better than 6...exd4
as recommended in *Chess Advantage*,
due partly to Short's 2003 game
with P.H.Nielsen with 7.♕b3.

7.♕b3
In the event of 7.0-0 ♗g4 8.♕b3
♗xf3 9.♗xf7+ ♔f8 10.gxf3 (after
10.♗xg8 ♖xg8 11.gxf3 exd4 12.♕xb7
♕e8 Black is much better) 10...♗b6
11.♗xg8 ♖xg8 12.d5 ♘a5 13.♕b5
♕h4 White's awful pawn structure
gives Black the edge.
7....♕d7

8.0-0
  A) 8.dxe5 ♗b6 9.♘bd2 (after
9.♗b5 a6 10.♗a4 ♗c5 11.c4 ♘ge7
12.♘c3 0-0 13.0-0 b5N 14.cxb5
♘xe5 15.♘xe5 dxe5 16.♖b1 ♕g4
17.♕c2 ♖d8 Black controls the open
center file in an otherwise balanced
position; 9...♘a5 10.♕c2 ♘xc4
11.♘xc4 d5 12.♗g5? h6 was Short-
Ponomariov, secret training match,
Yalta 2003, with Black's advantage,
but 12.♘cd2 would be equal, and
we're trying for a black edge here)
9...dxe5 10.♗a3 ♘a5 11.♕b4 c5
12.♕b2 ♕e7N 13.♗b5+ ♘c6. Since
Black can now play 14...♘f6 and
castle kingside, White has very
little compensation for the pawn;
  B) If 8.♘bd2 ♗b6, now 9.dxe5
transposes to the previous note,
while 9.0-0 transposes to the game.
8....♗b6 9.♘bd2

9.♗b5 a6 10.♗a4 (after 10.♗xc6 ♛xc6 11.♘bd2 f6N White is down a pawn and the bishop pair with no clear plan of attack) 10...♗a7 and the threat of ...b7-b5 ensures a good game for Black.

9....♘a5 10.♛c2

10.♛b1 f6 11.a4 ♘e7 12.♗a2 ♘ec6 13.♖e1 h5 (-0.09).

10...f6

10...♘e7 11.dxe5 0-0 was Short-Fressinet, Douglas 2015.

10...f6 aims for an edge.

11.a4

11....♘e7!N

The **actual game** went 11...♘h6 12.♗a3 (with 12.♗a2! ♘f7 White gets fair compensation for the pawn) 12...♘f7 13.♗d5 ♛e7 14.♗b4 c6 15.♗a2 0-0 16.♘h4 g6 17.♔h1 ♗e6 18.d5 ♗d7 19.c4 ♖ac8 20.♖ae1 ♛d8 21.♛d3 ♗d4 22.♘df3 c5 23.♗d2 b6 24.♗xa5 bxa5 25.♖b1 ♗xa4 26.♘xd4 cxd4 27.♛g3 ♔g7 28.♖b2 ♖b8 29.♖d2 ♗d7 30.f4 a4

31.fxe5 ♘xe5 32.♖xd4 ♖b2 33.♗b1 ♛b6 34.♖dd1 ♘xc4 35.e5 ♘xe5 36.♖de1 ♖b3 37.♛f4 ♖b4 38.♗e4 f5 39.g4 ♘xg4 40.♛g5 ♘f2+ 41.♖xf2 ♛xf2 42.♖g1 ♖xe4 43.♘xg6 ♛f3+ and White resigned.

12.♗a2 ♛c6

It is surprisingly hard for White to deal with the threat of 13...exd4. The knight on e7 prevents ♗d5, while 13.d5 ♛d7 lets Black castle with a safe extra pawn. 12...♘ec6 is also good though.

13.dxe5

13.♗a3 exd4 14.♗b4 dxc3 is better and equal.

13...dxe5

Next Black can play ...♗e6 with an extra pawn.

14.♗a3 ♗e6 15.♗b4 ♗xa2 16.♛xa2 ♘g6 17.g3 ♘f8 18.♗xa5 ♗xa5 19.♘c4 ♗b6 20.♖ad1 ♘d7 21.f5 0-0-0

White has some but not full compensation for the pawn.

CHAPTER 20

Scotch and Four Knights Opening

I group these two openings together because they often transpose: **1.e4 e5 2.♘f3 ♘c6 3.d4** (Scotch) **3...exd4 4.♘xd4 ♘f6 5.♘c3** and **3.♘c3 ♘f6** (the Four Knights) **4.d4 exd4 5.♘xd4** reach the same position, which is naturally enough called the Scotch Four Knights. In this chapter we look at all lines that typically begin with either the Scotch or the Four Knights.

In the Scotch, which was resurrected around 1990 by World Champion Garry Kasparov, 4.c3 is the Göring Gambit in the Gambit chapter, while the Scotch Gambit 4.♗c4 ♗c5 5.c3 ♘f6 is simply a transposition to the 4.c3 ♘f6 5.d4 exd4 line of the Italian Game. After **4.♘xd4** I recommend **4...♘f6** rather than 4...♗c5, mainly because after the latter move, 5.♘xc6 ♕f6 6.♕f3! seems to offer White a slight edge in most if not all lines. Now after 4...♘f6, **5.♘xc6** (Mieses) **5...bxc6 6.e5 ♕e7 7.♕e2 ♘d5 8.c4** my earlier book recommended 8...♗a6, which often leads to an endgame where White has rook, bishop, and knight vs two rooks and two extra but doubled pawns. This endgame is about equal but rather hard to win as Black, and since **8...♘b6** has been revitalized I now recommend that move.

If White responds with **9.♘d2** or **9.b3** we play **9...a5**, aiming to exchange off this pawn getting rid of an isolated pawn while giving White a backward one on b3 (see Game 20.1). I don't even see how White fully equalizes in this line. After the more aggressive **9.♘c3** the rare **9...♗b7** was played successfully by Kramnik and this seems to solve all of Black's opening problems (see Game 20.2).

The Scotch Four Knights Opening is not very promising for White, although Kramnik brought it back to some extent with the move 10.h3 (see note to Game 20.3). There are some tricks in the Scotch Four Knights so you need to study it. Black has to be willing (in the lines I recommend) to put up with a bad pawn structure in the endgame in return for the two bishops, but with queens off the bishops are a major plus so this is a good enough deal for Black. If White avoids this ending he may achieve a slightly better pawn structure but at the cost of conceding central domination to Black. See Game 20.3 for this as well as the Belgrade Gambit **5.♘d5!?**, which we meet by **5...♘b4** when I don't see how White equalizes.

Unusual fourth moves after the four knights come out, including **4.g3** (Glek) and **4.a3**, should lead to equality with correct play. In the former case simple development with **4...♗c5** and 5...d6 suffices, while after **4.a3** Black should respond with **4...d5** when White may find himself just playing the black side of the equal Scotch Four Knights with the useless move a2-a3 included.

The sacrificial Halloween Attack **4.♘xe5?** is unsound but tricky. Keeping the extra piece is probably theoretically best, but for practical play just retreat the knight to c6 when it is attacked and give back the piece by answering d4-d5 with ...♗b4, after which Black is just better. See Game 20.4 for these three lines.

Most novices play **4.♗c4** after the Four Knights Opening, until someone teaches them not to do so due to the 'fork trick' **4...♘xe4**. However, computer analysis fails to show full equality for Black in the traditional lines after that move. Fortunately I discovered a major novelty here (**5.♘xe4 d5 6.♗d3 ♘b4!**) which appears to give Black absolutely equal chances. There have been some games played with this line since then, confirming the conclusion.

The main line of the Four Knights is **4.♗b5**.

Recently **4...♗c5**, formerly thought bad due to the 'fork trick' (again!), now appears to be playable due to the discovery of the strength of 9...♗e7!. For both of these 'fork trick' lines see Game 20.5. However it does not seem to give total equality. Therefore my main recommendation vs the Four Knights is Rubinstein's **4...♘d4**, which does seem to give Black full equality (or more) in all lines. See Game 20.6.

Game 20.1   Scotch Opening –
                     Mieses Variation

Karel van der Weide   2512
Robert Ris   2395

Haarlem 2007 (9)

**1.e4 e5 2.♘f3 ♘c6 3.d4 exd4 4.♘xd4
♘f6 5.♘xc6 bxc6 6.e5**
6.♗d3 d5 7.exd5 cxd5 8.0-0 ♗e7
9.h3 (Jobava's line) 9...0-0 10.♘d2
(10.♖e1 c5) 10...a5 11.♖e1 ♗b7 12.♘f3
c5N.
6...♕e7 7.♕e2 ♘d5 8.c4
8.h4 (in fashion, don't ask me
why!) 8...♕e6 9.g3 (9.♘d2 a5 10.g3
♘b4 11.♘f3 ♗a6 12.c4 (Vocaturo-
Sargissian, Helsingør 2019) 12...♘b4
13.h5 ♕c2 14.♖h4 c5 favors Black
slightly) 10.c4 ♗a6 11.♗f4 d5
12.a3 ♗xc4 13.♕d1 was Tomczak-
Kramnik, Batumi 2018. Now
13...♕f5! 14.♗xc4 dxc4 15.0-0 ♘c2
16.♖a2 ♖d8 17.♕e2 ♖d3 is winning
for Black despite the tripled isolated
pawns!
8...♘b6

9.b3
9.♘d2 a5 and now:
A) 10.♕e4 d5 11.exd6 cxd6 12.♗e2
♕xe4 13.♘xe4 ♗e6 (-0.07);

B) 10.b3 a4 11.♗b2 transposes to
the game;
C) 10.g3 ♕e6 11.b3 a4 12.♗b2
♗b4 13.♗g2 0-0 (13...♕g6 14.♗e4
♕h6 is an untried and unclear
computer suggestion) 14.0-0 d5
15.♘f3 a3 16.♗d4 c5 17.cxd5 ♕xd5
18.♗e3 ♗a6 19.♕c2 ♗xf1 20.♖xf1
♖ad8 when White doesn't have full
compensation for the exchange
(-0.54).
**9....a5 10.♗b2 a4 11.♘d2 axb3
12.axb3 ♖xa1+ 13.♗xa1 ♕a3
14.♕d1 ♗b4**

15.♗d3
15.♕b1?? ♕a5 16.♕b2 ♗xd2+ 0-1
was a game I won from Russian
master Fayvinov in Washington
2002.
15....♕a2
15...♕a5 is far more common and
sufficient for equality after 16.♔e2
d6 (0.00), but the text aims to win a
pawn with some modest risk.
16.♗d4
In case of 16.♗c2 ♕a5 17.♔e2 d5
18.exd6 0-0 19.♘e4 cxd6 20.♕d4 f6
White has little to compensate him
for having his king in the center.
16....0-0 17.♗e3 ♕a5 18.0-0 ♕xe5

White has a slightly better development and a better pawn structure, but this is probably not quite full compensation for the pawn.

19.♘f3 ♕h5

The computer prefers 19...♕e7 (or 19...♕f6) 20.♗g5 ♕d6 to avoid the draw in the next note. Then on 21.♕c2 h6 (-0.14) is probably better than the usual 21...g6.

20.♕c2

Or 20.♕a1 d5 21.♕a7 ♗g4 22.♕xc7 ♗xf3 23.gxf3 dxc4 24.bxc4 ♕xf3 25.♕xb6 ♕g4+ with a draw by perpetual check.

20...c5N

In the **actual game** Black played 20...d6 21.♖a1 ♗g4 with equality, but White soon lost the exchange and yet managed to draw the endgame. The text is an engine suggestion which has the drawback of leaving the bishop on b4 a bit sidelined, but the other bishop becomes a monster.

21.♗e2 ♗b7

White has little compensation for Black's extra (doubled) pawn.

Game 20.2   Scotch Opening –
                    Mieses Variation
Alexey Shirov   2722
Vladimir Kramnik   2784
Wijk aan Zee 2011 (6)

1.e4 e5 2.♘f3 ♘c6 3.d4 exd4 4.♘xd4 ♘f6 5.♘xc6 bxc6 6.e5 ♕e7 7.♕e2 ♘d5 8.c4 ♘b6 9.♘c3

9....♗b7

This is rare but strong. Kramnik knows what he is doing in the opening.

10.♗d2

 A) 10.♗f4 g6 11.♕e3 ♗g7 12.♗d3 0-0 13.0-0 ♗a6 14.b3 d6 15.♖ae1 ♖fe8 16.♗e4 d5 17.♗f3 ♗b7 and the pressure on e5 prevents White from attacking by ♗g5 or ♗h6, while Black can play ...a7-a5 or ...dxc4 or ...♖ad8;

B) If White plays instead 10.b3
0-0-0 11.♗b2 ♖e8 12.f4 f6 13.0-0-0
fxe5 14.fxe5 g6 15.♖e1 ♗g7 16.♘d1
c5 (or also 16...d6) 17.h4 ♖hf8, Black
is better due to the pressure against
the isolani on e5.

10....g6 11.♘e4 0-0-0 12.a4

In the event of 12.f4 c5 13.0-0-0
♗g7 14.♗c3 ♘a4 15.♕c2 ♘xc3
16.♘xc3 d6 Black is better thanks to
his powerful bishop pair.

12....♗a6

13.♕e3

A) 13.a5 ♘xc4 14.♖a4 ♖e8 15.f3
♕xe5 16.♗c3 ♕f4 17.♖xc4 ♗xc4
18.♕xc4 d5 19.♕xc6 ♖xe4+ 20.♔d1
♖e6 21.♕a8+ ♔d7 22.♗b5+ c6
23.♗xh8 cxb5 24.♕xf8 ♕a4+
25.♔d2 ♕c4 26.♗c3 ♖e2+ 27.♔c1
♕d3 28.♕xf7+ ♔c6 29.♕f6+ and
White must give perpetual check;

B) 13.f3 ♗xc4 14.♕f2 ♗xf1 15.♔xf1
♕e6 16.a5 ♕c4+ 17.♔g1 ♕a6 18.♕d4
♘d5= 19.♗g5 ♗g7 20.♗xd8 ♖xd8
21.♘c3 ♘xc3 22.bxc3 d6 23.♕g4+
♖d7 24.e6 fxe6 25.♕xe6 ♗xc3
26.♕e8+ ♖d8 27.♕e6+ ♖d7 with a
draw by repetition;

C) 13.♕f3 ♖e8 14.♗d3 ♗g7 15.0-0
♗xe5 16.c5 ♗xd3 17.♕xd3 ♘d5
18.♖ae1 f5 19.♘g5 ♕f6 20.♘f3 ♔b7

21.♕b3+ ♔a8 22.♘xe5 ♖xe5 23.♗c3
♘xc3 24.♕xc3 ♖e6 25.♕xf6 ♖xf6
26.♖e7 ♖e6 27.♖xd7 ♔b7 28.h3 ♖e5
29.♖c1 g5 (+0.16).

**13....♕xe5 14.♗c3 ♗b4!! 15.♗xb4
♖he8 16.f3?!**

16.0-0-0 ♕xe4 17.a5 ♕xe3+ 18.fxe3
♘a8 19.♗d3 ♖xe3 (+0.10).

16....d5

It may already be too late for White
to equalize the game.

17.a5

17.cxd5 ♗xf1 18.♔xf1 f5 19.♕d3
fxe4 20.♕a6+ ♔d7 21.dxc6+ ♔xc6
22.♖c1+ ♔d7 23.♕b7 ♖e6 – both
sides have exposed kings but the
inability of the white king's rook to
join the battle tilts the evaluation in
favor of Black.

**17....♘xc4 18.♕xa7 ♕xb2 19.♕xa6+
♔d7 20.♖d1 ♕xb4+ 21.♔f2 ♖xe4
22.fxe4 ♕c5+ 23.♔e1 ♕b4+ 24.♔f2
♕c5+ 25.♔e1 ♘b2**

26.exd5?

26.♕e2 ♘xd1 27.♕xd1 ♖e8 28.♕d2
♖xe4+ 29.♗e2 ♖a4 30.a6 ♖a1+
31.♗d1 f5 and once Black gobbles
the a6-pawn he will have four
pawns for the bishop and so a slight
edge.

26....♕c3+ 27.♖d2 ♕c1+?

With 27...♖e8+! 28.♗e2 ♕c1+
29.♔f2 ♕xd2 30.♖xc6+ ♔d8
31.♕f6+ ♖e7 Black could have won
a piece.

**28.♔e2 ♖e8+ 29.♔f3 ♕xd2
30.♕xc6+ ♔d8 31.♕f6+ ♖e7**

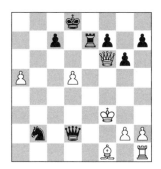

32.♔g4??

32.♔g3 ♘d3 33.♗xd3 ♕xd3+
34.♔h4 ♔e8 35.♖f1 ♕d2 – Black
is clearly better but White has
drawing chances.

**32....♘d1 33.♕h8+ ♔d7 34.♗b5+ c6
35.♗xc6+ ♔c7 36.d6+ ♕xd6**

36...♔xc6! 37.♕c8+ ♔d5 38.dxe7 f5+
wins the queen or mates.

**37.♖xd1 ♕xd1+ 38.♗f3 h5+ 39.♔g3
♕e1+ 40.♔h3 ♕e6+ 41.♔h4 g5+
42.♔xg5 ♕g6+ 43.♔f4 f6**

White resigned because if 44.♕xh5
♖e4+! wins the queen.

Game 20.3   Four Knights – Scotch
Ilja Schneider   2500
Stewart Haslinger   2529
Germany Bundesliga 2009/10 (10)

1.e4 e5 2.♘f3 ♘c6 3.♘c3
3.d4 exd4 4.♘xd4 ♘f6 5.♘c3
transposes.
3....♘f6 4.d4 exd4

5.♘xd4

This position is known as the
'Scotch Four Knights' as it can arise
from either the Scotch or the Four
Knights Opening.

5.♘d5 is the Belgrade Gambit. I
recommend 5...♘b4 and now:

analysis diagram

A) 6.♘xf6+ ♕xf6 7.♗c4 ♗c5 8.0-0
d6 9.e5 dxe5 10.♘xe5 0-0 11.♘d3
♘xd3 12.♗xd3 ♗d6 and Black is
just a pawn up;

B) 6.♘xd4 ♘xe4 7.♘b5 ♘xd5
8.♕xd5 ♕e7!N (also suggested
by Andrey Obodchuk in his 2011
book *The Four Knights Game*) 9.♕d4
(9.♘xc7+ ♔d8 10.♗f4 d6 11.0-0-0
♔xc7 12.♕c4+ ♔d8 13.♖e1 f5 14.f3
g5 15.♗e3 ♘c5 (0.00). White will
eventually regain the piece with
equality) 9...d5 10.♗f4 ♘d6+ 11.♔d1

♘xb5 12.♗xb5+ c6 13.♖e1 ♗e6 14.♗d3 ♕c5 – White has some development for the pawn but with his king stuck in the center that should not be enough;

C) 6.♗c4 ♘bxd5 7.exd5 ♗b4+ 8.♗d2 ♕e7+ 9.♕e2 ♗xd2+ 10.♔xd2 ♕xe2+ 11.♔xe2 0-0 12.♘xd4 a6 13.a4 ♖e8+ 14.♔d3 d6 15.♖he1 ♗d7 – Black has the better bishop, the safer king, and the option to play ...c7-c6 or ...c7-c5 at any moment.

5....♗b4 6.♘xc6 bxc6 7.♗d3 d5 8.exd5 cxd5 9.0-0 0-0

Here 9...♗g4 has caught on lately to avoid 10.h3, but I think the 'cure' is worse than the disease.

10.♗g5

Since 2012 the move 10.h3 has become the main line, postponing commitment of the bishop. Then after 10...c6 11.♕f3 ♖e8 12.♗f4 ♗d6 13.♖fe1 ♗e6 14.♘e2 ♕b8 15.b3 ♗d7 16.♗xd6 ♕xd6 17.c4 d4 18.♕f4 ♕xf4 19.♘xf4 g5! (+0.02) improves over Rublevsky-Najer, Eilat tt 2012, by kicking the knight before White can clear d3 for it.

10...c6

11.♕f3

A) After 11.♘a4 h6 12.♗h4 ♖e8 13.c4 ♗g4 14.♕xg4 ♘xg4 15.♗xd8

♖axd8 16.cxd5 ♖xd5= Black's better placed pieces offset his inferior pawn structure. The bishops of opposite color make a draw likely;

B) 11.♘e2 h6 12.♗h4 ♗d6 13.♘d4 c5 14.♘f5 ♗xf5 15.♗xf5 ♖b8 16.b3 ♗e5 17.♖c1 ♗f4 18.♖b1 ♕d6 19.g3 g5 20.gxf4 gxh4 21.♕f3 ♖b4 22.c4 ♔h8=. White and Black have equally bad pawns.

11....♗d6

11...h6, provoking 12.♗xf6 ♕xf6 13.♕xf6 gxf6, is fine if you want to draw, while 11...♗e7 is best if you must avoid a draw. The text is a good compromise, since White will have to lose a tempo to reach the above endgame and so rarely plays this way here.

12.♖fe1

A) 12.♖ae1 ♗e6 13.♘e2 ♗g4 14.♗xf6 ♗xf3 15.♗xd8 ♗xe2 16.♖xe2 ♖fxd8 17.c4 g6 (+0.07) but 9 out of 9 games were drawn from here in this obviously drawn ending;

B) 12.h3 ♖b8 13.♖ab1 h6 14.♗f4 ♖e8 15.b3 ♗b7 16.♗xd6 ♕xd6 17.♖fe1 ♖be7 and Black's control of the open file offsets his slightly inferior bishop.

12....♖b8 13.♘a4

13.♖ab1 h6 14.♗xf6 ♕xf6 15.♕xf6 gxf6 16.♘e2 c5 17.b3 ♗e6 18.♖ed1 ♖fc8=. Black's bishop pair compensates for the weakened pawns.

13....h6 14.♗f4

After 14.♗xf6 ♕xf6 15.♕xf6 gxf6 16.♖ad1 ♔g7 I prefer Black due to the offside white knight.

14....c5

In case of 14...♗g4! 15.♕e3 ♖e8 16.♕d2 ♗e6 17.b3 c5 (Black has a positive score in 20 games from here; Black is fine (-0.07)) 18.h3 ♗xf4N 19.♕xf4 c4 20.♗f1 ♕a5 the white knight on the rim gives Black the better chances.

15.b3 ♗e6 16.h3 ♖b4

16...♗xf4! 17.♕xf4 c4 18.♗f5 ♗xf5 19.♕xf5 ♕a5 is bad for White.

17.♗xd6 ♕xd6 18.c3

18.♖ad1 ♖e8=.

18....♖bb8 19.♖ad1 ♗d7 20.♘b2 ♖fe8

After 20...♗c6! Black has a better placed knight in an otherwise balanced position.

21.♖xe8+ ♖xe8 22.♘c4 ♕c7 23.♘e3 ♕e5 24.c4 d4 25.♘d5 ♘xd5 26.cxd5 ♕d6 27.♗c4

27....a5

In the **actual game** Black played 27...♗c8 28.♕d3 ♗b7 when White got in the equalizing 29.b4! and went on to win.

With the text move Black has a slight edge with his better bishop and control of the open file.

Game 20.4   Four Knights – Glek
Marijan Petrov   2526
Alexey Bezgodov   2497
Thessaloniki 2010 (9)

1.e4 e5 2.♘f3 ♘c6 3.♘c3 ♘f6 4.g3

This system is named the 'Glek' Four Knights after its chief exponent, GM Igor Glek.

   A) 4.a3 d5 and now:

analysis diagram

A1) 5.♗b5 ♘xe4 6.♘xe5 (if 6.♕e2 ♕d6! 7.♘xe4 dxe4 8.♕xe4 ♗d7 9.d3 0-0-0 10.0-0 ♖e8 Caruana-Kramnik, Paris blitz 2018 (-0.17) already favors Black due to his superior center) 6...♕f6 7.♘f3 ♗e6 8.♕e2 ♘xc3 9.dxc3 ♗d6 10.♗g5 ♕g6 11.♗d3 ♕h5 12.♗f5 ♘e5 13.♗xe6 fxe6 14.♘xe5 ♕xe2+ 15.♔xe2 ♗xe5 16.♖ad1 0-0. A balanced endgame has arisen;

A2) 5.exd5 ♘xd5 6.♗b5 ♘xc3 7.bxc3 ♗d6 8.d4 exd4 9.cxd4 0-0 10.0-0 ♗g4 11.c3 ♕f6=. White is playing the Black side of the Scotch Four Knights, with the extra but useless move a2-a3 included.

B) 4.♘xe5?! is the Halloween Attack: 4...♘xe5 5.d4 ♘c6 (5...♘g6 6.e5 ♘g8 7.♗c4 d5 8.♗xd5 ♘8e7 should also be good but is unnecessarily risky) 6.d5

analysis diagram

6...♗b4!. Black returns the piece to obtain a small but clear edge. After 7.dxc6 ♘xe4 8.♕d4 ♕e7 9.♗e3 0-0 10.♗d3 ♘xc3 11.bxc3 ♗d6 12.cxb7 ♗xb7 13.0-0 ♖fe8 14.♖ab1 ♗c6 White has no compensation for his poor pawn structure.

4....♗c5 5.♗g2 d6 6.d3
6.0-0 a6 7.d3 transposes to the game.
6....a6
This is to prevent 7.♘a4, winning the bishop pair, though Black can also allow this by playing either 6...h6 or 6...♘d4, since he obtains automatic compensation after 7...♗b6 8.♘xb6 axb6.
7.0-0
7.♗e3 ♗xe3 8.fxe3 0-0 9.0-0 ♗g4 (or 9...♘e7=, planning ...♘g6) 10.h3 ♗xf3 11.♕xf3 ♘e7. In a closed position a knight is at least as good as an unpaired bishop. White has slight pressure on the f-file but a slightly damaged pawn structure. The computers like Black due to the less safe white king, but I'll call it equal.
7....♘d4
In general in the 1.e4 e5 openings, this knight exchange favors Black slightly, as the c6-knight blocks the c7-pawn while the f3-knight guards the king.
7...0-0, 7...♗e6 or 7...h6 – all of these moves are satisfactory for Black.
8.♘xd4 ♗xd4

9.♘d5

If White instead plays 9.h3 ♗e6
10.♘e2 ♗a7 11.b3 ♕d7 12.♔h2, 12...
h5!? looks interesting for Black.
**9....♘xd5 10.exd5 0-0 11.c3 ♗a7
12.♗e3 ♗xe3 13.fxe3 ♕g5 14.♕d2**

14....f5=

14...♗g4!? is the computer's
preference: 15.h4 ♕h6 16.♖f2 f5=.
**15.♖f2 ♗d7 16.♖af1 ♖f6 17.e4 ♕xd2
18.♖xd2 fxe4 19.dxe4 a5 20.♖df2
♔f7 21.c4 ♔e7 22.h4 ♖af8 23.♖xf6
♖xf6 24.♖xf6 ♔xf6 25.♔f2 g5
26.♗f3 ½-½**

Game 20.5   Four Knights – Spanish
Mark Esserman   2439
Oleg Korneev   2573
Forni di Sopra 2011 (2)

1.e4 e5 2.♘f3 ♘c6 3.♘c3 ♘f6 4.♗b5

After 4.♗c4 ♘xe4 5.♘xe4 d5 6.♗d3:

analysis diagram

A) Everyone plays 6...dxe4?!
7.♗xe4 ♗d6 8.0-0 0-0 here, but
after 9.♖e1 (9.c3 is also good) we
reach the position discussed in
the note to move 8 below, but with
colors reversed. I call it slightly
better for Black there, which
means White is slightly better here,
e.g. 9...♖e8 (9...♘b4! 10.a3 f5 may
equalize) 10.d3 and White has a
slight pull – less than in main line
openings, so Black can play this, but
it seems that the following novelty
gives full equality;

B) 6...♘b4! 7.♘g3 (7.♘c3 e4 8.♗xe4
dxe4 9.♘xe4 transposes, while
after 7.♘eg5 e4 8.♗e2 ♗d6 9.d3
exf3 10.♘xf3 0-0 11.c3 ♘c6 12.0-0
♖e8 Black has slightly superior
development) 7...e4 8.♗xe4 dxe4
9.♘xe4 ♗f5 10.d3 ♗xe4 11.dxe4
♕xd1+ 12.♔xd1 ♗c5 13.a3 (13.c3!
♘d3 14.♔c2 0-0-0) 13...0-0-0+
14.♘d2 (after 14.♗d2 ♘c6 15.♔e2
♖he8 Black regains the pawn
favorably) 14...♘c6 15.f3 ♗e3 16.♖e1
♗f4 17.c3 ♘e5 18.♔c2 ♘d3 19.♖e2
♗xh2 (0.00). Black has regained his
pawn with a pleasant position.

4....♗c5

This obvious move has rarely
been seen due to the coming 'fork
trick'. In the previous edition I
recommended this for Black, but
I see some problems now so I
recommend Rubinstein's 4...♘d4 in
the following game. I leave this line
in as an option for variety.

5.0-0

5.d3 0-0 6.0-0 transposes to the
next note.

In his book *The Four Knights Game*,
Andrey Obodchuk opts for 5.♘xe5!
as the best way to fight for an
advantage, but the game Najer-
Landa, Novokuznetsk 2008, showed
that Black can equalize: 5...♘xe5
6.d4 ♗d6 7.f4 ♘c6! 8.e5 ♗b4 9.exf6
♕xf6 10.♗e3 (10.a3 ♗xc3+ 11.bxc3
d5 12.0-0 ♗f5 13.♖e1+ ♗e4 14.♗d3
♕g6 15.♗xe4 dxe4 16.f5 ♕xf5
17.♕d3 0-0-0 18.♖xe4 ♕d7 (-0.06),
Lc0 +0.03) 10...d5 11.0-0 ♗xc3
12.bxc3 ♗f5.

5....0-0

6.♘xe5

A) 6.♗xc6 dxc6 7.d3 ♗g4 8.h3
♗h5 9.♗g5 h6 10.♗xf6 ♕xf6 11.g4
♗g6 – with two bishops for two
knights at the price of having one

bishop shut in for now, Black must
be preferred;

B) 6.d3 ♘d4 (6...♖e8= is also
fine) 7.♘xd4 (in case of 7.♘xe5?! d6
8.♘f3 ♗g4 9.♗e3 ♗xf3 10.gxf3 c6
11.♗a4 b5 12.♗b3 ♘h5 13.♔h1 ♕h4
14.♖g1 ♕h3 Black regains the pawn
with the better chances) 7...♗xd4
(7...exd4 is also good) 8.♗g5 c6
9.♗c4 h6 10.♗h4 b5 11.♗b3 a5 12.a4
b4 13.♘e2 ♗a7 (13...♗b6 is similar
and just as good) 14.♔h1 g5 15.♗g3.
This was Petrisor-Nielsen, Aix-
les-Bains Ech 2011, and now after
15...♖e8 16.f3 ♘h5 17.♗f2 ♗xf2
18.♖xf2 d5 Black looks better, with
the white bishop obstructed and
the plan of ...♗e6, ...♕d6, and ...c6-
c5.

6....♘xe5

6...♖e8!? was tried in Paulsen-
Morphy, New York 1857. Then
White's best try is 7.♘f3!, when after
the exchange on e4 White will have
a superior version of the line I give
for him in the White book against
the Berlin Defense.

7.d4 ♗d6 8.f4

If 8.dxe5 ♗xe5 9.♗d3 ♖e8

analysis diagram

Black now has the position White would have if in the Four Knights he plays 4.♗c4 ♘xe4 5.♘xe4 d5 6.♗d3 dxe4 7.♗xe4 ♗d6 8.0-0 0-0 9.♖e1, because White wasted a tempo here by ♗b5-d3. This line is regarded as equal, but the computers slightly prefer White in that line (so Black here), and grandmaster Roman Dzindzichashvili told me that he agreed with the computers here.

8....♘eg4 9.e5

In case of 9.♗e2 ♗b4 10.♗xg4 ♗xc3 11.bxc3 ♘xe4 12.♗f3 d5=, Black's outposted knight and better pawn structure fully offset the bishop pair.

9....♗e7

9....♗b4 now looks best here: 10.f5 ♖e8 11.♘d5 ♘xe5 12.♘xb4 ♘c6 13.a3 a6 14.♗d3 a5 15.♘xc6 dxc6 16.c3 c5 17.dxc5 (Kovalev-Aronian, Batumi ol 2018) 17...♕d5.

10.♗e2

After 10.h3 d6 11.exf6?! (11.hxg4 ♘xg4N 12.♗e2 h5=) 11...♘xf6 12.g4 d5 13.♗d3 c6 14.♕f3 ♕b6 15.a3 ♘e8 16.♗e3 f5 17.g5 ♘d6 Black is better with the knight coming to e4, and

won in Berbatov-Hammer, Aix-les-Bains Ech 2011.

10....d6 11.exf6

Here 11.h3! dxe5 12.fxe5 ♘xe5 13.dxe5 ♘d7 14.♗f4 has an overwhelming score for White after the usual 14...c6. 15.♘e4 The computers prefer 14...♘c5 but 15.♘d5 wins the bishop pair and keeps at least a tiny edge (+0.14) due to that. So this is quite playable for Black but Rubinstein's 4...♘d4 is more clearly equal, although the note to move 9 may change that opinion.

11...♘xf6 12.f5?! d5 13.♗g5 ♖e8 14.♕d3 c6 15.♖ae1

15....b5!N

The **actual game** went 15...♗d7 16.♗d1 h6 17.♗h4 ♘h7 18.♗g3 ♕b6 19.♖xe7?! ♖xe7 20.f6?! ♘xf6 21.♖xf6 gxf6 22.♗h4 ♕c7 23.♕d2 ♖ae8 24.♕xh6 ♖e1+ 25.♗xe1 ♖xe1+ 26.♔f2 ♖e8 27.♘e2 ♕d6 28.c3 ♗f5 and Black eventually won.

16.♘b1 h6 17.♗h4 b4 18.♘d2 a5

Black is better. He has more space and a queenside initiative, while White has no real attack on the kingside.

Game 20.6   Four Knights – Spanish
Wei Yi   2743
Ding Liren   2777
China tt 2017 (20)

1.e4 e5 2.♘f3 ♘c6 3.♘c3 ♘f6 4.♗b5 ♘d4!

This Rubinstein Variation seems to be the only way for Black to reach full equality after the Four Knights Opening. Black will usually offer a gambit pawn next.

5.♗c4

A) 5.♗a4 c6 6.♘xe5 d6 7.♘f3 ♗g4 8.d3 ♗h5! 9.h3 ♘xf3+ 10.gxf3 d5 11.exd5 ♘xd5 12.♕e2+ ♗e7 13.♕e5 ♘xc3 14.bxc3 ♗xf3 15.♖g1 ♕d6 16.♗f4 ♕xe5+ 17.♗xe5 f6 18.♗h2 ♗f8 19.♔d2 g6 20.♖ge1+ ♔d7∓ (-0.29). Black has a better pawn structure at no cost;

B) 5.♘xd4 is a well-known drawing line: 5...exd4 6.e5 (6.♘d5 ♘xd5 7.exd5 ♕e7+ 8.♕e2 ♕xe2+ 9.♗xe2 b6=) 6...dxc3 7.exf6 ♕xf6 8.dxc3 ♗c5 9.♕e2+ ♕e6 10.0-0 ♕xe2 11.♗xe2 d6 12.♗f3 ♖b8 13.♖e1+ ♗e6=;

C) 5.0-0 ♘xb5 6.♘xb5 c6 7.♘c3 d6 8.d4 ♕c7 9.a4 ♗e7 10.h3 0-0 11.♗g5 h6 12.♗h4 ♗e6 (+0.12), Lc0 +0.10;

Black's bishop pair offsets White's space advantage.

5...♗c5 6.♘xe5

6.d3 d6 7.♘a4 b5 8.♘xd4 bxc4 9.♘e2 cxd3 10.♕xd3 ♗b4+ 11.c3 ♕d7 12.b3 ♗a5 13.0-0 ♗b7 14.f3 ♗c6 15.♕a6 ♗b6+ 16.♘xb6 axb6 17.♕d3 d5 18.exd5 ♕xd5 19.♖d1 ♕xd3 20.♖xd3 0-0 21.c4 ♖fe8= ½-½ Svidler-Giri, Wijk aan Zee 2018 (+0.08).

6...♕e7

7.♘f3

7.♘d3 d5 and now:

analysis diagram

A) 8.♘xd5 ♕xe4+ 9.♘e3 ♗d6 10.f3 (if 10.0-0? b5 11.♗b3 0-0∓ Black's development is worth way more than one pawn) 10...♕h4+ 11.♘f2 0-0 12.g3 ♕h5 13.g4 ♕c5 14.c3 ♖e8= 15.d3 b5 16.cxd4 ♕xd4 17.♗b3 ♗f4 18.♘e4 ♗xe3= (0.00). Black regains his piece but the resultant endgame is balanced;

B) 8.♗xd5 ♗b6 9.f3 c6 10.♗c4 0-0 11.a4 a5 12.♘f2 ♕c5 13.d3 ♘b3 14.d4 ♘xd4 15.♗a2 ♗e6∓ (-0.22). Black's superior piece placement is obviously worth more than the pawn he is down.

7...d5 8.♗xd5

8.♘xd5 ♕xe4+ 9.♘e3 ♗g4 10.♗e2 ♘xe2 11.♕xe2 0-0-0 12.d3 ♕e6 13.♘xg4 ♕xe2+ 14.♔xd2 ♘xg4 15.♗e3 ♖he8 (-0.02), Lc0 +0.02.

8...♗g4 9.d3 0-0-0 10.♗e3 ♘xd5 11.♘xd5 ♖xd5 12.exd5 ♖e8

13.c3

13.0-0 ♗xf3 14.gxf3 ♗d6 15.f4 (15. c3 ♕h4 16.f4 transposes) 15...♕h4 16.c3 g5 17.cxd4 ♕h3 18.♖e1 gxf4

19.♗xf4 ♗xf4 20.♖xe8+ ♔d7 21.♕a4+ c6 22.dxc6+ bxc6 23.♕xa7+ ♔xe8 24.♖e1+ ♔f8 25.♕c5+ ♔g7 26.♕c2 ♗xh2+ 27.♔h1 ♗g3+ 28.♔g1 ♗h2+ =. Neither side can avoid this perpetual check.

13...♘xf3+ 14.gxf3 ♕h4 15.♔d2 ♖xe3 16.fxe3 ♕f2+ 17.♔c1 ♗xf3 18.♕e1 ♗xe3+ 19.♔b1 ♗xh1 20.♕xh1 ♕e2 21.a4 ♕xd3+ 22.♔a2

22...♕c4+ 23.♔b1 ♕d3+ 24.♔a2 ♕c4+ 25.♔b1 ♕d3+ 26.♔a2 ♕c4+ My database has eleven games that ended in perpetual check this way. As a matter of fact Wei Yi and Ding Liren repeated the line in the Abidjan Grand Prix blitz in May 2019.

27.♔b1 ♕d3+ 28.♔a2 ½-½

CHAPTER 21

Italian Game

The Italian Game, or Giuoco Piano, is the favorite opening of novice players, but it is also now often chosen by grandmasters and even World Champions. In my opinion, it is the most promising alternative to the Spanish for White, and should keep at least a tiny edge.

After **1.e4 e5 2.♘f3 ♘c6 3.♗c4**, I recommend the safe **3...♗c5** rather than the Two Knights 3...♘f6, which is a risky gambit due to 4.♘g5. The main gambit line stats are +18 Elo for White in the Hiarcs db, which is satisfactory for Black, and Black certainly has decent practical chances. But since the two moves usually transpose after 4.d3, there isn't a compelling reason to learn all the variations after 3...♘f6 4.♘g5 or 4.d4.

In Game 21.1 we examine the gambit line **4.0-0 ♘f6 5.d4 ♗xd4 6.♘xd4 ♘xd4 7.f4**. The recommended response (after **7...d6 8.fxe5 dxe5 9.♗g5 ♕e7 10.♘a3**) is an astonishing computer suggestion, the ridiculous looking **10...♖g8!**. I will do my best to explain it. Note that I don't cover 4.d4, because 4...exd4 transposes to the Scotch Gambit, although 4...♗xd4 is also a good move.

Now after 3...♗c5 **4.c3** (for 4.b4 see the Evans Gambit in the Gambit chapter, while 4.♘c3 ♘f6 5.d3 h6 is a safe line for Black) **4...♘f6** White usually plays 5.d3 in master chess, because the obvious 5.d4 has supposedly been analyzed to equality. However as I show in Games 21.2 and 21.3, Black has to know what he is doing to equalize. As the positions after **5.d4 exd4 6.cxd4 ♗b4+ 7.♗d2** (Greco's ancient 7.♘c3 is a dubious gambit) are rather open, tactics prevail and there's not much point in talking about strategy, except that when White accepts an isolated d-pawn in return for piece play, Black should generally seek equal exchanges. However the **7.♘bd2** gambit has recently caught on and should be taken seriously (Game 21.3).

After **5.d3,** I recommended 5...a6 in the first edition of this book, but since then **5...0-0** has been shown to be a good move and is popular with the elite, since the pin **6.♗g5** is well met by **6...h6 7.♗h4 ♗e7!**, **6.b4** is met by **6...♗e7!**, and **6.♗b3** (or 6.c3) by **6...d5**. Inducing White to castle cuts out some options like ♘b1-d2-f1-g3 (without the need for ♖e1) and also takes the sting out of the pin 7.♗g5 after 6...d6, since White can no longer attack an early ...g7-g5 by h2-h4 with a rook behind it.

After **4.d3 ♘f6 5.0-0 0-0**

Black reacts to different sixth moves in different ways; **6.c3** by ...d7-d5, **6.♖e1** by ...♘g4, **6.a4** by ...h7-h6 followed by ...a7-a5, and **6.♘bd2** by ...d7-d6. Then play can take on a symmetrical nature if both players bring their queenside knights to the kingside, White by ♖e1 and ♘b1-d2-f1-g3, Black by ...♘c6-e7-g6. This results in positions where White's edge due to having the move is really tiny. Moreover, with all the pieces on the board and a fluid pawn structure Black has every right to play for a win if he is the stronger player. See Games 21.4 thru 21.6.

Game 21.7 incorporates the latest findings as of mid 2019. It seems that Black has finally settled on a way to neutralize the slow Italian, as follows: Castle only after White castles. Otherwise play ...d7-d6, ...a7-a6, ...h7-h6, ...♗a7, ...♖e8, and only then ...♗e6, planning to recapture on e6 with the rook to avoid doubled pawns. Then aim for ...♘g8-e7-g6, or ...♕d7, with perhaps a timely ...d6-d5. Whether White finds any antidote to this plan remains to be seen; as of this writing I detect a trend back to the Spanish for White perhaps due to this scheme.

Game 21.1   Italian Game

Sergey Movsesian   2751
Michael Adams   2712

Wijk aan Zee 2009 (2)

1.e4 e5 2.♘f3 ♘c6 3.♗c4 ♗c5 4.0-0 ♘f6 5.d4?!

This is a somewhat dubious gambit.

5....♗xd4 6.♘xd4 ♘xd4

7.f4

A) 7.♗g5 h6 8.♗h4 d6 9.f4 ♗g4 10.♗xf6 (after 10.♕d2 g5 11.fxe5 dxe5 12.♗g3 ♕e7 13.♘c3 0-0-0 Black is better) 10...♗xd1 11.♗xd8 ♖xd8 12.c3 ♗e2 13.cxd4 ♗xc4 14.♖c1 ♗d3 15.♖xc7 0-0 16.dxe5 ♗xe4 17.♘d2 ♗d5 18.♘f3 ♖fe8 19.♖e1 dxe5 20.fxe5 ♔f8 21.♔f2 ♖e7 22.♖c2 b6 and Black's bishop dominates White's knight, and White has a weak e-pawn;

B) Komodo considers the simple 7.♗e3N to be best, although no one plays it: 7...♘c6 8.♘c3 d6 9.f3 h6 10.♕d2 0-0 11.♖ae1 ♗e6 12.♘d5 (to retain the bishop pair, his main compensation for the pawn) 12...♗xd5 13.exd5 ♘e7 and White has the bishop pair, better development, and a much more active queen for the pawn, but the closed position favors knights so Komodo's eval of (-0.50) seems right to me.

7....d6 8.fxe5 dxe5 9.♗g5 ♕e7

The **actual game** went 9...♗e6?! (this natural move lets White equalize) 10.♘a3 ♕e7 11.c3 ♘c6 12.♔h1 ♖d8?! (12...♖g8! – again this computer move is best, and equalizes) 13.♕e2?! (13.♕b3! was strong) 13...h6?! 14.♗xf6 gxf6 15.♖f2 ♖g8 16.♖af1 ♖g6 17.♘c2 ♔f8 18.♘e3 ♘b8 19.♕h5 ♔g7 20.♕f3 ♔h7 21.♘d5 ♗xd5 22.exd5 e4 23.♕f4 ♖d6 24.♖e2 ♘d7 25.♖xe4 ♘e5 26.♗b3 ♔g8 27.c4 b6 28.♗c2 ♕f8 29.♖e3 ♖g5 30.♗f5 ♔h8 31.♖fe1 a5 32.b3 c6 33.dxc6 ♖xc6 34.h4 ♖g8 35.♖d1 a4 36.♖d8 ♕g7 37.♖xg8+ ♔xg8 38.♖g3 and Black resigned.

10.♘a3

A) Young prodigy Gukesh beat veteran Alexandrov with 10.c3 in Mumbai 2019, but 10...♘e6 favors Black;

B) 10.♖f2 ♕c5 11.♗xf6 gxf6 12.♘d2 (-0.42) is a decent alternative for White, but 12...♘e6 13.♕h5 ♗d7, planning to castle queenside, still favors Black.

10....♖g8!

This is a computer move if ever there was one! This move was called to the attention of the chess world in New In Chess *Yearbook* 91, where Genna Sosonko described how Roman Dzindzichashvili discovered it when analyzing with Rybka. The drawback is that if you play this move you may be accused of cheating, so be prepared to cite this book as your source for the idea! The idea is that Black does not yet know if he should play ...♗e6, ...♘e6, or ...♗d7, so he plays a move that is non-committal but will be fully useful whenever White takes on f6, which is pretty much inevitable. So White responds with a useful non-committal move of his own.

A human continuation (also favored by Lc0) is 10...♗d7 11.♕e1 ♘e6 12.♗xf6 gxf6 13.♕e3 ♖g8 14.♖f2 ♖g6 15.♖af1 ♘f4 16.♔h1 a6 17.g3 ♘e6N 18.♘b1 ♘d4 (-0.57) and White's compensation looks inadequate.

11.♔h1

Lc0 says 11.♕d3 h6 12.♗e3, while favoring Black, is less favorable than the 10...♗d7 line above, so it doesn't approve of 10...♖g8, and I'm inclined to agree.

11...♗d7 12.♕e1 0-0-0 13.♕h4

13.♕f2! ♗e6 14.♖ae1 a6 15.c3 ♘c6 16.♕e2 ♔b8 (-0.31). White has insufficient compensation for the pawn.

13...♗c6 14.♖ae1 ♘e6 15.♗xf6 gxf6 16.♕xf6 ♕xf6 17.♖xf6 ♘g5 18.♗d3 ♘xe4 19.♖xf7 ♘c5 20.♗f1 ♖d2 21.♖xe5 ♖dxg2 22.♗xg2 ♗xg2+

23.♔g1 ♗d5+ 24.♔f2 ♗xf7 25.♖xc5 b6 26.♖e5 a6

Black is better for two reasons. Rook and bishop are considered a better 'team' in the endgame than rook and knight (though I have never been able to prove this with statistics), and of course the knight is badly placed on the rim. Of course White has good drawing chances.

Game 21.2   Italian Game
Jose Fernando Cubas   2430
Sandro Mareco   2470
Santos 2008 (8)

1.e4 e5 2.♘f3 ♘c6 3.♗c4 ♗c5 4.c3 ♘f6 5.d4 exd4

6.cxd4

6.e5 d5 7.♗b5 (7.♗e2 ♘e4 8.cxd4 ♗b6) 7...♘e4 8.cxd4 ♗b6 9.♘c3 0-0 10.♗e3 ♗g4 11.♕c2 (11.h3 ♗h5 12.♕c2 is a slight improvement and rather critical, see White book for analysis) 11...♗xf3 12.gxf3 ♘g5 13.♗xc6 bxc6 14.0-0-0 ♘xf3 15.♕e2 ♘h4 16.♖hg1 f6 17.♕h5 ♘g6 18.♖g3 ♖e8N 19.f4 fxe5 20.fxe5 ♕h4 21.♕e2 ♕e7 22.♕h5 with a draw by repetition.

6....♗b4+ 7.♗d2

This simple line is rarely seen at high level any more, as it is considered drawish. I think that it is rather underestimated, as there appear to be two ways for White to obtain at least a microscopic edge, as noted in this game.
Greco's 7.♘c3?! is a dubious gambit: 7...♘xe4 8.0-0 ♗xc3 9.d5 (after 9.bxc3 d5 White's only compensation for the pawn is the bishop pair – not enough) 9...♗f6 10.♖e1 ♘e7 11.♖xe4 d6 12.♗g5 (in case of the bayonet attack 12.g4 0-0 13.g5 ♗e5 14.♘xe5 ♗f5! Black is clearly better) 12...♗xg5 13.♘xg5 h6 14.♕e2 hxg5 15.♖e1 ♗e6 16.dxe6 f6 17.♖e3 c6 18.♖h3 ♖xh3 19.gxh3 g6

analysis diagram

20.♕f3 (or 20.♖d1 ♔f8 21.h4 gxh4 22.♖d4 ♔g7 23.♖xh4 ♕a5, and Black plans to exchange rooks on h8 with a solid extra pawn) 20...♕a5 21.♖e2 (in case of 21.♕xf6 ♕xe1+ 22.♗f1 0-0-0 23.♕xe7 ♕e4 24.b4 d5N Black is up a safe exchange) 21...♕f5 22.♕a3 ♕b1+ 23.♔g2 ♘f5 24.f3 ♕d1N – Black is winning, with an attack plus an extra pawn.

7....♗xd2+

In my first book I recommended 7...♘xe4 (Black should probably choose this line if he must avoid a draw, as explained in the note to move 12) 8.♗xb4 ♘xb4 9.♗xf7+ ♔xf7 10.♕b3+ ♔f8! (probably better than 10...d5 11.♘e5+ ♔e6 12.♕xb4 as given in that book) 11.♕xb4+ ♕e7 12.♕xe7+ ♔xe7 13.0-0 ♘f6 14.♖e1+ ♔d8 15.♘c3 d6 16.d5 ♖e8 17.♘d4 ♖xe1+ 18.♖xe1 ♗d7 19.f3 c5 20.dxc6 bxc6 21.♔f2 c5 22.♘de2 ♖b8 23.b3 ♖b4 (-0.06). Although this is a drawn endgame, Black has some practical chances since bishop vs knight favors the bishop when there are opposing pawn majorities. So in this revised edition I'm back to recommending 7...♘xe4, but I still give the main line as well for those who don't mind a draw as Black.

8.♘bxd2

The gambit 8.♕xd2?! was played and recommended by GM Ian Rogers, who wrote a favorable article on it in *Secrets of Opening Surprises* 13. It looks to me quite unsound for multiple reasons:

8...♘xe4 9.♕e3 d5! 10.♗xd5 ♕xd5
11.♘c3 and now:

A) 11...♕f5 12.♘xe4 0-0 13.0-0
♗e6 14.♖fe1. So far this is given by
Rogers in SOS. Now 14...h6 seems
to give Black the better chances,
rather than his 14...♗d5, when
15.♘g3 cannot be met by 15...♕b5.

B) 11...♕c4!N 12.♕xe4+ ♗e6
13.♘e5:

B1) 13...♕xd4 14.♘xc6 ♕xe4+
15.♘xe4 ♗d5! 16.♘a5 ♗xe4 17.0-0-0
♗xg2 18.♖hg1 ♗h3 19.♖xg7 (19.♘xb7
0-0 with a safe extra pawn) 19...♖b8
20.♘b3 b6 White has some but not
sufficient compensation for the
missing pawn;

B2) Also strong, but only my
second choice, is 13...♘xe5 14.♕xe5
(if 14.dxe5?! 0-0-0 and Black is
much better, as he has good bishop
for knight with opposing majorities,
and White cannot castle) 14...f6
15.♕c5 ♕xc5 16.dxc5 0-0-0 17.0-0
♖d2 and Black is surely better with
his rook on the 7th rank. Also after
a rook trade Black will have the
favorable combination of rook and
bishop vs rook and knight.

8....d5 9.exd5 ♘xd5

10.♕b3

10.0-0 0-0 11.♖c1 (I recommended
this line for White in New In Chess
Yearbook 95) 11...♘b6 12.♗b3 a5 13.a4
♘d5 14.♖e1 ♘db4 – Black's knight
is strong on b4 and White has an
isolated d-pawn, but White has
much better development. I would
choose White if given the choice,
but I think his advantage is tiny.
10....♘a5 11.♕a4+ ♘c6 12.♘e5

A) If 12.♗b5 ♗d7 13.0-0 0-0
White's slight development edge
offsets his isolated pawn;

B) 12.♕a3! (this strong move has
been played and recommended
by GM Roman Dzindzichashvili)
12...♕e7+ 13.♕xe7+ ♘cxe7 14.0-0
(White has a par +37 Elo result from
here in 22 games) 14...♗d7 15.♖fe1
0-0-0.

analysis diagram

White's knights have good squares
on e4, e5, and c5, but he has an
isolated center pawn. I would rather
play White here, but it is very close
to equal;

C) 12.♕b3 amounts to offering
a draw. If Black doesn't want to
repeat, he must try 12...♘ce7.
Practical results from this position
are slightly below par for Black,

and the engines love White as his development edge is worth more than enough to offset the isolated pawn. So if you must avoid a draw, play this slightly worse position or else vary as noted on move 7.

12....0-0 13.♘xc6?!

After 13.♗xd5 ♘xe5 14.♗e4 ♘g4 15.0-0 ♕d6 16.♘f3 ♘f6 17.♗c2 ♗e6 18.♖fe1 a5N it's hard to see much compensation for White's isolated pawn.

13....♕e8+ 14.♔f1

If 14.♔d1 ♘b6 15.♕b5 bxc6 16.♕e5 ♕d8, Black is better due to king safety.

14....♘b6 15.♕b5 bxc6 16.♕c5

16....♘xc4N

The **actual game** went 16...♗e6 17.b3 ♖d8 18.♖e1 ♘xc4 19.♘xc4 ♖d5 20.♕xa7 ♕a8 (20...♕d8!) 21.♕xa8 ♖xa8 22.♔e2 ♖xa2+ 23.♔f3 ♖b5 (23...♖f5+!) 24.♖b1 ♗f5 (24...♖f5+!) 25.♖bf1? (25.♖a1 ♖xb3+ 26.♘e3) 25...♖xb3+ 26.♔f4? (26.♘e3 h5) 26...g6 27.♘e5 c5 28.dxc5 ♖a4+ 29.♔g5 ♔g7 30.♘d7 and White resigned in view of 30...h6 mate.

17.♘xc4

After 17.♕xc4 ♗e6 18.♕c3 ♖d8 Black's much better development

and potential bishop outpost on d5 trump his bad pawns.

17....♕e4 18.♖e1 ♕c2 19.♘e5 ♕xc5 20.dxc5 ♗a6+ 21.♔g1 ♖fe8

White's undeveloped rook is a bigger problem than Black's poor pawn structure.

Game 21.3   Italian Game

Hikaru Nakamura   2799
Anish Giri   2776
Khanty-Mansiysk 2015 (3)

1.e4 e5 2.♘f3 ♘c6 3.♗c4 ♗c5 4.c3 ♘f6 5.d4 exd4 6.cxd4 ♗b4+ 7.♘bd2

This modern gambit has been championed by Jonny Hector, but it just simplifies to a draw.

7...♘xe4

7...♗xd2+ is a better choice for a must-win game, but the game move is safer. After 8.♗xd2 ♘xe4 9.d5 ♘e7 10.♗b4 0-0 11.0-0 d6 12.♖e1 ♘c5 13.♕d2 b6 14.♗c3 a5 (+0.06) Black is up half a pawn, but his backward c-pawn and White's space advantage make the game equal.

8.d5

8.0-0 ♘xd2 9.♗xd2 ♗xd2 10.♕xd2 ♘e7∓ (-0.31). Without the bishop pair, White's space advantage isn't worth a pawn.

8...♘xd2 9.♗xd2 ♗xd2+ 10.♕xd2 ♘e7 11.d6 cxd6 12.0-0 d5 13.♗xd5 0-0 14.♖ad1 ♘xd5 15.♕xd5 d6 16.♕xd6 ♕xd6 17.♖xd6 ♗e6 18.a3 ♖fd8 19.♖d4 ♖xd4 20.♘xd4 ♖d8 21.♖d1 f6 22.f3 ♔f7 23.♔f2 ♖d5

Although rook and bishop tend to be superior to rook and knight, the symmetrical pawns favor the knight so this endgame is fully equal.

24.♔e3 ♖e5+ 25.♔d3 ♖c5 26.♖e1 ♗d7 27.♔d2 ♖d5 28.♔c3 ♖c5+ 29.♔d2 ♖d5 30.♔c3 ♖c5+ 31.♔d2

Repetition (0.00).

½-½

Game 21.4 Italian Game
Shakhriyar Mamedyarov 2804
Vladimir Kramnik 2787
Wijk aan Zee 2018 (9)

1.e4 e5 2.♘f3 ♘c6 3.♗c4 ♗c5 4.c3 ♘f6 5.d3 0-0 6.0-0

6.b4 ♗e7! 7.0-0 d5 8.exd5 ♘xd5 9.♖e1 a6 10.a4 ♗g4 11.h3 ♗h5. Black has no problems (0.00). The pawns on b4 and a4 make more sense when the black bishop is on the queenside.

6...d5

This is a good reaction when White has played c2-c3 early, as the d3-pawn or square may become weak.

7.exd5 ♘xd5

8.a4

8.♖e1 ♗g4 9.h3 ♗h5 10.♘bd2 ♘b6 11.♗b5 ♗d6 12.♘e4 f5 13.♘g3 ♗xf3 14.♕xf3 ♕d7 15.a4 a6 16.♗xc6 ♕xc6 17.♕xc6 bxc6 18.♘f1 a5 19.♘d2 ♘d7 20.♘c4 ♘c5= (+0.05). Black's pawn structure is worse, but his pieces are better placed to annoy the opponent's pawns.

8...♗f5

Rare but satisfactory.

9.♖e1 ♘b6 10.♗b5 ♘e7 11.a5 c6 12.axb6 cxb5 13.♗e3 axb6 14.♖xa8 ♕xa8

15.♗xc5

15.♘xe5 ♕a2 16.b4 ♗d6 17.♗d4
♘d5= (-0.16). Black's bishop pair
and superior development offset
the tripled pawns, which are on a
closed file so not fatally weak.
15...bxc5 16.♖xe5 ♕d8 17.d4 cxd4
18.♘xd4 ♗xb1 19.♕xb1 b4 20.♖b5
bxc3 21.bxc3 ♘d5 22.♕d3 ♘f4
23.♕f3 ♘e6= (+0.07) 24.♖xb7 ♘xd4
25.cxd4 ♕xd4 26.g3 g6 27.h4 h5
½-½

Game 21.5   Italian Game
Sergey Karjakin   2773
Le Quang Liem   2739
St Louis 2017 (17)

1.e4 e5 2.♘f3 ♘c6 3.♗c4 ♗c5 4.0-0
♘f6 5.d3 0-0

This move order with quick castling
for White is fashionable, but it has
the drawback of making ♗g5 less
effective due to ..h7-h6 and ...g7-g5.
6.c3 allows 6...d5 as in the previous
game. 6.a4 is met by 6...a5 or by
6...h6 7.c3 a5 as in the next game;
normally White plays a2-a4 only in
response to ...a7-a6.
6.h3

6.♖e1 ♘g4 7.♖e2 ♘d4, exchanging
his offside knight for White's better
knight, eases Black's problems:
8.♘xd4 ♗xd4 9.h3 ♘f6 10.c3 ♗b6
11.♗g5 h6 12.♗h4 g5 13.♗g3 d6
14.♖e1 h5 15.d4 h4 16.♗h2 g4
17.♕d3 ♘h5 18.hxg4 ♗xg4 19.♘d2
♕f6 20.♘f1 ♗e6= (0.00). Black's
kingside initiative offsets his
inferior pawn structure.
6...d6 7.c3 ♘e7 8.d4 ♗b6 9.♗d3
9.♖e1 ♘g6 10.♗d3 transposes to the
game.
9...♘g6 10.♖e1 c6 11.♘bd2
11.♗e3 d5= (0.05).
11...exd4 12.cxd4 d5 13.e5 ♘h5

14.♘f1
14.♘b3 ♘hf4 15.♗xf4 ♘xf4 16.♕d2
♘e6 17.♗f5 ♕e7 18.♕c2 ♔h8=
(+0.08). Black's bishop pair offsets
White's space advantage.
14...♘hf4 15.♗xg6 fxg6
Black actually took back with the
knight and was worse and went on
to lose. The test is an equalizing
improvement.
16.♗xf4 ♖xf4 17.♖e3 ♕e7= (0.00)
The bishop pair and f-file pressure
easily offset White's protected
passed pawn.

Game 21.6   Italian Game
Viswanathan Anand   2782
Wesley So   2788

London 2017 (9)

1.e4 e5 2.♘f3 ♘c6 3.♗c4 ♗c5 4.0-0 ♘f6 5.d3 0-0

6.a4
6.♘bd2 d6 (White has avoided 6.c3 d5, but has lost the chance to meet ...d7-d6 by ♗g5, making ...h7-h6 unnecessary) 7.c3 a6, and now:

A) 8.a4 ♗a7 9.h3 ♘e7 10.♖e1 ♘g6 11.d4 c6 12.♗d3 ♘h5 13.♗c2 ♘hf4 14.♘f1 exd4 15.♘xd4 d5 16.♘g3 dxe4 17.♘xe4 ♗xd4 18.cxd4 ♗f5 19.♕f3 ♗xe4 20.♖xe4 ♘e6 21.♕e3 ♘e7 22.♕d3 g6 23.♗d2 ♘d5 24.♗b3 ♕d7= (+0.13).

White's weak d-pawn and Black's outposted knight offset the bishop pair;

B) 8.♗b3 ♗a7 9.h3 h6 (an immediate 9...♗e6 is playable, but then White might trade bishops to double the pawns. So Black plays a useful move and waits for ♖e1 before offering the trade) 10.♖e1 ♗e6 (now trading bishops on e6 is less attractive for White as f2 is weak) 11.♘f1 ♗xb3 12.♕xb3 ♕d7 13.♗e3 ♗xe3 14.♘xe3 ♖fe8 15.♖ad1 ♘e7 16.♕c2 ♘g6= (+0.07).

White has only a cosmetic advantage.
6...h6 7.c3 a5 8.♘bd2 d6 9.h3

9...♗e6
9...♘e7 10.♖e1 ♘g6 11.♘f1 c6 12.♗b3 ♖e8 13.♘g3 d5 14.exd5 ♘xd5 15.d4

exd4 16.♖xe8+ ♕xe8 17.♗xd5 cxd5
18.♘xd4 ♗d7= (+0.03).

The bishop pair offsets the isolani.
**10.♖e1 ♗xc4 11.♘xc4 ♖e8 12.♗e3
♗xe3 13.♘xe3 ♕d7 14.♕b3 ♘e7
15.♘c4 ♘g6 16.♖ad1 b6 17.♕c2
d5 18.exd5 ♕xd5 19.b3 ♖ad8 20.d4
exd4 21.♖xd4 ♖xe1+ 22.♘xe1
♕a8=**

23.♖xd8+?!
23.♘e3 ♖xd4 24.cxd4=.
**23...♕xd8 24.♕d3 ♕e7 25.♘c2 ♘f4
26.♕d2 ♘6d5 27.♔f1**

27...♘xc3
27...♕e4∓.
28.♘4e3?
28.♘xb6! cxb6 29.♕xc3 ♕e2+
30.♔g1 ♕e4 31.f3 ♕g6 32.♕c8+
♔h7 33.♘e1 h5∓ (-0.20) Black is
obviously for choice, but a draw is
still likely.

28...♘e4–+ 29.♕d4 c5 30.♕d1 ♕f6
31.♘g4 ♕c3 32.♘ce3 h5 33.♘h2
♕b2 0-1

Game 21.7   Italian Game
Anish Giri   2779
Wesley So   2754
Zagreb 2019 (3)

1.e4 e5 2.♘f3 ♘c6 3.♗c4 ♗c5 4.0-0
4.c3 ♘f6 5.d3 d6 6.0-0 0-0
(Caruana-So, Zagreb 2019) 7.h3
transposed to this game. Wesley So
seems to be following the rule of
castling for Black only after White
castles, which takes the sting out of
♗g5 ideas.
**4...♘f6 5.d3 0-0 6.h3 d6 7.c3 a6
8.♖e1**
8.a4 h6 9.♖e1 ♗a7 Caruana-So,
Zagreb 2019, when 10.♘bd2
transposes back to this game.
**8...h6 9.♘bd2 ♗a7 10.a4 ♖e8 11.b4
♗e6 12.♗xe6 ♖xe6**

13.♗b2
  A) 13.♘b3 ♘e7 14.♘h4 d5 15.♕e2
(15.♕c2 ♖c8=) 15...♕d7!= (0.00).
This is better than 15...♖d6 as in
Caruana-So, Zagreb 2019, which was
drawn in 33 moves;

B) 13.♕c2 ♛d7 14.♘f1 d5 15.♗e3 ♗xe3 16.♘xe3 ♖ae8 17.b5 ♘e7 18.♖eb1 ♘g6 19.c4 d4 20.♘f5 ♖a8= (+0.00). Black can challenge the knight on f5 by ...♘e7, possibly leading to a repetition of position.

13...b5?!

13...♘e7! 14.♘f1 (14.d4 ♘g6 15.♕c2 ♛d7=) 14...♘g6 15.c4 (15.♘g3 d5 16.c4 dxc4 17.dxc4 ♕f8 18.♗c3 ♖d8= (+0.03), Lc0 +0.05. White has just a bit more space) 15...♘h7 16.♘g3 ♘g5 17.♘f5 ♘xf3+ 18.♕xf3 ♘h4 19.♕g3 ♘xf5 20.exf5 ♖f6 21.♕f3 ♖b8= (-0.09), Lc0 +0.10. White has more space but a worse pawn structure.

14.d4 ♖e8 15.axb5 axb5 16.♕e2 exd4 17.♕xb5 dxc3 18.♗xc3 ♘e5

19.♕b7

19.♘xe5 dxe5 20.♘f3 ♗b6 21.♖xa8 ♕xa8 22.♗xe5±.

19...♗b6 20.♗xe5 dxe5 21.♖xa8 ♕xa8 22.♕xa8 ♖xa8 23.♘xe5 ♗d4 24.♘c6 ♗c3 25.♖d1 ♗xd2 26.♖xd2 ♘xe4 27.♖e2 ♘d6 28.♖c2 ♖a1+ 29.♔h2 ♔f8 30.♘e5 ♖a7 31.♘c6 ♖a1 32.♘e5 ♖a7 33.♘c6 ♖a1 ½-½

CHAPTER 22

Spanish offshoots

In this chapter we consider all the ways White can vary from the main line of the Spanish (Ruy Lopez) Opening from moves four through nine. These are sidelines for a reason; generally speaking Black can achieve approximate equality if he follows my recommendations. Moreover Black has fair winning chances in most of these lines; my own record as Black in these sidelines is extremely good. But if you are unprepared, they can be rather dangerous.

The idea of the Spanish move 3.♗b5 is to exert indirect pressure on the e5-pawn, hoping to wring a concession from Black. It turns out that the 'threat' to win a pawn is an illusion, because after 4.♗xc6 dxc6 5.♘xe5? ♕d4 6.♘f3 ♕xe4 Black will just be up the bishop pair in an open position with queens exchanged, which favours the bishop pair. But once e4 is guarded Black usually responds to the threat by ...b7-b5, which at least gives White the option of a queenside attack starting with a2-a4. In general I recommend meeting a2-a4 with ...♗d7, assuming it is legal. Black should not play ...b7-b5 too early, because of potential problems on f7 if he is not yet ready to castle.

Let's look at the moves one by one now.
1.e4 e5 Beginners are taught that this is the best move, for good reason.
2.♘f3 ♘c6 and now:
3.♗b5

This, the Spanish or Ruy Lopez, is the main white weapon in master play. There is no easy route to equality for Black.

3...a6 For the Berlin 3...♘f6 see *Chess Advantage*. The text gives Black the option of chasing off the bishop later.

4.♗a4 A very important alternative is 4.♗xc6 dxc6 5.0-0, which I recommended for White in my first book.

analysis diagram

It was a favorite of Bobby Fischer and is still moderately popular in grandmaster play. The defense 5...f6 6.d4 ♗g4 comes close to equality (Game 22.1). In my opinion there is only one path to full equality for Black, namely 5...♗g4, which I give in Game 22.2. The idea is to offer the bishop after 6.h3 h5. White can't accept immediately but may do so later, or may choose to provoke an early endgame.

4...♘f6 5.0-0 White invites Black to play the 'Open' defense by taking on e4. White will win back the pawn, with a slight edge in general. I'm not recommending the Open Spanish for Black. Instead White can defend the pawn by 5.d3, which we meet by 5...d6 followed by ...g7-g6 and ...♗g7 (Game 22.3) (5...♗c5 is also fine and in the notes), which should give us something like an improved version of the Breyer. The Center Attack 5.d4 (Game 22.4) peters out to at least equality for Black. The Wormald Attack 5.♕e2 (or its brother the Worrall Attack 6.♕e2) is well met by playing as in the Marshall Attack, which is totally sound in this case. See Game 22.5.

5...♗e7 This is the conservative move; I don't believe in early aggression for Black, although I added a chapter on 5...♗c5 to this edition.

analysis diagram

6.♖e1 White hopes for 6...0-0 7.♗xc6 dxc6 8.♘xe5, winning a pawn. Instead 6.d3 is met by 6...b5 7.♗b3 d6! 8.a4 ♗d7 (see Game 22.6), while 6.d4 and 6.♕e2 transpose to lines mentioned in the previous note. The Deferred Exchange Variation 6.♗xc6 dxc6 (Game 22.7) requires some study, as each white seventh move requires different treatment, but Black has equality if he learns the lines.

6...b5 7.♗b3 d6 Black can also choose the move order 7...0-0 to 'bluff' White into avoiding 8.c3 for fear of the Marshall Attack 8...d5 even if his real intent is to play the Breyer, not the Marshall. See Chapter 24 for this. The only real drawback is that 8.a4 cannot be answered by 8...♗d7, but 8...b4 is probably just as good.

8.c3 Instead, 8.h3 or 8.d3 loses the bishop pair to 8...♘a5, while 8.d4 could land White in the famous Noah's Ark trap after Black exchanges twice on d4 and plays ...c7-c5 and ...c5-c4 (I fell into that trap as a teenager and won the game anyway!). So White just prepares d2-d4 and makes a retreat for his bishop.

8...0-0 9.h3 Here 9.d3 is met by ...♘a5, ...c7-c5, ...♘c6, ...♖e8, ...h7-h6, ...♗e6, and ...♗f8 with equality (see Game 22.8), while 9.d4 is met by 9...♗g4. Then 10.d5 ♘a5 11.♗c2 c6 12.h3 ♗c8! 13.dxc6 ♕c7 (to recapture on c6 with the queen) equalizes (Game 22.9). Instead, 10.♗e3 may be the most dangerous of White's Spanish offshoots. I meet it with 10...exd4 11.cxd4 d5 12.e5 ♘e4, which is at least pretty close to equal (Game 22.10).

Now we reach the most important ninth move position in chess. Black usually plays either 9...♘a5 (Chigorin) or 9...♗b7 (Zaitsev) or 9...♘b8 (Breyer), which I recommend.

Game 22.1   Ruy Lopez/Spanish –
             Exchange Variation

Jan Smeets   2647
Ivan Sokolov   2645

Boxtel ch-NED 2011 (2)

1.e4 e5 2.♘f3 ♘c6 3.♗b5 a6 4.♗xc6 dxc6 5.0-0 f6

I prefer 5...♗g4 as in the next game, but I give this as a backup line.

6.d4 ♗g4 7.dxe5 ♛xd1 8.♖xd1 fxe5

9.♘bd2

9.♖d3 ♗d6 10.♘bd2 ♘f6 (10...
b5 11.h3 ♗e6 12.a4 ♘f6 13.b3
♘d7 14.♗b2) 11.♘c4 0-0 12.♘fxe5
(12.♘cxe5 ♗h5) 12...♗e2 13.♖e3
♗xc4 14.♘xc4 ♘g4 (14...♗c5 15.♖e1
♘g4 16.♗e3 ♗xe3 17.♘xe3 ♘xf2
18.♘c4 ♖ae8 19.e5 ♘g4 20.h3 ♘h6
21.♖ad1 ♖e6) 15.♖f3 (15.♖e2 ♗xh2+
16.♔h1 ♗g3 17.f3 ♘e5 (17...♖f6
18.♗d2 ♖af8 19.♔g1 ♗h2+ 20.♔f1
♗g3 21.♖d1 ♖d8 22.♔g1 ♘e5 23.♘e3)
18.♘xe5 ♗xe5 19.♗e3 ♖ad8 20.♔g1
b6 21.c3 ♗g3 22.♔f1 c5) 15...♗c5N
16.♖xf8+ ♔xf8 17.♗e3 ♘xe3
18.♘xe3 ♖e8 19.♖d1 ♖xe4 20.♖d7
♗xe3 21.fxe3 ♖xe3 22.♖xc7 ♖e7
23.♖c8+ ♔f7=.

**9....0-0-0 10.♖e1 ♖e8 11.h3 ♗h5
12.b3**

12.g4 ♗f7 13.♘g5 ♘h6N (13...♗g6
14.♘df3 h6 15.♘h4 ♗h5 16.♘gf3
♗f7 17.b3 ♗d6 18.♘f5 g6 19.♘xd6+
cxd6 20.♘h4 ♘f6 21.♗d2) 14.♘xf7
(14.b3 ♗g6 15.♘df3 ♘f7 16.♘xf7
♗xf7 17.♗b2 ♗d6 18.♔g2 h5=)
14...♘xf7 15.♘f3 ♗b4 16.c3 ♗c5
17.♔g2 ♖hf8=. The backward pawn
on f2 and hole on f4 offset the black
crippled majority.

**12....♗b4 13.g4 ♗f7 14.♗b2 ♘f6
15.♖ad1 ♘d7 16.a3 ♗d6 17.♘g5
♗g8 18.♔g2 ♖f8 19.♘f1 g6 20.♘f3
h5 21.♘g5 b5 22.♖d2**

22....hxg4N

In the **actual game** Black omitted
this exchange, and after 22...♖f4
23.f3 he was reluctant to exchange
because White could take back with
the f-pawn, and soon White played
gxh5 and won.

The text move avoids this and
equalizes.

**23.hxg4 ♖f4 24.f3 ♔b7 25.♖ed1
♖f6=**

Black's bishop pair offsets White's
better pawn structure. It is hard for
either side to initiate action here,
though Black can try ...a7-a5 and
...a5-a4.

**Game 22.2   Ruy Lopez/Spanish –
Exchange Variation**

Maxime Vachier-Lagrave   2718
Alexey Shirov   2730

Germany Bundesliga 2009/10 (14)

1.e4 e5 2.♘f3 ♘c6 3.♗b5 a6 4.♗xc6 dxc6 5.0-0

After 5.♘c3 f6 6.d4 exd4 7.♘xd4 c5 8.♘de2 ♕xd1+ 9.♘xd1 ♗e6 10.♗f4 0-0-0 11.♘e3 ♘e7 12.♖d1 ♖xd1+ 13.♔xd1 g5 14.♗g3 f5 15.♗e5 ♖g8 16.♘c3 ♖g6N 17.b3 ♗d7 Black's bishop pair more than compensates for his crippled majority.

5....♗g4

I've played 5...♕f6 here, which is not bad but not quite equal.

6.h3 h5

I believe that this line is the only full equalizer to the Spanish Exchange Variation, which I recommended for White in my previous book. I have also played the gambit line with 6...♗h5 which offers good practical chances for a pawn, but White can return the pawn and keep a slight edge.

7.d3

7.c3 ♕d3 8.hxg4 hxg4 9.♘xe5 ♗d6 10.♘xd3 ♗h2 leads to perpetual check. This draw has happened in at least 400 games, first in Adorjan-Karpov, Groningen Ech-jr 1967/68. If a draw just won't do for Black, 7...♕f6 8.d4 ♗xf3 9.♕xf3 ♕xf3 10.gxf3 exd4 11.cxd4 ♘e7 has a near-zero eval by both engines and a 4 to 3 plus score for Black in my database.

7...♕f6

This line was considered the 'refutation' of 5.0-0 until Bobby Fischer took up the White side and showed that the existing analysis was wrong. However now things have gone full circle and this line once again looks best and rather pleasant for Black.

8.♘bd2

8.♗e3 ♗xf3 9.♕xf3 ♕xf3 10.gxf3 ♗d6 11.♘d2 ♘e7 12.♖fd1 ♘g6 13.♔f1 ♘f8 14.♘b3 ♘e6 15.d4 (Meier-Ganguly, Germany Bundesliga 2018/19) 15...0-0-0 16.c4 ♖he8 (+0.08).

8....♘e7

Noteworthy is 8...g5 9.♘c4 ♗xf3 10.♕xf3 ♕xf3 11.gxf3 f6 12.h4 (12.♖d1 ♘e7 13.♘e3 was agreed drawn here in Solak-Sethuraman, Novi Sad 2016, but Black is already slightly for choice after 13...♖d8) 12...gxh4 13.f4 b5 14.♘a5 exf4 15.♗xf4 ♔d7. Black plans ...♗d6 when his extra pawn and good king position for the endgame offset his poor pawn structure. Engine scores near zero.

9.♖e1

A) If 9.hxg4 hxg4 10.g3 gxf3
11.♕xf3 ♕e6 Black has a much safer
king at no cost;

B) 9.♘c4 ♗xf3 10.♕xf3 ♕xf3
11.gxf3 ♘g6 12.♗e3 ♗e7 13.♖fd1
0-0-0 14.♔f1 c5 15.c3 b6 16.a3 a5
(0.00). White's only active plans,
d3-d4 and b2-b4, both allow Black
to undouble his pawns and equalize.
9....♘g6 10.d4

In case of 10.hxg4 hxg4 11.g3 ♗c5
12.♘b3 ♗b6 13.♗g5 ♕xf3 14.♕xf3
gxf3 15.♘d2 f6 16.♗e3 ♗xe3 17.♖xe3
♘f8 18.♘xf3 ♘e6 Black's superior
piece placement outweighs his
doubled pawns.
10....♘f4!?

Fischer investigated Barendregt's
discovery 10...♗d6 11.hxg4 hxg4
12.♘h2 ♖xh2 13.♕xg4.

11.hxg4

11.dxe5 ♕g6 12.♘h4 ♗xd1 13.♘xg6
♘xg6 14.♖xd1 0-0-0 15.♖e1
(perhaps better is 15.e6 fxe6 16.♖e1
♘e5 17.♘b3 ♗e7 18.♗d2 ♗f6 19.♗c3
b6 20.♘d4 ♖he8 21.♖ad1 c5 22.♘e2
b5 23.b3 h4= (+0.07). Black's better
piece placement and space edge
make up for his inferior pawn
structure) 15...♘xe5 16.♘f1?! (after
16.♘f3 ♗b4 17.c3 ♘xf3+ 18.gxf3
♗c5 19.♔f1 ♖d3 both sides have
bad pawns but Black has more
active pieces) 16...♗b4 17.c3 ♘d3
18.♖e2 ♗c5 19.♗e3 ♗xe3 20.♘xe3
♘f4 21.♖c2 ♖he8 22.f3 ♖d3 23.♖e1
♖ed8 – Black's domination of the
open file and his knight outpost
count for more than the crippled
majority.
11....hxg4 12.g3

12.♘h2? ♘xg2!.
**12....gxf3 13.♕xf3 ♘e6 14.dxe5
♕xe5**

14...♕g6 15.♘b3 ♖h5 16.♔g2 0-0-0
17.♗f4 ♘xf4+ 18.♕xf4 ♕e6 19.♖ad1
♖e8 is also fully equal, because
20.♕e3 ♔b8 21.f4 g5! favors Black.

15.♕f5

After 15.♘b3 ♗d6 16.♔g2 0-0-0
17.♗d2 ♔b8 18.♖h1 ♘g5 19.♗xg5

♕xg5 Black's safer king and better minor piece offset his crippled majority.

15....♕b5 16.♘f3 g6 17.♕xb5 axb5 18.c3 b4 19.cxb4 ♗xb4 20.♖e2 ♖d8=

Black's more active pieces offset the crippled majority. The doubled pawn may prove useful after ...c6-c5 and ...♘d4.

21.♗e3 ♗c5 22.♗xc5 ♘xc5 23.♖c1 ♘e6 24.♖cc2

24....♖d1+

24...♔e7, planning ...c6-c5, looks fine.

25.♖e1 ♖d3 26.♘e5 ♖d8 27.♔g2 ♔e7 28.f4 ♖h5 29.♔f2 ♘c5 30.♖e3 ♖d1 31.f5 ♔f6 32.♘g4+ ♔g5 33.♘e5 ♔f6 34.♘g4+ ♔g5 35.♘h2 gxf5 36.♖xf5+ ♔g6 37.♘f3 ♖xf5 38.exf5+ ♔f6 39.g4 ♘d3 40.♔g3 b5

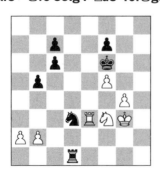

41.g5+ ♔xf5 42.♖e7 ♔g6 43.♖xc7 ♖c1 44.b3 ½-½

Game 22.3   Ruy Lopez/Spanish
Alexander Areschenko   2694
Zahar Efimenko   2701
Kiev ch-UKR 2011 (8)

1.e4 e5 2.♘f3 ♘c6 3.♗b5 a6 4.♗a4 ♘f6 5.d3 d6

Also fine is 5...♗c5 6.c3 b5 7.♗b3 (7.♗c2 d5!=) 7...d6 8.0-0 h6 9.♘bd2 0-0 10.♖e1 ♗b6 11.♘f1 ♖e8 12.♘g3 ♗e6 (+0.03).

This is almost identical to our main line defense to the quiet Italian, except ...b7-b5 is on the board for free.

6.c3 g6!

This shows the drawback to playing d2-d3 before Black plays ...♗e7. In the Breyer Black often plays ...♖e8, ...♗f8, ...g7-g6, and ...♗g7. Here Black gets to do this maneuver saving two or three tempi!

7.0-0

7.♗g5 ♗g7 8.♘bd2 h6 9.♗h4 0-0 10.♘f1 d5 (a good alternative is 10...♘e7 11.♘e3 c6 12.♗b3 ♘h5, which is balanced) 11.exd5 ♕xd5

12.♘e3 ♕d6 13.♘c4 ♕d5 14.♘e3
♕d6 leads to a draw by repetition,
which Black can avoid by 14...♕e6
or 12...♕e6.

7....♗g7 8.♖e1 0-0 9.♘bd2

9.♗g5 h6 10.♗h4 b5 11.♗c2 ♕d7
12.♘bd2 ♘h5 13.♘f1 ♗b7 14.♘e3
♖ae8 15.a4 ♘f4=.

9....b5

10.♗b3

10.♗c2 ♗b7 11.♘f1 (11.a4 b4 12.a5
♖b8 13.♘c4 d5 14.♘cd2 ♗a8=)
11...♘b8 12.♘g3 ♘bd7 13.d4 ♖e8
with equality. Black has reached a
main line position of our Breyer
Defense two tempi up (he has
already played ...♗g7 and White
lacks h3).

10....♘a5 11.♗c2 c5 12.♘f1

In case of 12.d4 cxd4 13.cxd4
exd4 14.♘xd4 ♖e8 15.♘f1 ♗b7
16.♘g3 ♕b6N 17.♘f3 ♘c4 Black is
much better due to his superior
development and pressure on e4.

12....h6 13.♗d2

13.♘g3 ♖e8 14.h3 ♗e6 15.♗e3 ♖c8
16.♕d2 ♔h7=.

**13....♘c6 14.a4 ♗e6 15.♘e3 ♕d7
16.♗b3 ♖fb8 17.♗xe6 ♕xe6 18.h3
c4 19.♕e2 ♘a5 20.axb5 axb5=
21.♖ad1?!**

21....cxd3!

The **actual game** continued 21...♖c8
22.♗c1 ♖ab8= 23.dxc4 bxc4 24.♘d5
♘d7 25.♘b4 ♘c6 26.♘d5 ♘e7
27.♘xe7+ ♕xe7 28.♗e3 ♘f6 29.♕c2
♖c6 30.♖e2?! ♕b7 31.♗c1 ♕b3
32.♕xb3 cxb3 33.♘e1 ♘e8 34.♘d3 f5
35.♘b4 ♖cc8 36.f4 ♔f7 37.fxe5 dxe5
38.exf5 gxf5 39.♖f1 ♔g6 40.♘d5
♖b7 41.♘e3 ♘d6 42.♖d1 ♖c6 43.♘f1
♖a6 44.♘d2 ♗f6 45.♘f3 e4 46.♘d4
♖a1 47.♘e6 ♘c4 48.♘f4+ ♔f7
49.♖f1 ♗g5 50.♖ee1 ♖xb2 51.g4 ♘c4
52.gxf5 ♗xf4 and White resigned.

**22.♕xd3 ♘b3 23.♕c2 ♘c5 24.♘d5
♘xd5 25.exd5 ♕c8**

Black is better due to the artificially
isolated d5-pawn.

Game 22.4   Ruy Lopez/Spanish –
              Center Attack
Samvel Ter Sahakyan   2575
Vladimir Akopian   2675
Aix-les-Bains Ech 2011 (8)

**1.e4 e5 2.♘f3 ♘c6 3.♗b5 ♘f6 4.d4
exd4 5.0-0 a6 6.♗a4 ♗e7**

We would reach this position by
3..a6 4.♗a4 ♘f6 5.d4 exd4 6.0-0
♗e7 or 5.0-0 ♗e7 6.d4 exd4. This
line is called the Center Attack.

7.♖e1

7.e5 ♘e4 8.♘xd4 0-0 9.♘f5 d5 and now:

A) 10.exd6 ♗xf5 11.dxe7 ♕xe7 12.♗xc6 bxc6 13.♕f3;

B) 10.♘xe7+ ♘xe7 11.c3 ♘c5 12.♗c2 ♗f5=. No more bishop pair here means no advantage, as White's remaining bishop is not a good one;

C) 10.♗xc6 bxc6 11.♘xe7+ ♕xe7 12.♖e1 ♖e8 13.f3

analysis diagram

13...♘d6 (New York master Paul Brandts surprised me with this move back in the 1960s) 14.b3 (14.♗f4 ♘f5 15.♕d2 a5N is pleasant for Black) 14...f6 15.♗b2 ♘f7 16.f4 fxe5 17.fxe5 ♗f5 18.♘d2 ♘g5 – Black will be better once his knight blockades on e6, as his bishop is clearly more active than White's.

7....b5 8.♗b3

8.e5 ♘xe5 9.♖xe5 (if 9.♘xe5 bxa4 10.♕xd4 0-0 11.♕xa4 ♖b8 Black's bishop pair compensates for his isolated pawn and White's space advantage) 9...d6! 10.♖e1 bxa4 11.♘xd4 ♗d7 12.♕f3 0-0 13.♘c6 ♗xc6 14.♕xc6 d5 15.♕xa4 (after 15.♗f4 ♗d6 16.♗xd6 ♕xd6 17.♕xd6 Black is better. His extra pawn is almost worthless, but he will be well ahead in development after the tempo-gaining ...♖ab8 and ...♖fc8) 15...♗c5N 16.♘c3 ♖b8 17.a3 (else ...♖b4 and ...♘g4) 17...♕d6 and Black has superior development and more central pawns.

8....d6 9.♗d5 ♘xd5 10.exd5 ♘e5 11.♘xd4 0-0

12.♘c3

12.a4 ♗g4 13.♕d2 (in case of 13.f3 ♗d7 14.♘c3 b4 15.♘e4 ♖e8 16.b3 ♗h4 17.g3 f5 18.♘f2 ♗f6 19.♗b2 ♕b8 White has a weakened king and is down the bishop pair) 13...♗d7 14.♘c3 b4 15.♘ce2 ♕b8 and White has no compensation for the bishop pair.

12....♗g4 13.f3

13.♕d2 ♖e8 14.b3 ♕c8 15.♗b2 ♗d7=; White's space advantage offsets Black's bishops.

13....♗d7 14.f4

14.a4 b4 15.♘e4 transposes to the note to move 12.

14....♗g4 15.♘ce2

15....♘c4

15.c5!? 16.dxc6 ♗h4 17.fxe5 dxe5 18.h3 ♗xe2 19.♘xe2 ♕b6+ 20.♔h2 ♗xe1 21.♕xe1 ♕xc6 22.♘g3 ♖ae8=. Although Black is down ¾ of a pawn, his twin threats of ...♕xc2 and ...f7-f5 plus his lead in development and strong passed pawn give him equality.

16.b3 ♘b6 17.♘c6 ♕d7 18.♗b2

18....♖ae8

Better was 18...♗h4! 19.g3 ♗f3 20.♕d3 ♗xd5 21.♘b4 ♗f6 22.♗xf6 ♗b7 23.c4 bxc4 24.bxc4 gxf6 and White has insufficient compensation for the pawn.

19.h3 ♗h5 20.♘xe7+ ♕xe7 21.g4 ♕e3+ 22.♔g2 ♕e4+ 23.♔h2 ♕f3

24.gxh5 ♖e3 25.♘g1 ♕xf4+ 26.♔h1 ♕e4+ 27.♔h2 ♕f4+ 28.♔h1 ♕e4+ Draw agreed.

Game 22.5   Ruy Lopez/Spanish – Worrall Attack

Rainer Polzin 2491
Zahar Efimenko 2654
Germany Bundesliga 2009/10 (2)

1.e4 e5 2.♘f3 ♘c6 3.♗b5 a6 4.♗a4 ♘f6 5.0-0

5.♕e2 (the Wormald Attack) 5...b5 6.♗b3 ♗e7 7.c3 (for 7.0-0 0-0 see the game) 7...d5 8.d3 (for 8.exd5 ♘xd5 9.♘xe5 ♘xe5 10.♕xe5 ♘f6 11.0-0 0-0 see the note to move 9) 8...0-0 9.0-0 – see the game.

5...♗e7 6.♕e2

This is the Worrall Attack, favored by among others grandmaster Sergey Tiviakov.

6....b5 7.♗b3 0-0 8.c3 d5

This is the Marshall Attack when White has played 6.♖e1 rather than 6.♕e2, but in this position few players accept the gambit, as Black gets a better version of the Marshall.

9.d3

9.exd5 ♘xd5 10.♘xe5 (after 10.d3 ♗b7 11.♘xe5 ♘xe5 12.♕xe5 ♕d7 13.♘d2 ♗d6 14.♕e4 c5 15.♗xd5 ♗xd5 Black has the bishops and a big lead in development for the pawn, more than enough. His pieces point menacingly towards White's king) 10...♘xe5 11.♕xe5 ♘f6 12.d4 ♗d6 (in the real Marshall White would retreat his rook to the first rank. But here a queen retreat will lose more time after 13...♖e8) 13.♕g5 ♖e8 14.♘a3 ♗b7N 15.f3 c5 16.♕h4 cxd4 17.cxd4 ♗e7 18.♗d2 ♘d5 19.♕f2 ♗h4 20.g3 ♗f6=. Black has full compensation for the pawn, which is isolated and under attack. Black has a safer king and a much better knight.

9....♗b7 10.♘bd2

10.♖d1 ♖e8 11.♘bd2 transposes to the next note.

10.♗g5 dxe4 11.dxe4 ♘xe4! 12.♕xe4 ♗xg5 13.♗d5 ♗e7N 14.c4 (if 14.♗xc6 f5 15.♕xe5 ♗xc6 16.♘d4 ♗d7 17.a4 ♗d6 18.♕d5+ ♔h8 Black is better with the two bishops in an open position) 14...♕d6=. White should eventually regain his lost pawn and equalize.

10....♖e8 11.♖e1

11.♖d1 ♗f8 12.♘f1 ♘a5 13.♗c2 c5 14.♘g3 h6 15.h3 ♕c7 16.♘h2 ♖ad8 17.♘g4 ♘xg4=. Black's queenside

play should offset White's kingside initiative.

11....♕d7

12.exd5

A) After 12.♘f1 h6N 13.♘g3 ♖ad8 14.h3 ♗f8 15.♗c2 g6 16.♘h2 d4N Black is doing well as he should gain access to the key square d4 by ...d4xc3 b2xc3 b5-b4;

B) 12.a3 ♗f8 13.exd5 ♘xd5 14.♘e4 f5 15.♗a2 ♔h8 16.♘fg5 h6 17.♕h5 fxe4 18.dxe4 ♘f6 19.♘f7+ ♔h7 20.♘g5+ with a draw by perpetual check.

12....♘xd5=

Says the computer – I even prefer Black.

13.♘e4 h6 14.♗d2 ♖ad8 15.♖ad1 ♕g4

16.h3?!

This gives Black a target. 16.a4 b4=.

**16....♕g6 17.a3 ♚h8 18.♕f1 f5
19.♘g3 ♗f6 20.h4?! f4 21.♘e4 ♗c8
22.♗c2? ♗g4 23.♕e2**

23....♘de7
23...♕h5 wins the h-pawn for
nothing.
24.d4?!
24.♘c5 a5 25.♖c1 ♕h5 favors Black
but White still has chances to
survive.
**24....exd4 25.♗xf4 ♘f5 26.♗xc7 ♖c8
27.♗b6?**
After 27.♕d3 ♖xc7 28.h5 ♗xh5
29.♘xf6 ♖xe1+ 30.♖xe1 gxf6 31.♕xf5
♕xf5 32.♗xf5 ♗xf3 33.♖e8+ ♚g7
34.gxf3 ♘e5 Black should emerge a
pawn ahead.
**27....dxc3 28.♕d3 ♘e5
29.♘xe5 ♗xe5 30.f3 ♕xb6+ 0-1**

Game 22.6   Ruy Lopez/Spanish
Vasil Durarbeyli   2487
Predrag Nikolic   2602
Sarajevo 2010 (5)

**1.e4 e5 2.♘f3 ♘c6 3.♗b5 a6 4.♗a4
♘f6 5.0-0**
Note that 5.d3 requires different
handling, as explained earlier in
Game 22.3.
5....♗e7 6.d3

This is probably White's best
option in the Spanish if he wants
to avoid the main lines, and is my
recommendation for White in the
White book. It makes more sense
here than after 6.♖e1, as with d2-d3
played that move is not urgent.
6....b5
Of course 6...d6 is playable, but then
after 7.c3 White can answer a later
...b7-b5 by ♗c2 instead of ♗b3.
7.♗b3 d6
If Black castles here he cannot
answer 8.a4 by my recommended
8...♗d7. However I now think that
castling here (7...0-0) and meeting
8.a4 by 8...b4 is slightly preferable.
Then 9.♘bd2 (9.♖e1 transposes
to Chapter 25) 9...d6 (9...♗c5 is
also OK but a bit less logical here
than after 9.♖e1) 10.a5 ♗e6 11.♘c4
h6 12.♗e3 ♕c8 13.h3 was Popov-
Maiorov, Voronezh 2018, when
13...♕b7 14.♘fd2 ♖ad8 15.♗a4 d5!
16.♗xc6 ♕xc6 17.♘xe5 ♕b5 gives
Black full compensation for his
half-pawn sacrifice (-0.04), Lc0
-0.01. If White meets castling by
8.c3 d5! equalizes, while if 8.h3 ♗b7
9.♖e1 d5! transposes to my Anti-
Marshall chapter.

8.a4

8.c3

A) 8...♘a5 9.♗c2 c5 10.d4 cxd4 11.cxd4 0-0! 12.h3 ♖e8 13.d5 (13.♘c3! exd4 14.♘xd4 ♗d7 15.b3 ♖c8 16.♗b2 ♘c6 17.♖c1 ♗f8 leaves White with a normal opening edge. It seems that only castling on move 7 avoids this, by keeping the option of ...d6-d5 open) 13...♗d7 14.♘c3 Carlsen-Ding Liren, St Louis 2019 playoff blitz, 14...♕c7! (0.00);

B) 8... 0-0 9.♖e1 transposes to the game with 9.d3 in the main line, while 9.h3 ♘a5 10.♗c2 c5 11.d4 cxd4 12.cxd4 transposes to the above Carlsen-Ding Liren game. But 9.a4 ♗d7 10.♗c2 may give White a slim edge, so Ding Liren's move order may be designed to avoid this.

8....♗d7!

This is a better square for the bishop than b7 when White has the d3-e4-pawn chain. If Black had castled instead of ...d7-d6 his best option would now be 8...b4, but I think the developing ...♗d7 is more useful here.

9.c3

After 9.♗d2 b4 10.c3 0-0 11.h3 ♖b8 12.♗c4 ♕c8 Black is doing well

because the bishop on d2 impedes the development of the knight. 9.♘c3 ♘a5 10.♗a2 b4 11.♘e2 0-0 12.♘g3 c5=. Black may sacrifice a pawn by ...b4-b3 next against routine moves, or may simply bring his knight back to c6. The game Erenburg-Kaufman, US Chess League (internet game) 2011, continued 13.♘h4 b3!N 14.cxb3 ♘c6 15.b4 ♘xb4 16.♗c4 and now 16...♘xe4 would have given me the advantage after 17.dxe4 ♗xh4 18.♕xd6 ♘c2 followed by ...♗e6.

9....0-0

10.♘bd2

A) 10.♖e1 ♘a5 11.♗c2 c5 12.♘bd2 transposes to the game.

B) However 10.♗c2! ♖e8 11.♖e1 h6 12.♘bd2 ♗f8 (+0.17) gives White a slim statistical and computer edge, so my preference has switched to the 7....0-0 8.a4 b4 line of Chapter 25.

10....♘a5 11.♗c2

11.♗a2 c5 12.♖e1 ♕c7 13.axb5 axb5 14.♘f1 c4 15.♗g5 ♗e6 16.♘e3 ♘g4=. The black knight on a5 and the white bishop on a2 are both poorly placed.

11....c5 12.♖e1 ♘c6

I prefer this to a quick ...b5-b4 as White may take advantageously on b4 if no piece guards that square.

13.♘f1 ♖e8 14.h3
14.♘e3 b4 15.♗b3 ♘a5 16.♗a2 ♖b8 17.d4?! exd4 18.cxd4 ♘xe4 19.♘d5 ♗f8 is a dubious pawn sacrifice by White.
14....h6 15.♘g3
15.♘e3 ♗f8 16.♘h2 b4 17.♕f3 ♖b8 18.♗d2 ♕c7 19.♘hg4 ♘xg4 20.hxg4 ♗e6=. With ideas of ...♕d7 or ...♘a5 or ...♗e7 Black has adequate counterplay.
15....♗f8 16.d4 cxd4 17.cxd4 ♘b4 18.♗b3

Now 18...a5? was played in the **actual game** when 19.axb5 ♗xb5 20.dxe5 dxe5 21.♕xd8 ♖exd8 22.♘xe5 won a pawn and eventually the game. The text is much better.

18....bxa4 19.♗xa4 exd4 20.♘xd4 ♗xa4 21.♖xa4 a5=
Black's pressure on e4 and his strong knight on b4 offset the isolated d6-pawn.

**Game 22.7   Ruy Lopez/Spanish _
            Deferred Exchange**
Lev Milman   2476
Larry Kaufman   2413
ICC 2010 (2)

1.e4 e5 2.♘f3 ♘c6 3.♗b5 a6 4.♗a4 ♘f6 5.0-0 ♗e7 6.♗xc6 dxc6

7.d3
A) 7.♕e1 ♗e6 8.b3 ♘d7 9.♗b2 f6 10.d4 ♗d6 11.♘bd2 ♕e7 12.♕e2 0-0-0 – with the bishop pair and a potential pawn storm Black has a slight edge;
B) 7.♘c3 ♗g4 8.h3 ♗h5 9.g4 ♘xg4 10.hxg4 ♗xg4 11.♔g2 ♕d6 – with two pawns, the bishop pair, better development, and the enemy king exposed, Black clearly has enough for a knight;
C) 7.♕e2 ♗g4 8.h3 ♗h5 9.d3 ♘d7 10.♘bd2 0-0 11.♘c4 f6=;
D) 7.♖e1 ♗g4 8.h3 ♗h5 9.g4 ♘xg4 10.hxg4 ♗xg4 11.d3 (11.♕e2 ♗g5 12.♔g2 ♕f6 13.♘a3 ♗f4 14.d4 ♗h3+

15.♔xh3 ♕e6+ 16.♔g2 ♕g4+ is a draw by perpetual check) 11...f6 12.♘bd2 ♕d7 13.♕e2 0-0-0 14.♘f1 h5 15.♘e3 g5 16.♗d2 ♗e6. As in the 7.♘c3 line, Black has two pawns, the bishop pair, and an attack for the knight. Komodo likes Black whereas Houdini likes White.

7....♘d7 8.♘bd2 0-0 9.♘c4 f6 10.♘h4 ♘c5 11.♘f5

11.♕f3 ♘e6 12.♘f5 ♘d4 13.♘xd4 ♕xd4=.

11....♘e6 12.♗e3

12.♕f3 ♘d4 13.♘xd4 ♕xd4= transposes to the last note.

12....c5 13.♕d2 ♘d4 14.♘xe7+ ♕xe7 15.f4 exf4 16.♗xf4 ♗e6 17.♘e3 ♖ad8 18.♕f2 ♖f7 19.♔h1 ♕d7

19...f5! 20.exf5 ♘xf5=.

20.b3 b6 21.a4 ♕c6

21...♖df8=. Black prepares ...f6-f5.

22.♖ae1 ♖fd7

23.e5

I think this helps Black more than White.

23....f5 24.♕g3 ♖f7 25.♗g5 ♖df8 26.♖f4?! ♗c8

Now Black is better, with the long diagonal in his possession.

27.♖h4?! ♘e6 28.♗f4? g5

Black wins a piece.

29.♗xg5 ♖g7 30.♖xh7 ♖xh7 0-1

Game 22.8   Ruy Lopez/Spanish
Sasho Nikolov   2429
Alexander Delchev   2625
Bankia 2011 (4)

1.e4 e5 2.♘f3 ♘c6 3.♗b5 a6 4.♗a4 ♘f6 5.0-0 ♗e7 6.♖e1 b5 7.♗b3 d6

8.c3

A) If White plays 8.d3 (or 8.h3) first, then 8...♘a5 nets the bishop pair;

B) An alternative is 8.a4 ♗d7 (I like this move here more than the pinning move 8...♗g4, as then after c2-c3, d2-d3, and ♘bd2 White will gain time by h2-h3) 9.c3 0-0 10.d4 h6 11.♘bd2 ♖e8 and now:

analysis diagram

B1) 12.h3 ♗f8 13.♗c2 exd4 14.♘xd4 ♘e5 (I chose the inferior 14...♘e7 against grandmaster Zapata at the 2011 U.S. Open and I lost) 15.♘f1 c5 16.♘e2 ♗c6 17.♘f4 c4=;

B2) 12.♘f1 ♗f8 13.♘g3 ♘a5 14.♗c2 c5 15.d5 c4 16.h3 ♕c7 17.♗e3 ♖eb8=. Black can aim for ...♘a5-b7-c5 or perhaps ... ♘f6-h7, ...♗e7, and ...♘h7-g5, or simply ...b5-b4.

C) 8.a3 0-0 9.c3 (9.h3 ♗e6 10.♗xe6 fxe6 11.d3 ♕e8=) 9...♘a5 10.♗c2 c5 11.d4 cxd4 12.cxd4 ♕c7 13.h3 ♗b7=. This is a normal Spanish position where White has played an inferior move (a2-a3);

D) 8.d4 0-0 9.c3 ♗g4 transposes to the 8.c3 0-0 9.d4 ♗g4 line.

8....0-0 9.d3
For 9.a4 ♗d7, see the note to move 8.

9....♘a5 10.♗c2 c5 11.♘bd2 ♘c6 12.♘f1 ♖e8

13.♘g3
13.h3 h6 14.d4 cxd4 15.cxd4 exd4 16.♘xd4 ♘xd4 17.♕xd4 ♗e6 18.♘e3 (18.♘g3 transposes to the game) 18...♖c8 19.♗d2 ♘h5 20.♖ad1 ♗f6 – Black has the initiative with ...♗e5 and ...♘f4 and ...♕g5 or ...♕h4 in prospect.

If 13.♘e3 ♗f8 – now the priority is to uncover the rook to deter d3-d4.

13....h6
This prepares ...♗e6 without allowing ♘g5 in response.

14.h3 ♗e6!
This is better than the routine 14...♗f8 as it allows Black to attack the c2-bishop by ...♖c8 after a mass exchange on d4 as in this game.

15.d4
After 15.a4 ♗f8 16.d4 cxd4 17.cxd4 exd4 18.♘xd4 ♘xd4 19.♕xd4 ♖c8 20.♕d1 ♕c7 21.♗d3 bxa4!N 22.♕xa4 ♘d7, Black is doing great with ...♘c5 coming next.

15....cxd4 16.cxd4 exd4 17.♘xd4
17.♘e2 d3 18.♗xd3 ♘e5 19.♘ed4 ♗d7 20.♗c2 ♖c8=.

17....♘xd4 18.♕xd4 ♖c8 19.♗b3 d5 20.e5 ♘d7 21.♗d2
After 21.♘h5 ♗f8 Black has a queenside initiative and a safe king.

21....♗c5 22.♕d3
22.♕f4 ♘f8 – with ideas like ...d5-d4 or ...♘g6 Black is better.

22....♕h4
22...♕c7 wins the e-pawn for little compensation.

23.♖ad1 ♕d4 24.♕xd4 ♗xd4 25.♗xh6 ♗xe5

25...♗xb2 was even better
objectively, but the text sets a nice
trap, which worked.

26.♗xd5??

26.♗e3 ♗xb2 27.♗xd5 ♗xd5
28.♖xd5 ♘e5 and with ...♘c4
coming Black has the better
endgame.

26....gxh6

White resigned, because he realized
that after 27.♗xe6 ♖xe6 28.♖xd7
♗xg3 29.♖xe6 Black has 29...♖c1+
with mate to follow.

Game 22.9   Ruy Lopez/Spanish
David Navara   2708
Alexander Beliavsky   2622
Vilnius rapid 2010 (1)

**1.e4 e5 2.♘f3 ♘c6 3.♗b5 a6 4.♗a4
♘f6 5.0-0 ♗e7 6.♖e1 b5 7.♗b3 0-0
8.d4 d6**

With this move order I now
prefer 8...♘xd4 as in Chapter 25,
but if White is willing to risk the
Marshall he can avoid this by 8.c3
d6 9.d4, transposing to the game
while avoiding ...♘xd4.

9.c3 ♗g4 10.d5 ♘a5 11.♗c2 c6

Also satisfactory is 11...♕c8 to meet
12.h3 by 12...♗d7.

12.h3

12.dxc6 ♕c7 13.♘bd2 ♕xc6 14.♘f1
♗e6 15.♘g5 ♗d7 16.♘e3 h6 17.♘f3
♘c4=. Black has solved the problem
of his bad knight on a5.

12....♗c8!

Note that the more natural 12...♗d7
loses the bishop pair to 13.♘xe5!
dxe5 14.d6.

13.dxc6 ♕c7 14.♘bd2

14.a4 ♕xc6 15.♘bd2 transposes to
the next note.

14....♕xc6 15.♘f1

After 15.a4 ♗e6 16.♘g5 ♗d7 17.♘f1
h6 18.♘f3 ♖fc8 19.♘e3 ♗e6 20.♘h4
g6 21.♕f3 ♔h8 White's kingside
play is running out of steam while
Black retains a queenside initiative.

15....♗e6 16.♘g3

16.♘g5 ♗d7 17.a4 transposes to the
note to move 15.

16....♖ac8

17.♘h4

17.♘g5 ♗d7 18.♘f5 ♗xf5 19.exf5
♖fe8=. The black pawn center and
White's doubled pawn offset the
bishop pair.

17....g6 18.♗h6

In case of 18.♗g5 ♘c4 19.♖b1 ♖fd8
20.♘f3 d5, Black has the initiative
and better placed pieces.

18....♖fd8 19.♕f3?

Now White is forced to make an
incorrect piece sacrifice. He should
have admitted his mistake by
retreating 19.♘f3 with slightly the
worse of it.

**19....♘e8 20.♘gf5 ♗xf5 21.♘xf5
gxf5 22.♕g3+ ♚h8 23.exf5 ♗f6**

White's sacrifice was unsound and
Black is already winning in this
position.

24.♖e4

24....♘c7

24...d5! 25.♖g4 ♘c7 and Black will
consolidate with ...♖g8.

**25.♗g5 ♗xg5 26.♕xg5 ♖g8
27.♕h5? f6 28.♖ae1 ♘c4 29.♕h6
♕d7**

29...d5!.

**30.♕xf6+ ♕g7 31.♕xg7+ ♖xg7
32.f4 ♘d5 33.fxe5 dxe5 34.♗b3 ♘f4
35.♗xc4 bxc4 36.♚h1**

36....♘d3

Black in the **actual game** played
the inferior 36...♖cg8, which was
still good enough to win the game,
but the text would have been much
simpler.

37.♖1e2 ♖b7 38.♚h2 ♚g7−+

Game 22.10 Ruy Lopez/Spanish
Sergey Pavlov   2508
Sergey Azarov   2609
Alushta tt 2010 (7)

**1.e4 e5 2.♘f3 ♘c6 3.♗b5 a6 4.♗a4
♘f6 5.0-0 ♗e7 6.♖e1 b5 7.♗b3 d6
8.c3 0-0 9.d4**

This is a serious try for an
advantage, played by Bobby Fischer
in 1962 and now by many strong
grandmasters. It can also be

reached by the move order 7...0-0 8.d4 d6 9.c3. It avoids the Breyer 9...♘b8 (and Chigorin's 9...♘a5) by the pressure on e5. But it makes the following pin rather effective.

9....♗g4 10.♗e3

Less popular is 10.d5, for which see the previous game. This ♗e3 line is statistically quite good for White, but Black should be able to reach near-equality with precise play. If you are a Marshall player I think it's wise to avoid this line as explained in Chapter 25.

In case of 10.a4 ♗xf3 11.gxf3 ♘a5 12.♗a2 c5 13.♘a3 exd4 14.cxd4 c4, and Black plans ...d6-d5. White will have great trouble utilizing his a2-bishop, so his bad kingside pawn structure should count for more than the bishop pair.

10....exd4 11.cxd4 d5

Also respectable is 11...♘a5 12.♗c2 c5, or first 12...♘c4 13.♗c1 and then ...c7-c5, but I'm not sure that either fully equalizes.

12.e5 ♘e4 13.♘c3

13.h3 (it's not clear that including this move is helpful, as the black bishop gets the option to go to g6. Sometimes Black even plays 10...♗h5 earlier, planning to meet 11.h3 as in this game, but White may choose something other than 11.h3) 13...♗h5 14.♘c3 ♘xc3 15.bxc3 ♘a5 16.♗c2 ♘c4 17.g4 ♗g6 18.♗f5 transposes to the note to move 16. But 13.♘bd2 ♘xd2 14.♕xd2 ♗xf3 15.gxf3 ♗b4 16.♕c2 ♘a5 17.♖ed1 ♕d7 18.♔h1 has good stats for

White, although Komodo calls it dead even (0.00) after 18...♖ac8.

13....♘xc3 14.bxc3 ♘a5

Here 14...♕d7, planning ...♘d8 and ...♘e6, is also popular.

15.♗c2 ♘c4

16.♕d3

16.h3 ♗h5 17.g4 ♗g6 18.♗f5 a5 19.♗f4 b4 20.h4 ♗xh4 21.♔g2 ♗e7 is a highly risky gambit by White. My game against Sammour Hasbun (US Chess League, Internet 2011) continued 22.♖h1 ♖a6 23.♕g1 and now I should have played 23...c5 24.♕h2 h5 25.♖ag1 ♕e8. It seems I can defend the kingside and calmly utilize my extra queenside pawn.

16....g6 17.♗h6 ♖e8 18.♕e2

After 18.h3 ♗e6 19.♕e2 ♖c8 20.♖ad1 ♘a3 21.♗d3 c5 (0.00).

18....a5 19.h3 ♗e6 20.♘h2

Or 20.♗d3 b4 with near-equality.

20....b4

20...c5 is equal per Komodo and Stockfish, while Lc0 likes White.

21.♘g4

Draw agreed; 21...♕d7 is roughly equal. Maybe 21.♗a4 was a tad better for White, so Black should go for 20...c5.

Breyer Variation

The Breyer is in my view the best all-purpose defense to the main line of the Spanish ending in 9.h3. When I wrote my first book in 2003 it was just one of many defenses to the Spanish, but now it is the most successful such defense in high-level play along with the Zaitsev Variation, which invites an immediate draw and so is not always suitable. It has been played many times in the past decade by World Champion Magnus Carlsen and by ex-World Champion Anand and title contenders Kamsky, Mamedyarov, Svidler, and Adams. It was also a favorite of World Champion Boris Spassky. It does not allow any quick forced draw by repetition, nor any quick queen trade. In fact it usually leaves all the pieces on the board for the first 20 moves or so, making it pretty much ideal if you must win on the Black side of the Ruy Lopez. My own results with it have been excellent. I recommended the Berlin in my first book, which still looks pretty decent, but defending a slightly inferior endgame from the opening is not everyone's cup of tea. Another factor in my choice is that some sidelines in the Berlin, especially 5.♖e1, leave Black pretty much just fighting for a draw. One final factor in favour of the Breyer for amateur players is that if your opponent is not familiar with it, when you play 9...♞b8 (the Breyer move) he will think you are a hopeless patzer and will underestimate you!

To be honest, the position after 9.h3 where the Breyer is played is already rather favourable for White, and in recent years most of the elite players have chosen to avoid this position by aiming for the Marshall Attack (see next two chapters). I cannot prove full equality with the Breyer, but it is probably a better winning try than the Marshall because it keeps the wood on the board, and doesn't give White too much of an edge even with perfect play. Lc0, being rather more space-oriented than material-oriented, clearly prefers the Marshall over the Breyer, but then it assumes that Black's goal is a draw.

The defense is credited to Gyula Breyer, a Hungarian master who was among the top ten players in the world in 1918 (per Chessmetrics website) but who died in 1921 at only age 27 from a heart attack. To come up with the move 9...♞b8 at that time took a real genius, as the belief in 'development' was very strong since the time of Morphy. The basic idea behind the move is that the knight has fulfilled its function on c6 and now is just in the way of the c-pawn and the bishop when it goes to b7.

Previously this problem was solved by 9...♞a5, chasing the bishop back to c2, and then ...c7-c5, but the knight normally had to return to c6. The beauty of the Breyer is that White still must retreat his bishop to c2 in the main line in order to complete the maneuver ♞d2-f1-g3, but Black's knight will be on d7 rather than c6, which makes the bishop fianchetto to b7 attractive. Black will usually fianchetto both bishops, will usually answer a2-a4 by ...c5-c4 and ...♞c5, will aim for ...c7-c6 against an early d4-d5, and will sometimes get in the shot ...d6-d5 himself.

Now let's look at the moves of the Breyer Variation. For comments on the first nine moves see the Spanish offshoots chapter.

1.e4 e5 2.♞f3 ♞c6 3.♝b5 a6 4.♝a4 ♞f6 5.0-0 ♝e7 6.♖e1 b5 7.♝b3 d6 8.c3 0-0 9.h3 ♞b8(!)

This makes it a Breyer. It only makes sense now as a response to h2-h3, because h2-h3 rules out the strategy of answering d2-d4 by ...♝g4, so pressure on d4 is now pointless.

10.d4 The quiet move 10.d3 is a serious alternative, designed to avoid the need for an unprovoked ♝c2 to defend the e4-pawn. It is likely to lead to the same position as 10.d4 but with the extra move b2-b4 included for White, which may be either good or bad. See Game 23.1.

10...♞bd7 This comes just in time to defend the e5-pawn.

11.♞bd2 See Game 23.2 for 11.♞h4 ♖e8 12.♞f5 ♝f8. See Game 23.3 for 11.c4 c6.

11...♝b7 12.♝c2 White doesn't really want to play this, as the bishop is currently active on b3. He does this for three reasons: he wants to play ♞f1, which would lose a pawn if played now. Also, he may want to play a2-a4 and then attack the b5-pawn by ♝d3. Finally, he may want to advance his b-pawn. For the alternative 12.a3 c5 see Game 23.4.

12...♖e8 Now that the bishop doesn't attack f7, there is no drawback to this move, which prepares to put indirect pressure on e4 by retreating ...♝f8.

13.♘f1 The alternative 13.a4 ♗f8 14.♗d3 is often seen, to force Black to block his bishop by playing ...c7-c6. On the plus side, ...c7-c6 lets out the queen and controls the center. See Game 23.5.

13...♗f8 14.♘g3 (in time to defend e4) **14...g6** This keeps out the white knight and enables a black fianchetto to defend the king strongly. For the alternative pin 14.♗g5 h6 15.♗h4 g6 see Game 23.6.

15.a4 For 15.♗g5 h6 16.♗d2 ♗g7 see Game 23.7. For 15.b3 ♗g7 16.d5 ♖c8 see Game 23.8.

15...c5 This move is triggered by a2-a4 because now after **16.d5 c4** the black knight will attack the a-pawn, restrain the b-pawn and can sometimes land on the b3-square.

17.♗g5 Experience has shown that if Black chases the bishop back to e3 by playing ...h7-h6, that move gives White a target, while if he doesn't, the bishop is more active on g5 than on e3. Most players do chase the bishop back, but I vote with the minority in this instance, choosing Spassky's **17...♗e7**.

See Game 23.9.

Game 23.1   Ruy Lopez/Spanish – Breyer

Alexander Lastin   2622

Elisabeth Pähtz   2449

Baku 2008 (3)

1.e4 e5 2.♘f3 ♘c6 3.♗b5 a6 4.♗a4 ♘f6 5.0-0 ♗e7 6.♖e1 b5 7.♗b3 d6 8.c3 0-0 9.h3 ♗b7 10.d3 ♘b8 11.♘bd2 ♘bd7

We would get this position by 9...♘b8 10.d3 ♘bd7 11.♘bd2 ♗b7. This is a sensible line for White against the Breyer, as the bishop on b7 bites on granite. Still, h2-h3 is not essential here.

12.♘f1 ♖e8

Usually Black plays 12...♘c5 13.♗c2 ♖e8, which transposes to the game after 14.♘g3, because the game order allows 13.♗g5, as discussed after the next move.

13.♘g3

If 13.♘g5 d5 14.exd5 ♘xd5 15.♕h5 ♗xg5 16.♗xg5 ♘7f6 17.♕f3 ♕c8 18.♘d2 h6 19.♗xf6 ♘xf6 20.♘e4 ♗xe4 21.♖xe4 c5 22.♖g4 ♖a7 23.♕xf6 ♕xg4 24.♕xf7+ ♖xf7 25.hxg4 ♖d8 26.♗xf7+ ♔xf7 27.a4 b4 28.♖d1 bxc3 29.bxc3 e4 30.d4 cxd4 31.cxd4 ♔e6 32.f3 ♔d5 33.♖b1

♖d6. Black will regain his pawn with a drawn endgame.

13....♘c5

13...♗f8!? 14.♘g5 d5 15.exd5 ♘c5 16.c4 c6 (+0.16) is a valid option.

14.♗c2 ♗f8

15.b4

A) 15.♘h2 and now:

A1) 15...d5 is the most frequent move, but it is second-best. I played it in this game because I forgot the analysis here, which I had already written. 16.♕f3 ♘e6 (16...g6 17.♗g5 ♗e7 18.h4 a5 19.h5 ♖a6=) 17.♘f5 ♕d7?!N (better is 17...♔h8!) 18.♕g3 dxe4 19.dxe4 ♖ad8? 20.♘f3. This was the game Shankland-Kaufman, US Chess League 2011, won quickly by White. Black is already losing;

A2) 15...g6 16.♘g4 (after 16.f4 exf4 17.♗xf4 ♘e6 18.♗e3 c5N) 16...♘xg4 17.♕xg4 ♗g7 18.♗g5 ♕d7 19.♖ad1?! ♘e6∓ (-0.34). Black has ideas of ...d6-d5, ...h7-h5, or ...a6-a5.

B) 15.♘f5 d5 16.exd5 ♕xd5 17.♗g5 ♕c6 (-0.13). I prefer Black – compare the light-squared bishops;

C) 15.♗d2 d5= (0.00).

15....♘cd7 16.d4

We now have a position from the main line of the Breyer (with 10.d4), with the sole difference that White has gotten to play b2-b4 'for free', since he has wasted one move with the d-pawn while Black has wasted two with his queen's knight. But is b2-b4 a plus or a minus? If White intends kingside play it's probably a minus as on b4 the pawn is a target for ...a7-a5 or ...c7-c5. On balance it's probably neutral.

A) 16.a4 c5 17.bxc5 ♘xc5 18.axb5 axb5 19.♖xa8 ♗xa8= (0.00);

B) If 16.♗b3 h6 17.♘h4?! d5 18.♘hf5 a5 19.♗d2 dxe4 20.dxe4 axb4 21.cxb4 c5 Black has the initiative;

C) 16.♗d2 c5 17.a4 d5= (-0.03).

16....a5 17.♗d2

17.a3 axb4 18.cxb4 c5 19.bxc5 dxc5= (0.00).

17....axb4 18.cxb4

Now the **actual game** went 18... g6 19.♗c3 and White took the initiative and went on to win. The text is a Rybka novelty.

18....d5! 19.exd5?! exd4 20.♖xe8 ♕xe8 21.♘xd4 ♕e5 (-0.10)

Black will regain the pawn and have somewhat the better chances due to the c-pawn's superiority over the a-pawn plus the long diagonal.

On an unrelated personal note, the loser of this game and I have in common that we are both members of the only two parent-child GM/IM combinations to my knowledge, her father being GM Thomas Pähtz while my son is IM Raymond Kaufman. [Editor's note: GM Viacheslav Zakhartsov's son Vladimir was an IM but turned GM in 2019; GM Evgeny Sveshnikov's son Vladimir is also an IM.]

Game 23.2   Ruy Lopez/Spanish – Breyer
Robert Byrne   2570
Josip Rukavina   2460
Leningrad izt 1973 (2)

1.e4 e5 2.♘f3 ♘c6 3.♗b5 a6 4.♗a4 ♘f6 5.0-0 ♗e7 6.♖e1 b5 7.♗b3 d6 8.c3 0-0 9.h3 ♘b8 10.d4 ♘bd7 11.♘h4 ♖e8

12.♘f5

12.♘d2 ♗b7 13.♘f5 ♗f8 (Dueball-Tukmakov, Kiev tt 1970) transposes to the next note.

12....♗f8 13.f3?!

A) 13.♘d2 ♗b7 14.♗c2 g6 15.♘g3 exd4 16.cxd4 c5 17.d5 ♗g7 – Black is doing well due to the loss of time by White's ♘f3-h4-f5-g3 maneuver;

B) 13.g4?! exd4 14.g5 ♘xe4 15.♗d5 ♘b6! 16.♗xa8 ♘xa8 17.♘xd4 ♘xg5, and Black gets way too much for the exchange;

C) 13.♕f3 exd4! 14.cxd4 ♗b7 15.♗c2 c5 16.dxc5 ♘xc5 and Black's pressure on e4 fully offsets the strong knight on f5;

D) 13.♗c2 d5= 14.exd5 exd4 15.♖xe8 ♕xe8 16.♘xd4 ♗b7 17.a4 ♗xd5 18.♗f4 c5 19.♘f5 ♘b6=. Black's pieces are well-placed and the pawns are symmetrical.

13....♗b7

An excellent alternative was 13...d5 14.♗g5 ♘b6 15.♘g3 (15.dxe5) ♗b7 16.♘d2 h6 17.♗e3 ♘bd7. Black is better, with a safer king and better placed king's knight.

But best was 13...c5! 14.♗g5 ♕b6 (-0.08) which already looks better for Black.

14.♗g5 h6 15.♗h4

15....g6!

In the **actual game** Black played 15...d5? 16.exd5 exd4 17.cxd4 g6 18.♘e3, after which White had a clear advantage and won: 18...♘b6 19.♘c3 g5 20.♗g3 ♘fxd5 21.♘exd5 ♖xe1+ 22.♕xe1 ♘xd5 23.♕e4 ♘xc3 24.♕g6+ ♗g7 25.♕xf7+ ♔h8 26.bxc3 b4 27.♗e5 ♗xe5 28.dxe5 bxc3 29.♖d1 ♕f8 30.♕xc7 ♖c8 31.♕xb7 c2 32.♖c1 ♖d8 33.♗xc2 and Black resigned.

16.♘e3 ♗g7 17.♘d2 exd4 18.cxd4 c5 19.dxc5 dxc5

Black is clearly better, with ...c5-c4 and ...♘c5 coming up.

As an aside, I drew games with both of the players in this game, but forty years separated those two games!

Game 23.3   Ruy Lopez/Spanish – Breyer
Hikaru Nakamura   2774
Magnus Carlsen   2815
Medias 2011 (6)

1.e4 e5 2.♘f3 ♘c6 3.♗b5 a6 4.♗a4 ♘f6 5.0-0 ♗e7 6.♖e1 b5 7.♗b3 0-0 8.c3 d6 9.h3 ♘b8 10.d4 ♘bd7 11.c4
There were only two grandmaster games in the first decade of this

century with 11.c4, but computers like it so it is coming back now. Bobby Fischer played it, and Khalifman is a great theoretician, so his choice here is interesting . Lu Shanglei, Grandelius, Adhiban, Sevian, and Shirov, all strong GM's, have played it in 2018 or 2019.

11....c6

12.♘c3?!

Both Nakamura in this game and Shabalov against me chose this inferior move, after which White has no prospects of getting the advantage.

A) 12.♘bd2 ♗b7 13.♗c2 exd4 (or 13...♖e8 directly) 14.♘xd4 (so far Khalifman-Short, Bazna 2008. Black continued 14...♖e8?! and had to struggle for a draw; the text is better) 14...g6 15.b3 c5 16.♘4f3 ♖e8 17.♗b2 ♗c6=. The pressure on e4 offsets White's pressure on the long diagonal;

B) 12.cxb5 axb5 13.♘c3 was played by Bobby Fischer against Spassky during their return match in Sveti Stefan 1992, but 13...b4 looks like a full equalizer;

C) 12.c5 ♕c7 13.cxd6 ♗xd6 14.♗g5 ♗b7=;

D) 12.♗g5 h6 13.♗h4 ♘h5=. The bishop exchange should favor Black as the fixed pawns on e4 and e5 leave Black with the better bishop;

E) Probably 12.a3 (or 12.♕c2, see below) is best, e.g. 12.a3 exd4 13.♘xd4 ♘e5 14.♗f4 ♕b6 15.cxb5 axb5 16.♘c3 ♖e8 17.♗e3 ♕b7 18.f4 b4! 19.fxe5 dxe5 20.♘xc6 bxc3 21.♘xe5 cxb2 22.♗xf7+ ♔f8 23.♖b1 ♖d8 24.♕f3 ♕xe4 25.♕xe4 ♘xe4 26.♖xb2 ♗f6 27.♗f4 ♗xe5 28.♗xe5 ♔xf7 29.♖xe4 ♖xa3 with an obviously drawn ending;

F) 12.♕c2 ♗b7 13.♘c3 exd4 14.♘xd4 b4 15.♘e2 (15.♘a4 c5 16.♘f5 ♖e8 (+0.11), White's great knight on f5 cancels his awful one on a4) 15...c5 16.♘f5 ♗xe4 17.♘xe7+ ♕xe7 18.♕d1 ♖fe8 19.♗f4 ♗c6 20.♕xd6 ♕xd6 21.♗xd6 ♖e6 22.♗f4 ♘h5 23.♗e3 ♖g6 (0.00).

12....b4 13.♘a4

13.♘b1 c5 14.d5 ♘b6 15.a3 a5 16.axb4 axb4 (+0.15) is a better try. White gets a space advantage but no more than that.

13...c5

14.d5

14.dxc5 dxc5 was Shabalov-Kaufman, Arlington 2010, in which

we agreed to a draw a few moves later when Black was already a bit better.

14....♖e8 15.♗c2 ♘f8 16.a3 a5 17.b3 ♘g6 18.♘b2 ♗d7 19.♘h2

White usually prefers 19.♘d3 h6 20.♖a2, when 20...♘h7 is most popular and equal (+0.11), Lc0 +0.07. It's just hard for White to do anything constructive. 20.♗d2 ♘h7 21.♕e2 ♘g5 22.♖a2 was Frolyanov-Shirov, Riga rapid 2019, when 22...bxa3 23.♖xa3 f5, as played later in the game, would have made for an interesting battle (+0.05), Lc0 -0.02.

19...h6 20.♘f1 ♘h7

21.♘e3

The computer prefers 21.♘d3 with an even game, to avoid the knight vs bad bishop scenario which occurs in the game.

21....♗g5 22.axb4 axb4 23.♖xa8 ♕xa8 24.♘f5 ♗xc1 25.♕xc1 ♗xf5 26.exf5 ♘gf8

Black should be a bit better here since he has the better knight versus White's bad bishop, though White's space advantage is probably enough to hold the draw.

27.♘d1 ♘f6 28.f3 ♕a2 29.g4 ♖a8 30.♘f2

30....♕a3 31.♕b1 ♕a2 32.♕c1 ♕a3 33.♕b1 ♕a2 34.♕c1

Draw agreed.

Game 23.4   Ruy Lopez/Spanish – Breyer
Ray Robson   2559
Gata Kamsky   2702
Philadelphia 2010 (5)

1.e4 e5 2.♘f3 ♘c6 3.♗b5 a6 4.♗a4 ♘f6 5.0-0 ♗e7 6.♖e1 b5 7.♗b3 d6 8.c3 0-0 9.h3 ♘b8 10.d4 ♘bd7 11.♘bd2 ♗b7

Mind your steps: 11...♖e8?? 12.♗xf7+! (in practice the majority of players have failed to pick up on this ploy when given the opportunity, including Judit Polgar!) 12...♔xf7 13.♘g5+ ♔g8 14.♘e6+–.

12.a3 c5 13.♗c2 ♖e8

13...♕c7= instead would discourage 14.b4, but Black didn't fear it.
14.b4 exd4 15.cxd4 cxd4 16.♘xd4
16.♗b2! ♗f8 17.♗xd4 ♗f8 (0.00).
16....♗f8 17.♗b2 ♖c8= 18.♕b1
18.♘4f3 ♘e5 19.♖c1 g6=.

18....g6
After 18...♘e5! 19.f4 ♘c4 20.♘xc4 bxc4 21.♗c3 ♘h5 22.♘e2 f5 23.exf5 ♕b6+ 24.♘d4 ♘xf4 Black has an attack at no cost.
19.♕a2?!
In case of 19.♘4f3 ♘h5 Black's pieces are a bit better placed than White's.
19....♖e7
19...♗h6! 20.♖ad1 d5 would have given Black the advantage.
20.♖ad1

20....♕e8

20...♗g7 21.a4 ♘e5 looks better for Black.
21.a4 bxa4
21...♘xe4 22.♘xe4 ♗xe4 23.♗xe4 ♖xe4 24.♕b1=.
22.♗xa4 ♘xe4 23.♗xd7 ♕xd7 24.♘xe4 ♖xe4 25.♖xe4 ♗xe4 26.♕xa6

26....♕b7= ½-½
With 26...♗g7 Black could have kept a small edge.

Game 23.5   Ruy Lopez/Spanish – Breyer
Alexander Shabalov   2606
David Navara   2707
Khanty-Mansiysk 2009 (2)

1.e4 e5 2.♘f3 ♘c6 3.♗b5 a6 4.♗a4 ♘f6 5.0-0 ♗e7 6.♖e1 b5 7.♗b3 d6 8.c3 0-0 9.h3 ♘b8 10.d4 ♘bd7 11.♘bd2 ♗b7 12.♗c2
12.a4 c5 13.♗c2 (13.d5 c4 14.♗c2 ♘c5=) 13...♕c7=.
12....♖e8 13.a4 ♗f8 14.♗d3
A few years ago engines and many top GM's favoured this line, but now the engines and top players have mostly returned to 13.♘f1 and 14.♘g3.
14....c6

15.b3

A) 15.♕c2 g6 16.b3 transposes; 16.axb5 axb5 17.♖xa8 ♕xa8 18.b4 exd4 19.cxd4 ♕a4=;

B) 15.♘f1 is a pretty good line for White, e.g. 15...exd4 16.cxd4 c5 17.d5 c4 18.♗c2 ♘c5 19.♘g3 g6 20.♗d2 ♘fd7 21.♗c3 ♘e5N 22.♘d4 ♘cd3 23.♗xd3 ♘xd3 24.♖e3 ♗h6 25.♖xd3 cxd3 26.♕xd3 ♗f4. White will end up with two pawns for the exchange, but Black has the bishop pair. Komodo calls it even (+0.03), while Lc0 likes White +0.38 perhaps due to his space advantage. I would say White has a par advantage.

C) 15.b4 ♖c8 (in earlier games Carlsen played 15...♘b6. The text is his improvement. The idea is to discourage axb5 though Anand played it anyway) 16.axb5?! (16.♗b2 ♘b6=) 16...cxb5 17.♗b2 d5 18.exd5 exd4. This was Anand-Carlsen, London 2010. Black is already a bit better here but White won after an oversight by Carlsen.

15....g6

15...♕c7 16.♕c2 ♖ac8 17.♗b2 ♘h5 18.♗f1 ♘f4 19.b4 ♘b6= was Karjakin-Carlsen from the 2010

World Blitz Championship in Moscow. Whether 15...♕c7 or 15...g6 is better is hard to say, but 15...g6 is the main line.

16.♕c2

16.♗b2 ♘h5 17.♗f1 ♘f4 18.♕c2 exd4 19.cxd4 b4 20.♘c4 ♘e6 (+0.09). White has just a little more space.

16....♖c8 17.♗a3

17.♗b2 ♘h5 18.♗f1 exd4 19.cxd4 d5 20.e5?! b4 Black is better due to ideas like ...♘g7 and ...c6-c5.

17....♘h5!

17...exd4 18.cxd4 ♘h5 19.g3 ♘g7 20.♗f1 ♘e6 is likely to transpose to the game. It does have the merit of avoiding the equalizing dxe5 at any point.

18.g3

18.♗f1 ♘f4 19.g3 ♘e6 transposes.

18...♘g7 19.♗f1 ♘e6=

20.♖ad1

In an earlier game with Navara (in their Khanty-Mansiysk, rapid playoff, 2009), Shabalov played 20.h4 but lost after 20...♕b6 21.♗h3 ♖cd8, though 20...exd4 21.cxd4 ♗g7 (-0.02) might have been better.

20....♕b6 21.♗a2?!

21.dxe5 ♘xe5 22.♘xe5 dxe5 23.♗xf8 ♖xf8= (+0.10).

21....exd4 22.cxd4 ♗g7 23.♗xd6 ♘xd4 24.a5 ♕a7

A) 24...♕d8 25.♘xd4 ♗xd4 also favors Black;

B) 24...♘xf3+ 25.♘xf3 ♕a7 transposes to the game.

25.♘xd4 ♗xd4 26.♘f3 ♗g7 27.b4?
27.♕c2 c5 and Black's queenside play is more effective than White's kingside play.

27....c5∓ 28.♗f4?! ♗xe4?
28...♗c6! 29.bxc5 ♘xc5 30.♗e3 ♕e7 wins a pawn.

29.♘g5 ♘f6 30.♗e3?
30.bxc5 ♗a8 31.♖xe8+ ♖xe8 32.♖d6 h6 33.♘xf7 ♕xf7 34.♕xf7+ ♔xf7 35.♖xa6 ♗d5 36.c6 g5 37.♗e3 and White's two far advanced passers offer full compensation for the knight.

30....♗a8−+ 31.bxc5 ♕b7 32.c6 ♕xc6 33.♕xf7+ ♔h8 34.f3

Now in the **actual game** Black erred by 34...h6? which led to a draw after 35.♖c1 ♕d7 36.♕xd7 ♘xd7. He should have played as follows:

34....♖c7 35.♖c1
35.♕b3 h6 36.♖c1 ♕d6−+.

35....♖xf7 36.♘xf7+ ♔g8 37.♖xc6 ♗xc6 38.♘g5 h6 39.♘e4 ♘xe4 40.fxe4 ♗xe4

With an extra protected passed pawn and a superior position, Black is winning.

Game 23.6   Ruy Lopez/Spanish – Breyer
Vugar Gashimov   2733
David Navara   2708
Reggio Emilia 2010/11 (8)

1.e4 e5 2.♘f3 ♘c6 3.♗b5 a6 4.♗a4 ♘f6 5.0-0 ♗e7 6.♖e1 b5 7.♗b3 d6 8.c3 0-0 9.h3 ♘b8 10.d4 ♘bd7 11.♘bd2 ♗b7 12.♗c2 ♖e8 13.♘f1 ♗f8

14.♗g5
The late elite GM Vugar Gashimov played this move several times so it clearly deserves to be taken seriously.

14....h6 15.♗h4 g6

Probably best is 15...exd4 16.cxd4 c5 17.d5 (17.e5 dxe5 18.dxe5 ♗xf3 19.♕xf3 ♘xe5 20.♕f5 ♘ed7 21.♘e3 g6 22.♕f3 ♕b6 23.♗xg6 ♘e5!) 17...g6 18.♗g3 ♘h5 19.♗h2 c4 20.b3 cxb3 21.axb3 ♖c8 (+0.02). White has one more pawn in the center, but Black's pieces are active.

16.♘1h2

16.dxe5 dxe5 17.♘3h2 ♗e7 18.♕d2 ♔g7 19.♖ad1 ♗c6 20.♘e3 ♘h5 21.♗xe7 ♕xe7 22.c4 ♘f4 23.♘f3 ♖ad8 24.♕c3 b4 (+0.28). White will get an edge by ♘d5, so Black should avoid this by the trade on move 15.

16....♗g7

17.dxe5

17.♘g4 exd4 18.cxd4 ♕c8 19.♘xf6+ ♘xf6= 20.e5 dxe5 21.dxe5 ♘h5 22.♗e4 c5 and now Black is a bit better due to the weakness of the e5-pawn.

17....dxe5 18.♘g4 g5 19.♗g3 ♘xg4 20.hxg4 ♕e7 21.a4 ♘c5

In the **actual game** Black played 21...c5 22.♘d2 ♘f6 23.♘f1 ♕e6 24.f3 h5. White now could have gotten an edge by 25.♕d2 but he played the unclear 25.gxh5 and won anyway.

22.♘d2 ♖ed8 23.axb5 axb5 24.♕e2 b4 25.♖xa8 ♗xa8 26.cxb4 ♘e6 27.b5 ♘f4 28.♗xf4 exf4=

With the bishop pair in an open position for a doubled isolated pawn, Black has full compensation.

Game 23.7   Ruy Lopez/Spanish – Breyer
Csaba Balogh   2613
Victor Mikhalevski   2607
Austria Bundesliga 2009/10 (3)

1.e4 e5 2.♘f3 ♘c6 3.♗b5 a6 4.♗a4 ♘f6 5.0-0 ♗e7 6.♖e1 b5 7.♗b3 d6 8.c3 0-0 9.h3 ♘b8 10.d4 ♘bd7 11.♘bd2 ♗b7 12.♗c2 ♖e8 13.♘f1 ♗f8 14.♘g3 g6 15.♗g5

15....h6

Here this is more logical than after 15.a4 c5 16.d5 c4 17.♗g5, because now the bishop should not retreat to e3 due to 16...exd4 17.cxd4 ♘xe4.

16.♗d2 ♗g7 17.a4 c5 18.d5 c4 19.b4

A) 19.♗e3 is often played but puts Black a tempo up (...♗g7) on a standard line in the 15.a4 c5 branch. Black replies 19...♕c7 with equality;

B) 19.♕c1 ♔h7 20.b4 cxb3 21.♗xb3 ♕c7 22.♕a3 ♖eb8 is a bit more pleasant for White due to his space advantage, but acceptable for Black (+0.12).

19....cxb3 20.♗xb3

20....♘c5 21.c4 ♕d7 22.♗a5 ♖ec8

Better is 22...♖eb8! 23.♗c2 ♗c8 24.♗b4 ♘e8 25.axb5 axb5 26.♗xc5 dxc5 27.cxb5 ♘d6 28.♗a4 ♖a5 29.♘d2 ♕a7 (+0.14). Black has good compensation for his half-pawn, with pressure on b5 and a4.

23.♗c2 bxc4 24.♘d2

24....♗xd5?!

24...h5!? 25.♘xc4 (but 25.♖b1 or 25.♖a3 give White an edge) 25...♘cxe4 26.♘b6 ♘xf2 27.♘xd7 ♘xd1 28.♘xf6+ ♗xf6 29.♗xd1 ♗xd5 30.♘e4 ♗xe4 31.♖xe4 d5 32.♖e1 ♖ab8=. Although a bishop (especially when part of a pair) is stronger than three pawns in general, here Black has two connected passers and control of both open files, so he is not worse.

25.exd5 ♘b7 26.♗b6?!

After 26.♗c3! ♘xd5 27.♘b1 ♕e6 28.♗e4 ♖c5 29.♗f3 White is slightly better. The bishop looks better than the three pawns here.

26....♘xd5 27.a5 ♘b4

27...♘xb6 28.axb6 d5=.

28.♗e4 d5 29.♖b1 ♘d3 30.♗xd3 cxd3 31.♖b3 e4 32.♘dxe4 dxe4 33.♘xe4 d2= 34.♕xd2 ♕xd2 35.♘xd2 ♗c3 36.♖e7 ♗xa5 37.♖xb7 ♗xd2 38.♖f3 ♖ab8 39.♖fxf7 ♖xb7 40.♖xb7 ♗f4 41.g3 ♖b8 42.♖a7 ♖xb6 43.gxf4 ♖f6 44.♔g2 ♖xf4 45.♖xa6 ½-½

Game 23.8   Ruy Lopez/Spanish – Breyer
Sanan Sjugirov   2610
David Navara   2731
Peristeri tt 2010 (5)

1.e4 e5 2.♘f3 ♘c6 3.♗b5 a6 4.♗a4 ♘f6 5.0-0 ♗e7 6.♖e1 b5 7.♗b3 d6 8.c3 0-0 9.h3 ♘b8 10.d4 ♘bd7 11.♘bd2 ♗b7 12.♗c2 ♖e8 13.♘f1 ♗f8 14.♘g3 g6 15.b3

The idea is to play d4-d5 next and be able to answer ...c7-c6 by c3-c4.

15...♗g7 16.d5 ♖c8

This permits ...c7-c6 next as the rook can recapture to defend d6.

17.c4 c6 18.♗d2?!

18.♗e3 ♘b6 19.♕e2 cxd5 20.cxd5 ♘bxd5 21.exd5 ♘xd5 22.♖ac1 ♘xe3 23.fxe3 d5 is an interesting line where Black gets two pawns, the bishop pair, better pawn structure, and center control for a knight. White is slightly better based on results and engine eval (+0.45). Black can avoid this by 18...♕c7 19.♖c1 b4, but the evals and results are similar so why not go for the wild line rather than suffer?

18....a5 19.♗e3

19....♕c7

Better was 19...♗a6! 20.dxc6 ♖xc6 21.cxb5 ♗xb5 22.♗d3 ♗xd3 23.♕xd3 ♘c5 24.♗xc5 ♖xc5 25.♖ad1

d5 26.exd5 ♖xd5 and Black has the initiative thanks to his extra center pawn.

20.♗d3 b4 21.a3 bxa3

21...♖a8=.

22.♖xa3 cxd5 23.cxd5 ♗xd5 24.exd5 e4 25.♗f1

A) 25.♗a6 ♖a8 26.♗b5 exf3 27.♕xf3 ♕b7 28.♗c6 ♕b4 29.♖ea1 ♘e5 30.♕d1 ♘xc6 31.dxc6 ♖ec8 32.♘e2 ♖xc6 33.♖a4 ♕b7 34.♖xa5 ♖xa5 35.♖xa5±;

B) 25.♗b5 exf3 26.♕xf3 ♕b7 27.♖xa5 ♖c5 28.♗c6 ♘e5 29.♕d1 ♘xc6 30.dxc6 ♖xc6=.

25....exf3 26.♕xf3 ♕c3 27.♖ea1 ♖xe3!?

27...♘c5=.

28.♕xe3?!

In case of 28.fxe3 ♖c5 29.♘e2 ♕b4 30.♖a4 ♕b6 31.b4 axb4 32.♘d4 Black has a pawn and a better bishop for the exchange, which is not quite enough to claim equality.

28....♕xe3 29.fxe3 ♘xd5 30.♖xa5 ♗xa1 31.♖xd5 ♘f6

White has returned his material advantage, hoping to draw this slightly worse position by bishops of opposite color.

32.♖d1

32.♖xd6 ♗e5 33.♖a6 ♖c1 34.♘e2
♖b1 35.♖a4 ♖xb3∓.
32....♗e5 33.♘e2

33....♖c2

Black played 33...♘e4 in the
actual game and White eventually
reached a draw. The text keeps a
serious advantage for Black, though
of course White retains decent
drawing chances.

Game 23.9   Ruy Lopez/Spanish – Breyer
Alberto David   2585
Evgeny Postny   2674
Belgium tt 2008/09 (9)

1.e4 e5 2.♘f3 ♘c6 3.♗b5 a6 4.♗a4
♘f6 5.0-0 ♗e7 6.♖e1 b5 7.♗b3
d6 8.c3 0-0 9.h3 ♘b8 10.d4 ♘bd7
11.♘bd2 ♗b7 12.♗c2 ♖e8 13.♘f1
♗f8 14.♘g3 g6 15.a4 c5 16.d5 c4
17.♗g5

17....♗e7

Usual is 17...h6 18.♗e3 ♘c5 19.♕d2
h5, but lately 20.♗xc5 has been
annoying. Normally giving up
a good paired bishop like this
for a knight is dubious, but the
protected passer and the crippled
black majority justify it. So I prefer
Postny's move introduced in 1973
by Boris Spassky.

18.♗e3

White reasons that he has provoked
a worsening of Black's bishop
location, but it's a minor point
here. More common is 18.♕d2 ♘c5
19.♗h6 ♘fd7 20.♘h2 ♘xa4 21.♗xa4
bxa4 22.♖xa4 a5 23.♘g4 ♗a6 (+0.13).
White's space and pawn structure
advantages offset Black's bishop
pair.

18....♕c7

This makes a later ...♘c5 safe while
preparing Black's next move. It is
generally accepted now that Black
should not play ...♘c5 if ♗xc5 has
to be met by ...dxc5.

19.♘h2

White aims for f2-f4 or ♘g4.

19....♖eb8

This prepares to reactivate the
bishop by ...♗c8, while preparing
...b5-b4. Another way to activate
the bishop was 19...♘c5, planning
...♗b7-c8-d7, e.g. 20.f4 (20.♘g4
♘xg4 21.♕xg4 ♗c8 22.♕e2 ♗d7=)
20...exf4 21.♗xf4 ♗f8 22.♘f3 ♘fd7
and Black is doing well, with ideas
of ...♘b6 or if 23.♘d4 ♘e5. But
20.♖f1! ♗d8 21.♗h6 ♔h8 gives
White some advantage (+0.30).

20.f4

20.♘g4! ♘xg4 21.♕xg4 ♘f6 22.♕e2
♗c8 23.♘f1 ♘h5 24.♕d2 ♗f8
(+0.24).
20....exf4 21.♗xf4 ♘e5 22.♘f3

22....♘xf3+

22...♘fd7 was probably better, and
Black is doing well.
**23.♕xf3 ♘d7 24.♖f1 ♗f8 25.♘e2
♘e5 26.♕g3**

26.♕f2 ♗c8 27.♘d4 b4 is perhaps a
tad better for White.
**26....♗g7 27.♔h1 ♗c8 28.♘d4 b4
29.♘c6 bxc3 30.bxc3 ♖b2 31.♗xe5
dxe5**

32.♖f2?
32.♕f2=.
**32....♗b7 33.♘d4 ♕a5 34.♘c6
♕c7 35.♘d4 ♕c5 36.♘c6 ♗xc6
37.dxc6 ♕xc6 38.♖d1 ♖f8 39.♕h4
♕b6 40.♖e2 ♗f6 41.♕e1 ♗g5
42.♖d5 ♗f4 43.a5 ♕f6 44.♗d3 ♖fb8
45.♗xc4 ♖b1 46.♖d1 ♖xd1 47.♕xd1
♕c6 48.♗d5 ♕xc3−+**

As there are attacking chances the
bishops of opposite color do not
presage a pawn-down draw.
49.♗xf7+?
This regains the pawn but makes
Black's attack much stronger.
**49....♔g7 50.♗a2 ♕g3 51.♕g1 ♖c8
52.♖e1 ♖c2 53.♗d5 ♖xg2 54.♕xg2
♕xe1+ 55.♕g1 ♕xa5 56.♕a7+ ♔h6
57.♕f2 ♕c7 58.♔g2 a5 59.♕h4+
♔g7 60.♕g4 ♕c2+ 61.♔f1 ♕d3+
62.♔g2 h5**
And White resigned. If he moves
the queen forward, he will get
mated.

CHAPTER 24

Marshall Attack

The Marshall Attack in the Spanish arises when Black plays **7...0-0** rather than 7...d6 in the main line, and answers **8.c3** with **8...d5!?** (rather than 8..d6, when 9.h3 transposes to the normal Spanish lines).

The statistics are overwhelmingly in favor of the Marshall. In the Hiarcs book, Black performs at just nine Elo below his average rating, compared to minus 62 Elo for the normal Spanish (thru 9.h3) or minus 49 for the Breyer (my preferred defense 9...♘b8 to the normal Spanish). If White avoids the Marshall with 8.a4 or 8.h3 his edge in the Hiarcs book is 29 or 25 Elo respectively with my chosen defense to each, which explains why White usually avoids the Marshall and why Black invites these Anti-Marshall systems. If you don't trust engine vs engine games, then look at the stats from my high-level human games (2500+ average rating OTB games plus 2000+ minimum rating correspondence games). The Marshall is minus 12 Elo, normal Spanish minus 57, Breyer minus 53. If White avoids the Marshall on move 8 by a2-a4 or h2-h3 and Black plays my recommended defense, White's edge is 10 or 11 Elo, about the same as in the Marshall proper. So statistically the Marshall is about forty Elo better than the Breyer, a huge difference, with Anti-Marshall lines somewhere in between, while the Breyer is another ten Elo better than the combined results of all the Spanish defenses to 9.h3. I should also mention that the super-strong neural network engine Lc0 considers the Marshall (or Anti-Marshall) to come significantly closer to equalizing than the Breyer or any other ninth move Spanish alternative for Black, probably because neural net engines tend to be less materialistic than normal (so-called alpha-beta) engines.

These statistics are so impressive that few GMs as White allow the Marshall, avoiding it with the lines in Chapter 25. In general, the Anti-Marshall stats are better for White than the Marshall, but worse than any normal Spanish defenses. So even if you don't want to play the Marshall, it makes sense to 'bluff' the Marshall with 7...0-0, when most players will avoid the Marshall by 8.a4 or 8.h3. I have hardly ever played the Marshall myself, because most of my opponents avoid it this way. I have never been much of a gambit player, but with the above stats and lots of engine analysis showing how Black can reach near-equality with the right lines, I think I'll play it more in the future if given the chance. It's true that if White knows enough theory he should be able to reach a theoretically drawn position if that is his goal, but that's probably true with any Spanish defense.

So what does Black get for the pawn? He gets a lead in development and some threats against White's king. Although these threats are not enough to win the game against good defense, they are usually enough either to win back the pawn, or to win the bishop pair with enough other favorable factors to get enough compensation for the pawn. Sometimes with precise play White can keep the pawn while allowing bishops of opposite colors, but these positions are usually clear draws.

White doesn't have to accept the gambit after 8...d5, he can strike with **9.d4**. After which Black must play a few precise moves to equalize. See Game 24.1.

After accepting the gambit pawn (**9.exd5 ♘xd5 10.♘xe5 ♘xe5 11.♖xe5**), Black defends his knight by **11...c6**.

White can play 12.d3 or 12.d4 (other moves usually transpose). Historically 12.d4 is the main (and obvious) move, but recently **12.d3** has overtaken it at the top level, with the idea of supporting a later ♖e4. Black usually manages to regain his pawn by attacking d3, but White keeps a minute edge, which normally leads to a draw. I recommend a rare but so far unbeaten line in the notes to Game 24.7 (I save the best for last).

After the traditional **12.d4** the next few moves are virtually forced: **12...♗d6 13.♖e1 ♕h4 14.g3 ♕h3**. Then White has some options on move 15.

He can **trade on d5** with the idea of winning a second pawn, but Black gets a bigger lead in development, the bishop pair, and threats against White's king, which is enough to at least draw with correct play, as in Game 24.2. He can play **15.♕e2**, which became popular early in this century when it looked like White at least kept a small plus by returning the pawn to win the bishop pair, but as Game 24.3 shows even that can be avoided by Black. He can play **15.♖e4**, but with the trick move 15...g5! (relying on a queen fork if the pawn is taken) Black can reach equality; see Game 24.4. It is precisely to avoid this 15...g5 trick that White often now plays 12.d3, but Black won't play this way in that case.

The traditional main line **15.♗e3 ♗g4 16.♕d3 ♖ae8 17.♘d2** is explored in Games 24.5 and 24.6, where I recommend the subtle move 17...♕h5!. This is now pretty much analyzed to equality.

Game 24.1   Ruy Lopez/Spanish –
                Marshall Attack

Alexander Areschenko   2649

Frode Urkedal   2541

Khanty-Mansiysk 2017 (4)

**1.e4 e5 2.♘f3 ♘c6 3.♗b5 a6 4.♗a4
♘f6 5.0-0 ♗e7 6.♖e1 b5 7.♗b3 0-0
8.c3 d5 9.d4**

This is the most frequent way to
decline the Marshall, but Black can
fully equalize.

9...exd4 10.e5 ♘e4 11.cxd4

11...♗g4

11...♗f5 is more often played, but
probably not as good: 12.♘c3 ♘xc3
13.bxc3 ♕d7 14.♗g5. This achieves
the trade of bad bishop for good
bishop with a tiny white plus,
because 14...♗a3 15.♘h4 favors
White.

**12.♘c3 ♘xc3 13.bxc3 ♕d7 14.h3
♗h5 15.♗c2**

15...♖ae8

15...♘d8 16.♗e3 ♘e6 17.♕e2 c6=
(-0.04). Black has a queenside
initiative which fully offsets
White's slight kingside plus.

16.♗f4 ♘d8 17.♕d3 ♗g6 18.♕d2

18...♘e6

18...♗xc2 19.♕xc2 ♘e6 20.♗e3 ♖b8
21.♕d3 a5 22.a3 c5 23.dxc5 ♖fc8=
(-0.06). Black regains the pawn with
no problems.

19.♗xg6 fxg6

The engines prefer to take with the
h-pawn to avoid giving White a
passed pawn, but in this case I agree
with the human that the activity
of the rook on the f-file is more
important.

20.♗e3

20...罝f5?!

20...a5! 21.a4 bxa4 22.豐d1 a3 23.奧c1 a4=.

21.罝f1?

21.a4! bxa4 22.豐d1±.

21...罝ef8= 22.公e1 c5 23.dxc5 罝xe5 24.公d3 罝h5 25.罝ad1 豐c8 26.豐e2 奧xc5 27.奧xc5?!

27.公xc5 公xc5 28.奧xc5 豐xc5= was the correct way to reach the same position.

27...公xc5 28.公xc5 豐xc5?!

28...罝e8!∓.

29.豐e6+ 當h8 30.豐xa6 罝hf5 31.當h1 g5 32.罝b1 罝xf2 33.罝xf2 豐xf2 34.豐xb5 豐xa2 35.罝d1 豐f2 36.豐xd5 g4 37.hxg4 豐h4+ 38.當g1 豐f2+ 39.當h1 豐h4+ 40.當g1 豐f2+

½-½

Game 24.2   Ruy Lopez/Spanish –
Marshall Attack

Alena Lukasova   2268
Frank Grube   2322
ICCF 2017

1.e4 e5 2.公f3 公c6 3.奧b5 a6 4.奧a4 公f6 5.0-0 奧e7 6.罝e1 b5 7.奧b3 0-0 8.c3 d5 9.exd5 公xd5 10.公xe5 公xe5 11.罝xe5 c6 12.d4 奧d6

13.罝e1

13.罝e2 奧g4 14.f3 奧f5 15.奧xd5 cxd5 16.公d2 b4 17.cxb4 豐b8 18.公f1 豐xb4 19.公e3 奧e6 20.g3 罝fe8 21.豐d3 罝ac8 22.豐xa6 奧d7 23.a3 豐b8 24.a4 h5 25.公xd5 奧xg3=. Black's attack on the weak white king and on the three isolated pawns offsets his 1.5 pawn deficit (0.00). Repetition is likely soon.

13...豐h4 14.g3 豐h3

15.奧xd5

This attempt to win a pawn is nowadays only played in correspondence games. Black can reach full equality.

15.豐f3 奧g4 16.豐g2 豐h5 17.奧e3 罝ae8 18.公d2 奧e7 19.a4 罝fe8 20.axb5 axb5 21.奧xd5 cxd5 22.豐f1 f5 23.f3 奧h3 24.豐xb5 f4 25.奧f2 fxg3 26.hxg3 奧d7 27.豐f1 奧h3 28.豐d3

409

♗f5=; perpetual 'check' to the queen!

15...cxd5 16.♕f3 ♗f5 17.♕xd5 ♖ae8 18.♗d2 ♗f4!

19.♖xe8

19.gxf4 ♖xe1+ 20.♗xe1 ♕g4+ 21.♔h1 ♗e6 22.♕e4 ♕d1 23.h3 ♖e8 24.♔h2 ♗d7 25.♕g2 ♕xe1−+ (−6.32). White is still up two pawns, but due to the pin he is effectively down two pieces and hopelessly lost.

19...♖xe8 20.♕c6 ♗d7

21.♕f3

If 21.♕g2 ♕h5 22.f3 ♗c6 23.g4 ♕g6 24.♗xf4 ♖e1+ 25.♔f2 ♕c2+ 26.♗d2 ♖e8 27.d5 ♗b7 28.a4 ♕xb2 29.♖a3 ♕xb1 30.♕f1 ♕g6 31.c4 ♕d6 32.♖e3 ♕xh2+ 33.♔e1 ♕g3+∓ Black will win a pawn.

21...♗g5

22.♗e3

22.c4 h6 23.♗e3 ♗g4 24.♕g2 ♕xg2+ 25.♔xg2 ♗xe3 26.fxe3 ♖xe3 27.♘c3 bxc4 28.h3 ♗f3+ 29.♔f2 ♖d3 30.h4 ♗g4 31.d5 ♔f8 32.♖c1 ♖f3+ 33.♔g2 ♖e3 (0.00). This is a drawn endgame, but White has to be more careful than Black. The rook + bishop combo is a bit stronger than the rook + knight with pawns on both wings.

22...♗g4 23.♕g2 ♕xg2+ 24.♔xg2 ♗xe3 25.fxe3 ♖xe3 26.a4 ♖e2+ 27.♔f1 bxa4

28.h3

28.♖xa4? ♖xh2 29.♘a3 ♖xb2 30.c4 g5∓ (−0.82). This is much worse for White than the game, as he has one pawn less in a similar position.

28...♗f3 29.♖xa4 ♖xb2 30.♘a3 g5 31.c4 ♗g2+=

A draw was agreed here. The following moves are a likely continuation. Keep in mind that this was a correspondence game; in an over-the-board game this would probably have been played out.
32.♔e1 ♗xh3 33.c5 ♖a2 34.d5 f5 35.d6 f4 36.gxf4 gxf4 37.c6 f3 38.♖f4 ♖xa3 39.♔d2 ♖a5 40.♖d4 ♖a2+ 41.♔c3 f2 42.d7 f1♕ 43.d8♕+ ♕f8 44.♕g5+ ♕g7 45.♕d5+ ♕f7 46.♕d8+ ♕f8 47.♕g5+ ½-½
Perpetual check.

Game 24.3   Ruy Lopez/Spanish – Marshall Attack

Hou Yifan   2603
Peter Leko   2735

Wijk aan Zee 2013 (13)

1.e4 e5 2.♘f3 ♘c6 3.♗b5 a6 4.♗a4 ♘f6 5.0-0 ♗e7 6.♖e1 b5 7.♗b3 0-0 8.c3 d5 9.exd5 ♘xd5 10.♘xe5 ♘xe5 11.♖xe5 c6 12.d4 ♗d6 13.♖e1 ♕h4 14.g3 ♕h3 15.♕e2
This formerly obscure move became a main line in the current century.
15...♗g4 16.♕f1 ♕h5 17.♘d2 ♖ae8 18.f3

18...♗h3
This is the way to play for a win, refusing to regain the pawn at the price of the bishop pair. But both moves should lead to a draw.
18...♖xe1 19.♕xe1 ♗xf3 20.♘xf3 ♕xf3 21.♗d2 ♕g4 22.a4 ♕d7 23.♕f2 ♖e8 24.♕f3 ♗f8 25.♖f1 g6= (+0.05) Lc0 +0.09. White has the bishop pair 'for free', but Black has a knight outpost on d5 and a very good bishop, and it is hard to see how White will make progress. All 14 games in my database were drawn from here.
19.♕f2 ♖xe1+ 20.♕xe1 ♗f4
20...♔h8 21.♕f2 f5 22.a4 ♖e8 23.♘f1 f4 (+0.16) is a way to play for a win, but not objectively better.

21.♗xd5

21.gxf4 ♘xf4 22.♗d1 ♘d3 23.f4 ♗g4
24.♕g3 ♗xd1 25.♕xd3 ♖e8 26.♕g3
f5 27.♘f1 ♖e6 28.♕f2 ♖e2 29.♘g3
♕g4 30.♕f1 h5 31.♕xd1 ♖g2+
32.♔xg2 ♕xd1= (0.00) since White
has more material but Black has
perpetual check.
**21...♗xd2 22.♗xd2 ♕xd5 23.♕e4
♕d7 24.♖e1 ♗e6 25.a3 ♖e8**
White has almost no chance of
capitalizing on his extra pawn due
to the bishops of opposite colors,
the bad white bishop, and the good
d5 outpost for the black bishop
(+0.13) but even that seems too
high; Lc0 gives just +0.02.
**26.g4 f6 27.h3 ♗f7 28.♕f4 ♖xe1+
29.♗xe1 h6 30.♕e4 ♗d5 31.♕e3
♕e6 32.♔f2 ♕xe3+ 33.♔xe3 ♔f7
34.h4 g6 35.♗g3 h5 36.gxh5 gxh5
37.♗d6 ½-½**

Game 24.4   Ruy Lopez/Spanish –
                     Marshall Attack

Viktor Stronsky   2393
Robert Leemans   2377
Correspondence game, 2016

**1.e4 e5 2.♘f3 ♘c6 3.♗b5 a6 4.♗a4
♘f6 5.0-0 ♗e7 6.♖e1 b5 7.♗b3 0-0
8.c3 d5 9.exd5 ♘xd5 10.♘xe5 ♘xe5
11.♖xe5 c6 12.♖e1 ♗d6 13.d4 ♕h4
14.g3 ♕h3 15.♖e4**
This move plans 16.♖h4.
15...g5!
This is protected by the ...♕f5 fork
if White takes. It is precisely for
this reason that 12.d3 has become
the main line, since 15.♖e4 is too
strong here with 15...g5 impossible.

16.♕f1

16...♕h5
16...♕xf1+ 17.♔xf1 ♗f5 18.♘d2 h6
19.♖e1 ♖ae8 20.♘f3 g4.

analysis diagram

This is Bologan's choice for Black,
which scores well in practice, but
Komodo gives White a par (+0.15)
after 21.♘g1 so I'm recommending
the retention of queens, although
you can fall back to this line in case
17...♗h3 gets refuted.
17.♘d2 ♗h3!
This has pretty much been played
only in correspondence games, but
seems to be fully satisfactory for
Black.
18.♕e2
18.♕d1 ♕g6 19.♗c2 (19.♖e1 ♖ae8
20.a4 b4 21.♘c4 bxc3 22.♘e5 ♕f6
23.♕e2 ♕e6 24.bxc3 f6 25.♘xc6

♕xe2 26.♖xe2 ♖xe2 27.♗xd5+ ♔g7 28.♗e3 ♖c8= (0.00). With queens off a rook is equal to a knight and two pawns generally) 19...♗f5 20.♗b1 ♔h8 21.a4 ♘f4 22.f3 g4 23.♘f1 ♗xe4 24.fxe4 ♘h3+ 25.♔g2 f5 26.e5 ♗c7∓. Although bishop pair and pawn for the exchange with queens on is about even material, Black's obvious development lead gives him a clear edge.

18...♕g6

19.♘f3

19.♘f1 ♗f5 20.f3 ♘f6 21.♖e3 ♗f4 22.♖e7 ♗d6 23.♖b7 (White should probably offer to repeat by 23.♖e3). 23...g4 24.f4 ♗d3 25.♕d1 ♖ae8 26.♘e3 ♗e4 27.♗c2 ♗xc2 28.♘xc2 ♖e4 29.♕d3 ♖fe8∓ (-1.40). Black has obviously way too much compensation for the pawn here.

19...f6 20.♘e1

A) 20.a4 ♔h8 21.♗c2 ♗f5 22.♗d2 ♖ab8 (22...♗xe4 23.♗xe4 ♕h5 24.♗f5 ♖ad8= (+0.13). This should be Black's choice if he doesn't want a quick draw. With a pawn, bishop pair, and better kingside pawn structure White has full compensation for the exchange, but not more) 23.axb5 axb5 24.♖a6 ♖fc8

25.h4 ♘f4 26.♕e3 ♘d5 27.♕e2=. Draw by repetition.

B) 20.♗c2 (an untried Lc0 novelty) 20...♗f5 21.♗d2 ♔h8 22.b3 ♖ab8 +0.08. White will have pawn and bishop pair plus a pleasant position for the exchange, enough for an interesting game but not enough to claim advantage.

20...♔h8 21.♗d2 ♗f5 22.f3 g4

23.♗xd5

23.♗c2 gxf3 24.♕xf3 ♗xe4 25.♗xe4 f5 26.♗xd5 cxd5 27.♘d3 ♖ae8 28.♗f4 ♖e4 29.♗xd6 ♕xd6 30.a3 a5 31.♖f1=. Black is up the exchange for a pawn, but his 3 isolated pawns and weaker king are enough for White to hold the balance.

23...cxd5 24.♖e3 ♗f4 25.♖e7 ♗d6 26.♖e3 ♗f4 27.♖e7 ♗d6 28.♖e3
½-½

Game 24.5   Ruy Lopez/Spanish –
Marshall Attack

Aleksandar Kovacevic   2549
Ivan Ivanisevic   2645
Mako 2013 (6)

1.e4 e5 2.♘f3 ♘c6 3.♗b5 a6 4.♗a4 ♘f6 5.0-0 ♗e7 6.♖e1 b5 7.♗b3 0-0 8.c3 d5 9.exd5 ♘xd5 10.♘xe5 ♘xe5

11.♖xe5 c6 12.d4 ♗d6 13.♖e1 ♕h4 14.g3 ♕h3 15.♗e3 ♗g4 16.♕d3 ♕h5 17.♘d2 ♖ae8 18.a4 ♖e6 19.axb5 axb5

This may be considered the main variation of what was the main line of the Marshall Attack in the 20th century.

20.♘f1

A) 20.♕f1 ♖fe8 21.♗xd5 ♕xd5 22.h3 ♗h5 23.♕g2 ♕xg2+ 24.♔xg2 f5 25.♘f3 f4 26.♘g5 fxe3 27.♘xe6 ♖xe6 28.♖a8+ ♔f7 29.♖xe3 ♗d1 30.♖xe6 ♔xe6 31.♖a7 ♗e7= (0.00).

analysis diagram

Two bishops are usually at least equal to rook and two pawns, and this position is no exception. If White's two extra pawns could become connected passed pawns he might be better, but that is not the case here;

B) 20.♘e4 ♗f5 21.♗d2 ♖xe4 22.♖xe4 ♘f6 23.f3 ♕g6 (if my memory serves me, this line was discovered by GM Leonid Shamkovich (from whom I took some lessons nearly 40 years ago), and it brought the Marshall to full respectability) 24.♕f1 ♘xe4 25.fxe4 ♗xe4 26.♗f4 ♗d3 27.♕f2 ♗xf4 28.♕xf4 h6= (0.00). With both material and positional equality, and various possible repetitions;

C) 20.♗xd5 ♕xd5 21.c4 bxc4 22.♕xc4 ♖b8 23.♖a6 ♗f8 24.b3 h6 25.♖ea1 ♗b4 26.♕xd5 cxd5 27.♖xe6 ♗xe6= (-0.07). White cannot avoid the drawing ...♗xd2 and ...♖xb3, while Black can choose to play on instead since his bishop pair, White's bad bishop, and White's weak pawns give full compensation for the pawn anyway.

20...♗f5 21.♕d2 ♗h3 22.♗d1 ♕g6

23.♗f3

23.♗c2 ♕h5 24.♕d1 (24.♗d1 ♕g6 repeats) 24...♗g4 25.♕d3 f5 26.♗d2 f4 27.♖xe6 ♗xe6 28.♗d1 ♕f7 29.♗c2 ♕h5 30.♗d1 ♕f7 31.♗c2 ♕h5 32.♗d1 ♕f7 33.♗c2 ½-½ Shirov-Aronian, Moscow 2010.

23...♕f5

24.♕d1

24.♗h1 ♖fe8 25.♖e2? (25.♖a6 h5!N 26.♖xc6 h4 27.♖a6 ♗g6 28.♗h6 ♖xe1 29.♕xe1 ♘c7 30.♖xd6 ♖xd6 31.♗f4 ♖e6 32.♗e5 ♗xf1 33.♕xf1 ♘e8= (0.00). Although two pawns and the bishop pair are worth more than the exchange, the missing pair of rooks favors Black, and Black's queen is much more active than White's. The game is likely to end in some repetition) 25...h5 26.♕c2 ♕g4 (26...♕f6! ∓) 27.♖ee1 h4 28.♕d1? (28.♗d2=) 28...♕f5 29.♕f3?? (29.♕b1 ♕h5∓) 29...♕g6 0-1 Shirov-Aronian, Bilbao 2009.

24...h5 25.♗e2

25.♖a6 ♗c7 26.♗h1 ♖fe8 27.♕f3 ♕g6 28.♖xc6 ♖xc6 29.♕xd5 ♖b6 30.♗f3 h4 31.♗h5 ♕f6 32.♖d1 ♖d8 33.♕f3 ♕xf3 34.♗xf3 ♖a6= (+0.03). With queens gone, rook vs knight and two pawns is about even as long as the rooks have open lines, as they do here.

25...♕e4 26.♗f3 ♕f5 27.♗e2 ♕e4 28.♗f3 ♕f5 29.♗e2

Repetition.

½-½

Game 24.6   Ruy Lopez/Spanish – Marshall Attack

Ilan Rothman   2230
Alois Kyhos   2266

Correspondence game, 2014

1.e4 e5 2.♘f3 ♘c6 3.♗b5 a6 4.♗a4 ♘f6 5.0-0 ♗e7 6.♖e1 b5 7.♗b3 0-0 8.c3 d5 9.exd5 ♘xd5 10.♘xe5 ♘xe5 11.♖xe5 c6 12.d4 ♗d6 13.♖e1 ♕h4 14.g3 ♕h3 15.♗e3 ♗g4 16.♕d3 ♖ae8 17.♘d2

17...♕h5

Whether Black plays this or ...♖e6 first won't matter if White plays 18.a4, but the text avoids the unpleasant endgame in the following note.

17...♖e6 18.♕f1 ♕h5 19.f3 ♘xe3 20.♕f2 ♘d5 21.fxg4 ♕xg4 22.♕f3 ♕g6 23.♖xe6 fxe6 24.♕e4 ♗xg3 25.♕xg6 ♗f2+ 26.♔g2 hxg6 27.♘f3 (+0.18). This endgame is a bit more pleasant for White due to the many weak black pawns.

18.♗c2

This is the attempt to avoid transposing to the old main line, 18.a4. See the previous game.

18...f5 19.f3 ♗h3

19...♗xf3 20.♘xf3 ♕xf3 21.♗d2
♕xd3 22.♗xd3 f4 23.♔g2±. White
gets to play an endgame up the
bishop pair for nothing.

20.♗f2 ♘f4 21.♗b3+
White can postpone this check but
it won't change anything.

**21...♔h8 22.gxf4 ♗xf4 23.♗g3 ♕g5
24.♘f1 h5**

Although White is up a piece in this
position, it turns out that he can't
retain it.

25.♕c2
25.♖xe8 ♖xe8 26.♗f7 ♖e7 27.♗xh5
♗xf1 28.♕xf1 ♗e3+ 29.♔h1 ♕xh5
30.♗e5 ♖e6 31.♖e1 f4 32.♖e2 ♖g6=
(-0.01). Black's pressure on the
weakened white king offsets the
one pawn deficit.

**25...h4 26.♕f2 ♗xf1 27.♕xf1 hxg3
28.♕h3+ ♕h6 29.♕xh6+ gxh6
30.hxg3 ♗xg3 31.♖e6**
Ten out of ten games from this
position were drawn, and the
Komodo eval is 0.00. White may
win a pawn, but Black will obtain
enough counterplay to insure the
draw with bishops of opposite color.

**31...♔g7 32.♔g2 ♗f4 33.♔f2 ♖xe6
34.♗xe6 ♔f6 35.♗d7 h5 36.♗xc6
♖c8 37.d5**

37.♗b7 ♖b8 38.♗xa6 ♖b6 39.♗c8 b4
40.a4 bxa3 41.♖xa3 ♖xb2+ 42.♔f1
♗g3= (0.00). Black will win the
f-pawn and reach material equality
with opposite bishops.

37...h4 38.♖h1 ♗g3+ 39.♔g2 ♔e5
Black's strong king insures the
draw with bishops of opposite color
despite the pawn deficit.

**40.♔h3 ♔d6 41.a4 bxa4 42.♖a1 ♖b8
43.♖a2 ♖b6 44.♔g2 ♔e5 ½-½**

Game 24.7   Ruy Lopez/Spanish –
                    Marshall Attack

Maxime Vachier-Lagrave   2796
Levon Aronian   2785

Sharjah 2017 (5)

**1.e4 e5 2.♘f3 ♘c6 3.♗b5 a6 4.♗a4
♘f6 5.0-0 ♗e7 6.♖e1 b5 7.♗b3 0-0
8.c3 d5 9.exd5 ♘xd5 10.♘xe5 ♘xe5
11.♖xe5 c6 12.d3**

This is considered to be the main
line now. The idea is that a later
♖e4 will be defended. Statistically
12.d3 at least has a plus score for
White, which 12.d4 can't even
claim.

12...♗d6 13.♖e1 ♗f5!
This highlights the drawback of
12.d3, the pawn is a target there.

14.♕f3

14...♕h4

14...♕f6 is the main alternative, recommended by Bologan. But it leads to Black having to defend an endgame down the bishop pair for nothing, which although drawn is not quite equal.

New analysis suggests that the rare 14...♗g6 may be a good alternative.

analysis diagram

15.d4 (15.♗xd5 cxd5 16.♗f4 d4 17.cxd4 ♗b4 18.♘c3 ♕xd4 19.♗e3 ♕d7 20.♖ec1 ♗d6 21.♘e4 ♗e5 22.♘c5 ♕e7 23.d4 ♗xd4 24.♗xd4 ♖xd4 25.♘xa6 ♗e4= (+0.08), Lc0 +0.16. Black's strong bishop vs knight on the edge offsets White's extra pawn) 15...♕c7 16.g3 ♖ae8 17.♗e3 ♗e4 18.♕d1 ♗f5 19.♗xd5 cxd5 20.♘d2 ♕c8 (to prevent 21.a4

b4 22.c4) 21.♘f1 ♕d7 22.♕d2 h6 23.♗f4 ♗e7 24.♕d1 ♗g4 (+0.29), but I think Black has enough compensation for the pawn with the bishop pair and White having a bad bishop and weak light squares near his king. Lc0 gives just +0.13, and Black has drawn all ten games from here.

15.g3

A) 15.♕xf5 ♕xh2+ 16.♔f1 ♖ae8 17.♖xe8 ♖xe8 18.♗e3 ♘xe3+ 19.fxe3 ♕h1+ 20.♔e2 (20.♔f2 ♗g3+!!) 20...♖xe3+! leads to perpetual check;

B) 15.♗xd5? ♗xh2+ 16.♔f1 ♗g4 17.♕e3 ♗f4 gives Black a better endgame.

15...♕h3

16.♗e3

White returns the gambit pawn to catch up in development and claim a tiny plus.

Or 16.♘d2 ♖ae8 17.♘e4 ♗g4 18.♕g2 ♕xg2+ 19.♔xg2 f5 20.h3 ♗h5 21.♗f4 ♗xf4 22.gxf4 fxe4 23.dxe4 ♗f3+ 24.♔xf3 ♖xf4+ 25.♔g3 ♖fxe4 26.♖xe4 ♖xe4 has occurred about 200 times with White scoring about a par plus, but Black can draw if he studies the position. The first game

417

Radjabov-Ding Liren in the final of the 2019 World Cup in Khanty-Mansiysk saw 27.a4 ♖e2 28.axb5 axb5 29.♗xd5+ cxd5 30.♖d1 ♖xb2 31.♖xd5 ♖b3 32.f3 ♖xc3 33.♖xb5 draw. After 27.f3 ♖e2 28.c4 bxc4 29.♗xc4 ♖xb2 30.♗xa6 g5 31.a4 ♔g7 32.a5 ♘f4 33.♗f2 ♔g6 34.h4 ♔f5 35.hxg5 ♔xg5 White cannot avoid perpetual check.

16...♗xd3 17.♘d2 ♕f5 18.♗d4

18...♖fe8

A good alternative is 18...♖fd8 19.a4 h6 20.h4 ♖ac8 21.♕xf5 (21.axb5 axb5 22.♗xd5 cxd5 was seen in two previous games by Ding Liren) 21...♗xf5 22.♘e4 (+0.05, Lc0 +0.21, both sub-par for White) 22...♗f8 (or 22...c5! 23.♘xd6 ♖xd6 24.♗e5 ♖d7 25.c4 ♘b4 26.axb5 axb5 27.cxb5 c4 28.♗a4 ♘d3 (+0.03), Lc0 +0.17. After trading on e5 and playing ...g7-g6, Black should have little trouble drawing despite White's extra but doubled pawn) 23.♘c5 ♘b4 24.♗e5 g6 25.axb5 cxb5 26.♘e6 ♗xe6 27.♖xe6 fxe6 28.♗xe6+ ♔h7 29.♗xc8 was the third match game Radjabov-Ding Liren, Khanty-Mansiysk 2019. Black has to lose a pawn, but 29...♘c2! 30.♖c1 ♘xd4

31.cxd4 a5 32.♖c7+ ♔g7 33.♗a6 ♖d5 should draw due to bishops of opposite color whereas 29...♖xc8? as played by Ding Liren left the bishops on the same color making the draw problematic, and he ultimately lost.

19.a4 h6

20.♔g2

I should point out that Lc0 gives both this move and 20.h4 around +0.40, and White does score a par 55% from here, so I would seriously consider the above suggestion of 14...♗g6, which has a 50% score. (20/20 draws) 20.h4 ♗f8 (20...♖xe1+ 21.♖xe1 ♕xf3 22.♘xf3 ♗g6 23.axb5 (23.♗e5 ½-½ (38) Vachier-Lagrave-Aronian, Stavanger 2017) 23...axb5 24.♘e5±) 21.axb5 ♖xe1+ 22.♖xe1 axb5=.

20...♕xf3+ 21.♘xf3 ♖ac8

White has a slight plus score and positive computer evals here, but his edge is tiny, surely sub-par, and Black should not have much trouble holding. This seems to be the best he can achieve against the Marshall, which is why Aronian and Carlsen play the Marshall against other top pros when they can. Most if not all other defenses to 1.e4 allow White a larger plus than this.

22.axb5 axb5

23.♖a6

A) 23.♗xd5 cxd5 24.♖xe8+ ♖xe8 25.♖a6 ♖e6 26.♗e5 ♖xe5 27.♖xd6 ♗e4 28.g4 h5= (0.00);

B) 23.♘d2 ♘c7 24.♖e3 ♗f5= (0.00);

C) 23.♔g1 ♗f5 24.♖xe8+ ♖xe8 25.♖a6 ♘e7 26.♘d2 ♖d8 27.♗b6 ♘c7 28.♗e3 c5 29.♖a7 ♗d6= (+0.06). White's pieces are a bit more active so he is 'for choice', but it's nearly equal.

23...♖xe1 24.♘xe1 ♘c7 25.♖b6 ♗f5 26.♗c2 ♗e6 27.♗e4 ♘d5 28.♖a6 b4 28...♗f8= (0.00).

29.c4 ♘f6 30.♗f3 ♗xc4 31.♖xc6 ♖xc6 32.♗xc6 ♔f8 33.♘c2 ♘d5 34.♔f3 g6 35.♘e3 ♘xe3 36.♗xe3 g5 37.♔e4 ♔e7 38.♔d4 ♗e2 39.♗b7 f6 40.f4 gxf4 41.♗xf4 ♗xf4 42.gxf4 ♔d6 43.h4 ½-½

CHAPTER 25

Anti-Marshall

There are three serious attempts by White to avoid the Marshall (excluding deviations before move 6). He can play 6.d3 before Black even hints at playing the Marshall by 7...0-0. This is better than playing it at move 8, because with d2-d3 played the move ♖e1 is not high-priority. This line played a big role in the 2016 World Championship (Carlsen vs Karjakin). Alternatively, White can wait for 7...0-0 and then choose 8.a4 or 8.h3 to avoid the Marshall. However, as we shall see, 8.h3 avoids the Marshall only in name, not in spirit.

The idea behind **6.d3** is that by threatening to take on c6 and then on e5, White pretty much obliges Black to choose between **6...d6**, which allows 7.c3 permitting the bishop to retreat directly to c2 when it is attacked, or **6...b5** to avoid this, which is my recommendation. After **7.♗b3 0-0** (note that 7...d6 8.a4 ♗d7 was analyzed in Game 22.6, but I now slightly prefer castling here). White can choose between **8.♘c3 d6 9.a3** (to avoid the loss of the bishop, which is Game 25.1 by transposition of moves (7...d6 8.a3 0-0 9.♘c3, an equally valid move order), and 8.a4 b4 9.a5 d6, transposing to Game 25.2. While the overall stats for White are good here, after the recommended **9...♘a5 10.♗a2 ♗e6** my strong human database has Black at just minus 7 Elo with 48 games, an excellent result, while the Hiarcs db has Black actually +4 Elo after 58 games.

After **6.♖e1 b5 7.♗b3 0-0** the idea of **8.h3** is that 8...d5 is less good than in the Marshall proper, while 8...d6 9.c3 transposes to the normal Spanish.

So Black must choose another move or else everyone would prefer 8.h3 to 8.c3. The move is **8...♗b7**, which makes 8.h3 look a bit unnecessary. Now White must play **9.d3** (9.c3? d5 would be much better for Black than the Marshall, since ...♗b7 is clearly more useful than h2-h3), when it turns out that **9...d5!** is every bit as good as the real Marshall. This was not so clear when I wrote the previous edition, which was a major reason that I didn't recommend the Marshall then. The stats in my strong human database are just minus 12 Elo for Black here (533 games), while after my preferred sub-variation, **10.exd5 ♘xd5 11.♘xe5 ♘xe5 12.♖xe5 ♕d6! 13.♖e1 ♖ae8 14.♘d2 c5** the database shows zero Elo (!) after 109 games. The Hiarcs book shows minus 24 Elo (over 30,000 games) in the position after 9...d5 and minus 12 Elo (507 games) after 14...c5. So even with engines playing both sides, this 'pseudo-Marshall' Attack scores very well for Black compared to normal defenses. See Game 25.3.

Because of the above, attention has turned back to **8.a4**, when Black can reply either 8...♗b7 or 8...b4.

I recommend the latter move, as chosen repeatedly by Aronian, the most consistent Marshall practitioner among top players. After **8...b4** White's edge is 10 Elo in my human database and 29 Elo in the Hiarcs book, which are better stats for White than in the Marshall proper or in other Anti-Marshalls but still worse for White than in the normal Spanish or in any other normal defense to 1.e4. See Games 25.4 thru 25.6.

Finally, White can play **8.d4**, intending to transpose to a fairly strong line in the normal Spanish after 8...d6 9.c3 ♗g4 10.♗e3. We avoid this by **8...♘xd4**, which seems to equalize more clearly than the 8...d6 variation. See Game 25.7.

Game 25.1   Ruy Lopez/Spanish

Sergey Karjakin	2773
Levon Aronian	2799

St Louis rapid 2017 (7)

1.e4 e5 2.♘f3 ♘c6 3.♗b5 a6 4.♗a4 ♘f6 5.0-0 ♗e7 6.d3 b5 7.♗b3 d6 8.a3 0-0 9.♘c3 ♘a5 10.♗a2 ♗e6 11.b4

11.♗xe6 fxe6 12.b4 ♘c6 13.♗d2 d5 14.♖e1 ♕d6 15.♘a2 dxe4 16.dxe4 ♘d4 17.♘xd4 ♕xd4 18.♗c3 ♕d6=. White has a better pawn structure, but Black has play on the f-file, a better posted knight, and the ...c7-c5 lever, so only +0.06.

11...♗xa2

12.♘xa2

12.♖xa2 ♘c6 13.♗g5 ♘d7 14.♗e3 (14.♗d2 ♘f6 15.♖e1 ♕d7 16.♘d5 ♘xd5 17.exd5 ♘a7 18.a4 c6 19.axb5 axb5 20.♕a1 cxd5 21.♗e3 d4 22.♘xd4 exd4 23.♗xd4 ♗f6 24.♗xf6 gxf6 25.♖e3 ♖fe8 (+0.10); White will probably settle for a perpetual check soon) 14...♘f6 15.♗g5 ♘d7 16.♗e3 ♘f6 17.♕b1 (17.♖e1 h6 18.h3 ♕d7 19.♘d5 ♘xd5 20.exd5 ♘d8 21.a4 f5 (+0.05). Black's kingside advantage offsets White's queenside play) 17...d5 18.exd5 ♘xd5 19.♘xd5

♕xd5 20.c4 bxc4 21.dxc4 ♕e6 ½-½ (51) Vachier-Lagrave-Mamedyarov, Sharjah 2017. Black is fine, his better center offsets his inferior pawn structure (0.00).

12...♘b7

Lately play has favored 12...♘c6 13.c4 ♘d4 14.♘xd4 (14.♗e3 ♘e6 15.♘c3 c6) 14...exd4 (+0.21) but White's edge is mostly cosmetic.

13.c4 bxc4 14.dxc4 a5

15.♗b2

A) 15.♕c2 axb4 16.axb4 ♕d7 17.♗g5 h6 (17...♘d8 18.♘c3± Nepomniachtchi-Aronian, chess.com 2017) 18.♗xf6 ♗xf6 19.♘c3 c6 20.g3 ♖fb8 21.♕d3 ♘d8 22.♖xa8 ♖xa8 23.♘e1 ♘e6 24.♘c2 ♗d8 25.♖d1 ♗c7 (+0.06). Black's bishop for knight doesn't quite offset White's space advantage, but White's edge is minimal;

B) 15.♗e3 axb4 16.axb4 ♘xe4 17.♕d5 ♖xa2 18.♖xa2 ♘c3 19.♕xb7 ♘xa2 20.♖a1 (20.♗d2? ♕b8∓ Nepomniachtchi-Aronian, chess.com 2017) 20...♘c3 21.♖a3 ♕d1 22.♗c1 d5 23.♖d3 e4 24.♖xd1 exf3 25.b5 ♕d6 26.♕xd5 ♕xd5 27.♖xd5 ♖a8 28.♗b2 ♖a2 29.♗d4 ♖c2 30.gxf3 ♖xc4 31.♖d7 ♔f8 32.♗xg7+ ♔xg7

33.♖xe7 ♖c5= (0.00) with a surely drawn endgame;

C) 15.♕e2 ♕d7 16.♗g5 axb4 (16...♘d8 17.♘c3 Nepomniachtchi-Aronian, chess.com 2017) 17.axb4 h6 18.♗xf6 ♗xf6 19.♘c3 c6 20.g3 ♖fb8 21.♖xa8 ♖xa8 22.♖d1 ♘d8 23.♘e1 ♘e6 24.♘c2 ♗d8 25.♕d3 ♗c7 We have transposed to the 15.♕c2 variation above.

15...♕b8

15...c6 is a good alternative.

16.♘c3 axb4 17.axb4 ♖xa1 18.♕xa1 ♘d8 19.♕a4 ♘e6 20.♘d5 ♘xd5 21.cxd5

21.exd5 ♘f4 22.♖a1 ♕c8 23.♘e1 ♕g4 24.♕c2 e4 (+0.13). Black has counterplay on the kingside.

21...♘f4 22.g3 ♕c8 23.♕d1 ♘h3+ 24.♔g2 f5 25.exf5 ♕xf5 26.♗c1 g5 27.♕e2 g4 28.♘d2 ♘g5

29.f3?

29.h4 gxh3+ 30.♔h2 ♖a8=.

29...gxf3+ 30.♘xf3 ♕e4 31.♕xe4 ♘xe4∓ 32.♗h6 ♖f6 33.♗d2 ♖xf3 34.♖xf3 ♘xd2 35.♖a3 ♔f7 36.♖a8?

36.♖a2 ♘c4∓.

36...♘c4−+ 37.♔f3 ♘b6 38.♖a5 ♔g6 39.♔e4 ♘d7 40.♔d3 ♔f5 41.♖a7 e4+ 42.♔e2 ♗d8 43.♖a8 ♗f6 44.♖a7 ♘b6 45.♖xc7 ♘xd5

46.♖b7 ♘c3+ 47.♔d2 d5 48.b5 d4 49.b6 e3+ 50.♔d3 e2 51.♔d2 d3 52.♖f7 ♘e4+ 53.♔e1 ♘g5 0-1

Game 25.2   Ruy Lopez/Spanish
Fabiano Caruana   2807
Magnus Carlsen   2822
St Louis 2017 (1)

1.e4 e5 2.♘f3 ♘c6 3.♗b5 a6 4.♗a4 ♘f6 5.0-0 ♗e7 6.d3 b5 7.♗b3 d6 8.a4

This was supposed to be the main point of the 6.d3 system, and is my choice for the White book, but lately 8.a3 and 9.♘c3 has been preferred at the top level. See the previous game.

8...b4

8...♗d7 has been more popular lately at the top, but I think Black has had more problems in the latest games with ...♗d7 than with the text move.

9.a5 0-0 10.♘bd2 ♖b8 11.♖e1 ♗e6

12.♗xe6

Such bishop trades on e6 were considered bad and the sign of a novice player in my youth, but now we see top players making the trade quite often. The old books would say that strengthening Black's center and giving him the f-file could not be good, but now I think there is greater awareness of the drawbacks to doubled pawns, as well as the potential for a white space advantage after a pawn exchange on d4.

12.♕e2 ♗xb3 13.♘xb3 ♘d7= (+0.04) or 12.♗c4 ♗xc4 13.♘xc4 ♖e8 14.b3 h6 (-0.13). Black will play ...♗f8 and ...♖b5, when space is equal but a5 is weaker than b4.

12...fxe6

13.♘b3

13.c3 ♖b5 14.d4 (14.c4 ♖b8 15.♘b3 ♕c8 (+0.12)) 14...bxc3 15.bxc3 exd4 16.cxd4 ♘b4 17.♖a3 ♕d7= (+0.13).

13...♕c8 14.♕e2

14.d4 ♘d7 15.♕d3 exd4 16.♘bxd4 ♘xd4 17.♘xd4 ♘c5 18.♕e2 ♕b7 19.f3 ♖fe8 20.♗e3 ♘d7= (0.00). Quite balanced.

14...♘d8

14...♘d7 15.♗e3 ♗f6 is more common and scores well for Black, though Komodo prefers Carlsen's choice.

15.d4

15.♘fd2 ♘c6 16.h3 ♘d7= (0.00). Black's better pieces offset his worse pawns.

15...exd4 16.♘bxd4 c5 17.♘b3

17...e5

17...♘d7! 18.♖d1 ♘c6 19.♗g5 ♖xf3 20.♗xe7 ♖xb3 21.cxb3 ♘xe7 22.♖xd6 ♘c6 23.♖xe6 ♘de5= (0.00). Although rook and two pawns are a bit stronger than two knights, the bad white pawn structure and the well-placed knights keep the balance.

18.♘bd2 ♘e6 19.♘c4 ♘d4 20.♘xd4 cxd4 21.♘b6

21.♗g5! ♕c6 22.♗xf6 gives White an edge – therefore Black should play what we saw in the note to move 17.

21...♕c6 22.♗g5 ♗d8 23.♗xf6 ♗xb6 24.axb6 ♖xf6 25.♖xa6 h6 26.♕d3 ♖xb6 27.♖ea1 ♖xa6 28.♖xa6 ♕c5 29.♖a8+ ♔h7 30.h3 b3 31.♕xb3 d3 32.cxd3 ♕xf2+ 33.♔h2 ♕f4+ 34.♔h1 ♕c1+ 35.♔h2 ♕f4+ 36.♔h1 ♕g3 37.♕g8+ ♔g6 38.♖f8 ♕xd3 39.♖xf6+ ♔xf6 40.♕f8+ ♔e6 41.♕e8+ ♔f6 42.♕f8+ ♔e6 43.♕e8+

Draw.

Game 25.3   Ruy Lopez/Spanish –
Anti Marshall

Matei Cornel   2441
Viorel Craciuneanu   2452

Correspondence game, 2015

**1.e4 e5 2.♘f3 ♘c6 3.♗b5 a6 4.♗a4
♘f6 5.0-0 ♗e7 6.♖e1 b5 7.♗b3 0-0
8.h3**

This move-order is designed to
avoid the Marshall Attack, which
it technically does, but it allows a
very similar ...d7-d5 gambit which
is just as good as the Marshall if not
better.

This has led to a decline in the
popularity of 8.h3, and was a
major factor in my decision to
recommend the Marshall in this
edition.

8...♗b7 9.d3 d5

9...d6 10.a3 ♕d7 11.♘bd2 ♘d8 is
quite playable, and only (+0.04)
according to Komodo, but the
database stats are above par for
White so I prefer the gambit.

10.exd5 ♘xd5 11.♘xe5

11.♘bd2 ♕d7 12.♘f1 ♗c5 13.♘xe5
♘xe5 14.♖xe5 ♗d4 15.♖e1
♖ae8 (-0.10). Black's superior
development and pressure on

White's kingside fully compensate
for the missing pawn.

11...♘xe5

11...♘d4 is the main line and
also satisfactory, but I prefer the
game move. 12.♗d2 (12.♘d2 c5
13.♘df3 ♘xb3 14.axb3 f6 15.♘g4
♖e8 16.♘e3 ♗f8 17.♘xd5 ♕xd5=
(+0.05). The bishop pair, the
dominant black queen, and the
doubled white pawns give Black
full compensation for the pawn)
12...♖e8 13.♘c3 ♘xb3 14.axb3 ♗d6
15.d4 ♘b4 16.♘e4 ♗xe5 17.dxe5
♖xe5 18.♗xb4 ♖xe4 19.♕xd8+
♖xd8 20.♖ad1 ♖xd1 21.♖xd1 h5
22.♖d8+ ♔h7 23.♗c3 ♖e6= (+0.18).
This endgame should be an easy
draw, but Black has to be a bit more
careful than White.

**12.♖xe5 ♕d6 13.♖e1 ♖ae8 14.♘d2
c5**

I believe Kamsky resurrected this
formerly obscure line. Black's
much better development and
possibilities of attacking g2 or
getting in ...c5-c4 offset the missing
pawn.

15.♘e4

15.a4 c4 16.dxc4 ♘f4 17.♘f3 ♘xg2
18.♕xd6 ♘xe1 19.♕b6 ♘f3+ 20.♔f1

♘h2+ with perpetual check has been played in many games, including one of mine.

15...♕c6 16.c4 ♘b6 17.f3 ♗h4 18.♖e3

18.♖e2 bxc4 19.dxc4 ♕c7 20.♕f1 ♗xe4 21.♖xe4 ♖xe4 22.fxe4 ♗f6 (+0.01). White is up 1.5 pawns counting the bishop pair, but his unopposed bishop is quite bad, e4 is weak, and Black's bishop will be quite powerful on d4.

18...♕c7 19.♕e2 bxc4 20.dxc4

20...♖e7

This line seems to have been played mostly in correspondence games so far, but Black has 28 draws and two wins in 30 games.

20...♖e6 21.♗d2 ♖fe8 22.♗c2 ♕e7 23.♖d1 g6 24.g3 ♗xe4 25.♖xe4 ♖xe4 26.♕xe4 ♕xe4 27.fxe4 ♗xg3 28.b3 ♗e5 29.♗e3 ♖c8 30.♔f2 ♔g7 31.♗d3 ♘d7 32.♗e2 ♘f6 33.♗f3. Because White is up the bishop pair 'for free' the eval is about +0.30, but there doesn't appear to be a plan for White to make progress, so this line should also be a safe draw.

21.♗d2 ♖fe8 22.♖d1 ♗xe4 23.♖xe4 ♖xe4 24.fxe4 ♗f6 25.♗e1 g6 26.♗f2 a5 27.♖f1 ♕c6

27...♗e5, 27...♖e7, and 27...a4 all appear fully equal too (0.00). White is up a pawn plus the bishop pair, but it looks impossible for White to make progress after the inevitable exchange of dark-squared bishops.

28.♖e1 ♕d6 29.♗d1 ♗d4 30.b3 ♘d7 31.♕d2 ♘e5

31...♕b6 is a simpler equalizer. The point is that after the dark-squared bishops are exchanged, Black will have a strong knight vs bad bishop and will probably regain the pawn on e4.

32.♗xd4 ♖d8 33.♕xa5 ♕xd4+ 34.♔h2 ♕d6 35.♔h1 ♕d2 36.♕xd2 ♖xd2 37.♗f3 ♖xa2 38.♖d1 ♖b2 39.♖d5 ♖b1+ 40.♔h2 f6 41.♖xc5

The game was drawn here. The remaining moves show the likely finish: 41...♖xb3 42.♖c8+ ♔f7 43.♖c7+ ♔e6 44.♖xh7 ♘xf3+ 45.gxf3 ♖xf3 46.♖g7 ♖c3 47.♖xg6 ♖xc4 48.h4 ♖xe4=.

Game 25.4   Ruy Lopez/Spanish – Anti-Marshall

Leinier Dominguez Perez   2739
Levon Aronian   2785
Doha 2016 (12)

1.e4 e5 2.♘f3 ♘c6 3.♗b5 a6 4.♗a4 ♘f6 5.0-0 ♗e7 6.♖e1 b5 7.♗b3 0-0 8.a4 b4

This is generally preferred to the older 8...♗b7. Generally modern GMs don't like to place the bishop on b7 when White can defend e4 by d2-d3 without having spent a move on h2-h3.

9.d4

This is considered the most testing line by White, but as the text shows Black can equalize with a few precise moves.

9...d6 10.dxe5 dxe5

Taking back with the knight instead is also okay, but Aronian consistently prefers this pawn capture, and I am inclined to agree. It is preferred by about 2 to 1 in my strong human db. Komodo and Stockfish prefer the pawn capture, Lc0 prefers the knight capture. It's a close choice.

11.♘bd2

11.♕xd8 ♖xd8 12.♘bd2 ♗d6 13.a5 h6 14.h3 ♖b8 15.♗c4 ♗e6 16.♗xe6 fxe6 17.♘c4 ♖b5 18.♗d2 ♖f8 19.b3 ♗c5 20.♗e3 ♗d4= (0.00). Black's d4 outpost and f-file play offset the theoretical weakness of the doubled isolated e-pawns.

11...♗c5 12.♕e2

12.a5 ♗e6 13.♕e2 (13.♗xe6 fxe6 14.♕e2 ♘g4 15.♖f1 ♘d4 16.♕c4 ♕d6 17.h3 ♘xf3+ 18.♘xf3 ♘f2 19.♖xf2 ♕d1+ 20.♕f1 ♕xc2 21.♕e1 ♗xf2+ 22.♕xf2 ♕xe4. The engines rate White about half a pawn plus here, but this is a rare case where

I disagree. I don't see why White is better, and all four games from here were drawn) 13...♕e7 14.♗c4 ♘d4 15.♘xd4 ♗xd4 16.♘b3 ♖fd8 (16...♗xc4! 17.♕xc4 c5 18.c3 ♘g4 19.♘xd4 exd4 20.♕e2 ♘e5 21.cxd4 cxd4 22.f4 d3 23.♕d1 ♘c6 24.♕xd3 ♖fd8 25.♕c4 ♘d4 26.♗e3 (White must surrender the exchange with this move or else worse things will happen) 26...♖ac8 27.♕xa6 ♘c2 28.e5 ♘xe1 29.♖xe1 ♕d7= (-0.04). White's two pawns are worth a bit more than Black's exchange, but Black controls the open files and has better piece coordination, so is doing fine) 17.♘xd4± Dominguez Perez-Aronian, St Louis 2017.

12...♕e7 13.h3

13.♗d5 ♘xd5 14.exd5 ♘d4 15.♘xd4 ♗xd4 16.♘b3 ♕d6 17.♘xd4 exd4 18.♕e4 ♗b7 19.♕xd4 ♕xd5 20.♕xd5 ♗xd5 21.♗f4 ♖fd8 22.♖e7 c5= (+0.11). White has the sunny side of a nearly certain bishops of opposite color draw.

13...♖d8 14.♘c4 ♘d4 15.♘xd4 ♖xd4 16.♗e3 ♖xe4 17.♕f3 ♗b7 18.♘a5 ♖xe3 19.♕xb7 ♖xe1+ 20.♖xe1 ♖e8 21.♕xa6 e4 22.♘c4

22...e3?

22...♖d8! 23.♘e3 g6 24.♕e2 c6=
(0.00). Black's central dominance
offsets White's passed pawn.
23.♘xe3± ♘e4 24.♕c4 g6??
24...♘xf2 25.♕xf7+ ♕xf7 26.♗xf7+
♔xf7 27.♔xf2±.
25.♘g4+– ♘d2 26.♕xf7+ 1-0

Game 25.5   Ruy Lopez/Spanish –
             Anti-Marshall

Alexander Grischuk   2761
Ding Liren   2781

China 2017 (8)

──────────────

**1.e4 e5 2.♘f3 ♘c6 3.♗b5 a6 4.♗a4
♘f6 5.0-0 ♗e7 6.♖e1 b5 7.♗b3 0-0
8.a4 b4**

9.a5
This is the principal alternative to
9.d4 and 9.d3. It prevents ...♘a5 and
leaves b4 a bit weak, but a5 is also
weak.
**9...d6 10.d3 ♗e6 11.♗xe6 fxe6
12.♘bd2 ♖b8 13.c3 bxc3**
I think it's more accurate to defer
...bxc3 with 13...♖b5, since c3-c4
isn't much of a threat: 14.c4 (14.h3
♘d7=; 14.d4 bxc3 15.bxc3 transposes
to the game) 14...♖b8 15.♘b3 ♕c8=
(+0.05).

14.bxc3 ♖b5

15.d4
15.♘f1 ♕d7 16.♗g5 ♖xa5 17.♖xa5
♘xa5 18.d4 exd4 19.cxd4 ♘c6!∓
(19...h6 ½-½ (60) Vachier-Lagrave-
Wojtaszek, Dortmund 2017). White
doesn't have enough for the pawn.
15...exd4 16.cxd4 ♘b4

17.♘f1
  A) 17.♗a3 ♘d3 18.♖f1 c5 19.♕c2
♘b4 20.♗xb4 cxb4 21.♖fc1 ♕e8
22.♕b3 d5 23.e5 ♘e4 24.♘xe4 dxe4
25.♕xe6+ ♕f7 26.♕xf7+ ♔xf7
27.♘d2 b3 28.♖ab1 b2 29.♖c7 ♖fb8
30.♘c4 ♗e6 31.g3 ♗d8 32.d5+ ♖xd5
33.♖c6+ ♔d7 34.♖xa6 ♖b4 35.e6+
♔e7 36.♖c6 ♗xa5 37.♖xb2 ♖d1+
38.♔g2 ♖xb2 39.♘xb2 e3 40.♖c2
♖d2 41.♖xd2 ♗xd2 42.fxe3 ♗xe3
43.♔f3 ♗d4 44.♘d3 ♔xe6=. Zero
score, draw certain;

B) 17.♖a3 ♕d7 18.h3 d5 19.exd5 ♘bxd5= (0.00). White has one fewer weak pawns, but Black has better piece placement.

17...c5 18.dxc5 dxc5 19.♕b3 ♕c8 20.♕c4 ♘c6 21.♗d2

21...♘g4

21...♘d4 22.♖a3 ♖d8= (0.00). The outpost makes up for the inferior pawn structure.

22.♗c3 ♖xf3 23.gxf3 ♘ge5 24.♕e2 c4 25.f4 ♘d3 26.♕g4 g6 27.f5 ♘xe1 28.♖xe1 ♘e5 29.♗xe5 ♖xe5 30.♘g3 c3

30...exf5 31.♘xf5 ♕c5∓.

31.fxg6 ♖g5 32.gxh7+ ♔h8 33.♕f3 c2 34.♖c1 ♖c5 35.♕f7 ♕f8 36.♕xf8+ ♗xf8 37.♘f1 ♗h6 ½-½

Game 25.6   Ruy Lopez/Spanish – Anti-Marshall

Magnus Carlsen   2838
Levon Aronian   2774
Karlsruhe 2017 (2)

1.e4 e5 2.♘f3 ♘c6 3.♗b5 a6 4.♗a4 ♘f6 5.0-0 ♗e7 6.♖e1 b5 7.♗b3 0-0 8.a4 b4 9.d3

This used to be the main move, but now 9.a5 is preferred so as to meet

9....♗c5 by 10.c3 planning d2-d4, without the loss of a tempo.

9...♗c5

10.c3

A) 10.♘bd2 d6 11.h3 h6 12.c3 ♖b8 13.♘c4 (13.♗c4 ♗b6 14.♘b3 ♖e8 15.♕c2 ♗a7 16.♗d2 bxc3 17.bxc3 ♘h5 18.d4 ♕f6= (0.00); White's pieces look a bit clumsy, but his pawn center makes it even) 13...♗a7 14.♗e3 ♗xe3 15.♘xe3 ♖e8 16.a5 ♘a7 (16...♘e7! 17.♕c2 ♘g6=; zero score; fully balanced) 17.♗c2 bxc3 18.bxc3 ♘b5 19.♕d2 ♗d7 20.♘c4 (20.♖eb1±) 20...♗e6 21.♘e3 ♗d7 22.♘c4 ♗e6 23.♘e3 ♗d7 ½-½ Wei Yi-Tomashevsky, Wijk aan Zee 2016;

B) 10.♗e3 ♗xe3 11.♖xe3 (11.fxe3 d6 12.♖f1 ♘a5 13.♗a2 ♕e8 14.♕e1 ♖b8 15.♘bd2 ♕c6 16.♘b3 ♘xb3 17.♗xb3 ♗e6= (0.00); as usual the active white rook on the f-file just balances the doubled pawns) 11...d6 12.♘bd2 ♘a5 13.♗a2 c5 14.♘c4 ♘c6 15.♖e1 ♗e6 16.♘fd2 ♖e8= (0.00). Fully balanced.

10...bxc3 11.bxc3 ♖b8 12.♗g5 h6 13.♗h4 g5 14.♗g3 ♘h5 15.♘bd2 ♘xg3 16.hxg3 ♕f6 17.♘c4 d6 18.♘e3 ♗e6

19.♗xe6

19.♘d5 ♗xd5 20.exd5 ♘e7 21.d4 ♗a7 22.♖c1 ♘g6= 23.dxe5 ♘xe5 24.♗c2 ♘xf3+ 25.gxf3 ♔g7=. A zero score here, but I'd rather play Black since Black can attack the king while White can only attack the a6-pawn.

19...fxe6 20.♕c2 h5 21.♖ab1 ♖xb1 22.♖xb1 h4 23.gxh4 gxh4 24.♖b7 h3?!

24...♖f7! (-0.16). Black needlessly sacrificed c7 in the game and still drew.

The text move keeps the initiative for free.

25.♖xc7 hxg2 26.♕e2 ♘e7

Game eventually drawn, but White could have kept an edge.

½–½

Game 25.7   Ruy Lopez/Spanish –
              Anti-Marshall

Lu Shanglei   2614
Daniil Dubov   2666

Moscow 2016 (4)

1.e4 e5 2.♘f3 ♘c6 3.♗b5 a6 4.♗a4 ♘f6 5.0-0 ♗e7 6.♖e1 b5 7.♗b3 0-0 8.d4

8...♘xd4

8...d6 9.c3 ♗g4 10.♗e3 is much more frequently played, transposing to a major line of the normal Spanish, but White has pretty good stats from this position so I recommend taking advantage of the Marshall move-order by 8...♘xd4 instead.

9.♘xd4

9.♗xf7+ ♖xf7 10.♘xe5

analysis diagram

10...♖f8 (unfortunately moves that save the d4-knight lose to 11.♘xf7 followed by e4-e5, so Black is forced to sacrifice half a pawn. But it turns out to be fine) 11.♕xd4 ♗b7 12.♕d1 c5 13.♘c3 b4 14.♘d5 ♘xd5 15.exd5 ♗d6 16.f4 (16.c4 bxc3 17.bxc3 was Nepomniachtchi-Aronian, Moscow 2019, when 17...♕f6 was best and near-zero eval per Komodo, Lc0, and Stockfish) 16...♕c7 17.♕d3 ♖ae8 18.♕c4 ♕b8 19.♗d2 ♗xe5 20.d6+ ♖e6 21.fxe5 ♕a8 22.♖e2 a5 23.♕xc5 ♖g6 24.g3 ♕a6 25.♖ae1 ♖c8 26.♕f2 ♕c6 27.♖e4 ♕d5 28.♗f4 ♖e6 29.♕d4 ♕b5 30.♕d3 ♕c5+ 31.♖d4 ♕c6 32.♖de4 ♕b6+ 33.♗e3 ♗xe4 34.♗xb6 ♗xd3 35.cxd3 ♖ce8 36.d4 ♖xd6∓ (-0.90). White is down the exchange for a pawn in an endgame without much compensation.

9...exd4 10.e5 ♘e8

11.c3

11.♕xd4 c5 12.♕e4 ♖b8 13.c4 ♗b7 14.♕d3 d5 15.♗c2 f5 16.cxd5 ♕xd5 17.♕xd5+ ♗xd5 18.♘c3 ♗c6∓ (-0.27). Black's space and better development easily offset White's passed pawn.

11...dxc3

11...c5 is much less common, probably because it's more tempting to win a pawn, but it is a satisfactory alternative. 12.cxd4 c4 13.♗c2 d5 14.♘c3 ♘c7 15.♗e3 b4= (0.00) looks pretty balanced, with each side dominating one wing. Although having the advantage on

the side where the kings are favors White, Black's queenside initiative is much further along.

12.♘xc3 ♗b7

12...d6 is the usual move, but the stats favor White after this move, so I prefer the game move. 13.♕f3 (13.♘d5 ♗e6 14.♕f3 transposes) 13...♗e6 14.♘d5 ♖c8 15.♗f4 dxe5 16.♘xe7+ ♕xe7 17.♗xe5 c5 18.♖ad1 ♗xb3 19.axb3 ♕a7 and White has obvious and full compensation for the pawn. Zero score per Komodo, but it is surely easier to play White from here.

13.♘d5 ♗xd5 14.♕xd5 c6 15.♕e4

15...a5!

15...g6 16.♗h6 ♘g7 17.♖ad1± was the **actual game** continuation, drawn after 36 moves. Black should wait for White to play ♗e3 before playing ...g7-g6, to save a tempo in case of ♗h6 as happened in the game.

16.♗e3 g6 17.♖ad1 ♘g7 18.♕g4 ♘f5=

White has some pressure on d7 and f7 which compensates for his half-pawn deficit (0.00).

CHAPTER 26

Møller Defense

I have added one more chapter to the Black book in June of 2019, as some very recent games (especially by ex-World Champion Vishy Anand) and analysis make it look like a good option for Black against the Spanish if he hopes to have some winning chances without undue risk. It is a close relative of the Neo-Archangel (5...b5 and 6...♗c5), but Black plays the bishop to c5 directly on move 5.

This has the downside of giving White the option to retreat to c2 after 6.c3 b5, but it seems that the b3 retreat is probably better. The upside is that White can't attack b5 with a2-a4 without playing c2-c3 first, which takes away options based on playing ♘c3 at some point. This defense looks almost ideal in most variations, but there is one line, given in the final game, that poses huge practical problems for Black even though they can be solved. So my current opinion is that the Møller Defense may be excellent for correspondence play, but is probably not suitable for over-the-board play against a well-prepared opponent, unless a simpler defense can be found to the final game.

After **6.c3 b5**, first I consider **7.♗c2**, the attempt to 'punish' Black's move-order, but Black in turn 'punishes' White by **7...d5!** (7...d6 is playable but not quite equal). Game 26.1 features the rather rare but good move **8.a4** when after **8...dxe4 9.dxe5** I recommend a sideline (**9...♗g4**) based on a sacrificial novelty on move 14 which seems to give Black a strong attack for the sacrificed material, enough to say that all three results are plausible. I doubt that many players as White would knowingly allow this. I also include the 'fork trick' 6.♘xe5 in the notes, Black fully equalizes. Game 26.2 shows the standard **8.d4**, when the main line results in an endgame where White has two rooks and knight for one rook and two bishops, roughly a one pawn advantage, but Black has all the positional advantages and is fully equal. I also give the rare but somewhat tricky **7.d4** line, where I also recommend an exchange sacrifice that looks fully correct. It seems that after 7.♗c2 d5 almost all lines end in some kind of material imbalance for compensation, but Black looks fine everywhere.

Next comes the more standard **7.♗b3 d6 8.a4 ♗b7**. In general in the Spanish the bishop is not so well placed on b7 when White has pawns on c2 and d3, but with the pawn already on c3 the bishop is okay there.

If **9.d3** Black has time for **9...h6** (preventing the pin) before castling. This leads to balanced play with no particular problems for Black, though he should play a couple precise moves to fully equalize. See Game 26.3.

Game 26.4 features **9.d4 ♗b6 10.♗g5**, when **10...h6** more or less obligates White to give up the bishop pair on f6 (11.♗h4 g5 is fine for Black when he hasn't castled yet). White counts on **11.♗xf6 ♕xf6 12.♗d5** to compensate, but eventually Black untangles and reaches full equality. This line is easy for Black.

After **9.d4 ♗b6** White can exchange pawns on b5 and rooks on a8. Both recaptures are satisfactory for Black. Anand chose the bishop, the engines prefer the queen. Take your pick! See Game 26.5.

Now we come to the scariest line for Black, **10.♖e1!**, waiting for Black to castle before pinning, so that the unpinning ...h7-h6 and ...g7-g5 can be met by the sacrifice ♘xg5. Although this forces Black to play many accurate moves to survive, he can apparently reach equality and draw in Game 26.6 and the notes, at least in correspondence play. I give some options for Black along the way if he must play for a win, but objectively White is better in those lines. This is the line to play for White.

Game 26.1   Ruy Lopez/Spanish –
Møller Defense

Alan Pichot   2552
Yu Yangyi   2760

PRO League Stage rapid 2018 (4)

**1.e4 e5 2.♘f3 ♘c6 3.♗b5 a6 4.♗a4
♘f6 5.0-0 ♗c5**

6.c3
6.♘xe5 ♘xe5 7.d4 b5 8.♗b3 ♗xd4
9.♕xd4 d6 10.f4 ♘c6 11.♕c3 ♗b7
12.e5 ♘e4 13.♕e3 ♘a5 14.♘d2 ♘xb3
15.cxb3 ♘xd2 16.♗xd2 0-0 17.♖ad1
♖e8 18.♗c3 f5 19.♕f2 ♖e6 20.♖d3
b4 21.♗xb4 a5 22.♗c3 ♗a6 23.♖g3
♗xf1 24.exd6 ♖g6 25.♕xf1 ♖xg3
26.dxc7 ♕xc7 27.hxg3 ♕c5+ 28.♔h2
♕d5= (-0.03), Lc0 -0.13. With two
pawns for the exchange White is
nominally ¼ pawn up by my count,
but he has two sets of doubled
pawns, and the disappearance of
most of the other pieces favors
Black, so he is fine here.
6...b5 7.♗c2
7.d4 bxa4 8.dxc5 ♘xe4 9.♘xe5. I
lost a game as Black here about 20
years ago to GM Joel Benjamin,
but I didn't even consider the
following exchange sacrifice:
9...♘xe5 10.♕d5 ♘xc5! (instead

10...♗b7 11.♕xe5+ ♕e7 is only
slightly in White's favor, but the
exchange sacrifice is fully equal)
11.♕xa8 0-0 12.♗e3 ♘cd3 13.♕e4
d5 14.♕xa4 c5 15.♘d2 ♗f5= (-0.23).
Both engines actually prefer
Black here despite White's extra
exchange! Black has fantastic
minor pieces, ideas like ...♘xb2,
...♘g4, ...♕f6, ...d5-d4, and ...h7-h6.
White just can't activate his rooks.
7...d5 8.a4 dxe4 9.axb5

9...exf3
9...♗g4! (I recommend this line
because of the novelty on move 14)
10.bxc6 exf3 11.gxf3 ♗h3! 12.♖e1 0-0
13.♖a5 ♕d6 14.b4 ♗xf2+!N 15.♔xf2
e4

analysis diagram

16.♔g1 (16.♗xe4 ♖ae8 17.d3
♕xh2+ 18.♔e3 ♘xe4 19.fxe4 f5∞

(+0.02). Black is a knight down but has a very powerful attack. The engines rate it equal, seeing lots of repetition draws. In an over-the-board game, I would rather play Black here, it's too hard to defend a position like this as White) 16...♖ae8 17.♖e3 ♘h5 18.♖g5 ♕h6 19.♖g3 ♘xg3 20.hxg3 exf3 21.♕xf3 ♖e6 22.♗d3 ♖d8 23.♗e2 ♕g6 24.♖xe6 ♗xe6 25.♘a3 h5= (-0.02). White is up 1.5 pawns, but has poor development and an unsafe king. In OTB play this looks easier to play as Black.

10.♕xf3 e4 11.♗xe4 ♘e5 12.♕e2 0-0 13.d4 ♗g4 14.♕c2 ♘xe4 15.♕xe4 ♘f3+ 16.gxf3 ♗h3 17.dxc5 ♗xf1 18.♔xf1 ♕d1+ 19.♕e1 ♕xf3 20.♗e3 axb5 21.♖xa8 ♖xa8 22.♘d2 ♕h1+ 23.♔e2 ♕xh2 24.♘f3 ♕h3 25.♕d1 ♕e6 26.♕d3

26...♕b3

26...c6 27.♕d6 ♕c4+ 28.♔d2 b4 29.cxb4 ♕xb4+ 30.♔d3 ♕xb2 31.♕xc6± (+0.49). White has a half pawn material edge, and his advanced passed pawn offsets his exposed king.

27.♘g5 ♕c4 28.♕xc4 bxc4 29.♘f3 ♖a2

30.♘e5?

30.♘d4! ♖xb2+ 31.♔f3 ♖b3 32.♔e4 ♖xc3 33.c6 ♖xe3+ 34.♔xe3 ♔f8 35.♘b5 h5 36.♘xc7 ♔e7 37.♔d4−+.

30...♖xb2+ 31.♔f3 ♖b3= 32.♗d4 f6 33.♘xc4 ♔f7 34.♘e3 ♔e6 35.♔e4 ♖b1 36.♘g2? g5

36...f5+−+.

37.♘e3 ♖e1∓ 38.f4 f5+ 39.♔f3 g4+ 40.♔f2 ♖h1 41.♗e5 c6 42.♔g2 ♖c1 43.♔g3 h5 44.c4 ♖g1+ 45.♔f2 ♖h1 46.♔g2 ♖c1 47.♔g3 ♖g1+ 48.♔f2 ♖h1 49.♔g2 ♖e1 50.♔f2 ♖c1?

50...♖b1∓.

51.♔g3 ½-½

Game 26.2   Ruy Lopez/Spanish –
             Møller Defense

Hrvoje Stevic   2587
Ante Brkic   2596

Pozega 2018 (5)

1.e4 e5 2.♘f3 ♘c6 3.♗b5 a6 4.♗a4 ♘f6 5.0-0 ♗c5 6.c3 b5 7.♗c2 d5 8.d4 dxe4 9.♘xe5

9.dxe5 ♕xd1 10.♖xd1 exf3 11.exf6 gxf6 12.♗e4 ♗d7 13.♘d2 fxg2 14.♘b3 ♗b6 15.♘d4 ♗xd4 16.cxd4 0-0-0 17.♗f4 ♖hg8 18.♗g3 ♘e7 19.♗xh7 ♖g5 20.♗e4 ♗e6 21.a4 bxa4= (+0.02). White can't retain the bishop pair and regain his lost pawns.

9...♘xe5

10.dxe5

10.dxc5 ♘d3 11.♘d2 ♘xc5 12.b4 e3 13.bxc5 exd2 14.♗xd2 0-0 15.♗f4 ♗e6 16.♕xd8 ♖fxd8 17.♗xc7 ♖d2 18.♖fc1 ♖c8 19.♗d6 ♘d7 20.♗f4 ♖e2 21.c4 ♘xc5 22.cxb5 axb5 23.♗e3 ♘a6 24.♗b3 ♖xc1+ 25.♖xc1 h6 26.♔f1 ♖b2 27.♗d4 ♖d2 28.♗c3 ♖d6= (+0.08). White can't avoid the exchange of bishops, after which a draw is pretty much inevitable.

10...♕xd1 11.♖xd1 ♘g4 12.♗xe4 ♘xf2 13.♗c6+ ♔e7 14.♖d5 ♗b6

15.♗xa8

15.♗g5+ f6 16.exf6+ gxf6 17.♗h4 ♘g4+ 18.♔h1 ♖b8 19.♘d2 ♗e6

20.♖h5 ♘f2+ 21.♗xf2 ♗xf2 22.♖f1 ♗e3= (+0.04). White's more active rooks and better pawn structure offset Black's bishop pair.

15...♘d3+ 16.♔f1 ♘xc1 17.♘a3

17.♖d1 ♗f5 18.♖xc1 ♖xa8 19.♘d2 ♗d3+ 20.♔e1 ♖e8 21.a4 f6 22.♘f3 fxe5= (+0.02). It's similar to the game.

17...♗e6 18.♖xc1 ♖xa8 19.♖d3 ♗f5

In general, rook + two bishops + pawn equals two rooks + knight. Since the pawn count is equal here, Black is down one pawn, but he has huge positional compensation. White has a weak exposed center pawn, his knight is on the rim, and the bishops and king are very active. Black is fully equal here.

20.♖dd1

20.♖g3 ♖d8 21.♘c2 ♖d2 22.♘d4 ♗e4 23.♖e1 ♗d5 24.♖xg7 ♔f8 25.♖xh7 ♖xb2=.

20...♗e3 21.♖a1 h5!= 22.g3 f6

22...♔e6= (0.00). Although it's equal, this is a better choice to play for a win.

23.♖e1 ♗d3+ 24.♔g2 ♗e4+ 25.♔h3 ♗f5+ 26.♔g2 ♗e4+ 27.♔f1

Draw agreed.

Game 26.3   Ruy Lopez/Spanish –
Møller Defense

Wesley So 2754
Viswanathan Anand 2767

Stavanger 2019 (6)

1.e4 e5 2.♘f3 ♘c6 3.♗b5 a6 4.♗a4
♘f6 5.0-0 ♗c5 6.c3 b5 7.♗b3 d6
8.a4 ♗b7 9.d3 h6

It seems that as long as Black meets
d2-d3 by ...h7-h6 in this line, he has
no worries.

10.♖e1 0-0

11.♘bd2

11.axb5 axb5 12.♖xa8 ♗xa8
(12...♕xa8! (-0.13). Black aims to
play ...♕a7, already Black is for
choice) 13.♘h4?! ♘a5! (already
winning the bishop pair because
of the threat of ...♘xe4. It should
be noted that this was a 10' to 7'
Armageddon game, hence the bad
play) 14.♘f5 ♘xb3 15.♕xb3 ♗c6
16.♘a3 ♗d7 17.♘e3 ♕b8 18.♕d1 b4
19.♘ac4 bxc3 20.bxc3 ♕a7 21.♕f3
♖b8 22.♗d2 ♕a2 ½-½ (40) Vachier-
Lagrave-Anand, Stavanger 2019.
Black is already winning and only
gave a draw later as Black had draw
odds in the game.

11...♘e7 12.♘h4

12.♘f1 ♘g6 13.♘g3 d5 14.d4 exd4
15.e5 ♘e4 16.cxd4 ♗b4 17.♖e2 c5
18.dxc5 ♗xc5 19.♗e3 bxa4= (0.00).
The outposted knight offsets the
isolated d-pawn.

12...♖b8

12...b4 13.♘df3 a5 14.h3 ♗b6=
(+0.08). White's only plus is a
slightly more active queen's bishop,
it's really nothing: Lc0 +0.02.

13.axb5 axb5 14.♘f1

14...♗c8

14...d5! 15.d4 exd4 16.e5 ♘e4 17.cxd4
♗b4 18.♖e2 c5 19.♘e3 ♗c8 20.♘xd5
♘xd5 21.♖xe4 c4 22.♗c2 f5 23.exf6
♕xf6 24.♕e2 ♗d6= (0.00). Black
has full compensation for the
pawn, a better pawn structure, a
blockading central knight, and
pressure on f2.

15.h3 ♗e6 16.♗xe6 fxe6 17.♘f3 b4
17...♗b6 18.♘g3 ♘g6 19.d4 ♘d7
20.b4 ♕e7 (+0.09). Black has
adequate counterplay on the f-file.
18.♘g3
White is just marginally better
around here due to the option to
play the push d3-d4 at will, but
Black was never in any trouble in
the game.
**18...bxc3 19.bxc3 ♘g6 20.d4
♗b6 21.♗e3 ♘d7 22.♘d2 exd4
23.cxd4 e5 24.♘f3 ♕f6 25.♘f5 ♘e7
26.♘xe7+ ♕xe7 27.♖c1 ♖f7**

28.d5
In the line 28.dxe5 ♗xe3 29.♖xe3
♘xe5 30.♕d5 c6 31.♕a2 ♘xf3+
32.♖xf3 d5 33.♖e3 ♕a7 34.♕xa7
♖xa7 35.♖xc6 dxe4 36.♖xe4 ♔h7
Black has a pawn down but easily
drawn endgame.
**28...♗xe3 29.♖xe3 ♘c5= 30.♕e2
♖ff8 31.♖ec3 ♖b4 32.♖c4 ♖fb8
33.g3 ♖xc4 34.♖xc4 ♕e8 35.♔g2
♖b7 36.♘h4 ♕f7 37.♘f5 ♔h7
38.h4 ♘d7 39.♕c2 ♘c5 40.♕e2
♘d7 41.♕c2 ♘c5 42.♘e3 ♘b3
43.♕d1 ♘d4 44.♘c2 ♖b2 45.♖c3
h5 46.♕d3**
Draw agreed.

Game 26.4   Ruy Lopez/Spanish –
Møller Defense
Dmitry Svetushkin   2563
Nichita Morozov   2437
Anogia 2017 (7)

**1.e4 e5 2.♘f3 ♘c6 3.♗b5 a6 4.♗a4
♘f6 5.0-0 b5**
We would transpose to the game by
5...♗c5! 6.c3 b5 7.♗b3 d6 8.a4 ♗b7.
**6.♗b3 ♗c5 7.a4 ♗b7 8.c3 d6 9.d4
♗b6 10.♗g5 h6**

11.♗xf6
If White wants to retain this bishop
by 11.♗h4 he needs to wait for
Black to castle before playing ♗g5,
since here there is no objection to
11...g5.
11...♕xf6 12.♗d5
White reasons that eventually the
knight must move so Black can't
retain the two bishops, and White
has a slight central edge. But the
bishop on b6 is an excellent piece
even if the other bishops are traded.
12.axb5 axb5 13.♖xa8+ ♗xa8 14.d5
♘a7 15.♘a3 0-0 16.♕d3 ♖b8 17.♖a1
g6 18.♕e2 ♔g7= (0.00). Black
plans ...♗b7 and ...♗c8 or ...c7-c6
if White's bishop retreats to c2 or
d1. White has space and the open

file for his rook, but Black has the bishop pair, and the unopposed bishop is super strong.

12...0-0 13.♘a3 ♖fb8

13...exd4 14.cxd4 ♖fb8 15.♘c2 bxa4 16.♖xa4 transposes to the game.

14.♘c2 bxa4 15.♖xa4 exd4 16.cxd4 ♘e7 17.♗xb7 ♖xb7

18.♕d3

18.♘e3 a5 19.♖e1 ♖ab8 20.b3 c6 21.♘c4 ♗c7 22.♘xa5 ♗xa5 23.♖xa5 ♖xb3 24.e5 dxe5 25.dxe5 ♕g6= (+0.05). Black has an isolated but passed pawn. Otherwise it's quite equal.

18...a5 19.♘e3

19...♕g6?!

19...♖ab8!N 20.♘c4 d5 21.exd5 ♘xd5 22.♕e4 c6 23.g3 ♖e7 24.♕g4 g6 25.♘fe5 h5 26.♕f3 ♕xf3 27.♘xf3 ♗c7 28.♘fe5 ♗xe5 29.♘xe5 ♖xb2 30.♖xa5 ♘c3 31.♘xc6 ♖c7 32.♘e5 ♘e2+ 33.♔g2 ♘xd4= (0.00). Clearly an equal and drawn endgame, although a weaker player could still get outplayed and lose from either side.

20.♘h4

20.b4 d5 21.♘f5 c6 22.♘e5 ♕e6 23.♘xe7+ ♖xe7 24.bxa5 dxe4 (+0.01). It will be a drawn endgame, but Black has to play a few good moves to reach it.

20...♕f6 21.♘hf5 ♘xf5 22.exf5 c6 23.♘g4 ♕g5= 24.d5?! ♗c5?!

24...cxd5! 25.♕xd5 ♖ab8∓ (-0.50). Black's bishop is a lot stronger than White's knight here.

25.dxc6 ♖xb2 26.♕f3 ♖b4 27.c7 ♖c8 28.♖xb4 axb4 29.h4 ♕e7 30.f6 ♕e6 31.♕g3 ♔h7 32.fxg7 ♖g8?

32...♔xg7=.

33.♕f4 ♔xg7

34.♘xh6?

34.♔h2+−.

34...♕xh6 35.♕g4+ ♕g6 36.c8♕ ♖xc8 37.♕xc8 b3 38.♕h3 ♕c2 39.♕g4+ ♔f8 40.♕c8+ ♔g7 41.♕g4+ ♔f8 42.♕a4 ♕c3 43.h5 b2 44.♕e4 ♔g7 45.♕g4+ ♔h7 46.♕f4 ♔g7 47.h6+ ♔g6 48.h7 ♔g7 49.♕f5 ♗d4 50.♕h5 ♕c8 51.♕g5+

♔h8 52.♕f4 ♕c4 53.♕f5 ♕e6
54.♕d3 ♗g7 55.f4 f5 56.♔f2 ♕a2
57.♔f3 ♕e6 58.g4 fxg4+ 59.♔g3 d5
60.♖h1 d4 61.♖b1 ♕e3+ 62.♕xe3
dxe3 63.♔xg4 ♔xh7 64.♔f3 ♔g6
65.♖g1+ ♔f7 66.♔xe3 ♗f6 67.♔e4
♗c3 68.♖h1 ♔g7 69.♔d3 ♗f6
70.♖d1 ♔f7 71.♔e4 ♔e6 72.f5+
♔e7 73.♖h1 ♔d6 74.♖d1+ ♔c5
75.♔d3 ♔d5 76.♖e1 ♗h4 77.♖f1
♗f6 78.♔c2 ♔e4 79.♖f2 ♔e3
80.♖h2 ♔f4 ½-½

Game 26.5   Ruy Lopez/Spanish –
              Møller Defense

Maxime Vachier-Lagrave   2779
Viswanathan Anand   2767

Stavanger 2019 (3)

**1.e4 e5 2.♘f3 ♘c6 3.♗b5 a6 4.♗a4
♘f6 5.0-0 ♗c5 6.c3 b5 7.♗b3 d6
8.d4 ♗b6 9.a4 ♗b7 10.axb5 axb5
11.♖xa8**

11...♗xa8
11...♕xa8 12.d5 ♘e7 13.♕d3 0-0
14.♗g5 ♘g6 15.♗xf6 gxf6 16.g3 ♗c8
17.♘a3 ♗h3 18.♖e1 ♕c8= (-0.04).
White can win a pawn on b5, but
Black's ideas of ...♘f4, ...♕g4, ...f7-f5
are full compensation.
12.♘a3

12...♘xe4?
12...exd4! 13.cxd4 ♘xe4 14.♖e1 d5
15.♘xb5 0-0 16.♘c3 ♘e7 17.♗c2
h6 18.♘xe4 dxe4 19.♗xe4 ♗xe4
20.♖xe4 ♘c6 21.♕d3 ♕d5 22.h4
f5 23.♖f4 ♘b4 24.♕c3 ♘c6 25.♗e3
♘d8 26.g4 fxg4 27.♖xf8+ ♔xf8
28.♘e5 ♘e6= (+0.04). Black
has regained his pawn with no
problems.
13.♘xb5?
13.♕e2± (+0.65). Black will probably
emerge a pawn down for minimal
compensation.
**13...0-0 14.♕e2 ♘f6 15.dxe5 ♘xe5
16.♘xe5 ♕e8 17.♘d4**

17...♕xe5
17...dxe5! 18.♘f5 ♗c5 19.♗e3 ♕c6
20.f3 e4 (-0.07). It's already more
pleasant to be on the black side
here.

18.♕xe5 dxe5 19.♘f3 ♖e8?!

19...♗xf3 20.gxf3 ♖e8 (+0.13).
White's awful pawns offset the two
bishops.

20.♗a4 c6 21.♘d2

21.h3±.

**21...♗b7 22.♘c4 ♗c7 23.♖d1 ♘d5
24.♘e3 ♖d8 25.c4?! ♘f4= 26.♖xd8+
♗xd8 27.♗d2 c5 28.b4 cxb4
29.♗xb4 ♘d3 30.♗d6 ♗b6 31.♔f1
♗c5 32.♗xc5 ½-½**

Game 26.6   Ruy Lopez/Spanish –
             Møller Defense

Alan Pichot   2562
Lorenzo Lodici   2458

Manavgat 2018 (6)

**1.e4 e5 2.♘f3 ♘c6 3.♗b5 a6 4.♗a4
♘f6 5.0-0 b5 6.♗b3 ♗c5 7.a4 ♗b7
8.c3 d6 9.d4 ♗b6 10.♖e1!**

This is a very scary line for Black to
meet over the board. White waits
for castling before pinning the
knight, so he can sacrifice on g5
after ...h7-h6 ♗h4 g5.

10...0-0

I wish I could recommend 10...
h6?! to avoid the dangerous line in
the game, but Black just can't spare
the tempo here: 11.♗e3 0-0 12.d5

♘a7 13.♗xb6 cxb6 14.axb5 ♘xb5
15.♘bd2± (+0.49). White has more
space and more center-controlling
pawns.

11.♗g5 h6 12.♗h4 exd4 13.cxd4 g5

14.♘xg5!

This sacrifice requires several
precise moves by Black but appears
to lead to a draw with correct play.
It is certainly the best choice in a
practical over-the-board game. The
defense is quite difficult. So perhaps
the Møller Defense is best reserved
for correspondence games due to
this line.

14.♗g3 ♖e8 (Black's pressure on
the center gives him full equality
in this line) 15.d5 ♘a5 16.♗c2 c6
17.dxc6 ♗xc6 18.♘c3 ♘c4 19.♖b1
♕d7 20.♘d4 b4 21.♘xc6 bxc3
22.a5 cxb2 23.♘e7+ ♖xe7 24.axb6
♖c8 25.♗d3 ♘xb6 26.♖xb2 ♘a4
27.♖c2 (27.♖b4 ♘c3 28.♕a1 a5
29.♕xa5 ♘cxe4∓) 27...♘c5 28.f3
♘xd3 29.♖xc8+ ♕xc8 30.♕xd3 d5
31.♕d4 ♕c6 32.♗e5 ♘d7 33.exd5
♕b5 34.♗g3 ♖xe1+ 35.♗xe1 ♕b6
36.♕xb6 ♘xb6 37.d6 f6= (-0.01).
Black has the more pleasant side of
a drawn endgame.

14...hxg5 15.♗xg5 ♘xd4 16.♗d5

16...♘e6

Objectively 16...c6? is a bad move, but if you absolutely have to win with black this is a try, as it is ridiculously complicated and not clearly losing: 17.♖a3 ♖e8 18.♗g3 ♔f8 19.♗h6+ ♔e7 20.♗xf7 ♖f8 21.♗a2 ♔d7 22.♘c3 c5 23.♖g6 ♕e8 24.♗g5 c4 25.e5 ♘h7 26.♗g7+ ♖f7 27.♖g6 ♗c5 28.♖xd6+ ♗xd6 29.♕xd4 ♖f6 30.♗b1 ♖xh6 31.♗f5+ ♔c6 32.axb5+ axb5 33.♗e4+ ♔c7 34.exd6+ ♖xd6 35.♕c5+ ♖c6 36.♘xb5+ ♔b8 37.♕f5 ♖aa6 38.♕xh7 ♖ab6 39.♘c3 ♖xb2 40.♕f5± (+0.72). This is just a sample line, there are countless other tries for both sides along the way.

17.♗h4 ♗xd5

17...c6? 18.♕f3 ♘d4 19.♕f4 ♘e6 20.♗xe6 fxe6 21.♖a3 ♗d4 (+0.34). Although this may be defensible for Black, he should avoid it by following the game.

18.exd5 ♘g7 19.♕f3 ♖e8 20.♘c3

20.♘d2 ♖xe1+ 21.♖xe1 ♗d4 22.♘e4 transposes to the game.

20...♖xe1+ 21.♖xe1 ♗d4 22.♘e4

22.♖e4 ♗xf2+ 23.♕xf2 ♘xe4 24.♘xe4 ♕c8 25.♘f6+ ♔f8 26.g4

♘e8 27.♕f4 ♘xf6 28.♗xf6 ♕b8 29.♕h6+ ♔e8 30.♕e3+ ♔d7 31.♕e7+ ♔c8 32.♕e8+ ♔b7 33.♕c6+ ♔c8 34.♗d4 (34.axb5 axb5 35.♕e8+ ♔b7 36.♕xb5+ ♔c8 37.♕e8+ ♔b7 38.♕xb8+ ♔xb8 39.♔f2 ♖a5 40.h4 ♖xd5 41.h5 ♖d2+ 42.♔g3 ♖d3+ 43.♔h4 ♖d1 44.♔g5 d5= (+0.05). Black's extra exchange offsets White's more advanced passed pawn and king. A draw is inevitable) 34...♔d8 35.h4 ♘e7 36.♕c1 c5 37.dxc6 ♕c8 38.♕g5+ ♔e8 (0.00), but Lc0 +0.45. This is probably defensible in correspondence chess, but over the board it looks too difficult for Black.

22...♘ge8 23.h3

White has strong pressure on the pinned knight and the black king, but he is down a knight for a pawn with no immediate way to achieve more than a drawn position. 23.♖e3!? bxa4 24.♕f4 ♗xe3 25.fxe3 ♔g7= (0.00). White doesn't have more than perpetual check.

23...bxa4

24.♕f4

A) 24.♕g3+ ♘g7 25.♕g5 ♘xe4 26.♕xd8+ ♖xd8 27.♖xe4 ♗xf2+ 28.♔xf2 ♖b8 29.♗f6 ♘h5 30.♗c3

a3 31.bxa3 ♖b3 32.♗d4 f5 33.♖e8+
♔f7 34.♖c8 ♖xa3 35.♖xc7+ ♔e8=
(0.00). Some repetition is likely
soon, it's too balanced to avoid that
result;

 B) 24.♘xf6+ ♗xf6 25.♖xe8+ ♕xe8
26.♗xf6 ♕e1+ 27.♔h2 ♕b1 28.h4
♖f8 29.h5 ♔h7 30.♕f4 (30.g4 ♖e8
31.♗c3 f5 32.g5 ♕e4 33.g6+ ♔h6
34.♗d2+ ♔g7= White can take
the perpetual or try for more with
35.♕g3 ♕g4 and trading queens,
but that's probably also a draw)
30...♕d3 31.♗e7 ♖g8 32.♕xf7+ ♖g7
33.♕e6 ♕c2 34.♗f6 ♕xf2 35.♗xg7
♔xg7 36.♕g4+ ♔h7 37.♕e4+ ♔h8
(0.00), Lc0 +0.27. White has the
only winning chances, but it seems
that Black can draw by taking the
b2-pawn and then using his passed

pawn to force perpetual check or to
win the white h-pawn.
**24...♖b8 25.♘xf6+ ♗xf6 26.♖xe8+
♕xe8 27.♗xf6 ♕e1+ 28.♔h2 ♕b1**

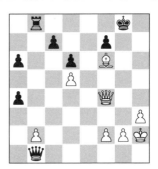

29.♕g4+
29.♕xa4 ♕f5 30.♕h4 ♕h7 31.♕g5+
♕g6 32.♕h4= (0.00). Neither side
can avoid repetition profitably.
**29...♕g6 30.♕h4 ♕h7 31.♕g4+
½-½**

Index of variations (Black)

Unusual opening moves

1.c4 g6 – English Opening

1.♘f3 ♘f6 2.c4 b6 – Queen's Indian vs Réti

1.♘f3 ♞f6 2.c4 g6 3.♘c3 d5 – Anti-Grünfeld and Symmetrical English

1.d4 ♞f6 – Queen's Pawn Openings

1.d4 ♞f6 2.c4 g6 – Neo-Grünfeld

1.d4 ♘f6 2.c4 g6 3.♘c3 d5 – Grünfeld Defense – Non-Exchange lines

1.d4 ♘f6 2.c4 g6 3.♘c3 d5 4.cxd5 ♘xd5 – Grünfeld Exchange

1.e4 e5 – Center Game, Ponziani, Bishop's Opening, Vienna Game, and Gambits

1.e4 e5 2.♘f3 ♘c6 – Other Gambits and Scotch and Four Knights Opening

1.e4 e5 2.♘f3 ♘c6 3.♗c4 ♗c5 – Italian Game

1.e4 e5 2.♘f3 ♘c6 3.♗b5 a6 – Spanish Offshoots

1.e4 e5 2.♘f3 ♞c6 3.♗b5 a6 4.♗a4 ♞f6 5.0-0 ♗e7 6.♖e1 b5 7.♗b3 d6 8.c3 0-0 9.h3 ♞b8 – Breyer Defense

1.e4 e5 2.♘f3 ♞c6 3.♗b5 a6 4.♗a4 ♞f6 5.0-0 ♗e7 6.♖e1 b5 7.♗b3 0-0 8.c3 d5 – Marshall Attack

1.e4 e5 2.♘f3 ♘c6 3.♗b5 a6 4.♗a4 ♘f6 5.0-0 ♗e7 – Anti-Marshall

1.e4 e5 2.♘f3 ♘c6 3.♗b5 a6 4.♗a4 ♘f6 5.0-0 ♗c5 – Møller Defense

Index of names (Black)

(numbers refer to pages)

Bibliography

Books

The Safest Grünfeld Reloaded, Alexander Delchev, Chess Stars 2019

Keep It Simple 1.e4, Christof Sielecki, New In Chess 2018

Bologan's Ruy Lopez for Black, Victor Bologan, New In Chess 2015

Rossolimo and Friends, Alexei Kornev, Chess Stars 2015

Chess Developments – the Grünfeld, David Vigorito, Gloucester Publishers Ltd 2013

The Four Knights Game, Andrey Obodchuk, New In Chess 2011

Secrets of Opening Surprises Vol. 13, Jeroen Bosch (ed.), New In Chess 2011

The Safest Grünfeld, Alexander Delchev & Evgenij Agrest, Chess Stars 2011

Grandmaster Repertoire 8: The Grünfeld Defence (Volume One), Boris Avrukh, Quality Chess 2011

Grandmaster Repertoire 9: The Grünfeld Defence (Volume Two), Boris Avrukh, Quality Chess 2011

The Scotch Game, Yelena Dembo & Richard Palliser, Everyman Chess 2011

The English Opening, Mihail Marin, Quality Chess 2010

The Scotch Game for White, Vladimir Barsky, Chess Stars 2009

The Pirc in Black and White, James Vigus, Everyman Chess 2007

Chess Openings For White, Explained, Lev Alburt, Roman Dzindzichashvili & Eugene Perelshteyn, Chess Information and Research Center 2007

Challenging the Grünfeld, Edward Dearing, Quality Chess 2005

The Chess Advantage in Black and White, Larry Kaufman, Random House 2004

Periodicals

New In Chess Magazine

New In Chess Yearbook

Databases

MegaDatabase 2019

Hiarcs PowerBook 2019

ChessBase 15

Engines

Komodo 13

Lc0 (networks thru 42858)

Stockfish 10

Houdini 6.03

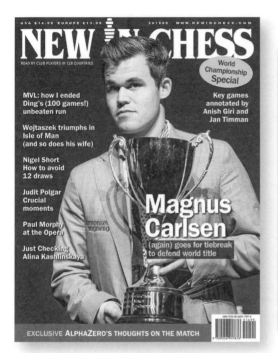
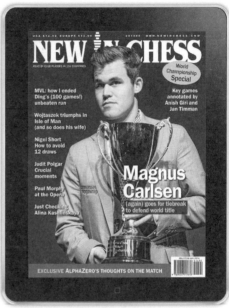

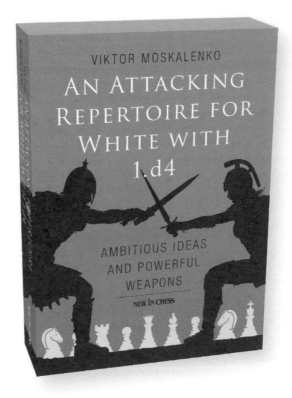